OXFORD STUDIES IN ANCIE

8 —

7 · 1 0

# OXFORD STUDIES IN ANCIENT PHILOSOPHY

EDITOR: DAVID SEDLEY

VOLUME XXXIII

WINTER 2007

OXFORD
UNIVERSITY PRESS

# OXFORD
## UNIVERSITY PRESS

Great Clarendon Street, Oxford OX2 6DP

Oxford University Press is a department of the University of Oxford.
It furthers the University's objective of excellence in research, scholarship,
and education by publishing worldwide in

Oxford New York

Auckland Cape Town Dar es Salaam Hong Kong Karachi
Kuala Lumpur Madrid Melbourne Mexico City Nairobi
New Delhi Shanghai Taipei Toronto

With offices in

Argentina Austria Brazil Chile Czech Republic France Greece
Guatemala Hungary Italy Japan Poland Portugal Singapore
South Korea Switzerland Thailand Turkey Ukraine Vietnam

Oxford is a registered trade mark of Oxford University Press
in the UK and in certain other countries

Published in the United States
by Oxford University Press Inc., New York

British Library Cataloguing in Publication Data

Data available

Library of Congress Cataloging in Publication Data

Oxford studies in ancient philosophy.—
Vol. xxxiii (2007).—Oxford: Clarendon Press;
New York: Oxford University Press, 1983–
v.; 22 cm. Annual.
1. Philosophy, Ancient—Periodicals.
B1.O9      180.'5—dc.19      84–645022
AACR 2      MARC-S

Typeset by John Waś, Oxford
Printed in Great Britain
on acid-free paper by
Biddles Ltd, King's Lynn, Norfolk

ISBN 978–0–19–923801–9
ISBN 978–0–19–923802–6 (Pbk.)

1 3 5 7 9 10 8 6 4 2

# ADVISORY BOARD

Contributions and books for review should be sent to the Editor (from 1 October 2007), Professor Brad Inwood, Department of Classics, University of Toronto, 125 Queen's Park Crescent, Toronto, ON, M5S 2C7, Canada (e-mail brad.inwood@utoronto.ca).

Contributors are asked to observe the 'Notes for Contributors to Oxford Studies in Ancient Philosophy', printed at the end of this volume.

Up-to-date contact details, the latest version of Notes to Contributors, and publication schedules can be checked on the *Oxford Studies in Ancient Philosophy* website:

www.oup.co.uk/philosophy/series/osap

# CONTENTS

viii                        *Contents*

# WISDOM IN HERACLITUS

ALEX LONG

HERACLITUS frequently draws attention to a hidden connection between opposites, and his examples are richly varied. In some fragments the connection lies in mutual succession (B 57, 88); elsewhere it is to be found in a single thing which is characterized by opposite properties or gives rise to opposite results (B 59, 60, 61, 67).[1] These fragments have long been read as not merely terse observations but instances of a general principle: the unity of (or in) opposites. The mere variety of Heraclitus' examples suggests that he thought the phenomenon ubiquitous, and on occasion he apparently generalizes about a divergent 'connection' (B 51) and claims that *all* things are unified (B 10, 50). And so he has been credited with the thesis that every unity embodies an opposition and that every pair of opposites is connected.

In what way are opposites connected? Perhaps Heraclitus means merely that for every pair of opposites there is *some* case of coinstantiation or mutual succession.[2] But it is not clear why the promise of a single coinstantiation should prevent us from habitually, if cautiously, treating the opposites as distinct. And Heraclitus offers not one but several connections between a single pair of opposites, life and death, and claims that life arises because of death and vice versa

© Alex Long 2007

My thanks to David Sedley for his comments on an earlier draft of this paper, and to St Catharine's College for supporting my research.

[1] Unless indicated otherwise, the references and texts are those of H. Diels, *Die Fragmente der Vorsokratiker*, 6th edn., rev. W. Kranz [*Fragmente*] (3 vols.; Berlin, 1951). 'Connection' might seem a rather limp description of Heraclitean unity, but compare Heraclitus' ἁρμονίη (B 51, 54). For a table of the opposites in Heraclitus see M. Marcovich, *Heraclitus: Greek Text with a Short Commentary*, 2nd edn. [*Heraclitus*] (Sankt Augustin, 2001), *Table* after p. 160.

[2] So J. Barnes, *The Presocratic Philosophers* [*Philosophers*], rev. edn. (London, 1982), 70. On Barnes's account, however, Heraclitus saw succession as evidence for, rather than an alternative to, coinstantiation; see *Philosophers*, 72. For a riposte see D. W. Graham, 'Heraclitus' Criticism of Ionian Philosophy', *Oxford Studies in Ancient Philosophy*, 15 (1997), 1–50 at 7–12.

(B 62, 76).[3] So it is more likely that he regarded opposites as mutually entailing.[4] A member of a pair of contrary predicates imports a simultaneous or prospective connection with its twin.

If this principle is true of the Heraclitean world, is it also true of Heraclitean wisdom, that is, of knowledge of this world? If so, Heraclitus would seem to face difficulties for both his cosmology and his programme. Heraclitus' world is governed intelligently, and its ruler is a wise god; if god's wisdom makes him foolish, why should his rule be consistently intelligent, or indeed consistent at all? Heraclitus' programme is to educate a reader and prime him for the insights of wisdom, and yet, on the unity thesis, not only would that wisdom doom the reader to folly, but his initial folly would already have equipped him—and his ignorant peers—with wisdom (or at least the promise of wisdom).[5] Heraclitus might have responded by distinguishing between different forms of wisdom and folly;[6] for example, he could have suggested that the uncomprehending men of B 1 enjoy a limited kind of wisdom, but have not achieved that insight which would grant them understanding of the world. But it is difficult to see why they could then be characterized as wise at all, and in any case Heraclitus denies himself such a route when he declares there to be *one* sort of insight that constitutes wisdom, and so *one* way to be wise (B 41).

In this paper I shall argue that Heraclitus opts for a more radical response: he suggests that no wise man or god is foolish and so exempts wisdom from the unity of opposites. I first discuss two fragments which may suggest that wisdom is an exception to the

---

[3] For life and death see also B 15, 26, 48, 88. See also B 126, which seems to claim not merely that there is a cold thing that becomes hot, but that it is cold things that become hot.

[4] Barnes, *Philosophers*, 601 n. 27, notes this interpretation, suggesting that it is as probable as that on which every pair of opposites is *somewhere* coinstantiated.

[5] If, on a weaker unity thesis, wisdom and folly are only *somewhere* coinstantiated, Heraclitus could argue that god and the successful human enquirer, at least, are shielded from folly by their wisdom, and that wisdom and folly are coinstantiated elsewhere. But what other creature could possess wisdom (as well as folly) and so serve as Heraclitus' example?

[6] M. M. Mackenzie argues that the unity thesis applies to epistemic properties and distinguishes between a private, mortal understanding and a divine grasp of the common; see her 'Heraclitus and the Art of Paradox' ['Heraclitus'], *Oxford Studies in Ancient Philosophy*, 6 (1988), 1–38 at 23. On her account, both the human perspective and 'the god's eye view' are needed for wisdom. But if so, a wise creature, armed with both perspectives, would not be foolish by either criterion, and so would not fall under the unity thesis.

unity thesis. I then turn to a fragment which claims that Homer was wiser than his fellow Greeks and yet in error; I argue that Heraclitus' description of Homer as 'wiser' is sincere, and yet that Heraclitus does not see in Homer the coinstantiation of wisdom and folly. Finally, I suggest that while Heraclitus does not provide an explicit argument to show that wisdom is exempt from the unity of opposites, he at least provides the resources with which we could construct such an argument. So I intend to offer not only a fresh point about Heraclitean wisdom, but a fresh example of Heraclitus' oblique way of arguing.

## 1. Wisdom an exception to the unity thesis

ὁκόσων λόγους ἤκουσα, οὐδεὶς ἀφικνεῖται ἐς τοῦτο, ὥστε γινώσκειν ὅτι σοφόν ἐστι πάντων κεχωρισμένον. (B 108)

Of all those whose accounts I have heard, none gets as far as this: to know that the wise is different from everything.[7]

Heraclitus does not explain how the wise is different. Some have argued that his point is theological and his contrast is between god and world: god transcends all things, because of his unity,[8] his material character or location,[9] or his role as Zeus or 'thunderbolt'.[10] Alternatively, on a second theological construal, the fragment states that god is different from all traditional *conceptions* of the divine.[11] To the first reading one might object that the very notion of a *tran-*

[7] Parallels for κεχωρισμένος having the sense 'different' (rather than 'separated') are set out by Marcovich, *Heraclitus*, 441; the translation 'separated' might seem to favour taking σοφόν to refer to a transcendent god. With the omission of the article before σοφόν compare B 18, B 88, and B 126. With different punctuation the end of the fragment could be translated 'know what is wise, different from everything', but this does not jeopardize my suggestion about the way in which the wise differs.

[8] 'Die ἀφανὴς ἁρμονία Gottes (B 67) und seine im λόγος verkörperte Einheit tritt der irdischen Dissonanz und ihrem steten Wechsel als das Absolute gegenüber' (Diels–Kranz, *Fragmente*, 175). Compare E. Hussey, *The Presocratics* [*Presocratics*] (London, 1972), 36.

[9] W. K. C. Guthrie suggests that in B 108 Heraclitus may have in mind the 'transcendence' of his god, whom Guthrie describes as 'the Logos-fire (or *aither*) surrounding the cosmos in its purity, inextinguishable and invisible, mind and soul in their highest form' (*A History of Greek Philosophy*, i. *The Earlier Presocratics and the Pythagoreans* (Cambridge, 1962), 471–2).

[10] T. M. Robinson, *Heraclitus: Fragments* [*Heraclitus*] (Toronto, 1987), 152. For the claim that B 108 refers to a transcendent god see also O. Gigon, *Untersuchungen zu Heraklit* [*Heraklit*] (Leipzig, 1935), 138.

[11] So Marcovich, *Heraclitus*, 441–2, arguing that, unlike traditional conceptions of

*scendent* god sits awkwardly with Heraclitus' description of god in B 67. And to both such readings one might object that they make the mention of wisdom redundant, implying that the fragment would be no poorer, and would indeed gain greater clarity, if 'god' were substituted for 'wise'. Unless Heraclitus is being uncharacteristically casual about wording in B 108, it must be *wisdom* that sets god apart, and not material constitution or some other aspect of his nature.[12]

But Heraclitus' point need not be exclusively theological at all, for 'the wise' encompasses not only god but also the successful student of Heraclitus' account. Heraclitus invites his reader to achieve wisdom after hearing the account (B 50), and his description of the wisest soul (B 118) surely describes the wisest *human* soul. And while Heraclitus frequently belittles humans in comparison with gods (B 70, 78, 79), these disparagements do not categorically deny that humans are capable of wisdom.[13] In B 83 Heraclitus is recorded by Plato (*H. Ma.* 289 B 3–5) as having said that 'the wisest man will appear an ape in comparison with god, in wisdom, beauty, and everything else'.[14] But it is not certain that this report comprises or even contains verbatim quotation.[15] As M. Conche

god, Heraclitus' god is 'the non-anthropomorphic, shapeless and almost immaterial purest Fire (or *aither*)'. As Marcovich seems to concede, if Heraclitus is contrasting truth and tradition about god, Xenophanes could fairly complain that he and his λόγος have 'got this far'. With Marcovich's reading compare A. Nehamas' suggestion that B 108 draws a Parmenidean contrast between the truths revealed by wisdom and 'ordinary views of the world'; see 'Parmenidean Being/Heraclitean Fire', in V. Caston and D. W. Graham (eds.), *Presocratic Philosophy: Essays in Honour of Alexander Mourelatos* (Aldershot, 2002), 45–64 at 47 n. 9.

[12] Compare Philolaus B 20 DK, where presumably the description of the 'god' sets out the respects in which he is ἕτερος τῶν ἄλλων.

[13] In B 78 human character is said to have no understanding, and in B 79 humans are compared to infants, but, as Hussey, *Presocratics*, 36, neatly observes, 'men may, uncharacteristically, come to understanding, just as children can be educated'. Compare Hussey, 'Heraclitus', in A. A. Long (ed.), *The Cambridge Companion to Early Greek Philosophy* (Cambridge, 1999), 88–112 at 104. B 113 and 116 suggest that understanding is available to all people; see H. Granger, 'Heraclitus' Quarrel with Polymathy and *Historiē*' ['Polymathy'], *Transactions of the American Philological Association*, 134 (2004), 235–61 at 259. Contrast D. Rankin, 'Limits on Perception and Cognition in Heraclitus' Fragments', *Elenchos*, 16 (1995), 241–52.

[14] ἦ οὐ καὶ Ἡράκλειτος αὐτὸ τοῦτο λέγει, ὃν σὺ ἐπάγῃ, ὅτι ἀνθρώπων ὁ σοφώτατος πρὸς θεὸν πίθηκος φανεῖται καὶ σοφίᾳ καὶ κάλλει καὶ τοῖς ἄλλοις πᾶσιν;

[15] It has been suggested that B 82 (*H. Ma.* 289 A) and B 83 are merely creative recollections of B 79; see Marcovich, *Heraclitus*, 485–9 (who reaches the same verdict about B 70), and J. Bollack and H. Wismann, *Héraclite ou la séparation* (Paris, 1972), 249. It also seems possible to me that in B 83 Socrates is imaginatively spelling out

notes,[16] the talk of beauty in B 83 could have been supplied by Plato, given the nature of the discussion in the *Hippias Major*; clearly so, but the same is also true of its mention of wisdom, given that Socrates has just ironically described Hippias as wise (289 A 5–6), and repeatedly does so in this dialogue (281 A 1, B 6; 282 E 9–283 A 2; 283 C 3; 286 D 5; 300 D 1; 304 C 3). Heraclitus' dictum, as spelt out by Socrates, would have unwelcome consequences both for Hippias' account of beauty and for his pretensions to wisdom.

B 83 is thus unreliable evidence for radical pessimism about the human potential for wisdom. It has been suggested that Heraclitus acknowledged the possibility of human wisdom, but distinguished it from divine, 'true', or 'absolute' wisdom.[17] But, as noted above, his claim that wisdom consists of *one* insight (and one apparently available to humans) (B 41) suggests that he drew no such distinction.[18] And so in B 108 he need not mean merely that *god* is set apart by his wisdom, and cannot mean that wisdom is set apart from all *men* (with πάντων masculine rather than neuter).[19]

I suggest then that B 108 does not describe god alone, but claims that whatever is wise is different from 'everything'. Where does the difference lie? Let us consult Heraclitus' description of 'everything' for guidance: all things (and, in his examples, all opposites) are unified (B 50). Given this characterization of everything else, the peculiarity of wisdom—or rather, given Heraclitus' use of σοφόν rather than σοφίη, the peculiarity of being wise—would lie in separation from its opposite. No man or god is foolish as well as wise, much less foolish because of being wise, or oscillates between states

---

Heraclitus' meaning in B 82 (with λέγει at *H.Ma.* 289 B 3 meaning 'means', as in Fowler's Loeb translation); Heraclitus explicitly compared apes and humans, but his *real* point was an analogous comparison between humans and gods.

[16] 'Socrate et Hippias discutent de la beauté, non de la science' (*Héraclite: Fragments* [*Héraclite*] (Paris, 1986), 87).

[17] See G. S. Kirk, *Heraclitus: The Cosmic Fragments* [*Heraclitus*] (Cambridge, 1954), 394, and n. 21 below.

[18] Marcovich, *Heraclitus*, 450, claims that τὸ σοφόν in B 41 refers *exclusively* to human wisdom, but the text contains no such suggestion. If in B 41 Heraclitus is contrasting wisdom with 'much-learning' (as is suggested by D.L. 9. 1, where B 41 immediately succeeds B 40), he must have in mind a sort of expertise which human polymaths should have sought, but he need not view this expertise as an exclusively human preserve.

[19] See Kirk, *Heraclitus*, 399. C. H. Kahn suggests that B 108 claims *both* that wisdom cannot be attained by men *and* that Heraclitus' 'divine principle', foreshadowing Anaxagoras' νοῦς, is 'separate or transcendent'; see *The Art and Thought of Heraclitus* [*Heraclitus*] (Cambridge, 1979), 115.

of wisdom and folly. On this reading, the fragment qualifies his characterization of all things, and is thus not an isolated claim but very much a part of Heraclitus' programme. This would explain why Heraclitus' predecessors, despite their reverence for (or delusions of) wisdom, failed to appreciate its distinctiveness; if one is to see why wisdom is different from everything else, one needs to understand not only wisdom but also the nature of everything else, and that is to see the world as Heraclitus did. Another fragment may confirm this interpretation of B 108:

ἓν τὸ σοφὸν μοῦνον λέγεσθαι οὐκ ἐθέλει καὶ ἐθέλει Ζηνὸς ὄνομα. (B 32)

One thing, the wise only, is unwilling and willing to be spoken of by the name of Zeus.

This fragment has been read, like B 108, as putting wisdom beyond the reach of mortals, but should be read, like B 108, as exempting wisdom from the unity of opposites. The syntax and punctuation are uncertain, but μοῦνον has most frequently been taken to belong with the preceding phrase and to restrict the attribution of wisdom to a single subject: only this god is wise.[20] Here again it has been noted that elsewhere Heraclitus envisages humans becoming wise, and here again scholars have devised a distinction between human and divine wisdom to explain the discrepancy.[21]

Stokes has made a more promising suggestion: μοῦνον does indeed restrict the attribution of wisdom, but restricts the attribution not to a single subject but to a single predicate.[22] On this reading, Heraclitus' suggestion is not that only god should be character-

[20] So Kirk, *Heraclitus*, 393–5; Marcovich, *Heraclitus*, 445. Kahn suggests that μοῦνον could be taken with both the preceding and the following phrases, and concludes that *both* readings should be understood as parts of 'the expression of a total view' (*Heraclitus*, 268–71).

[21] 'Wisdom in the full sense is accessible only to the divine ruler of the universe, since it means mastering the plan by which the cosmos is governed. For human beings such wisdom can serve only as an ideal target, a goal to be pursued by *homologein*, by agreement with the *logos*: putting one's own thought, speech, and action in harmony with the universal course of things' (Kahn, *Heraclitus*, 268). Marcovich, *Heraclitus*, 445, suggests that τὸ σοφόν in B 32 refers to 'the divine principle', 'the only *truly* wise being' (emphasis original). Compare Gigon, *Heraklit*, 138; Robinson, *Heraclitus*, 102.

[22] M. C. Stokes, *One and Many in Presocratic Philosophy* (Washington, 1971), 300 n. 75. As Stokes argues, the position of μοῦνον supports his reading over Kirk's, for μόνος takes attributive position when it is an attribute. See R. Kühner, *Ausführliche Grammatik der griechischen Sprache*, pt. 2. *Satzlehre*, rev. B. Gerth (2 vols.; Hanover, 1898–1904), i. 621; H. W. Smyth, *Greek Grammar* (Cambridge, Mass., 1956), 296.

ized as wise, but that god should be characterized only as wise.
As Stokes notes, traditionally anthropomorphic descriptions of the
god would thus be excluded, which would explain god's reluctance
to be called 'Zeus'. But the fragment would also suggest that god's
only *epistemic* property is wisdom; the god is only wise, and not
foolish as well.

B 32 thus provides both an example of, and a striking exception
to, the unity of opposites. The name 'Zeus' both misleads and informs us about god, given its association with traditional cult and
its suggestion of 'living', ζῆν.[23] God is like and unlike the Zeus of
cult and poetry,[24] and experiences both life and death. For B 62
suggests that even immortals undergo death as well as life; Heraclitus does not explain how this is true of god, but if god is day and
night, summer and winter (B 67), he may undergo death as he is
changed from one to the other, just as water 'dies' when it becomes
earth (B 36). So the very fact that 'Zeus' is only *partly* an accurate
name for god captures a powerful truth about his embodiment of
opposites, death and life; its partial aptness is itself informative.
But god is not only one thing, ἕν, but is wise without being foolish.
So god's wisdom exempts him from the unity of opposites, though
his immortality does not.

If this account of wisdom is correct, Heraclitus might concede
other exceptions to the unity thesis. Wisdom is 'speaking the truth',
as well as acting with understanding (B 112).[25] So if wisdom is
distinct from folly, the *truth* of what is known and disclosed by the
wise should be distinct from falsehood; we could of course surmise
as much from B 1, where Heraclitus promises to distinguish each
thing 'according to its constitution' and explain 'how it is', and
describes his account as true.[26] B 108 has itself been taken to make
this very point, to exclude the principles known by the wise from

[23] For the claim that Ζηνός in B 32 recalls ζῆν see Hussey, 'Heraclitus', 108; Kahn,
*Heraclitus*, 270. Kirk (*Heraclitus*, 392) and Marcovich (*Heraclitus*, 445–6) both note
that Heraclitus uses the alternative Διός in B 120 and so seem over-cautious in
denying that Heraclitus has etymology in mind when he opts for Ζηνός in B 32.

[24] See Marcovich, *Heraclitus*, 446.

[25] The authenticity of B 112 has been challenged by Kirk, *Heraclitus*, 390, but
see Kahn, *Heraclitus*, 120.

[26] Assuming ἐόντος to be veridical; see Marcovich, *Heraclitus*, 9. Compare later
Sceptical readings of Heraclitus, where the *principle* of conflicting appearances is
regarded as commonly accepted, and therefore true; see R. Polito, *The Sceptical
Road: Aenesidemus' Appropriation of Heraclitus* (Leiden, 2004), 56–9. My thanks to
Roberto Polito for bringing this comparison to my attention.

8    *Alex Long*

the unity of opposites.[27] If so, 'the wise' in B 108 would refer to what is known (as in B 41), as well as to the knower (as in B 32), and exempt both the truth of the former and the wisdom of the latter. Heraclitus might also except the product of wisdom. Whereas humans have supposed some things to be just, others unjust, for god *everything* is fair, good, and just (B 102); there is no suggestion that everything is also bad and unjust, or really a synthesis of justice and injustice.[28] And our source suggests that the world's goodness is not merely apparent from the divine perspective, but produced by the divine administration;[29] if this is right, Heraclitus may believe that god's wise governance ensures that the world's goodness is not tainted by injustice. This may have an analogue for the human sage: if wisdom is to have a practical application, as B 112 suggests, we would expect the wise man to bring about consistently *good* results when he acts from knowledge. If so, Heraclitus would hold a rather Socratic view on the essential connection between wisdom and goodness,[30] whereby wisdom, free from folly, would ensure that its products are not contaminated by badness and injustice.

## 2. Poetic wisdom?

In two fragments Heraclitus might be thought to describe a poet as both wise and foolish and so to countenance epistemic cases of the unity thesis. But neither poet, I shall argue, is really granted wisdom. The first claimant, Hesiod, can be quickly dismissed:

διδάσκαλος δὲ πλείστων Ἡσίοδος· τοῦτον ἐπίστανται πλεῖστα εἰδέναι, ὅστις ἡμέρην καὶ εὐφρόνην οὐκ ἐγίνωσκεν· ἔστι γὰρ ἕν. (B 57)

---

[27] So Conche, *Héraclite*, 238–9. (Contrast Mackenzie, 'Heraclitus', where she argues that the unity thesis applies to itself and to other principles about the world.) P. K. Curd also seems to read σοφόν in B 108 as the *object* of knowledge, arguing that the fragment contrasts 'the phenomena of the everyday world' with 'the world of knowledge and wisdom'; see her 'Knowledge and Unity in Heraclitus', *Monist*, 74 (1991), 531–49 at 535.

[28] As Marcovich has noted (*Heraclitus*, 482). It is not clear to what extent men are misguided in their division of just and unjust things; for discussion see Kirk, *Heraclitus*, 181; Marcovich, *Heraclitus*, 484. The authenticity of B 102 has been disputed, but see Marcovich, *Heraclitus*, 481–2.

[29] συντελεῖ γὰρ ἅπαντα ὁ θεὸς πρὸς ἁρμονίαν τῶν ὅλων, οἰκονομῶν τὰ συμφέροντα: Porph. *Qu. Hom.* ad *Il.* 4. 4; *Scholia Graeca in Homeri Iliadem*, ed. W. Dindorf (6 vols.; Oxford, 1877), iii. 194. We might of course compare B 41 and B 64.

[30] Compare *Meno* 87 C–89 A and *Euthd.* 279 D–282 D.

Hesiod is the teacher of most. They are sure that he knows the most, he who did not recognize day and night—for they are one.

It has been noted that Heraclitus uses ἐπίσταμαι (usually translated 'know') to describe the conviction of Hesiod's admirers, and the conclusion has been drawn that they are right, in Heraclitus' eyes, to ascribe knowledge of 'the most' to the poet. On the other hand, Hesiod is said not to have recognized day and night, which hardly befits the author of a poem entitled *Works and Days*,[31] and so he seems to have been scandalously ignorant as well as widely knowledgeable.[32] But, as Kirk notes, ἐπίσταμαι need not be veridical in Heraclitus' Greek, for Herodotus uses the verb of clearly mistaken convictions (1. 122; 3. 139; 8. 25).[33] And so, given Heraclitus' disparagement of Hesiod elsewhere (B 40), there seems no reason to believe that Heraclitus endorsed the view of the poet's enthusiasts, and so no reason to read B 57 as a paradox about combined knowledge and ignorance.[34]

The second claimant, Homer, will detain us for longer:

ἐξηπάτηνται οἱ ἄνθρωποι πρὸς τὴν γνῶσιν τῶν φανερῶν παραπλησίως Ὁμήρῳ, ὃς ἐγένετο τῶν Ἑλλήνων σοφώτερος πάντων. ἐκεῖνόν τε γὰρ παῖδες φθεῖρας κατακτείνοντες ἐξηπάτησαν εἰπόντες· ὅσα εἴδομεν καὶ ἐλάβομεν, ταῦτα ἀπολείπομεν, ὅσα δὲ οὔτε εἴδομεν οὔτ᾽ ἐλάβομεν, ταῦτα φέρομεν. (B 56)

People are deceived in recognizing the obvious, like Homer, who was wiser than all the Greeks. For he was deceived by boys killing lice, who said: 'We leave behind what we saw and caught, but we carry what we didn't see or catch.'

Homer (foolishly) failed to decipher a simple riddle, and yet, in an apparent instance of the unity thesis, he is described as 'wiser' than

[31] But Heraclitus' polemic is also directed at *Theogony* 123–4 and (perhaps) 748–57; see Kahn, *Heraclitus*, 109; Kirk, *Heraclitus*, 155–7.

[32] See Mackenzie, 'Heraclitus', 19–20; on her account, 'Hesiod both knows and does not know', as he has grasped the opposition between night and day (an instance of 'the opposition of unity') but failed to grasp their unity (an instance of 'the unity of opposites'). Her conclusion (23): 'the unity of opposites/opposition of unity applies also in the epistemological sphere'.

[33] See Kirk, *Heraclitus*, 155; Marcovich, *Heraclitus*, 223. For other examples see J. E. Powell, *A Lexicon to Herodotus*, 2nd edn. (Hildesheim, 1960), s.v. 3.

[34] Mackenzie, 'Heraclitus', 18 n. 30, takes the description of Hesiod as a 'teacher' to support her reading of B 57 as a paradox about knowledge, stressing the contrast between B 57 and B 40, where, on her account, Hesiod and others 'are said to have been taught nothing by their polymathy'. But there Hesiod is said specifically not to have been taught 'intellect' or 'understanding'; his polymathy could still have taught him *something* (albeit something of dubious value) to pass on to his followers.

other Greeks. It is tempting simply to dismiss the attribution of wisdom as ironic and so to read the fragment as purely contemptuous of Homer; we might compare B 129, where Pythagoras is said to have devised a (clearly bogus) 'wisdom of his own' (ἑαυτοῦ σοφίη).[35] Or we might take Heraclitus to have in mind merely Homer's *reputation* as a sage.[36] But these temptations should be resisted. For the text does not present its ascription of wisdom as ironic or dialectical, and Heraclitus' point is strongest if the ascription is correct; if Homer really was wiser than any other Greek, then confusion in *him* gives us a compelling reason to doubt our own ability to understand the obvious.

But then to what extent was Homer wise, and in what did the poet's pre-eminence consist? I suggest that Heraclitus found in Homer recognition of the pervasiveness of conflict, and that he thought that this insight gave Homer better understanding of the world than that enjoyed by any other Greek; unfortunately, in Heraclitus' eyes, Homer failed to take proper advantage of this insight, and so failed to achieve wisdom. For while Homer recognized that conflict is pervasive, he taught us to lament rather than to welcome its ubiquity, failing to appreciate that conflict is integral to the preservation of the world.

Homer's insight is recognized in B 80, where Heraclitus alludes to the *Iliad*:

εἰδέναι δὲ χρὴ τὸν πόλεμον ἐόντα ξυνόν, καὶ δίκην ἔριν, καὶ γινόμενα πάντα κατ' ἔριν καὶ χρεών. (B 80)

One must know that war is common and justice is strife, and that everything happens in accordance with strife and necessity.

ξυνὸς Ἐνυάλιος, καί τε κτανέοντα κατέκτα. (*Il.* 18. 309)

The War-god is common, and kills the man that would kill.[37]

In the Homeric passage Hector claims that the War-god and his

---

[35] See Granger, 'Polymathy', 250; Kahn, *Heraclitus*, 172. M. C. Nussbaum, 'ψυχή in Heraclitus', *Phronesis*, 17 (1972), 1–16, 153–70, suggests that Heraclitus frequently, but 'implicitly', faults Homer.

[36] So Marcovich, *Heraclitus*, 82, where ὃς ἐγένετο τῶν Ἑλλήνων σοφώτερος πάντων is rendered 'although he was (considered) wiser than any other Greek'.

[37] The overlap between the Heraclitean fragment and the Homeric passage is slim, but in A 22 Heraclitus clearly refers to another passage from *Iliad* 18, which suggests that in B 80 the echo of *Il.* 18. 309 is unlikely to be an accident. Kirk, *Heraclitus*, 240, counts as possible evidence against a Homeric allusion the fact that Heraclitus does not use the personification 'Enyalios'. But Heraclitus could have omitted this personification in order to refer to two poets simultaneously; as Kahn,

help (or enmity) are 'common' to both sides and may overwhelm even the mighty Achilles. On Heraclitus' reading, this points to a deeper sense in which war is 'common': war is universal, and the whole world is pervaded by strife (B 53), albeit by different kinds of conflict from that illustrated in Homer's epic. For Heraclitus is interested in cosmic strife, as well as human warfare, noting the way in which opposed qualities are in tension with one another (A 22, B 51), and the way in which opposed sorts of stuff (such as earth and water) violently replace one another (B 31, B 36).

It has been suggested that B 80 is polemical not only in subject-matter but also in intent, faulting Homer's sayings about war.[38] But if B 80 indicates qualified approval of Homer's epic, we can explain why Heraclitus describes Homer as 'wiser' in B 56 and why Homer (unlike Hesiod) is omitted from the list of authorities chastised for their lack of understanding in B 40. So I suggest that B 80 indicates not censure but an idiosyncratically Heraclitean understanding of Hector's pronouncement; for Heraclitus, the *Iliad*'s reflections on human conflict, correctly understood, point to the dominance of strife in our world.

Such a creative interpretation of Homer is intelligible and can be paralleled. Intelligible, because the *Iliad* is saturated with conflict; not only does conflict dominate many of the scenes of the epic, but the setting of the entire work is a state of war. For Homer, famously, describes a short episode that takes place within the Trojan War, and does not narrate the conflict's beginning or end. So the *Iliad*'s scenes are dominated by, and its plot immersed in, a war. Little wonder, then, that Heraclitus attributed to Homer an insight that made him wiser than other Greeks. And the view of human war as an emblem of cosmic strife has parallels in Heraclitus' fragments. Adomėnas has argued persuasively that Heraclitus values human religious traditions for the way in which they embody the cosmic unity of opposites.[39] For example, the paradoxical way in which blood can both defile and ritually purify (B 5) points to a deeper

---

*Heraclitus*, 205, notes, in B 80 Heraclitus also alludes to Archilochus fr. 38 Diehl, where Archilochus echoes *Il*. 18. 309 but replaces 'Enyalios' with 'Ares'.

[38] Kahn, *Heraclitus*, 205, 207; Marcovich, *Heraclitus*, 137. Whether or not the fragment has polemical intent against Anaximander is of course another matter; see G. Vlastos, 'On Heraclitus' ['Heraclitus'], in id., *Studies in Greek Philosophy*, i. *The Presocratics*, ed. D. W. Graham (Princeton, 1995), 127–50 at 141–3; Marcovich, *Heraclitus*, 138–40.

[39] M. Adomėnas, 'Heraclitus on Religion', *Phronesis*, 44 (1999), 87–113.

cosmic paradox about opposites. Traditional religious observances, properly decoded, contain powerful truths about the world. I suggest that Heraclitus values this traditional literature in a similar way. But despite perceiving the rule of strife, Homer failed to understand its role. For Heraclitus, we are told, took the poet to task for having Achilles pray that strife might be eradicated from gods and men (A 22);[40] in Heraclitus' view, Homer failed to grasp that the world is maintained by, as well as infused with, conflict. This error may explain Heraclitus' declaration that Homer (and Archilochus) should be violently expelled from public recitals (B 42).[41] Homer encourages us to bemoan the very phenomenon to which he alludes; since he (like Archilochus) draws attention to the universal presence of strife, his misguided plea for strife to cease calls all the more urgently for punishment and censorship.

So for Heraclitus Homer was wiser than his compatriots, and yet mistaken. But this is not to say that Homer was both wise and foolish, for Heraclitus would not grant that Homer was 'wise' at all. Heraclitus reserves 'wisdom' for those who understand how everything is governed (B 41) and thus have *complete* understanding of the world; the positive σοφός is, so to speak, implicitly superlative.[42] But with the comparative he shows more lenience, allowing someone who has achieved a particular insight to be 'wiser' than others.

There is a celebrated parallel for this liberal use of comparative and stringent use of positive. In Plato's *Apology* Socrates believes himself to be wiser than his fellow Athenians, and yet is unsure whether he really is wise.[43] When Socrates claims that he is wiser than his fellow citizens (21 D 2–3, 22 C 6–8), he does so with apparent confidence,[44] given the oracle's verdict (21 A) and the evidence gathered in his enquiry. He calls one human 'wiser' than another

---

[40] The ancient accounts offer a variety of explanations for Heraclitus' rebuke; see Kirk, *Heraclitus*, 242–4. Marcovich, *Heraclitus*, 140–2, suggests that the testimonies in A 22 are merely recollections of B 80, but it seems unlikely that the entire quotation of *Il.* 18. 107 would have been added by Aristotle as a 'commentary' on B 80.

[41] Marcovich, *Heraclitus*, 152, cautiously suggests that in B 42 Heraclitus has in mind his conception of war. For Archilochus see n. 37 above. The neat play on 'rhapsody' in ῥαπίζεσθαι is noted by G. W. Most, 'The Poetics of Early Greek Philosophy', in A. A. Long (ed.), *The Cambridge Companion to Early Greek Philosophy* (Cambridge, 1999), 332–62 at 338.

[42] I owe this wording to David Sedley.

[43] Compare also Plato, *Phdr.* 243 B (where Socrates calls himself 'wiser' than Homer and Stesichorus) with 278 D (where Socrates says that only god is 'wise').

[44] But his claim to be wiser is put more tentatively at *Ap.* 21 D 6–7 (ἔοικα) and 29 B 4–6.

when the first enjoys a particular piece of knowledge which the second does not have (22 D 3–4), or when the second suffers from a particular delusion from which the first is free (21 D 2–8, 29 B 4–6). However, he is uncertain whether any human is *wise*, proposing that it is really god who is wise (23 A 5–6).[45] Socrates of course suggests that he possesses *human* wisdom (20 D 6–9), but then he seems to doubt whether this really constitutes wisdom (20 E 6–7),[46] despite all the evidence that he is wis*er* than his contemporaries.

So too in Heraclitus' fragments Homer is said to be 'wiser' than his fellow Greeks and yet is not portrayed as wise. But, unlike Socrates, Heraclitus does not even entertain the notion of distinct *human* wisdom, and attributes wisdom only to those who have achieved full knowledge of the world's governance. Given his claim that wisdom is unitary, he cannot demarcate a separate wisdom for humans,[47] and in any case he simply has no need for such a recourse, for he grants that full understanding of the world is within our grasp.[48] Heraclitus cannot grant and need not grant that Homer was wise, let alone both wise and foolish. And so his subtle reading and qualified praise of Homer do not supply us with an epistemic case of the unity of opposites.

### 3. Wisdom as unitary

In my introduction I set out reasons why Heraclitus might have been motivated to exempt wisdom from the unity thesis. Does he ever argue for this exemption? Not explicitly. But I shall conclude by briefly suggesting that his characterization of wisdom provides the basis for such an argument; the nature of wisdom and the nature of the world guarantee that the wise person will not be foolish.

There has been some recent controversy about the extent to

[45] For Socrates god's claim to wisdom may rest on his knowledge of the most important subjects. *Ap.* 20 D 9–E 2 and its reference to the knowledge claimed by sophists (described at 20 B 2–5) suggest that divine wisdom is or at least involves knowledge of human and civic virtue.

[46] See also 38 C 3–4, where Socrates states that others will call him 'wise' even if he is not. Stokes suggests that in 38 C Socrates grants only that he may lack conventional expertise or knowledge of the natural world, but I cannot see such circumscription in the text. See M. C. Stokes, *Plato:* Apology (Warminster, 1997), 21.

[47] Compare p. 2 and n. 18 above.

[48] See pp. 4–5 above. In n. 54, however, I suggest a contrast between the ways in which humans and gods can *exercise* their wisdom.

14                    *Alex Long*

which Heraclitus uses argument. Although in some fragments he offers directly an explanation or premiss for his claim (as in, for example, B 1, B 57, B 85, B 88, B 114), these passages are not the norm. Barnes rightly notes that Heraclitus uses arguments, though he seems to go too far in claiming that we are promised 'a continuous and systematic treatise' by the style and content of B 1.[49] But happily we need not take such a view of Heraclitus' book if we are to read Heraclitus as a philosopher who argues; as Barnes himself would later note, even though Heraclitus' work may have contained some isolated passages without inferential or even connective particles, 'often enough the connection of thought is visible despite the lack of connectives'.[50] There may thus be more to Heraclitus' argumentation than the scarceness of explicit arguments would suggest.[51] And I propose that his discussion of wisdom contains an example of indirect argumentation.

Heraclitus claims not only that wisdom consists in grasping the way in which the world is directed, but that the content of wisdom is unitary:

ἓν τὸ σοφόν· ἐπίστασθαι γνώμην ὅκη κυβερνᾶται[52] πάντα διὰ πάντων. (B 41)

The wise is one, knowing how the judgement steers all things through all.

[49] Barnes, *Philosophers*, 600 n. 6; see also 75. For a judicious *via media* between aphoristic and continuous readings of Heraclitus, see H. Granger, 'Argumentation and Heraclitus' Book' ['Argumentation'], *Oxford Studies in Ancient Philosophy*, 26 (2004), 1–18.

[50] Barnes, 'Aphorism and Argument', in K. Robb (ed.), *Language and Thought in Early Greek Philosophy* (La Salle, 1983), 91–109 at 105.

[51] So Granger, 'Argumentation', 14; Mackenzie, 'Heraclitus', 4–7. A reason for Heraclitus' coyness with explicit arguments has been set out already in the literature; to understand the world we need to rethink what is already common and obvious to us all (B 2, B 56), rather than to be convinced of a wholly unfamiliar thesis, and so Heraclitus' programme is to help us 'to redescribe or find the meaning in what we know already' (M. Schofield, 'Heraclitus' Theory of Soul and its Antecedents', in S. Everson (ed.), *Psychology* (Cambridge, 1991), 13–34 at 18).

[52] The transmitted texts (ὁτέη κυβερνῆσαι/ὅτε ἢ κυβερνῆσαι/ὅτ᾽ ἐνκυβερνῆσαι) are corrupt, and emendations vary; for alternatives see Marcovich, *Heraclitus*, 449. I have followed Kirk's emendation, but read κυβερνᾶται as middle rather than passive. Heraclitus may thus be stressing that the divine judgement steers everything relying simply on itself; compare Cleanthes' Zeus, who steers everything 'relying on the γνώμη' (*Hymn.* 34–5). As Kahn, *Heraclitus*, 54, notes, Heraclitus' use of ὅκη in B 117 gives some support for emending ὁτέη to ὅκη in B 41; see also ibid. 321 n. 204. Plutarch's recollection of B 41 (ὅπως [emended to ὅτῳ] κυβερνᾶται, *De Iside* 382 B) also gives some support for emending κυβερνῆσαι to κυβερνᾶται rather than to ἐκυβέρνησε. For these and other possible recollections of B 41 see Marcovich, *Heraclitus*, 447–8; none has a form of κυβερνάω in the aorist, as Kirk, *Heraclitus*, 388, notes. Kirk took ἐπίστασθαι γνώμην to mean merely 'to be skilled in true judgement', but Marcovich,

The divine pilotage is universal, steering all things through all the stages of their development, and this can explain why wisdom is one. For if everything is directed by the same agent and in the same way, knowledge of this governance will enable us to understand any instance or product of it in the world. One and the same insight will prepare us for all our encounters with the world, thanks to the fundamental homogeneity of the world's regime; the monism of Heraclitus' wisdom follows from the monism of his world. Heraclitus may have this in mind when he describes the wisest soul as a ray or gleam of light (αὐγή, B 118).[53] The wise soul's insight into the world's governance will illuminate and enable her to understand whatever she encounters; she will both light up and intelligently perceive any object of her scrutiny, just as αὐγή is not only light but also the eye that would perceive in that light.[54]

It follows that the wise will not be foolish; the simplicity of wisdom ensures that it is never embodied together with its opposite. God both maintains and thoroughly understands the pilotage of all things, and a wise soul, although she will not directly encounter or know about everything in the world, will none the less understand anything she does encounter, because the principles and traits in her grasp are common to all things. One such principle is of course the unity of opposites. So Heraclitus' very conception of the world as unified by common characteristics exempts wisdom from that characterization.

*St Catharine's College, Cambridge*

---

*Heraclitus*, 451–2, and Vlastos, 'Heraclitus', 138–9, argue effectively against this reading.

[53] I follow Bollack–Wismann, Conche, and Kahn (and now S. N. Mouraviev, *Heraclitea: III.3.B*, i. *Textes, traductions, apparats I–III* (Sankt Augustin, 2006)) in retaining Stobaeus' full text; for defence of this reading see Kahn, *Heraclitus*, 245–6.

[54] Most famously in Plato, *Rep.* 540 A 7; for an earlier use of αὐγή to mean 'eye' see the Homeric *Hymn to Hermes* 361. The plural of αὐγή often means 'rays' of light (rather than merely 'gleams' of light); should Heraclitus have this sense in mind, B 118 may suggest a contrast between god and humans. Like a ray of light, at any one time a soul's attention must always be focused on or directed at a specific part or aspect of the world, whereas in that time god will be considering and directing the entire world. But a basic kinship remains; the wise soul will understand anything she considers, thanks to the insights she shares with god.

## BIBLIOGRAPHY

Adomėnas, M., 'Heraclitus on Religion', *Phronesis*, 44 (1999), 87–113.

Barnes, J., *The Presocratic Philosophers* [*Philosophers*], rev. edn. (London, 1982).

—— 'Aphorism and Argument', in K. Robb (ed.), *Language and Thought in Early Greek Philosophy* (La Salle, 1983), 91–109.

Bollack, J., and Wismann, H., *Héraclite ou la séparation* (Paris, 1972).

Conche, M., *Héraclite: Fragments* [*Héraclite*] (Paris, 1986).

Curd, P. K., 'Knowledge and Unity in Heraclitus', *Monist*, 74 (1991), 531–49.

Diels, H., *Die Fragmente der Vorsokratiker*, 6th edn., rev. W. Kranz [*Fragmente*] (3 vols.; Berlin, 1951).

Dindorf, W. (ed.), *Scholia Graeca in Homeri Iliadem* (6 vols.; Oxford, 1877).

Gigon, O., *Untersuchungen zu Heraklit* [*Heraklit*] (Leipzig, 1935).

Graham, D. W., 'Heraclitus' Criticism of Ionian Philosophy', *Oxford Studies in Ancient Philosophy*, 15 (1997), 1–50.

Granger, H., 'Argumentation and Heraclitus' Book' ['Argumentation'], *Oxford Studies in Ancient Philosophy*, 26 (2004), 1–18.

—— 'Heraclitus' Quarrel with Polymathy and *Historiē*' ['Polymathy'], *Transactions of the American Philological Association*, 134 (2004), 235–61.

Guthrie, W. K. C., *A History of Greek Philosophy*, i. *The Earlier Presocratics and the Pythagoreans* (Cambridge, 1962).

Hussey, E., *The Presocratics* [*Presocratics*] (London, 1972).

—— 'Heraclitus', in A. A. Long (ed.), *The Cambridge Companion to Early Greek Philosophy* (Cambridge, 1999), 88–112.

Kahn, C. H., *The Art and Thought of Heraclitus* [*Heraclitus*] (Cambridge, 1979).

Kirk, G. S., *Heraclitus: The Cosmic Fragments* [*Heraclitus*] (Cambridge, 1954).

Kühner, R., *Ausführliche Grammatik der griechischen Sprache*, pt. 2. *Satzlehre*, rev. B. Gerth (2 vols.; Hanover, 1898–1904).

Mackenzie, M. M., 'Heraclitus and the Art of Paradox' ['Heraclitus'], *Oxford Studies in Ancient Philosophy*, 6 (1988), 1–38.

Marcovich, M., *Heraclitus: Greek Text with a Short Commentary*, 2nd edn. [*Heraclitus*] (Sankt Augustin, 2001).

Most, G. W., 'The Poetics of Early Greek Philosophy', in A. A. Long (ed.), *The Cambridge Companion to Early Greek Philosophy* (Cambridge, 1999), 332–62.

Mouraviev, S. N., *Heraclitea: III.3.B*, i. *Textes, traductions, apparats I–III* (Sankt Augustin, 2006).

Nehamas, A., 'Parmenidean Being/Heraclitean Fire', in V. Caston and D. W. Graham (eds.), *Presocratic Philosophy: Essays in Honour of Alexander Mourelatos* (Aldershot, 2002), 45–64.

Nussbaum, M. C., 'ψυχή in Heraclitus', *Phronesis*, 17 (1972), 1–16, 153–70.

Polito, R., *The Sceptical Road: Aenesidemus' Appropriation of Heraclitus* (Leiden, 2004).

Powell, J. E., *A Lexicon to Herodotus*, 2nd edn. (Hildesheim, 1960).

Rankin, D., 'Limits on Perception and Cognition in Heraclitus' Fragments', *Elenchos*, 16 (1995), 241–52.

Robinson, T. M., *Heraclitus: Fragments [Heraclitus]* (Toronto, 1987).

Schofield, M., 'Heraclitus' Theory of Soul and its Antecedents', in S. Everson (ed.), *Psychology* (Cambridge, 1991), 13–34.

Smyth, H. W., *Greek Grammar* (Cambridge, Mass., 1956).

Stokes, M. C., *One and Many in Presocratic Philosophy* (Washington, 1971).

—— *Plato: Apology* (Warminster, 1997).

Vlastos, G., 'On Heraclitus' ['Heraclitus'], in id., *Studies in Greek Philosophy*, i. *The Presocratics*, ed. D. W. Graham (Princeton, 1995), 127–50.

# ANAXAGORAS ON PERCEPTION, PLEASURE, AND PAIN

## JAMES WARREN

ALTHOUGH he is known primarily for his thesis of universal mixture and his use of *Nous* as some kind of cosmogonic principle, Anaxagoras also offered more detailed accounts of various topics in natural philosophy. Like many other early natural philosophers, he gave an account of humans' interaction with the world via the powers of perception. On this matter, he offered the arresting slogan that 'every perception is accompanied by pain' (πᾶσαν αἴσθησιν μετὰ λύπης).[1] Like other famous Anaxagorean pronouncements, this is a deliberately paradoxical expression. It chimes with the general thesis of universal mixture at least to the extent that just as we might be surprised to learn that everything in the world is composed of every other thing, so too we are surprised to learn that every perception, even those which appear to be most pleasant, is accompanied by pain.

Our primary evidence for this Anaxagorean doctrine is Theophrastus' *De sensibus*, in which Theophrastus outlines what he takes to be Anaxagoras' reasons for holding such a view (27–30) and offers his own rebuttal of the idea (31–5). This is followed by a section which discusses the specific question of the nature of visual images, colour, and reflection (36–7). Further, Theophrastus contrasts Anaxagoras' view with that of Empedocles. Empedocles, we are told, insisted that pleasure and perception are both caused by the interaction of like with like (16–17), whereas Anaxagoras insisted

© James Warren 2007

My thanks in particular to Malcolm Schofield, who shared some of his Anaxagorean expertise in discussing an earlier draft. I received generous and helpful comments also from Jim Porter and David Sedley. A version of part of this paper was given at the Institute of Classical Studies, London, in October 2006.

[1] Thphr. *De sens.* 17: καίτοι πολλάκις αἰσθανόμενοι λυπούμεθα κατ᾽ αὐτὴν τὴν αἴσθησιν, ὡς ⟨δ᾽⟩ Ἀναξαγόρας φησίν, ἀεί· πᾶσαν γὰρ αἴσθησιν εἶναι μετὰ λύπης; 29: ἅπασαν δ᾽ αἴσθησιν μετὰ λύπης, ὅπερ ἂν δόξειεν ἀκόλουθον εἶναι τῇ ὑποθέσει.

that perception is caused by the interaction of unlikes (27). This contrast allows Theophrastus to underline his primary criterion for the categorization of these early accounts of sense-perception and the principal organizing strategy of his work (1–2). Theophrastus attempts to convict Anaxagoras of giving a false account of pain and of failing to be able to give a satisfactory account of pleasure. It appears, however, that Anaxagoras would have reasonable grounds for a complaint of unfair treatment by Theophrastus and that his attempt to claim a close link between pain and each and every act of perception has something to be said for it.

## 1. The evidence

Apart from Theophrastus' *De sensibus*, the primary pieces of evidence for this assertion by Anaxagoras are collected at A 94 DK, and foremost among those is a passage from Aspasius' commentary on Aristotle's *Nicomachean Ethics*. This is important because it both contains a number of Theophrastan objections to Anaxagoras and also leads us back to the Aristotelian source text and to some questions about an important additional note to Anaxagoras' theory:

τὸ δὲ "μηδέτερον" τὸ μήτε ἥδεσθαι μήτε λυπεῖσθαι "πολλοῖς λυπηρὸν" †καὶ τὸ δοκεῖν ἡ κρατίστη αὐτῷ εἶναι κατάστασις· ὃ δέ φησι πολλοῖς ἀλγεινὸν εἶναι, τοῦτο "διὰ τὴν φύσιν. ἀεὶ γὰρ πονεῖ τὸ ζῷον, ὥσπερ καὶ οἱ φυσιολόγοι" λέγουσιν. ὁ γὰρ Ἀναξαγόρας ἔλεγεν ἀεὶ πονεῖν τὸ ζῷον διὰ τῶν αἰσθήσεων. ταῦτα δὲ οὐχ ὡς συγκατατιθέμενος λέγει ἀλλ' ἱστορῶν· ἐπεὶ οὐκ ἐδόκει γε αὐτῷ ἀεὶ ἐν πόνῳ εἶναι τὸ ζῷον. καὶ τὸν Ἀναξαγόραν αἰτιᾶται Θεόφραστος ἐν Ἠθικοῖς λέγων ὅτι "ἐξελαύνει ἡδονὴ λύπην ἤ γε ἐναντία", οἷον ἡ ἀπὸ τοῦ πίνειν τὴν ἀπὸ τοῦ διψῆν, "καὶ ἡ τυχοῦσα", τουτέστιν ἥτις οὖν ἂν εἴη "ἰσχυρά", ὥστε ἐνίοτε πεῖναν ἐξελαύνει καὶ ἀκοῆς ἡδονή, ὅταν ᾄσμασιν ἢ ἄλλοις τισὶν ἀκούσμασι διαφερόντως χαίρωμεν. "καὶ διὰ ταῦτα ἀκόλαστοι" γίνονται ἄνθρωποι· ἵν' ὅλως γὰρ μὴ λυπῶνται μηδὲ ἀλγῶσι, μεγάλας καὶ σφοδρὰς ἡδονὰς ἑαυτοῖς πορίζουσι. (Aspas. *In EN* 1154ᵇ6–15, 156. 11–22 Heylbut = Thphr. fr. 555 FHS&G)

The 'neither', (i.e.) neither experiencing pleasure nor pain, is 'painful to many' . . . the best condition . . . And what he (Aristotle) says is grievous to many, this is 'on account of (their) nature. For an animal is always toiling, just as also the natural philosophers say.' For Anaxagoras used to say that an animal is always toiling through the senses. He (Aristotle) says this not as one agreeing but investigating, since it does not seem to him[2] that an animal is always toiling. And Theophrastus in the *Ethics* criticizes Anaxagoras by saying that 'pain is driven out by pleasure, at least that opposed (to it)', e.g. the pain resulting from thirst by the pleasure from drinking, 'and by any chance pleasure', i.e. by whatever pleasure might be 'strong'. Consequently hunger is sometimes driven out even by the pleasures of hearing, when we take exceptional delight in songs or something else we hear. 'And on account of this intemperance' develops in men. In order that they may not in any way experience pain or grief, they provide themselves with great and intense pleasures. (Translation based on FHS&G)

This evidence shows that Theophrastus returned to this Anaxagorean notion on at least two occasions, once in *De sensibus*,[3] and again in a work here referred to as *Ethics*.[4] There is also good evidence to suggest that he wrote at least one other work specifically about Anaxagoras.[5] Here, he is being used by Aspasius to help to elucidate a passage from Aristotle's *Nicomachean Ethics*, 7. 14, 1154[b]6–15, which does not itself mention Anaxagoras by name. Rather, Aristotle there refers more generally to 'natural philosophers' who claimed that animals are always toiling (ἀεὶ γὰρ πονεῖ τὸ ζῷον: 1154[b]7). Indeed, it is hard to imagine that without Theophrastus' and Aspasius' later discussions anyone would have thought that Anaxagoras in particular was in Aristotle's mind at this point. The only other reference to 'natural philosophers' in the

---

[2]  Reading αὐτῷ with Fortenbaugh rather than the MS αὐτοῖς printed by FHS&G.

[3]  There is some debate over the original place of what we know as *De sensibus* in Theophrastus' works. Diels, following Usener, classified it as part of a larger work, the *Phys. op.* Cf. H. Baltussen, 'Peripatetic Dialectic in the *De sensibus*' ['Peripatetic Dialectic'], in W. W. Fortenbaugh and D. Gutas (eds.), *Theophrastus: His Psychological, Doxographical and Scientific Writings* (New Brunswick, 1992), 1–19, and id., *Theophrastus against the Presocratics and Plato: Peripatetic Dialectic in the De sensibus* [*Theophrastus*] (Leiden, 2000), 239–45, who concludes that the evidence is inconclusive.

[4]  For evidence of a Theophrastan work by this name see Thphr. fr. 436 2a–b FHS&G. I accept Aspasius' attribution of the remark to Theophrastus, but for some scholars' doubts on the point see C. Natali in this volume, p. 365 n. 36.

[5]  Diogenes Laërtius lists two works at D.L. 5. 42: a Πρὸς Ἀναξαγόραν ᾱ and a Περὶ τῶν Ἀναξαγόρου ᾱ. Each seems to have been one book in length. Simpl. *In Phys.* 166. 15 ff. Diels (A 41 DK) refers to 'the second book of Theophrastus' *On Anaxagoras*', so perhaps these were also considered to be two books of the same work. Here and at 27. 2 ff. (also A 41 DK) Simplicius cites Theophrastus' discussion of Anaxagoras' claims that 'in everything there is a portion of everything' (B 12) and that there is no limit to division or extension and that all things are in every quantity, however large or small (B 3). It is possible, therefore, that in this work (or these works) Theophrastus limited himself to the discussion of Anaxagoras' physical theory and left discussion of perception and pleasure/pain to other works.

*Nicomachean Ethics* (at 7. 3, 1147ᵇ8–9) tells us that we should ask
them for an explanation of the physiology of the process by which
a drunk man can later shake off the temporary ignorance on which
akratic behaviour can be blamed; it is unlikely that Anaxagoras
alone is in Aristotle's mind on that occasion.[6]

In *NE* 7. 14 Aristotle is interested in explaining the nature and
value of physical pleasures and, in particular, the reasons why some
people are mistaken in their evaluation of them. There are two
important points for our purposes. First, Aristotle notes that some
people think physical pleasures particularly choiceworthy because
they drive out or displace (ἐκκρούει) pain (1154ᵃ25–6).[7] He also notes
at 1154ᵃ30–1 that some people pursue physical pleasures 'because
they appear opposed to the opposite' (i.e. pain). Aristotle agrees that
physical pleasures displace their opposite, pain, but denies that this
is a good reason to pursue intensely all physical pleasures; some
physical pleasures are neither desirable nor necessary, and their
intense pursuit can even be harmful to one's character. The two
claims, (i) that physical pleasure drives out or counteracts physical
pain, and (ii) that pleasure and pain are in this sense opposites, are
taken up by Theophrastus and used prominently in his criticisms
of Anaxagoras. We have already seen that, in the passage from
Aspasius, Theophrastus happily uses the idea that pleasure 'drives
out pain, being its opposite' (ἐξελαύνει ἡδονὴ λύπην ἤ γε ἐναντία)
and, again following Aristotle, diagnoses this as one of the causes
of wanton characters (ἀκόλαστοι).

Shortly after, at *NE* 1154ᵇ4–9, comes the passage which Aspasius
feels the need to explain and which prompts his references both to
Anaxagoras and to Theophrastus' criticisms. It is worth citing this
in full:

ὅταν μὲν οὖν ἀβλαβεῖς, ἀνεπιτίμητον, ὅταν δὲ βλαβεράς, φαῦλον. οὔτε γὰρ ἔχουσιν
ἕτερα ἐφ' οἷς χαίρουσιν, τό τε μηδέτερον πολλοῖς λυπηρὸν διὰ τὴν φύσιν. ἀεὶ

---

[6] Aristotle refers to Anaxagoras by name only in connection with his ethical pronouncements. At *NE* 1141ᵇ3–8 he and Thales are used as examples of the 'practically
wise' (φρόνιμοι), as distinct from the wise (σοφοί). At 1179ᵃ13–15 he is noted as saying that the happy man is not necessarily rich or powerful and, indeed, might seem
peculiar to many people. See *EE* 1215ᵇ5–14 for a longer discussion of this same
point, and cf. *EE* 1216ᵃ10–16.

[7] Compare *NE* 1119ᵇ8–10, where Aristotle discusses cases in which large and
intense appetites 'displace' reasoning (τὸν λογισμὸν ἐκκρούουσιν), and *NE* 1175ᵇ8,
where Aristotle notes that a greater pleasure can displace (ἐκκρούει) a lesser one.

γὰρ πονεῖ τὸ ζῷον, ὥσπερ καὶ οἱ φυσιολόγοι μαρτυροῦσι, τὸ ὁρᾶν, τὸ ἀκούειν
φάσκοντες εἶναι λυπηρόν· ἀλλ᾽ ἤδη συνήθεις ἐσμέν, ὡς φασίν.

When they [sc. the bodily pleasures they pursue] are harmless, then they
are not to be blamed; but when they are harmful, this is bad. For they have
no other objects of enjoyment, and to many what is neither pleasure nor
pain is painful, because of their nature. For an animal is always toiling—as
the natural philosophers testify when they say that seeing and hearing are
painful. But, as they say, we are now accustomed to it.

Aristotle is continuing his explanation of the potential pitfalls of a
mistaken evaluation of physical pleasures. Sometimes the pursuit
of physical pleasures, while not in fact contributing to the good life,
is at least blameless; some people are unable to enjoy other more
noble pleasures and contrive to enjoy various new physical pleasures instead. This is acceptable provided the physical pleasures
involved are harmless. But in other cases the constant search for
physical pleasures is not blameless. Some people are led to pursue
physical pleasures because they find themselves—owing to some
failing in their nature—in the position of being pained when in fact
they are in a state of feeling neither pleasure nor pain. This is, no
doubt, a deliberately paradoxical claim and there is no wonder that
Aspasius felt the need to offer some explanation of it. But Aristotle's
own explanation is reasonably clear. Some people are so corrupted
that when they are in fact in no need or lack and, moreover, are undergoing nothing which would properly produce either a pleasure
or pain, they find this state painful. We can imagine a person who,
unless he is at that moment experiencing some pleasure, finds his
state painful whether or not he is undergoing any real distress.[8] This
is the cause of their constant drive for pleasure and is the root of
their being self-indulgent and base (ἀκόλαστοι καὶ φαῦλοι, 1154ᵇ15).

Aristotle's reference here to the views of various 'natural philosophers' in order to account for such people is, nevertheless, puzzling.
The natural philosophers claim that we—as perceiving animals—
are in fact undergoing various kinds of exertion but tend not to
notice this because it is such a constant and necessary part of our
lives. Aristotle appears prepared to endorse their view. This is odd

---

[8] The 'objective' notion of what is pleasant will be grounded in Aristotle's normative conception of human nature and activity and therefore of what is naturally
pleasant and good for a human. Corrupted people enjoy what is pleasant *for them*
but not what is pleasant *by nature* or without qualification, i.e. what is pleasant to
the virtuous person. See S. Broadie, *Ethics with Aristotle* (Oxford, 1991), 357–63.

because it suggests that therefore the people we have just been discussing are in fact not in a neutral state of feeling neither pleasure nor pain. Instead, they—like the rest of us—are experiencing this constant background pain as they perceive. But, whereas for most of us this is simply a fact of our lives which we now fail significantly to register because we are so used to it, these people are led constantly to pursue physical pleasures since they feel pain even in the state where most people are content feeling neither pleasure nor pain. Perhaps these people are simply more prone to noticing this pain than the rest of us. Aristotle's overall argument wants to claim that the people afflicted with this particular and damaged nature are in fact in a neutral state but feel that they are in pain. They are mistaken about their true hedonic state and are therefore led to pursue unnecessary and potentially damaging pleasures. However, if the natural philosophers are right to think that perception is a kind of toil and therefore painful, perhaps it is those who do not feel pain who are mistaken, since what we might have thought of as a neutral state is in fact characterized by constant pain, only this pain is so constant that most people have come not to notice it. In that case, it is those who feel this pain who seem to be the best judges of what actually is the case; the rest of us simply fail to notice the constant pain of perception and mistakenly think that we are in a neutral state. The passage therefore presents, albeit in very compressed form, two symmetrical ways in which it is possible to feel. First, there are those whose natures are such as to feel pain while in a neutral state. Second, there is the view that all animals are in pain although most are so accustomed to this that they fail to register it.

  The consequences of this paragraph for the overall interpretation of Aristotle's argument in this chapter of the *Nicomachean Ethics* are relatively minor. But it is important to recognize that on any interpretation the argument in this brief section relies to a large degree on the second of two claims attributed by Aristotle to the 'natural philosophers'. Not only does he report their claim about the exertion of perception, but he adds their reply to the obvious objection to this claim. If, as they say, seeing and perceiving are such painful exertions, then why do we not always find ourselves in pain? Because, they reply, we—at least most of us—are now so accustomed to this that we simply fail to notice it any longer. This is what differentiates most of us from those whose nature is such that they do in fact feel in constant need of counteracting physical pleasures. If the first claim, about the pain of perception, is attributed to Anaxagoras, then it will be worth asking if the second claim, about our general failure to notice this pain, is also Anaxagorean. Aspasius is much less interested in this second claim than in the arresting slogan that 'an animal is always in distress'; his emphasis again follows Theophrastus, whose *De sensibus* contains no mention of the idea that most people are simply accustomed to the constant pain.

Before we move away from Aristotle, let us register a point about terminology. Aristotle explains that these 'natural philosophers' say that animals are constantly toiling (ἀεὶ γὰρ πονεῖ) because they say that 'seeing and hearing are painful' (τὸ ὁρᾶν, τὸ ἀκούειν φάσκοντες εἶναι λυπηρόν). The close connection made by Aristotle—and attributed by him to these natural philosophers—between 'toil' or 'exertion' (πόνος) and 'pain' (λύπη) explains the presence in our sources of two formulations of the Anaxagorean dictum. Aristotle and Theophrastus clearly felt that it was sufficiently legitimate to move between talk of πόνος and talk of pain for them to do so without comment. However, Aëtius' report of this Anaxagorean thesis retains a reference to πόνος without mention of λύπη.[9] It is difficult to know whether either of these formulations retains any original Anaxagorean vocabulary. Aristotle clearly felt there to be little significant distinction in meaning between λύπη and πόνος, and Theophrastus follows his lead. However, we might think that Anaxagoras could have insisted on some distinction between the two, and a consequence of this would be that Theophrastus' presentation of an Anaxagorean view that all perception involves, specifically, *pain* might be inaccurate. As we shall see, Theophrastus is very eager to show the difficulties faced by Anaxagoras as a result of the idea that all perception is caused by opposites, and all such interaction of opposites produces pain. How can this allow for pleasant sensations? But if Anaxagoras in fact held only that all perception involves exertion (that the animal does some work every time it perceives), then this is not clearly incompatible with holding that some perceptions are pleasant and others painful. In the *Eudemian Ethics* Aristotle himself, speculating on what might be the ideal life according to Anaxagoras, suggests that it might be one in which one lives 'painlessly [ἀλύπως] and purely with respect to what is just or sharing in some divine contemplation' (*EE*

[9] Aëtius 4. 9. 16 (Stob. *Ecl.* 1. 50. 32): Ἀναξαγόρας πᾶσαν αἴσθησιν μετὰ πόνου.

$1215^{b}11-14$). It would seem that if Aristotle, Theophrastus, and Aspasius interpret Anaxagoras correctly, the first of these conditions is impossible to fulfil while still doing any sort of perceiving. Now, perhaps Anaxagoras would simply say that the ideal life is impossible for humans to attain, given that they are perceivers, or perhaps this painlessness is compatible with our experiencing—but not noticing—the constant pain of perception. But there are still, I think, sufficient grounds for us to keep in mind the possibility that all the talk about pain in connection with Anaxagoras' views of perception is the product of a Peripatetic interpretation and not part of his own original thesis about the 'exertion' or 'toil' involved in perception.[10]

## 2. Theophrastus' presentation of Anaxagoras' argument

Theophrastus' first reference to the Anaxagorean thesis comes in a discussion of Empedocles. Empedocles, Theophrastus tells us, thought that perception came about through the interaction of 'likes' which enter the organs of sense through various passages. The arrangement and size of these passages may vary, which is supposed to account for differences in perceptual abilities between individuals and species.[11] Whatever the accuracy of this interpretation, it is relied upon by Theophrastus to highlight what he takes to be an inconsistency in Empedocles' thought. Empedocles also, we are told, considered pleasure and pain to be types of perception or concomitants of perception, but explained pleasure as caused by

[10] The relation between πόνος and λύπη is complicated, but there is room to argue for a distinction between the two. Xenophanes' god, for example, in B 25 governs everything ἀπάνευθε πόνοιο, which seems to suggest that his control is 'effortless' rather than 'without pain'. Yet the Epicureans designate the state of highest bodily pleasure, the removal of all bodily pains, ἀπονία. Also note Hipp. *Loc.* 7. 1: πόνος καὶ ὀδύνη . . . E. Craik, *Hippocrates: Places in Man* (Oxford, 1998), ad loc., comments that this is likely to be a hendiadys and notes the use of various terms for pain through the text. The choice of word in a given context appears to be driven by stylistic reasons. Cf. J. Prost, *Les Théories hellénistiques de la douleur* (Louvain, 2004), 20, on πόνος in Cynicism: 'Le terme désigne à la fois la douleur subie et l'effort produit notamment pour surmonter la douleur, notions distingués en latin par les termes *dolor* et *labor*.'

[11] For more on Empedocles on perception see D. N. Sedley, 'Empedocles' Theory of Vision' ['Empedocles'], in Fortenbaugh and Gutas (eds.), *Theophrastus*, 20–31, and K. Ierodiakonou, 'Empedocles on Colour and Colour Perception' ['Empedocles'], *Oxford Studies in Ancient Philosophy*, 29 (2005) 1–37.

'likes' and pain by 'opposites' (16).[12] Either, therefore, perception is not all caused by 'likes', since pain—a kind of perception—is not caused by likes, or we should say that pleasure is a kind of perception but pain is not. This latter option is rejected by Theophrastus since 'in the very act of perception we often feel pain as we perceive—and according to Anaxagoras we *always* feel pain. For he says that every perception is accompanied by pain' (17).[13]

This opportunity to use Anaxagoras as a weapon in the criticism of Empedocles suits Theophrastus' overall dialectical strategy very well. Although he has no intention of endorsing the extreme Anaxagorean claim that every perception is accompanied by pain, he is happy to refer to it here since it can serve to highlight the extreme opposition between these two great Presocratic natural philosophers: Empedocles receives the longest discussion of all those, including Plato, in the 'like-by-like' camp and Anaxagoras appears to be regarded by Theophrastus as the champion of the 'opposites' party. One way to reconcile the two Empedoclean claims—that pleasure is a kind of perception caused by likes and that all perception is caused by likes—is to conclude that therefore every perception is pleasant. That would generate the extreme opposite claim to the Anaxagorean view. Of course, neither such view is in the least bit plausible to Theophrastus, who holds that any acceptable account must be able to accommodate the reasonable thought that some perceptions are pleasant and some are painful. Revealing the odd commitments or consequences of these philosophers' mistaken conceptions of pleasure and pain in particular and perception in general is an integral part of his own philosophical argument begun at the very beginning of the work. There, Empedocles and Anaxagoras are listed on opposing sides in the basic division between theories basing perception on likes and those basing perception on unlikes or opposites (1–3). The difficulties that both these theories turn out to face in offering a plausible account of the nature of pleasure and pain is just one more reason, Theophrastus argues, for us to be wary of accepting either of these species of explanation.

We should also note that this early reference to Anaxagoras' the-

---

[12] ἀλλὰ μὴν οὐδὲ τὴν ἡδονὴν καὶ λύπην ὁμολογουμένως ἀποδίδωσιν ἥδεσθαι μὲν ποιῶν τοῖς ὁμοίοις, λυπεῖσθαι δὲ τοῖς ἐναντίοις.

[13] καίτοι πολλάκις αἰσθανόμενοι λυπούμεθα κατ᾽ αὐτὴν τὴν αἴσθησιν, ὡς ⟨δ᾽⟩ Ἀναξαγόρας φησίν, ἀεί· πᾶσαν γὰρ αἴσθησιν εἶναι μετὰ λύπης.

sis comes very shortly after the closest thing we have in the text to an account of what pleasure and pain are. After announcing Empedocles' idea that pleasure is brought about by likes and pain by opposites, and having cited Empedocles B 22. 4–5 in support, Theophrastus comments in *De sensibus* 16:

αἰσθήσεις γάρ τινας ἢ μετ' αἰσθήσεως ποιοῦσι τὴν ἡδονὴν καὶ τὴν λύπην . . .

For they make pleasure and pain kinds of perceptions or accompaniments of perception . . .

Theophrastus' argument against Empedocles, like his later criticisms of Anaxagoras, will work only if he can rely on the strong claim that, according to Empedocles, pleasure and pain are perceptions, perhaps of a special sort. Only then do pleasure and pain have to conform to Empedocles' general conception of perception coming about through the interaction of likes. Some debate has centred around the identity of the 'they' to whom this view is to be attributed, since it might refer to both Empedocles and Anaxagoras, who will be named two sentences later. Certainly, it is a little odd for Theophrastus to move to the plural here given that he has consistently used singular verbs up to this point to describe Empedocles' position and has not yet introduced Anaxagoras into the discussion. Clearly, it would be of importance for our present enquiry if this account of the nature of pleasure and pain can be ascribed to Anaxagoras also.[14] The additional note that pleasure and pain might also be, according to these people, 'accompaniments of perception' perhaps suggests a lack of clarity on their part. This phrasing allows a certain indeterminacy in the relationship between pleasure, for example, and perception since it is not committed to any particular causal relationship between the two. It does not, more specifically, insist that pleasures are caused by perceptions of a certain sort. We would like to press for more information at this point, since the question of the precise relationship between pleasure, pain, and perception is one to which we shall return. But, infuriatingly, this is as close as we get to an explicit account. For his part, Theophrastus moves on as if he were able to rely on the idea that for both Empedocles and Anaxagoras pleasure

---

[14] Cf. G. M. Stratton, *Theophrastus and the Greek Physiological Psychology before Aristotle* (London, 1917), 170. Diels's apparatus to this passage in *Dox.* notes 'ποιοῦσι: simul intellegitur Anaxagoras.' A note in the text when it appears as DK A 86 (i. 303) leaves the question open.

and pain are perceptions of a sort, or at least conform to the same explanatory mechanism as other perceptions.

When Theophrastus next invokes the Anaxagorean claim that all perception is accompanied by pain, he is in the middle of a dedicated discussion of Anaxagoras' general theory of sense-perception. As in the case of Empedocles, here he attempts to show that the consequences of Anaxagoras' theory fail to fit some basic and unquestionable facts about our perception of the world. The thesis that perception is always accompanied by pain is introduced at 29 and noted as being consistent with the guiding principle that perception is caused by opposites:

ἅπασαν δ' αἴσθησιν μετὰ λύπης, ὅπερ ἂν δόξειεν ἀκόλουθον εἶναι τῇ ὑποθέσει· πᾶν γὰρ τὸ ἀνόμοιον ἁπτόμενον πόνον παρέχει. φανερὸν δὲ τοῦτο τῷ τε τοῦ χρόνου πλήθει καὶ τῇ τῶν αἰσθητῶν ὑπερβολῇ. τὰ γὰρ λαμπρὰ χρώματα καὶ τοὺς ὑπερβάλλοντας ψόφους λύπην ἐμποιεῖν καὶ οὐ πολὺν χρόνον δύνασθαι τοῖς αὐτοῖς ἐπιμένειν.

[He says that] every perception is accompanied by pain, which would appear to follow from his hypothesis. For every unlike we contact causes distress. And this is made clear by both extended length of time and excessive objects of perception. For bright colours and excessively loud noises produce pain and we are unable to withstand the same ones for very long.

Whereas for Empedocles the possibility of experiencing pain was threatened by his guiding principle that perception is caused by likes, Anaxagoras has no difficulties in explaining pain. However, he will suffer from a problem symmetrical to that faced by Empedocles: How, given his overall conception of perception, can Anaxagoras account for experiences of pleasure? But before we turn to consider Theophrastus' criticisms in more detail, we should note that here not only do we have a report of the by now familiar Anaxagorean thesis that all perception is accompanied by pain, but also we have a report of an Anaxagorean argument in favour of accepting what is an admittedly paradoxical thesis. The argument has two parts. The first part is a deduction based on two premises and the second is an attempt to offer some empirical support for the thesis based on our experience of certain extreme cases of perception.

From *De sensibus* 27–8 comes the first premiss, that all perception occurs via the interaction of opposites because 'the like is unaffected by the like' (τὸ γὰρ ὅμοιον ἀπαθὲς τοῦ ὁμοίου). Touch and taste provide further support for this explanation because (i) we feel neither

heat nor cold from the proximity of an object which is of a similar temperature to ourselves and (ii) we do not perceive sweetness
by sweetness or sourness by sourness. The first of these claims is
likely to be the more persuasive.[15] The second is a restatement of
the general thesis that perception occurs via opposites emphasizing the Anaxagorean view that all the opposites nevertheless are
'in us', which allows us to perceive each of the opposed qualities
in some external object. We are told that it is impossible to feel
the temperature of something which is of the same temperature as
our hand, but both the object and the hand contain 'the hot' and
'the cold', each of which interacts with its opposite. The details are
left unexplored, and leave open room for various conceptions of
the structure of Anaxagorean matter and the relationship between
the opposites. Perhaps when we feel the temperature of something
there are two independent processes occurring: the hot in the object interacting with the cold in the hand and the hot in the hand
interacting with the cold in the object. In cases where the ratio of
hot to cold is the same in the object and the hand these two will
somehow cancel each other out and the net result will be no overall
perception of temperature. Or, perhaps when he claims that 'the
hot' is never entirely separated from 'the cold' (B 8), he means
that everything has some temperature between two indefinitely extendible extremes: nothing, however hot, could not be hotter. In
that case there is a single interaction between the temperature of
the object and that of the hand. When the two are equal, no perceptions occurs. Nothing in Theophrastus' account determines which
of these two we should accept, and the choice matters little at present for the overall understanding of the theory. However, the issue
will resurface in Section 3 below.

The Anaxagorean argument then proceeds with the claim in 29
that 'every unlike we contact causes distress' (πᾶν γὰρ τὸ ἀνόμοιον
ἁπτόμενον πόνον παρέχει). The full argument therefore can be expressed as follows:

(1) The like is unaffected (ἀπαθές) by the like.
(2) (Perception is or involves an affection (πάθος).) [Implicit]

---

[15] The principle is used in sensory deprivation, isolation, or flotation tanks. These
allow the user to float in temperature-controlled water the density of which has been
altered by dissolving Epsom salts. Light and sound are also removed. The overall
effect is intended to be extremely relaxing. Anaxagoras would presumably note this
as an absence of πόνος.

(3) Therefore all perception occurs via opposites.
(4) Every unlike with which we come into contact causes exertion/toil (πόνος).
(5) Therefore all perception involves exertion/toil.
(6) (Toil is painful.) [Implicit]
(7) Therefore all perception involves pain.

We have seen some support offered for (1) and (3), and this is what we would expect given that this is precisely the way in which Anaxagoras differs markedly from other philosophers such as Empedocles and this difference is the central organizing distinction in Theophrastus' work. (4), however, receives no support in the text. Further, we can note once again that there is a very swift transition from a claim that perception involves πόνος to the conclusion that perception involves pain. In the initial survey of the evidence I noted that Aristotle makes a similar move in *NE* 7. 14 but also suggested that we might wish to reserve judgement over whether Anaxagoras was similarly inclined to use πόνος and λύπη more or less interchangeably. That same issue becomes important here. Theophrastus wants to secure a conclusion involving the attribution of pain to all perceptions, partly because this will drive his charge of inconsistency against Anaxagoras and also serve to make a clear contrast with Empedocles. Anyone inclined to be suspicious of Theophrastus could say that it is prudent to view (5) as Anaxagoras' own conclusion and the further move to (7) as a Peripatetic addition.[16] Whatever reservations we might have about Theophrastus, he remains by far our best source for this element of Anaxagoras' thought. I shall therefore continue on the assumption that (7) is a genuine Anaxagorean conclusion since it is consistent with other aspects of Anaxagoras' thought and is an interesting thesis which is well worth investigating. In any case, Theophrastus himself gives some reason for thinking that (7) is Anaxagoras' own conclusion by reporting in *De sensibus* 29 Anaxagoras' own response to the most obvious objection to (7). The problem is that (7) fails to accord with the phenomenology of our everyday lives: we do not feel constant pain. Anaxagoras replies by asking us to pay attention to the discomfort we all feel in certain extreme circumstances, namely cases

---

[16] One might think that the claim in (4) (πᾶν γὰρ τὸ ἀνόμοιον ἁπτόμενον πόνον παρέχει) has the ring of at least a paraphrase of an original Anaxagorean jingle, and Aëtius' version of Anaxagoras' thesis gives us the conclusion in (5), not (7): Aëtius 4. 9. 16 (Stob. *Ecl.* 1. 50. 32): Ἀναξαγόρας πᾶσαν αἴσθησιν μετὰ πόνου.

in which the perception is excessively prolonged or the particular object is excessively bright or loud. Then we are asked to imagine that this discomfort, so evident in these cases, is present in every case of perception but varies according to the length or nature of the object perceived. On most occasions the discomfort is too small to be noticed. Only in the particular cases highlighted here does the ever-present discomfort make itself noticed.

Theophrastus himself objects to this method of argumentation, claiming that Anaxagoras is illicitly drawing inferences about what is always the case in normal acts of perception from thinking about these rare and unusual circumstances (33). Yet it is a recognizable Anaxagorean tactic. Let us compare the famous experiment described by Sextus Empiricus at *M.* 7. 90, which includes Anaxagoras fragment B 21:

ὁ μὲν φυσικώτατος Ἀναξαγόρας ὡς ἀσθενεῖς διαβάλλων τὰς αἰσθήσεις "ὑπ᾽ ἀφαυρότητος αὐτῶν, φησιν, οὐ δυνατοὶ ἐσμεν κρίνειν τἀληθές", τίθησί τε πίστιν αὐτῶν τῆς ἀπιστίας τὴν παρὰ μικρὸν τῶν χρωμάτων ἐξαλλαγήν. εἰ γὰρ δύο λάβοιμεν χρώματα, μέλαν καὶ λευκόν, εἶτα ἐκ θατέρου εἰς θάτερον κατὰ σταγόνα παρεκχέοιμεν, οὐ δυνήσεται ἡ ὄψις διακρίνειν τὰς παρὰ μικρὸν μεταβολάς, καίπερ πρὸς τὴν φύσιν ὑποκειμένας.

Anaxagoras, the greatest natural philosopher, in order to show how weak the senses are, says, 'we are unable to distinguish the truth because of their lack of strength'. And he offers as evidence of their lack of reliability the gradual change between two colours. For if we take two colours, black and white, and then pour out one into the other drop by drop, sight will be unable to distinguish the gradual changes, although they underlie the nature of things.

Sextus is interested in offering evidence of early and widespread philosophical distrust of the senses as criteria of truth, and therefore concentrates on the apparent scepticism expressed in B 21.[17] But the evidence (πίστις) which Anaxagoras goes on to offer shows a more nuanced view of the role of the senses in guiding us to the truth about nature, quite in keeping with his other famous pronouncement that what appears to us is a 'glimpse of what is not evident'.[18] The illustration of the gradual but imperceptible change

---

[17] Cf. Cic. *Acad.* 1. 44 (A 95 DK); J. Barnes, *The Presocratic Philosophers* [*Presocratic*], rev. edn. (London, 1982), 540–1.

[18] B 21a (at S.E. *M.* 7. 140): ὄψις τῶν ἀδήλων τὰ φαινόμενα. Some have questioned the authenticity of this fragment, arguing that it should instead be ascribed to Democritus (who is said to have approved of it) or perhaps the Diotimus also mentioned

from white to black as black pigment is introduced drop by drop is not only evidence for the weakness of the senses, but also evidence for Anaxagoras' contention that 'in everything there is a portion of everything'. Two related but distinct points might be made about the senses' inability to discern the true nature of things. Early on in the mixing process, what appears to be a perfectly good pot of white paint, say, must be agreed to contain at least some black paint since some black has been seen being introduced. But also, each drop of black added to the mix will make an imperceptible difference to the overall colour. What began as white will eventually be a grey, although at no particular stage will it have been possible to detect a perceptible change.[19]

These observations are clearly intended as some kind of support for Anaxagoras' theory of universal mixture and the idea that we generally perceive only the properties of the predominant elements in any given object. The substances we perceive contain not only evident but also latent elements. What appears to be a perfectly pure white substance contains portions of black, undetectable because of their being a relatively small proportion of the whole. There are two ways in which we could understand this claim. Perhaps Anaxagoras means to say that if only our eyesight were more acute, we would be able to detect the tiny portion of black in a large pot of white paint. In this case, the black is in principle perceptible, but there is an insufficient proportion of it for our human eyesight to be able to register it. (In the colour-change experiment this would amount to saying that the very first drop added does in fact make a difference to the colour of the whole, but that the change is not such that human sight can detect it.) Strong support for this view comes from the observations reported by Theophrastus at *De sensibus* 29–30, in which Anaxagoras claims that the power of sense-perception varies according to the size of an animal.[20] However he explained the differences in perceptual ability, this clearly leaves room for

---

by Sextus. See G. E. R. Lloyd, *Polarity and Analogy* (Cambridge, 1966), 338–41, and D. Sider, *The Fragments of Anaxagoras: Introduction, Text, and Commentary* [*Anaxagoras*], 2nd edn. (Sankt Augustin, 2005), 165–6. Cf. also Democritus B 125.

[19] Cf. Barnes, *Presocratic*, 538–40.

[20] Confusingly, Anaxagoras' account apparently combines the claim that larger sense-organs are able to detect all their proper sensibles to a greater degree and the claim that larger ears, for example, are better at detecting loud sounds and smaller ears are better at detecting delicate sounds. Theophrastus rightly objects at *De sensibus* 34–5.

him to claim that certain things are imperceptible by humans but perceptible by other animals. Alternatively, he could take his theory of universal mixture to mean that latent elements such as the tiny portion of black in what appears to be pure white paint are not even in principle perceptible. Even the most powerful and acute visual apparatus would be unable to detect a change since no change in the colour of the whole has yet occurred. Only when the proportion of black within the whole has reached a certain level will there be any actual—not just any detectable—change in the colour of the whole.[21]

Whatever its precise relationship to Anaxagoras' more general theory of matter, this famous discussion of colours is a close analogue to the observations reported by Theophrastus and designed to lead us to accept the view that all perception is accompanied by pain. In both instances Anaxagoras offers something which does not 'prove' his own theory since there are a number of other compatible explanations of the phenomenon in question. Rather, these cases are noted in order to show that the Anaxagorean view in question is not incompatible with observed phenomena and therefore cannot simply be dismissed on empirical grounds. Theophrastus objects that the evidence from extended or excessive perceptions offers no support for Anaxagoras' view, but rather supports an alternative account which claims that pain occurs as a result of exceeding the 'symmetry and blending' required for perception (*De sensibus* 32). Since perception is natural, under normal circumstances it occurs either painlessly or with pleasure. Theophrastus is wrong to think that his objection is fatal to Anaxagoras' project, since Theophrastus' rival explanation of this evidence of itself is no more persuasive unless one is already convinced of his own preferred Peripatetic theory of perception.[22]

---

[21] The difficulty of deciding between the two understandings of 'imperceptible' occurs throughout Anaxagoras' work, notably in the appearances of the terms ἔνδηλον and ἄδηλον. In B 21a it is not clear whether the ἄδηλα are things merely unobservable 'by us' or are things which are absolutely imperceptible. Similarly, when in B 1 Anaxagoras describes all the various elements in the original homogeneous cosmic mixture as not ἔνδηλα because of their 'smallness', we might wonder whether this is imagining some hypothetical observer who would have been unable to distinguish any elements or whether it is a claim that none of these elements were at all manifest in the intrinsic nature of the whole. We might note that in B 12 *Nous* is credited with knowledge of all things, whether combined, mixed, or separated.

[22] Baltussen, *Theophrastus*, 170: '[T]he *paradoxon* that pain is natural is countered by the *endoxon* that pleasure is according to nature.'

In the remarks on painful perceptions, as in the colour-change example, Anaxagoras wants us to realize that our senses are sometimes insufficiently sensitive to what is in fact the case. Just as they are unable to register small amounts of black in a large amount of white, so they are generally unable to register the discomfort caused by each and every act of perception. Further, just as the senses are unable to detect tiny gradual changes, but agree that once a large amount of black has been added the colour has indeed changed, so too the senses may be unable to detect at what point a light, gradually increasing in brightness, becomes painful to look at. If it is painful at the end, then perhaps there was some— albeit unnoticed—discomfort earlier on in the process just as there must have been some unnoticed colour change early on in the other experiment.[23] If a large amount of black paint were to be mixed straight away into the white, then the change would be obvious. Similarly, if the particular act of perception is prolonged or directed at an object able to exert an extremely large effect on the sense (such as when we suddenly look at a very bright light), the discomfort is immediately noticeable. Our senses are not, therefore, absolutely hopeless guides to the reality of things, but we need to be careful to recognize that sometimes they are unable to provide evidence of something which is in fact taking place. The senses are, in that sense, 'weak', and once we have noted their weakness we ought to be wary of assuming that the lack of immediate empirical evidence of some process or state of affairs is a reason to doubt that the process is taking place or the state of affairs is the case. We know, after all, that *some* black paint has been added to the white paint, even when we cannot see any change in colour.[24] The two Anaxagorean observations can be seen to offer complementary and consistent elements of this view. The colour-change example tries to make plausible the idea that the senses are unable to detect real but gradual changes or small elements within a greater mixture. The case of seeing an extremely bright light shows that the senses, although weak, can in the right circumstances detect changes or states which otherwise go unnoticed.

We can now return to the additional comment attributed by Aristotle to the 'natural philosophers' in *NE* 7. 14, namely that this con-

---

[23] Compare R. M. Hare, 'Pain and Evil', in J. Feinberg (ed.), *Moral Concepts* (Oxford, 1969), 29–42, esp. 31.

[24] Cf. B 10: καὶ γὰρ ἐνεῖναι τῷ λευκῷ τὸ μέλαν καὶ τὸ λευκὸν τῷ μέλανι.

stant pain is not generally noticed by us. It is reasonable to assume that Aristotle's source for this comment is the same as for the claim that perception is accompanied by pain, so there is good reason to think that it is something which might be attributed to Anaxagoras. Aristotle's report makes this lack of attention the result of simple habituation, and perhaps Anaxagoras could indeed endorse such an explanation. Consider an experiment in which someone looks at a light, which begins by being rather dim and gradually increases in intensity. Perhaps the viewer would not feel quite so much pain at the very end of the process if the increase has been gradual; at each step he has been able to become accustomed to the slight increase in the intensity of the light. Of course, had the light been switched immediately to a very intense from a rather dim level, it would have been very uncomfortable to look at. Perhaps in this way Anaxagoras might claim that even our everyday levels of perception are painful, but we are so accustomed to it that we fail to notice. Only when sudden changes occur or extremely intense objects present themselves to us do we notice what is always the case.[25]

If that is a plausible interpretation of his view, two difficulties remain for Anaxagoras. First, it is not clear what account he could provide of pleasure, particularly if we accept Theophrastus' account of his theory. Second, he will need to answer the objection that it is absurd to say that we are in pain but fail to feel or notice it: an unfelt pain is not a pain at all. These two problems will be the focus of the remainder of my discussion.

### 3. Anaxagoras and pleasure

It is clear why Theophrastus thinks that Anaxagoras has a problem in finding what to say about pleasure. Pleasure, like pain, is surely some kind of perception or affection (a view which is not only plausible itself, but might also be ascribed to Anaxagoras on the basis of *De sensibus* 16 and the assumption that if pain is a πάθος

---

[25] Compare 'Boiling frog syndrome', a term applied to an analogy for a number of phenomena, from people's acceptance of rising interest rates and the gradual increase of workplace stress to declining environmental conditions. The story is as follows: 'Throw a frog into a pan of boiling water and it will jump out. Place a frog in a pan of tepid water and gradually increase the heat. The frog will remain in the pan until it is boiled to death.' (The story is false; any real frog will certainly try to get out once the water is uncomfortably warm.)

then there is no reason to think that pleasure is any different). But if only opposites cause perceptions and all opposites produce pain when we come into contact with them, how can a perception ever be pleasant?

  Are there any reasons to doubt Theophrastus' account and therefore leave room for some alternative Anaxagorean explanation? It might be helpful to offer in comparison the account given by Theophrastus of Empedocles' analysis of pleasure and pain (*De sensibus* 9):

ἥδεσθαι δὲ τοῖς ὁμοίοις κατά τε ⟨τὰ⟩ μόρια καὶ τὴν κρᾶσιν, λυπεῖσθαι δὲ τοῖς ἐναντίοις.

[He says that we] feel pleasure because of the likes both in terms of their parts and their mixture, and that we feel pain because of the opposites.

This gives a symmetrical account of pleasure and pain. Since the two seem in some sense to be opposite sensations, then their causes must be similar in kind but also relevantly dissimilar. So here pleasure is said to occur when items are perceived which are similar to the perceiver either in terms of their constituents or in terms of the arrangement of their constituents. Pain occurs when the items are opposite in terms of their constituents or arrangement.[26] For Empedocles, as we saw, this leads to a difficulty because it conflicts with his general view that all perception comes about through likes (see *De sensibus* 16–17). Since he explains pleasure in terms of a mechanism common to all perceptions, either pain is not a perception or we never experience pain. Anaxagoras' problem is the mirror image: since he explains pain in terms of a mechanism common to all perceptions, either pleasure is not a perception or we never experience pleasure.

  There is some reason to think that Theophrastus has been overkeen to engineer a formal similarity between Empedocles and Anaxagoras in order to cast them as mirror images of one another, certainly in so far as they offered similar but contrasting accounts of perception and pleasure or pain. This contrast suits Theophrastus' aim of demonstrating the failings of all previous accounts of sense-perception by showing that the whole preceding tradition of natural speculation was based on a misconception of the kind of ex-

---

[26] Compare the account of the causes of pain in Hipp. *Loc.* 42. There it is claimed that pain is caused by opposites—by heat affecting cold parts of the body, moisture affecting dry parts of the body, and so on.

planation required. The entire project, as Theophrastus has cast it, of explaining perception in terms of likes or unlikes was poorly thought out, and even those, such as Democritus, who tried to offer a different account fall foul of a shared malaise.[27]

There are also signs that, in the case of Empedocles, Theophrastus has not given us the whole story of his account of pleasure and pain. Two reports from Aëtius, collected in 31 A 95 DK, replace the Theophrastan account of pleasure being based on the perception of likes with a different process of the body being affected by some deficiency and then subsequent satisfaction.[28] The first report (Aëtius 4. 9. 15) tells us that Empedocles explained pleasure as arising from the satisfaction of a desire caused by some kind of deficiency. The organism suffering a lack feels a desire to be replenished by external sources which are like what is needed. We can imagine hunger being a desire brought about by the absence of certain kinds of substance needed by the body. Pleasure arises when the right kind of object is found to satisfy the desire—the 'like'—while pain is caused by 'the opposites'. The second report (Aëtius 5. 28) adds that pleasures arise because of the input of what is 'appropriate' (οἰκεῖον) according to the mixtures of likes. This account avoids the problems generated by Theophrastus since it leaves aside the idea that pleasure and pain are kinds of perception. Rather, it explains the two in terms of the input of material appropriate for replenishing the organism. The phenomenal experience of pleasure and pain is not emphasized at all, and its place is taken by an account based on general physical processes. Such accounts are fairly common,

---

[27] Cf. Ierodiakonou, 'Empedocles', 30–1. A. A. Long, 'Theophrastus' *De sensibus* on Plato' ['Theophrastus'], in K. A. Algra, P. W. van der Horst, and D. T. Runia (eds.), *Polyhistor: Studies in the History and Historiography of Ancient Philosophy Presented to J. Mansfeld on his Sixtieth Birthday* (Leiden, 1996), 345–62, considers Theophrastus' treatment of Plato, the one philosopher tackled in *De sensibus* from whom we have the original text, and the *Timaeus*, on which Theophrastus bases his interpretation. Long sounds a general note of caution against relying on Theophrastus as an accurate reporter of early Greek philosophy. For a full account of Theophrastus' dialectical method see Baltussen, 'Peripatetic Dialectic', and id., *Theophrastus*, esp. 177: 'Theophrastus' treatment of Anaxagoras is aggressive and may represent an implied value-judgement. The intrusion of Peripatetic notions occurs early in the criticisms.' (Baltussen, *Theophrastus*, 136–9, gives his reaction to Long, 'Theophrastus'.) Cf. Sedley, 'Empedocles', 26–31, esp. 29, on his treatment of Empedocles: 'The trouble seems to be that Theophrastus is the prisoner of an over-schematized doxographical view, according to which Empedocles has *got* to come out as a like-by-like theorist.'

[28] Cf. J. C. B. Gosling and C. C. W. Taylor, *The Greeks on Pleasure* [*Pleasure*] (Oxford, 1982), 21–2.

since a popular method of explaining the physiology of pleasure and pain was to use some such account of the natural or normal state of the body and its maintenance. Any destruction or impediment of that state is used to account for pain, and pleasures are identified with its restoration. Similar views are found in a number of ancient authors, and an example can be found in Theophrastus' account of the philosophy of Diogenes of Apollonia, in *De sensibus* 43.[29] The central notion in such accounts is not the mechanism of perception but some natural state of the body or sense-organ.

Indeed, just as there is evidence from Aëtius of an Empedoclean view not reported by Theophrastus, so there is some other evidence of Anaxagoras' view on pleasure and pain. Diels–Kranz include in their collection of testimonia as 59 A 117 a section of a Latin work they refer to as [Arist.] *De plantis*. This is from a work probably by Alfredo de Sareshel (twelfth–thirteenth century), which is one of a number of translations of a Syriac version of a work Περὶ φυτῶν by the Augustan Peripatetic Nicolaus of Damascus, itself probably based on works by Aristotle and Theophrastus. The Latin translation includes the following observation early in the text (at §3):

Anaxagoras animalia esse has [sc. plantas], laetarique et tristari dixit fluxum foliorum argumentum assumens.

Anaxagoras said that plants are living things too and that they feel both pleasure and pain. He drew this conclusion from the shedding and growth of their leaves.

The status of the text is such that we should be wary of placing too much weight on this report.[30] Nevertheless, it does indicate that

---

[29] Thphr. *De sens.* 43: ἡδονὴν δὲ καὶ λύπην γίνεσθαι τόνδε τὸν τρόπον. ὅταν μὲν πολὺς ὁ ἀὴρ μίσγηται τῷ αἵματι καὶ κουφίζῃ κατὰ φύσιν ὢν καὶ κατὰ πᾶν τὸ σῶμα διεξιών, ἡδονήν· ὅταν δὲ παρὰ φύσιν καὶ μὴ μίσγηται συνιζάνοντος τοῦ αἵματος καὶ ἀσθενεστέρου καὶ πυκνοτέρου γινομένου, λύπην. ὁμοίως καὶ θάρσος καὶ ὑγίειαν καὶ τἀναντία. κριτικώτατον δὲ ἡδονῆς τὴν γλῶτταν· ἁπαλώτατον γὰρ εἶναι καὶ μανὸν καὶ τὰς φλέβας ἁπάσας ἀνήκειν εἰς αὐτήν· διὸ σημεῖά τε πλεῖστα τοῖς κάμνουσιν ἐπ' αὐτῆς εἶναι, καὶ τῶν ἄλλων ζῴων τα χρώματα μηνύειν· ὁπόσα γὰρ ἂν ᾖ καὶ ὁποῖα, τοσαῦτα ἐμφαίνεσθαι. τὴν μὲν οὖν αἴσθησιν οὕτω καὶ διὰ τοῦτο γίνεσθαι.

[30] See H. J. Drossaart Lulofs and E. L. J. Poortman, *Aristoteles Semitico-Latinus: Nicolaus Damascenus De plantis. Five Translations* (Amsterdam, 1989). There are four extant translations of the work, one of each into Arabic, Greek, Latin, and Hebrew together with fragments of and brief quotations from the Syriac. The anonymous Greek version is a translation of the Latin. It renders the section quoted as: ὁ μὲν Ἀναξαγόρας καὶ ζῷα εἶναι [τὰ φυτὰ] καὶ ἥδεσθαι καὶ λυπεῖσθαι εἶπε, τῇ τε ἀπορροῇ τῶν φύλλων καὶ τῇ αὐξήσει τοῦτο ἐκλαμβάνων (815ᵃ18–20). The report tallies with other remarks in the testimonia. See Plut. *Quaest. phys.* 911 D (A 116): ζῷον

Anaxagoras was prepared to explain pleasure and pain in various ways, and the process described here looks like a description of the disruption and restoration of the plants' natural, leafy state. The text also says that Anaxagoras and Empedocles ascribed various other psychological capacities to plants, including perception (Latin: §3, Greek: 815ᵃ15–18), but even if we are to imagine that plants are pained because they somehow perceive their leaves falling off or perceive their growth, nevertheless there is no reason to discount the possibility of an Anaxagorean account of pleasure and pain which makes no immediate reference to the interaction of opposites involved in the basic process of perception.[31]

It would not be difficult to imagine an Anaxagorean account of the human experience of pleasure and pain which either posits some normal state for a human and accounts for pleasure and pain in terms of the disruption and restoration of the natural state or else, like Aëtius' version of Empedocles' theory, relies on some notion of what is 'appropriate' for a particular organism. Just as plants are pained by the disruption of shedding their leaves, so humans would be pained by analogous physical loss or disruption. (We have evidence for other, roughly contemporary, explanations of pain based on accounts of physiological disruption.)[32] However, it would be charitable to try to retain a link in his theory between pleasure and pain and perception. Not only is Theophrastus himself quite insistent that there was such a link in both Anaxagoras' and Empedocles' discussions, but we might well think that there ought to be such a link in any credible theory of pleasure and pain. In fact, the difficulty with the physiological accounts of pleasure and pain which make no reference to perception is that they seem oblivious to the fact that there is a phenomenology of pleasure and pain. There is no direct evidence for Anaxagoras' preferred expla-

ἔγγειον τὸ φυτὸν εἶναι οἱ περὶ . . . καὶ Ἀναξαγόραν . . . οἴονται. Anaxagoras may have held that there are airborne seeds which are brought to earth by rain, where they germinate (Thphr. *Hist. plant.* 3. 1. 4; *Caus. plant.* 1. 5. 2; A 117). Perhaps this refers to an early stage in the development of the cosmos: Irenaeus 2. 14. 2 (A 113). Cf. Sider, *Anaxagoras*, 94–5.

[31] It is unclear whether Anaxagoras assigned ψυχή or νοῦς or both to all living things and indeed whether he identified ψυχή and νοῦς. Apart from this evidence about plants, see also Aristotle's comments at *DA* 404ᵇ1 ff., 405ᵃ13 ff. (A 100), and cf. B 4a: . . . τὰ ἄλλα ζῷα ὅσα ψυχὴν ἔχει, and B 11. Cf. Sider, *Anaxagoras*, 97–8.

[32] See e.g. Hipp. *Nat. hom.* 4: pain is caused by an excess or deficiency or separation of one of the four humours in some part of the body, whereas health requires them to be balanced and mixed appropriately.

nation of pleasure, of course, but we have good grounds for offering on his behalf a set of possible responses to the Theophrastan accusation.

Consider two examples of pleasant experiences: (i) eating an ice cream and (ii) sitting in a warm bath. Let us simplify matters by concentrating on two of the opposites in the ice cream, 'the sweet' (τὸ γλυκύ) and 'the sour' (τὸ ὀξύ), and two opposites in the bath, the hot (τὸ θερμόν) and the cold (τὸ ψυχρόν).[33] Both the sweet and sour are present in the ice cream and both the hot and the cold are present in the bathwater because, as Anaxagoras notoriously insists, 'in everything there is a portion of everything'. Further, we experience the sweet by means of the sour in us and vice versa.[34] At this point we face an important complication: our account runs into a more general debate about the correct view of Anaxagoras' conception of the structure of matter and about precisely how we are to understand such claims as 'ice cream contains both "the sweet" and "the sour"'. Specifically, there is some debate over whether Anaxagoras holds a 'particulate' or, more popular in recent discus-

---

[33] I think this claim about two of the opposites in ice cream is fairly uncontroversial, despite the long-running dispute over whether the basic stuffs in Anaxagoras' cosmology are (i) the opposites (see F. Cornford, 'Anaxagoras' Theory of Matter' ['Anaxagoras'], in R. E. Allen and D. J. Furley (eds.), *Studies in Presocratic Philosophy*, ii (London, 1975), 275–322, first published in *Classical Quarterly*, 24 (1930), 14–30, 83–95; G. Vlastos, 'The Physical Theory of Anaxagoras' ['Anaxagoras'], *Philosophical Review*, 59 (1950), 31–57, repr. in Allen and Furley (eds.), *Studies in Presocratic Philosophy*, ii. 323–53, and in Vlastos, *Studies in Greek Philosophy*, i (Princeton, 1995), 303–27; M. Schofield, *An Essay on Anaxagoras* [*Anaxagoras*] (Cambridge, 1980), 100–44; and D. N. Sedley, *Creationism and its Critics in Antiquity* (Berkeley and Los Angeles, forthcoming)), (ii) some more expanded range of stuffs which are sometimes identified as the 'homoiomeries' (see W. Mann, 'Anaxagoras and the *homoiomerē*', *Phronesis*, 25 (1980), 228–49; D. Graham, 'The Postulates of Anaxagoras' ['Postulates'], *Apeiron*, 27 (1994), 77–121)), sometimes identified as 'seeds' (Sider, *Anaxagoras*, e.g. 171–2), or (iii) an even more expansive group (see D. Furley, 'Anaxagoras in Response to Parmenides', in id., *Cosmic Problems* (Cambridge, 1989), 47–65). For a good discussion of the various interpretations of Anaxagorean matter see P. Curd, *The Legacy of Parmenides* (Princeton, 1998), 131–54, and cf. Curd, 'The Metaphysics of Physics: Mixture and Separation in Empedocles and Anaxagoras', in V. Caston and D. W. Graham (eds.), *Presocratic Philosophy* (Aldershot, 2002), 139–58 at 140, 153–5. Those who do not think that the opposites are the fundamental elements in Anaxagorean cosmology should nevertheless agree that they are the primary objects of sense-perception.

[34] See *De sens.* 28: τὸ γὰρ ὁμοίως θερμὸν καὶ ψυχρὸν οὔτε θερμαίνειν οὔτε ψύχειν πλησιάζον οὐδὲ δὴ τὸ γλυκὺ καὶ τὸ ὀξὺ δι᾽ αὐτῶν γνωρίζειν, ἀλλὰ τῷ μὲν θερμῷ τὸ ψυχρόν, τῷ δ᾽ ἁλμυρῷ τὸ πότιμον, τῷ δ᾽ ὀξεῖ τὸ γλυκὺ κατὰ τὴν ἔλλειψιν τὴν ἑκάστου· πάντα γὰρ ἐνυπάρχειν φησὶν ἐν ἡμῖν.

sions, a 'continuum' view of matter.[35] On the former, particulate
view, when Anaxagoras says that there is 'the sweet' and 'the sour'
in the ice cream (and in everything else, for that matter), he means
that there are portions or particles of all of these opposites in everything. For the most part, however, many of these are not manifest
(ἄδηλα) because of the vast preponderance of the other opposites.
On this view, importantly, the sense-organ comes into contact with
a wide range of distinct opposites but the vast preponderance of
one or more of them creates the impression of the overall character
of the object.[36] On the latter, continuum view, when Anaxagoras
claims that, for example, 'the hot' is never entirely separated from
'the cold', he means that everything has some temperature between
two indefinitely extendible extremes: nothing, however hot, could
not be hotter. Similarly, an ice cream is sweet but not absolutely
so, since the presence of 'the sour' places it somewhere along a
continuum between absolute sweetness and absolute sourness.

On the particulate view, since both an ice cream and a warm bath
contain portions or particles of 'the sweet' and 'the sour', we can
imagine Anaxagoras claiming that just as it is evidently painful to
view a bright light directly, so it is also painful to perceive these
extreme opposites. But since every act of perception is the receipt
of such opposites, every act of perception is painful. The difficulty
he would face on this account, as no doubt Theophrastus would be
quick to point out, is how to explain the pleasure we might expect
to feel from eating an ice cream or slipping into a warm bath.
Here Anaxagoras would have two possibilities open to him. First,
he might try to argue that pleasure emerges from the simultaneous
perception of pairs of opposites—each of which is a source of pain—
provided that these pairs are perceived in some particular ratio. For

[35] For some concerns about assigning a particulate theory to Anaxagoras see
Barnes, *Presocratic*, 323–6, and the reply by Graham, 'Postulates', 101–12.

[36] This view may accommodate the idea that none of the 'portions' of, say, black
and white in a pot of white paint is of a pure colour. A strip of white paint contains portions of white and fewer portions of black. Each white portion comprises a
series of smaller portions, of which the vast majority are white. And each of these
white portions is similarly composed. There is a regress, but not, I think, a vicious
one. Cf. the account in Graham, 'Postulates', esp. 104–5 (and see also Cornford,
'Anaxagoras', 309–10; Vlastos, 'Anaxagoras', 49–50; C. Strang, 'The Physical Theory of Anaxagoras', in Allen and Furley (eds.), *Studies in Presocratic Philosophy*, ii.
361–80 at 361–2, first published in *Archiv für Geschichte der Philospohie*, 45 (1963),
101–18; Schofield, *Anaxagoras*, 74–5). Compare the account of colour-perception
attributed to Empedocles by Ierodiakonou, 'Empedocles', 3–22, which relies to a
large extent on the juxtaposition of certain basic colours.

example: a warm bath is pleasant whereas a bath which is too hot and a bath which is too cold are both not pleasant. The pleasure of a warm bath is the product of a balance between the two opposed painful perceptions of hot and cold. The pleasant ratio between opposite perceptions need not be one in which they are both equally present, of course: an ice cream tastes pleasant because the ratio of sweet to sour is one in which the sweet predominates. But the ice cream is not entirely sweet (there is some sour in it) and were this sour not present to some degree, the ice cream would not be pleasant to eat. The obviously paradoxical claim here is that pleasure is the product of certain pairs of pains and that sometimes opposed pains can balance one another out and result in us noticing no particular discomfort. Whether such a thought is so intolerably paradoxical that we should not even be tempted to offer it to Anaxagoras is another matter.

Alternatively, Anaxagoras might argue that the experience of pleasure is best explained by a mechanism different from that by which perception generates pain. Rather than pleasure being caused by the direct interaction between an object of perception and a perceiver, he might, for example, say that pleasure arises when the perceiver's physiology is altered in some beneficial way, perhaps by restoring some necessary balance between the perceiver's constituent elements. This beneficial fulfilment of certain physiological needs then, in turn, generates a perception of pleasure. Our evidence for Anaxagoras' discussion of plants suggested that the plants flourish and take pleasure as their leaves grow but also feel pain as they fall. In that case, one would expect that if humans take pleasure in some promotion of a flourishing state, so too they would feel pain from the disruption of that state. There is no reason why Anaxagoras might not accept this too. His controversial claim, we should remember, is that 'every perception is accompanied by pain'; there is no evidence that he claimed that perception of the external world is the only source of pain. In any event, it might be that the perception of opposites always causes some physiological disruption since it involves some physical interaction between the perceiver and the object perceived.[37] Eating an ice cream, there-

---

[37] Note again Thphr. *De sens.* 29: πᾶν γὰρ τὸ ἀνόμοιον ἁπτόμενον πόνον παρέχει. The physics of distance senses are somewhat obscure: see *De sensibus* 27 on sight and 28–30 on smell and hearing. These latter do involve some kind of direct contact between perceiver and object.

fore, would be painful in so far as it is an instance of perceiving the opposites in some external object (which might disrupt one's physiology) but pleasant in so far as overall it contributes to some physiological benefit.

The continuum account of Anaxagorean matter could not accommodate the first of these possible explanations of pleasure since, on its view, the perception of a warm bath does not involve two simultaneous perceptions of 'the hot' in the bath and of 'the cold' in the bath. But it could accommodate a version of the second explanation. Experiencing a warm bath is painful in so far as it is the perception of some external object, and Anaxagoras has tried to persuade us that all such perceptions are painful although only in some extreme cases are they noticeably so. However, the warm bath may also cause various other physiological changes (relaxing the muscles, for example) which can produce a feeling of pleasure. A bath which is too hot or too cold would be more noticeably painful and would not cause the accompanying physiological benefits.

Much of this remains necessarily speculative. But whatever the plausibility of these suggestions for an Anaxagorean account of pleasure, and whichever view of Anaxagorean matter is favoured, I see no reason to doubt that Anaxagoras would be capable of offering some explanation of pleasant perceptions in a manner consistent with his general theory of matter and with the thesis that all perception is accompanied by pain.[38] In doing so, however, Anaxagoras must be prepared to argue for a notion of pain which accepts the following two controversial consequences:

(*a*) It is possible for a perceiver to be simultaneously in pain and experiencing pleasure, a possibility which Theophrastus and

---

[38] Compare A. Mourelatos, 'Quality, Structure and Emergence in later Pre-Socratic Philosophy', *Proceedings of the Boston Area Colloquium in Ancient Philosophy*, 2 (1987), 127–94 at 148–52, who rejects a particulate analysis of the perception of some tepid water as the combined perception of stretches of hot and stretches of cold because (i) it would posit a 'veil of appearances', since the appearance of the water being tepid is superimposed over what is really the case, namely that the water is composed of stretches of the hot and the cold, and (ii) it would show that our senses are extremely limited, hardly ever perceiving the true composition of objects. To the second objection, we might reply by referring to Thphr. *De sensibus* 29–30 and Anaxagoras' claim that human senses may well be limited in comparison with other animals. To the first, I see no reason to accept Mourelatos' insistence that B 21a denies the possibility of an 'appearances/reality' split. B 21a was, after all, applauded by Democritus, who is happy with such a split.

Aristotle deny.[39] In Theophrastus' case, so Aspasius tells us in the passage discussed above, this denial was aimed explicitly at Anaxagoras. In the *Ethics* Theophrastus objected to Anaxagoras on the grounds that pleasure 'drives out' pain, being its opposite (ἐξελαύνει ἡδονὴ λύπην ἥ γε ἐναντία). We can assume, therefore, that the compresence of pleasure and pain was a thesis which either Anaxagoras himself explicitly espoused or else was easily deducible from his other claims, and it is a virtue of any proposed interpretation of Anaxgoras' view of pleasure and pain if it allows the possibility of their compresence. In any case, the compresence of these two opposites, pleasure and pain, sounds like a plausibly Anaxagorean thought. All the opposites are thoroughly intermingled in his general cosmology, and we can imagine that he extended this motif even to affective states such as pleasure and pain.

(*b*) It is possible for a perceiver to be in pain but not be aware of it. This is a difficulty faced by any attempt to explain Anaxagoras' view since it is an essential part of his claim that perception is always accompanied by pain, although we are aware of it only on certain occasions (bright lights, excessively prolonged sensations). Any account has to accept that Anaxagoras is happy for there to be 'unperceived pains' in some sense—pains which we experience but of which we are unaware. The next section discusses this claim in more detail.

### 4. Can there be unnoticed pains?

Anaxagoras needs to defend the notion that there are unnoticed pains. This task remains whatever the preferred account of Anaxagoras' view of the cause of pain and of the structure of matter underlying the causes of pain. Whether the constant pain which accompanies perception is unnoticed through simple habituation (as Aristotle claims was the view of the 'natural philosophers') or whether there is some other account which holds that the pain is constantly present but very small except in certain special circumstances, we can still demand a defence of the notion of an unnoticed pain.

One response is to defend Anaxagoras by pointing to common physiological explanations of pleasure and pain and to say that

---

[39] Cf. Arist. *NE* 1154[a]25–6.

Anaxagoras uses 'perception' and 'pain' to mean both some physiological process—the contact between an object and a sense-organ—
and some psychological state or awareness.[40] In that case, the pain
which we undergo but do not notice is a perception in so far as it is
a physiological process, but it is not a subjective or affective state.
Only in extreme cases, such as prolonged perceptions or perceptions of excessive objects, is the pain a perception in the second
sense, since only then do we *feel* pain. It might be objected that
this is simply to equivocate on the meaning of 'pain' or to install
two very different senses of the word, one physiological and the
other psychological, without making clear any connection between
the two. Anaxagoras' argument in *De sensibus* 28–9 remains valid if
'perception' and 'distress' or 'pain' are throughout read in a physiological sense with no commitment to any claims about the state
of awareness of any agent. But this validity comes at the price of
making it unclear what the argument is intended to show. It merely
defines both perception and pain as physical processes involving
contact between opposites, from which it follows that all perceptions in this sense must involve pain in this physiological sense.
It also makes the subsequent discussion of felt pains arising from
prolonged or excessively intense perceptions seem merely to muddy
the waters since, although it might provide evidence that perception can indeed *feel* painful, it can hardly offer support for the
physiological view of 'pain' as some sort of disruption or alteration
of one's state which is caused by each and every external object of
perception.[41]

Anaxagoras' argument might on this account become consistent,
but at the price of being hard to accept as a satisfying analysis of
what we generally think of as pain. There is widespread (but not, it

---

[40] Cf. Gosling and Taylor, *Pleasure*, 17, who detect an ambiguity in the use of the
term *aisthēsis*: 'The thesis that Empedocles and Anaxagoras regarded pleasure as a
kind of *aisthēsis*, or alternatively as something always accompanying *aisthēsis* will
then be undifferentiated between whether they regarded it as a kind of perception
and the thesis that they regarded it as a kind of internal impression, as something
"perceived" rather than the perceiving of something.'

[41] G. Casertano, *Il piacere, l'amore e la morte nelle dottrine dei Presocratici* (Naples,
1983), 50: 'Se vivere è avere sensazioni, e se avere sensazioni è modificarsi, essere
cambiato da qualcosa di contrario, da qualcosa cioè che non fa parte già dell'equi-
librio consitutivo del nostro organismo, finché vive—*in quanto* vive—l'individuo è
sempre questo tipo di dolore. *Non quindi una generica concezione pessimistica ma una
precisa dottrina fisiologica*' (emphasis original). Casertano goes on to say that this
general physiological pain nevertheless occasionally erupts into pain of a 'second
level', namely perceived and noticed pain, as in the cases of extreme perceptions.

has to be said, universal) agreement among modern philosophers that pain, whatever it is, must be felt.[42] Beyond that general agreement, however, various views have been proposed by modern philosophers about what pain is, ranging from those who take pain to be a certain form of perception of a certain kind of object—perhaps a special sense which is able to perceive the state of one's own body[43]—to those who instead prefer an adverbial analysis whereby to feel a pain in one's foot is not to perceive some peculiar object (a pain) in that part of one's body, but to 'be appeared to' in a certain manner, i.e. painfully.[44] Those who favour the latter view point to the fact that pains are private: I cannot feel the pain of my friend's cut hand by looking at it. They also might claim that a pain and the awareness of a pain are so intimately connected that they should not be separated into distinct act and object. Those who favour the former view emphasize the fact that pains seem to be located in particular places in a person's body: when I feel the pain of a cut hand I seem to be feeling something *in* my hand.[45] Pain appears

---

[42] Cf. G. Ryle, *The Concept of Mind* (Oxford, 1949), 194: 'A pain in my knee is a sensation that I mind having, so "unnoticed pain" is an absurd expression, where "unnoticed sensation" has no absurdity.' G. Pitcher, 'Pain Perception', *Philosophical Review*, 79 (1970), 368–93 at 370: 'A pain lasts only as long as it is felt, and it is nonsense to speak of having a pain that one cannot feel or there being a pain that no one has.' D. Lewis, 'Mad Pain and Martian Pain', in D. Rosenthal (ed.), *The Nature of Mind* (Oxford, 1991), 229–35 at 233, first published in N. Block (ed.), *Readings in the Philosophy of Psychology*, i (Cambridge, Mass., 1980), 216–22: 'Pain is a feeling. Surely that is uncontroversial. To have a pain and to feel pain are one and the same. For a state to be pain and it to feel painful are likewise one and the same. A theory of what it is for a state to be pain is inescapably a theory of what it is like to be in that state, of how that state feels, of the phenomenal character of that state.' The International Association for the Study of Pain (www.iasp-pain.org) defines pain as: 'An unpleasant sensory and emotional experience associated with actual or potential tissue damage, or described in terms of such damage', and notes: 'Pain is always subjective. Each individual learns the application of the word through experiences related to injury in early life. Biologists recognize that those stimuli which cause pain are liable to damage tissue. Accordingly, pain is that experience we associate with actual or potential tissue damage. It is unquestionably a sensation in a part or parts of the body, but it is also always unpleasant and therefore also an emotional experience. Experiences which resemble pain but are not unpleasant, e.g., pricking, should not be called pain. Unpleasant abnormal experiences (dysesthesias) may also be pain but are not necessarily so because, subjectively, they may not have the usual sensory qualities of pain.'

[43] See Pitcher, 'Pain Perception', and N. Everitt, 'Pain and Perception', *Proceedings of the Aristotelian Association*, 89 (1988–9), 113–24.

[44] See V. Tsouna, *The Epistemology of the Cyrenaic School* (Cambridge, 1998), 45–53, on the adverbial analysis of perception and Cyrenaic epistemology.

[45] For a helpful introduction to philosophical discussions of pain see M. Aydede,

to be tied to localized parts of the body and generally to be correlated with some kind of damage. It also, of course, has important
emotional, intentional, evaluative, and qualitative aspects. Tying
together the physiological and intentional aspects is very tricky;
there are cases both of pain arising with no obvious object (e.g.
'phantom limb pain') and also cases of serious tissue damage with
no accompanying feelings of pain.[46]

Anaxagoras shows signs of struggling with the same general difficulty of combining physiological and phenomenological accounts
of pain. His preferred solution holds that I might now be in pain,
since all perception is accompanied by pain, but not realize it. That
certainly puts him outside the general modern consensus, but is it
enough to say that he is simply mistaken or else wilfully misusing
the word 'pain'? It might be instructive to compare another ancient
account which attempts to bridge the gap between physiological and
phenomenological aspects of pleasure and pain. In Plato's *Timaeus*
(64 B ff.) the account of bodily pleasure and pain retains the notion
that they are, respectively, restorations or disruptions of the body's
natural state.[47] However, Timaeus adds a further factor. These disruptions and restorations are thought of in terms of motions which
vary in intensity and duration. Some motions are too gradual, too
small, or else too easily instigated to produce the experience of
pleasure or pain. Timaeus expresses this by saying that in those
cases the motion itself is not perceived, although it is made quite
clear that the motion in question may be one produced in an act
of perceiving. For example, motions involved in the act of seeing
cause neither pleasures nor pains (at least in usual circumstances)
because they occur so readily (64 D–E). However, a cut to the hand,
because motions in that part of the body are less easily instigated,

'Pain', in N. Zalta (ed.), *The Stanford Encyclopedia of Philosophy* (http://plato.stan-
ford.edu/entries/pain/ ⟨accessed 5 Oct. 2005⟩) and his bibliography available online
at: http://www.clas.ufl.edu/users/maydede/pain/.

[46] There are people who feel no pain. Such people do not feel nothing at all, but
they do not register, say, a burning sensation in the hand when it is placed over a
candle, *as painful*. This can lead to significant damage over time since such people
lack the trigger for avoiding certain objects or behaviours. See V. Hardcastle, *The
Myth of Pain* (Cambridge, Mass., 1999), 58–60, for a case study. Cf. R. Trigg, *Pain
and Emotion* (Oxford, 1970), 166–76.

[47] Cf. Thphr. *De sens.* 84, which Long, 'Theophrastus', 155, calls a 'clear and
accurate paraphrase': ἡδὺ δὲ καὶ λυπηρόν, τὸ μὲν εἰς φύσιν ἀθρόον πάθος, τὸ δὲ παρὰ
φύσιν καὶ βίᾳ [λυπηρόν], τὰ δὲ μέσα καὶ ἀναίσθητα ἀνὰ λόγον. διὸ καὶ κατὰ τὸ ὁρᾶν οὐκ
εἶναι λύπην οὐδ' ἡδονὴν τῇ διακρίσει καὶ συγκρίσει. Cf. Baltussen, *Theophrastus*, 112–15.

causes motions to be passed on to the entire body and produce pain (64 E). Here, it seems, pain is explained by emphasizing the effort required to set up these internal motions and recognizing that only certain motions are sufficient to be communicated to the central seat of consciousness (τὸ φρόνιμον, 64 B 5). Others, though still *pathē*, are insufficient to be communicated and are therefore unperceived (ἀναίσθητον παρέσχεν τὸ παθόν, 64 C 3). Timaeus then uses this model to explain various common phenomena. Two examples are offered: fragrances can produce pleasures when smelt by offering a rapid restoration of an unperceived (and therefore not painful) prior gradual disturbance and lack;[48] in contrast, cuts to a person's flesh can produce pains by setting up rapid intense disturbances which are followed by slow gradual restorations—healing—which do not produce pleasures.

 This account aims to do justice both to a common physiological basis for pain and also to the intuition that only certain physiological changes or acts of perception are noticed as painful or pleasant. It might appear to do a much better job than Anaxagoras in this regard, principally because it introduces a further factor—the *phronimon*—which has the function of registering only some of the motions set up in the rest of the body as being pleasures or pains. Timaeus notably describes the awareness of these motions on the part of the *phronimon* as itself a kind of perception:

ὅσα δὲ κατὰ σμικρὸν τὰς ἀποχωρήσεις ἑαυτῶν καὶ κενώσεις εἴληφεν, τὰς δὲ πληρώσεις ἀθρόας καὶ κατὰ μεγάλα, κενώσεως μὲν ἀναίσθητα, πληρώσεως δὲ αἰσθητικὰ γιγνόμενα, λύπας μὲν οὐ παρέχει τῷ θνητῷ τῆς ψυχῆς, μεγίστας δὲ ἡδονάς· ἔστιν δὲ ἔνδηλα περὶ τὰς εὐωδίας. (Plato, *Tim.* 65 A 1–6)

All those bodies which receive their disruptions and depletions little by little, but whose restorations are intense and large, fail to perceive the depletion but do perceive the restoration, and they provide no pains, but the greatest pleasures to the mortal soul. This is clear in the case of pleasing fragrances.

Timaeus apparently recognizes two kinds of perception: the first is the standard means of becoming aware of the external world; the second is some kind of internal awareness of the motions of one's own body, including the motions involved in perception: proprio-

<hr/>

[48] Cf. Plato, *Phileb.* 51 B 3–7: τὰς περί τε τὰ καλὰ λεγόμενα χρώματα καὶ περὶ τὰ σχήματα καὶ τῶν ὀσμῶν τὰς πλείστας καὶ τὰς τῶν φθόγγων καὶ ὅσα τὰς ἐνδείας ἀναισθήτους ἔχοντα καὶ ἀλύπους τὰς πληρώσεις αἰσθητὰς καὶ ἡδείας [καθαρὰς λυπῶν] παραδίδωσιν. See also Gosling and Taylor, *Pleasure*, 180–1.

ception. Pleasure and pain are perceptions in this second sense: they
are perceptions of certain internal bodily motions, and some of these
motions are caused by perceptions in the standard sense.[49] It therefore allows there to be cases of perception which are not painful, but
at the price of introducing the complication—not deeply pursued
in Timaeus' exposition—of a further kind of internal awareness of
changes in one's own body. Timaeus retains what is recognizably
a kind of perceptual account of pain while restricting the sorts of
motions that are perceived as painful and retaining the common
idea that it is absurd to allow that there are unperceived pains.

Although, as we noted, there is a widespread agreement that
pains are always felt, there are some philosophers who have made
a case for the view that it is possible to feel a pain but not be
aware of it, or to feel a pain and not notice it.[50] Their case will rest
on the plausibility of particular descriptions of our experiences of
pain. I can imagine, for example, having a toothache which, when
I focus my attention on it, is rather painful. However, if I become
distracted or engrossed in some other activity, I might not notice
the pain and only later, when I focus on it again, do I notice it
once more. The most reasonable view of this sort of experience, it
is claimed, is not that the pain of the toothache disappears and then
returns and when I choose to focus upon it, but that the pain
is present throughout but not noticed for a time. We could even
say that the pain is felt, but not noticed. The necessary additional
factor here is the faculty of being able to focus or divert one's

---

[49] Cf. Thphr. *De sens.* 32: ἀλλὰ μὴν οὐδὲ αἱ τῶν αἰσθητῶν ὑπερβολαὶ καὶ τὸ τοῦ χρόνου
πλῆθος οὐδὲν σημεῖον ὡς μετὰ λύπης ἐστίν, ἀλλὰ μᾶλλον ὡς ἐν συμμετρίᾳ τινὶ καὶ κράσει
πρὸς τὸ αἰσθητὸν ἡ αἴσθησις. διόπερ ἴσως τὸ μὲν ἐλλεῖπον ἀναίσθητον, τὸ δ' ὑπερβάλλον
λύπην τε ποιεῖ καὶ φθείρει.

[50] See e.g. D. Armstrong, *A Materialist Theory of the Mind* (London, 1968), who
claims (141) that pains can exist when we are not aware of them and holds that
this is consistent with saying (311) that 'A pain or an itch is a felt pain or felt itch,
and an unfelt pain or itch is nothing.' For a full defence of the view that there can
be unfelt pains see D. Palmer, 'Unfelt Pains', *American Philosophical Quarterly*,
17 (1975), 289–98. P. Wall, *Pain: the Science of Suffering* (London, 1999), 170–4,
uses a distinction between sensation and attention: 'The central nervous system
receives steady reports of all the events the sense organs are capable of detecting.
Obviously, it would be a disaster of excess if we were continuously aware of the entire
mass of arriving information' (170). He notes that the sensation of pain particularly
demands a person's attention, presumably for good reasons to do with the survival
of the individual, and discusses pain-alleviation therapies concerned with relaxation
and the diversion of attention. (He also discusses (4–17) cases of injuries which
are, at least initially, painless. In these cases the victim's attention is immediately
directed away from the pain to concerns about escaping the threatening situation.)

attention or consciousness. The philosophical disagreement now becomes rather complicated. Where Timaeus, for example, draws a distinction between disturbances which are painful and perceived and those which are not perceived and not painful, Anaxagoras can happily draw a rival distinction between those which are painful and noticed and those which are painful but not noticed. If this distinction is at all plausible, then his only remaining contentious claim will be that each and every perception is painful. And with this claim he will part company even with most of his philosophical allies. For example, David Palmer, who otherwise offers a spirited defence of the view that there can be unfelt pains, draws a line at this point:

If the foregoing account is correct then we may be faced with a problem that the traditional account [sc. that there can be no unfelt pains] does not have to contend with. That is the criticism that if, as I have claimed, one could be in pain but not notice it, then one might always be in pain, when he isn't attending to whether he is in pain. I think the suggestion that we *might* always be in pain when we are not attending whether we are in pain is correct, but the suggestion that this is a *problem* for this account is mistaken.

Clearly nothing *guarantees* that there are not many more unnoticed pains than anyone would ever have thought. It is in a certain sense *conceivable* (i.e., it is not self contradictory to assert) that one usually has pains he never has any inkling of whatsoever—just as it is *conceivable* that in the standard case of headache our headaches flee and then return between noticings. But there is no reason whatever to suppose that this is the case. It violates the principle of sufficient reason and, as well, may threaten perfectly acceptable causal accounts of pain. (Palmer, 'Unfelt Pains', 298)

To this last argument Anaxagoras may simply reply that, to his mind, there is a sufficiently plausible causal account of pain— namely that it is produced in every act of perception by the interaction of opposites—to make it more than just conceivable that we are always in pain when we perceive. If some acts of perception are painful, then, so Anaxagoras argues, we should think that all acts are, albeit to different degrees. Then he can point to habituation or lack of attention to explain why we are not always aware of the pain we undergo.[51] So even if we accept Theophrastus' presentation of Anaxagoras' views on perception and pain, there is no

[51] Let us note in passing that, if my interpretation is correct, Anaxagoras deserves consideration in the ongoing debate over whether there is in any ancient philosopher the notion that there is truth or knowledge to be had of one's own subjective states (see M. Burnyeat, 'Idealism and Greek Philosophy: What Descartes Saw and

reason to dismiss them on the grounds of obvious absurdity or to accuse him of a gross misuse of the notion of pain. His view can be ranked well among many other ancient theories for attending to both the physiological and the affective aspects of pain.

*Corpus Christi College, Cambridge*

## BIBLIOGRAPHY

Armstrong, D., *A Materialist Theory of the Mind* (London, 1968).

Aydede, M., 'Pain', in N. Zalta (ed.), *The Stanford Encyclopedia of Philosophy* (http://plato.stanford.edu/entires/pain/) ⟨accessed 5 Oct. 2005⟩.

Baltussen, H., 'Peripatetic Dialectic in the *De sensibus*' ['Peripatetic Dialectic'], in W. W. Fortenbaugh and D. Gutas (eds.), *Theophrastus: His Psychological, Doxographical and Scientific Writings* (New Brunswick, 1992), 1–19.

—— *Theophrastus against the Presocratics and Plato: Peripatetic Dialectic in the* De sensibus [*Theophrastus*] (Leiden, 2000).

Barnes, J., *The Presocratic Philosophers* [*Presocratic*], rev. edn. (London, 1982).

Broadie, S., *Ethics with Aristotle* (Oxford, 1991).

Burnyeat, M., 'Idealism and Greek Philosophy: What Descartes Saw and Berkeley Missed', in G. Vesey (ed.), *Idealism Past and Present* (Cambridge, 1982), 19–50.

Casertano, G., *Il piacere, l'amore e la morte nelle dottrine dei Presocratici* (Naples, 1983).

Cornford, F., 'Anaxagoras' Theory of Matter' ['Anaxagoras'], in R. E. Allen and D. J. Furley (eds.), *Studies in Presocratic Philosophy*, ii (London, 1975), 275–322; first published in *Classical Quarterly*, 24 (1930), 14–30, 83–95.

Craik, E., *Hippocrates:* Places in Man (Oxford, 1998).

Curd, P., *The Legacy of Parmenides* (Princeton, 1998).

—— 'The Metaphysics of Physics: Mixture and Separation in Empedocles

Berkeley Missed', in G. Vesey (ed.), *Idealism Past and Present* (Cambridge, 1982), 19–50, and, recently, G. Fine, 'Subjectivity, Ancient and Modern: The Cyrenaics, Sextus, and Descartes', in J. Miller and B. Inwood (eds.), *Hellenistic and Early Modern Philosophy* (Cambridge, 2003), 192–231). Of course, Anaxagoras makes no explicit distinction between a subjective state (a feeling of pain) and an objective fact about how one is being affected. Nevertheless, it is a consequence of his view that a person is not necessarily an incorrigible authority about his own *pathē*; in fact, those of us who believe that we are perceiving but feeling no pain are in that respect wrong about our *pathē*.

and Anaxagoras', in V. Caston and D. W. Graham (eds.), *Presocratic Philosophy* (Aldershot, 2002), 139–58.

Drossaart Lulofs, H. J., and Poortman, E. L. J., *Aristoteles Semitico-Latinus: Nicolaus Damascenus De plantis. Five Translations* (Amsterdam, 1989).

Everitt, N., 'Pain and Perception', *Proceedings of the Aristotelian Society*, 89 (1988–9), 113–24.

Fine, G., 'Subjectivity, Ancient and Modern: The Cyrenaics, Sextus, and Descartes', in J. Miller and B. Inwood (eds.), *Hellenistic and Early Modern Philosophy* (Cambridge, 2003), 192–231.

Furley, D., 'Anaxagoras in Response to Parmenides', in id., *Cosmic Problems* (Cambridge, 1989), 47–65.

Gosling, J. C. B., and Taylor, C. C. W., *The Greeks on Pleasure* [*Pleasure*] (Oxford, 1982).

Graham, D., 'The Postulates of Anaxagoras' ['Postulates'], *Apeiron*, 27 (1994), 77–121.

Hardcastle, V., *The Myth of Pain* (Cambridge, Mass., 1999).

Hare, R. M., 'Pain and Evil', in J. Feinberg (ed.), *Moral Concepts* (Oxford, 1969), 29–42.

Ierodiakonou, K., 'Empedocles on Colour and Colour Perception' ['Empedocles'], *Oxford Studies in Ancient Philosophy*, 29 (2005), 1–37.

Lewis, D., 'Mad Pain and Martian Pain', in D. Rosenthal (ed.), *The Nature of Mind* (Oxford, 1991), 229–35; first published in N. Block (ed.), *Readings in the Philosophy of Psychology*, i (Cambridge, Mass., 1980), 216–22.

Lloyd, G. E. R., *Polarity and Analogy* (Cambridge, 1966).

Long, A. A., 'Theophrastus' *De sensibus* on Plato' ['Theophrastus'], in K. A. Algra, P. W. van der Horst, and D. T. Runia (eds.), *Polyhistor: Studies in the History and Historiography of Ancient Philosophy Presented to J. Mansfeld on his Sixtieth Birthday* (Leiden, 1996), 345–62.

Mann, W., 'Anaxagoras and the *homoiomerē*', *Phronesis*, 25 (1980), 228–49.

Mourelatos, A., 'Quality, Structure and Emergence in Later Pre-Socratic Philosophy', *Proceedings of the Boston Area Colloquium in Ancient Philosophy*, 2 (1987), 127–94.

Palmer, D., 'Unfelt Pains', *American Philosophical Quarterly*, 17 (1975), 289–98.

Pitcher, G., 'Pain Perception', *Philosophical Review*, 79 (1970), 368–93.

Prost, J., *Les Théories hellénistiques de la douleur* (Louvain, 2004).

Ryle, G., *The Concept of Mind* (London, 1949).

Schofield, M., *An Essay on Anaxagoras* [*Anaxagoras*] (Cambridge, 1980).

Sedley, D., 'Empedocles' Theory of Vision' ['Empedocles'], in W. W. Fortenbaugh and D. Gutas (eds.), *Theophrastus: His Psychological, Doxographical and Scientific Writings* (New Brunswick, 1992), 20–31.

—— *Creationism and its Critics in Antiquity* (Berkeley and Los Angeles, forthcoming).

Sider, D., *The Fragments of Anaxagoras: Introduction, Text, and Commentary* [*Anaxagoras*], 2nd edn. (Sankt Augustin, 2005).

Strang, C., 'The Physical Theory of Anaxagoras', in R. E. Allen and D. J. Furley (eds.), *Studies in Presocratic Philosophy*, ii (London, 1975), 361–80; first published in *Archiv für Geschichte der Philosophie*, 45 (1963), 101–18.

Stratton, G. M., *Theophrastus and the Greek Physiological Psychology before Aristotle* (London, 1917).

Trigg, R., *Pain and Emotion* (Oxford, 1970).

Tsouna, V., *The Epistemology of the Cyrenaic School* (Cambridge, 1998).

Vlastos, G., 'The Physical Theory of Anaxagoras' ['Anaxagoras'], *Philosophical Review*, 59 (1950), 31–57; repr. in R. E. Allen and D. J. Furley (eds.), *Studies in Presocratic Philosophy*, ii (London, 1975), 323–53, and in Vlastos, *Studies in Greek Philosophy*, i (Princeton, 1995), 303–27.

Wall, P., *Pain: The Science of Suffering* (London, 1999).

# SOCRATIC MIDWIFERY:
# A SECOND *APOLOGY*?

## ZINA GIANNOPOULOU

PLATO's *Theaetetus* is a peculiar dialogue. While it has generally
been regarded as either middle/late or late, it possesses several
features traditionally associated with Plato's early philosophical
works.[1] The most important of them centre around the figure of
Socrates: he is a self-proclaimed ignoramus who asks for the definition of a difficult term (knowledge), dialectically examines a variety
of answers, rejects them all, and ends at an impasse (*aporia*). This
preoccupation with the figure of Socrates of the early dialogues is
reinforced by the dramatic date of the conversation, which is mentioned twice in the dialogue.[2] In the preface, Eucleides remarks
that Socrates met Theaetetus shortly before Socrates' death (142 C
6) and, at the end, Socrates tells Theaetetus that he must go to
the King Archon's porch to meet the indictment that Meletus had

© Zina Giannopoulou 2007

I wish to thank Tony Long, Mark McPherran, David Sansone, Gerry Santas, Nick
Smith, and Harold Tarrant for helpful comments on various drafts of this paper. I
owe a special debt of gratitude to David Sedley for patient and generous criticism.
Responsibility for any remaining errors is my own.

[1] For a useful collection of the main early and late features of *Theaetetus*, see R.
Blondell, *The Play of Character in Plato's Dialogues* [*Play of Character*] (Cambridge,
2002), 251 nn. 1 and 3. Although I use such entrenched chronological rubrics as
'early' and 'late', I must say that my argument does not subscribe to a develop-
mentalist agenda. This does not necessarily betoken any deep-seated ideological
disagreement with the tenets of developmentalism. Rather, inasmuch as my reading
relates *Theaetetus* to *Apology*, it simply invites us to consider the putative benefits
of a unitarian approach to the dialogue's interpretation. For a well-balanced study
that acknowledges that *Theaetetus* is a middle/late or late dialogue that harks back
to Socrates' early aporetic dialectic, see D. Sedley, *The Midwife of Platonism: Text
and Subtext in Plato's* Theaetetus [*Midwife*] (Oxford, 2004).

[2] When I refer to Socrates, I mean the fictionalized character populating Plato's
dialogues. I shall make no claims about the historical Socrates, even when I deal
with *Apology*, the dialogue traditionally viewed as offering a picture of the historical
figure. For the Socratic dialogue as a fundamentally fictional genre, see C. Kahn,
*Plato and the Socratic Dialogue* (Cambridge, 1996), 1–35.

brought against him (210 D 2–4). These references place the dramatic date of the conversation in 399, the year of Socrates' trial and execution. Socrates' interest in the intellectual progress of the Athenian young men, which belies the charge of corrupting the youth levelled at him in *Apology*, occurs at the very beginning of Eucleides' reported conversation (143 D 4–8). And, above all, the dialogue contains the most elaborate presentation of Socrates' elenctic practice, his divinely mandated spiritual midwifery (149 A 1–151 D 6).[3] As a barren midwife of the intellect, Socrates delivers his pregnant interlocutors' psychic children and, after he has subjected them to scrutiny, retains or rejects them on the basis of their epistemic worth. His maieutic art enjoys divine support, indeed the god affects the execution of Socrates' elenctic practice.

These features of *Theaetetus*, situated prominently at its beginning, invite a comparison with *Apology*. Although the two works differ in many respects, they unmistakably place Socrates and his philosophic mission against the backdrop of his death. Anthony Long has cast the relation between them in the language of defence. 'What is remarkable about the *Theaetetus*', he writes, 'is the explicitness of Socrates' defence, its chronology, and its allusions to, and recasting of, the official *Apology*.'[4] In this paper I would like to flesh out and substantiate this line of thought by concentrating on Socratic midwifery, the justly celebrated and unique image of Socrates *qua* mental obstetrician, and in particular on two of its constitutive elements, the midwife's intellectual barrenness and the divine underpinnings of spiritual maieutics.[5] I shall broadly claim that both these traits set up the elenctic art as essentially antithetical to sophistry, from whose practitioners Socrates undertook to distinguish himself in *Apology*.[6] His emphatic assertions of

---

[3] In the midwifery passage the word 'elenchus' is not used, but there are good reasons for identifying Socrates' elenctic practice with spiritual midwifery. See S. R. Slings, *Plato: Clitophon* (Cambridge, 1999), 132–3.

[4] See A. A. Long, 'Plato's Apologies and Socrates in the *Theaetetus*', in J. Gentzler (ed.), *Method in Ancient Philosophy* (Oxford, 1998), 113–36 at 122.

[5] For the novelty of Socrates' midwifery in the *Theaetetus*, see M. F. Burnyeat, 'Socratic Midwifery, Platonic Inspiration' ['Socratic Midwifery'], *Bulletin of the Institute of Classical Studies*, 24 (1977), 7–16. Considerations of space prevent me from treating Socratic matchmaking, the third and last component of mental obstetrics, whereby Socrates marries off sterile young men to 'Prodicus . . . and to other wise and inspired persons' (151 B 5–6). It will become obvious, I hope, that its examination would only strengthen the interpretation of spiritual midwifery I am here expounding.

[6] At this point I should make it clear that I am not concerned with the sophists as

ignorance in *Theaetetus* contrast sharply with the ostensible wisdom of Protagoras and a host of other reputed authorities, such as Heraclitus and Empedocles, all of whom are taken collectively to support Theaetetus' phenomenalist conception of knowledge (152 E 2–9). By performing midwifery directly on the young man, Socrates indirectly delivers, elenctically tests, and finally discards the false beliefs of purportedly wise men, thereby showing in practice his fundamental difference from them. This difference is further underscored by the divine support Socratic midwifery enjoys. According to Socrates, he and the god collaborate (150 D: 'it is I, *with God's help*, who deliver them of this offspring'), and at the end of every divinely assisted obstetric event Socrates determines the epistemic value of the idea borne by the pregnant interlocutor, whether it is 'a phantom, that is, an error, or a fertile truth' (150 C 2–3). His confidence in the assessment of the elenctic result derives, in my view, from the divine underpinnings of the art itself, from the fact that god, and, by extension, Socrates *qua* his mortal assistant, cannot 'wish evil to man', and so cannot accept that a lie, and not the truth, would ever emerge from the performance of mental midwifery (151 D 1–3). The divine backing of the elenchus, then, grants its results indisputable epistemic authority, of which the ordinary beliefs of men, so dear to Protagoras and his ilk, are deprived.

The notion that *Theaetetus* attacks Protagoras' ideas is found in an ancient testimony. Proclus reports a view that it is a peirastic dialogue directed against Protagoras.[7] Concerning the thematic structure of the dialogue, he takes Part II, Socrates' exploration of false belief, to be a continuation of Part I's critique of Protagoras.[8] David Sedley describes Proclus' understanding of the function of these two parts as follows:

Part I explores the problematic consequences of supposing all opinions to be true, that is, of agreeing with Protagoras; part II explores the problematic consequences of supposing some opinions to be false, that is, of disagreeing with Protagoras.[9]

historical figures or with Plato's occasionally sympathetic treatment of some of them (e.g. Protagoras in the homonymous dialogue), but with his inimical stance towards Protagoras and sophistry in the *Theaetetus*. The fact that some sophists resembled the Socrates of the *Theaetetus* in that they eschewed theoretical commitments does not weaken the contrast for which I argue, since the Protagorean dictum under scrutiny here is treated as a *thesis* of important epistemological ramifications.

[7] Proclus, *In Parm.* 631 Cousin.                [8] Ibid. 654. 15–26 Cousin.
[9] D. Sedley, 'Three Platonist Interpretations of the *Theaetetus*' ['Platonist In-

Even if one does not entirely agree with Proclus' construal of these two segments or of the dialogue as a whole, one may see in his views a promising interpretation of *Theaetetus*, the seeds of which are sown, in my opinion, in the midwifery analogy.

Before I present my argument, I should briefly address an issue that is central to my approach to the dialogue. Why, it might be asked, should one expect to find in *Theaetetus* a recast of the contrast between Socrates and the sophists? Given that one can look to either *Protagoras* or *Gorgias* for Plato's concern to differentiate Socrates from the sophists, or to *Euthydemus* for a caustic representation of his difference from the practitioners of eristics, why should one suppose that *Theaetetus* in particular revisits this old, and perhaps tired, subject?[10] The answer, in my view, lies in the very topic under investigation in this dialogue, the definition of knowledge. For the ultimate distinction between Socrates and the sophists lies precisely in their respective views of, and claims to, knowledge or wisdom.[11] While Socrates categorically and repeatedly asserts that the only sort of wisdom he possesses is awareness of his own ignorance, the sophists pride themselves on, and profit from, the possession of 'some more-than-human wisdom' (*Ap.* 20 E 1). In *Apology* the distinction between the all too ignorant Socrates and the all too knowledgeable sophists emerges at length in 19 D– 20 C, but almost every page of the text is strewn with expressions of Socrates' appropriately human belief in his ignorance. But whereas in *Apology* the contrast is primarily a notional tool in Socrates' rhetorical arsenal, in *Theaetetus* it acquires philosophical and dramatic poignancy. For here Socrates dramatically embodies, so to speak, that which in *Apology* and elsewhere he merely claims to be: he is a self-proclaimed barren midwife of the intellect who undertakes to examine the validity of a host of definitions of knowledge brought to him by Theaetetus, a youth acquainted with sophistic discourse. The late *Theaetetus*, then, by virtue of its very subject, offers a unique opportunity for the articulation of important conceptual and methodological differences between Socrates and the sophists.

---

terpretations'], in C. Gill and M. M. McCabe (eds.), *Form and Argument in Late Plato* (Oxford, 1996), 79–103 at 81. He also offers a useful account of Proclus' understanding of the structure of the dialogue as a whole.

[10] Thanks to Tony Long for raising this question.

[11] The two are seen as semantically coextensive at 145 E 6–7. See also *Prot.* 330 B 4 and *Phdr.* 247 D 6–E 2.

In the first section of this paper I argue that Socrates' intellectual barrenness is best seen as the deliberate suppression of any convictions of his own. By presenting himself as the empty midwife of the intellect, he creates the sharpest possible contrast between himself and his purportedly wise opponents. His awareness of the inferior epistemic value of his beliefs, which underlies his mental sterility, further distinguishes him from those who never question their wisdom, the sophists and their ilk, since they take it to be unarguably authoritative.[12] In the second section, I argue that the religious garb in which Socrates dresses his mission is meant to legitimize the validity of the obstetric result. Socrates' pronouncement on the epistemic worth of his associate's mental child is true, since it is the product of a divinely mandated and assisted art. Truth thus ceases to be, *à la Protagoras*, a quality possessed by every mortal utterance and, instead, becomes associated with god's indisputably wise authority.

## 1. Socratic barrenness

Barrenness is the most important maieutic trait. Midwives, Socrates says, practise their skill only after they have lost their ability to procreate. The reason for this is that Artemis, the virgin goddess of childbirth, has entrusted midwifery to those women who resemble her in being unable to conceive their own offspring. The barrenness of these women follows a period of fertility, as 'human nature is too weak to acquire skill where it has no experience' (149 C 1–2).[13] The limitations of human nature, then, prevent a complete identification of the secular with the divine, allowing only for a certain degree of 'likeness' (ὁμοιότητα, 149 C 3): the exercise of the medical midwife's skill is made possible by her previous experience with childbirth, while Artemis' knowledge of obstetrics requires no such experi-

---

[12] Although I shall here argue and provide evidence for the distinction between Socrates and the sophists in the context of the second definition of knowledge as perception, I believe that traces of it may also be found in the third and fourth definitions of *epistēmē* as true judgement and as true judgement accompanied by *logos*, respectively. I make a case for its presence there in my book-length study of *Theaetetus*, currently in progress.

[13] For the sake of convenience, all translations of the Greek, unless otherwise noted, come from M. F. Burnyeat, *The* Theaetetus *of Plato* [*Theaetetus*] (Indianapolis, 1990).

ence.[14] But if having had the ability to have children of one's own is a necessary precondition for *mortals'* practising obstetrics, it is at least odd to find Socrates claiming not to have given birth. His barrenness is described first as inability to birth wisdom (150 C 4, 6, D 1–2, where psychic infertility is equated with the absence of wise progeny) and then as compatible with the possession of some sort of wisdom (150 D 1, in which case, and quite paradoxically, barrenness is associated with some wise possessions).[15] These admissions seem to render Socratic midwifery a hopelessly complicated affair. For if mortal obstetrics presupposes *prior* experience with childbirth but Socrates has not given birth to wisdom, how can he be a *midwife* of the intellect? Conversely, if he now possesses 'rudiments of wisdom', how can he be a *barren* midwife of the intellect?[16] Scholars have attempted to resolve this impasse by viewing Socrates' barrenness as an inability to birth wisdom, not ordinary beliefs.[17] They claim that *qua* begetter of mortal beliefs, Socrates has personal experience in birthing, and may thus be said to lay a legitimate claim to mental midwifery. The association of Socrates' barrenness with lack of wisdom receives confirmation from his repeated and emphatic claims of ignorance throughout the Platonic corpus.[18] It

[14] Cf. the digression's main preoccupation with *homoiōsis theōi* at 176 B.

[15] The most common interpretation of οὐ πάνυ τι σοφός postulates a total rejection of any Socratic claim to wisdom ('I am not at all wise'), while the anonymous commentator on the *Theaetetus*, at 55. 42–5, takes the adverbial phrase as *qualifying* the rejection of wisdom ('I am not entirely wise'). For a defence of the latter rendering, which I am here adopting, see J. Riddell, *A Digest of Platonic Idioms* (Amsterdam, 1967), §139; Sedley, 'Platonist Interpretations', 98; and H. Thesleff, *Studies on Intensification in Early and Classical Greek* (Helsingfors, 1954), 76–8.

[16] I borrow this expression from Sedley, *Midwife*, 31.

[17] See e.g. R. M. Polansky, *Philosophy and Knowledge: A Commentary on Plato's Theaetetus* (London and Toronto, 1992), 62.

[18] For Socrates' proclamations of his ignorance see *Ap.* 20 C 1–3; 21 D 2–7; 23 B 2–4; *Charm.* 165 B 4–C 2; 166 C 7–D 6; *Euthph.* 5 A 7–C 5; 15 C 12; 15 E 5–16 A 4; *La.* 186 B 8–C 5, D 8–E 3; 200 E 2–5; *Lys.* 212 A 4–7; 223 B 4–8; *H.Ma.* 286 C 8–E 2; 304 D 4–E 5; *Gorg.* 509 A 4–6; *Meno* 71 A 1–7; 80 D 1–4; *Rep.* 337 E 4–5. For reports of it in ancient sources, see Arist. *SE* 183ᵇ6–8; Ael. Arist. *Or.* 45. 21, ii. 25 Dindorf; Antiochus of Ascalon ap. Cic. *Acad.* 1. 4. 16; Arcesilaus ap. Cic. *Acad.* 1. 12. 45; Plut. *Adv. Col.* 117 D. For those construing Socrates' disavowal of knowledge as ironic or strategic, as did Thrasymachus at *Rep.* 331 A, see N. Gulley, *The Philosophy of Socrates* (New York, 1968), 62; H. Teloh, *The Development of Plato's Metaphysics* (University Park, PA, 1981); and L. Versenyi, *Socratic Humanism* (New Haven, 1963), 118. For those who take the disclaimer at face value, see S. Austin, 'The Paradox of Socratic Ignorance (How To Know That You Don't Know)', *Philosophical Topics*, 15 (1987), 23–34; T. C. Brickhouse and N. D. Smith, *Plato's Socrates* (Oxford, 1994); T. H. Irwin, *Plato's Moral Theory: The Early and Middle Dialogues [Moral*

runs, however, counter to the essential prerequisite for midwifery, the temporal discontinuity between *past* fertility and *present* barrenness.[19] For the obstetric skill requires, as we have seen, that the midwife's past ability to conceive children be lost in the present, whereas this view suggests that Socrates-*qua*-midwife is still able to engender ordinary mental offspring. Furthermore, this interpretation must obviously concede that Socrates' lack of wisdom is an abiding feature of his epistemic make-up, not the necessary concomitant of spiritual midwifery, so that, once again, no distinction is permissible between a previously wise but currently non-wise Socrates. What has not been seriously entertained as a viable construal of Socratic barrenness is that, if psychic sterility is intended *both* to connote mental emptiness *and* to succeed a period of intellectual fertility, it must pertain to ordinary beliefs. For the advent of mental midwifery necessarily entails the elimination of the sort of opinions Socrates was able to produce during his pre-obstetric period, i.e. mortal opinions.

Now, on the face of it, this suggestion seems patently absurd. After all, does not Socrates ordinarily express a great number of his own, properly human beliefs in his conversations with others?[20] How can his intellectual barrenness be so radical as to signify a complete psychic emptiness? One may rejoin that the fact that Socrates is elsewhere depicted as both having and submitting personal convictions does not *by itself* prove that this is how he must be dramatically presented in *Theaetetus*. It is at least conceivable that for reasons peculiar to this dialogue Socrates' mental infertility is here painted more starkly than one might expect.[21] In any case, the unique appearance of the midwifery analogy in *Theaete-*

*Theory*] (Oxford, 1977), 39–40; J. H. Lesher, 'Socrates' Disavowal of Knowledge', *Journal of the History of Philosophy*, 25 (1987), 275–88; G. Vlastos, 'Socrates' Disavowal of Knowledge' ['Disavowal'], *Philosophical Quarterly*, 35 (1985), 1–31; and P. Woodruff, 'Plato's Early Theory of Knowledge' ['Early Theory'], in S. Everson (ed.), *Companions to Ancient Thought*, i. *Epistemology* (Cambridge, 1990), 60–84.

[19] To my knowledge, the only modern commentator who has been puzzled by this temporal discontinuity is R. G. Wengert, 'The Paradox of the Midwife', *History of Philosophy Quarterly*, 5 (1998), 3–10.
[20] For a detailed analysis of this view see, among others, T. H. Irwin, *Plato's Ethics* (Oxford, 1995), ch. 2, and Vlastos, 'Disavowal'.
[21] Cf. Sedley, *Midwife*, 31: 'As a matter of fact, I doubt that any one interpretation [of Socrates' claims of ignorance] will work for all the Socratic dialogues, if only because Plato himself may have had considerable trouble deciding what spin to put on Socrates' disavowal.'

*tus* renders plausible a depiction of Socrates that differs to some extent from the way in which his philosophic persona is crafted in other dialogues.[22] Before I proceed fully to formulate and adduce evidence for this view, let me simply mention that an obvious attraction of this interpretation is that it preserves a crucial feature of the analogy between physical and mental midwifery, as it renders both medical and spiritual midwives barren in respect of the same type of offspring, i.e. ordinary, *mortal* children. This feature is missing from the alternative interpretation, which conceives of Socrates' barrenness as the inability to birth a more-than-human epistemic offspring, *wisdom*.

I submit that Socrates' barrenness is best conceived as the conscious eschewing of any strongly held beliefs. *Theaetetus* invites us to countenance his disavowal of knowledge, not only as yet another expression of his well-known inability to birth wisdom, but rather as a deliberate arrest of his eagerness to communicate any convictions of his own in the form of *logoi*, i.e. conceptual definitions of knowledge and theories offered in their support.[23] From the point of view of his publicly conducted midwifery, Socrates is barren; bereft of wisdom and reluctant to propound theories of his own, he simply elicits his interlocutors' ideas.[24] These ideas may take the form of full-fledged definitions ready to be put to the elenctic test, or may be unrefined assumptions of those participating in the

---

[22] For the various guises Socrates assumes in the Platonic corpus, see Blondell, *Play of Character*, 8–11.

[23] My construal of Socratic barrenness does not pertain to Socrates' knowledge of midwifery. On this point, see Sedley, *Midwife*, 32.

[24] There are two cases that seem to threaten a radical construal of Socratic barrenness. First, in the digression Socrates offers his own views on godlikeness (176 A 9–B 2) and the objective standards that govern human happiness and misery (176 E 3–177 A 3). These positive assertions need not undermine his spiritual barrenness, since they appear in a digression and thus lie outside the scope of the argument proper. See J. Annas, 'Plato the Sceptic', in J. C. Klagge and N. D. Smith (eds.), *Methods of Interpreting Plato and his Dialogues* (*OSAP* suppl.; Oxford, 1992), 32–52. Secondly, in his examination of false judgement Socrates announces his conviction that thinking takes the form of silent internal question and answer (189 E 6–190 A 7), and is quick to tell Theaetetus that this is said 'in all ignorance' (μὴ εἰδώς, 189 E 7), a proper reminder of his obstetric barrenness. I suggest that we ought to take the reminder seriously: by endowing thinking with the mechanics of dialectic and by identifying judgement with its final stage or outcome, Socrates attributes to an internal cognitive event the characteristics of his own elenctic practice. Making a judgement, then, mirrors the process of Socratic midwifery, knowledge of which I have exempted from the cognitive range of Socrates, the barren midwife of the intellect.

conversation. In this latter case, Socrates helps his interlocutors to articulate their rudimentary sayings and to transform them into testable positions. And although helping them may require of him to express opinions of his own, he firmly refrains from advancing any definitions of knowledge or from supporting those submitted by his interlocutors with strongly held convictions of his own.

There is ample textual evidence for the view that Socrates' barrenness is best understood as a suppression of the desire to articulate his own theoretical commitments. Sometimes he couches his barrenness in the strongest possible language of cognitive sterility, while at other times his admission of barrenness amounts to no more than a simple declaration of ignorance. In all cases, however, Socrates appears unwilling to voice a definition or to adduce his own support on behalf of a definition advanced by others.[25] The passage that most clearly shows this to be the case is 185 B 8–9.[26] In the argument about the role of the senses and the mind in perception (184 B 3–186 E 12) Socrates begins by openly suggesting ideas to Theaetetus, but then stops and asks his young interlocutor to provide the requisite answers himself. Prompted by this suggestion, Theaetetus comments on the importance of the mind in grasping 'the commons', upon which Socrates says: 'this was what I thought myself, but I wanted you to think it too'. Here we see a Socrates who holds beliefs, but is reluctant to voice them. The same attitude is manifested, both theoretically and practically, at other points in the dialogue. On a theoretical level, Socrates' reiteration and endorsement of the popular reproach against him, according to which he makes no *assertions* of his own about anything (αὐτὸς δὲ οὐδὲν ἀποφαίνομαι περὶ οὐδενός, 150 C 5–6), constitutes a strong expression of his unwillingness to advance doxastic commitments.

The force of this declaration is further borne out by his enquiring practice in the dialogue, which displaces his personal voice and accords to him the role of a reporter of theories in support

---

[25] The obvious exception is Socrates' definition of clay at 147 C 5–6. But note that (*a*) this is not a definition of knowledge *per se*, but one that illustrates a methodological point, i.e. how to define knowledge; and (*b*) Socrates prefaces its formulation by calling it a 'simple, commonplace statement' (φαῦλόν που καὶ ἁπλοῦν εἰπεῖν), which suggests that it involves an idea readily available to anyone, hardly requiring the difficult labour in which Theaetetus is about to engage. See also 147 A 1–2.

[26] Already noted by Annas, 'Plato the Sceptic', 56, and Sedley, 'Platonist Interpretations', 101.

of the various definitions under consideration.[27] In the first part of the dialogue Theaetetus' *logos* of knowledge as perception, for example, is immediately linked to the theories of absent *sophoi*, i.e. Protagoras' homo–*mensura* theory (151 E 8–152 C 7) and Heraclitus' flux doctrine (152 D 2–E 10), while a little later the 'mysteries of the *kompsoteroi*' are invoked to clarify the enigmatic utterances of Protagoras-cum-Heraclitus (156 A 2–157 C 1). Socrates explicitly associates Protagoras' theory with 'all the wise men of the past, with the exception of Parmenides', namely, Heraclitus, Empedocles, Epicharmus, and Homer (152 E 3–5), an association which he repeats towards the end of his exposition (160 D 5–E 2).[28] When Theaetetus is asked to appraise the 'tempting meal' of *logoi* Socrates has put together for him, but cannot tell 'whether the things [Socrates is] saying are what [he] thinks [himself], or whether [he is] trying [him] out', Socrates reiterates his barrenness:

You are forgetting, my friend. *I don't know anything about this kind of thing myself, and I don't claim any of it as my own. I am barren of theories* [αὐτῶν]:[29] my business is to attend you in your labour. So I chant incantations over you and offer you little titbits from each of the wise till I succeed in assisting you to bring your own belief forth into the light. When it has been born, I shall consider whether it is fertile or a wind-egg. (157 C 7–D 3)

A similar reluctance to procreate *logoi* emerges at 161 A 7–B 6: when Theodorus asks Socrates to point out the potential defects of Theaetetus' newborn, Socrates responds:

You are the complete lover of discussion, Theodorus, and it is too good of you to think that I am a sort of bag of arguments [λόγων], and can easily pick one out which will show you that this theory is wrong. But you don't realize what is happening. The arguments never come from me [οὐδεὶς τῶν λόγων]; they *always* come from the person I am talking to. *All that I know, such as it is, is how to take an argument* [λόγον] *from someone else, and give it a*

[27] The sceptical implications of Socrates' *ad hominem* enquiring practice have been ably examined by Annas, 'Plato the Sceptic'. This is not the place to reopen this issue. In the second section of this paper it will become clear that my reading of Socrates' barrenness opposes a sceptical understanding of his elenctic practice.

[28] At *Prot.* 316 D–E Protagoras claims to be a sophist, a specialist in wisdom, and enlists to his cause poets such as Homer and Hesiod.

[29] One may object that Levett's rendering of the quite general αὐτῶν as 'of theories' is an overtranslation. However, I think that it accurately captures the meaning of what Socrates intends to say here: he is barren of the things he has been spewing forth to his interlocutors, i.e. the various *logoi* of the wise. Note the equally general and ultimately synonymous pronouns used immediately prior to it, τῶν τοιούτων (157 C 8) and αὐτά (157 C 6).

*fair reception.* So, now, I propose to try to get our answer out of Theaetetus, *not to make any contribution of my own.*

The preponderance of the term *logos* and its cognates in these passages suggests that Socrates disclaims the ability to construct definitions, such as Theaetetus' *logos* of knowledge as perception, and to expound theories, i.e. explanatory *logoi*, in their support. By making the theoretical constructs under examination the offspring of well-known wise thinkers of the past, he invites us to see the reluctance to voice his own *logos* as lack of wisdom (*sophia*): the wise confidently submit their *logoi* to an avowedly barren and non-wise Socrates, who proceeds to test and disprove the viability of their progeny.[30]

The suppression of Socrates' voice is also demonstrated by the frequent invocation of unnamed extra-dialogic voices whose imaginary utterances provide fodder for the discussion. In the first section of the dialogue, where knowledge is defined as perception, these imaginary interlocutors emerge as various embodiments of sophistic or eristic discourse, for example 'Protagoras or anyone else' (154 C 7; 162 D 4–5), 'people who propose it as a rule that whatever a man thinks at any time is the truth for him' (158 E 5–6), or 'some intrepid fellow' who 'has you "trapped in the well-shaft" as they say, with a question that leaves you no way out' (165 B 8). The indignant complaints of Protagoras *redivivus* at 166 A 2–168 C 2 offer the most extensive variant of this sort of oblique argumentative technique, which is also at work in the second part of the dialogue, during the interlocutors' examination of false judgement. There the external voices belong to an anonymous examiner (188 D 7: τις) and 'our friend the expert in refutation' (200 A), an invocation that harks back to the faceless surrogate of the previous section. The two elaborate and constructive models Socrates presents in this section are also occasioned by external reports. The Wax Tablet is offered as an illustration of why 'they claim' (φασίν, 194 C 5) false judgements arise when perception and memory-knowledge come together. In likening the soul to 'wax', Socrates alludes to Homer (194 C 8–9), whose name he brings up again in reference to a man's heart as 'shaggy, the kind of heart our marvellously knowing poet praises' (194 E 1–2). In setting up the Aviary's heuristic distinction

---

[30] For Socrates' reliance on the interlocutors' arguments as a standard feature of the elenchus see Blondell, *Play of Character*, 138 n. 135.

between 'having' and 'possessing' knowledge, Socrates relies on a definition of knowing as 'the having of knowledge' provided by certain unnamed individuals (φασίν, 197 B 1). Socrates' appeal to an external authority becomes less prominent in the last section of the dialogue, where knowledge is defined as true judgement accompanied by *logos*. But even there, the definition advanced is proposed by Theaetetus as the oral report of an unidentified 'someone' (τοῦ, 201 C 7), while the theory of elements that informs the interlocutors' investigation is attributed to 'some people' talking to Socrates in a 'dream' (ἄκουε δὴ ὄναρ ἀντὶ ὀνείρατος. ἐγὼ γὰρ αὖ ἐδόκουν ἀκούειν τινῶν, 201 D 9–E 1; cf. also 'the author of our theory'—τὸν εἰπόντα, 202 E 7, and τὸν ἀποφηνάμενον, 206 E 5).[31] The same tendency to construct theories out of unidentified people's *logoi* is evident in Socrates' attempt to come up with a viable definition of *logos* ('account') towards the end of the dialogue. The first definition of it as 'vocalization of thought' is generated by Socrates, but is basic enough to be readily available to all competent users of speech, as he himself admits (206 D 7–9). The second definition of *logos* as 'answering in terms of the elements' is hedged by use of the adverb 'perhaps' (ἴσως, 206 E 6), and Hesiod is immediately brought up as the author of a *logos* that illustrates the meaning of the definition (207 A 3–7).[32] The last definition, 'saying the distinguishing mark', is clearly introduced as 'what the majority of people would say' (ὅπερ ἂν οἱ πολλοὶ εἴποιεν, 208 C 7).[33] It is, of course, possible to dispute the legitimacy of an appeal to voices external to the dialogue proper as evidence for Socrates' mental barrenness, on the grounds

[31] Admittedly, Socrates is rather elusive as to the provenance of his dream. He introduces it as something he *thought* he heard from some 'people'. But Theaetetus' confident attribution of his third definition, the materials for which are supplied by the Dream Theory, to a 'man' lends plausibility to its being derived from someone other than Socrates. In fact, the Dream Theory has been connected with Antisthenes and Protagoras. For the former, see Burnyeat, *Theaetetus*, 165–73. The latter seems to underlie Damascius, *Princ.* 3, 169. 5–22 Westerink–Combès. Sedley, *Midwife*, 160, traces in Socrates' presentation of the theory 'the epistemological implications of Presocratic reductionist physics', which he ultimately rejects. For the idea that Socrates may have been the originator of the Dream Theory, see A. Koyré, *Discovering Plato* (New York, 1945). For Socrates' tendency to attribute creative or novel ideas to an unspecified 'someone', see e.g. *Euthd.* 290 D–291 A; *Gorg.* 493 A; 524 A; *Meno* 81 A–B; *Phaedo* 61 D; 108 C; *Phileb.* 16 C; 20 B; *Phdr.* 235 B–D; *Sym.* 201 D.

[32] Sedley, *Midwife*, 170, suggests that the second definition of *logos* echoes the atomists' theory of knowledge, figures 'whom Plato notoriously never once names in his writings'.

[33] Sedley, *Midwife*, 174, calls this definition of *logos* 'the most commonplace and therefore unphilosophical of those considered'.

that the invocation of these imaginary interlocutors should not obscure the fact that the ultimate originator of their thoughts is none other than Socrates himself: he is the one endowing them with a particular mental disposition or moral fibre and allowing them to come to life or disappear as he pleases. Thus, it may be claimed, their voices are not their own, but the product of Socrates' dramatic inventiveness. Although this sort of reductive reading seems eminently reasonable, it ought, in my view, to be resisted. While it is trivially true that these characters are animated by Socrates, their theories are presented as their own. Each time Socrates invokes an absent interlocutor, he either places the words attributed to him in direct discourse or unequivocally associates them with him, thereby preserving for himself the role of a mere reporter of others' ideas, as is suitable for a barren midwife of the intellect.

That Socrates claims to be and acts as a barren psychic midwife simply states the nature of his intellectual condition without accounting for its provenance. How are we to understand the sudden lapse into psychic sterility of an individual known to make all sorts of assertions in dialogues outside *Theaetetus*? In this regard, a comparison with the emergence of the medical midwife's physical sterility is not particularly instructive. For while a sudden elimination of one's physical ability to beget children is easily attributable to the advancement of age (149 c 2), the positing of a similar break in the production of mental children is less readily conceivable. After all, human experience speaks against the naturalness of such a supposition, and even medical expertise shows that intellectual activity can go on unimpaired until the end of a person's life, unless impeded by brain damage or some other serious medical ailment. If then old age, an involuntary and inescapable factor of human life, causes physical but not intellectual barrenness, how are we to understand the inception of Socrates' psychic emptiness?

I suggest that the deliberate silencing of Socrates' voice emerges from the acute realization that his mortal opinions are inferior to divine wisdom.[34] This explanation of Socratic barrenness preserves

---

[34] One of the three interpretations of Socrates' disavowal of wisdom suggested by the anonymous author of the partially extant commentary on the *Theaetetus* echoes mine: 'or, if "having no wisdom" is to be understood in an absolute sense, it will be that he is not wise in the wisdom which he attributes to god.' Anon. does not, however, establish a causal link between Socrates' intellectual stance and his awareness of the inferior epistemic quality of his mortal wisdom. See H. Diels and W. Schubart, *Anonymer Kommentar zu Platons 'Theaitet'* (Berlin, 1905). A new edition

an important similarity between physical and mental obstetrics, as it places barrenness exclusively within the human realm: sterility is something that occurs to the midwife either as the result of her advancement in age (physical) or as a conscious desisting from birthing opinions (mental). At the same time, however, it foregrounds an important difference between the two mortal practitioners of midwifery: while the medical *maia* does not will her barrenness but suffers it as the inevitable corollary of old age, Socrates embraces it freely. His choice, a clear manifestation of personal agency, must result from a certain kind of thinking apparently denied to physical midwives. My claim is that Socrates' mental barrenness emerges precisely from his awareness of the epistemic inferiority of his mortal offspring, an awareness of which his medical counterpart is deprived. The assumption of the obstetric art signifies the loss of the midwife's ability to procreate the sort of children she would birth in her procreative past, i.e. ordinary progeny whose genuineness she took for granted. However, Socrates-*qua*-midwife inhibits his procreative capacity *because* he is aware of the limited epistemic value of his mental children. He therefore possesses what the medical *maia* lacks, namely the ability to reflect critically on the quality of his offspring, an ability that leads him to the deliberate avoidance of any definitions of *epistēmē*.

Evidence for the claim that Socratic midwifery is predicated on the *conscious* awareness of the inferior epistemic quality of his mental offspring may be found in the following passage:

For one thing which I have in common with the ordinary midwives is that I myself am barren of wisdom [ἄγονός εἰμι σοφίας]. The common reproach against me is that I am always asking questions of other people but never make any assertions about anything [αὐτὸς δὲ οὐδὲν ἀποφαίνομαι περὶ οὐδενός], because there is no wisdom in me [διὰ τὸ μηδὲν ἔχειν σοφόν]; and that is true enough. And the reason of it is this [τὸ δὲ αἴτιον τούτου τόδε], that god compels me [ἀναγκάζει] to attend the travail of others, but has forbidden me [ἀπεκώλυσεν] to procreate. (150 C 3–8)

of the text has been provided by G. Bastianini and D. Sedley, 'Commentarium in Platonis *Theaetetum*', *Corpus dei papiri filosofici*, pt. iii. *Commentari* (Florence, 1995), 227–562. See also Anon. *Proleg.* 10. 60–5: 'When he says "I know nothing", he is comparing his own wisdom with that of the gods, the latter being in a different class from the former. Ours is mere knowledge, while god's is practically applied. And god's knowledge knows by simple attention, whereas we know through causes and premisses.' For the composition of Anon.'s commentary, see H. Tarrant, 'The Date of Anon. *in Theaetetum*', *Classical Quarterly*, NS 33 (1983), 161–87.

Here Socrates makes five interdependent moves: (1) he glosses his obstetric barrenness as lack of wisdom, on a par with the physical midwife's infertility (150 c 3–4); (2) he submits the popular conception of himself as someone who tends always to ask questions but never to supply answers (150 c 4–6); (3) he reports people as attributing (2) to his being devoid of wisdom (150 c 6); (4) he accepts that they are right (150 c 7); and (5) he provides his own reason for the whole of (2)–(4), namely that he is divinely compelled to act as a mental midwife but has been forbidden to procreate (150 c 7–8). Two causal connections are established in this passage. First, Socrates makes no assertions *because* he has no wisdom (*per* 3). This admission directly corroborates my view that his habit of withholding his doxastic commitments is causally linked with a prior awareness of his intellectual poverty: it is *on account of his lack of wisdom* (διὰ τὸ μηδὲν ἔχειν σοφόν) that he asserts nothing. Secondly, Socrates has no wisdom *because* god has willed it so (*per* 5). This statement both points up a mere fact, that god compels him to perform midwifery but has forbidden him to engender wisdom, and betrays Socrates' awareness of it. By conjoining these two causal connections, we obtain the following result: Socrates knows that god has endorsed his inability to birth wisdom, and the knowledge of his sorry epistemic state prevents him from making any assertions of his own. His tense-usage in this regard is suggestive: while use of the present tense 'compels' (ἀναγκάζει) refers to his *current* practice of midwifery in obedience to god's ordinance, use of the aorist 'forbade' (ἀπεκώλυσεν) underscores the fact that god has *always* prevented him from birthing wisdom.[35] As a *technē* practised in the present, midwifery post-dates Socrates' realization that he is unable to beget wisdom, and marks his systematic undertaking of mental midwifery.

The notion that Socrates had been aware of his lack of wisdom

[35] While the imperfect tense would more precisely capture the sense that god has *always* prevented Socrates from generating wisdom, the nature of the meaning of the verb (ἀπο)κωλύειν makes the aorist a more appropriate choice. For while the aorist conveys the notion that god 'succeeded in preventing' Socrates from acquiring wisdom—and that, therefore, Socrates was and, presumably, continues to be bereft of wisdom—the imperfect would mean that god 'tried, or kept trying, to prevent him'. Use of the imperfect would leave open two interpretative possibilities, both at odds with the image of midwifery and our general understanding of Socrates' religiosity: (a) Socrates keeps struggling against the god's attempts to prevent him from giving birth; and (b) Socrates' struggle may some day prove successful. Thanks to David Sansone for helping me see this point.

before he picked up mental midwifery echoes *Ap.* 21 B 3–6. For there, and upon reception of the puzzling divine revelation that he is the wisest of men, Socrates says that he thought to himself:

> What on earth is the god saying? What is his hidden meaning? *I'm well aware that I have no wisdom, great or small* [ἐγὼ γὰρ δὴ οὔτε μέγα οὔτε σμικρὸν σύνοιδα ἐμαυτῷ σοφὸς ὤν]. So what can he mean by saying I am so wise?

He supplies the answer a little later:

> It looks as though the god is really wise and what he is saying in this oracle is this: human wisdom is worth little or nothing. By referring to this 'Socrates' he seems to be using my name as an example, as if he were saying, 'That one of you, O men, is wisest, who, like Socrates, *has understood* [ἔγνωκεν] that in relation to wisdom he is truly worthless.' (23 A 5–B 4)

These two passages make it clear that the oracle's declaration confirmed Socrates' *prior* awareness of his lack of wisdom, while his elenctic practice brought out the particular force of that declaration.[36] His procreative years, which preceded the purposeful testing of his fellow Athenians' beliefs, were infused with a heightened sense of self-awareness that prevented him from committing the hubris of appearing to be blithely content with the kind of knowledge he possessed.[37] The midwifery passage in *Theaetetus* corroborates this view by presenting us with a Socrates who desists from self-confidently offering definitions of *epistēmē*, because he is aware of being devoid of wisdom, thereby showing the worthlessness of man's pretensions to knowledge.

[36] For Socrates' awareness of his ignorance, see *Phdr.* 235 C 7. Cf. his poignant self-criticisms at *H.Ma.* 304 D–E, and 286 C–D in conjunction with 298 B. For a brief discussion of Socrates' awareness of his ignorance in the context of expert knowledge, see Woodruff, 'Early Theory', 68–9.

[37] That Socrates' divine mission began only after he had discovered the real meaning of the oracle is suggested by *Apology*. This is not to say, however, that Socrates had not acquired a reputation for wisdom prior to the oracle's pronouncement, which was based on the ostensible inerrancy of his mortal beliefs. Socrates' testing of the meaning of the oracle, however, yielded the correct understanding of his mortal wisdom, and necessitated the inception of a quest that would induce in others an awareness of their true epistemic state. For an interpretation of the origin of Socrates' mission similar to mine, see T. C. Brickhouse and N. D. Smith, 'The Origin of Socrates' Mission', *Journal of the History of Ideas*, 44 (1983), 657–66. For the claim that the oracle simply confirmed Socrates' belief in the necessity of his mission, but failed to contribute to that mission's origin, see M. L. McPherran, 'Elenctic Interpretation and the Delphic Oracle', in G. A. Scott (ed.), *Does Socrates Have a Method? Rethinking the Elenchus in Plato's Dialogues and Beyond* (University Park, PA, 2002), 114–44.

Socrates' deliberate avoidance of doctrinal commitments serves
effectively to distinguish him, the barren practitioner of spiritual
midwifery, from the purportedly wise advocates of Protagorean and
eristic sophistic.[38] His barrenness is thus a methodological device
that separates him from his 'wise' opponents.[39] In the first part of
the dialogue both Theodorus and Theaetetus are explicitly associated with Protagoras' thought, the former through his friendship
with the sophist, the latter through direct exposure to Protagoras'
man-as-measure doctrine (152 A 5), as well as Theodorus' teaching.[40] As we saw earlier, Theaetetus' definition of knowledge as
perception bears obvious Protagorean connotations, and Socrates
links it with the theories of an array of wise men of the past, chief
among whom stands Protagoras himself (152 E 3). All these present
and absent interlocutors come pregnant with *logoi* to an avowedly
barren Socrates, who proceeds to extract, test, and finally discard
their offspring as inauthentic. Even after the Protagorean and Heraclitean underpinnings of Theaetetus' definition have been properly
disposed of, the contrast between sophistic and Socratic thought
is still evident in the final refutation of Theaetetus' view of knowledge: by making the soul the single agent of all cognitive activity,
Socrates implicitly places his mental midwifery, a soul-oriented art,
over and above any system of thought which, like Protagorean relativism, valorizes perception. Furthermore, by attributing to the
soul the ability to perform calculations regarding the being and
advantageousness of bodily experiences, he both reiterates and ex-
pands on his earlier critique of the appeal of the Protagorean man-
as-measure doctrine to the notion of utility (177 D 2–179 A 8). While

[38] Lack of space prevents me from analysing the various ways in which sophistic
discourse is castigated in the dialogue. I shall here restrict myself to pointing out
a few examples of Socrates' tendency to refer to—explicitly or implicitly—and
critique sophistic conceptual categories, while I intend to provide a more thorough
treatment of the topic elsewhere.

[39] Anon. similarly sees Socrates' barrenness as methodological in nature, but gives
it a different spin. According to him, Socrates suppresses his personal beliefs in order
to make his interlocutors engender their own progeny (47. 31–48). For a discussion
of his view, see Sedley, 'Platonist Interpretations', 99–101.

[40] Unlike Theodorus, who is presented as a 'friend of Protagoras' and as a mostly
unwilling participant in Socratic dialectic, Theaetetus has not yet been fully immersed in sophistic views or rhetorical methods; Protagoras *redidivus*, for example,
dismisses him as an inadequate spokesman for his ideas (166 A). From this point
of view, Socratic midwifery may be seen as an attempt to guide a youth ambiva-
lently poised between philosophy and sophistry. For an interesting discussion of this
issue, see Blondell, *Play of Character*, 282–3.

in the earlier passage he simply asserts the obvious fact that only the expert is able correctly to predict the future outcome of present experiences, he now provides a reason for this state of affairs, namely the expert's ability to appraise 'being' and 'advantageousness', an appraisal which results from his participation in a 'long and arduous development involving a good deal of trouble and education' (186 C 3–4).[41] The expert's education echoes the philosopher's training, as described in *Republic*, while reference to its length subtly contrasts with the immediacy with which perceptual stimuli, Protagoras' cognitive realm, are received.[42]

The barren midwife's conducting of a verbal exchange with a view to assessing reliably the legitimacy of the interlocutor's mental offspring further distinguishes Socratic midwifery from eristic, a sophistic practice traditionally viewed as similar to elenchus.[43] For it shows that the essential difference between Socrates and his inauthentic counterpart is that the latter is uninterested in the veridical status of the interlocutor's opinions: the truth may or may not emerge from an eristic set-to, but discovering it is not the objective of the verbal jousting.[44] With a rapid series of questions

---

[41] For the Socratic elements of the critique's use of the predictive powers of expertise, see Sedley, *Midwife*, 87–8.

[42] This contrast is one of the main themes of the digression, where Socrates opposes the philosopher's enjoyment of leisure to the orator's pressure for time. See also 201 A–B. This topic is also present at *Ap.* 19 A, 24 A, and 37 A.

[43] The claim that the Socratic elenchus is similar in many ways to sophistic eristic is no longer a disputed issue. Even if one is not willing to agree with H. Sidgwick, 'The Sophists', *Journal of Philology*, 4/8 (1872), 288–307, who argues that eristic originated entirely with Socrates, there are well-documented similarities between the two modes of verbal exchange, of the kind that led Campbell to call eristic 'the ape of the Socratic elenchus'. *Rep.* 537 D–539 C speaks of the dangers of *dialegesthai* degenerating into *antilogia*; cf. 487 B–D; 497 E–498 C; *Phileb.* 15 D–16 A. For useful discussions see, among others, H. H. Benson, 'A Note on Eristic and the Socratic Elenchus' ['Note'], *Journal of the History of Philosophy*, 27 (1989), 591–9; W. K. C. Guthrie, *Socrates* (Cambridge, 1971), 27–54; T. H. Irwin, 'Coercion and Objectivity in Plato's Dialectic', *Revue internationale de philosophie*, 156 (1986), 49–74 at 61–3; id., 'Plato: The Intellectual Background', in R. Kraut (ed.), *The Cambridge Companion to Plato* (Cambridge, 1992), 51–89 at 63–9; G. B. Kerferd, *The Sophistic Movement* [*Sophistic Movement*] (Cambridge, 1981), 59–67; P. Moraux, 'La joute dialectique d'après le huitième livre des *Topiques*', in G. E. L. Owen (ed.), *Aristotle on Dialectic: The Topics* (Oxford, 1968), 277–311; J. Poulakos, *Sophistical Rhetoric in Classical Greece* (Columbia, SC, 1995); H. D. Rankin, *Sophists, Socratics, and Cynics* (London, 1983), 13–29; and R. Wardy, *The Birth of Rhetoric: Gorgias, Plato and their Successors* (London, 1996).

[44] Cf. *Euthd.* 272 A 8–B 1, where Socrates describes the skill of the formidable brothers Euthydemus and Dionysodorus as the ability 'to fight in words and refute whatever is said, whether it happens to be false or true'. See also *La.* 196 B;

the skilled sophist knocks down his respondent's mental children, thereby reducing him to self-contradiction and silence.[45] By the end of the verbal exchange, the interlocutor is left feeling benumbed and ashamed of his ostensible lack of mental resources, while the eristic enjoys the applause his verbal acrobatics have earned him. The purpose of the eristic's exchange is to ensure victory at all costs, and one of his tactical weapons is the formulation of disjunctive questions, which drastically restrict the respondent's freedom to answer as he sees fit. These 'inescapable questions' are receptive of contradictory answers, which the skilled sophist has prepared in advance and to which he owes his reputation for wisdom.[46] But the epistemic validity of the final answer to any given debate is never assessed: it is accepted as valid merely on the strength of its having won the day. The ensuing victory confirms the eristic's false belief in his wisdom; for without the desire or the ability to test the correctness of the result of the conversation, he, as well as those observing the disputation, easily mistakes the verbal victory he has scored for a demonstration of his indubitable intellectual superiority. However, Socrates' spiritual barrenness and active interest in the epistemic validity of the interlocutor's opinions are in stark contrast with the eristic's smug display of his purported wisdom through the upholding of untested beliefs.

*Gorg.* 457 C; 470 C–472 C; *Rep.* 454 A; 499 A; *Phaedo* 91 A. At *Soph.* 231 D–E eristic is described as 'disputational in relation to speeches'. These passages agree with the frequently argued position that the main difference between eristic and the Socratic elenchus is that the former, unlike the latter, is concerned only to establish consistency, never truth or falsity. See, among others, E. R. Dodds, *Plato: Gorgias* (Oxford, 1959), 213; T. H. Irwin, *Plato: Gorgias* (Oxford, 1979), 122–3; Kerferd, *Sophistic Movement*, 59–68; R. K. Sprague, *Plato's Use of Fallacy* (New York, 1962), 3; H. Teloh, *Socratic Education in Plato's Early Dialogues* (Notre Dame, 1986), 195–210; and G. Vlastos, 'The Socratic Elenchus' ['Socratic Elenchus'], *Oxford Studies in Ancient Philosophy*, 1 (1983), 27–58 at 31 n. 14.

[45] For the eristic's interest in verbal contentiousness for securing victory in the debate, as opposed to Socrates' philosophical search for the truth, see Vlastos, 'Socratic Elenchus', 31. For the antilogician's readiness to refute whatever his opponent asserts, regardless of its epistemic worth, see *Euthd.* 275 E.

[46] Aristotle provides evidence that practising controversialists were advised to memorize a vast number of arguments based on primary theses and first principles, and to classify them according to a system (*Top.* 100$^a$–164$^b$). At *SE* 164$^a$–184$^b$ he alludes to the sort of intellectual barrenness I am imputing to them here by describing the sophistic art as the practice of leading one's partner to the kind of statement against which one is already well armed with arguments oneself. For the eristic technique of asking 'inescapable questions' see *Euthydemus*, *passim*.

This contrast between Socratic midwifery and sophistic eristic emerges at various junctures in the first section of the dialogue.[47] At 154 C 10–E 5 Socrates notes that in verbal duelling there is a lack of correspondence between the sophists' words and their thoughts, and that the entire practice is jocular and aims solely at verbal consistency.[48] By contrast, Socrates' and Theaetetus' aim should be to 'look at [their] thoughts themselves in relation to themselves, and see what they are—whether, in [their] opinion, they agree with one another or are entirely at variance'. With his customary irony, he also brings out the temporal discontinuity between the sophists' *past* examination of their thoughts ('[they] had already analysed all the contents of [their] minds') and their *present* engagement in playful and meaningless testing ('[they] should now spend [their] superfluous time trying each other out') (154 D 8–E 1).[49] The eristic's concern with verbal, as opposed to doxastic, consistency emerges also at 164 C 8–D 2, where Socrates berates himself and his interlocutor for adopting the 'methods of professional conversationalists: we've made an agreement aimed at getting words to agree consistently'. He attributes this practice to 'champion controversialists' (ἀγωνισταί), whom he explicitly dissociates from 'philosophers' (φιλόσοφοι). At 165 B 2–E 4 Socrates offers a parodic demonstration of an eristic exchange, which consists in the employment of one 'inescapable question' after another (ἀφύκτῳ ἐρωτήματι, 165 B 8; cf. also τὸ δεινότατον ἐρώτημα, 165 B 2).[50] But perhaps the most delightful inveighing against the argumentative tools of contentious debate appears in the mouth of Protagoras *redivivus* at 167 E 2–168 A 6, where the renowned sophist implores Socrates to abstain from resorting to injustice in the way in which he treats another's words and to try, instead, to keep controversy (ἀγωνιζόμενος τὰς διατριβὰς ποιῆται) distinct from

---

[47] For references to eristic practices in other dialogues see *Lys.* 211 B; 216 A; *Meno* 75 C–D; 80 E; 81 D; *Rep.* 454 A; 499 A; 537 D–539 D; *Phaedo* 90 B–C; *Euthd.* 272 B and *passim*; *Soph.* 225 B–C; 268 B.

[48] For the eristic's indifference to the correspondence between verbal construct and objective reality see H. Keulen, *Untersuchungen zu Platons 'Euthydem'* [*Untersuchungen*] (Wiesbaden, 1971), 64–5; and E. S. Thompson, *The* Meno *of Plato* (London, 1901), 91 n. 12.

[49] The interlocutor's commitment to an honest expression of his beliefs is an indication of his serious investment in the elenctic process, and is to be contrasted with the eristic's argumentative playfulness. See *Gorg.* 500 B–C and *Rep.* 349 A. Cf. Vlastos, 'Socratic Elenchus', 36.

[50] For the role of verbal inconsistency in eristic discourse see Benson, 'Note'.

dialectic (διαλεγόμενος).[51] For, he says, in controversy a man 'may play about and trip up his opponent as often as he can, but in discussion he must be serious, he must keep on helping his opponent to his feet again, and point out to him only those slips which are due to himself or to the intellectual society which he has previously frequented' (167 E 6–168 A 2). These passages reveal the major methodological flaws of eristic discourse: the transformation of the debate into a verbal game and the deployment of tricks that trip up the opponent, so that he may eventually be reduced to a shameful state of unmitigated ignorance.[52] One also glimpses in them the epistemological assumption of the eristic art, namely, the dissociation of thought from its verbal expression, which underlies the sophist's indifference towards the truth-content of his own and his interlocutor's opinions. For if what guarantees victory in a debate is simply the avoidance of verbal inconsistency, the participants will strive to make their words agree with one another, rather than examine the contents of their thoughts, in order to assess their epistemic value and place in the broader nexus of their beliefs.

In this section I have argued that Socrates' intellectual barrenness may fruitfully be seen as the conscious suppression of his own theories about knowledge, so that he may devote all his efforts to extracting the mental progeny of his pregnant interlocutors. The midwifery passage shows that Socrates silences his personal voice because he is aware of the limited epistemic value of his opinions: he is a self-consciously non-wise man who performs obstetrics on the ostensibly wise, only to discover that they have given birth to wind-eggs. His interlocutors, both real and imaginary, claim to know, but the Socratic midwifery to which they submit their intellectual children shows their ignorance. Socrates' awareness of his ignorance

---

[51] According to Diogenes Laertius (9. 55), Protagoras wrote an *Art of Eristics*, which, if true, would only exacerbate the existing ironic effect of having a sophist adopt for himself and praise principles of philosophic discourse. For arguments for and against Diogenes' testimony see Gulley, *The Philosophy of Socrates*, 206 n. 23. See also Keulen, *Untersuchungen*, 84–90.

[52] Some of the tricks the eristic has at his disposal are as follows: he may disallow qualifications made by his interlocutor (*Euthd.* 295 B–296 A; *Rep.* 454 A–B), force him to respond before he has had time to consider what he really believes, use ridicule (*Gorg.* 467 B 10 and 473 E 2–3) or peer pressure (*Gorg.* 471 C 8–D 2; 473 E 4–5; 474 B 6) or even fallacies of ambiguity (*Euthd.* 275 D–278 E). For the respondent's feeling of a loss of dignity at his failure to sustain the verbal onslaughts of the eristic, see *Theaet.* 165 B.

contrasts sharply with others' pretensions to wisdom and, more importantly, becomes the very instrument that reveals the hollowness of their assertions. These 'others' are practitioners of sophistry whose epistemic assumptions Socrates methodically and successfully undermines. The question that now arises is: what, if anything, ensures the validity of the obstetric result? For unless spiritual midwifery compels confidence in the outcome of the delivery, unless, in other words, it somehow ensures the epistemic reliability of the assessment of the interlocutors' mental foetus, it will appear indistinguishable from the intellectual practices from which it strives to be dissociated. I shall tackle this important question, and the issues arising from it, in the next section.


## 2. Socratic piety

Socrates describes his practice as a divinely inspired mission. In the context of the midwifery passage, he appeals to divine authority six times: in five cases he uses the noun 'the god' (ὁ θεός) and once he invokes his customary 'divine sign' (to daimonion).[53] The most striking feature of the role of the divine in mental maieutics is its governing almost every aspect of the practice: the god 'compels' Socrates to attend the travail of others but 'has forbidden' him to procreate (150 C 7–8); he 'permits' (ἂν . . . παρείκῃ, 150 D 4–5) some of his associates to make progress; he is the 'cause' (αἴτιος, 150 E 1), along with Socrates, of the delivery; he somehow lurks behind Socrates' guesses concerning the choice of the best educational couples (σὺν θεῷ εἰπεῖν, 151 B 3); and he serves as the paradigm of benevolence with which Socrates compares his own lack of malice in disabusing his interlocutors from their ignorance (οὐδεὶς θεὸς δύσνους ἀνθρώποις, 151 D 1). The divine sign both 'forbids' (ἀποκωλύει, 151 A 4) Socrates from associating with some of those who seek his company after they have prematurely left him and 'permits' (ἐᾷ, 151 A 4) him to do so, presumably on the basis of a predictive assessment of that individual's potential for a future

---

[53] One more reference to the divine origin of the elenchus appears at 210 D. The secondary literature on the *daimonion* is vast. For good samples of it, see P. Destrée and N. D. Smith (eds.), *Socrates' Divine Sign: Religion, Practice, and Value in Socratic Philosophy* (Kelowna, BC, 2005); M. L. McPherran, *The Religion of Socrates* (University Park, PA, 1996); and A. Patzer, *Bibliographia Socratica* (Freiburg, 1985).

moral improvement.[54] How are we supposed to understand this divine participation in Socrates' elenctic practice? Does it consist in some sort of direct communication between god and his mortal servant that enables the latter to perform his obstetric function? Or is it rather felt as an internal injunction to perform mental obstetrics in accordance with the god's command?

To countenance the divine role as a direct participation in the proceedings of the elenchus would be patently absurd. A strong interpretation of divine assistance, according to which god and Socrates wield the elenchus in harmonious collaboration, is nowhere attested in the Platonic corpus.[55] On the contrary, Socrates and his interlocutors, all fallible human beings, are the only participants in a dialectical procedure whose aim is to reveal the limitations of human knowledge. Nor do we have any indication that the god dictates to Socrates the kinds of question he needs to ask, or their value for his enquiry. Socrates alone chooses the material to be used throughout the elenctic process, on the basis of a solid understanding of his interlocutors' psychic disposition and the particular goal of the discussion. But, then, his firm conviction of god's interest in mental obstetrics must have a psychological foundation: Socrates must somehow believe that his art of midwifery, as well as the means whereby its end result is secured, enjoys divine sanction.[56] It is this belief that grounds the religious nature of his elenctic mission, not some sort of direct divine intervention in the particularities of his practice. Socrates' defence in *Apology*, at whose heart is the claim that the very activities for which he has been brought to trial con-

[54] H. Tarrant, 'Socratic *Synousia*: A Post-Platonic Myth?', *Journal of the History of Philosophy*, 43/2 (2005), 131–55, attributes the fact that god allows some of Socrates' partners to make progress to their potential for future progress (139). I think that this consideration also governs the *daimonion*'s intervention in Socratic midwifery. For discussions of the *daimonion*'s apparently protreptic role in the *Theaetetus*, see M. Joyal, 'Socrates, *Daimonios Anēr*: Some Textual and Interpretive Problems in Plato', in id. (ed.), *In Altum: Seventy-Five Years of Classical Studies in Newfoundland* (St John's, Newfoundland, 2001), 343–57; and id., *The Platonic* Theages: *An Introduction, Commentary and Critical Edition* (Stuttgart, 2000); and J. Opsomer, 'Plutarch's Defence of the *Theages*, in Defence of Socratic Philosophy?', *Philologus*, 141 (1997), 114–36, esp. 116–18.

[55] Not even Socrates' divine monitor, his *daimonion*, appears to be of much assistance in his examinations. In all cases of the *daimonion*'s activity, not once do we find Socrates adjusting his questioning on the basis of its intervention.

[56] Cf. W. K. C. Guthrie, *A History of Greek Philosophy*, iii. *The Fifth-Century Enlightenment* (Cambridge, 1969), 408: 'Having learned the lesson [of the oracle] himself he *felt* it to be the god's will that he should impart it to others' (emphasis added).

stitute a religious mission, undergirds his belief in the divine origin of the elenchus as evidenced in *Theaetetus*. For at his trial Socrates reiterates his conviction that he examines others at god's command (23 B 5; 28 E 4; 30 A 5, E 3; 33 C 5), that he is god's gift to the city of Athens (30 D 8; 31 A 8), that his elenctic practice is his particular way of coming to god's aid and serving him (23 B 7, C 1), and that failure to philosophize would be tantamount to disobeying the god (37 E 6). Common to all these assertions is the personal nature of his belief in the divine underpinnings of the elenchus: the fact that the god entrusted to him the difficult task of freeing people from their pretence of wisdom (23 B 7; 37 E 5–38 A 6) is not an unambiguous and incontestable divine declaration but Socrates' *own* interpretation of an oracular pronouncement which, on the face of it, revealed a simple fact (that Socrates is the wisest of men), but withheld any injunction to a particular course of action (elenctic method as the means of validating the divine message).[57] Similarly, in *Theaetetus* Socrates interprets mental midwifery as a divinely inspired *technē* aiming to disabuse his interlocutor of his false epistemic pretensions. In both *Apology* and *Theaetetus* the conscious and systematic undertaking of the elenctic process is coupled with an explicit awareness of the practitioner's lack of wisdom. In *Apology* Socrates claims that by proving his interlocutor's inability to display his wisdom by means of a valid definition of a concept that falls within the parameters of his expertise, he succeeds in showing that the man's epistemic pretensions are unfounded, thereby indirectly corroborating the god's pronouncement that he, Socrates, is the wisest man: his wisdom lies in his awareness of his epistemic barrenness, which is the very foundation of his art of midwifery.[58] Although in *Theaetetus* the eponymous character lacks the customary intellectual smugness of the Socratic interlocutor, he

---

[57] The fact that there is nothing obviously jussive in the Delphic oracle has been widely observed. See, among others, T. C. Brickhouse and N. D. Smith, *Socrates on Trial* (Oxford, 1989), 88; R. Hackforth, *The Composition of Plato's Apology* (Cambridge, 1933), 89; C. D. C. Reeve, *Socrates in the Apology: An Essay on Plato's Apology of Socrates* [*Apology*] (Indianapolis, 1989), 25; and G. Vlastos, *Socrates: Ironist and Moral Philosopher* (Cambridge, 1991), 171, who emphasizes the subjective aspect of Socrates' interpretation.

[58] The elimination of the false conceit of knowledge is explicitly represented as the function of the elenchus. See e.g. *Ap.* 23 A; 28 D; 39 C; *Meno* 80 A–D with 84 A–C; 85 C; *Soph.* 229 E–230 E. For the view that human piety is predicated on the god's assistant's conscious awareness of his lack of divine wisdom see R. Weiss, 'Virtue without Knowledge: Socrates' Conception of Holiness in Plato's *Euthyphro*', *Ancient Philosophy*, 14 (1994), 263–82.

has uncritically absorbed the importance of traditional education and its representatives, such as Theodorus' mathematical expertise, and has come to think of geometry as a branch of knowledge without feeling the need to examine its potential epistemic limitations (146 C–D). His reliance on authority may also be detected in his subsequent definitions, all of which have their origin in external sources. By subjecting these definitions to dialectical scrutiny, Socrates' obstetric mediations could be seen as aiming to enhance Theaetetus' critical attitude towards the various practitioners of wisdom and the kind of knowledge they claim to impart.

   Although Socrates' mental sterility resembles the physical barrenness of the medical midwife, it is endowed with a function that effectively distinguishes his art from its bodily counterpart. While the medical obstetrician is unable to distinguish the true from the false offspring (150 A 9–B 4), Socrates can determine 'whether the young mind is being delivered of . . . an error or a fertile truth' (150 C 2–3), an ability which clinches the superiority of his *technē* over that of physical maieutics. Two interrelated questions arise from this admission: how can Socrates, a mentally barren man, assess the veracity of the beliefs expressed by an ostensibly wise interlocutor, if he lacks any wisdom of his own? And why should Socrates expect the elenctically defeated and vexed associate to accept the result of his obstetric ministration, if he lacks the epistemic credentials that would legitimize his pronouncement on the pregnant interlocutor's beliefs? These questions not only foreground the need for a justification of the end result of the Socratic elenchus, but also have a direct bearing on my suggestion that the midwifery analogy distinguishes elenctic enquiry from sophistic practices. In fact, these two claims inform one another: for unless the validity of Socrates' final appraisal of his interlocutor's mental child is secured by means of an appeal to an indisputably rational and supremely wise authority, it will appear to be as subjective as the sophists' purportedly wise utterances or as arbitrary as the eristics' capricious refutations of their interlocutors' opinions.

   The requisite justification, I submit, is inextricably tied with Socrates' belief in the divine underpinnings of his mission: his firm conviction that the god (1) has given him the art of intellectual midwifery, (2) is a contributory cause of the delivery, (3) influences the progress of his interlocutors, (4) assists Socrates in choosing suitable conversational partners, and (5) affords him the highest moral paradigm of benevolence, guarantees the veracity of the elenctic result.[59] While it is true that the ideas never come from the barren Socrates but always from the pregnant interlocutor, their delivery is made possible by a procedure sanctioned by god and administered by his chosen mortal servant. The divine backing of the elenchus gives Socrates a confidence he would otherwise lack in the validity of the assessment of the interlocutor's mental child: a procedure that enjoys god's unreserved support can only reveal truth, never falsity.[60] The two elenctic requirements, that the interlocutor say what he believes and carry on courageously a potentially distressing conversation, further the divinely approved aim of Socratic midwifery.[61] For unless the opinion put forth, as well as those elenctically induced that corroborate it, is the associate's genuine child and not a mere plausibility, chosen *ad hoc* and designed to support beliefs that do not meet with the interlocutor's approval, there is no pregnancy and, consequently, no need for midwifery.[62] Socrates alludes to the necessity for doxastic ownership by explicitly situating 'a multitude of beautiful things' in his interlocutor's soul (150 D

[59] The fact that Socrates models his benevolence towards his fellow Athenians upon that of the god is particularly instructive, for it underscores the other-directed dimension of his inner goodness: just as the god cares for humans' welfare (*Ap.* 31 A 6–7 and 41 D 2), so has Socrates dedicated his life to the betterment of those who converse with him.

[60] For a similar interpretation of Socrates' trust in the products of the elenchus, see T. C. Brickhouse and N. D. Smith, 'Socrates' Elenctic Mission', *Oxford Studies in Ancient Philosophy*, 9 (1991), 131–59 at 148.

[61] For the 'say-what-you-believe' constraint of the elenchus, a term coined by Vlastos ('Socratic Elenchus', 35), see *Euthph.* 9 D 7–8; *Crito* 49 C 11–D 1; *Prot.* 331 C 4–D 1; *Rep.* 349 A 4–8; *Gorg.* 458 A 1–B 1; 495 A 5–9; 499 B 4–C 6; 500 B 5–C 1. The importance of this principle is not diminished by Socrates' willingness to relax it at times: see *Gorg.* 499 B 4–C 6; 501 C 7–8; 505 C 5; *Rep.* 349 A 9–B 1; 350 E 1. Socrates invites his interlocutor to withdraw or amend his opinions if he does not think that they have been accurately represented. See e.g. *Euthph.* 11 B 2; 13 C 11–D 3; *Crito* 49 D 9–E 2; *Prot.* 354 B 7–355 A 5; *Gorg.* 461 C 8–D 3; 462 A 3; 482 D 7–E 2; *Rep.* 348 B 8–10. Among those who have questioned the importance of this constraint see H. H. Benson, *Socratic Wisdom: The Model of Knowledge in Plato's Early Dialogues* (Oxford, 2000), 38; J. Beversluis, *Cross-Examining Socrates: A Defense of the Interlocutors in Plato's Early Dialogues* (Cambridge, 2000), 37–58; C. Kahn, 'Vlastos' Socrates', *Phronesis*, 37 (1992), 233–58 at 255–6; D. Nails, 'Problems with Vlastos' Platonic Developmentalism', *Ancient Philosophy*, 13 (1993), 272–91 at 286–8; and ead., *Agora, Academy and the Conduct of Philosophy* (Dordrecht, 1995), 92–5.

[62] Note that the delivery of Theaetetus' child is proclaimed complete only after both Protagorean relativism and Heraclitean flux have been brought forth as corollaries of his initial identification of knowledge with perception (160 E).

7–8).[63] Later on, towards the end of the digression, he comments on the importance of 'standing one's ground like a man', as opposed to 'running away like a coward', when it comes to giving and taking an account in a private discussion (177 B 3–4).[64] The midwife's job lies in drawing the ideas out from within, a task reminiscent of the theory of recollection expounded in *Meno*.[65] Even though, as Myles Burnyeat has convincingly argued, the assimilation of the midwifery analogy to the method of learning suggested by the theory of recollection should be resisted, both metaphors foreground the notion that the propositions discovered in the interrogation of the interlocutor by Socrates are begotten by the former and extracted by the latter.[66]

At this point I must address the important issue of the epistemic status of Socrates' findings. Can they properly be called knowledge or are they, rather, mere beliefs? If the latter is the case, what sort of beliefs are they? On this issue, scholars have been divided between the so-called non-constructivists, who claim that the elenchus can demonstrate only the inconsistency of the interlocutors' belief, and the so-called constructivists, who think that it can yield truth.[67] My interpretation supports a form of constructivism that views the elenctic result as true belief, not knowledge. Nowhere in the dialogue do the interlocutors claim that their conversation has yielded knowledge. They do, however, express their belief in the veracity

[63] For the use of the sincerity requirement as the requirement of ownership of one's beliefs, see M. M. McCabe, 'Measuring Sincerity', *Dialogos*, 5 (1998), 40–64.
[64] See also 151 D and 204 B. [65] Cf. *Meno* 81 E–82 A; 82 B, E; 84 C–D; 85 B–D.
[66] For the important dissimilarities between the two metaphors, see Burnyeat, 'Socratic Midwifery'.
[67] For a discussion of the former view see, among others, H. H. Benson, 'The Problem of the Elenchus Reconsidered', *Ancient Philosophy*, 7 (1987), 67–85; M. C. Stokes, *Plato's Socratic Conversations: Drama and Dialectic in Three Dialogues* (London, 1986), 1–35 and 440–3; and Teloh, *Socratic Education*. The latter view has been propounded most forcefully by Vlastos, 'Socratic Elenchus', 27–58, and id., 'Afterthoughts on the Socratic Elenchus', *Oxford Studies in Ancient Philosophy*, 1 (1983), 71–4. Different versions of constructivism have been advanced by T. C. Brickhouse and N. D. Smith, *Plato's Socrates*, 30–71; R. Kraut, *Socrates and the State* (Princeton, 1984); M. L. McPherran, 'Socratic Piety in the *Euthyphro*', *Journal of the History of Philosophy*, 23 (1985), 283–309; Reeve, *Apology*. For various attacks on Vlastos's interpretation of constructivism, see T. C. Brickhouse and N. D. Smith, 'Vlastos on the Elenchus', *Oxford Studies in Ancient Philosophy*, 2 (1984), 185–95; R. Kraut, 'Comments on Gregory Vlastos, "The Socratic Elenchus"', *Oxford Studies in Ancient Philosophy*, 1 (1983), 59–70; and R. M. Polansky, 'Professor Vlastos's Analysis of the Socratic Elenchus', *Oxford Studies in Ancient Philosophy*, 3 (1985), 247–59.

of the elenctic result. In the context of *Theaetetus*, the eponymous
character's three identifications of knowledge with perception, true
judgement, and true judgement accompanied by *logos* are all shown
to be wind-eggs with no life in them, a pronouncement accepted
both by the pregnant interlocutor and by the midwife (186 E 11–12,
201 C 6, and 210 A 6–9, respectively; the negation of Theaetetus'
three definitions is summarily expressed at 210 A 9–B 3). If, then,
the assessment of Socratic midwifery is not a piece of knowledge,
it must be an opinion whose truthfulness is ensured by its being
the product of a dialectical process endorsed by the omniscient and
benevolent god. Aided by him, the mentally sterile Socrates subjects Theaetetus' psychic progeny to the elenctic scrutiny and ends
up rejecting it as false. The divine origin of the obstetric art guarantees the validity of the final assessment of the foetus' genuineness,
so that at the end of the encounter both parties may rest assured that
a true, second-order pronouncement on its worth has been reached.
But that is all they can ever be assured of.[68] Socrates expresses his
confidence in the result of his midwifery as follows: 'Well then, our
art of midwifery tells us that all of these offspring are wind-eggs and
not worth bringing up?', and Theaetetus wholeheartedly agrees:
'Undoubtedly' (210 B 8–10). Both interlocutors are convinced that
Theaetetus' mental children have been proven false.

The product of the elenchus, then, is a true human *doxa*, not
a piece of wisdom. The language of 'seeming', in which Socrates
and Theaetetus couch their final assessment of the three definitions, lends support to this view.[69] Regarding the first definition,
Theaetetus receives Socrates' assertion that 'perception and knowledge could never be [οὐκ ἄρ' ἂν εἴη ποτέ] the same' with the rejoin-
der 'Evidently not [οὐ φαίνεται], Socrates; it has become by now as
clear as possible [καταφανέστατον γέγονεν] that knowledge is different
from perception' (186 E 9–12).[70] Theaetetus' use of the superlative

---

[68] For the view that Socrates desiderates wisdom but adheres to true belief
see M. F. Burnyeat, 'Examples in Epistemology: Socrates, Theaetetus, and G. E.
Moore', *Philosophy*, 52 (1977), 381–98; Irwin, *Moral Theory*, 39–42, 62; G. X. Santas, *Socrates: Philosophy in Plato's Early Dialogues* (London, 1979), 120, 311 n. 26.

[69] In attempting to show that, starting with *Gorgias*, the elenctic result is intended
to be seen as 'proven', Vlastos appeals to Socrates' use of the verb 'to prove' (*Gorg.*
479 E; 508 E–509 A), as opposed to the prevalent use of weaker forms of conviction
in earlier dialogues (e.g. *Rep.* 1, 335 E: 'it has been made clear to us'; *La.* 199 E: 'it
appears to be so').

[70] In rendering Theaetetus' response, I prefer this translation to Levett's, 'we
have now got the clearest possible proof that knowledge is something different from

notwithstanding, both statements convey strongly held beliefs, not steadfast knowledge. Similarly, Socrates' rejection of the second definition is based on the way things 'seem' (νῦν δὲ ἔοικεν, 201 C 6), and the same expression of a firmly held belief is used in Theaetetus' agreement with Socrates' rejection of all definitions, 'it seems not' (οὐκ ἔοικεν, 210 B 3).

Associating the truthfulness of the elenctic result with a dialectical procedure that enjoys divine support corroborates the distinction I have argued for between Socratic midwifery and sophistry in two important ways. First, whereas Protagorean relativism guarantees the infallibility and irrefutability of the individual's opinion, Socratic midwifery is predicated on the notion of the inherent errancy of human *doxa*, which it exposes with god's help. Thus it posits something external to the human condition, i.e. god, as the absolute standard of wisdom and the objective foundation of the meaning and value of men's beliefs. God is not, as the Protagorean *dictum* seems to imply, simply as wise as men (162 C 3–6), but wiser, indeed the wisest of creatures. Secondly, truth does not necessarily accompany every mortal utterance by virtue of its having been formed, but is assessed through a human interaction guided by the divine. Socratic midwifery, far from being 'an extremely tiresome piece of nonsense' (161 E 5–6), requires that a pregnant interlocutor engender ideas and then work together with the obstetrician to assess their worth. The emerging interaction is then an essentially collaborative enterprise, and is thus to some extent similar to the kind of collaboration Socrates envisages between himself and god: the collaboration between god and Socrates enables the latter to locate truth, and elenctic *synousia* makes possible the discovery of truth in the dialectical exchange of ideas. For Protagoras, however, intellectual collaboration is unnecessary for the discovery of truth, as individual *logoi* are indisputably veridical.

## 3. Conclusions

In the midwifery passage Socrates connects his art of spiritual obstetrics with the divine in such a way as to suggest that the god

perception', as the latter seems to me to overstate the case. If 'proof' were what Socrates and Theaetetus had furnished, we would naturally expect a verbal form of the verb ἀποδεικνύναι, rather than the phrase φανερὸν γίγνεσθαι. See also 162 E.

crucially affects its function and outcome. Seen from this point of view, the midwife's assessment of the interlocutor's mental children can only be true, and thus the belief reached at the end of the dialogue, that Theaetetus' three definitions of knowledge are false, is true. Socrates' appeal to the divine underpinnings of his *technē* helps further to distinguish his art from that of his sophistic competitors: while they either acknowledge no higher source of truth and knowledge than the opining individual (Protagoras) or refute all arguments irrespective of their epistemic worth (eristic), Socrates invites us to countenance the elenctic outcome as true *qua* the result of a divinely sanctioned conversational practice. Socrates' mental barrenness and religiosity, then, interpenetrate and create a dialectical tool that differs, in function and aim, from the sophistic method of conversation. The midwifery analogy affords Socrates the opportunity to present his philosophical practice as a divinely inspired mission infused by the keen awareness of the limited epistemic value of his beliefs. By claiming that divine wisdom vouchsafes the truthfulness of the elenctic outcome, Socrates makes god the measure of the correctness of men's beliefs, and in so doing he conclusively shows that the elenchus is essentially different from sophistry and its epistemic presuppositions.

*University of California, Irvine*

## BIBLIOGRAPHY

Annas, J., 'Plato the Sceptic', in J. C. Klagge and N. D. Smith (eds.), *Methods of Interpreting Plato and his Dialogues* (*OSAP* suppl.; Oxford, 1992), 32–52.
Austin, S., 'The Paradox of Socratic Ignorance (How To Know That You Don't Know)', *Philosophical Topics*, 15 (1987), 23–34.
Bastianini, G., and Sedley, D., 'Commentarium in Platonis *Theaetetum*', *Corpus dei papiri filosofici*, pt. iii. *Commentari* (Florence, 1995), 227–562.
Benson, H. H., 'The Problem of the Elenchus Reconsidered', *Ancient Philosophy*, 7 (1987), 67–85.
—— 'A Note on Eristic and the Socratic Elenchus' ['Note'], *Journal of the History of Philosophy*, 27 (1989), 591–9.
—— *Socratic Wisdom: The Model of Knowledge in Plato's Early Dialogues* (Oxford, 2000).
Beversluis, J., *Cross-Examining Socrates: A Defense of the Interlocutors in Plato's Early Dialogues* (Cambridge, 2000).

Blondell, R., *The Play of Character in Plato's Dialogues* [*Play of Character*] (Cambridge, 2002).

Brickhouse, T. C., and Smith, N. D., 'The Origin of Socrates' Mission', *Journal of the History of Ideas*, 44 (1983), 657–66.

—— 'Vlastos on the Elenchus', *Oxford Studies in Ancient Philosophy*, 2 (1984), 185–95.

—— *Socrates on Trial* (Oxford, 1989).

—— 'Socrates' Elenctic Mission', *Oxford Studies in Ancient Philosophy*, 9 (1991), 131–59.

—— *Plato's Socrates* (Oxford, 1994).

Burnyeat, M. F., 'Socratic Midwifery, Platonic Inspiration' ['Socratic Midwifery'], *Bulletin of the Institute of Classical Studies*, 24 (1977), 7–16.

—— 'Examples in Epistemology: Socrates, Theaetetus, and G. E. Moore', *Philosophy*, 52 (1977), 381–98.

—— *The* Theaetetus *of Plato* [*Theaetetus*] (Indianapolis, 1990).

Destrée, P., and Smith, N. D. (eds.), *Socrates' Divine Sign: Religion, Practice, and Value in Socratic Philosophy* (Kelowna, BC, 2005).

Diels, H., and Schubart, W., *Anonymer Kommentar zu Platons 'Theaitet'* (Berlin, 1905).

Dodds, E. R., *Plato: Gorgias* (Oxford, 1959).

Gulley, N., *The Philosophy of Socrates* (New York, 1968).

Guthrie, W. K. C., *A History of Greek Philosophy*, iii. *The Fifth-Century Enlightenment* (Cambridge, 1969).

—— *Socrates* (Cambridge, 1971).

Hackforth, R., *The Composition of Plato's Apology* (Cambridge, 1933).

Irwin, T. H., *Plato's Moral Theory: The Early and Middle Dialogues* [*Moral Theory*] (Oxford, 1977).

—— *Plato: Gorgias* (Oxford, 1979).

—— 'Coercion and Objectivity in Plato's Dialectic', *Revue internationale de philosophie*, 156 (1986), 49–74.

—— 'Plato: The Intellectual Background', in R. Kraut (ed.), *The Cambridge Companion to Plato* (Cambridge, 1992), 51–89.

—— *Plato's Ethics* (Oxford, 1995).

Joyal, M., *The Platonic* Theages: *An Introduction, Commentary and Critical Edition* (Stuttgart, 2000).

—— 'Socrates, *Daimonios Anêr*: Some Textual and Interpretive Problems in Plato', in id. (ed.), *In Altum: Seventy-Five Years of Classical Studies in Newfoundland* (St John's, Newfoundland, 2001), 343–57.

Kahn, C., *Plato and the Socratic Dialogue* (Cambridge, 1996).

—— 'Vlastos' Socrates', *Phronesis*, 37 (1992), 233–58.

Kerferd, G. B., *The Sophistic Movement* [*Sophistic Movement*] (Cambridge, 1981).

Keulen, H., *Untersuchungen zu Platons 'Euthydem'* [*Untersuchungen*] (Wiesbaden, 1971).

Koyré, A., *Discovering Plato* (New York, 1945).

Kraut, R., 'Comments on Gregory Vlastos, "The Socratic Elenchus"', *Oxford Studies in Ancient Philosophy*, 1 (1983), 59–70.

—— *Socrates and the State* (Princeton, 1984).

Lesher, J. H., 'Socrates' Disavowal of Knowledge', *Journal of the History of Philosophy*, 25 (1987), 275–88.

Long, A. A., 'Plato's Apologies and Socrates in the *Theaetetus*', in J. Gentzler (ed.), *Method in Ancient Philosophy* (Oxford, 1998), 113–36.

McCabe, M. M., 'Measuring Sincerity', *Dialogos*, 5 (1998), 40–64.

McPherran, M. L., 'Socratic Piety in the *Euthyphro*', *Journal of the History of Philosophy*, 23 (1985), 283–309.

—— *The Religion of Socrates* (University Park, PA, 1996).

—— 'Elenctic Interpretation and the Delphic Oracle', in G. A. Scott (ed.), *Does Socrates Have a Method? Rethinking the Elenchus in Plato's Dialogues and Beyond* (University Park, PA, 2002), 114–44.

Moraux, P., 'La joute dialectique d'après le huitième livre des *Topiques*', in G. E. L. Owen (ed.), *Aristotle on Dialectic:* The Topics (Oxford, 1968), 277–311.

Nails, D., 'Problems with Vlastos' Platonic Developmentalism', *Ancient Philosophy*, 13 (1993), 272–91.

—— *Agora, Academy and the Conduct of Philosophy* (Dordrecht, 1995).

Opsomer, J., 'Plutarch's Defence of the *Theages*, in Defence of Socratic Philosophy?', *Philologus*, 141 (1997), 114–36.

Patzer, A., *Bibliographia Socratica* (Freiburg, 1985).

Polansky, R. M., 'Professor Vlastos's Analysis of the Socratic Elenchus', *Oxford Studies in Ancient Philosophy*, 3 (1985), 247–59.

—— *Philosophy and Knowledge: A Commentary on Plato's* Theaetetus (London and Toronto, 1992).

Poulakos, J., *Sophistical Rhetoric in Classical Greece* (Columbia, SC, 1995).

Rankin, H. D., *Sophists, Socratics, and Cynics* (London, 1983).

Reeve, C. D. C., *Socrates in the* Apology: *An Essay on Plato's* Apology of Socrates [*Apology*] (Indianapolis, 1989).

Riddell, J., *A Digest of Platonic Idioms* (Amsterdam, 1967).

Santas, G. X., *Socrates: Philosophy in Plato's Early Dialogues* (London, 1979).

Sedley, D., 'Three Platonist Interpretations of the *Theaetetus*' ['Platonist Interpretations'], in C. Gill and M. M. McCabe (eds.), *Form and Argument in Late Plato* (Oxford, 1996), 79–103.

—— *The Midwife of Platonism: Text and Subtext in Plato's* Theaetetus [*Midwife*] (Oxford, 2004).

Sidgwick, H., 'The Sophists', *Journal of Philology*, 4/8 (1872), 288–307.

Slings, S. R., *Plato:* Clitophon (Cambridge, 1999).

Sprague, R. K., *Plato's Use of Fallacy* (New York, 1962).

Stokes, M. C., *Plato's Socratic Conversations: Drama and Dialectic in Three Dialogues* (London, 1986).

Tarrant, H., 'The Date of Anon. *in Theaetetum*', *Classical Quarterly*, NS 33 (1983), 161–87.

—— 'Socratic *Synousia*: A Post-Platonic Myth?', *Journal of the History of Philosophy*, 43/2 (2005), 131–55.

Teloh, H., *The Development of Plato's Metaphysics* (University Park, PA, 1981).

—— *Socratic Education in Plato's Early Dialogues* (Notre Dame, 1986).

Thesleff, H., *Studies on Intensification in Early and Classical Greek* (Helsingfors, 1954).

Thompson, E. S., *The* Meno *of Plato* (London, 1901).

Versenyi, L., *Socratic Humanism* (New Haven, 1963).

Vlastos, G., 'The Socratic Elenchus' ['Socratic Elenchus'], *Oxford Studies in Ancient Philosophy*, 1 (1983), 27–58.

—— 'Afterthoughts on the Socratic Elenchus', *Oxford Studies in Ancient Philosophy*, 1 (1983), 71–4.

—— 'Socrates' Disavowal of Knowledge' ['Disavowal'], *Philosophical Quarterly*, 35 (1985), 1–31.

—— *Socrates: Ironist and Moral Philosopher* (Cambridge, 1991).

Wardy, R., *The Birth of Rhetoric: Gorgias, Plato and their Successors* (London, 1996).

Weiss, R., 'Virtue without Knowledge: Socrates' Conception of Holiness in Plato's *Euthyphro*', *Ancient Philosophy*, 14 (1994), 263–82.

Wengert, R. G., 'The Paradox of the Midwife', *History of Philosophy Quarterly*, 5 (1998), 3–10.

Woodruff, P., 'Plato's Early Theory of Knowledge' ['Early Theory'], in S. Everson (ed.), *Companions to Ancient Thought*, i. *Epistemology* (Cambridge, 1990), 60–84.

# PLEASURE'S PYRRHIC VICTORY: AN INTELLECTUALIST READING OF THE *PHILEBUS*

## J. ERIC BUTLER

> For the goddess, Philebus, saw everyone's arrogance and wide-spread wickedness, with no limit to pleasures and indulgences, and she established law and order as limits. You will say she destroyed them, but I claim, on the contrary, that she saved them.
>
> (*Philebus*, 26 B 7–C 2)

## 1. Introduction

SCHOLARS often suggest that in his late dialogues Plato becomes something like what Søren Kierkegaard calls the knight of infinite resignation. There is some ideal—be it rule by philosopher-king or the life of pure intellection—which is unattainable; as things stand, we are stuck with some second-best. The Stranger's conclusion in the *Statesman* might be delivered with a sigh:

But as things are, when—as we say—a king does not come to be in cities as a king bee is born in a hive, one individual immediately superior in body and mind, it is necessary—so it seems—for people to come together and write things down, chasing after the traces of the truest constitution (301 D 8–E 4)

—as if he were compromising.[1] The *Philebus*, too, seems to dis-

© J. Eric Butler 2007

I must acknowledge the patient and thorough advice of Professor Sedley, in matters philosophical and editorial, during the completion of this paper. Thanks also to the audience at the APA, Western division (2006), where this work was first presented, especially Sarah Brill, Ryan Drake, Jena Jolissaint, and Adriel Trott.

[1] On the topic of political idealism vs. realism in the late dialogues, see T. Saunders, 'Plato's Later Political Thought', in R. Kraut (ed.), *The Cambridge Companion to Plato* [*Companion*] (New York, 1992), 464–92, and the provocative but highly speculative biographical account in R. Hackforth, *Plato's Examination of Pleasure* [*Pleasure*] (New York, 1945), 1–10.

play this kind of resignation, because at 33 B 3–7 Socrates says that
the life of intellection and reason, having 'joys neither great nor
small', is 'perhaps . . . the most godlike [ἴσως . . . θειότατος]'.[2] Yet
with the rather malleable hedonist Protarchus he concludes that
a life including some pleasures is, somehow, also good. Through
this contrast of an ideal life and one that is also good but less than
ideal, Plato seems to have resigned himself to a compromise with
the real exigencies of this mortal life. For this reason, Dorothea
Frede has called pleasure a 'remedial good' in the *Philebus*. Others
have argued for a more sanguine reading. Against Frede, Carone
claims that Plato sees at least some redemptive potential in pleasure
(understood in the right way), and that a mortal life can be good
because (rather than in spite) of the pleasures available to it.[3] My
interpretation cuts across this dichotomy.

Though the good life is called 'mixed', I argue that knowledge
is the *exclusive* cause of its goodness (Section 2). I do not think
that Socrates makes any significant hedonist concessions. And yet
I also want to argue that the inclusion of pleasure in the mixed life
[=ML] does not make it any less ideal, as if it were tainted (Section
3). The burden, then, lies in showing how the dialogue can consis-

---

[2] Translations of the *Philebus* are my own, though I have benefited from li-
beral consultation of the following: D. Frede, *Plato: Philebus, Translated, with
Introduction and Notes* [*Philebus*] (Indianapolis, 1993); J. Gosling, *Plato: Philebus,
Translated with Notes and Commentary* [*Philebus*] (Oxford, 1975); and Hackforth,
*Pleasure*. Citations follow the lineation of the OCT.

On 'likeness to god' in Plato's ethical theory generally see J. Armstrong, 'After
the Ascent: Plato on Becoming like God', *Oxford Studies in Ancient Philosophy*, 26
(2004), 171–83; D. Russell, *Plato on Pleasure and the Good Life* (Oxford, 2005), 138–
65. For constraints of space, I have not been able to engage with Russell's recent
book as thoroughly as I would have liked in this paper. I find myself in agreement
with most of his conclusions, especially his arguments against both hedonistic and
ascetic readings of the *Philebus*.

[3] See Frede, *Philebus*, p. lvi, and G. Carone, 'Hedonism and the Pleasureless Life
in Plato's *Philebus*' ['Hedonism'], *Phronesis*, 45 (2000), 257–83. Though Carone
especially refers to Frede as the advocate of the 'remedial good' reading, she offers
the following quote from Gosling to exemplify just what such a reading entails: 'we
get the suggestion that pleasure is only part of the good for *man*, and only because
man is an inferior sort of being. It would be better to be a god, and so better to
be able to live a perfect life without pleasure' (from Gosling, *Philebus*, 103; quoted
by Carone, 'Hedonism', 260 n. 9). Presumably Frede's description of pleasure as
a 'necessary evil' also captures the meaning of 'remedial good' ('Rumplestiltskin's
Pleasures: True and False Pleasures in Plato's *Philebus*' ['Rumplestiltskin'], *Phronesis*, 30 (1985), 151–80 at 151). Throughout this article I usually refer specifically to
the arguments in Carone, 'Hedonism'. She advances, generally, the same arguments
(with helpful elaborations) in *Plato's Cosmology and its Ethical Dimensions* [*Cosmology*] (New York, 2005).

tently claim (*a*) that knowledge is the cause and the sole measure of goodness, and (*b*) that a life characterized by some pleasure(s) is no less good because of them. The key lies in a new interpretation of the status of pleasure itself. As the analysis of false and true pleasures shows, far from being antithetical to knowledge, pleasure is ontologically parasitic upon it. Because knowledge is a necessary condition for the existence of pleasure, the necessary presence of pleasure testifies to the importance of knowledge. And if one could take random samples of the mixed life, one would never come up with a knowledge-free slice. Because knowledge must be present in order for pleasure to obtain, every instance of pleasure is also an instance of knowledge. This interpretation of the status of pleasure may be seen as deflationist or reductive. But if pleasure's status is thin, it is thereby redeemed.

When the real is subordinated to the ideal, one argumentative strategy is to maintain their strict separation, but to argue that the real has some overlooked, intrinsic value.[4] But another strategy is to call into question the supposed difference between that which is posited as real and that which is posited as ideal. If it can be shown that (*a*) knowledge is the cause of the good life, and (*b*) pleasure places no limit on the potential for knowledge, then in principle the (real) mixed life is no worse off than the (ideal) life of pure pleasure. This, I want to claim, is the upshot of the argument(s) in *Philebus*.

In Section 2 I argue that knowledge is the cause of the mixed (i.e. good) life—both the cause of its being and the cause of its goodness. First I examine the dialogue's 'initial skirmish', and the one/many problems that are raised there (2*a*). Then I turn to Socrates' set-up of the dialogue's central question: the side-by-side comparison of the life of pure pleasure and the life of pure knowledge, and the ultimate victory of the mixed life (2*b*). Next I employ the Aristotelian causes, in order to show that knowledge functions as both the formal and the efficient cause of the mixed life (2*c*). Though arguably anachronistic, the use of Aristotelian causal terminology to talk about causality in Plato is hardly unprecedented.[5] But I do hope to show that the conceptual tools by which one might identify at least

---

[4] This, on my reading, is Carone's tactic in 'Hedonism' and *Cosmology* (ch. 5).

[5] T. Irwin makes cautious use of Aristotelian causal terminology in *Plato's Ethics* [*Ethics*] (New York, 1995), 318–38. So do Carone, *Cosmology*, 94–7; Frede, *Philebus*, 23 n. 3; Hackforth, *Pleasure*, 36; and C. Hampton, *Pleasure, Knowledge, and Being: An Analysis of Plato's* Philebus [*Pleasure*] (Albany, NY, 1990), 45.

formal and efficient types of cause are present in the *Philebus*, and in much of the rest of Plato's corpus, such that one is not using heavy-handed importation when referring to them. I take it that something is a remedial good if it is the best thing attainable to a certain subset (mortals), which subset is barred from attaining some absolute (ideal, immortal) good. Thus I argue that the question whether pleasure is a remedial good comes down to the question whether its necessary attainment bars one from attaining knowledge (by which the ideal life would be wholly characterized). In Section 3 I offer a close textual reading of the *Philebus*, with the goal of proving that it does not. In that section I divide up the dialogue into sections, following most traditional commentaries. Thus 3*b* treats the discussion of pleasure in general, 3*c* false pleasures, 3*d* true pleasures, 3*e* the final mixture, and 3*f* the final ranking of goods.[6]

## 2. The good life and the cause of the good life

### (a) *Intellectualism vs. hedonism*

In the *Philebus* Socrates and Protarchus set out 'to prove some condition [ἕξις] or state [διάθεσις] of the soul to be the one that can render life happy for all human beings' (11 D 4–6). The discussion is initially framed as a simple dialectic: a competition between two antithetical types of life. Protarchus will argue that the life of pleasure fulfils such requirement, while Socrates will argue on behalf of the life of intellection.[7]

At 12 C 4 Socrates begins a short-lived attack on the hedonist position: 'I know that pleasure is multi-faceted [ποικίλον] and, as I said before, we must start by taking it up and examining what kind of nature it has' (12 C 4–6). Despite appearances, Socrates never suggests in what follows that pleasure is not a coherent, or unitary, concept. Instead, he questions the relationship between pleasure

---

[6] My division of the dialogue into sections largely follows the divisions of Frede, *Philebus*.

[7] Plato is not particularly consistent in his employment of the various Greek knowledge terms. I have made every effort to translate them consistently, as follows: νοῦς = intellect/intellection; φρόνησις = reason; ἐπιστήμη = knowledge. νοῦς occurs most frequently, and my 'intellection' doubtlessly sounds a bit awkward. But I am convinced (*a*) that 'reason' is a better translation of φρόνησις, and (*b*) that Plato has in mind an activity, rather than a capacity, for which 'intellection' is preferable to 'intellect'. 'Intelligence', of course, has too many problematic connotations (IQ tests etc.).

and goodness by arguing, essentially, that given the radical diversity of kinds of pleasure, the hedonist needs—but in fact lacks—some strong warrant for positing that pleasure and goodness are coextensive. 'There is one thing', he says of pleasure, 'which sounds simple on the one hand, but which takes on many diverse forms which are somehow unlike each other' (c 6–8).[8] Soon enough we find Socrates and Protarchus engaged in a discussion about some familiar-sounding one/many problems. But the fact that the ensuing metaphysical discussion has a familiar ring (reminiscent, for instance, of the *Parmenides*) might lead us to draw hasty conclusions about what, exactly, the problem with pleasure is. The more familiar one/many problems (i.e. as expressed in the middle dialogues) concern the way in which a form such as pleasure can be one, and yet also dispersed among the many particular instances of pleasure. This, as Moravcsik points out, is not the problem Socrates has in mind with respect to pleasure.[9] To exemplify pleasure's multifacetedness, he turns not to individual instances of pleasure, but to *kinds* of pleasure, each of which might, in turn, be embodied in individual instances: the pleasure of the philanderer vs. the pleasure of the sober-minded fellow, the pleasure of the ignoramus vs. the pleasure of the wise man (12 D 1–4).[10] Surely, says Socrates, 'if someone were to say that these [kinds of] pleasure are similar to each other, he would justly seem to be a fool' (D 4–6). The problem, then, lies not

---

[8] ἔστι γάρ, ἀκούειν μὲν οὕτως ἁπλῶς, ἔν τι, μορφὰς δὲ δήπου παντοίας εἴληφε καί τινα τρόπον ἀνομοίους ἀλλήλαις. Compare Gosling's translation: 'mentioned by itself like that, it sounds like a single thing, but it no doubt takes all sorts of forms, which in some way are unlike each other'. Based on the arguments that follow, I do not think that Socrates wants to say that pleasure merely *sounds* like some unity. Rather, it really *is* ἔν τι, but the relevant ambiguity arises in that it sounds simple on the one hand and yet takes on a multiplicity of forms on the other hand.

[9] That the one/many problems discussed in the *Philebus* 'have nothing to do with sensible particulars' is argued by J. Moravcsik, 'Forms, Nature, and the Good in the *Philebus*' ['Forms'], *Phronesis*, 24 (1979), 81–101 at 81–2 *et passim*, and also by H. Teloh, *The Development of Plato's Metaphysics* [*Development*] (University Park, PA, 1981), 176–88. But compare K. Sayre, 'The *Philebus* and the Good: The Unity of the Dialogue in Which the Good is Unity' ['Unity'], *Proceedings of the Boston Area Colloquium in Ancient Philosophy*, 2 (1987), 45–71. Irwin concedes that the *Philebus* question is, strictly, different from the question of the universal and the particulars, but shows how Plato plausibly conceived the earlier and the later one/many problems to be closely related to each other (*Ethics*, 322).

[10] I agree with Hackforth's conclusion that, throughout the dialogue, Socrates always takes pleasures to be inseparable from their source, and that 'what really occurs is always "my pleasure in this"', though I see neither a lack of cogency nor a gross fallacy here, as he does (*Pleasure*, 16 n. 1).

in explaining how many particular instances of pleasure somehow participate in one form of pleasure; rather it is to see how several different species of pleasure, which seem antithetical to each other, can have anything other than pleasantness in common. The most intuitive answer is the circular one offered up by Protarchus: wisdom and folly may be antithetical to each other, but the pleasures derived from each are none the less identical *qua* pleasure. Pleasure, he protests, should be 'most like [ὁμοιότατον]' pleasure (D 8–E 2). Socrates' strategy in refuting this claim is instructive: pleasure should be compared to colour and shape. *Qua* colour, black and white are similar. Yet no one can deny that, in some *real* sense, black and white are opposites. Likewise, although shape is not a category that readily admits of opposites, it is easy to see that while circle and triangle are both shapes, they are very different.[11] Thus the question he finally puts to Protarchus, now bringing the discussion back to the topic at hand: 'What is it about bad and good pleasures alike that makes you call [προσαγορεύεις] all pleasures good?' (13 B 3–5). Again, Socrates has never argued against the coherence of a unitary concept pleasure. Indeed, 'no argument will dispute that all pleasant things are pleasant' (13 A 10–B 1). The only time he has used a plural noun, τῶν ἡδονῶν at 12 D 4, he might just as well have meant 'these types of pleasure' or 'these pleasant things', which still accords with his observation above that pleasure 'is one thing [ἔστι . . . ἕν τι]' which, on the one hand, sounds simple (ἀκούειν μὲν οὕτως ἁπλῶς) but takes on many different forms (μορφὰς δὲ δήπου παντοίας εἴληφε) (12 C 6–8). On the metaphysical status of the concept pleasure, Socrates remains quite agnostic in this passage; he neither acknowledges a form Pleasure, nor denies that such a form exists. For his concern is a simpler one: he means just to deny that goodness is concomitant with pleasantness. The latter does not necessarily imply the former.

But there is more to be said about the analogy to shape and colour. Circle and triangle are different from each other in that they are different *shapes*—one has every peripheral point equidistant from the centre, while the other has three sides. Applying the analogy as closely as possible to the main theme, Protarchus wants to predicate goodness of the various pleasure species, just as one predicates shape of the circle, triangle, etc. Socrates, however, presses for a middle term that will warrant that predication: by

---

[11] On opposition in Plato see N. Cooper, 'Pleasure and Goodness in Plato's *Philebus*', *Philosophical Quarterly*, 18 (1968), 12–15.

virtue of *what* are (all) pleasures good? Protarchus' initial strong hedonism ('all pleasant things are good') can still be vindicated if there is some category *I* whose extension is broader than pleasure but narrower than (or coextensive with) goodness, such that one can predicate *I* of all pleasure, and goodness of all *I*. Such a simple, nested *Barbara*-type relationship is exactly what the shape analogy leads us to expect. For there is obviously some middle term that links circles and triangles with shape: two-dimensional finite extension or some such. Indeed the initial skirmish at 12 A 4–14 B 7 serves only to show that Protarchus cannot warrant any immediate inference from pleasantness to goodness.[12] If Socrates wanted radically to sever the link between pleasure and the good, he would need to show that there are some goods that are not pleasant, such that there is some goodness criterion that is truly independent of the category pleasure. But that would be a terrible strategy for converting a hedonist. Instead, what he ends up demonstrating is that the goodness of pleasure is mediated by, and dependent on, some other category (*I*), so that any connection between pleasure and goodness (even if it just so happens that all goods are pleasant) is neither direct nor causal. I have obviously rigged the demonstration, for, as I shall proceed to argue, the middle term sought—that by virtue of which one has warrant for predicating goodness of pleasure—is intellection (*I*). Specifically, all pleasures are intellectual, and their goodness comes from *that* fact (not the fact that they are pleasant).[13]

Socrates' initial attack on Protarchus' inference from pleasant-

[12] Irwin notes that 'Red and green do not differ simply in properties external to what is necessary and essential for being colour; they do not, for instance, differ only insofar as red happens to be found on berries and green on leaves' (*Ethics*, 321). He wants to argue that there are relevant immanent differences within the category pleasure itself, such that Socrates will end up converting the hedonist on hedonist ground (rather than appealing to some extra-hedonistic ethical criterion). This interpretation is commensurate with mine; I take the false-pleasures section to show that the hedonist cannot discriminate genuine from impostor pleasures without appeal to something extra-hedonistic (namely, reason). Thus the hedonist position is immanently self-refuting.

[13] Despite what the opening skirmish might lead us to expect, Socrates does not end up arguing that *some* pleasures are good. We might expect something like: all intellectual things are good, some pleasures are intellectual, therefore some pleasures are good (by *Darii*). I argue that, as the dialogue proceeds, Socrates wants to claim that *only* pleasures that are intellectual deserve the name 'pleasures'—only they are *real* pleasures. Therefore, it ends up being true to assert that all pleasures are intellectual, and so all pleasures are good, provided one accepts Socrates' final, tricky conception of real pleasure (cf. 3*b–f* below).

ness to goodness is interrupted by a discussion of the one and the
many, which occasions his introduction of a new method of investigation involving the one, the limited, and the unlimited (16 c
5 ff.). I leave the details of this so-called 'heavenly tradition' to one
side, for its conclusions are somewhat peripheral to my main concerns.[14] That discussion concludes with another tantalizing false
start. Socrates has asked how knowledge and pleasure can be both
one and many (18 E 9), and Protarchus concludes: 'It seems to me
that Socrates is now asking us whether or not there are forms [εἴδη]
of pleasure, and [if there are] how many and what kinds there are'
(19 B 2–3). To which Socrates responds: 'You are most correct' (19 B
5). This is indeed an interesting question, but the conversation gets
waylaid before it can be addressed. Exasperated, Protarchus chides
Socrates for his perceived obfuscation, and demands:

> *You* decide, with respect to this [point], whether it is necessary to divide
> up the forms of pleasure and knowledge, or whether you can just let it
> go if, through some other means, you are able and willing to resolve the
> present conflict. (20 A 5–9)

In response to this demand, Socrates suggests that the good is neither pleasure nor knowledge, but some third thing. The rest of the
dialogue will bear out this suggestion, and as we look at the following arguments, it is crucial to keep in mind that the lingering
question—the unanswered query that led into the suggestion of a
third kind of life—is: 'Are there forms [εἴδη] of pleasure, and if so
what kind and how many are they?'

### (b) The good and the cause of the good

At 20 c 8 Socrates begins to lead Protarchus in a side-by-side comparison of pleasure and knowledge, with the goal of determining
which one ranks as 'the good' (20 D 1).[15] The good should be both
perfect (τέλεον: D 1) and sufficient (ἱκανόν: D 4), and these requirements warrant a unique method of comparison: each candidate will

[14] But see: Striker, *Peras und Apeiron: Das Problem der Formen in Platons Phile-
bus [Peras]* (Göttingen, 1970); Carone, *Cosmology*, 81–6; Hampton, *Pleasure*, 13–50;
Teloh, *Development*, 176–88; K. Sayre, *Plato's Late Ontology: A Riddle Resolved*
(Princeton, 1983), 118–55.

[15] τἀγαθοῦ, which must be equivalent to the ἕξις ψυχῆς καὶ διάθεσις which, at 11 D
4–6, makes one's life εὐδαίμων. There is plenty of room for debate about what kind of
good such an ingredient is, for which see Gosling, *Philebus*, 139–42; Frede, *Philebus*,
pp. xvi–xix); Sayre, 'Unity', *passim*.

be examined separately (χωρίς: 20 E 2). In this context, to examine something 'separately' means to examine a life characterized by it alone, and not at all by its rival, for 'if either of them is the good, it must have no need of anything else to be added to it' (E 5–6). Such is the very definition of sufficiency.[16] This simple dialectical approach is short-lived, as the interlocutors quickly agree that no one wants to live a life that consists purely either of pleasure or of knowledge (22 A 1–6).[17]

And so Socrates suggests that the condition of the soul that renders life happy for all human beings is a mixed life, one with some pleasures but also a healthy dose of intellection and reason (22 A 1–2). But the debate does not end with this temporary agreement. For Socrates further suggests that although the mixed life has taken the prize, we may still debate over second place. The remainder of the dialogue, then, will be devoted to the debate for this second place. But what, exactly, does second place *mean*? Socrates explains that, between intellection and pleasure, second place should go to whichever is the *cause* (αἴτιον) of the mixed life, which has taken first prize:

οὕτω τὸ μὲν ἀγαθὸν τούτων ἀμφοτέρων οὐδέτερον ἂν εἴη, τάχα δ᾽ ἂν αἴτιόν τις
ὑπολάβοι πότερον αὐτῶν εἶναι. τούτου δὴ πέρι καὶ μᾶλλον ἔτι πρὸς Φίληβον διαμαχοίμην ἂν ὡς ἐν τῷ μεικτῷ τούτῳ βίῳ, ὅτι ποτ᾽ ἔστι τοῦτο ὃ λαβὼν ὁ βίος
οὗτος γέγονεν αἱρετὸς ἅμα καὶ ἀγαθός, οὐχ ἡδονὴ ἀλλὰ νοῦς τούτῳ συγγενέστερον
καὶ ὁμοιότερόν ἐστι, καὶ κατὰ τοῦτον τὸν λόγον οὔτ᾽ ἂν τῶν πρωτείων οὐδ᾽ αὖ
τῶν δευτερείων ἡδονὴ μετὸν ἀληθῶς ἄν ποτε λέγοιτο. (22 D 3–E 1)

[1] Neither [intellection nor pleasure] would be the good, but it could be assumed that one or the other of them is its *cause*. [2] But I would be even more ready to contest this point against Philebus. I should hold that, [a] whatever that thing is upon whose presence the mixed life becomes choiceworthy and good, [b] intellection is more closely related to that thing and more like it than [c] pleasure; and if this can be upheld, neither first nor second prize could really ever be claimed for pleasure.[18]

---

[16] The procedure is somewhat similar to that suggested by Glaucon in examining the extremes of justice and injustice at *Rep.* 2, 360 E 1–361 D 3. To see if justice is choiceworthy, we should look at the life characterized only by justice, without any admixture of either injustice *or even the concomitant benefits of justice itself* (i.e. reputation etc.).

[17] Socrates' assertion at 21 C 4–5 that without true *doxa* one would not even be able to recognize pleasure *while one was pleased* serves as a preliminary indication of the arguments that follow: that genuine pleasure requires some intellectual operation. For what could it mean to be pleased *and not know it*?

[18] I have inserted artificial divisions into the translation in order to facilitate the explication that follows. I have followed Gosling in inserting a full point in the

This claim seems straightforward, but several comments are called for. First, how many assertions (or potential assertions) are contained in this passage? Is the second clause [2] simply explicative of the first [1], or are there two potential contentions, the first of which Socrates bypasses, but the second of which he would much rather take up? Secondly, should we understand that the subject of [2*a*] is different from the subject of [2*b*], or might [2*b*] represent a reiteration of [2*a*]?

The first question concerns the relationship between [1] and [2]. One interpretation holds that [2] represents an amendment or correction of [1], such that Socrates has mentioned two separate claims, bypassing the first in favour of the second. This interpretation may be attractive if one takes the particle δή as strictly adversative, and Hackforth offers it, calling the second clause a correction or modification of the first suggestion, that intellection *is* the cause of the good.[19] But if these are two different possible contentions, and if Socrates neglects the first in favour of the second, it is odd that he never justifies his neglect of it. If these are two different contentions, just *why* would Socrates 'much rather' make the second against Protarchus than the first? What would the first contention look like, and what is wrong with it? Plato may be employing some rhetorical trickery here. If, as Hackforth assumes, [1] and [2] are two different potential arguments, and Socrates makes it sound as though he will argue for [2] but not for [1], this makes the ensuing argument a little easier. It would be less intellectualist to claim that intellection is not the cause of the good, but that it is close to it. It would be easier to persuade a committed hedonist of [2] than of [1], and this may be why Socrates explicitly says that he would rather make such a contention *against Philebus* (πρὸς Φίληβον διαμαχοίμην ἄν: 22 D 5). But his preference for arguing [2] against hedonistic Philebus does not necessarily entail that he cannot or will not argue [1]. Here I shall claim that the actual arguments that follow confirm [1] (that intellection is *the cause of the good life*) rather than [2]. Whether

---

second clause, which preserves the ambiguity inherent in the sentence. For 'this point' in the translation might refer either to the antecedent claim that reason is the cause of the good, or to the forthcoming one that reason is more like the cause of the good than pleasure. It loses that ambiguity when placed in the same sentence with the latter claim.

[19] *Pleasure*, 36.

Protarchus understands that such a conclusion results is another question.

Which brings me to the second point of ambiguity in the passage. In the second clause [2], what, exactly, is the status of intellection for which Socrates intends to argue? One possibility is this: there is [a] something in the mixed life that makes it choiceworthy and good, and then there is [b] intellection, and then there is [c] pleasure, and [b] is συγγενέστερον καὶ ὁμοιότερον to [a] than [c] is. Another possibility is that this is a pleonastic way of saying just that intellection *is* the thing in ML that makes it good and choiceworthy. The Greek is so ambiguous that it would be difficult to construct a structurally parallel sentence in English, but it might sound something like the following: 'Whatever it is you're looking for, Target is more likely to have things like that than Wal-Mart.' Such a (cumbersome) construction does not imply that the thing you are looking for is different from the thing you are more likely to find at Target. Rather, it implies that you will find *exactly the thing you are looking for* at Target. But of course in Plato's Greek there is even more ambiguity because of the ostensibly technical context of the statement. Here one might expect to find precision, but instead the claim is ambiguous. Again, it is just possible that Socrates is being somewhat ambiguous on purpose, but I shall claim that, based on the arguments that follow, he ends up proving that intellection *is* that thing in the mixed life that makes it good and choiceworthy.

Now Gosling argues for the first interpretation, where there is the thing [a] that makes ML good and choiceworthy, and this thing is different from both [b] intellection and [c] pleasure, though intellection is more closely related to it than pleasure. He offers *peras* as the first thing—the thing that is responsible and to which intellection is more closely related: 'In the present section intelligence is only shown to be responsible for the good life in the sense of being its producer. *Peras* is responsible (cf. 64 D) in another sense, and intelligence is just more close[ly] related to that.'[20] His reference to 64 D is indeed instructive, as there Socrates returns to ask:

What [ingredient] in the mixture would appear to us to be the most honourable and at the same time most properly a cause of this state's being well regarded by everyone? When we know this, we shall enquire further

[20] *Philebus*, 185.

whether it is more like the nature of, and akin to, pleasure or intellection in the cosmos as a whole. (64 c 5–9)

Let us briefly examine this later discussion, with an eye towards the earlier (22 d 1–e 1), to which I shall return below. The ingredients that make the mixture most valuable and precious turn out to be measure and proportion (64 d 9),[21] which ally themselves with beauty and virtue (64 e 5–7). So here it appears that there *is* some ingredient—ingredient [a] in the earlier text (22 d 1–e 1)—which is different from intellection and which Protarchus will now proceed to compare with intellection and pleasure.[22] Socrates asks Protarchus to take these terms individually, comparing each one to intellection and pleasure. When compared to truth, pleasure is the 'greatest impostor [ἀλαζονίστατον]', while intellection 'either is the same as truth or of all things it is most like it and most true' (65 c 5–d 3). But which is it? Is intellection the same as truth or is it most like it and most true? Or do these amount to the same thing?[23] Again, if intellection is the same as truth, then we would be justified in reading 22 d 1–e 1 as a statement by Socrates that intellection is actually *the same* as the ingredient in ML that makes it good and choiceworthy. But even here in the latter passage, we still have the simultaneous possibility that intellection and the constitutive ingredient are different, and that intellection is closer to it than pleasure. As Protarchus continues his comparisons, we learn, with respect to measure, that 'nothing more measured than intellection and knowledge could ever be found' (65 d 9–10), and that intellection is more beautiful than pleasure, because 'no one could ever regard reason and intellection as ugly' (65 e 1–7). In summary, three terms now characterize the constitutive ingredient: truth, measure/proportion, and beauty. Protarchus has compared

[21] More precisely 'measure and that which is of the nature of proportion [μέτρου καὶ τῆς συμμέτρου φύσεως]'.

[22] We might wonder if the four terms listed—measure, proportion, beauty, and virtue—are explicative of each other, or if they are meant to be held apart as four distinct terms, all of which apply individually to the constitutive ingredient. Note, though, that virtue drops off the list when Socrates repeats it at 65 a 2.

[23] This kind of construction is quite common in the *Philebus*. Notice 59 c 2–6: true scientific results belong to things ἀεὶ κατὰ τὰ αὐτὰ ὡσαύτως ἀμεικτότατα ἔχοντα, ἤ . . . ἐκείνων ὅτι μάλιστά ἐστι συγγενές. Does he *really* mean that there are two different classes of things, those that are always self-same and then those that are most closely related to them? He never spells out what the second class of objects would be. One gets the impression that this has become a pleonastic trope for Plato, where the second clause reiterates the first.

each of them with intellection and pleasure, and pleasure is immediately discounted from bearing much (or any) resemblance to any
of them. Intellection, on the other hand, is either the same as truth,
or it is most like it and most true; intellection is the most measured/
symmetrical thing; and intellection is on all accounts beautiful.

Things get even more interesting at 66 A 4, where, having heard
Protarchus' comparisons of intellection and pleasure to the three
terms that describe the constitutive ingredient, Socrates asks:

So you will announce everywhere, both by sending messengers and saying
it in person to those present, that pleasure is not a property of the first
rank, nor again of the second, but that first comes what is somehow connected with measure, the measured and the timely, and whatever else is
considered similar. (66 A 4–8)

There is nothing particularly unclear about this text. First place
goes to 'the measured',[24] and we learnt just above (65 D 9–10) that
intellection/reason is the most measured thing that could ever be
found. The obvious conclusion of this passage is that intellection
wins first place. It does not matter whether we draw that conclusion because of Protarchus' suggestion at 65 D 2–3 that intellection
and truth are the same ($\tau\alpha\dot{v}\tau\acute{o}\nu$), or from Socrates' later assertion
that first rank goes to that which is measured (66 A 7) coupled with
the earlier assertion that nothing is more measured than intellection
(65 D 9–10). Both lines of argument lead to the same conclusion: intellection *is* the ingredient that makes the mixture most valuable and
precious. Which means that, within clause [2] in the earlier passage
(22 D 1–E 1), there is no difference between [a] and [b]: intellection
*is* that thing which makes the mixed life choiceworthy and good.

So Gosling is right to compare these two passages (22 D 1–E 1;
64 C 5–66 A 8), and while there is a healthy dose of ambiguity in the
first, I want to claim that the arguments that intervene between it
and the second recommend that we understand Socrates to claim
that intellection is the cause of the good life. The alternative interpretation sets a lower bar: the claim that intellection is more closely
related than pleasure to the cause of the good life is more populist—
less intellectualist—than the second. And in that sense it goes along
with the 'correction' interpretation, whereby one understands that

---

[24] I take it that 'the measured [$\tau\grave{o}$ $\mu\acute{e}\tau\rho\iota o\nu$]' is a more accurate specification of 'that
which is somehow connected with measure [$\pi\eta$ $\pi\epsilon\rho\grave{\iota}$ $\mu\acute{e}\tau\rho\iota o\nu$]'. I do not know what to
make of 'the timely/punctual [$\tau\grave{o}$ $\kappa\alpha\acute{\iota}\rho\iota o\nu$]'. As to the ranking that follows (66 B 1 ff.),
where $\nu o\hat{v}s$ $\kappa\alpha\grave{\iota}$ $\phi\rho\acute{o}\nu\eta\sigma\iota s$ are explicitly said to take third place, see below, sect. 3*f.*

[2] is a different claim from [1] such that Socrates decides to argue not that intellection is the cause of the good life but that it is more akin to the ingredient that causes the good life. But if 22 D 4–6 [2] does not constitute a correction but rather an explication—if, that is, being the cause of the good *means* being the ingredient in the mixed life that makes it choiceworthy—then the bar has been set much higher. In short, the passage as a whole admits of two distinct readings: (A) intellection is the cause of the good life, which is equivalent to intellection's being that ingredient in ML that makes it good and choiceworthy; (B) we are strictly focusing on a comparison between intellection [*b*] and pleasure [*c*], determining which of them wins second place, behind [*a*], whatever [*a*] turns out to be. The second possibility (B) has, justly, received its hearing in the scholarship. In what follows, I shall argue for (A).[25]

### (c) *Intellection as formal, efficient cause*

A consequence of (A) is that Socrates is being explicative, not disjunctive, when he moves from 'the cause of the good' (22 D 4 = [1]) to 'the [ingredient] in the mixed life that makes it choiceworthy and good' (22 D 6–7 = [2*a*]). Two more results follow. First, if 'the good' in D 4 (= [1]) is short for 'the good life', and 'the good life' is ML, then intellection is the cause (*aition*) of ML. In general, the *Philebus* is one of the best places to turn to for an examination of Plato's understanding of causality, and in this section I shall examine the various ways that intellection plays a causal role in the mixed life, beginning with the passage already under consideration. A second consequence of (A) is that the cause of the good life *is*, at least in the context of 22 D 1–E 1, the ingredient in a life that makes it true to predicate 'good' of it. We might then formulate the following definition of cause, as that term is being used in this passage: $x$ is the cause of S's being P if, once S has acquired (λαβών) $x$ it is true to predicate P of S. If I may be permitted a minor anachronism, it seems that we have something quite close to a formal cause. Again, at 64 C 5 the ingredient that makes the mixed life precious to all mankind seems to refer to a formal cause—that factor which, once it obtains

---

[25] I do not assume that I have definitively proven that (A) is the only right interpretation. In fact I think that both (A) and (B) are defensible. But my goal is to present a new interpretation of the dialogue as a whole, and (A) is necessary in order to secure the coherency of that interpretation.

in the mixed life, makes it true to predicate of it προσφιλής.[26] And the language of 64 D 3–5 is even more indicative: 'It doesn't seem difficult to see the cause, through which [τὴν αἰτίαν, δι' ἥν] every mixture becomes either priceless or valueless.' And it is, of course, interesting that Aristotle uses ratio or proportion (specifically 1 : 2) and number generally to exemplify his own formal cause.[27]

Socrates also presents arguments to the effect that intellection functions as the formal cause of the mixed life. At 26 E 2–8 he queries:

soc. . . . Tell me, then, if you think that everything that comes to be must [do so] on account of some cause [διά τινα αἰτίαν] of the coming-to-be?
PROT. I do; how should it come about otherwise?
soc. Don't the nature of the maker [ἡ τοῦ ποιοῦντος φύσις] and the cause [τῆς αἰτίας] differ in no way other than in name, such that it would be correct to call the maker [τὸ ποιοῦν] and that which is responsible [τὸ αἴτιον] 'one'?

Here, Gosling argues, Plato 'seems to equate explanans with producer [i.e. form with mover] and explanandum with product'.[28] It is true that the passage does not distinguish the explanation from the moving cause, and so in some sense it is true to say that Plato does not offer a systematic distinction between the formal and the efficient cause. But overall this passage does not aim to argue that intellection is the formal cause or the *explanans*—that argument is accomplished both earlier (22 D 1–E 1) and later (64 C 5–66 A 8). Here Plato has moved on, and he will now have Socrates argue that intellection is the *archē kinēseōs* of the good life, which is to say, of ML.

In order to see how intellection turns out to be the efficient cause of ML, it is necessary to examine the complicated and obscure ontological division—a division of 'everything that now exists' (πάντα τὰ νῦν ὄντα; τὰ ὄντα: 23 C 4; C 9)—into four classes.[29] Guided by Socrates, the interlocutors come up with the following division:

---

[26] Here governed by διάθεσις at 64 C 7, hence the feminine.

[27] *Phys.* 2. 3, 194[b]27–9; *Metaph.* Δ 1, 1013[a]26–9.

[28] *Philebus*, 95. Indeed, Plato does not generally proceed systematically—at least not in the sense that Aristotle proceeds systematically in the individual treatises (such as *Physics* 2). So it is not unusual that he should fail to spell out, all in one place, whatever distinctions between types of cause he may be alive to. But this is independent of the question whether Plato *had* a conception of the distinction between formal and efficient causes. I shall argue here that he did.

[29] In this section I have tried to limit my remarks on the ontological fourfold to the bare letter of the text. For responsible and thorough interpretation of the division, see Moravcsik, 'Forms'.

- The UNLIMITED[30] includes hot and cold, which always contain the more and the less, and have no end (τέλος: 24 B 1–8). Such beings are 'always in flux and never remain [προχωρεῖ γὰρ καὶ οὐ μένει . . . ἀεί]' (24 D 4).
- LIMIT includes mathematical concepts such as 'the equal', 'equality', 'double', and 'all that is related as number to number and measure to measure' (25 A 6–B 2).
- MIXTURE results when LIMIT is imposed on the UNLIMITED (23 C 12–14). Such mixture brings about health from sickness, musical perfection from dissonance, and in general moderation and harmony result (25 E 7–26 A 8).[31]
- The CAUSE of the mixture is the fourth ontological category. CAUSE is immediately called 'craftsman [δημιουργός]' (27 B 1) and, later, the 'soul [ψυχή]' (30 A 6 ff.) of the cosmos.

From the demonstration that reality in general (i.e. everything that is) is divided into these four kinds, Socrates moves discretely to a microcosmic analysis of the human being. The individual human constitution, it will turn out, mirrors the cosmological constitution in its fourfold nature. This will allow the candidates intellection, pleasure, and ML to be slotted into the fourfold division as well, since they are features of the individual human constitution. But the transition from the macroscopic to the microscopic is subtle. Having laid out the fourfold ontological distinction, Socrates reminds his audience of 'the issue that started our whole debate' (27 C 10): to determine the first and the second prize. He recalls that ML was previously declared the winner (D 1–2), and asks into which of the four divisions it falls. Obviously, it falls into the category MIXTURE (D 7–11). Turning next to pleasure, Philebus readily admits that it falls into the UNLIMITED class (E 7–28 A 4), and so Socrates turns to the assignment of reason, knowledge, and intellection (φρόνησις, ἐπιστήμη, νοῦς: 28 A 4). The conversation is interrupted here, both

[30] To avoid confusion, I have placed the names of the four ontological kinds in SMALL CAPITALS, in order to distinguish the specific ontological use of MIXTURE from the ordinary descriptive use of the noun 'mixture': ML is a mixture of reason and pleasure, so it falls into the category MIXTURE.

[31] Though the examples here (health, good weather) would imply otherwise, Sayre ('Unity') argues that the bare fact of being a mixture does not necessarily imply being a good mixture (or 'right combination [ὀρθὴ κοινωνία]'—cf. 25 E 7). In this claim he follows H. Jackson, 'Plato's Later Theory of Ideas', *Journal of Philology*, 10 (1882), 253–98, and Irwin also concurs (*Ethics*, 324). Frede seems to disagree (*Philebus*, 23 n. 3), as does Carone (*Cosmology*, 92–3).

by an oddity in the manuscripts and by some playful banter between the interlocutors.[32] When he mentioned reason, knowledge, and intellection at 28 A 4, Socrates had employed what he later describes as a 'playful interruption [ἐν τῷ παίζειν ἐθορύβησα]' (28 C 3), which led Philebus to roll his eyes in admonishment (28 B 1). After some minor squabbling, the discussion gets back on track at 28 C 6. 'All the wise are agreed', claims Socrates, 'that intellection is our king, over both heaven and earth' (28 C 6–8). But the collective agreement of the wise serves merely as a kind of *endoxa*, for Socrates suggests that they undertake a lengthier investigation into the class of things that includes intellection. This is appropriate because at this point in the discussion intellection could be assigned to either of the two remaining categories: LIMIT or CAUSE.

At 28 D 7 Socrates asks if 'our forebears' were correct in claiming that the universe is 'governed by the order of a wonderful intelligence [νοῦν καὶ φρόνησίν τινα θαυμαστὴν συντάττουσαν διακυβερνᾶν]'. To which Protarchus consents: 'intellection arranges it all [νοῦν πάντα διακοσμεῖν]' (28 E 3). At this point it appears that intellection, by virtue of its governing and arranging, belongs in the CAUSE category. But that question is not answered right away. Instead we enter into a conversation about the elements (fire, earth) that compose our mortal bodies, and their relationship to the cosmic elements (the 'fire of the cosmos [τὸ ἐν τῷ παντὶ πῦρ]' (29 C 2), 'earth of the cosmos [ἡ ἐν τῷ παντὶ γῆ]' (29 D 2), etc.). As it turns out, the comparison between our elements and the cosmic ones is meant to establish a strict analogy, such that Socrates can move at 29 E 2 to talking about the ordered universe as a body (because the combination of 'our' elements constitutes a body, and they have been shown to be analogous in all ways to those of the cosmos). Also like each of the elements considered individually, the body of the universe 'provides for the sustenance of [τρέφεται] what is body in our sphere' (29 E 5–7). Sticking to the microcosm/macrocosm analogy rather (too?) strictly, Socrates can next move from the observation that our body has a soul to the conclusion that the cosmos as a whole must have a soul (30 A 6).[33] More specifically, the cosmos as a whole must have an

---

[32] The oddity is actually somewhat relevant to my point. I assume τοῦτο at 28 A 3 with MS Ven. 189, and most modern translators. This against the τούτων of the other manuscripts and the τούτῳ of the OCT. I assume the antecedent is the ἄλλο τι of 28 A 1–2: whatever it is that allows pleasure to partake of the good will remain unsaid for now, but it will turn out to be reason!

[33] Note the logic here: the analogy is supposed to be so tight as to allow two-way

ordering cause, and that cause 'would justly be called wisdom and intellection [σοφία καὶ νοῦς]' (30 C 6–7), but there cannot be wisdom and intellection without a soul (30 C 9–10), therefore the cosmos as a whole must have a soul. Thus it has become apparent that 'intellection is akin to cause and is part of that family' (31 A 7–10).

There are four kinds—UNLIMITED, LIMIT, MIXTURE, and CAUSE—and three candidates—pleasure, intellection, and mixture—so one of the kinds is bound to be left out of the pairing exercise that the interlocutors have been engaged in. The odd kind out has been limit, which might seem a bit counter-intuitive. ML is a mixture of pleasure and intellection and MIXTURE is a mixture of UNLIMITED and LIMIT. So *prima facie* we might expect intellection to be paired with LIMIT. But it is not. I would suggest that this is because intellection is *elsewhere* paired with limit, and in *that* pairing intellection is shown to be the formal cause of the good life (cf. above, pp. 102–3). Here, the point has been to show that intellection is the cause of the good life in the sense of *efficient cause*. Looking back over the discussion, the cause under consideration 'leads [ἡγεῖται]' (27 A 5), 'rules over everything [τοῦ παντὸς νοῦς ἄρχει]' (30 D 8), and so on. The same cause as in *Phaedrus* 245 C–E and *Laws* 10 (894 E ff.), this is a cause *qua archē kinēseōs*.


## 3. Pleasure, and its role in the good life

### (a) *Concerns about pleasure remain*

So far, I have focused on the relationship between intellection and the good life, with the goal of showing that the former is the cause of the latter. Now I want to focus on the relationship between intellection and *pleasure*. The arguments in the later two-thirds of the dialogue reveal that knowledge is the cause not only of the ML, but of pleasure. Pleasure is, I shall argue, ontologically dependent on intellection. This parasitic conception of pleasure puts the hedonist in a nearly impossible situation. For in making any claims about the importance of pleasure, one will simultaneously be propping up intellection. Because intellectual activity is the condition of possibility for pleasure, the ingredients of ML have not an inversely

---

movement between the micro- and the macrocosmic level. Carone tries generously to make the micro-/macrocosm logically coherent (*Cosmology*, 96–100).

proportionate relationship, but a scalar, proportionate one, in so far as an increase in pleasure demands an increase in intellection (though not necessarily vice versa). Beginning with the analysis of pleasure in general (31 B ff.), Socrates systematically demonstrates that it cannot exist—cannot have any status whatsoever in a human life—in the absence of intellection.[34] This is why I call my reading 'intellectualist', and why, I argue, pleasure is neither a remedial good nor an independent kind of 'thing' that needs to be (or could be) saved from degradation.

The exact relationship between pleasure and the good life is a lingering concern, left over from the opening skirmish. Socrates' concise query at 13 B 3–5—'What is it about bad and good pleasures alike that makes you call all pleasures good?'—alerted us to the demands that the hedonist seems unable to meet. First, it remains unclear that the diverse species of 'pleasure' (philandering, sobriety, etc.) have enough in common to be grouped under a real genus. And second, even if they can be, we will need some middle term to warrant the conclusion from 'all these species of activity qualify as pleasures' to 'therefore they all qualify as good'. Socrates had pressed Protarchus for an answer to the question 'By virtue of *what* is one warranted to predicate "good" of a class of things?' I have intended to argue above that the answer is: by virtue of the presence of intellection (since intellection is both the formal and the efficient cause of the good). Now we return to the connection between pleasure and intellection: either only some pleasures are intellectual, and so only some pleasures are good, or all pleasures are intellectual, such that Protarchus' initial hedonism is redeemed, although in a version that he might no longer recognize. I intend to show that the dialogue's remaining arguments confirm the latter possibility.

### (b) *Pleasure in general*

Having slotted pleasure, intellection, and ML into their respective ontological categories, Socrates proposes at 31 B 2 that, with respect to these three terms, 'We should see where each is found and what the conditions of their occurrence are. As we examined its category first, we might as well start this enquiry with pleasure.' Socrates first draws some general conclusions about the nature of pleasure,

---

[34] Though that argument has already been suggested by the dismissal of the life of pleasure (see above, n. 17).

and then proceeds to the much-discussed examination of true and false pleasures. As to the more general discussion (31 B 2–36 C 3), two points prove crucial. Firstly, Socrates offers (finally) a relatively precise definition of pain and pleasure:

I would suggest that when we have the harmony of a living thing undone, then there simultaneously occurs a dissolution of its nature and the coming into being of pain . . . but when the harmony comes back and the same [i.e. the previous] nature obtains, we must say that pleasure comes about. (31 D 4–9)

Now Socrates claims to have in mind two kinds of pleasure, each of which falls under this general definition. The first is characterized in terms of the body: 'the power of liquid to replenish a parched throat is a pleasure', for instance (33 E 10–32 A 1). The second involves 'the soul alone, separate from the body [χωρὶς τοῦ σώματος αὐτῆς τῆς ψυχῆς]' (32 C 4). The example of such a purely psychic pleasure is the pleasure that accompanies the expectation of a future pleasurable experience. Now it should be noted that this is not a distinction between purely psychic or mental pleasures and purely bodily pleasures. Both kinds involve the soul(/mind)—one involves the soul *and* the body, while the other involves the soul alone.[35] And this is what we should expect, based on the agreements Socrates has already extracted from Protarchus. The thrust of 20 E 4–21 D 5, where Protarchus rejected the life of pleasure, is that 'intellection, memory, knowledge, and true opinion' (all psychic operations) are necessary for present-tense enjoyment.[36] So there can be no pleasure without some minimum of intellectual activity, and this is confirmed in the present discussion by the fact that, in his response, Protarchus emphasizes that the second kind of pleasure involves the soul alone, without the body. The obvious implication is that the other class involves the soul *with* the body. But beyond implication, the present discussion includes a rigorous argument whose point is to show that intellectual operations are necessary in order for pleasure to obtain. At 33 C 5 Socrates suggests that the second class of pleasures is 'entirely dependent on memory [διὰ μνήμης πᾶν ἐστι γεγονός]', and in order to get clear on them an account of memory is called for. But the account of memory

---

[35] So Frede, *Philebus*, 33 n. 3, but compare Gosling, *Philebus*, 100.
[36] Precisely, the passage does not necessarily suggest that all of these capacities (activities?) are necessary, but at least some of them are.

evidently requires a preliminary account of perception (αἴσθησις) (c 8–9). Some bodily affections (παθήματα) are extinguished before they reach the soul, while others succeed in reaching the soul. The ones that never reach it are 'insensible' (ἀναισθησίαν: 34 A 1), while the joint arousal of the soul and the body is perception proper. Now the purely psychic pleasures depend on perception because memory depends on perception (you cannot remember what you have not perceived), recollection depends on memory, and anticipatory psychic pleasures depend on recollection. Socrates is now able to clarify the process by which we experience pleasures that involve the soul by itself: 'when the soul of itself, without the [mediation of the] body, recovers as far as possible what it once underwent *through* the body, we call this recollection' (34 B 6–8). A pleasure that results from recollection—one of the kind Socrates mentioned at 32 B 9–c 2—thus depends on the aforementioned process of recollection, and it is a purely psychic pleasure. So we see that several intellectual operations (perception, memory, recollection) are necessary conditions for psychic pleasure to obtain.

What of the first category of pleasure—the one that involves the body as well as the soul? This section of the dialogue provides ample argumentation to suggest that for joint pleasures, too, some minimum of psychic operation is a necessary prerequisite. At 34 D 10 Socrates reminds Protarchus that 'just now [νυνδή] we said that hunger and thirst and many other such things are some sort of desire [ἐπιθυμία]'. The 'just now' in question must be the example of the first kind of pleasure—the one that involves both the body and the soul—from 31 E 10 ff.[37] There the first example was thirst, 'a deterioration and a form of pain, while the power of liquid to replenish a parched throat is pleasure'. To be thirsty, notes Socrates, means to be lacking (κενοῦται)—when someone is thirsty, the body is lacking water. But the thirst itself, which accompanies the bodily condition of thirstiness, is a mental condition. The proof for this point proceeds along the same lines as that for the spirited part of the soul in *Republic* 4. In short, the thirsty person 'doesn't desire what he is suffering, for he is thirsty and this is a lack [κένωσις]. But he desires fulfilment' (35 B 3–4). Somehow, then, the thirsty

---

[37] In fact, though, Socrates' 'reminder' at 34 D 10 is the first time hunger (πεῖνα) has been mentioned in the dialogue, and while 31 E 10 mentions δίψος, he does not call it ἐπιθυμία; that term does not come up until 34 C 7. So he must be (ironically) misremembering.

man must 'have contact [ἐφάπτοιτο]' with fulfilment, contact being
necessary for desire (B 6–7). Since the body is in a state of lack,
it must be the soul that 'has contact' with fulfilment, and it is,
predictably, *memory* through which such contact is made. Desire,
then, is just that state of the soul where it makes contact through
memory with an object that would fulfil a lack suffered by the body.
How, then, does desire relate to pleasure? Socrates describes these
joint conditions as a 'mid-point [μέσῳ]' between pleasure and pain,
because the psychic memory of the fulfilling object is pleasant, but
the bodily suffering is painful (35 E 9–36 A 1). If the memory of the
fulfilling object cannot be conjured up, then the suffering person
will be doubly pained (36 B 13–C 1). But the conclusion to be drawn
from this discussion is that the pleasures under consideration (joint
soul/body pleasures) are *not at all* a function of the body, but of the
soul, since the soul is responsible for memory (on which these pleasures depend) and memory is explicitly intellectual.[38] The body is
the source of pain—either pain that combines with psychic pleasure
(when the fulfilling object is remembered) to produce a middle condition, or pain that is compounded when the soul cannot remember
the fulfilling object. Socrates has conspicuously neglected any pleasure that might belong to the body alone, or even one that might
belong to the body *in combination with the soul*. What he originally
mentioned as joint body/soul pleasure (at 31 E 10 ff.) turns out (from
31 B 2 to 36 C 1) to be just as mental (psychic) as the so-called *purely*
mental (psychic) pleasures. The whole general account of pleasure,
from 31 B 2 to 36 C 1, then, confirms what was suggested by the dismissal of the life of pleasure at 21 B 6–D 2: all pleasure is dependent
on intellectual activity. There is simply no such thing as pleasure
that is not conditioned by memory (which is decidedly intellectual,
as Socrates makes clear at the very beginning of the dialogue, 11 A
7). The intellect, in short, is a necessary condition for pleasure.[39]

The second important point established in this general section of
the dialogue is the brief admission at 33 A 8–B 7, seemingly at odds
with the primary thesis of the entire dialogue:

---

[38] I take it that, from the beginning, both sides have conceded the point that
memory is intellectual. See Socrates' initial framing of the debate at 11 B 4–C 3.

[39] Most of my analysis seems to agree with that of Frede on this point ('Rumplestiltskin', 163–5). She refers to 'immediate pleasure which is an *aisthēsis*' (165),
which I can accept, so long as *aisthēsis* is understood as inherently propositional.
See also T. Penner, 'False Anticipatory Pleasures: *Philebus* 36 A 3–41 A 6' ['Anticipatory'], *Phronesis*, 15 (1970), 166–78 at 171.

SOC. You realize that there is nothing to prevent one living such a life of reason?

PROT. You mean the one that is neither joyful nor painful?

SOC. It was said in the comparison of lives that it is necessary to enjoy neither large nor small [pleasures] when opting for the life of intellection and reason.

PROT. Indeed that was said.

SOC. And that kind of life *would* be like that, and perhaps there is nothing unusual if it were the most divine of all lives.

Protarchus takes Socrates' superlative description literally: such a life is the kind lived by gods, because they probably do not experience pleasure and pain (33 B 8–9). This passage has given rise to some of the most interesting, and relevant, criticism of the *Philebus*, and it is perhaps necessary to consider its implications. Most surprising is the fact that Protarchus is willing to cede this point to Socrates. If a pure life of intellection is possible, then very little hope remains for his modified hedonist position. We should note, though, that Protarchus does not concede that a pleasure-neutral life is available to human beings, only that it is probably lived by the gods. Less surprising is the fact that Socrates should make the suggestion. We should note that his claims are not put in positive terms; he employs litotes: 'nothing prevents [οὐδὲν ἀποκωλύει]' such a life and there is 'nothing unusual [οὐδὲν ἄτοπον]' if it were most divine. In fact, little more is admitted here than was admitted in Protarchus' original dismissal of the life of intellection: though thinkable, or possible, it is not evidently choiceworthy. The divine description perhaps puts desirability back on the table, but the possibility of a life of pure intellection, unlike that of a life of pleasure *devoid* of intellection, has never been in question.

## (c) False pleasures

The next major section of the dialogue is the long discussion of false pleasures. By now we should expect that it will bear out the general thesis for which I have been arguing: that all pleasures *depend on* intellectual operations. They have no independent status, because the intellect must be in place as a condition of possibility for their existence. In fact, the point is most obvious in this section, because Socrates establishes right away that all pleasures are ontologically dependent on propositional judgements or beliefs (which are decidedly intellectual).

As Socrates makes clear at 35 E 5–7, the topic of the section will be false positive pleasures—thinking one is pleased when one is not. Again, nowhere is it suggested that there can be false negative-pleasure judgements—thinking one is not pleased when one in fact is. Now the topic, true/false pleasures, is interestingly ambiguous, and Socrates shows himself alive to this ambiguity at 37 A 11:

> With a subject judging, whether or not he is judging correctly, at least that he is really [ὄντως] judging he never loses . . . Similarly with someone who is pleased, whether he is rightly pleased or not, at least that he is really [ὄντως] pleased he never loses . . . Then we must examine how it is that judgement is commonly false, as well as being true [ἀληθής], while pleasure is only true [τὸ δὲ τῆς ἡδονῆς μόνον ἀληθές], although in these cases both remain genuine [ὄντως] examples of judgement and pleasure. (37 A 11–B 8, following Gosling)

Though confusingly worded, these concerns are indeed fleshed out in what follows. It turns out that pleasures can be false in both ways—they can be propositionally false (ψευδής), which will depend on their content, and they can be impostors (μὴ ὄντως), which will also depend on their propositional content.

The varieties of false pleasure that Socrates proceeds to spell out have been thoroughly analysed elsewhere,[40] but a few points are worth dwelling on. We should expect, based on the remarks at 37 A 11–B 8, that the analysis of false pleasures will depend somehow on the distinction between truth and genuineness signalled by the difference between the adjective ψευδής and the adverb ὄντως. In fact it takes some work to see how that distinction operates in

---

[40] See especially Frede ('Rumplestiltskin', *Philebus*, and 'Disintegration and Restoration: Pleasure and Pain in Plato's Philebus' ['Disintegration'], in Kraut (ed.), *Companion*, 425–63); J. Gosling, 'False Pleasures: *Philebus* 35 C–41 D' ['False Pleasures'], *Phronesis*, 4 (1959), 44–54, and 'Father Kenny on False Pleasures' ['Father Kenny'], *Phronesis*, 6 (1960), 41–5; A. Kenny, 'False Pleasures in the *Philebus*: A Reply to Mr. Gosling' ['Reply'], *Phronesis*, 5 (1960), 45–52; J. Dybikowski, 'False Pleasure and the *Philebus*' ['Pleasures'], *Phronesis*, 15 (1970), 147–65; Penner, 'Anticipatory'. The literature on this topic has grown to enormous proportions, and while immanently interesting, it cannot thoroughly be discussed in an article such as this. A distinctive feature of my analysis is that I have not devoted any space to the scribe/painter image at 39 A 1 ff. While I think that the image is important, it seems to have been overemphasized in the literature on false pleasures. I suspect that most commentators have tried to squeeze it too hard for answers to the several difficulties arising from the pleasure/belief relationship.

the ensuing discussion. We might expect that, once a 'pleasure' is exposed as an impostor—as being μὴ ὄντως—the question of its propositional falsity—whether or not it is ψευδής—becomes irrelevant. Surely *really* being a pleasure is a necessary prerequisite for being a *true* pleasure. If we remain as faithful as possible to the analogy with judgements, this is how the analysis would have to play out, for something that is not *really* a judgement can hardly be a *false* judgement. But the text actually confounds this expectation.[41] Crucial is the line where Socrates summarizes the first kind of false pleasure (actually during the discussion of the second type): 'we then [i.e. with respect to the first kind of false pleasure] found that true and false beliefs at the same time infected [ἀνεπίμπλασαν] the pleasure or pain with their own condition [πάθημα]' (42 A 8–9).[42] The suggestion here is that a pleasure's genuineness *depends* on the propositional truth or falsity of its attendant judgement. So the case is not like that of judgements considered on their own. Whereas the question of a judgement's truth-value can be raised only after its status as a *genuine* judgement has been secured, with pleasure the

---

[41] Of the different interpretations of the pleasure/judgement analogy, I agree fully with Kenny that Socrates never accepted the claim that a pleasure is (or can be) still a pleasure, regardless of whether its attendant belief is true or false: 'the fact that [Socrates] is later prepared to admit the existence of a very large class of ἡδοναὶ εἶναι δοκοῦσαι, οὖσαι δ' οὐδαμῶς (51 A 5) makes it clear that the assertion is never really accepted, but merely left as a *datum non concessum* in the passage concerned with the first type of false pleasures' ('Reply', 46). This goes against the claims of Gosling ('False Pleasures', 'Father Kenny'). The rest of my account differs from Kenny's, though; especially, I argue that there can be no ἡδοναὶ μὲν ψευδεῖς, ὄντως δὲ οὖσαι ἡδοναί, whereas he thinks there can be, since otherwise all pleasures would be true. Suitably modified, this is a consequence I am willing to accept, as I think Plato was in the *Philebus*. The modification should be: all pleasures are true and genuine, but not all 'pleasures' are true, and the ones that are not true are not genuine so they do not really qualify as pleasures.

[42] I understand the 'infection' of pleasures by judgements in the same way as Frede ('Rumplestiltskin', 166 ff.), and thus I concur that the English word may be too weak to capture the nature of their relationship. I have kept it for lack of a better idea. As will become clear in what follows, I do not think that Plato wants to recognize the possibility of the kind of pleasure that would be independent of a propositional belief—the kind mentioned by Dybikowski ('Pleasure', 158), and thoroughly analysed by Penner ('Anticipatory'). In Penner's article, the type of pleasures that do not 'involve', or are not 'infected by', the accompanying belief simply accompany the propositional belief, but do not depend on it. He claims that 'there is no need to deny that Socrates would have accepted' this kind of non-propositionally dependent pleasure 'sometimes', only that he would deny that the pleasure is independent of the belief in the pathological cases he is analysing in the section on false anticipatory pleasure (174). This is where my reading departs from that of Penner, for I *do* think that Socrates wants to deny the possibility of such an accidental relationship between pleasure and belief.

case will be quite the opposite. A pleasure's propositional truth must be guaranteed before the question of its genuineness can be raised.[43] Instead of reality being a necessary condition for truth, truth is a necessary condition for reality. This is indeed how the various examples of false pleasure are treated. The first class of false pleasures occurs when I am pleased about an imagined state of affairs, which state of affairs does not correspond with reality.[44] The falsity of the judgement (about the state of affairs) *makes* the resultant pleasure an impostor, 'infecting' the pleasure with its (false) condition. This criterion sets a rather high bar for a pleasure to be genuine (ὄντως): it must be based on a true (ἀληθής) judgement. What is often overlooked is that this criterion should carry through to all of the other kinds of false pleasure. In so far as they are all based on false (ψευδής) judgements, *none* of them will be genuine (ὄντως) pleasures. And their non-genuine status will not need to be proven or argued in any other way. So as Socrates proceeds to explain the other three kinds of false judgement, his goal is not to give three other explanations for their falseness—the first explanation is all he needs. Rather, his goal is to mention some of the most common mistakes people make about pleasure. All of them will be mistaken in the same way: propositionally mistaken.[45]

We should have expected this criterion for genuine pleasures, based on what had come before in the dialogue. Socrates has just shown that all pleasures are dependent on mental (psychic) operations (3*b*)—that there are no pleasures that do not derive from

---

[43] Thus against Penner ('Anticipatory') and with Frede ('Rumplestiltskin'), I understand the truth-value of product-pleasure as primary, and that of process-pleasure as derivative and dependent on the former. Though it is beyond the scope of this paper, I do not see the need to make the same claim about judgements—saving the analogy does not necessitate such an epistemological move.

[44] The futural nature of the first kind of false pleasures is often stressed: they are strictly 'anticipatory', and the judgement that infects them with truth/falsity is a judgement about a future state of affairs. Their future-oriented judgement does not set them apart in any radical sense from the other types, though. Just because the judgement in the first type is about the future, that has no bearing on its falsity. The other types of false pleasure are based on judgements as well, and this results in their falsity. But the fact that they are not anticipatory does absolve them from the criterion for truth/genuineness set by the first example.

[45] That this is Plato's strategy—to catalogue some (all?) varieties of hedonist mistakes—is supported by the fact that proper names can be surmised for them: the hedonistic calculus of the *Protagoras* (gone awry) for the second, Speusippus for the third, Callicles (of the *Gorgias*) for the fourth. Frede ('Rumplestiltskin', 158–9) demonstrates that the third and fourth types of false pleasures treated in the *Philebus* parallel those proposed (and partially rejected) in *Republic* 9 and *Gorgias*.

judgements. An apparent difficulty arises, however, when Socrates begins to analyse the fourth class of false pleasure. He suggests a peculiar methodology for examining the proposed class:

If we wanted to get clear about the nature of the class of pleasures, we should have to examine not those examples that are only just pleasures, but ones at the top of the scale that are said to be the most intense . . . And surely the familiar pleasures, that are also greatest, are, as we repeat, the physical ones. (44 E 7–45 A 5)

This seems to suggest that there *are* purely physical pleasures, which would run counter to the claims Socrates has made earlier, linking pleasure intrinsically to intellectual activity. The suggestion is reconfirmed at 46 B 8–C 1, where he claims that some of the states that lead to the candidates for pleasure currently under consideration 'are bodily [κατὰ τὸ σῶμα] and are in the body itself [ἐν αὐτοῖς τοῖς σώμασι], but there are also ones of the soul, in the soul itself [ἐν τῇ ψυχῇ]'. In fact, Socrates is not betraying his earlier arguments, which established that nothing confined to the body alone (without some attendant intellectual operation) qualifies as a pleasure. For this entire section of the dialogue is a counterfactual, hypothetical confrontation with *hoi dyschereis*.[46] It is *they* who are suggesting that there are certain intense, purely bodily pleasures, *they* who are suggesting this method of investigation. Since Socrates thinks they are wrong in their suggestion that these are pleasures in the first place, he is in no way committed to agreeing with them that there are purely bodily pleasures. At the end of the discussion of false pleasures, then, we are left with an even stronger and more thoroughly argued claim that the *very being* [ὄντως εἶναι] of pleasure depends on activity of the intellect (here, *doxa*).

## (d) True pleasure

After the discussion of false pleasures, Socrates turns to a discussion of genuine ones. Tellingly, he begins the examination of true pleasures by referring to what preceded as a discussion of 'mixed' pleasures (τὰς μειχθείσας ἡδονάς), and what will follow as a discussion of 'unmixed' (τὰς ἀμείκτους) ones (50 E 5–6). There is a certain sliding going on here with respect to the meaning of 'mixed'. In

---

[46] See the thorough analysis of M. Schofield, 'Who Were οἱ δυσχερεῖς in Plato, *Philebus* 44 A ff.?', *Museum Helveticum*, 28 (1971), 2–20; also Hackforth, *Pleasure*, 85–8; A. Taylor, *A Commentary on Plato's* Timaeus (London, 1928), 456.

the prior discussion at 44 B 6 ff., 'mixed' was used to refer to the pleasures proposed by *hoi dyschereis*—the morbid pleasures that are mixed with pain (46 A 12 ff.). The mixture in question there was a mixture of pleasure and pain, and the whole class turned out to be false (impostor) pleasures. Since 'mixed' evidently just means 'false' (that was the conclusion of the previous discussion to which Socrates refers at 50 E 5), 'unmixed' will mean 'true' (that is the topic of the ensuing discussion).[47] Only what is unmixed or pure deserves the name 'pleasure' after all, and there are not really such things as 'mixed pleasures'.

These true (=pure, =unmixed) pleasures will turn out to be ones 'having an imperceptible and painless need, the fulfilment being perceptible and pleasant' (51 B 5), such that they 'are not mixed with a requisite pain' (51 E 2). Note that there *is* a need or a lack involved in these pleasures, but because it is imperceptible, it does not count as a pain. Further, true pleasures must be pure, which means that the object that occasions the pleasure must be pure. The example here is the pleasure taken in a patch of pure white colour. This is a notorious example, as are the first two (earlier) examples of true pleasure: those whose objects are 'smooth, clear sounds', and 'smells' (51 B 2–E 5; 53 A 5–C 2). But perhaps the least surprising of the examples of true pleasure are the pleasures of learning (τὰς περὶ τὰ μαθήματα ἡδονάς: 51 E 7–B 8). Sometimes we reflect on the fact that we have forgotten something, and this reflection causes some pain. This reflective (and unusual) condition is not the one Socrates has in mind. He has in mind what we might think of as the 'natural attitude', one where we are not being critically self-reflexive (χωρὶς τοῦ λογισμοῦ διαπεραίνομεν) about our state of ignorance. When, out of such a pre-reflexive state of forgetfulness we recover the lost knowledge, the attendant pleasure is genuine and pure, because it was not accompanied by any painful lack.[48]

*(e) Mixture*

My goal has been to discuss the ontological status of pleasure in

---

[47] With Carone, *Cosmology*, 235 n. 7.

[48] We are discussing the kind of learning that occurs when we recover lost knowledge that we do not even remember having lost. Is this what becomes of the more familiar theories of *anamnēsis* from the middle period? Any speculative answer would have to take account of Protarchus' conclusion in the present dialogue that such pleasures belong only 'to a very few [τῶν σφόδρα ὀλίγων]' (52 B 8).

the *Philebus*, and so I skip forward here to the final sections of the dialogue, leaving to one side the discussion of true intellection and knowledge (55 C 4–59 D 9). Having examined pleasure and intellection on their own, Socrates now proposes to find the proper mixture of the two, the final result of which will presumably constitute the ML, which is to say the good life for human beings. The mixture section begins with Socrates' suggestion that:

It would be a fairly accurate account if, with respect to the mixture of intelligence and pleasure, someone were to say that we are like craftsmen [δημιουργοί] who have the things out of which or in which to construct and build. (59 D 10–E 3)

It cannot be a coincidence that, during the discussion of true intellection/knowledge, Socrates had praised the builder's craft: 'I think that building [τεκτονική], in making use of greater measures and instruments, is given lots of accuracy and is more calculative [τεχνικωτέραν] than the other branches of knowledge' (56 B 4–6). Of course, the builder's art is less precise than that of the philosophical mathematician (56 E 7–57 A 4), but it still admits of an admirable amount of precision. The mixing that follows, then, will be reasonably precise and well measured.

In building the mixture that will constitute the good life, Socrates and Protarchus must select the proper ingredients—a task for which the entire dialogue has presumably been preparing them. Instead of letting in 'every pleasure with every form of intelligence', Socrates proposes a more cautious method for selection. The following line is crucial; here is Frede's translation: 'Didn't we find that one pleasure turned out to be truer than another, just as one art was more precise than the other?' (61 D 7–8).[49] I think that this way of distributing the comparative betrays something about the arguments that have preceded. It suggests that there have been *degrees of reality* when it comes to pleasure. But the account of false pleasures showed not that some pleasures were more, others less, real. It showed that many things going by the name 'pleasure' are not pleasures at all. Are there degrees of *pleasantness*? This is another question, but it is not what the builders will consider when making the mixture. A pleasure is either genuine (ὄντως) or not, and its genuineness depends on a preceding true (ἀληθής) belief and on its precipitating

---

[49] ἦν ἡμῖν ἡδονή τε ἀληθῶς, ὡς οἰόμεθα, μᾶλλον ἑτέρας ἄλλη καὶ δὴ καὶ τέχνη τέχνης ἀκριβεστέρα; Gosling gives the same sense as Frede.

lack being imperceptible. If Plato had wanted to indicate degrees of being-pleasure, such that $x$, $y$, and $z$ are all pleasures, but that they can be ranked in terms of their pleasure-reality, it would have been open to him to use the comparative or superlative of ἀληθής, as he does just a few lines later at 61 E 4–6. Here, the comparative clause μᾶλλον ἑτέρας ἄλλη can just mean 'rather than others': certain things (pleasures), rather than others ('pleasures'), are *truly* plea-sures. Incidentally, types of knowledge/skill (τέχνη) are not, in this passage, ranked on a scale of reality, or genuineness, either. They are ranked on a scale of accuracy such that some are ἀκριβέστερος than others. Of course, nothing in the preceding arguments has suggested that there *cannot* be degrees of reality when it comes to intellection/knowledge. On the contrary, the entire discussion from 55 D 1 ff. suggests that there can be. This is exactly what happens in the next passages, where branches of knowledge that take un-changing things as their objects are truer (ἀληθέστερος) than those that consider changing objects (61 D 10–E 4).

The mixture will include all the branches of knowledge—both the more and the less true. But which pleasures will be included? Both interlocutors agree that only the 'true' (ἀληθεῖς) ones should be let in (62 E 3–8). Again, the language is not comparative, such that only the tru*est* ones will count. There is some infelicity in the language here, since technically there are no false pleasures. If something is not true, it is only a 'pleasure', but not a real pleasure. In other words, when Socrates suggests that only the true pleasures be allowed in the mixture, he is essentially saying that *all* pleasures should be admitted.[50] The set of pleasures is, strictly, coextensive with the set of true pleasures. That Socrates is aware of this issue is confirmed by his strange aside at 63 B 2–3. Speaking directly to the personified group of all 'pleasures', he asks which branches of knowledge *they* would prefer to have included in the mixture. They will answer that they want every branch of knowledge to be in-cluded. But especially relevant is the way Socrates addresses them: 'O friends, whether we must address you as "pleasures" or by some other name . . .' What does this mean? Presumably Socrates means here to address all those things that go by the name 'pleasure'—even

_____

[50] Hence Dybikowski's observation that 'in constructing his hierarchy of goods, Socrates makes no use at all of the distinction between true and false pleasures in the ranking. The important distinction for this purpose is the one between pure and mixed pleasures ('Pleasure', 160).

those that have been exposed as impostors. But the impostors, the false pleasures, do not deserve the name 'pleasure', hence the hesitation. That this motley group is the intended addressee is again demonstrated by the fact that when he later asks all the branches of knowledge which pleasures they would prefer to cohabit with, they reject the Calliclean 'pleasures' (which are no pleasures at all) at 63 D 1–64 A 3. In short, during the dialectical querying of pleasure and knowledge, the false pleasures are not excluded. This is not a backsliding on Socrates' part; it functions like an independent argument which will reach the same conclusion as the investigation of false pleasures: only a select group of what we formerly thought of as 'pleasures' will make it into the ML.

## (*f*) *Ranking*

Having discussed the next section above (2*b*–*c*), I move now to the very final scene of the *Philebus*: the ranking of goods. I have wanted to argue that knowledge/intellection is, in all ways, the cause of the good life (ML). Above I argued that, when Socrates claimed that intellection was either the cause of the good or most like the cause of the good, he really meant that intellection *is* the cause of the good. Further, I argued that when he shows that intellection is the most measured thing, and that 'the measured [τὸ μέτριον]' is the cause of the good life (66 A 4–8), he really meant that intellection is the cause of the good life (see Section 2*b*). I am left, finally, with the undeniable fact that Socrates and Protarchus agree to rank νοῦς and φρόνησις as the *third* most prized possession (in the ML), behind (1) the measured and the things concerning measure (πῃ περὶ μέτρον) and the punctual (τὸ καίριον) (ibid.) and (2) proportion, beauty, perfection, sufficiency, and 'those kinds of thing' (66 B 1–3). Based on everything that has preceded, I find it exceptionally difficult to believe that intellection should receive third place. Plato's language may provide the key here. Notice the precise wording of the announcement of third place: 'now for third place, if I am [any kind of] prophet, [if] you proffer wisdom and intelligence you would not be wandering a great [distance] from the truth' (66 B 5–6).[51] He might have been more committal, to say the least. Is it possible that Protarchus is still just a little

[51] τὸ τοίνυν τρίτον, ὡς ἡ ἐμὴ μαντεία, νοῦν καὶ φρόνησιν τιθεὶς οὐκ ἂν μέγα τι τῆς ἀληθείας παρεξέλθοις.

way from the truth? Might he be closer to it if he were to realize that the first three rankings are, based on everything Socrates
has shown him, just various names for intellection, reason, and
knowledge?

## 4. Conclusion

Reason and intellection play a major role in *all* the final rankings of
the *Philebus*. Fourth place goes to 'those things we placed in the soul
itself, branches of knowledge and skills and so-called correct opinions' (66 в 8–9). Why these should be in a different category from
νοῦς and φρόνησις could also have been more clear (but presumably
it is based on the distinctions between more and less precise kinds
of knowledge at 55 Е 1 ff.). Pleasures are admitted at fifth place,
but only 'those pleasures we designated as painless, named 'purified' [and belonging to] the soul itself, some following knowledge,
others perception' (66 с 4–6).[52]

   Is pleasure a 'remedial good?' The *Philebus* shows us that, while
a life might not be choiceworthy if it includes no pleasures at all,
the inclusion of pleasure does not place a limitation on intellectual
capacity.[53] It *may* be true that more intellectual achievement results
necessarily in more pleasure. And it is certainly true that because
intellection is a necessary condition for pleasure, the necessity of
pleasure in the good life testifies to the necessity of intellection—in
fact, any increase in pleasure demands an increase in intellection.[54]
And if you take any slice of the good life, even though it is a mixture
of pleasure and intellection, there is no chance that you will end up
with an intellect-free slice. Plato's presentation of these conclusions
is, as always, strategic. He makes explicit the fact that the mixed
life includes some pleasures, but it remains, perhaps, less explicit
that he is redefining 'pleasure' to refer to something much more fa-

---

[52]  That the pleasures that 'follow perception' are dependent on intellectual activity was argued during the discussion of pleasure in general (see above, sect. 3*b*).

[53]  Perhaps, when compared with some sort of divine life, mortal life is limited in
its capacity for intellectual achievement. But if so, that limitation comes from some
other criterion besides the need for pleasure.

[54]  Precisely, the relationship between pleasure and knowledge for which I have
been arguing is scalar, such that an increase in pleasure demands an increase in
intellection. But this is not necessarily reversible. None of the arguments, so far as
I can see, shows that an increase in intellection guarantees an increase in pleasure.

miliar to an intellectualist than to a hedonist. But that is a brilliant strategy for converting a hedonist to Platonism.

When Hegel showed that the Kantian 'real' (noumenal) is rational, and the rational real, the conclusion to be drawn was not that the real world was, sadly, merely apparent. The conclusion was more sanguine: what was formerly demoted to the status of 'mere' appearance was now redeemed, winning the status of reality.[55] Something similar happens in the *Philebus*. If Plato has shown that pleasure is not something antithetical to the ideality of pure intellection, then he has shown that a life that includes pleasure should not be seen as remedial. But what should also be noticed is that there is no need to work on behalf of pleasure, trying to redeem it, as does Carone. She is surely correct to assert that 'at least pure pleasures will be capable of being intrinsically good, and . . . Plato considers it possible to view them under an unqualifiedly positive light.'[56] But once we look closely at Socrates' (intellectualist, deflationary) conception of pure pleasures, we see how very far from any recognizable hedonism this admission leaves us. To try and redeem pleasure is to insist on giving it a fundamentally different ontological status from intellection. True, pure pleasure—anything that genuinely deserves the name— is intellect-based. One can still be a good (Phileban) Platonist and live a life that includes pleasure. If it makes a malleable hedonist like Protarchus feel better to call such a life 'mixed', that is fine. But however mixed, it is still characterized fully—completely, perfectly, and sufficiently—by intellection. The intelligent can be pleasant, but the pleasant is, in all ways, intelligent.

*Villanova University*

BIBLIOGRAPHY

Armstrong, J., 'After the Ascent: Plato on Becoming like God', *Oxford Studies in Ancient Philosophy*, 26 (2004), 171–83.
Bury, R. G., *The* Philebus *of Plato* (Cambridge, 1897).
Carone, G., 'Hedonism and the Pleasureless Life in Plato's *Philebus*' ['Hedonism'], *Phronesis*, 45 (2000), 257–83.

---

[55] So Nietzsche: 'We have done away with the true world: what world is left over? The apparent one, maybe? . . . But no! *Along with the true world, we have also done away with the apparent!*' (*Twilight of the Idols*, trans. R. Polt (Indianapolis, 1997), 24).                    [56] 'Hedonism', 264.

—— *Plato's Cosmology and its Ethical Dimensions* [*Cosmology*] (New York, 2005).

Cooper, N., 'Pleasure and Goodness in Plato's *Philebus*', *Philosophical Quarterly*, 18 (1968), 12–15.

Dybikowski, J., 'False Pleasure and the *Philebus*' ['Pleasure'], *Phronesis*, 15 (1970), 147–65.

Frede, D., 'Disintegration and Restoration: Pleasure and Pain in Plato's *Philebus*' ['Disintegration'], in Kraut (ed.), *Companion*, 425–63.

—— *Plato's Philebus, Translated, with Introduction and Notes* [*Philebus*] (Indianapolis, 1993).

—— 'Rumplestiltskin's Pleasures: True and False Pleasures in Plato's *Philebus*' ['Rumplestiltskin'], *Phronesis*, 30 (1985), 151–80.

Gosling, J., 'False Pleasures: *Philebus* 35 C–41 D' ['False Pleasures'], *Phronesis*, 4 (1959), 44–54.

—— 'Father Kenny on False Pleasures' ['Father Kenny'], *Phronesis*, 6 (1960), 41–5.

—— *Plato: Philebus, Translated with Notes and Commentary* [*Philebus*] (Oxford, 1975).

Hackforth, R., *Plato's Examination of Pleasure* [*Pleasure*] (New York, 1945).

Hampton, C., *Pleasure, Knowledge, and Being: An Analysis of Plato's Philebus* [*Pleasure*] (Albany, NY, 1990).

Irwin, T., *Plato's Ethics* [*Ethics*] (New York, 1995).

Jackson, H., 'Plato's Later Theory of Ideas', *Journal of Philology*, 10 (1882), 253–98.

Kenny, A., 'False Pleasures in the *Philebus*: A Reply to Mr. Gosling' ['Reply'] *Phronesis*, 5 (1960), 45–52.

Kraut, R. (ed.), *The Cambridge Companion to Plato* [*Companion*] (New York, 1992).

Moravcsik, J., 'Forms, Nature, and the Good in the *Philebus*' ['Forms'], *Phronesis*, 24 (1979), 81–101.

Nietzsche, F., *Twilight of the Idols*, trans. R. Polt (Indianapolis, 1997).

Penner, T., 'False Anticipatory Pleasures: *Philebus* 36 A 3–41 A 6' ['Anticipatory'], *Phronesis*, 15 (1970), 166–78.

Russell, D., *Plato on Pleasure and the Good Life* (Oxford, 2005).

Saunders, T., 'Plato's Later Political Thought', in Kraut (ed.), *Companion*, 464–92.

Sayre, K., *Plato's Late Ontology: A Riddle Resolved* (Princeton, 1983).

—— 'The *Philebus* and the Good: The Unity of the Dialogue in Which the Good is Unity' ['Unity'], *Proceedings of the Boston Area Colloquium in Ancient Philosophy*, 2 (1987), 45–71.

Schofield, M., 'Who Were οἱ δυσχερεῖς in Plato, *Philebus* 44 A ff.?', *Museum Helveticum*, 28 (1971), 2–20.

Striker, G., *Peras und Apeiron: Das Problem der Formen in Platons Philebus* (Göttingen, 1970).

Taylor, A., *A Commentary on Plato's* Timaeus (London, 1928).

Teloh, H., *The Development of Plato's Metaphysics* [*Development*] (University Park, PA, 1981).

# SUBSTANTIAL UNIVERSALS
# IN ARISTOTLE'S *CATEGORIES*

CASEY PERIN

ARISTOTLE in the *Categories*, but not elsewhere, presents the distinction between individual substances such as Socrates or Bucephalus and their species and genera as the distinction between *primary* (πρῶται) and *secondary* (δεύτεραι) substances (2ᵃ11–19).[1] The distinction between primary and secondary substances, in turn, is a distinction between substances that are *particulars* and substances that are *universals*. In chapter 7 of *De interpretatione* Aristotle tells us:

I call universal [καθόλου] that which is by its nature predicated of a plurality of things [ὃ ἐπὶ πλειόνων πέφυκε κατηγορεῖσθαι], and particular [καθ᾽ ἕκαστον] that which is not; human being, for instance, is a universal, Callias a particular [οἷον ἄνθρωπος μὲν τῶν καθόλου Καλλίας δὲ τῶν καθ᾽ ἕκαστον]. (17ᵃ38–ᵇ1)

In the *Categories* Aristotle defines a primary substance as that which is neither SAID OF nor IN a subject (2ᵃ11–13). Being SAID OF a subject and being IN a subject are the only relations of *metaphysical* predication Aristotle recognizes in the *Categories*—they are the only ways in which one being or entity (τὸ ὄν) can be predicated of another being or entity as its subject.[2] If a primary substance is neither

© Casey Perin 2007

Thanks to David Sedley for his comments on an earlier version of this paper.

[1] I am assuming that Aristotle's δεύτεραι οὐσίαι λέγονται means 'are called "secondary substances"'. As S. Menn, 'Metaphysics, Dialectic, and the *Categories*', *Revue de métaphysique et de morale*, 100 (1995), 311–37 at 324 n. 23, notes, the only alternative is to treat δεύτεραι 'quasi-adverbially' and take δεύτεραι οὐσίαι λέγονται and its parallels to mean 'are, in a secondary way, called "substances"' (as e.g. M. V. Wedin, *Aristotle's Theory of Substance: The* Categories *and* Metaphysics Zeta [*Aristotle's Theory of Substance*] (Oxford, 2000), 96–7, does). But, as Menn points out, Aristotle does in fact call the species and genera of primary substances δεύτεραι οὐσίαι (e.g. at 2ᵇ7).

[2] I follow F. Lewis, *Substance and Predication in Aristotle* [*Substance*] (Cambridge,

SAID OF nor IN a subject, then a primary substance is not predicated of anything. *A fortiori* it is not predicated of a plurality of things. Therefore, according to the definitions of 'universal' and 'particular' Aristotle gives in *De interpretatione*, a primary substance is not a universal but a particular. In the *Categories* a secondary substance is the species or genus of a primary substance ($2^a14-19$). The species human being, for instance, is SAID OF, and so predicated of, all individual human beings (Socrates, Callias, Coriscus, etc.). The genus animal is SAID OF, and so predicated of, its species (human being, horse, dog, etc.) as well as all individual animals (Socrates, Bucephalus the horse, Fido the dog, etc.). Since a secondary substance is predicated of more than one being or entity as its subject, it is not a particular but a universal.[3] The question I want to try to

1991), and W. R. Mann, *The Discovery of Things: Aristotle's* Categories *and their Context* [*Discovery*] (Princeton, 2000), in capitalizing the names of the predication relations introduced in chapter 2 of the *Categories* in order to indicate that these names are technical terms. For the relations being SAID OF and being IN a subject as relations of metaphysical (or, as it is sometimes called, ontological) rather than linguistic predication, see especially J. L. Ackrill, *Aristotle's* Categories *and* De interpretatione [*Aristotle's* Categories] (Oxford, 1963), 75–6; A. Code, 'On the Origins of Some Aristotelian Theses about Predication' ['Origins'], in J. Bogen and J. McGuire (eds.), *How Things Are* (Dordrecht, 1985), 101–31 at 103–4; id., 'Aristotle: Essence and Accident' ['Essence'], in R. Grandy and R. Warner (eds.), *Philosophical Grounds of Rationality: Intentions, Categories, and Ends* (Oxford, 1986), 411–39 at 414–23; and Lewis, *Substance*, 4 n. 4 and 54–6. The use of 'metaphysical predication' for the genus of which the relations being SAID OF and being IN are the species is *my* usage (and the usage of other commentators on the *Categories*). However, this usage reflects the way in which Aristotle sometimes, though not always or even usually, uses κατηγορεῖσθαι in the *Categories*. Aristotle often uses κατηγορεῖσθαι as a variant of λέγεσθαι in its technical sense as denoting the SAID OF relation: $1^b10-15$, $2^a37$, $2^b15$, $3^a3-^b4$, and possibly $1^b22$. He no less often uses κατηγορεῖσθαι to denote the relation of *linguistic* predication, i.e. the relation which a linguistic item (a name (ὄνομα) or account (λόγος)) bears to a non-linguistic item: $2^b22-5$, $2^b28-30$, $3^a16-20$. But on at least two occasions he uses κατηγορεῖσθαι to denote the genus of which the relations being SAID OF and being IN are the species. At $2^b31$ he says that 'of the things predicated' (τῶν κατηγορουμένων) of a primary substance, only secondary substances reveal that primary substance. Here, as Aristotle indicates at $2^b35-6$, the things that are κατηγορεῖται of a primary substance include non-substantial items, e.g. paleness or running. But non-substantial items are IN a primary substance. So here κατηγορεῖσθαι is used in a way that includes the being IN relation. At $3^a4$ κατηγορεῖσθαι denotes the relation in which, on the one hand, both secondary substances and all non-substantial items stand to primary substances, and, on the other hand, all non-substantial items stand to secondary substances. That relation can only be the relation—metaphysical predication—of which being SAID OF and being IN are the species.

[3] This point is made explicitly by Aristotle at $3^b17-18$: secondary substances such as the species human being and the genus animal are 'said of many things' (κατὰ

answer here is why, according to Aristotle in the *Categories*, certain universals such as the species human being or the genus animal are *substances*.

Aristotle appears to answer this question in the following passage (2ᵇ29–37):

> It is reasonable [εἰκότως] that, after primary substances, their species and genera should be the only other things called secondary substances [δεύτε-ραι οὐσίαι]. For only they, of things predicated, reveal the primary substance [μόνα γὰρ δηλοῖ τὴν πρώτην οὐσίαν τῶν κατηγορουμένων]. For if someone is to say of the individual human being [τὸν τινὰ ἄνθρωπον] what he is [τί ἐστιν], it will be proper to give the species or the genus [τὸ μὲν εἶδος ἢ τὸ γένος ἀποδιδοὺς οἰκείως ἀποδώσει] (and more informative to give 'human being' than 'animal'). But to give any of the other things will be improper [ἀλλοτρίως], for example to give 'pale' or 'runs' or anything like that. So it is reasonable that these should be the only other things called substances.⁴

According to Aristotle here something is a substance, albeit a se-condary one, if it 'reveals' or 'discloses' (δηλοῖ) a primary substance. Call this *the disclosure condition for secondary substance*. Something 'reveals' or 'discloses' a primary substance if and only if mention of that thing constitutes a correct answer to the question 'What is it?' (τί ἐστιν;) asked about that primary substance. Aristotle in this pas-sage claims that *only* the species and genera of primary substances satisfy the disclosure condition for secondary substance, but he fails to explain why this is so. Suppose I ask about some primary substance, e.g. Socrates, 'What is it?' Strictly speaking this ques-tion is *not* a request for a definition of Socrates. For on Aristotle's view in the *Categories*, and throughout the *Organon*, the objects of definition—that is, those beings or entities that are definable—are universals, not particulars, and Socrates is a particular.⁵ None the less, Socrates or any other particular is something essentially, and in asking the question 'What is it?' about Socrates I am asking what Socrates is essentially. So a being or entity will be mentioned in a

---

πολλῶν . . . λέγεται). Cf. *Pr. An.* 1. 27, 43ᵃ25–42; *Metaph. Z* 13, 1038ᵇ11–12; and T. H. Irwin, *Aristotle's First Principles* (Oxford, 1988), 56 and 503 n. 22.

⁴ Translations from the *Categories* draw on those by Ackrill in Ackrill, *Aristotle's Categories*, and S. M. Cohen and G. B. Matthews in S. M. Cohen, P. Curd, and C. D. C. Reeve (eds.), *Readings in Ancient Greek Philosophy: From Thales to Aristotle*, 3rd edn. (Indianapolis, 2005), 656–62.

⁵ For this point see especially Code, 'Origins', 112–13.

correct answer to this question, and so will satisfy the disclosure condition for secondary substance, only if that being or entity is something that Socrates is essentially. Now let lower-case letters (*x*, *y*) be beings or entities, i.e. non-linguistic items, and let upper-case letters (*X*, *Y*, *L*) be linguistic items. So let *X* be the name of *x*, *Y* be the name of *y*, and *L* be the account of *y*.[6] In the *Categories* the SAID OF relation is the relation of essential predication: if *y* is SAID OF *x*, then *y* is something *x* is essentially.[7] Aristotle claims by implication that this is so when he claims that 'if something is said of a subject [τῶν καθ' ὑποκειμένου λεγομένων] both its name [τοὔνομα] and its account [τὸν λόγον] are necessarily predicated of the subject [κατηγορεῖσθαι τοῦ ὑποκειμένου]' (2ᵃ19–21). According to Aristotle here, if *y* is SAID OF, and so *metaphysically* predicated of, *x*, then both the *name* of *y* (= *Y*) and the *account* of *y* (=*L*) are *linguistically* predicated of *x*. Linguistic predication is a relation between a linguistic item—a name or an account—and a being or entity.[8] The name *Y* is linguistically predicable of *x* if and only if the sentence

(1)  *X* is *Y*

is true; and the account *L* is linguistically predicable of *x* if and only if the sentence

(2)  *X* is *L*

is true. Aristotle's claim at 2ᵃ19–21 is that if *y* is SAID OF *x*, then (1) and (2) are true, and consequently the name *Y* and the account *L* are linguistically predicable of *x*.

What follows from the fact that the account of *y* is linguistically predicable of *x*? The account of *y* is a *complete* answer to the question 'What is it?' asked about *y*. The question 'What is it?' is a request for a description of what it is to be *y* or, equivalently, of the essence of *y*. This description has the form of a list of *all* of the beings or entities that are *essentially* predicated of *y*. If the account of *y* is linguistically predicable of *x*, then all of the beings or entities that are essentially predicated of *y* are essentially predicated of *x*. According to Aristotle, then, if *y* is SAID OF *x*, everything that is

⁶ I borrow this useful notation from Mann, *Discovery*, 42.
⁷ See Code, 'Origins', 103–4, and 'Essence', 429–31.
⁸ On the distinction between metaphysical and linguistic predication, see Code, 'Origins', 111–12, and 'Essence', 422–3; Lewis, *Substance*, 4.

essentially predicated of *y* is essentially predicated of *x*: what it is
to be *y* (=the essence of *y*) is, or at least is part of, what it is to
be *x* (= the essence of *x*). That is why the account that answers the
question 'What is it?' asked about *y* (= *L*) is linguistically predicable
of *x*, and so is the answer, or at least part of the answer, to the
question 'What is it?' asked about *x*.⁹ If this is so, then the SAID OF
relation is the relation of essential predication. (The qualifications
here are required because it does not follow from the fact that
everything essentially predicated of *y* is essentially predicated of *x*
that everything essentially predicated of *x* is essentially predicated
of *y*, i.e. that the essence of *y* exhausts the essence of *x*. For Aristotle
this is sometimes the case: if *y* is an *infima* species (e.g. the species
human being) and *x* is a member of the species (e.g. Socrates), then
the essence of *y* just is, and so exhausts, the essence of *x*. That is
why, as Aristotle indicates in the *Topics*, the account of what the
species human being is—i.e. the definition of the species—is the
same as the account of what Socrates or any other human being
is.¹⁰ But if *x* is a species (e.g. human being) and *y* is a genus to
which that species belongs (e.g. animal), then the essence of *y* is
part, but only part, of the essence of *x*.)

Both the species and the genus of a primary substance are SAID
OF that primary substance. Since the SAID OF relation is the relation
of essential predication, its species and genus are each something
a primary substance is essentially. If this is so, then the question
'What is it?' asked about a primary substance can be answered correctly by mentioning the species or genus of that primary substance.
Both the species and the genus of a primary substance, therefore,
satisfy the disclosure condition for secondary substance.

In this context, as in others, Aristotle's treatment in the *Categories* of differentiae is problematic.¹¹ For, on the one hand, dif-

---

⁹ Cf. the remarks on 2ᵃ19–21 in M. Furth, *Substance, Form, and Psyche: An
Aristotelian Metaphysics* [*Substance, Form, and Psyche*] (Cambridge, 1988), 23.
¹⁰ *Top.* 6. 1, 139ᵃ26–7: 'the definition of human being must be true of every human
being' (δεῖ γὰρ τὸν τοῦ ἀνθρώπου ὁρισμὸν κατὰ παντὸς ἀνθρώπου ἀληθεύεσθαι). See also
*Top.* 7. 4, 154ᵃ17–18, where Aristotle says that a species is a synonym (συνώνυμον) of
its members. The definition of the species human being is not the same as the definition of Socrates—for, according to Aristotle, there is no definition of Socrates or
of any other particular. But since the species human being is the essence of Socrates,
the definition of that species will be an account of what Socrates is essentially. For
this point see especially Code, 'Origins', 112–13.
¹¹ On the problems with the status of differentia in the *Categories*, see Ackrill,
*Aristotle's* Categories, 85–7; H. Granger, 'Aristotle on Genus and Differentia' ['Aris-

ferentiae are *not* secondary substances—that is the clear implication
of Aristotle's remark at 3ª21–2, and it is no less clearly implied by
Aristotle's claim at 2ᵇ36–7 that the species and genera of primary
substances are the *only* secondary substances. Yet, on the other
hand, a differentia is SAID OF, not IN, the primary substance of which
it is predicated, and so it is something that primary substance is
essentially. Since this is so, it appears that the question 'What is
it?' asked about a primary substance can be answered correctly by
mentioning a differentia predicated of that primary substance and,
therefore, that differentiae satisfy the disclosure condition for secondary substance.[12] Now according to Aristotle in the *Categories*,
and elsewhere, a differentia occurs in only one genus.[13] For this
reason it is not possible to mention a differentia without thereby
referring to the genus in which that differentia occurs. So an answer to the 'What is it?' question that mentions a differentia also
refers to, even if it does not mention, the genus in which that differentia occurs. Since the combination of a genus and differentia
is a species, any answer to the question 'What is it?' that mentions
only a differentia, but thereby refers to the genus in which that differentia occurs, is equivalent to an answer that mentions a species.
So Aristotle's view in the *Categories might* be that while the question 'What is it?' asked about a primary substance can be answered
correctly by mentioning a differentia predicated of that primary
substance, strictly speaking it is not that differentia but the species
which it in part constitutes that satisfies the disclosure condition
for secondary substance.[14]

If we bracket the problems raised by Aristotle's treatment of differentiae, then in the *Categories* the species and genera of primary
substances satisfy the disclosure condition for secondary substance,
and they are the *only* things that do so. For, first, the question 'What

totle'], *Journal of the History of Philosophy*, 22 (1984), 1–24 at 9–11; and Mann,
*Discovery*, 194–5.

[12] Cf. *Top.* 7. 3, 153ª17–18, and 7. 5, 154ª27–8, where Aristotle claims that both
the genus and the differentia are predicated in the what-it-is (ἐν τῷ τί ἐστι . . .
κατηγοροῦνται). For a discussion of these and other passages in the *Topics* where
Aristotle assimilates differentiae to genera, see Granger, 'Aristotle', 7–9.

[13] *Cat.* 1ᵇ16–17; *Top.* 1. 15, 107ᵇ19–20; 6. 6, 144ᵇ12–13. See also the comments
in Ackrill, *Aristotle's* Categories, 76–7.

[14] See Irwin, *Aristotle's First Principles*, 64–5, for a similar point made in the
context of arguing that Aristotle has good reasons in the *Categories* for taking differentiae to be secondary substances.

is it?' asked about a primary substance is not answered correctly simply by giving the proper name of that primary substance.[15] (Suppose, for example, that someone pointing at a horse asks 'What is it?' and I answer 'Bucephalus'.) The proper name of a primary substance denotes a primary substance and not a *predicable*—a being or entity that is predicated of another being or entity as its subject. *A fortiori*, the proper name of a primary substance does not denote anything that is essentially predicated of that primary substance. If this is so, then in giving the proper name of a primary substance I do not thereby mention something that primary substance is essentially. Second, according to Aristotle any answer to the question 'What is it?' asked about Socrates that mentions a predicable other than Socrates' species or genus—for instance, a quality of Socrates such as his paleness or something Socrates is doing, e.g. running—will be incorrect. For it mentions something Socrates happens to be rather than something Socrates is essentially: Socrates can cease to be pale or to be running without ceasing to be Socrates.

So, to sum up this part of the discussion, Aristotle claims that the only things that satisfy the disclosure condition for secondary substance are the species and genera of primary substances. He also claims that the species and genera of primary substances are the only secondary substances. It follows that according to Aristotle satisfaction of the disclosure condition is not only sufficient, but also necessary, for something to be a secondary substance. So the fact that in the *Categories* some universals but not others are substances, albeit secondary ones, is to be explained by the fact that some universals but not others satisfy the disclosure condition for secondary substance.[16]

I want to suggest, however, that in the *Categories* the status of the species and genera of primary substances as themselves substances is a more complicated matter. For why, we might ask, does something qualify as a substance, albeit a secondary one, in virtue of satisfying the disclosure condition? What is the connection between, on the one hand, being something that can be mentioned as a correct answer to the question 'What is it?' asked about a pri-

---

[15] Thanks to David Sedley for bringing this possibility to my attention.
[16] Cf. Wedin, *Aristotle's Theory of Substance*, 94.

mary substance and, on the other hand, being a *substance*, albeit a secondary one? 

In the absence of any connection of this sort it might appear as though for Aristotle in the *Categories* there is not one but two ways in which something can be a substance. For any primary substance $x$, there is some species $\epsilon$ and some genus $\gamma$ such that $x$ belongs to $\epsilon$ and $\gamma$. In virtue of belonging to $\epsilon$ and $\gamma$, $x$ is not just a particular but a particular such-and-such, e.g. a particular human being or horse or animal. The species and genus of a primary substance are each something that primary substance is essentially: a human being is something Socrates is essentially, an animal is something Bucephalus the horse is essentially, etc. That is why the species and genus of a primary substance—and, again bracketing the problems raised by differentiae, only these—satisfy the disclosure condition for secondary substance. So for Aristotle in the *Categories* something can be a substance *either* by being a primary substance like Socrates *or* by being what a primary substance is essentially, that is, by being the being or substance (οὐσία) *of* a primary substance.[17]

On this line of thought the term 'substance' (οὐσία) applies both to Socrates and to his species or genus. But the account of what it is to be a substance that is true of Socrates is different from the account of what it is to be a substance that is true of his species or genus.[18] For what it is for Socrates' species or genus to be a substance is for it to be what something else—Socrates and his ilk—is essentially, and that is *not* what it is for Socrates to be a substance. So Socrates and his genus or species are homonyms (ὁμώνυμα) with respect to the term or name (ὄνομα) 'substance', and 'substance' has one meaning when it is applied to Socrates and a different meaning when it is applied to his species or genus. This, however, cannot be Aristotle's view in the *Categories*. For there he claims that primary substances such as Socrates or Bucephalus are substances 'most of all' (μάλιστα, $2^{a}11$–$12$, $2^{b}17$). Now the claim that $x$ is an $F$ 'most of all' is, or at least implies, the claim that there

---

[17] If I have understood it correctly, something like this is the view in G. B. Matthews and S. M. Cohen, 'The One and the Many', *Review of Metaphysics*, 21 (1968), 630–55 at 632, who write: 'Every individual is an individual such-and-such. And so the such-and-such of an individual is also the being or substance (οὐσία) of the individual: it is what the individual is.'

[18] My use of the awkward locution 'the account of what it is to be' is meant to render Aristotle's phrase λόγος τῆς οὐσίας in the definitions of homonymy and synonymy he gives at $1^{a}1$–$12$.

is something else *y* such that *y* is an *F* and *x* is an *F* more than *y*. And for Aristotle in the *Categories x* is an *F* more than *y* only if *x* and *y* are *F*s in precisely the same sense, that is, only if the term or name '*F*' has the same meaning when it is applied to *x* as it has when it is applied to *y*.[19] If Socrates is a substance more than his species or genus, however, then the term 'substance' has the same meaning when it is applied to Socrates as it has when it is applied to his species or genus. And if that is so, then the account of what it is for Socrates to be a substance is the same as the account of what it is for his species or genus to be a substance.

We are still left, then, with the question why something qualifies as a substance, albeit a secondary one, in virtue of satisfying the disclosure condition. The answer to this question, I claim, comes in two parts. First, for Aristotle in the *Categories* the *general* notion of a substance is the notion of *a subject for inherence*. Inherence, or being IN a subject, is one of the two relations of metaphysical predication Aristotle introduces in chapter 2 of the *Categories*. A substance, primary or secondary, is something which other things inhere in or are IN. Second, a universal is a subject for inherence, and hence a substance, if and only if it satisfies the disclosure condition for secondary substance. So, on the view I shall now sketch, in the *Categories* certain universals but not others are substances because certain universals but not others are subjects for inherence.[20]

---

[19] For this point see G. E. L. Owen, 'Logic and Metaphysics in Some Earlier Works of Aristotle', in id., *Logic, Science, and Dialectic: Collected Papers in Greek Philosophy* (Ithaca, NY, 1986), 180–99 at 195, who cites *Cat.* 11ᵃ12–13 and *Phys.* 7. 4, 249ᵃ3–8. At *Cat.* 3ᵇ33–4ᵃ2 Aristotle claims that for any two substances that are specimens of the same species or genus, one substance cannot be more or less a specimen of that species or genus—more or less a human being or horse or animal—than the other substance. But that claim is compatible with the claim that a being or entity of one kind (Socrates) is a substance more than a being or entity of another kind (his species or genus).

[20] The view I defend here is, I think, similar to the one expressed by the remark in M. Frede, 'Individuals in Aristotle' ['Individuals'], in id., *Essays in Ancient Philosophy* (Minneapolis, 1987), 49–71 at 59, that 'Just as the individual objects are the subjects underlying all properties, so too the species and genera underlie all properties as subjects. Since this is what makes substances, species and genera also deserve to be called substances.' To say that the species and genera underlie all properties as subjects is just to say that all properties (except differentiae) inhere in or are IN the species and genera. Frede does not, however, discuss what I call the disclosure condition for secondary substance, and he does not discuss whether or how the species and genera of primary substances 'underlie all properties as subjects' in virtue of satisfying the disclosure condition. The view I defend here is also similar to one suggested by remarks in Lewis, *Substance*, 64, and Furth, *Substance, Form, and Psyche*, 28–9.

In the *Categories* something is a *primary* substance in virtue of
being an *ultimate* subject of predication.[21] An *ultimate* subject of
predication is something of which other things are predicated while
it itself is not predicated of anything. According to Aristotle 'it is
because the primary substances are subjects for all other things
and all other things are predicated of them or are in them, that they
are called substances most of all' ($2^b15$–$17$; see also $2^b37$–$3^a1$).[22] If
something is not a primary substance, then it is a predicable, that is,
a being or entity that is predicated of another being or entity as its
subject. Aristotle's view in the *Categories* is that any predicable—
any secondary substance, any non-substantial item—is predicated
of a primary substance. Since in the *Categories* there are only two
relations of metaphysical predication, being SAID OF a subject and
being IN a subject, Aristotle's view is that any predicable is either
SAID OF or IN a primary substance. And since a primary substance
is not itself a predicable, it is not predicated of any other being or
entity as its subject. In this way primary substances are *subjects* for
*all* other things, and Aristotle's claim is that this is the reason why
primary substances are substances in the *primary* sense.

However, primary substances are not the *only* subjects of predication in the *Categories*. Non-substantial items are subjects for the
SAID OF relation, and therefore are subjects of predication, because
they have essences.[23] If a non-substantial item *x* has an essence,
then there is some predicable *y* such that *y* is SAID OF, and so predicated of, *x*. White, for instance, is essentially a colour, colour is
SAID OF white, and so white is a subject of predication. Secondary
substances, too, are subjects for the SAID OF relation, and therefore are subjects of predication. For both the genus and the differentia of a species are SAID OF, and so predicated of, that species.
But secondary substances, like primary substances and unlike non-

---

[21] For this point see Code, 'Essence', 431, and M. Frede, 'Substance in Aristotle's
*Metaphysics*', in id., *Essays in Ancient Philosophy*, 72–80 at 73. Being an ultimate
subject of predication is one of the two principal senses of 'substance' (οὐσία) distinguished in *Metaph. Δ* 8. We might ask why the fact that something is an ultimate
subject of predication qualifies it as a primary substance. I cannot pursue that question here, but for one answer to it see Lewis, *Substance*, 67–73.

[22] $2^b15$–$17$: ἔτι αἱ πρῶται οὐσίαι διὰ τὸ τοῖς ἄλλοις ἅπασιν ὑποκεῖσθαι καὶ πάντα τὰ
ἄλλα κατὰ τούτων κατηγορεῖσθαι ἢ ἐν ταύταις εἶναι διὰ τοῦτο μάλιστα οὐσίαι λέγονται.
Here, as at $1^b10$–$15$ and elsewhere in the *Categories*, Aristotle uses κατηγορεῖσθαι as
a variant of λέγεσθαι in its technical sense as denoting the SAID OF relation.

[23] For this point see Code, 'Essence', 431, who notes that in the *Categories* 'Substances and non-substances alike are endowed with essential natures.'

substantial items, are also subjects for inherence or the being IN relation. After claiming that the species and genera of primary substances satisfy what I have called the disclosure condition for secondary substance, Aristotle continues:

Further [ἔτι], it is because the primary substances are subjects for every-thing else that they are called substances most strictly [κυριώτατα οὐσίαι λέγονται]. But as the primary substances stand to everything else, so the species and genera of primary substances stand to all the rest: all the rest are predicated of these [κατὰ τούτων γὰρ πάντα τὰ λοιπὰ κατηγορεῖται]. For if you will call the individual human being [τὸν τινὰ ἄνθρωπον] grammatical, it follows that you will call both human being and animal grammatical; and similarly in other cases. (2ᵇ37–3ᵃ6)

Three points are especially important in connection with this pas-sage. First, Aristotle claims here that every non-substantial item—every quality, quantity, etc.—is predicated not only of a primary substance but also of the species and genus of that primary sub-stance. Now some non-substantial items—differentiae—are SAID OF the species and genera of primary substances (3ᵃ21–4). But with the exception of differentiae, if a non-substantial item is predicated of a species or genus of a primary substance, then it is IN that species or genus. So if every non-substantial item is predicated not only of a primary substance but also of the species and genus of that primary substance, then the species and genera of primary substances are, like primary substances, subjects for inherence or the being IN re-lation. Second, and relatedly, a non-substantial item is IN a species or genus if it is IN a primary substance that belongs to that species or genus. So if paleness is IN Socrates—if it is the case that Socrates is pale—then paleness is also IN the species human being and IN the genus animal.[24] All that is required for a species or a genus to be a subject for inherence is that those primary substances that belong to the species or genus are subjects for inherence.

Third, this passage implies something it does not explicitly state: that the species and genera of primary substances are themselves substances, albeit secondary ones, *because* they are subjects of which all non-substantial items are predicated. The context of the pas-sage makes this implication clear. At 2ᵇ29–30 Aristotle claims that

[24] See Frede, 'Individuals', 61, for the point that any non-substantial item that is IN a subject is IN a plurality of subjects. For if a non-substantial item is IN a subject, it is IN a primary substance; and if a non-substantial item is IN a primary substance, then it is also IN the species and IN the genus of that primary substance.

among the things predicated of a primary substance only their species and genera are secondary substances. He then ($2^b30-7$) provides an argument for this claim: among the things predicated of a primary substance, only its species and genus 'reveal' or 'disclose' that primary substance. And then ($2^b37$) our passage begins with the adverb ἔτι, and this adverb indicates that Aristotle is offering a second argument for why the species and genera of primary substances, and only these, are secondary substances.[25] This argument comes in two steps. Aristotle first claims that primary substances are substances in the primary sense in virtue of the asymmetric relation in which they stand to everything else: they are subjects of which everything else is predicated while they are not themselves predicated of anything else. He then claims that the species and genera of primary substances stand in this same asymmetric relation to all non-substantial items: they are subjects of which all non-substantial items are predicated while they themselves are not predicated of any non-substantial item. Just as primary substances are substances in the primary sense because they are subjects for everything else, Aristotle implies, so the species and genera of primary substances are themselves substances, albeit secondary ones, because they are subjects for all non-substantial items.

Now, to repeat a point made earlier, with the exception of differentiae, any non-substantial item predicated of a species or genus of a primary substance is IN that species or genus. So to imply,

[25] See the same use of ἔτι at $2^b15$—introducing a second argument for the claim that the species is a substance more than the genus. Ammonius, in his commentary on the *Categories* (43. 15–44. 4 Busse), notices that at $2^b37-3^a6$ Aristotle is offering a second argument for the claim that the species and genera of primary substances, and only these, are secondary substances. Wedin, *Aristotle's Theory of Substance*, 95, misses this point. He writes that the passage at $2^b37-3^a6$ 'says neither that species and genera are called *substances* nor that they are substances *secondarily* because of qualifying as subjects . . . It says simply that, as primary substances are subjects, so also, in a certain way, are species and genera subjects. So while [$3^a1-6$] offers some kind of contrast between primary substances and their species and genera, it does not contrast the *bases* on which they are *called substances*. This has already been given in [$2^b30-7$]. [$3^a1-6$] simply records the fact that they are subjects to different kinds of items.' Wedin reads the passage from $2^b29$ to $3^a6$ in this way because he claims that the adverb ἔτι 'typically marks a fresh start' and presumably thinks it does so at $2^b37$. But if at $2^b37$ ἔτι marks a fresh start, that frest start consists in offering a new argument for the claim made at $2^b29-30$, viz. that the species and genera of primary substances, and only these, are secondary substances. This point is also missed by R. Bodéüs, *Aristote: Catégories* (Paris, 2001), 93, who takes the passage at $2^b29-3^a6$ to contain two arguments for the thesis that the species and genus of a primary substance are the only things that are essentially predicated of that primary substance.

as I claim Aristotle does at 2ᵇ37–3ᵃ6, that the species and genera of primary substances are themselves substances because they are subjects of which all non-substantial items are predicated is to imply that these species and genera are substances because they are subjects for inherence or the being IN relation. For clearly Aristotle does not imply here that the species and genera of primary substances are themselves substances because they are subjects for the SAID OF relation. For in the *Categories* both substances and non-substantial items are subjects for the SAID OF relation. Since this is so, something cannot be a substance simply in virtue of being a subject for the SAID OF relation. Moreover, in the *Categories* both primary substances *and* their species and genera are subjects for inherence, and they are the *only* subjects for inherence.²⁶ Being a substance of any sort in the *Categories* is a matter of being a subject for inherence.

It is true, of course, that at 2ᵇ37–3ᵃ6 Aristotle does not say that being a subject for inherence or the being IN relation is what makes something a substance. He instead emphasizes there, as I have indicated, that primary and secondary substances share something else, namely, being *ultimate* subjects with respect to *some* domain of items—though not with respect to the same domain of items. For primary substances are ultimate subjects with respect to everything else, while secondary substances are ultimate subjects with respect to all non-substantial items. So it might appear that according to Aristotle at 2ᵇ37–3ᵃ6 it is not being a subject for inherence or the being IN relation, but being an *ultimate* subject with respect to some domain of items, that makes something a substance. It seems to me, however, that this appearance is misleading for at least two reasons. First, in the *Categories* something can be an ultimate subject with respect to some domain of items without being a substance. For non-substantial individuals—those things which are IN a subject but are not SAID OF a subject—are ultimate subjects with respect to

²⁶ For the claim that in the *Categories* if *x* is IN *y*, then *y* is a substance, i.e. for the claim that substances are the only subjects for inherence, see Ackrill, *Aristotle's Categories*, 76, and cf. Furth, *Substance, Form, and Psyche*, 25. At 4ᵃ15–16 Aristotle denies that 'that same action, one in number, will be bad and good' (ἡ αὐτὴ πρᾶξις καὶ μία τῷ ἀριθμῷ οὐκ ἔσται φαύλη καὶ σπουδαία). As D. Devereux, 'Inherence and Primary Substance in Aristotle's *Categories*' ['Inherence'], *Ancient Philosophy*, 12 (1992), 113–31 at 128 n. 24, notes, Aristotle's remark might be taken to imply that certain things, e.g. bravery, can be predicated of an action, and so actions and other non-substantial items can be subjects for inherence.

their species and genera: the latter are predicated of the former, but the former are not predicated of the latter.

Second, and more importantly, it is necessary to distinguish, as it seems to me Aristotle does, what it is that makes something a substance rather than a non-substantial item from what it is that makes a substance more or less a substance. Although something is a substance because it is a subject for inherence or the being IN relation, in the *Categories* some subjects for inherence are substances more than others. So while something's status as a substance is a matter of its being a subject for inherence, something's place in the hierarchy of substances is a function of the predication relations in which it stands to other substances. For any two substances $x$ and $y$, if $y$ is SAID OF $x$ and $x$ is not SAID OF $y$, then $x$ is a substance more than $y$. A primary substance is a substance more than its species or genera because they are SAID OF it, but it is not SAID OF them. And, as Aristotle explains at $2^b15$–22, Socrates' species is a substance more than his genus because his genus is SAID OF his species but his species is not SAID OF his genus. (Matters are in fact more complicated, however, since the formula I have given here specifies a sufficient, but not a necessary, condition for one substance being a substance more than another substance. For in the *Categories* there are cases in which both $x$ and $y$ are substances, $x$ is a substance more than $y$, $x$ is not predicated of (and so not SAID OF) $y$, but $y$ is not predicated of (and so not SAID OF) $x$. So, for instance, Bucephalus, a primary substance, is a substance more than the species human being to which he does not belong and which is not predicated of (and so not SAID OF) him. The following formula is required to capture this kind of case: for any two substances $x$ and $y$, if there is some substance $z$ such that $y$ is SAID OF $z$, and there is no substance $w$ such that $x$ is SAID OF $w$, then $x$ is a substance more than $y$.) So on my account the fact that primary substances are ultimate subjects for *everything else*—that is, the fact that they are subjects for secondary substances as well as non-substantial items—is relevant not to the status of primary substances as *substances* but to their status as *primary* substances. And, in fact, at $2^b37$–$3^a1$ (and cf. $2^b15$–17) Aristotle cites the fact that primary substances are ultimate subjects, and therefore are subjects for both secondary substances and non-substantial items, not as the reason why primary substances are (or are called (λέγονται)) substances but as the reason why they are (or are called) substances *most strictly* (κυριώτατα), i.e. why they are (or are called) *primary* substances. Two additional points are worth making in this context. First, according to Aristotle in the *Categories* all and only substances are able to receive contraries (τῶν ἐναντίων δεκτικόν).[27] For this reason we might say that for Aristotle something is a substance *because* it is able to receive contraries. But in saying this we are saying no more than that something is a substance because it is a subject for inherence. For to say that *x* is able to receive contraries *F* and *G* is just to say that it is possible for both *F* and *G* to be IN *x* (though not necessarily at the same time.) Second, the claim that in the *Categories* something is a substance because it is a subject for inherence is not to be confused with the claim Aristotle makes at 3ª7–8 that 'Not being IN a subject is something common to all substances' (κοινὸν δὲ κατὰ πάσης οὐσίας τὸ μὴ ἐν ὑποκειμένῳ εἶναι). In making the latter claim Aristotle is *not* making a claim about why something is a substance. For since, as he himself notes, not being IN a subject is a characteristic not only of substances but also of differentiae (3ª21–2), and since differentiae are not substances, it cannot be his view that something is a substance because it is not IN any subject.[28]

But why, according to Aristotle, are the species and genera of primary substances subjects for inherence? Why is it that, as Aris-

[27] Though I am inclined to think that this is *not* the claim Aristotle makes in claiming at 4ª10–11 (and 4ª16–17) that it is (or is thought to be) μάλιστα ἴδιον of substance that, being the same and one in number, it is able to receive contraries (ταὐτὸν καὶ ἐν ἀριθμῷ ὂν τῶν ἐναντίων εἶναι δεκτικόν). The scope of Aristotle's claim here seems to be restricted to primary substances. For at 4ª29–30 Aristotle explicates his claim that substances are able to receive contraries by claiming that they do so by themselves changing (αὐτὰ μεταβάλλοντα), and that is the way in which primary, but not secondary, substances are able to receive contraries. So Aristotle's claim at 4ª10–11 seems to be that what is distinctive of *primary* substance is that among things that are the same and one in number it alone is able to receive contraries.
[28] So here I disagree with G. B. Matthews, 'Aristotelian Categories', in G. Anagnostopoulos (ed.), *A Companion to Aristotle* (forthcoming), who writes that 'Not being in a subject makes something a substance (*ousia*) . . . Because man and horse are not in any subject, they, too, count as substances, along with Socrates and Bucephalus.' Note that when in chapter 5 of the *Categories* Aristotle defines secondary substances, he does *not* (as he does in the case of primary substances) do so by reference to the predication relations introduced in chapter 2. In particular, he does not define a secondary substance as what is SAID OF but not IN a subject. (He instead defines secondary substances as the species and genera of primary substances.) The reason for this may be, as Ackrill, *Aristotle's* Categories, 81–2, noted, the fact that for Aristotle in the *Categories* some entities or beings that are SAID OF but not IN a subject—namely, differentiae—are *not* substances.

totle claims, if a non-substantial item is IN Socrates, it is also IN the species human being and the genus animal ($3^a1-6$)? Aristotle can answer this question only by appealing to the relation in which a species or genus stands to the primary substances that belong to it. It is Aristotle's view in the *Categories* that a primary substance is a subject for inherence, and that the species and genera of a primary substance are themselves subjects for inherence because they are what that primary substance is essentially. But this is just the view that the species and genera of primary substances are subjects for inherence in virtue of satisfying what I have called the disclosure condition for secondary substance: mention of its species or genus constitutes a correct answer to the question 'What is it?' asked about a primary substance. Socrates, for example, is essentially a human being. According to Aristotle, if it is true that

(1) Socrates is pale,

then it is also true, and true in virtue of the fact that Socrates is pale, that

(2) Human being is pale.

For Aristotle (2) is not equivalent to, though it does imply,

(3) A human being is pale.

(3) asserts that paleness is IN some member or other of the species human being. (2), by contrast, asserts that paleness is IN the species human being itself. (2) is true because the species human being is what some primary substance (Socrates) is essentially and paleness is IN that primary substance. To be clear: the view I am attributing to Aristotle in the *Categories* is that the species and genera of primary substances are themselves substances *not* because they are what primary substances are essentially, but because being what primary substances are essentially they, like primary substances, are subjects for inherence. But their status as subjects for inherence is parasitic on the status of primary substances as subjects for inherence. For a species or genus is a subject for inherence only because those primary substances that belong to it are subjects for inherence. Moreover, the various non-substantial items that inhere in a species or genus do so only because those same non-substantial

items inhere in primary substances that belong to that species or genus.²⁹

If any non-substantial item that is IN a primary substance is IN the species and genus of that primary substance as well, then it is possible for contraries (τὰ ἐναντία)—incompatible qualities, quantities, or other non-substantial items—to be IN a species or genus at one and the same time. If, for example, at time *t* Socrates is pale and Callias is dark, then at *t* the qualities paleness and darkness are both IN the species human being and the genus animal. But now, it might be argued, it is a condition of something's being a genuine subject for inherence that it is *not* possible for contraries to be IN that thing at one and the same time. Since the species and genera of primary substances fail to satisfy this condition, they are not genuine subjects for inherence.³⁰ And if this is so, then it is not the case that the species and genera of primary substances are themselves substances in virtue of being subjects for inherence.

This argument, however, is not one Aristotle accepts in the *Categories*. His view there is not

(A)  If *x* is a subject for inherence, then it is not possible for contraries to be IN *x* at one and the same time.

but rather

(B)  If *x* is a subject for inherence that is 'one in number' (ἓν ἀριθμῷ), then it is not possible for contraries to be IN *x* at one and the same time.

For Aristotle in the *Categories* the truth of (B) does not entail the truth of (A) because not all subjects for inherence are 'one in number'. Aristotle writes that 'It seems most distinctive of substance that being the same and one in number (ταὐτὸν καὶ ἓν ἀριθμῷ) it is able to receive contraries' (4ᵃ10–11), and he explains that a substance that is 'one in number' receives contraries by changing (4ᵃ29–30). So, for instance, someone who is pale at one time becomes (γίγνεται) dark at a later time. The clear implication of Aristotle's remarks here is that it is not possible for contraries at one and

---

²⁹ On this point—that any case of inherence that has a species or genus as its subject is grounded in a case of inherence that has a primary substance that falls under the species or genus in question as its subejct—see Lewis, *Substance*, 64–6.

³⁰ See Wedin, *Aristotle's Theory of Substance*, 98–100, for this argument.

the same time to be IN a substance that is 'one in number'. For if that were possible, then, contrary to what Aristotle claims here, it would be possible for a substance that is 'one in number' to receive contraries *without* changing. Since Aristotle elsewhere ($3^{b}10–13$) claims that a *primary* substance is 'one in number', his view is that it is not possible for contraries to be IN a *primary* substance at one and the same time.

But it is also Aristotle's view that, unlike primary substances, their species and genera are *not* 'one in number'. For Aristotle writes that 'things that are individual and one in number [τὰ ἄτομα καὶ ἓν ἀριθμῷ] are, without exception [ἁπλῶς], not said of any subject [κατ' οὐδενὸς ὑποκειμένου λέγεται], but nothing prevents them from being in a subject' ($1^{b}6–8$). So if *x* is 'one in number', there is no *y* such that *x* is SAID OF *y*.[31] But the species of a primary substance is SAID OF the primary substances that belong to it; and the genus of a primary substance is SAID OF both its species and the primary substances that belong to those species. So, according to Aristotle, neither the genus nor the species of a primary substance is 'one in number'. If this is so, and given that the species and genera of primary substances are subjects for inherence, then for Aristotle not all subjects for inherence are 'one in number'.

On Aristotle's view in the *Categories*, then, the species or genus of a primary substance is *both* a subject for inherence, and for this reason a substance, *and*, being a universal, a predicable predicated of (SAID OF) a plurality of subjects. The non-substantial items that inhere in the species or genus of a primary substance are *all* of those non-substantial items that inhere in the primary substances of which that species or genus is predicated. As a result the species or genus of a primary substance, unlike a primary substance itself, is a subject for inherence in which contraries can inhere at one and the same time. This view obviously invites a question that, as far

---

[31] This claim seems to be the import of Aristotle's remarks at $3^{b}13–18$ as well. For if κατὰ πολλῶν λέγεται at $3^{b}17$ denotes the SAID OF relation, as it does in chapter 2 of the *Categories*, then according to Aristotle in this passage a necessary condition for something's being 'one in number' is *not* that it is not predicated of a plurality of subjects, i.e. neither IN nor SAID OF a plurality of subjects, but rather that it is not SAID OF a plurality of subjects. If this is right, then *contra* Devereux, 'Inherence', 114–16, Aristotle's remarks at $3^{b}10–18$ are at least compatible with the view that a non-substantial individual—an item that is IN a subject but not SAID OF any subject— is *both* 'one in number', and therefore an individual, *and* predicable of a plurality of subjects in so far as it can be IN a plurality of subjects. Cf. Frede, 'Individuals', 53–4.

as I know, no commentator has yet answered: what kind of being or entity could *this* be?

*The University of Massachusetts, Amherst*

## BIBLIOGRAPHY

Ackrill, J. L., *Aristotle's* Categories *and* De interpretatione [*Aristotle's* Categories] (Oxford, 1963).

Bodéüs, R., *Aristote: Catégories* (Paris, 2001).

Code, A., 'Aristotle: Essence and Accident' ['Essence'], in R. Grandy and R. Warner (eds.), *Philosophical Grounds of Rationality: Intentions, Categories, and Ends* (Oxford, 1986), 411–39.

—— 'On the Origins of Some Aristotelian Theses about Predication' ['Origins'], in J. Bogen and J. McGuire (eds.), *How Things Are* (Dordrecht, 1985), 101–31.

Cohen, S. M. and Matthews, G. B. (trans.), *Categories*, in S. M. Cohen, P. Curd, and C. D. C. Reeve (eds.), *Readings in Ancient Greek Philosophy: From Thales to Aristotle*, 3rd edn. (Indianapolis, 2005), 656–62.

Devereux, D., 'Inherence and Primary Substance in Aristotle's *Categories*' ['Inherence'], *Ancient Philosophy*, 12 (1992), 113–31.

Frede, M., 'Individuals in Aristotle' ['Individuals'], in id., *Essays in Ancient Philosophy* (Minneapolis, 1987), 49–71.

—— 'Substance in Aristotle's *Metaphysics*', in id., *Essays in Ancient Philosophy* (Minneapolis, 1987), 72–80.

Furth, M., *Substance, Form, and Psyche: An Aristotelian Metaphysics* [*Substance, Form, and Psyche*] (Cambridge, 1988).

Granger, H., 'Aristotle on Genus and Differentia' ['Aristotle'], *Journal of the History of Philosophy*, 22 (1984), 1–24.

Irwin, T. H., *Aristotle's First Principles* (Oxford, 1988).

Lewis, F., *Substance and Predication in Aristotle* [*Substance*] (Cambridge, 1991).

Mann, W. R., *The Discovery of Things: Aristotle's* Categories *and their Context* [*Discovery*] (Princeton, 2000).

Matthews, G. B., 'Aristotelian Categories', in G. Anagnostopoulos (ed.), *A Companion to Aristotle* (forthcoming).

—— and Cohen, S.M., 'The One and the Many', *Review of Metaphysics*, 21 (1968), 630–55.

Menn, S., 'Metaphysics, Dialectic, and the *Categories*', *Revue de métaphysique et de morale*, 100 (1995), 311–37.

Owen, G. E. L., 'Logic and Metaphysics in Some Earlier Works of Aristotle', in id., *Logic, Science, and Dialectic: Collected Papers in Greek Philosophy* (Ithaca, NY, 1986), 180–99.

Wedin, M. V., *Aristotle's Theory of Substance: The* Categories *and* Metaphysics *Zeta* [*Aristotle's Theory of Substance*] (Oxford, 2000).

# THE STRUCTURE OF TELEOLOGICAL EXPLANATIONS IN ARISTOTLE: THEORY AND PRACTICE

MARISKA E. M. P. J. LEUNISSEN

IN the *Posterior Analytics* Aristotle discusses demonstrative knowledge. Despite the long tradition of Aristotelian scholarship on this treatise, many details concerning the nature of demonstration and its relation to explanation remain enigmatic, and are the subject of much controversy.[1] This paper aims to shed light on Aristotle's pivotal discussion of the relation of demonstration, explanation, and scientific knowledge in *Post. An.* 2. 11, and specifically on the structure of teleological explanations as presented in this chapter. In the first part (Sections 1–3) I shall clarify the examples Aristotle provides to illustrate his theoretical remarks about causal explanation. In particular, I hope to make sense of the teleological example of walking after dinner for the sake of health. In Section 4 I shall focus on the structure of the actual teleological explanations provided in Aristotle's *De partibus animalium*. This will show that Aristotle's

© Mariska E. M. P. J. Leunissen 2007

Versions of this paper were presented to the Joint Ancient Philosophy Program at the University of Texas at Austin and the Marquette Summer Seminar in Ancient and Medieval Philosophy on the *Posterior Analytics* and Aristotelian Sciences, at Marquette University; I am grateful to all those who asked critical questions and made helpful comments. I am also indebted to the participants of the Leiden research seminar on the *Posterior Analytics*, Frans de Haas, Pieter Sjoerd Hasper, and Marije Martijn, for their invaluable assistance in analysing *Post. An.* 2. 11. For help and comments on earlier drafts of this paper, I would like to thank Frans de Haas, Jim Hankinson, Pieter Sjoerd Hasper, and Jim Lennox. I also benefited greatly from comments by the editor of this journal. I thank Jeff Laux for correcting my English. The errors that remain are, of course, my responsibility, and the views expressed are not necessarily shared by those thanked above.

[1] For present purposes, I leave aside the question whether the *Posterior Analytics* presents a theory of scientific methodology and investigation or a theory of the organization and presentation of the finished scientific system. On this matter, see among others J. Barnes, *Aristotle: Posterior Analytics* [*Posterior*] (Oxford, 1993), xi–xix.

theory and practice of teleological explanation are in agreement with each other.

## 1. Causes, explanations, and middle terms

### 1.1. *The problem: the middle terms of the examples in* Post. An. 2. 11 *do not pick out all four causes*

In *Post. An.* 1. 2 Aristotle introduces demonstrations as being syllogistic in form and causal in content. Demonstrations are thus deductive arguments that produce scientific knowledge (*Post. An.* 1. 2, 71ᵇ17–19). For Aristotle, scientific knowledge consists ultimately in knowledge of the explanation of why things are the case (*Post. An.* 1. 2, 71ᵇ9–13):

ἐπίστασθαι δὲ οἰόμεθ' ἕκαστον ἁπλῶς, ἀλλὰ μὴ τὸν σοφιστικὸν τρόπον τὸν κατὰ συμβεβηκός, ὅταν τήν τ' αἰτίαν οἰώμεθα γινώσκειν δι' ἣν τὸ πρᾶγμά ἐστιν, ὅτι ἐκείνου αἰτία ἐστί, καὶ μὴ ἐνδέχεσθαι τοῦτ' ἄλλως ἔχειν. δῆλον τοίνυν ὅτι τοιοῦτόν τι τὸ ἐπίστασθαί ἐστι.

We think we have [scientific] knowledge of each thing without qualification (and not in the sophistic way, incidentally) when we think we know of the explanation because of which the state of affairs is the case, that it is its explanation, and also that it is not possible for this [state of affairs] to be otherwise. It is clear that something of this kind is what it is to have [scientific] knowledge.[2]

At the beginning of *Post. An.* 2. 11 Aristotle specifies—and, from our perspective, complicates—this assertion by introducing a 'doctrine' of four *aitiai*, which, he claims, are all to be demonstrated through the middle term (*Post. An.* 2. 11, 94ᵃ20–7):

ἐπεὶ δὲ ἐπίστασθαι οἰόμεθα ὅταν εἰδῶμεν τὴν αἰτίαν, αἰτίαι δὲ τέτταρες, μία μὲν τὸ τί ἦν εἶναι, μία δὲ τὸ τίνων ὄντων ἀνάγκη τοῦτ' εἶναι, ἑτέρα δὲ ἡ τί πρῶτον ἐκίνησε, τετάρτη δὲ τὸ τίνος ἕνεκα, πᾶσαι αὗται διὰ τοῦ μέσου δείκνυνται.

Since we think we have [scientific] knowledge when we know the explanation, and there are four types of explanation—one, what it is to be a thing, and another, given what things being the case it is necessary for that to hold;[3] another, what first initiated the motion; and fourth, the for the sake of what—all of them are brought out through the middle term.[4]

---

[2] All translations are mine, unless indicated otherwise.

[3] The expression used here to refer to material causation is puzzling; I believe Aristotle to imply that material causes for the most part necessitate their results, or

[*See opposite for* n. *3 cont. and* n. 4

After this short introduction to the topic of this chapter, Aristotle moves on to give syllogistic examples of how each of the four explanations (*aitiai*) is indeed brought out through the middle term.

In contrast to the apparent clarity of structure and argument in this chapter, its content has raised many interpretative problems for modern scholars, most of which pertain to the general purpose of the chapter and to the nature of the syllogistic examples. The sentence stating that 'all the *aitiai* are brought out through the middle term' has traditionally been interpreted as meaning that all four Aristotelian causes can or even must be picked out by the middle term in scientific demonstrations.[5] However, under this interpretation the syllogistic examples Aristotle gives to illustrate his introductory sentence present us with two major difficulties. In the first place, contrary to the expectations of many interpreters the syllogisms posited in no way constitute typical Barbara demonstrations (the required mood for science) where the predicates hold universally and necessarily of the subjects.[6] In the second place, it is not immediately clear how the middle terms in the given examples refer to the causes in question. In particular the section that shows how final causes are brought out

that they at least do so when picked out in demonstrations. For present purposes, I shall treat the expression and the example discussed below as a 'canonical' example of material explanation, taken in the broad sense as an explanation stating 'that out of which'. For the problems involved (which do not affect the interpretation presented here), see Barnes, *Posterior*, 226–7; W. Detel, *Aristoteles: Analytica Posteriora* [*Analytica*] (Berlin, 1993), 685, 690–4; and W. D. Ross, *Aristotle's Prior and Posterior Analytics: A Revised Text with Introduction and Commentary* [*Revised*] (Oxford, 1949), 638–42.

    [4] See the Appendix below for a complete translation of *Post. An.* 2. 11, 94$^a$20–94$^b$26.

    [5] This interpretation ultimately goes back to Philoponus, who criticizes this chapter in his commentary on the *Posterior Analytics* (*In An. Post.* 376. 12–14, 16–18, 31–2; 377. 21–2, 26–7 Wallies). He thinks that the examples are wrong and rebukes Aristotle for having set out the syllogisms in a confused way (*In An. Post.* 378. 16–19; 379. 4–9; 379. 33–380. 3 Wallies). In order to correct Aristotle, Philoponus rearranges the examples and thereby manœuvres the causes into the preferred position of the middle term (*In An. Post.* 378. 19–22; 379. 33–380. 3; 381. 35–6 Wallies). On these issues, see my 'Ancient Comments on *APo.* II. 11: Aristotle and Philoponus on Final Causes in Demonstrations', in F. A. J. De Haas and Mariska E. M. P. J. Leunissen, *Interpreting Aristotle's Posterior Analytics in Late Antiquity and the Byzantine Period* (forthcoming).

    [6] Cf. Barnes, *Posterior*, xvi ('In chapters *B* 11–12 the syllogism is, alas, a positive embarrassment and a bar to understanding'), 228; and Ross, *Revised*, 647.

through the middle term is notorious,[7] because the final cause is not picked out by the middle term, but rather by the major or predicate term.[8] Some scholars have taken up Aristotle's own suggestion that things will become clearer if we 'change the *logoi*' (94$^b$21–2: μεταλαμβάνειν τοὺς λόγους), taking it to mean that we as readers are supposed to rearrange the syllogism so that the middle term picks out the final cause after all.[9] However, it is not an easy undertaking to construct such a syllogism, let alone to do so while remaining close to the Aristotelian original. On the whole, the verdict of interpreters on this chapter has been very negative.[10]

1.2. *The hypothesis: the causality of the explanation and of the explanatory middle term can be different*

The hypothesis that I put forward in order to solve the problem outlined above is a fairly simple one. I submit that it is not the examples that are wrong, but rather our interpretation of what Aristotle means by saying that 'all the *aitiai* are brought out through

---

[7] For the difficulties modern commentators encounter in this section, see Ross, *Revised*, 642; Barnes, *Posterior*, 225, 229; Detel, *Analytica*, 695, 707.

[8] See Barnes, *Posterior*, 229 ff.; Detel, *Analytica*, 707 ff.; and Ross, *Revised*, 642–3. W. Detel, 'Why All Animals Have a Stomach: Demonstration and Axiomatization in Aristotle's *Parts of Animals*' ['Stomach'], in W. Kullmann and S. Föllinger (eds.), *Aristotelische Biologie: Intentionen, Methoden, Ergebnisse* (Stuttgart, 1997), 63–84 at 65–6, expresses the problem most emphatically: 'The syllogistic reconstruction of the first of these [two teleological] examples Aristotle seems to offer in the subsequent passage (94b12–20) turns out to be, at first sight, extremely problematic, though, since he represents the aim of being healthy, not by the middle term, B, but by the major term, A. This is *clearly incompatible* with his general claim, expressed in 94a20–24, that the aim too must be proved through the middle term' (emphasis added).

[9] See in particular Detel, *Analytica*, 684–716, and 'Stomach', 65–7. Most recently, Johnson has argued that 'changing the terms' should be read as entailing that 'health' and 'good digestion' are convertible in this explanation: see M. R. Johnson, *Aristotle on Teleology* (Oxford, 2005), 52–5. This, however, would be possible only if the terms were coextensive, which seems unlikely in this case. R. Bolton, 'The Material Cause: Matter and Explanation in Aristotle's Natural Science' ['Material'], in Kullmann and Föllinger (eds.), *Aristotelische Biologie*, 97–124 at 115, saves the example, but suggests that ultimately what is picked out by the major term (the final cause) is 'in its primitive definition' equal to what is picked out by the middle term (the material cause).

[10] This might explain why the chapter has largely been ignored by some recent studies on the *Posterior Analytics* (e.g. O. Goldin, *Explaining an Eclipse: Aristotle's Posterior Analytics 2. 1–10* (Ann Arbor, 1996), and R. McKirahan, *Principles and Proofs: Aristotle's Theory of Demonstrative Science* (Princeton, 1992)).

the middle term'. What is crucial for the understanding of this chapter is that within an Aristotelian demonstration there can be a difference between the type of causality expressed in the *explanation* of a state of affairs (i.e. the causality expressed by the whole demonstrative syllogism) and the type of causality expressed in the middle term that picks out the *explanans* of this state of affairs. In the case of teleological explanations, I shall even argue for the stronger case that the type of causality expressed by the middle term *must be* different from that expressed in the explanation. The upshot of this distinction for Aristotle's theory of demonstration is that all four types of explanation will be brought out through the middle term (because it is through the middle term that a demonstrative syllogism is construed), but that the middle term itself will not have to refer to the corresponding cause in all four cases.

I shall give an example to illustrate this distinction. Consider the *dia ti* ('Why?') question of what is ice. Aristotle takes this question (as presented in *Post. An.* 2. 12, 95ᵃ16–21) to be about the essence of ice—about what ice *is*. An adequate explanation thus needs to be a formal one. By assuming (the nominal definition) that ice is solidified water Aristotle makes a first move towards such a formal-cause explanation. However, this preliminary answer does not qualify as a demonstration yet, because we do not know why it is that 'solidified' belongs *per se* to 'water', or why there is ice. This is where the explanatory middle term comes in: the middle term picks out the *explanans* of why solidified belongs to water. The explanatory middle term that Aristotle proposes for this particular example is a complete cessation (ἔκλειψις) of heat: ice comes about when there is a complete cessation of heat. The middle term, which picks out the efficient cause[11] of the solidification of water, reveals the essence of ice: ice is solidified water resulting from a complete cessation of heat in water. While the explanation is a formal-cause explanation, the middle term bringing out this explanation picks out an efficient cause.

In sum, Aristotle's claim that 'all the *aitiai* are brought out through the middle term' means under this scheme that all four types of explanations are brought out through the middle term, but

---

[11] I here follow D. Charles, 'Aristotle on Substance, Essence and Biological Kinds' ['Substance'], in L. P. Gerson (ed.), *Aristotle: Critical Assessments* (London and New York, 1999), 227–55 at 233–5, who identifies ἔκλειψις as a process (the suffix -σις indicates a *nomen actionis*) and an efficient cause.

that these demonstrations may proceed through middle terms that pick out causes of a different type.

### 1.3. *The semantic distinction between* hē aitia *and* to aition

Within the context of the *Posterior Analytics* this philosophical distinction is supported by a semantic distinction between the terms *hē aitia* (fem.; pl. *aitiai*) and the term *to aition* (neut.; pl. *aitia*). Frede has argued that the two terms were used differently in the original legal context in which they arose: *to aition*, from the adjective *aitios* 'responsible', designated the agent responsible for a state of affairs, while *hē aitia* designated the accusation.[12] This distinction between *aition* as cause and *aitia* as causal account or explanation seems to be preserved in Plato's *Phaedo*,[13] and perhaps also in Chrysippus[14] and Diocles.[15]

Outside the *Posterior Analytics*, there is little or no evidence that Aristotle also endorsed this distinction,[16] but within the *Posterior Analytics* I believe there is. The semantic distinction is not crucial for the philosophical distinction, but a short sketch of the semantic distinction might help us to obtain a clearer view of the theory Aristotle is setting out in *Post. An.* 2. 11.

First *to aition*: usually, *to aition* is characterized as a condition for knowledge.[17] More specifically, in 'demonstrations of the reason why' the middle term must always refer to an *aition*.[18] This is

---

[12] M. Frede, 'The Original Notion of Cause' ['Cause'], in M. Schofield, M. Burnyeat, and J. Barnes (eds.), *Doubt and Dogmatism* (Oxford, 1980), 217–49 at 222–3.

[13] Frede, 'Cause', 223; J. G. Lennox, *Aristotle's Philosophy of Biology: Studies in the Origin of Life Science* [*Biology*] (Cambridge, 2001), 282–3; D. Sedley, 'Platonic Causes', *Phronesis*, 43 (1998), 114–32 at 115 and 115 n. 1.

[14] Frede, 'Cause', 222.          [15] Diocles, fr. 176 van der Eijk.

[16] In other treatises the distinction may be preserved only in 'technical discussions' of demonstrations such as *DA* 2. 2, 413ᵃ11–21; this, however, requires further research. Interpreters of the *Posterior Analytics* usually take the terms to be semantically equivalent, and translate them more or less randomly as cause, reason, or explanation. See e.g. Barnes, *Posterior*, 89–90: 'I . . . resolved to adhere to a single translation for all occurrences of the word [i.e. *aitia* and its cognates]; and I opted for "explanation".'

[17] Knowing why is to know *by means of* to aition (75ᵃ35); this knowledge proceeds *from aitia* (76ᵃ19–20) that are primitive (78ᵃ25–6). See also 93ᵃ4–8, ᵇ19, 21–6; 95ᵃ10–12, 22–5, ᵇ14.

[18] The middle term in demonstrations of the reason why always picks out the *aition* that is immediate and primitive (89ᵇ15; 90ᵃ7–9; 93ᵃ4–8; 95ᵃ10–12, 17; *passim* in 98ᵇ17–99ᵇ13). If the deduction does *not* proceed through the *aition* but through

what Aristotle points out at the end of the following passage (*Post. An.* 2. 2, 89ᵇ37–90ᵃ9):

ζητοῦμεν δέ, ὅταν μὲν ζητῶμεν τὸ ὅτι ἢ τὸ εἰ ἔστιν ἁπλῶς, ἆρ᾿ ἔστι μέσον αὐτοῦ ἢ οὐκ ἔστιν· ὅταν δὲ γνόντες ἢ τὸ ὅτι ἢ εἰ ἔστιν, ἢ τὸ ἐπὶ μέρους ἢ τὸ ἁπλῶς, πάλιν τὸ διὰ τί ζητῶμεν ἢ τὸ τί ἐστι, τότε ζητοῦμεν τί τὸ μέσον. . . . συμβαίνει ἄρα ἐν ἁπάσαις ταῖς ζητήσεσι ζητεῖν ἢ εἰ ἔστι μέσον ἢ τί ἐστι τὸ μέσον. τὸ μὲν γὰρ αἴτιον τὸ μέσον, ἐν ἅπασι δὲ τοῦτο ζητεῖται.

When we seek the fact or if something is without qualification, we are seeking whether or not there is a middle term for it. And when, having come to know either the fact or if it is—either partially or without qualification—we again seek the reason why or what it is, we are then seeking what the middle term is. . . . Thus it results that in all our searches we seek either whether there is a middle term or what the middle term is. For the middle term is the *aition*, and in all cases it is this which is being sought.

The middle term must pick out whatever is responsible for the connection between the two terms it mediates. In this way, the middle term clarifies the causal relation between the two terms by providing the real cause (and not merely the epistemic reason) of why the one extreme term holds of the other. I therefore translate the noun *to aition* as cause.[19]

The term *hē aitia* is used less frequently in the *Posterior Analytics*, and is usually part of the definition of scientific knowledge. Scientific knowledge is always knowledge of *hai aitiai*.[20] For instance, in *Post. An.* 1. 2, 71ᵇ20–33, Aristotle first picks up on his definition of scientific knowledge as being knowledge of *hē aitia* of something, and then continues by stating that this knowledge can be reached through things that are, among other things, *aitios* of the conclusion:

εἰ τοίνυν ἐστὶ τὸ ἐπίστασθαι οἷον ἔθεμεν, ἀνάγκη καὶ τὴν ἀποδεικτικὴν ἐπιστήμην ἐξ ἀληθῶν τ᾿ εἶναι καὶ πρώτων καὶ ἀμέσων καὶ γνωριμωτέρων καὶ προτέρων καὶ αἰτίων τοῦ συμπεράσματος· . . . αἴτιά τε καὶ γνωριμώτερα δεῖ εἶναι καὶ πρότερα, αἴτια μὲν ὅτι τότε ἐπιστάμεθα ὅταν τὴν αἰτίαν εἰδῶμεν.

If, then, to have [scientific] knowledge of something is what we have posited it to be, then demonstrative knowledge in particular must proceed from [items which are] true and primitive and immediate and more familiar

the more familiar of the (non-explanatory) converting terms, that is, when the middle term does not pick out the relevant cause, then the demonstration that follows is not a demonstration of the reason why, but of the fact (78ᵃ27–9, ᵇ4, 12, 15, 24; 79ᵃ4).

[19] See e.g. 78ᵇ17; 85ᵇ22; 94ᵇ8, 18; 95ᵇ20, 28; 98ᵃ35–ᵇ3; *passim* in 98ᵇ17–99ᵇ13.
[20] See 71ᵇ9–13, 30–1; 87ᵇ40; 94ᵃ21–4.

than and prior to and *aitios* of the conclusions. . . . They [the items that are constitutive of demonstrative understanding] must be *aitios* and more familiar and prior—*aitios* because we understand something only when we have knowledge of *hē aitia* . . .

Other passages (especially 78$^b$28–31) indicate that Aristotle conceives of these *aitiai* as being larger linguistic or syllogistic formulae that state the reason why in answer to the question 'why' (*to dioti* or *to dia ti*).[21] At least within the *Posterior Analytics* it is thus implied that *hē aitia* itself is a kind of *syllogismos* containing an explanatory middle term, where *to aition* is a subordinated element of *hē aitia*.[22] I therefore translate *hē aitia* with such terms as 'causal account' or 'explanation', and the adjective *aitios* as either 'causative' or 'explanatory' depending on the context.

Assuming that this semantic distinction between *aition* and *hē aitia* illustrates a philosophical distinction between the type of causality that is revealed through the middle term and the type of causality picked out by the middle term, I shall now present a new reading of *Post. An.* 2. 11.

## 2. Towards a new reading of *Posterior Analytics* 2. 11

### 2.1. *Making sense of the opening statement and the examples in* Post. An. 2. 11

In his opening statement of the chapter, Aristotle first recapitulates his definition of scientific knowledge. That is, we know something when we know its explanation, which is the syllogistic formula stating the *aition* of the state of affairs to be explained. He then specifies four kinds of explanation, which are formulated as four different questions as to the reason why (formal explanation is an explanation of *what* it is to be a thing; material explanation is an explanation

---

[21] These are explanations of the reason why, picking out *to aition* through the middle term (cf. 78$^b$12–34; 85$^b$23–7, 35–6). In 93$^b$33 *hē aitia* indicates a non-syllogistic causal account.

[22] One might object that in 85$^b$24–7 Aristotle uses the expressions 'of the *aitia* and of the *dia ti*' and 'of the *aition* and of the *dia ti*' interchangably. However, the first expression applies to the nature of the demonstrative syllogism (what is demonstrated is the explanation and the reason why), while the second applies to the nature of the universal premiss, which is more explanatory in the sense that it shows the *aition* more clearly (cf. 88$^a$5–6).

of *given what* things being the case it is necessary for that to hold; efficient explanation is an explanation of *what* initiated the movement; and teleological explanation is an explanation of the for the sake of *what*). As the 'since' (ἐπεὶ δέ) indicates, this should all be common knowledge.

The new information is that all of these explanations are brought out through the middle term. This is the process of demonstration: the explanations of the reason why are demonstrated through middle terms that explain why the predicate holds of the subject in the conclusion. The middle term thus reveals a causal connection underlying the *per se* relation between these two terms.[23] The point is that it is only by setting out the whole syllogism and thereby expressing explicitly the cause of why the predicate holds of the subject term that we come to reach true understanding of a phenomenon.

Aristotle then works out three examples of explanations (material, efficient, and final) that are brought out through the middle term. He gives no separate example of formal explanation, supposedly because that 'has already been proven' (*Post. An.* 2. 11, 94ª35–6) in earlier chapters.[24] For the sake of completeness, I shall supply a formal-cause explanation from an earlier chapter in my discussion below.

My reconstruction of the four examples and their formalizations into syllogisms is as follows:

**Example 1. Material explanation** (*Post. An.* 2. 11, 94ª27–35; cf. Eucl. *El.* 3. 31)

*Explanandum*:

  (i) [Why [*dia ti*] is there a right angle?]               [Why A?]
  (ii) Why [*dia ti*] is the angle in a semicircle a right angle?   [Why A of C?]

A = right
B = half of two rights (*aition* = *material cause*)
C = angle in a semicircle

AaC because of B: right holds of the angle in a semicircle because of being half of two rights.

---

[23] In 73ª10–17 Aristotle explicates the *per se* relation in terms of causation, i.e. as something holding because of itself (δι᾽ αὐτό).

[24] I take Aristotle to refer to chapter 2. 8, which is part of his larger investigation into the relation of definition and causal explanations in chapters 2. 8–10.

**Example 2. Formal explanation** (*Post. An.* 2. 8, 93$^{b}$8–13; 2. 11, 94$^{b}$ 34–6)

*Explanandum*:

  (i)  What is thunder?                                 [What is A?]

  (ii)  Why [*dia ti*] is there noise in the clouds?     [Why A of C?]

A = thunder (a sort of noise)

B = extinction of fire (*aition* = *efficient cause*)

C = cloud

AaC because of B: thunder is noise in the clouds because of fire being extinguished.

**Example 3. Efficient explanation** (*Post. An.* 2. 11, 94$^{a}$36–$^{b}$8)

*Explanandum*:

  (i)  [Why [*dia ti*] is there a Persian war?]        [Why A?]

  (ii)  Why [*dia ti*] did the Persian war come upon

       the Athenians?                             [Why A of C?]

A = war

B = being the first to attack (*aition* = *efficient cause*)

C = Athenians

AaC because of B: being warred upon holds of the Athenians because of being the first to attack.

**Example 4. Teleological explanation** (*Post. An.* 2. 11, 94$^{b}$8–26)

*Explanandum*

  (i)  Why [*dia ti*] does he walk?               [Why C?]

A = being healthy

B = food not floating (*aition* = *material cause*)

C = walking after dinner

AaC because of B: being healthy holds of walking after dinner because of the food not floating.

Before turning to an analysis of these examples, let me state from the outset that contrary to the traditional interpretation I see no decisive indications in the text as to why Aristotle should be concerned only with syllogisms in the Barbara mood. I submit that the introduction of the four types of explanation in *Post. An.* 2. 11 rather shows that he is concerned with laying out a general syllogistic structure into which *every* causal relation can be fitted. If we read the chapter in this way, the contingency and singularity of the examples noted by critics of Aristotle need no longer constitute a lingering problem. They can be accounted for within the larger framework of causal relations that Aristotle is interested in, and so can the other examples he mentions in the remainder of the chapter (*Post. An.* 2. 11, 94$^b$27–34).[25]

## 2.2. *The example of material explanation*

The first example of material explanation is developed in the context of a discussion of the necessary nature of demonstrative syllogisms (*Post. An.* 2. 11, 94$^a$24–7).[26] The example can be analysed as follows (for the proof see Figure 1). The *dia ti* question Aristotle poses is 'Because of what is the angle in a semicircle a right angle?' An adequate explanation should thus state the geometrical proof showing 'that out of which' it follows that the angle in a semicircle is right. This example of material explanation is in fact reflected in a theorem from Euclid (*El.* 3. 31), and the proof might be as well.

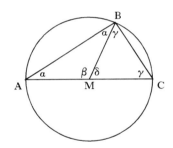

Demonstration: $\angle ABC = 90°$

$\angle MAB = \angle MBA$ ($a$)
$\angle MCB = \angle MBC$ ($\gamma$)

(i) $\beta + \delta = 180°$.
(ii) $2a + \beta = 180°$; $2\gamma + \delta = 180°$.
(iii) $2(a + \gamma) + \beta + \delta = 360°$.
(iv) $2(a + \gamma) = 180°$.
(v) $a + \gamma$ ('the angle in a semicircle') = $180°$ ('two rights') divided by 2 ('half') = $90°$ ('right').

F I G. 1. Material explanation

Here Aristotle introduces the search for the middle term by rephrasing the question explicitly in terms of material necessity: 'Given what being the case is it a right angle?' What we are looking for is a condition that necessitates the rightness of the angle in a semicircle—a condition, incidentally, that will be immediately

[25] These latter examples are rather more fanciful than serious, such as the Pythagorean belief that it thunders in order to frighten the inhabitants of Tartarus, or else they report scientific views that Aristotle rejects elsewhere, such as the explanation of thunder as being the extinction of fire in the clouds (this explanation is explicitly rejected at *Meteor.* 2. 9, 369$^b$12–24).

[26] Here Aristotle states that, given a middle term shared by two propositions, it is necessary for the conclusion of the syllogism to hold. The middle term, or the two premisses taken as one, literally bring about the conclusion, and are therefore in a sense the material causes of the conclusion (cf. *Phys.* 2. 3, 195$^a$18–19).

evident once the right mathematical figure has been discovered (cf. *Metaph.* Θ 9, 1051ᵃ21–9). Aristotle then formalizes the explanation, while introducing 'half of two rights' as the middle term (B) that explains why 'right' (A) holds of 'angle in a semicircle' (C).

The rationale Aristotle offers in this section is somewhat obscure, but is not too problematic once we presuppose the familiarity of Aristotle's readership with the relevant mathematical figure and the proof of the proposition as we know it from Euclidean geometry (Aristotle hints at both of them in the above-mentioned passage in *Metaph.* Θ 9). Important in this proof is that the geometrical relations between 'right angle' and 'angle in a semicircle' are discovered by *division*.²⁷ It is this division that Aristotle refers to when claiming that '[the term B] is equal to A, and C to B, because it [C] is of two rights—half.'²⁸ It is this 'being half' that necessitates the angle in a semicircle being a right angle. In sum, the angle in a semicircle is a right angle because it is half of two rights; 'being half of two rights' is the material cause of 'right' holding of 'the angle in a semicircle.' The angle in a semicircle is by necessity a right angle *given that it is two rights—divided in half*.

In this case, both the causation expressed by the explanation and the explanatory middle term that brings out this explanation are of the material type.

### 2.3. *The example of formal explanation*

The second example of formal explanation (taken from *Post. An.* 2. 8, 93ᵇ8–13) can be analysed as follows. The *dia ti* question Aristotle poses is why there is thunder. This is a reformulation of the question 'What is thunder?', which is a request for the definition of thunder (Aristotle answers the 'what is' question by stating that it is the extinction of fire in cloud, which is not a demonstration of the essence of thunder yet). For Aristotle, the question why there is thunder is equivalent to the question what thunder is, except that the first is a request for a demonstration and the latter for a definition (cf. *Post. An.* 2. 10, 94ᵃ1–8). An adequate explanation of why there is thun-

---

²⁷ Cf. *Metaph.* Θ 9, 1051ᵃ22–3: 'Mathematical figures, too, are discovered by actualization; for they find them by dividing [the figures] [διαιροῦντες].'
²⁸ Note the word order in the Greek: while B is defined as ½-2R (94ᵃ29: ἡμίσεια δυοῖν ὀρθαῖν; 94ᵃ32–3: ὄντος ἡμίσεος δύο ὀρθῶν), C is explained as 2R—½ (94ᵃ32: δύο γὰρ ὀρθῶν ἡμίσεια).

der thus needs to be a formal explanation expressing the essence of thunder through a middle term that brings out this essence.

However, as Aristotle indicates in another text where he discusses the same example (*Metaph. Z* 17, 1041ᵃ24–32),²⁹ the only way to get a demonstration is by converting the *explanandum* into a predicative relation.³⁰ This can be done, first, by taking the nominal definition of thunder (as being 'a sort of noise in the cloud': *Post. An.* 2. 8, 93ᵃ22–3). Secondly, one can do this by turning the request for a definition into a *dia ti* request for a demonstration, in which the object of enquiry is 'a something of something else' (i.e. why is there thunder in the clouds). Because the explanation in this case is already known (i.e. thunder comes about through the extinction of fire in the cloud), Aristotle sets out immediately to formalize the example: the subject term (C) is 'cloud'; the middle term (B) is 'extinction of fire'; and the predicate term (A) is 'thunder'. Now, B holds of C, because the extinction of fire takes place *in* the cloud (the cloud is the locus in which the phenomenon typically resides), and A—'thunder' (i.e. a sort of noise)—holds of B, because B is a definition of A.

In this case, the explanatory middle term picks out an efficient cause of why there is thunder or noise in the clouds: the origin of motion of the noise lies in the extinction of fire. It is through this efficient cause that the essence of thunder and thereby the formal explanation of why there is thunder are revealed: thunder is noise in the clouds caused by fire being extinguished.³¹

2.4. *The example of efficient explanation*

The third example of efficient explanation (*Post. An.* 2. 11, 94ᵃ36–ᵇ8) is fairly straightforward. Here Aristotle picks a historical example in asking why it is that the Persian war came upon the Athenians, rephrased as what the explanation is for the Athenians being warred upon. It is not clear from the outset which type of explanation will be demonstrated; a similar example at *Phys.* 2. 7, 198ᵃ18–19, shows that this question has different answers.

²⁹ For the thunder examples in the *Posterior Analytics* and *Metaphysics*, see Charles 'Substance', 233–5, 238–9.
³⁰ J. G. Lennox, 'Getting a Science Going: Aristotle on Entry Level Kinds', in G. Wolters (ed.), *Homo Sapiens und Homo Faber: Festschrift Mittelstrass* (Berlin, 2004), 87–100 at 90 n. 2.
³¹ Charles, 'Substance', 239; J. G. Lennox, 'Aristotle on the Unity and Disunity of Science', *International Studies in the Philosophy of Science*, 15 (2001), 133–44 at 141.

However, the short explanation Aristotle offers first ('because the Athenians attacked Sardis with the Eretrians') shows that he is looking for some state of affairs that initiated the movement, which is an efficient cause (and not for that for the sake of which, such as the desire of the Persians to gain an empire). Aristotle then formalizes the example in the following way: 'War, A; being the first to attack, B; Athenians C.' It is significant that Aristotle here adds the notion of 'first' to the attack: it is being the *first* to do wrong that is explanatory for being wronged, and this is the origin of motion.

In this case, the middle term picks out the efficient cause of why war came upon the Athenians: for 'people make war on those who first began', which is why being warred upon holds of those who first began. The Athenians were the ones who first began (they fall under this formal description), and this explains the origin of the Persian war.[32]

### 2.5. *The example of teleological explanation*

Aristotle introduces the section on teleological explanation (*Post. An.* 2. 11, 94ᵇ8–26) with a somewhat puzzling clause: ὅσων δ᾿ αἴτιον τὸ ἕνεκά τινος. From what follows it is clear that the explanations that are at stake are teleological ones: Aristotle gives two parallel examples ('For what reason does he walk? In order to be healthy. For what reason is there a house? In order to protect possessions'), and identifies the final cause or the purpose in each example ('In the one case it is in order to be healthy, in the other in order to protect'). He also explains that in these cases there is no difference between a 'because of what' question and a 'for the sake of what' question. However, it is not immediately clear whether or not Aristotle means that the final cause has to be picked out by the middle term.

The introductory clause (*Post. An.* 2. 11, 94ᵇ8) has often been read as implying just that (i.e. that in these cases the cause is that for the sake of which),[33] but it does not have to be read in this way. The Greek has τὸ ἕνεκά τινος, which means something different from τὸ

---

[32] Note that in all three examples the primary *explanandum* is the occurrence of a certain phenomenon (i.e. 'rightness', 'thunder', and 'war') that can be expressed in a predicative relation with a subject in which the phenomenon typically and for the most part inheres (i.e. 'angle in a semicircle', 'cloud', and 'Athenians'). In the demonstration that follows what is revealed is that there is always some aspect of this subject that explains the holding of its attributes.

[33] See e.g. H. G. Apostle, *Aristotle's* Posterior Analytics: *Translated with Commentaries and Glossary* (Grinnell, 1981), 59: 'Lastly, there is a final cause [or, that

οὗ ἕνεκα. The latter is the more common expression and is used more or less as a stock phrase designating the end (literally, 'that for the sake of which', in which οὗ is a relative pronoun).[34] τὸ ἕνεκά τινος/του designates rather the teleological relation of something being for the sake of something else (literally, 'that which is for the sake of something', where τινος is an indefinite pronoun). In this expression, the τό is not used as a definite article to substantivize the prepositional phrase, but to identify whatever is for the sake of something, or the relation as such.[35]

Under this interpretation, the point Aristotle makes here is not that the explanatory middle term in this case is the final cause, but that the causal relation involved is teleological, and that the middle term must pick out something that explains how something is for the sake of something. The teleological explanation is brought out through a middle term that need not itself be a final cause, but that rather shows how an end can hold of something. This causal relation is then illustrated by the two examples: walking is for the sake of health, and a house is for the sake of protection. The middle term that we are looking for needs to pick out a state of affairs that shows why this teleological relation between walking and being healthy obtains.

In a simplified version of the demonstrative syllogism, the predicate term (A) is being healthy, the middle term (B) is the food not floating, and the subject term (C) is walking after dinner. In this case, the middle term picks out the material cause of why being healthy holds of walking after dinner, because it identifies the physiological condition that is healthy—a condition that itself is initiated by walking that brings about health as an efficient cause.[36] For the identification of 'the food not floating' as a material cause, compare Aristotle's qualification of the boiling of the blood surrounding the heart as a material cause of anger at *DA* 1. 1, 403ᵃ25–ᵇ1.

for the sake of which]'; Barnes, *Posterior*, 60: 'suppose it is the purpose which is explanatory'.

[34] Cf. *Phys.* 2. 2, 194ᵃ27–30: 'Further, that for the sake of which [τὸ οὗ ἕνεκα], or the end, as well as whatever is for the sake of these [ὅσα τούτων ἕνεκα], belongs to the same study. But nature is an end and a that for the sake of which [οὗ ἕνεκα].' *De caelo* 2. 12, 292ᵇ6–7: 'For action always consists in two factors, when there is that for the sake of which [οὗ ἕνεκα] and that which is for the sake of something [τὸ τούτου ἕνεκα].'

[35] Cf. *Phys.* 196ᵇ17, 20–2; *DA* 434ᵃ32; *GA* 715ᵃ4, 778ᵇ13; *MA* 700ᵇ26–7; *Metaph.* 1065ᵃ31.

[36] As Bolton, 'Material', 113–15, suggested.

In all four examples the different explanations that are at stake are revealed through the middle term, which picks out a cause for the holding by the predicate term of the subject term. However, in my analysis of the example of teleological explanation I have left two important questions unanswered. First, if Aristotle did not intend the final cause to be picked out by the middle term, what does he mean by 'changing the *logoi*'? Secondly, one might wonder what it is about this example—or about teleological explanations in general—that makes it so hard to rewrite the demonstrations in such a way that the final cause is actually picked out by the middle term. The following sections address these questions.

### 3. Teleological explanations and what it means to 'change the *logoi*'

#### 3.1. *Why walking is for the sake of health*

The argument of the section on final causes is fairly long compared with the illustration of the other types of explanation, and it proceeds in a quite complicated way. Here I shall first separate the different steps in the argument and give a detailed interpretation of each; next, I shall propose two possible interpretations of 'changing the *logoi*'. Let me start by introducing the way Aristotle originally formulates the terms of the explanation (Table 1). For the sake of clarity, I also add the alternative formulations of the terms that Aristotle uses during the argument (Table 2).[37]

The argument itself proceeds in roughly the following four steps. First Aristotle asks us to suppose that to make the food not floating ($B_2$) holds of C, walking after dinner, and that this is healthy ($A_2$). Note that he changes the formulations of the terms A and B, presumably to show that walking (which is an activity) holds of another activity that produces the condition of the non-floating of food. It is this latter activity that Aristotle calls healthy, for healthy is just that which produces (or is useful to) the condition of being healthy. This is in fact the way Aristotle characterizes 'healthy' in the *Eudemian Ethics* (*EE* 1. 8, $1218^b16$–22):

---

[37] I shall retain the numbering in my discussion of the example of teleological explanation; where it is not clear which formulation Aristotle has in mind, the term is not numbered.

5

TABLE 1. *The original formulations of the terms*

| | | | | |
|---|---|---|---|---|
| A₁ | Being healthy | τὸ ὑγιαίνειν | Condition | Final cause |
| B₁ | The food not floating | τὸ μὴ ἐπιπολάζειν τὰ σίτια | Condition | *Aition* |
| C | Walking after dinner | περίπατος ἀπὸ δείπνου | Activity | *Explanandum* |

TABLE 2. *The alternative formulations of the terms*

| | | | |
|---|---|---|---|
| A₂ | Healthy | ὑγιεινός | Productive of condition |
| B₂ | To make the food not floating | τὸ ποιεῖν μὴ ἐπιπολάζειν τὰ σίτια | Activity productive of condition |

ὅτι δ᾽ αἴτιον τὸ τέλος τοῖς ὑφ᾽ αὑτό, δηλοῖ ἡ διδασκαλία. ὁρισάμενοι γὰρ τὸ τέλος τἆλλα δεικνύουσιν, ὅτι ἕκαστον αὐτῶν ἀγαθόν· αἴτιον γὰρ τὸ οὗ ἕνεκα. οἷον ἐπειδὴ τὸ ὑγιαίνειν τοδί, ἀνάγκη τόδε εἶναι τὸ συμφέρον πρὸς αὐτήν· τὸ δ᾽ ὑγιεινὸν τῆς ὑγιείας αἴτιον ὡς κινῆσαν, καὶ τότε τοῦ εἶναι ἀλλ᾽ οὐ τοῦ ἀγαθὸν εἶναι τὴν ὑγίειαν.

And that the end stands in a causal relation to the means subordinate to it is shown by teaching. For, having defined the end they show, regarding other things, that each of them is a good, because that for the sake of which is explanatory. For example, since 'being healthy' is such-and-such a thing, then necessarily this other thing will be what is useful for it. And *what is healthy will be the efficient cause of health*, though only the cause of its being, but not of health being a good.

By characterizing walking as an activity that is productive of the food not floating, and the latter as being productive of health, Aristotle implies that C is an efficient cause of A₁, being healthy: walking is productive of a healthy condition (cf. *Rhet.* 1. 6, 1362ᵃ31–4). Walking and health are thus causes of each other: while walking is the efficient cause of health, health is the final cause of walking (cf. *Phys.* 2. 3, 195ᵃ8–11). Now, if walking is a health-producing activity, it remains for the teleological demonstration to exhibit why it is that walking effects a change that is directed towards health. Accordingly, Aristotle continues the argument (and this is step 2) by explaining that it is thought that B₁, the material condition where the food is not floating on the surface, holds of C, walking, and healthy (A₂) holds of B (B₁). This opinion points towards the explanatory role of B₁.

Indeed, Aristotle now (thirdly) poses the question what the *aition* is that causally connects C, walking, and A, the 'that for the sake of which'.[38] The answer is $B_1$, the not floating. Aristotle adds that 'this is like a definition of that' (*Post. An.* 2. 11, 94$^b$19–20). Probably the first 'this' refers to $B_1$, the not floating, while 'that' refers to $A_1$, being healthy, 'for', Aristotle explains, 'in that way the A will be explained'. The not floating of the food is like a definition of being healthy in the sense that it shows how being healthy in this context (i.e. in the context of a person who has just had dinner) is to be understood. Part of what it means to be healthy in this case is to be in a condition where the food is not floating on the surface of the stomach.[39]

Finally, Aristotle turns to an account of the minor premiss: 'For what reason does B hold of C?' He answers that the reason is 'because that is what being healthy is: to be in such a condition.' The formulation of this response suggests that we have touched upon a premiss that is not further analysable but is immediately evident (that is, the premiss is immediate). At this point Aristotle ends his discussion of this particular example of teleological explanation.

### 3.2. *Two possible interpretations of 'changing the* logoi *'*

The section is completed by the enigmatic statement (Barnes called it the 'Delphic injunction')[40] that one needs to 'change the *logoi*' (μεταλαμβάνειν τοὺς λόγους), and that 'in that way each of them will become clearer' (*Post. An.* 2. 11, 94$^b$21–2). The traditional interpretation reads this sentence in an apologetic way: Aristotle realizes that his example of the final cause is ill-chosen and messy, and that by mistake the middle term does not pick out the final cause. In order to make sense of this example, we should therefore (stipulate that the terms are coextensive and) rearrange the order of the terms or of the premisses in such a way that the middle term will pick out health as the final cause. However, I see two problems with this reading that strongly suggest that we should look for a different interpretation.

First, Aristotle spends quite some time expounding the example of teleological explanation, and it seems not very charitable to assume that this is not the example he actually would have liked to

---

[38] The apposition 'the for the sake of which' at *Post. An.* 2. 11, 94$^b$18, belongs to A, not to the *aition*.

[39] Other definitions of health are having one's body in a uniform state (*Metaph.* Z 7, 1032$^b$6–8), or having fasted for a while (*Phys.* 194$^b$36).

[40] Barnes, *Posterior*, 229.

present to his readers. In fact, the explanation that walking is for the sake of health is a stock example in the Aristotelian corpus, and the rationale Aristotle provides for health holding of walking in this chapter is perhaps not entirely transparent, but very much in line with other accounts of the example. If my interpretation holds, then we might say that Aristotle succeeds quite well in demonstrating how the middle term, i.e. the food not floating, exhibits the teleological relation between walking and health. There is thus no need to rearrange the example.

Secondly, Aristotle uses the verb μεταλαμβάνειν as a technical term in the *Prior Analytics* and *Topics*, where it means without exception 'to substitute for'.[41] This suggests that we should expect μεταλαμβάνειν τοὺς λόγους to mean something like 'substituting the *logoi* (for something else)'. In fact, the use of μεταλαμβάνειν as some kind of technical procedure of substitution in these texts presents two options for how to interpret the expression in the context of the *Posterior Analytics*, neither of which implies a rearrangement of the example.

One possible interpretation[42] is that the substitution concerns the formulations (*logoi*) of the terms. This reading is based on Aristotle's use of μεταλαμβάνειν in chapter 34 of the first book of the *Prior Analytics* (*Pr. An.* 1. 34, 48ᵃ1–27):

πολλάκις δὲ διαψεύδεσθαι συμπεσεῖται παρὰ τὸ μὴ καλῶς ἐκτίθεσθαι τοὺς κατὰ τὴν πρότασιν ὅρους. . . . τούτου δ' αἴτιον τὸ μὴ καλῶς ἐκκεῖσθαι τοὺς ὅρους κατὰ τὴν λέξιν, ἐπεὶ μεταληφθέντων τῶν κατὰ τὰς ἕξεις οὐκ ἔσται συλλογισμός, οἷον ἀντὶ μὲν τῆς ὑγιείας εἰ τεθείη τὸ ὑγιαῖνον, ἀντὶ δὲ τῆς νόσου τὸ νοσοῦν. οὐ γὰρ ἀληθὲς εἰπεῖν ὡς οὐκ ἐνδέχεται τῷ νοσοῦντι τὸ ὑγιαίνειν ὑπάρξαι. τούτου δὲ μὴ ληφθέντος οὐ γίνεται συλλογισμός, εἰ μὴ τοῦ ἐνδέχεσθαι· τοῦτο δ' οὐκ ἀδύνατον· ἐνδέχεται γὰρ μηδενὶ ἀνθρώπῳ ὑπάρχειν ὑγίειαν. . . . φανερὸν οὖν ὅτι ἐν ἅπασι τούτοις ἡ ἀπάτη γίνεται παρὰ τὴν τῶν ὅρων ἔκθεσιν· μεταληφθέντων γὰρ τῶν κατὰ τὰς ἕξεις οὐδὲν γίνεται ψεῦδος. δῆλον οὖν ὅτι κατὰ τὰς τοιαύτας προτάσεις ἀεὶ τὸ κατὰ τὴν ἕξιν ἀντὶ τῆς ἕξεως μεταληπτέον καὶ θετέον ὅρον.

Mistakes frequently will happen because the terms in the premiss have not been well set out. . . . The reason for this is that the terms are not set out well

---

[41] R. Smith (trans. and comm.), *Aristotle: Prior Analytics* (Indianapolis, 1989), 137, 261. See *Pr. An.* 1. 17, 37ᵇ15; 1. 20, 39ᵃ27; 1. 22, 40ᵃ34–5; 1. 23, 41ᵃ39; 1. 29, 45ᵇ12–20; 1. 34, 48ᵃ1–27; 1. 38, 49ᵇ1–2; 1. 39, 49ᵇ3–6; 2. 4, 56ᵇ7–8; 2. 8, 59ᵇ1–11; *Top.* 2. 2, 110ᵃ4–9; 5. 2, 130ᵃ29–ᵇ10; 6. 4, 142ᵇ3; 6. 9, 147ᵇ12–14; 6. 11, 148ᵇ24–149ᵃ7 (*passim*).

[42] Already suggested by W. W. Fortenbaugh, '*Nicomachean Ethics* I, 1096b26–29', *Phronesis*, 11 (1966), 185–94 at 192.

with regard to formulation, since if the terms for being in the conditions are substituted [for the terms for the conditions themselves], there will not be a deduction; for example, if instead of 'health' 'healthy' is posited, and instead of 'disease' 'diseased'. For it is not true to say that being healthy cannot hold of someone diseased. But if this is not assumed, there is no deduction, except in respect of possibility: and that is not impossible. For it is possible that health holds of no man. . . . It is evident, then, that in all these cases the fallacy results from the setting out of the terms; for if the terms for being in the conditions are substituted, there is no fallacy. Thus, it is clear that in such premisses the term for being in the condition always needs to be substituted and posited instead of that of the condition itself.

In this passage Aristotle deals with fallacies that occur when the terms of the syllogisms have not been set out well with regard to formulation (48ᵃ9: κατὰ τὴν λέξιν).[43] The problem is solved by substituting terms 'for being in the conditions', i.e. adjectives such as 'healthy' (ὑγιαῖνον) and 'diseased', instead of the terms for the conditions themselves, i.e. nouns such as 'health' (ὑγίεια) and 'disease'. We might postulate that a similar kind of substitution of the formulation of the terms has taken place in *Post. An.* 2. 11: the terms indicating the conditions are replaced by terms indicating what is in the condition, or rather, by terms indicating what is productive of the condition. We have seen that Aristotle substituted 'healthy' (A₂) for 'being healthy' (A₁), and 'to make the food not floating' (B₂) for 'the food not floating' (B₁). Through these substitutions A and B could be predicated of C (a term indicating an activity), and furthermore the causal relations (in this case, both material causal and efficient causal ones) between the three terms would become more evident.

Another possible interpretation[44] is that the substitution concerns the replacement of words by their definitions. This is the stock use of the expression in the context of the *Topics*, and accordingly, we should supply ἀντὶ τῶν ὀνομάτων in the passage in *Post. An.* 2. 11. One context in which the expression 'to substitute the definitions for the words' is used in the *Topics* is that of the fallacy of repeating the word that is being defined or predicated in the definition or predication. The failure pertains to not having used the prior or better-known term in the definition or predication. The procedure

---

[43] For parallels for this method of μετάληψις in the ancient grammatical tradition, see I. Sluiter, *Ancient Grammar in Context: Contributions to the Study of Ancient Linguistic Thought* (Amsterdam, 1990), 111 ff.

[44] Suggested by Pieter Sjoerd Hasper in personal correspondence.

of substituting definitions for words is one of the recommended ways to detect the fallacy (*Top.* 6. 9, 147ᵇ12–14; 6. 4, 142ᵃ34–ᵇ6):

ἄλλος, εἰ αὑτῷ κέχρηται τῷ ὁριζομένῳ. λανθάνει δ' ὅταν μὴ αὑτῷ τῷ τοῦ ὁρι-
ζομένου ὀνόματι χρήσηται, οἷον εἰ τὸν ἥλιον ἄστρον ἡμεροφανὲς ὡρίσατο· ὁ γὰρ
ἡμέρᾳ χρώμενος ἡλίῳ χρῆται. δεῖ δ', ὅπως φωραθῇ τὰ τοιαῦτα, μεταλαμβάνειν
ἀντὶ τοῦ ὀνόματος τὸν λόγον, οἷον ὅτι ἡμέρα ἡλίου φορὰ ὑπὲρ γῆς ἐστιν.

Another [failure] is, if one has used the term defined itself. This passes unnoticed when the actual name of the object being defined is not used, e.g. supposing anyone had defined the sun as a star that appears by day. For in bringing in day he brings in the sun. To detect errors of this sort, substitute the definition for the word, e.g. the definition of day as the passage of the sun above the earth.

The expression is also used in the context of examining the correctness of definitions rendered of a complex term. For the definition to be correct, the words of the complex term have to be replaced by the definitions of the words (*Top.* 6. 11, 149ᵃ1–3). The substitution of definitions of words used in definitions also helps to clear up whether or not the predications hold non-accidentally (*Top.* 2. 2, 110ᵃ4–9):

λαμβάνειν δὲ καὶ ἀντὶ τῶν ἐν τοῖς λόγοις ὀνομάτων λόγους, καὶ μὴ προαφίστασθαι
ἕως ἂν εἴς τι γνώριμον ἔλθῃ· πολλάκις γὰρ ὅλου μὲν τοῦ λόγου ἀποδοθέντος οὔπω
δῆλον τὸ ζητούμενον, ἀντὶ δέ τινος τῶν ἐν τῷ λόγῳ ὀνομάτων λόγου ῥηθέντος
κατάδηλον γίνεται.

One should substitute definitions also for the words contained in the definitions, and not stop until one comes to something familiar; for often when the definition is given as a whole, the thing looked for is not cleared up, whereas if for one of the words used in the definition a definition be stated, it becomes obvious.

Under this interpretation, we need to replace the words set out in the syllogism—such as 'walking' or 'being healthy'—by their definitions (perhaps just as Aristotle did himself), until we find the more familiar terms, [45] and in that way the predications will become clearer. A striking parallel is provided by Galen, who—plainly fol-

---

[45] This type of substitution might be connected to the one Charles observes in the *Posterior Analytics* concerning the example of thunder: the predicative term 'thunder' is replaced by its nominal definition 'noise in the clouds', which both gives us more familiar terms and indicates how thunder is to be understood in the relevant syllogism. See Charles, 'Substance', 240.

lowing Aristotle—uses μεταλαμβάνειν in precisely this way while discussing scientific demonstrations.[46]

The expression μεταλαμβάνειν τοὺς λόγους may be too elliptical to help us decide which of the two possible interpretations we should favour, but this problem need not concern us too much. Both uses seem to be at play in the *Posterior Analytics* context: Aristotle probably meant some technical procedure of substitution that he applied himself in discussing the example, and through which the causal relations between the terms and the predications became clearer.

### 3.3. *Ends cannot be picked out by middle terms*

If my interpretation is right, then Aristotle has offered us an example of teleological explanation where the middle term picks out a material cause, while the final cause is picked out by the predicate term. This leaves us with the question why he did not simply provide us with an example of teleological explanation where the middle term picks out a final cause.

I believe that Aristotle indirectly addresses this question in the passage where he brings up the order of causation in different types of demonstration (*Post. An.* 2. 11, 94[b]23–6):

αἱ δὲ γενέσεις ἀνάπαλιν ἐνταῦθα καὶ ἐπὶ τῶν κατὰ κίνησιν αἰτίων· ἐκεῖ μὲν γὰρ τὸ μέσον δεῖ γενέσθαι πρῶτον, ἐνταῦθα δὲ τὸ Γ, τὸ ἔσχατον, τελευταῖον δὲ τὸ οὗ ἕνεκα.

Here the events occur in the opposite order from the cases where the causes are according to motion. For in the latter the middle term must occur first, while here C, the ultimate term, [must occur first], and last the for the sake of which.

In this passage Aristotle contrasts the order of causation in demonstrations of efficient causal explanations with those of teleological explanations. As we saw earlier, the middle term in the example of efficient explanation (i.e. being the first to attack) picked out an event that *later* initiated the war against the Athenians. The explanatory efficient cause thus precedes the *explanandum* in time.

---

[46] See Galen, *Meth. med.* x. 39. 5–10 Kühn: καί σοι τὸν ἑξῆς λόγον ἤδη ἅπαντα ποιήσομαι, χρώμενος ταῖς μεθόδοις ἃς ἐν τοῖς περὶ τῆς ἀποδείξεως ὑπομνήμασι κατεστησάμην. ὅτι τε γὰρ ἀρχαὶ πάσης ἀποδείξεώς εἰσι τὰ πρὸς αἴσθησίν τε καὶ νόησιν ἐναργῶς φαινόμενα καὶ ὡς ἐπὶ πάντων τῶν ζητουμένων εἰς λόγον χρὴ μεταλαμβάνεσθαι τοὔνομα [that with regard to every enquiry one needs to substitute the definition for the word], δι᾽ ἐκείνων ἀποδέδεικται. I am grateful to Jim Hankinson for bringing this parallel to my attention.

However, in the example of teleological explanation we saw that the action picked out by the subject term (i.e. walking) occurred first. The final cause, health, came about last. It seems that in teleological explanations the final causes are literally, in a temporal sense, the *telos* or the end (and culmination) of the events to be explained.

In later discussions of the temporal relations between the three terms (*Post. An.* 2. 12 and 16) Aristotle puts forward the requirement that the state of affairs picked out by the middle term must be simultaneous with the state of affairs it explains.[47] However, in the case of events that come about consecutively (*Post. An.* 2. 12, 95$^{b}$13: ἐφεξῆς) the middle term must be chronologically prior to the state of affairs it explains. As Aristotle points out (*Post. An.* 2. 12, 95$^{b}$33–8), there is no difference in demonstration between the two cases.

The upshot is that, given that demonstrations are to reflect the order of causation in the real world,[48] final causes of events cannot be picked out by the middle term, but must always be part of the conclusion that is demonstrated. Since an efficient cause of an event typically occurs before the event itself, the efficient cause can be picked out through the middle term as being causally prior to what needs to be explained. The final cause of an event—although logically prior—typically occurs in actuality after the event itself has already taken place and the necessary prerequisites have been fulfilled.[49] The demonstration then shows how the events to be explained actually bring about the end that constitutes the final cause. This is exactly what Aristotle has shown us, namely that the action of walking actually leads to health, because walking is what makes the food not floating, and being in a condition of having the food not floating is what being healthy is. On this account, ends are part of the conclusion that needs to be demonstrated, and cannot be picked out by the middle term through which the conclusion is demonstrated.

---

[47] See mainly *Post. An.* 2. 12, 95$^{a}$22: 'that which is causative in this way and that of which it is a cause come to be simultaneously [ἅμα γίνεται]', and *Post. An.* 2. 12, 95$^{a}$36–7, where Aristotle argues that the middle term must be ὁμόγονος with the state of affairs it explains.

[48] Cf. D. Charles, *Aristotle on Meaning and Essence* (Oxford, 2000), 198–204, on the dependence of the practice of definition on the order of causation in the *Posterior Analytics*.

[49] This might explain why in the case of the teleological explanation in *Post. An.* 2. 11 the *explanandum* is picked out by the subject term ('why does walking after dinner occur?'), rather than by the predicate term as in the other three types of explanation.

The question I shall focus on below is how this picture of the structure of teleological explanations as described in the *Posterior Analytics* relates to the structure of actual teleological explanations offered by Aristotle in *De partibus animalium*. I shall first turn briefly to his discussion of demonstration in the natural sciences, and then analyse three predominant types of explanation in biology that involve final causality. Without going into too much detail, I shall show that the actual teleological explanations illustrate our findings about the theory of explanation rather well.[50]

## 4. Teleological explanations in practice: evidence from *De partibus animalium*

### 4.1. *Demonstration in the natural sciences and conditional necessity*

The first book of *De partibus animalium* sets out the principles and standards for biological investigations. It discusses a great variety of scientific principles and also the causes involved in the study of nature, such that its student will be able to assess the 'manner of the things brought to light' (τὸν τρόπον τῶν δεικνυμένων: *PA* 1. 1, 639ª12–15). Aristotle proceeds mainly through discussing various methodological dilemmas, one of which pertains to the question of demonstration in the natural sciences. He states that the modes of demonstration in the theoretical sciences and in the natural sciences are different, because the modes of necessity are different (*PA* 1. 1, 640ª3–6):

ἡ γὰρ ἀρχὴ τοῖς μὲν τὸ ὄν, τοῖς δὲ τὸ ἐσόμενον· ἐπεὶ γὰρ τοιόνδε ἐστὶν ἡ ὑγίεια ἢ ὁ ἄνθρωπος, ἀνάγκη τόδ᾽ εἶναι ἢ γενέσθαι, ἀλλ᾽ οὐκ ἐπεὶ τόδ᾽ ἐστὶν ἢ γέγονεν, ἐκεῖνο ἐξ ἀνάγκης ἐστὶν ἢ ἔσται.

For the starting-point is in some [i.e. the theoretical sciences] what is, but in others [i.e. the natural sciences] what will be. For, 'since health or man

---

[50] This question touches upon the important debate on the relation between the ideal of scientific investigation and demonstration set out in the *Posterior Analytics* (the 'theory') and the methodological reflections and actual explanations Aristotle offers in his treatises on natural science (the 'practice'). Although I cannot defend my position here, I am more sympathetic to the approach defended *passim* in the works of, among others, Lennox and Gotthelf, who hold that Aristotle builds upon and elaborates his scientific standards for the different sciences, than to the approach defended by G. E. R. Lloyd, *Aristotelian Explorations* [*Explorations*] (Cambridge, 1996), who argues that Aristotle is a methodological pluralist, and that theory and practice cannot be reconciled with each other.

is such, it is necessary that this is or comes to be', but not 'since this is or has come about, that from necessity is or will be'.

The mode of necessity operative among natural perishable things is thus identified as conditional necessity, which Aristotle explains as the necessity of certain things being present first, if the end is to come to be.[51] Again, because demonstrations of the reason why have to reflect the true order of causality, the necessity that governs deductions of natural phenomena has to be conditional too. If the end has come to be or is (such and such), then its necessary prerequisites have had to come to be or be present first (or, in other words, its necessary prerequisites cannot not be; cf. *Phys.* 2. 9, 200ª19–22). The deduction is not of the consequences of a certain starting-point, but of the antecedents of the end.[52] The demonstration that results is not as strong as the demonstrations of the theoretical sciences, because the material-efficient prerequisites (though all in some sense being conditionally necessary for the end) do not ensure[53] the coming to be of the end. Of course, wherever a teleological relation obtains, the necessary material conditions will—for the most part, and if nothing impedes—bring about the end that constitutes the final cause.

These remarks about the nature and structure of demonstrations in the natural sciences present the following picture of what these demonstrations in practice would look like: first, it needs to be noted that the predominant form of demonstration is teleological demonstration. What needs to be demonstrated in the context of *De partibus animalium* is mainly why certain functions belong to the parts whose presence these final causes explain. The final cause of something is the realization of the form of that thing, and this is something that chronologically comes to be last. At the same time, this final cause is taken as a (heuristic and observational) starting-point, presumably as a part of the conclusion of the demonstration. Next, one has to work one's way back to the conditionally necessary

[51] See *PA* 1. 1, 639ᵇ26–30: 'It is necessary that a certain sort of matter be present if there is to be a house or any other end, and this must come to be and be changed first, then that, and so continuously up to the end and that for the sake of which each comes to be and is.'
[52] Lloyd, *Explorations*, 32; as Lloyd rightly points out, the antecedents that are deduced are antecedents of the final cause in a chronological or ontological sense, not in a logical one.
[53] This is because, as Aristotle explains (in *PA* 1. 1, 640ª6–9, and *GC* 2. 11), the necessity involved does not convert.

antecedents, which the realization of this end demands. These antecedents will be exhibited by material or efficient causes (or both) that are directed towards this final cause, and as such will be picked out by the middle term.

This picture is largely consistent with the example of why one walks after dinner in *Post. An.* 2. 11. The question why one walks after dinner parallels the biological question why, for instance, a certain part is present in a certain animal. The question is answered by identifying the final cause: in the case of walking, health; in the case of biological parts, the function of that part. In both cases, the middle term will have to pick out the conditionally necessary antecedents that for the most part will bring about the end that constitutes the final cause.

I shall strengthen this general picture by an analysis of the most common types of teleological explanation that Aristotle uses in *De partibus animalium*.

### 4.2. *The place of final causes in actual teleological explanations*

4.2.1. *The explanation of the presence of parts: final cause is subsumed under the formal cause*   The most common question in *De partibus animalium* is why a certain animal has a certain part, and Aristotle typically answers this question by pointing out the function that part plays within the particular animal kind that has that part. The presence of parts is thus explained teleologically through reference to their function, but usually the presence of these functions themselves is explained by reference to the definition of the substantial being of the animal.

Let me explain this by giving an example. The question why birds have wings is answered by reference to the function of flying as a part of the definition of the substantial being of birds: birds are essentially flyers, and flyers necessarily have wings.[54] In a formalization of this example, the middle term would be 'flyers' (which picks out a functionally defined essence), not 'flying' (which picks out the function or final cause). It is this definition of the substantial being of birds that is explanatorily basic, and which is thus picked out to explain why certain parts with certain functions hold of cer-

---

[54] *PA* 4. 12, 693$^b$10–14: 'For the substantial being of the bird is that of the blooded animals, but at the same time also that of the winged animals . . . and the ability to fly is in the substantial being of the bird.' (Cf. *PA* 4. 13, 697$^b$1–13; 3. 6, 669$^b$8–12.)

tain animal kinds.[55] From the definition of birds as blooded flyers not only the presence of wings can be demonstrated, but also many of the bird's other features, such as the having of two feet (rather than four, or six: *PA* 4. 12, 693ᵇ2–13).

Additionally, Aristotle sometimes explains the presence of parts in subspecies by reference to the functions that are part of the definition of the substantial being of the wider kind. The fact that birds are essentially flyers explains, according to Aristotle, why ducks have wings for the sake of flying. Here, the functions (the final causes) tend to be subsumed under the essence (the formal cause) of the animal or its wider kind. Wings belong to ducks because ducks are essentially birds.

In these cases, functions are picked out by the predicate term and only 'indirectly' through the middle term as being part of the definition of the substantial being of something—that is, as being included in the formal cause.[56] Final causes of parts are demonstrated to belong to parts through the functionally defined substantial being of an animal, and it is this formal cause that is explanatorily basic.

4.2.2. *The explanation of differentiations of parts: differentiae are causally basic*   Another common question in *De partibus animalium* is why a part has the structural and material properties it has in the particular animal that has it. Or, in other words, why the part is differentiated in the way it is in this particular animal, relative to other parts with the same name and approximately the same function in other animals.

Take the example of eyes: both birds and insects have eyes for the sake of vision, but birds have eyes made of fluid eye jelly, while insects have hard eyes. This material differentiation of eyes cannot be explained by reference to the function of vision as such, which only requires eyes to be made of some transparent stuff (the general function explains only the presence of parts, not their differentiations). Aristotle explains these differentiations by claiming that they are for the better: that is, they are for the sake of the functional optimization of that part within the particular animal kind (*PA* 2. 2, 648ᵃ14–19):

---

[55] For features belonging to the substantial being of animals, see A. Gotthelf, 'First Principles in Aristotle's *Parts of Animals*', in A. Gotthelf and J. G. Lennox (eds.), *Philosophical Issues in Aristotle's Biology* (Cambridge, 1987), 167–98 at 190–1.

[56] *PA* 1. 1, 640ᵃ33–5: 'Hence we must in particular say that since this is what it is to be a human being, on account of this it has these things; for it cannot be without these parts.' (Cf. *Phys.* 2. 9, 200ᵃ14; *PA* 1. 1, 639ᵇ13–14.)

ὑποληπτέον ἔχειν τὴν διαφοράν, τὰ μὲν πρὸς τὸ βέλτιον ἢ χεῖρον, τὰ δὲ πρὸς τὰ
ἔργα καὶ τὴν οὐσίαν ἑκάστῳ τῶν ζῴων, οἷον ἐχόντων ὀφθαλμοὺς ἀμφοτέρων τὰ
μέν ἐστι σκληρόφθαλμα τὰ δ᾽ ὑγρόφθαλμα, καὶ τὰ μὲν οὐκ ἔχει βλέφαρα τὰ δ᾽
ἔχει πρὸς τὸ τὴν ὄψιν ἀκριβεστέραν εἶναι.

They [i.e. parts] should be assumed to possess a differentiation, in some
cases relative to what is better or worse, in other cases relative to each animal's functions and substantial being. For instance, two animals may both
have eyes, but in one these eyes are hard, while in the other they are of fluid
consistency; and while the one does not have eyelids, the other does—both
being for the sake of a greater accuracy of vision.

Aristotle thus explains the (relative) fluidity of the eyes of birds as
being for the sake of *better* vision in birds: birds have fluid eyes
to be better able to see. However, Aristotle explains this functional
optimization by reference to the specific nature, habitat, and needs
of the animal in question. That is, the explanatorily basic features
in these explanations are the four differentiae of the animal kind,
which are the other parts (and functions) the animal has, the animal's *bios* (lifestyle and habitat), its activities, and its disposition.
These four *differentiae* immediately necessitate the variation among
parts through conditional necessity. The *differentiae* demand a
functional fine-tuning of the part, and this will in its turn conditionally necessitate material-structural changes or a relocation of
the part. This is clear in the following example (*PA* 2. 13, 657ᵇ22–9):

τὰ δὲ τετράποδα καὶ ᾠοτόκα οὐ σκαρδαμύττει ὁμοίως, ὅτι οὐδ᾽ ὑγρὰν αὐτοῖς
ἀναγκαῖον ἔχειν καὶ ἀκριβῆ τὴν ὄψιν ἐπιγείοις οὖσιν. τοῖς δ᾽ ὄρνισιν ἀναγκαῖον·
πόρρωθεν γὰρ ἡ χρῆσις τῆς ὄψεως. διὸ καὶ τὰ γαμψώνυχα μὲν ὀξυωπά (ἄνωθεν
γὰρ αὐτοῖς ἡ θεωρία τῆς τροφῆς, διὸ καὶ ἀναπέτονται ταῦτα μάλιστα τῶν ὀρνέων
εἰς ὕψος), τὰ δ᾽ ἐπίγεια καὶ μὴ πτητικά, οἷον ἀλεκτρυόνες καὶ τὰ τοιαῦτα, οὐκ
ὀξυωπά· οὐδὲν γὰρ αὐτὰ κατεπείγει πρὸς τὸν βίον.

The four-footed, egg-laying animals do not blink in the same way as the
birds, because since they are terrestrial, it is unnecessary for them to have
moist and accurate vision. But for the birds it is necessary, since they use
vision to see from a great distance. Accordingly, crook-taloned birds have
sharp vision (for they search their food from above, which is also why
these most of all soar to the heights), while those which are terrestrial and
incapable of flight, such as domestic fowl and the like, do not have sharp
vision. For nothing related to their way of life requires them to have it.
(Trans. Lennox)[57]

[57] J. G. Lennox (trans. and comm.), *Aristotle: On the Parts of Animals [Parts]*
(Oxford, 2001), 39–40.

A reconstruction of the premises involved in this example shows that the fact that crook-taloned birds search for their food from above explains why they need accurate vision, and it is this need for accurate vision that conditionally necessitates the moistness of the eyes of these birds. However, the ability of crook-taloned birds to see accurately *follows* from the material differentiation of eyes: the specific material disposition of each kind of eye explains the accurateness of vision of the animal that has those kinds of eye.[58] Again, the final cause is part of the conclusion of the demonstration, while the middle term refers to formal or material-efficient causes.

4.2.3. *The explanation of luxurious parts: secondary teleology* A third type of explanation that is fairly common in *De partibus animalium* is the so-called 'double-barrelled' explanation. In these cases Aristotle explains the presence of a part or its differentiation both by reference to a final cause and by reference to material necessity. This type of explanation usually pertains to parts or functions that are not of vital or essential importance for the animal (and therefore not necessary in a strict sense), but 'merely' contribute to its well-being. Examples of such parts are horns, spurs, hoofs, nails, teeth, hair, and eyebrows; these parts all serve the luxury function of defence or protection. The doubleness of the explanation indicates that these parts are due to what might be called 'secondary teleology'.[59] That is, the *coming to be* of the materials out of which the luxurious parts are constituted is due to material necessity (see e.g. *PA* 4. 3, 677ᵇ22–9; 4. 4, 678ᵃ3–10). The *presence* of these parts, on the other hand, and their organization and distribution in an animal's body are due to the goal-directed actions of the formal nature of the animal. Aristotle describes the action of the formal nature of the animal in these cases as *making use* of materials that are present of necessity for a good purpose, rather than as *producing* those materials for the sake of some function.

Take the example of horns (*PA* 3. 2). First, Aristotle explains that horns are present in the animals that have them for the sake

---

[58] For habitat being picked out as an explanatory basic feature, see A. Gotthelf, 'The Elephant's Nose: Further Reflections on the Axiomatic Structure of Biological Explanations in Aristotle', in Kullmann and Föllinger (eds.), *Aristotelische Biologie*, 85–95 at 85–9; and Charles, 'Substance', 249–50.

[59] My usage of the term 'secondary teleology' derives from Lennox's notion of 'indirect teleology' (Lennox, *Parts*, 248–9), although our interpretations of the causal pattern underlying this type of teleology are different.

of self-defence and attack (*PA* 3. 2, 663ᵇ21–2). Next, he poses the following question (*PA* 3. 2, 663ᵇ22–4):

πῶς δὲ τῆς ἀναγκαίας φύσεως ἐχούσης τοῖς ὑπάρχουσιν ἐξ ἀνάγκης ἡ κατὰ τὸν λόγον φύσις ἕνεκά του κατακέχρηται, λέγωμεν.

We must say what the character of the necessary nature is, and, how nature according to the account has made use of things present of necessity for the sake of something.⁶⁰

The necessary nature of the animal indicates, I submit, the amount and kind of materials that come to be as a result of material necessity, as a by-product or surplus of conditionally necessitated processes (without being themselves conditionally necessary). As Aristotle explains, large animals seem to produce more earthen material than is conditionally necessary (and necessitated) for the production of their bones, and it is this residue which is then 'used by nature for the sake of protection and advantage' (*PA* 3. 2, 663ᵇ25–35).

In cases like this, the function that explains the presence of the part *follows* from the potentials the available material has.⁶¹ The earthen residue is used by the formal nature of an animal to produce parts such as horns, *because* this kind of material has a defensive potential.⁶² Formalizations of examples like these are not easy, but for our purposes it suffices to notice that again a final cause is demonstrated to belong to some feature through another more basic feature, in this case the presence of materials with certain material potentials.

Let me end this exposition of common types of teleological ex-

---

⁶⁰ Here Ogle's translation (W. Ogle (trans.), *Aristotle: De partibus animalium* (Oxford, 1912): 'Let us now consider the character of the material nature whose necessary results have been employed by rational nature for a final cause') is grammatically closer to the Greek than Lennox's (*Parts*, 51: 'Since there is a necessary nature, we must say how the nature according to the account makes use of things present of necessity for the sake of something'). πῶς should be taken with ἐχούσης in the genitive absolute, *and* with κατακέχρηται: as soon as we know what kind of thing the necessary nature is, we can explain how nature makes use of the things that are present on account of this necessary nature.

⁶¹ This is what Aristotle explains in *PA* 2. 9, 655ᵇ4–12: 'All these [uniform parts, such as horns] the animals have for the sake of protection . . . Of necessity all of these parts have an earthen and hard nature; for this potential is of the defensive kind.' Cf. *GA* 2. 6, 744ᵇ12–27.

⁶² *Pace* Lennox, *Biology*, 194–5, who holds that 'such material is present for the sake of constituting parts which must have a material propensity suitable for defense'.

planation in *De partibus animalium* by pointing out that although the actual explanations are more complicated than the example of walking after dinner in the *Posterior Analytics*, the basic structure and the role of final causes seem to be the same. In biology, Aristotle attributes functions to (differentiations of) parts in order to explain the presence of the latter. However, the holding of these functions follows from other, more basic features, such as the animal's essence (that comprises functions), its lifestyle, or the availability of certain material potentials. It thus seems that in practice too, final causes are what is attributed to a subject, and not what can be picked out by an explanatory middle term.

## 5. Conclusion

In the preceding sections I have argued that *Post. An.* 2. 11 shows how each of the four types of explanation is brought out through an explanatory middle term, which need not express the same type of causality as the explanation does.

This interpretation, supported by the lexical difference between *aitia* and *aition*, takes away the need to rearrange Aristotle's syllogistic example of walking after dinner for the sake of health. Nothing in the text of the *Posterior Analytics* suggests that final causes *must* be picked out by the middle term in a teleological demonstration. A comparison with the use of μεταλαμβάνειν in the *Prior Analytics* and the *Topics* shows that the expression μεταλαμβάνειν τοὺς λόγους should be taken as referring to some kind of procedure of substitution that Aristotle has applied himself while setting out his example, rather than as an admonition to us to change the order of the terms or premisses. The fact that in teleological explanations the end for the sake of which the event is undertaken comes to be chronologically last, together with Aristotle's requirement that explanations have to reflect real causal sequences, explains why it is impossible to construct a syllogism in which the middle term picks out this end as a final cause.

A short analysis of Aristotle's methodological remarks about demonstration in the natural sciences and of his actual practice of teleological explanation in *De partibus animalium* confirms the general picture found in the *Posterior Analytics* with regard to the structure of teleological explanations. Functions explain the presence (or differentiations) of parts, but the holding of these functions by those parts is demonstrated through the discovery of some other basic explanatory feature. Final causes are the starting-points from which the conditionally necessary antecedents are to be traced back, but it is the presence of these prerequisites that causes—for the most part, and if nothing interferes—the coming to be of ends. This does not mean that final causes have only a heuristic value: because final causes are part of the conclusion that is being demonstrated, the demonstration demonstrates the very existence of natural teleology.

*Leiden University*


# APPENDIX
## Translation of *Post. An.* 2. 11, 94$^a$20–94$^b$26

Since we think we have [scientific] knowledge when we know the explanation, and there are four types of explanation—one, what it is to be a thing and another, given what things being the case it is necessary for that to hold; another, what first initiated the motion; and fourth, the for the sake of what—all of them are brought out through the middle term. For, 'given what thing being the case it is necessary for this to hold' does not occur when one proposition is assumed, but when at least two are. This is the case when they have one middle term. Thus when this one is assumed, it is necessary for the conclusion to hold. It is clear too in the following way. Because of what is the angle in a semicircle a right angle? Given what thing being the case is it a right angle? Suppose, then, that right is A, half of two rights B, the angle in a semicircle C. Thus of A's—right—holding of C—the angle in a semicircle B is the cause. For this [B] is equal to A and C to B, because it [C] is of two rights—half. Thus given B, half of two rights, being the case, A holds of C (for that was it that [necessitates] the angle in a semicircle being a right angle). And that [B] is the same as what it is to be it, since the definition signifies this [i.e. what it is to be it].

Now it has also been shown that the middle term is explanatory of the essence.

For what reason did the Persian war come upon the Athenians? What is an explanation of the Athenians' being warred upon? Because they attacked Sardis with the Eretrians. For that initiated the movement. War, A; being the first to attack, B; Athenians C. B holds of C, the Athenians being the first to attack, and A holds of B, because people make war on those who have wronged them first. Therefore A holds of B, being warred upon to those who first began, and this, B, holds of the Athenians—for they first began. And in this case, too, the cause, that which initiated the movement, is the middle term.

Regarding the cases in which the causal relation is that something is for the sake of something—for example: for what reason does he walk? In order to be healthy. For what reason is there a house? In order to protect the possessions. In the one case it is in order to be healthy, in the other in order to protect. There is no difference between for what reason it is necessary to walk after dinner and for the sake of what it is necessary. Call 'walking after dinner' C, 'the food not floating on the surface' B, and 'being healthy' A. Suppose, then, that to make the food not floating on the surface at the mouth of the stomach holds of walking after dinner, and suppose the first is healthy. For it is thought that B, the food not floating on the surface, holds of to walk, of C, and that thereof (of B) A, healthy, holds. What, then, is the causal factor for C of A's—the for the sake of which—holding of it? B, the not floating. This is like a definition of it [of A]; for A will here be explained in this way. And for what reason does B hold of C? Because that is what being healthy is: being in such state. Surely one must substitute the definitions, and in that way each of them will become clearer. Here the events occur in the opposite order from the cases where the causes are according to motion. For in the latter the middle term must occur first, while here C, the ultimate term, [must occur first], and last the for the sake of which.

## BIBLIOGRAPHY

Apostle, H. G., *Aristotle's* Posterior Analytics, *Translated with Commentaries and Glossary* (Grinnell, 1981).

Barnes, J., *Aristotle:* Posterior Analytics [*Posterior*] (Oxford, 1993).

Bolton, R., 'The Material Cause: Matter and Explanation in Aristotle's Natural Science' ['Material'], in Kullmann and Föllinger (eds.), *Aristotelische Biologie*, 97–124.

Charles, D., *Aristotle on Meaning and Essence* (Oxford, 2000).

—— 'Aristotle on Substance, Essence and Biological Kinds' ['Substance'], in L. P. Gerson (ed.), *Aristotle: Critical Assessments* (London and New York, 1999), 227–55.

Detel, W., *Aristoteles: Analytica Posteriora* [*Analytica*] (Berlin, 1993).

—— 'Why All Animals Have a Stomach: Demonstration and Axiomatization in Aristotle's *Parts of Animals*' ['Stomach'], in Kullmann and Föllinger (eds.), *Aristotelische Biologie*, 63–84.

Fortenbaugh, W. W., 'Nicomachean Ethics I, 1096b26–9', *Phronesis*, 11 (1966), 185–94.

Frede, M., 'The Original Notion of Cause' ['Cause'], in M. Schofield, M.

178          *Mariska E. M. P. J. Leunissen*

Burnyeat, and J. Barnes (eds.), *Doubt and Dogmatism* (Oxford, 1980), 217–49.

Goldin, O., *Explaining an Eclipse: Aristotle's Posterior Analytics 2. 1–10* (Ann Arbor, 1996).

Gotthelf, A., 'First Principles in Aristotle's *Parts of Animals*', in A. Gotthelf and J. G. Lennox (eds.), *Philosophical Issues in Aristotle's Biology* (Cambridge, 1987), 167–98.

——— 'The Elephant's Nose: Further Reflections on the Axiomatic Structure of Biological Explanations in Aristotle', in Kullmann and Föllinger (eds.), *Aristotelische Biologie*, 85–95.

Johnson, M. R., *Aristotle on Teleology* (Oxford, 2005).

Kullmann, W., and Föllinger, S. (eds.), *Aristotelische Biologie: Intentionen, Methoden, Ergebnisse* (Stuttgart, 1997).

Lennox, J. G. (trans. and comm.), *Aristotle: On the Parts of Animals* [*Parts*] (Oxford, 2001).

——— 'Aristotle on the Unity and Disunity of Science', *International Studies in the Philosophy of Science*, 15 (2001), 133–44.

——— *Aristotle's Philosophy of Biology: Studies in the Origin of Life Science* [*Biology*] (Cambridge, 2001).

——— 'Getting A Science Going: Aristotle on Entry Level Kinds', in G. Wolters (ed.), *Homo Sapiens und Homo Faber: Festschrift Mittelstrass* (Berlin, 2004), 87–100.

Leunissen, Mariska E. M. P. J., 'Ancient Comments on *APo.* II. 11: Aristotle and Philoponus on Final Causes in Demonstrations', in F. A. J. De Haas and Mariska E. M. P. J. Leunissen, *Interpreting Aristotle's Posterior Analytics in Late Antiquity and the Byzantine Period* (forthcoming).

Lloyd, G. E. R., *Aristotelian Explorations* [*Explorations*] (Cambridge, 1996).

McKirahan, R., *Principles and Proofs: Aristotle's Theory of Demonstrative Science* (Princeton, 1992).

Ogle, W. (trans.), *Aristotle: De partibus animalium* (Oxford, 1912).

Sedley, D., 'Platonic Causes', *Phronesis*, 43 (1998), 114–32.

Sluiter, I., *Ancient Grammar in Context: Contributions to the Study of Ancient Linguistic Thought* (Amsterdam, 1990).

Smith, R. (trans. and comm.), *Aristotle: Prior Analytics* (Indianapolis, 1989).

Ross, W. D., *Aristotle's Prior and Posterior Analytics: A Revised Text with Introduction and Commentary* [*Revised*] (Oxford, 1949).

# THE ASSIMILATION OF SENSE TO SENSE-OBJECT IN ARISTOTLE

## HENDRIK LORENZ

## 1. Introduction

ARISTOTLE holds that acts of sense-perception crucially involve some kind of assimilation of the perceiver to the relevant sense-object—say, a red flag, or a fragrant lavender bush. It has for some time been highly controversial how he conceives of this kind of assimilation. According to some scholars, what he has in mind is an alteration or change in quality whereby the perceiver's sense-organ in a straightforward way takes on the perceptible quality of the object that is being perceived.[1] According to others, such assimilation just is becoming aware of the perceptible quality in question.[2] On this view, the likeness between perceiver and sense-object in the act of perception depends on the fact that the perceptible form of the sense-object has in a certain way come to be present in the perceiver's sense-organ. However, the relevant notion of presence

[1] Different interpretations of this kind are on display, for instance, in T. Slakey, 'Aristotle on Sense Perception', *Philosophical Review*, 70 (1961), 470–84; R. Sorabji, 'Body and Soul in Aristotle', *Philosophy*, 49 (1974), 63–89; S. Everson, *Aristotle on Perception* (Oxford, 1997). Useful distinctions among different versions of this kind of interpretation are drawn in V. Caston, 'The Spirit and the Letter: Aristotle on Perception', in R. Salles (ed.), *Metaphysics, Soul, and Ethics in Ancient Thought: Themes from the Work of Richard Sorabji* (Oxford, 2005), 245–320 at 248–54.

[2] The protagonist of this kind of interpretation is M. Burnyeat. His main contributions to the topic are 'Is an Aristotelian Philosophy of Mind Still Credible? (A Draft)', in M. Nussbaum and A. Rorty (eds.), *Essays on Aristotle's* De anima (Oxford, 1992), 15–26; 'How Much Happens When Aristotle Sees Red and Hears Middle C? Remarks on De anima 2. 7–8', in Nussbaum and Rorty (eds.), *Essays on Aristotle's* De anima, paperback edn. (Oxford, 1995), 421–34; and '*De anima* II 5', *Phronesis*, 47 (2002), 28–90. Another statement of this kind of interpretation is T. Johansen, *Aristotle on the Sense-Organs* (Cambridge, 1998). Supporters also include S. Broadie, 'Aristotle's Perceptual Realism', in J. Ellis (ed.), *Ancient Minds* (*Southern Journal of Philosophy*, 31, suppl.; 1993), 137–59; and D. Murphy, 'Aristotle on Why Plants Cannot Perceive', *Oxford Studies in Ancient Philosophy*, 29 (2005), 295–339.

is a technical one. It is the notion of presence of perceptible form without matter, and such presence, at any rate in a sense-organ, is taken to come to no more and no less than perceptual awareness of the quality in question.[3] The two competing views that I have sketched are central, respectively, to one or the other of the two most prominent and influential interpretations of Aristotle's theory of perception. Those are known as 'literalism' and 'spiritualism'. I am convinced that neither of those interpretations is sustainable. Each disregards significant details of Aristotle's intricate discussion of perception in *De anima* 2. 5–3. 2, and in the related chapters of *De sensu*. Each fails to do justice to the complexity of Aristotle's theory of perception. Together they have stood in the way of a proper philosophical reconstruction and appreciation of that theory.

On the view for which I shall argue in what follows, Aristotle's mature theory of perception in *De anima* assigns prominent explanatory roles both to a technical notion of assimilation of sense to sense-object, according to which such assimilation is perceiving, or perceiving considered in a certain way, and to assimilation of a more ordinary kind, in which one thing comes to be like another by taking on one of its features in a straightforward way. The chief task that I want to accomplish in the present paper is to show in some detail that Aristotle's theory of perception does prominently employ a tolerably clear, though rather technical, conception of the likeness of some sensory power to the sense-object in the act of perception. I shall also call attention to at least some of the textual evidence, in the *De anima* and elsewhere, that shows it to be part of Aristotle's theory that one thing that happens when a perceiver encounters a sense-object in suitable circumstances is that the sense-object assimilates the relevant sense-organ to itself by causing it to undergo an ordinary change—for instance, a change whereby the sense-organ loses one attribute and gains another from the same range delimited by contrary qualities. However, I shall leave detailed engagement with that evidence, and with the questions it raises, for another occasion. My focus, for now, is on the assimilation of sense to sense-object.[4]

---

[3] Cf. M. Burnyeat, 'Aquinas on "Spiritual Change" in Perception', in D. Perler (ed.), *Ancient and Medieval Theories of Intentionality* (Leiden, 2001), 129–53 at 141.

[4] In effect, the present paper's main target is literalism. While I shall in what follows mount a serious challenge to spiritualism as well (see n. 73, together with Section 4, pp. 212–14), I propose to leave direct and full-scale confrontation with spiritualism for another occasion.

## 2. Non-destructive alteration in *DA* 2. 5

At the end of *DA* 2. 5 Aristotle says:

τὸ δ' αἰσθητικὸν δυνάμει ἐστὶν οἷον τὸ αἰσθητὸν ἤδη ἐντελεχείᾳ, καθάπερ εἴρηται. πάσχει μὲν οὖν οὐχ ὅμοιον ὄν, πεπονθὸς δ' ὡμοίωται καὶ ἐστιν οἷον ἐκεῖνο.

What perceives [τὸ αἰσθητικόν] is potentially such as the sense-object is already in actuality, as has been said. Not being like [sc. the sense-object], it is affected. Having been affected, it has been likened and is such as it. (*DA* 2. 5, 418ᵃ3–6)

Aristotle takes care to indicate that in characterizing the kind of assimilation he has in mind, he is using the language of being affected (πάσχειν) in a non-standard way. He has just said that since there is no terminology to mark a relevant distinction between two ways of being potentially something or other, 'it is necessary to use the terms "being affected" and "being altered" as if they were the proper terms' (417ᵇ33–418ᵃ3). This somewhat telegraphic remark relies on two related distinctions made earlier on in the chapter: a distinction between two ways of being potentially something or other, illustrated, first, by someone who is potentially a knower in virtue of being human and thereby endowed with the faculty of reason and, secondly, by someone who is potentially a knower in virtue of having mastered a body of knowledge (417ᵃ21–ᵇ2); and in addition a distinction, made on the basis of that earlier distinction, between two corresponding ways of being affected. The first of these is illustrated by being taught, so as to acquire mastery of a body of knowledge; the second way is illustrated by passing from merely having knowledge to exercising it, as one contemplates, say, a geometrical proof. This second way of being affected is presented as being either no alteration at all or an alteration of a different kind (417ᵇ6–7)—different in kind, I take it, from ordinary alterations. For reasons that are not immediately clear, Aristotle regards this second way of being affected as somewhat extraordinary.

He takes perceiving to be a matter of being somehow affected by, and assimilated to, a suitable sense-object. There is a question about what precisely it is that he claims, in *DA* 2. 5, to have been likened to the sense-object in the act of perception. The expression he uses in referring to what undergoes the relevant kind of affection, and which I translate as 'what perceives', might be meant to denote the animal in question ('the perceiver'), or that animal's power to perceive ('the sense').[5] For the moment I remain neutral about these possibilities, since for the purposes of the present section nothing hangs on the issue. In Section 3 I shall offer some reasons for favouring the second alternative. Something that does matter for present purposes is that Aristotle takes the assimilation of what perceives to the sense-object to be a case of being affected that is like the transition from merely having knowledge to exercising it. As we shall see, this places a significant constraint on how we are to interpret the assimilation of what perceives to the sense-object, never mind what precisely Aristotle might mean by 'what perceives'.

In rough outline, the conception that emerges by the end of the chapter is this. Prior to the act of perception, what perceives has already risen to a developed state of preparedness for perceptual activity, which is analogous to mastery of a body of knowledge. When a perceiver encounters a sense-object in suitable circumstances, the sense-object brings about a transition whereby that developed state of preparedness is put to use. What results is perceptual awareness of the sense-object. In some way or other, the transition also involves the assimilation of what perceives to the sense-object. This kind of assimilation, Aristotle holds, is a somewhat extraordinary case of being affected. Why?

One might think, and some have thought, that Aristotle's reason is that for a perceiver to be assimilated to a sense-object in the requisite way is a change that involves the exercise and preservation of the perceiver's capacity for perception.[6] After all, it is a change that can accurately be described as 'the preservation of what is potentially' ($417^{b}3-4$), and as a transition whereby the perceiver 'rises into itself and into actuality' ($417^{b}6-7$). If that is Aristotle's

[5] The former is Burnyeat's preferred alternative: '*De anima* II 5', 44 n. 41. (The word is clearly used in this way at *DA* 2. 3, $415^{a}6-7$.) The latter is adopted by R. D. Hicks, *Aristotle: De anima* (Cambridge, 1907); by W. D. Ross in his paraphrase in *Aristotle: De anima* (Oxford, 1961); and by E. Barbotin in his translation, *Aristote: De l'âme* (Paris, 1966). In using the expression 'what perceives', I mean to leave open the possibility that the item so referred to is one of the perceiver's senses, or the sense in general.

[6] A view of this kind is held, for instance, by Caston, 'The Spirit and the Letter', 268–9. Similarly Everson, *Aristotle on Perception*, 92: 'the second type of alteration is the realization of a capacity, where the capacity will be defined by reference to its realization'; the definition of the second type of alteration 'is such that the actualization of any capacity will fall under it' (93). Cf. J. Sisko, 'Alteration and Quasi-Alteration', *Oxford Studies in Ancient Philosophy*, 16 (1998), 331–52 at 335–6.

reason, then his insistence that the kind of assimilation he has in mind is a somewhat extraordinary case of being affected plainly allows him to accept that such assimilation consists in an alteration whereby a sense-organ loses, for instance, an intermediate degree of warmth and becomes somewhat cold, thus being assimilated to the ice cube on the perceiver's hand. On this view, Aristotle is merely insisting that such assimilation is also a change that exercises and preserves a perceptual capacity.

It is, however, clear that Aristotle does not think that the relevant kind of assimilation, as he conceives of it here at the end of *DA* 2. 5, consists in the loss of one quality and acquisition of another by whatever it may be that he takes to be assimilated to the sense-object. Crucially, it is part of his conception of this particular kind of assimilation that being affected in this way is not a matter of suffering the loss of a given quality by having it replaced with another quality from the same range.

To see this, one must first of all notice that the chapter offers not only one distinction between different ways of being affected, but in fact two such distinctions.[7] Aristotle first distinguishes between one way of being affected which is 'destruction of a sort by the agency of something contrary' ($417^b2-4$), and another way which is 'rather a preservation of what is potentially by the agency of what is in actuality, and of what is like it the way a potentiality is in relation to the actuality in question' ($417^b3-5$). The first of those two ways seems clear enough. When something or other is affected in this way, one of its attributes is destroyed or lost. If the change in question is an alteration, the thing that is changed suffers the loss of some quality.[8] It passes from being $F$, for some quality $F$-ness, to being not $F$. Being $F$ is the starting-point of the change, and to undergo the change is in part to suffer the loss of $F$-ness (cf. *Phys.* 7. 1, $242^a69-{}^b42$). Take, for instance, learning. Ignorance, being a disposition, is a quality (cf. *Cat.* 8, $9^a4-10$). When a process of learning is complete, the result is a completed alteration. Ignorance has been replaced with knowledge, and this has come about by the

---

[7] This is shown in great detail in Burnyeat, '*De anima* II 5', 53–67. It was clearly understood already by Philoponus (*In DA* 304. 29–305. 2 Hayduck).

[8] Cf. *GC* 1. 4, $319^b11-16$: 'alteration occurs when what underlies, which is perceptible, persists, but there is a change in its attributes [sc. in its qualities, $319^b34$], which are contraries or intermediates; for example, the body is healthy and then again sick, though it persists in being the same body, and the bronze is spherical and then again angular, remaining the same bronze.'

agency of a teacher or alternatively, and more perspicuously, by the agency of a teacher's knowledge.

The other one of the two ways of being affected that are initially pinpointed may seem somewhat obscure, especially given its characterization in terms of preservation. It may seem difficult to see how being affected in this second way amounts to being changed by being affected. Affecting something or other in this particular way is clearly not meant to be only a matter of preserving a potentiality. We should set aside as irrelevant an idea that one might think is suggested by Aristotle's characterization.[9] It is not part of his conception of this second way of being affected that the potentiality that is preserved is preserved or sustained specifically by being affected in this particular way, which crucially involves the exercise of the potentiality in question. Aristotle will go on to treat the activation of, for instance, sight by colour as an example of this second way of being affected. Now, such activation does preserve the sensory power in that it leaves it fully intact. But Aristotle does not think that a perceiver's capacity for colour perception is sustained specifically by being exercised. He takes that capacity to be in place right away from birth ($DA$ 2. 5, $417^{b}16-18$),[10] and he also takes it to be an essential characteristic of the relevant sense-organs, the eyes ($DA$ 2. 1, $412^{b}20-2$). Since it falls to the nutritive faculty to maintain the animal's organism and its parts, it must be Aristotle's view that, after an animal's birth, its nutritive faculty takes care of sustaining its capacity for colour perception, by maintaining its sense-organs, which requires maintaining them in a state of preparedness for operation. Being affected in this second way, then, crucially involves the preservation of a potentiality in the sense that the potentiality in question is left fully intact, and it also involves being brought into operation or actuality. In explaining why this way of being affected is either no alteration at all or at least no ordinary alteration, Aristotle adds that in being affected in this way, the thing that is so affected 'rises into itself' ($417^{b}6-7$). By this he must mean that in being affected in this way, what is so affected achieves a way of being active or actual that contributes to the completion of its nature.

---

[9] *Pace* Burnyeat, 'De anima II 5', 55.

[10] Cf. *NE* 2. 1, $1103^{a}26-31$, where Aristotle uses the senses as an example of features that we have by nature, having claimed just before (at $1103^{a}19-23$) that habituation has no impact on such features, any more than one can habituate a rock into moving upwards rather than downwards.

Having distinguished between these two ways of being affected, Aristotle adds a further distinction between different ways or manners of being altered, saying that

> that which from being potentially [sc. knowledgeable] learns and acquires knowledge by the agency of what is in actuality [sc. knowledgeable] and what is capable of teaching should either not be said to be affected,[11] or one should say that there are two manners of alteration [δύο τρόπους . . . ἀλλοιώσεως], on the one hand change into privative dispositions, and on the other hand change into states [ἕξεις] and into a thing's nature. (*DA* 2. 5, 417ᵇ12–16)

This is a distinction within the category of destructive alteration:[12] Aristotle is proposing to distinguish such alterations into ones which consist in transitions from being *F*, for some quality *F*-ness, to being not *F*,[13] and ones that are distinctive in that they lead to states which contribute to the altered thing's completion of its nature. Now it should be clear that every case of destructive alteration can correctly be described as a transition from being *F*, for some quality *F*-ness, to being not *F*. After all, such alterations are changes whereby one quality is lost and replaced with another from the same range. Thus it seems best to interpret Aristotle as

---

[11] Some of our manuscripts have the words ὥσπερ εἴρηται after φατέον at 417ᵇ14. On that reading of the text, Aristotle is implying that the acquisition of knowledge has been said not to be a case of being affected. But clearly no such thing has been said. Rather, learning has been characterized as a transition from one contrary state to another, and so it would seem that we have been given at least some reason for thinking that, so far from being no case of being affected, it is in fact a standard case! There is then good reason not to adopt the reading ὥσπερ εἴρηται. Moreover, several manuscripts do not include those words. Philoponus seems not to have read it either. At any rate, his interpretation is incompatible with thinking that the acquisition of knowledge has in what precedes been said not to be a case of being affected. He clearly recognizes (304. 29–305. 2 Hayduck) that the distinction between two manners of alteration at 417ᵇ12–16 is a fresh distinction, and one which distinguishes within the category of transition from one contrary quality to another, which in the initial distinction at 417ᵇ2–5 is contrasted with the preservative kind of alteration.

[12] This point is missed by Everson, *Aristotle on Perception*, 91. He thinks that Aristotle here 'makes explicit the difference between' the two types of alteration distinguished at 417ᵇ2–7. It should be obvious, however, that what now exemplifies 'change into states' in the initial distinction exemplifies 'destruction of a sort'. There is, moreover, no reason at all to think that it is characteristic of the preservative kind of alteration pinpointed at 417ᵇ3–5 that what is altered in that particular way changes into a new state (ἕξις). An Aristotelian ἕξις is a settled disposition. To do a bit of contemplating is not to acquire such a thing.

[13] As is pointed out by Burnyeat, '*De anima* II 5', 62 n. 88, the adjective στερητικός is used at 417ᵇ15 in its standard logical sense, in which it means 'to do with negation', 'of negative character'.

meaning to pinpoint a distinctive kind of destructive alteration: alterations of this particular kind consist not only in the loss of one quality and its replacement with another, but also, and crucially, in the acquisition of a quality that contributes to the altered thing's completion of its nature. When a person acquires some body of knowledge, that is an alteration that contributes to the completion of his or her rational nature. By contrast, when Socrates catches a suntan and thereby loses his paleness, that alteration is neither here nor there so far as the completion of his nature is concerned.

Thus the chapter pinpoints three, and not just two, distinct kinds of alteration or quasi-alteration. Two of these kinds are destructive in that they consist, at least partly, in the loss by what is altered of some quality or other. One of the destructive kinds is exemplified by a transition that involves not only the exercise and preservation of a potentiality, namely the learner's potentiality for knowledge that comes with his or her humanity; it also involves the acquisition by what is altered of a state which contributes to the completion of its nature. In that transition, too, what is altered 'rises into itself and into actuality'. Why, then, is learning not an example of the preservative form of being affected that is pinpointed at $417^b3$–$5$?[14] The reason can only be that learning is a matter of losing a certain quality by having it replaced with another. This makes clear what the flow of the discussion suggests in any case, which is that Aristotle conceives of the preservative kind of alteration or quasi-alteration pinpointed at $417^b3$–$5$ as non-destructive in the sense that being altered in this particular way is not a matter of losing a given quality by having it replaced with another. The second, and special, way of being affected that is introduced at $417^b3$–$5$ is not only conceived of in terms of the exercise and preservation of a

[14] According to Caston, 'The Spirit and the Letter', what is distinctive of the preservative kind of alteration is that 'in exercising a particular capacity C, I do not alter *with respect to* C in a way that destroys *that capacity*. On the contrary, exercising C generally preserves or even reinforces it' (269, emphasis original). This is inadequate, since learning is also a case of both exercising and preserving a capacity, namely the capacity for knowing that comes with being a rational animal. Besides, it is evidently Aristotle's view that the builder, in exercising his art, is not altered (period), not merely that he is not altered with regard to his art, in that the art remains intact (*DA* 2. 5, $417^b8$–$9$). Note also *DA* 2. 4, $416^b1$–$3$: οὐδ᾽ ὁ τέκτων [sc. πάσχει] ὑπὸ τῆς ὕλης, ἀλλ᾽ ὑπ᾽ ἐκείνου αὕτη· ὁ δὲ τέκτων μεταβάλλει μόνον εἰς ἐνέργειαν ἐξ ἀργίας ('nor is the carpenter affected by the matter, but it is affected by him; the carpenter only changes from inactivity to active operation'); note the word μόνον ('only'). This clearly is a remarkable claim for Aristotle to make. It is explained in S. Waterlow, *Nature, Change, and Agency in Aristotle's Physics* (Oxford, 1982), 195–9.

potentiality. It is also conceived of negatively, as not being a matter of losing a quality by having it replaced with another. Otherwise there would be no reason to treat learning as an example of the destructive way, rather than of the preservative way, of being affected.

The upshot for our purposes is that Aristotle, in *DA* 2. 5, conceives of the assimilation of what perceives to the sense-object as a non-destructive alteration, in the sense that such alteration, for the altered thing, whatever precisely it may be, is not a matter of losing a given quality by having it replaced with another. This need not entail that being altered in this particular way cannot in any way involve suffering the loss of a quality.[15] It surely does entail, however, that an alteration of this particular kind cannot properly be characterized as the kind of change it is in terms of the loss of a given quality and its replacement with another.[16]

That is enough to rule out the literalist interpretation of what sensory assimilation, so conceived of, comes to. On that view, what is assimilated in such assimilation is specifically the relevant sense-organ, and its assimilation to the sense-object consists in an alteration whereby it takes on the quality of the sense-object in a straightforward way. For instance, in the act of perceiving the coldness of an ice cube, the perceiver's organ of touch goes cold in a straightforward way. This cannot be what Aristotle has in mind in saying, at the end of *DA* 2. 5, that in the act of perception, what perceives has been likened to the sense-object and is such as it. When a bodily organ is cooled in a straightforward way, that is a destructive alteration of the organ whereby it passes from being warm, or from being at some intermediate point on the hot–cold range, to being cold.[17] Alterations of this kind can properly be characterized as the

---

[15] Ordinary alterations may be involved incidentally, or even as necessary concomitants, in the way thinking, for instance, may necessarily involve ordinary alterations in the thinker's perceptual apparatus. I thus think that Johansen, *Aristotle on the Sense-Organs*, 12, goes too far when, on the basis of what is said in *DA* 2. 5, he ascribes to Aristotle the view that perception involves 'no changes of attributes in the perceiver'.

[16] I am relying on the idea of classifying changes in a more fine-grained way than by categorial analysis. Aristotle offers the basis for such a more fine-grained classification at *Phys.* 7. 1, 242ᵃ69–ᵇ37: 'A change may be the same in genus, in species, or in number. It is the same in genus if it is of the same category, e.g. substance or quality; it is the same in species if it proceeds from something specifically the same to something specifically the same, e.g. from white to black or from good to bad, which is not of a kind specifically distinct.'

[17] I am using tactile perception as my example, since that yields an obvious and

kinds of change they are in terms of the loss of a given quality and
its replacement with another. It is irrelevant whether or not this is a
change that involves the exercise and preservation of a capacity. Nor
does it matter whether or not it is a change whereby the changed
thing advances towards the completion of its nature. What matters
is that changes of this kind are destructive alterations. By contrast,
the kind of assimilation whereby what perceives becomes like the
sense-object is supposed to be non-destructive. It is not supposed
to be a matter of losing a given quality by having it replaced with
another.

### 3. The likeness between sense and sense-object in the act of perception

At this stage we should turn to the question of what kind of change
the assimilation described at the end of *DA* 2. 5 could be. What
sense can be made a kind of assimilation that is not supposed
to be a matter of losing a given quality by having it replaced with
another?

I shall argue that the non-destructive alteration that Aristotle
describes at the end of *DA* 2. 5 is meant to consist in, and be exhausted by, a change or quasi-change that he ascribes to a sensory
power; and that he conceives of this kind of change or quasi-change
as the activation of the sense in question, or perhaps as that activation considered in a way that disregards any bodily process that
may be involved. My argument will proceed as follows. I begin by
showing that one thing that happens when a perceiver encounters
a suitable sense-object, according to Aristotle's theory, is that the
relevant sense is in some way affected by the sense-object. It will
emerge that this kind of affection is a beautifully clear and complete
example of the non-destructive kind of alteration that is introduced
and explained in *DA* 2. 5. There is good reason to think, then, that

clear-cut case of a quality being lost and replaced with a contrary quality from the
same range. The same point could be made about taste (Section 3, pp. 208–9) and
smell (Section 3, p. 191). In the case of vision, the starting-point is transparency,
rather than some colour or other; so it would seem that no colour is lost in the
transition to colour perception. However, the express purpose of *DA* 2. 5 is to make
comments about perception in general. These comments apply to all the senses.
If a literalist interpretation of these general comments is ruled out for the cases of
touch, taste, and smell, that is more than enough to rule it out as an interpretation
of these general comments.

this kind of affection is at least part of what Aristotle has in mind in describing, at the end of *DA* 2. 5, how what perceives has been assimilated to the sense-object in the act of perception. There is also good reason to think that the assimilation of what perceives to the sense-object, as described at the end of *DA* 2. 5, is meant to be exhausted by that kind of affection. Finally, I shall turn to the question of how to interpret the expression 'what perceives' (τὸ αἰσθητικόν) in the claim, at the end of *DA* 2. 5, that in the act of perception what perceives has been assimilated to the sense-object. I shall argue that Aristotle is using that expression so as to denote the power to perceive.

My first task, then, is to show that Aristotle's theory of perception is committed to the occurrence of changes or quasi-changes of a certain kind that are undergone by, or at any rate ascribed to, the senses.[18] This task is complicated by a number of factors, including the following. One complication is terminological. Aristotle distinguishes with admirable clarity between sense-organs and senses or sensory powers (*DA* 2. 12, 424ª24–8; 3. 2, 426ᵇ7–12). He conceives of the senses as unextended, immaterial items that are distinct from the bodily structures in which they reside, and together with which they constitute the sense-organs, conceived of as hylomorphic composites (*DA* 2. 12, 424ª24–8).[19] He also has terminology that is suitable for denoting specifically the sense-organs on the one hand and the senses on the other.[20] Unfortunately, though, he occasionally

---

[18]  I remain agnostic about the question of what Aristotle, in his final and most careful analysis, takes, or would take, to be the proper subject of this kind of change or quasi-change, the sense in question or the animal that is equipped with that sense. Perhaps we shall never know. I do think, however, that at the level of analysis at which Aristotle's discussion of cognition in *DA* 2. 5–3. 8 operates, it is the senses that are regarded as the proper subjects of changes or quasi-changes of this kind. As we shall see, that view reflects a straight and literal reading of a number of prominent passages throughout that discussion; and I see no decisive reason to reject the plain message of that straight, literal reading.

[19]  I recommend Hicks's helpful comments on 2. 12, 424ª24–8: 'The organ and the faculty are one and the same, but we can separate the two in thought. If we look at the organ (τὸ αἰσθανόμενον) as a concrete thing and take account of its matter, it is an extended magnitude: if we abstract from the matter and attend only to the form, it is a power or faculty residing in this extended magnitude, but itself unextended and immaterial.' I would only want to add that organ and faculty, for Aristotle, are separate not only in thought, but also in being (424ª25–6). Standing to each other as matter and form, they are ontologically distinct items, though together they make up the unified object that is the sense-organ in question.

[20]  The general term for 'sense-organ' is αἰσθητήριον; in addition there are the eyes, ears, nostrils, tongue, and the organ of touch, which Aristotle thinks is the

refers to the sense-organs by means of the very words that one would expect, or anyhow wish, to be reserved for the senses.[21] This does not happen very often, nor does it ever seem to happen in contexts in which the distinction between sense-organ and sense matters. None the less, it does make it somewhat hazardous to infer simply from the use of the words in question that Aristotle must have in mind specifically the relevant sensory power rather than the organ in which it resides. At any rate, Aristotle's looseness in the use of his terminology renders such inferences open to challenge.

A second complication stems from Aristotle's metaphysics. He conceives of sense-organs as necessarily equipped with sensory powers, just as he conceives of animal bodies as necessarily en-souled, and for the same reasons. An eye that has lost the capacity for seeing, he famously holds, is an eye in name only (*DA* 2. 1, 412ᵇ20–2). As a result, he can consistently ascribe to sense-organs attributes that belong to them because, and only in so far as, they are equipped with the relevant sensory power. He tells us in *DA* 2. 12 that specifically the senses are such as to receive perceptible forms without the matter (424ᵃ17–24), and proceeds right away to distinguish the senses from the organs in which they reside (424ᵃ24–8). A little later on, in *DA* 3. 2, he says that each sense-organ is such as to receive perceptibles without the matter (425ᵇ23–4). This need not mean that the sense-organs, considered separately from the sensory powers that reside in them, are such as to receive perceptible forms without the matter. It is perfectly compatible with thinking that specifically the senses are the primary bearers of this kind of receptivity, and that such receptivity belongs to the organs only

heart. (That the tongue is the organ of taste seems to be accepted at *DA* 2. 10, 422ᵃ34–ᵇ10, and rejected at 2. 11, 423ᵇ17–26. Aristotle's considered view might be that the organs of taste and touch are twofold, incorporating both the heart, which is the organ strictly speaking, and parts of the body that play the role of a perceptual medium, namely the tongue and the peripheral flesh; this idea is floated, for the case of touch, at *PA* 2. 8, 653ᵇ24–7. For discussion, see Johansen, *Aristotle on the Sense-Organs*, 199–203.) The general terms for 'sense' or 'sensory power' are αἴσθησις and τὸ αἰσθητικόν. The specific terms for the particular senses are ὄψις ('sight'), ἀκοή and τὸ ἀκουστικόν ('the sense of hearing'), ὄσφρησις and τὸ ὀσφραντικόν ('the sense of smell'), γεῦσις and τὸ γευστικόν ('the sense of taste'), and ἀφή and τὸ ἁπτικόν ('the sense of touch'). Note that it is important to distinguish between τὸ γευστικόν and τὸ γευστικὸν αἰσθητήριον (etc.): the former picks out the sense of taste, the latter the organ in which it resides.

[21] The words ἀκοή ('hearing') and ὄσφρησις ('smell') seem to be used to denote the relevant organs at *DA* 3. 1, 425ᵃ4–5; they clearly are so used at *GA* 2. 6, 744ᵃ2–5, where Aristotle says that 'smell and hearing are passages full of connate *pneuma*'.

derivatively, in virtue of the fact that the sensory powers reside in them.

Thirdly, Aristotle evidently does think that acts of perception crucially involve changes in which the sense-organs play the role of the patient, and do so in an immediate, non-derivative way. This is clearest in the cases of perception by smell and taste. For a perceiver to smell something, Aristotle thinks, the organ of smell must undergo a slight drying.[22] In the act of tasting something, the perceiver's tongue has been moistened (*DA* 2. 10, 422$^a$34–$^b$5). It is only to be expected, then, that we will find in the discussion of perception in the *De anima* references to changes that are undergone non-derivately by the sense-organs, rather than by the sensory powers that reside in them. To call attention to such changes will not by itself undermine the claim that Aristotle's theory is committed to the occurrence of changes or quasi-changes of a certain kind that the senses undergo by the agency of suitable sense-objects. Nor, for that matter, will it undermine the view that it is some sense or sensory power that is supposed to be the patient of the non-destructive kind of alteration that is described at the end of *DA* 2. 5.[23] Aristotle's theory takes acts of perception to involve different kinds of change or quasi-change undergone by distinct patients, which crucially include both the relevant sense-organs and the relevant sensory powers. Combine with this the terminological and metaphysical complications mentioned just now. The result is a complicated bit of philosophical discussion that has proved rather difficult to sort out.

None the less, Aristotle's discussion is not as untidy as might

---

[22] 'Odour', he says at the end of *DA* 2. 9, 'belongs to what is dry, just as flavour belongs to what is moist; and the organ of smell is potentially such' (ἐστι δὲ ἡ ὀσμὴ τοῦ ξηροῦ, ὥσπερ ὁ χυμὸς τοῦ ὑγροῦ· τὸ δὲ ὀσφραντικὸν αἰσθητήριον δυνάμει τοιοῦτον, 422$^a$6–7). The connection between odours and dryness is explained in *De sensu* 5: Aristotle takes odours to be formed and propagated by the action of suitable dry materials on materials characterized by moistness, including air (443$^b$3–6). This requires the presence of some source of heat (443$^b$14–16). As a result, at least some odours are not only dry, but also hot, so that, as they act on the perceiver, they bring about a slight, and beneficial, warming in the area around the brain (444$^a$28–$^b$2). The organ of smell is composed of *pneuma* (*GA* 2. 6, 744$^a$2–5), thus being actually moist and potentially dry, and therefore open to being affected by the dried materials in which olfactory forms reside.

[23] On the other hand, to show that the *DA* 2. 5 assimilation of what perceives to the sense-object is a non-destructive change or quasi-change is not, *pace* Burnyeat, '*De anima* II 5', 76, to show that Aristotle does not require ordinary changes for acts of perception to occur.

now be feared. It turns out that in all those contexts in *De anima* in which he discusses the ways in which he takes perceivers to be affected when they encounter suitable sense-objects, his language indicates accurately enough what he takes the patient of the change in question to be. It is part of the picture that emerges that the non-destructive alteration described at the end of *DA* 2. 5 is an alteration undergone by the perceiver's power to perceive. Or at any rate, that is what I now want to show.

One relevant question is how to interpret the four occurrences in *DA* 2. 5 of the expression 'what perceives' (τὸ αἰσθητικόν). Aristotle says about it that it is, or has being, in virtue of a potentiality rather than an actuality:[24] like burnable fuel, it is actualized only by suitable external causes;[25] that it rises to a developed state of preparedness, analogous to the possession of knowledge, by the agency of that which gives birth to the creature in question;[26] that it is potentially such as the sense-object is in actuality; and that, in the act of perception, it has been likened to the sense-object (418ᵃ3–6). Prior to *DA* 2. 5, Aristotle has used the expression τὸ αἰσθητικόν, in the singular, ten times.[27] Every single time, it denotes specifically the power to perceive. As has been noted already, in *DA* 2. 5 it is not clear whether the expression is meant to denote the power to perceive or the perceiver in question. It may seem that when Aristotle says, in the first occurrence of the expression at 417ᵃ6, that τὸ αἰσθητικόν is merely in potentiality rather than in actuality, 'the power to perceive' is a more likely candidate than 'the perceiver'.[28]

---

[24] 417ᵃ6–7: δῆλον οὖν ὅτι τὸ αἰσθητικὸν οὐκ ἔστιν ἐνεργείᾳ, ἀλλὰ δυνάμει μόνον. For the notion that certain things have being in virtue of a potentiality, see *Metaph.* Λ 6, 1071ᵇ17–19. Cf. *DA* 1. 1, 402ᵃ25–ᵇ1.

[25] Cf. *De sensu* 4, 441ᵇ19–23, where Aristotle recapitulates the doctrine of *DA* 2. 5 and says that flavour is such as to alter the sense of taste into operation or actuality (ἐνέργεια), adding that 'it brings into operation (or actuality) that which perceives [τὸ αἰσθητικόν], which, prior to this, exists potentially'.

[26] 417ᵇ16–17: τοῦ δ' αἰσθητικοῦ ἡ μὲν πρώτη μεταβολὴ γίνεται ὑπὸ τοῦ γεννῶντος.

[27] 402ᵇ13, 16; 408ᵃ13; 410ᵇ22, 26; 414ᵇ1 (twice); 415ᵃ2 (twice); 415ᵃ17. The same expression is used at 415ᵃ6 to pick out creatures capable of perception. There, however, the expression is in the plural: τῶν αἰσθητικῶν δὲ τὰ μὲν ἔχει τὸ κατὰ τόπον κινητικόν, τὰ δ' οὐκ ἔχει ('of animals capable of perceiving some have the capacity for locomotion, others do not').

[28] This seems to be accepted by Burnyeat, though not in his analysis of *DA* 2. 5 ('*De anima* II 5'). In his 'Introduction: Aristotle on the Foundations of Sublunary Physics', in F. De Haas and J. Mansfeld (eds.), *Aristotle: On Generation and Corruption, Book 1* (Oxford, 2004), 7–24 at 10, he reports Aristotle's claim at 417ᵃ6–7 as being that 'the senses are potentialities rather than actualities—they need an external cause to set them going'.

This in itself, however, does little to settle the question of what precisely is meant to play the role of the patient in the chapter's conception of the assimilation of what perceives to the sense-object. After all, Aristotle might employ the expression τὸ αἰσθητικόν in different ways even within *DA* 2. 5 Fortunately, a number of remarks later on in the *De anima*'s discussion of perception and cognition supply important clues as to the identity of the patient.

At the beginning of *DA* 2. 12 Aristotle returns to the topic of perception in general, having by now discussed each of the senses in turn. He says that a sense (αἴσθησις) is 'what is such as to receive perceptible forms without the matter'. He then compares the power to perceive to wax, which is such as to receive the imprint of a signet ring without receiving any of the ring's silver or gold. 'In a similar way', he continues,

the sensory power relative to each sense-object [ἡ αἴσθησις ἑκάστου] is affected [πάσχει] by what has colour, flavour, or sound, but not in so far as each of them is spoken of the way it is except as being of this or that quality,[29] and in accordance with the form [λόγος]. (*DA* 2. 12, 424ᵃ21–4)

As the passage shows, Aristotle is prepared to ascribe specifically to the senses affections brought about by suitable sense-objects. In what follows immediately, he distinguishes tidily between sensory power and sense-organ (αἰσθητήριον), the (primary) thing in which such a power resides. Given the presence of that careful distinction in the immediate context, the claim that it is the sense in question

[29] I depart from the text read by modern editors in reading ἡ rather than ᾗ at 424ᵃ24, adopting the reading of the 12th-/13th-cent. MS Ambrosianus H 50 sup., gr. 435. Caston, 'The Spirit and the Letter', 306 n. 120, notes the awkwardness of two construals of the standard text that have been proposed, including Hicks's. I agree that the difficulty is real, but reject the solution Caston proposes. According to his proposal, Aristotle is here claiming that it is not in so far as something is, say, crimson that it affects the sense of sight, but in so far as it embodies a certain proportion (306). I reject this as contradicting the view, which I take to be Aristotle's, that the special perceptibles, including colours, affect the senses as such, rather than incidentally. (Aristotle seems to specify what affects the senses both as, for instance, colour and as what has colour, in so far as it has colour. This, I take it, is part of the general pattern that the efficient cause may be specified either as the form in question, e.g. the art of building, or as the form–matter composite, e.g. the builder.) At *DA* 2. 6, 418ᵃ23–4, Aristotle says specifically about incidental perceptibles that perceivers, or the senses, are not affected by them as such, because they are perceived incidentally, which is to say that they are not perceived *per se* or in their own right. That explanation would be quite inadequate if perceivers, or the senses, were not affected by special perceptibles as such, either, even though the special perceptibles are evidently among those things that are perceived *per se* or in their own right (418ᵃ8–9, 24).

194        *Hendrik Lorenz*

that is affected by what has colour, flavour, or sound carries special weight. How could a sensory power be affected by a sense-object? Obviously it cannot undergo ordinary changes whereby it passes from having one perceptible quality in a straightforward way to having another. After all, it is not the right kind of thing to have any perceptible quality in a straightforward way. It is unextended and immaterial. The discussion in *DA* 2. 5 provides us with a conception of a type of change or quasi-change that can be ascribed to a sensory power with at least a measure of intelligibility. Aristotle evidently conceives of the senses as, so to speak, dynamic potentialities, capable of existing in mere potentiality as well as in actualized potentiality.[30] This enables one to see how sensory powers can be activated or actualized by suitable sense-objects. It remains to be seen how this peculiar kind of affection can be understood as some kind of alteration undergone by the sense, rather than simply a transition from potentiality to operation or actuality. But in any case there is at least some reason to think that we are meant to understand the claim in *DA* 2. 12 that the senses are affected by suitable sense-objects in the light of the conception of non-destructive alteration that is introduced and explained in *DA* 2. 5. Perception crucially involves, and perhaps in some sense just is, a peculiar kind of affection undergone by the sense in question in which it 'rises into itself and into actuality', without losing any quality, and does so by the agency of a suitable sense-object.

That this is along the right lines becomes somewhat clearer in *DA* 3. 2. That chapter includes a passage in which Aristotle applies the *Physics* 3. 1–3 model of causal agency and patiency to the case of perception. He begins with sound and hearing:

If change and acting and being affected are in that which is acted on, it is necessary also that sound and hearing in operation are in the sense of hearing [ἀνάγκη καὶ τὸν ψόφον καὶ τὴν ἀκοὴν τὴν κατ᾽ ἐνέργειαν ἐν τῇ κατὰ δύναμιν εἶναι].[31] For the operation of what is such as to act and to effect

[30] Note *De sensu* 4, 441ᵇ19–23: the senses are brought into operation or actuality by suitable sense-objects. Cf. M. Frede, 'Introduction', in M. Frede and D. Charles (eds.), *Aristotle's* Metaphysics *Lambda* (Oxford, 2000), 1–52 at 44: 'any soul . . . is in different states at different times, depending on whether the potentialities it is constituted by are actualized or exercised or not'.

[31] I reject Ross's extravagant decision, in his *editio maior* (Oxford, 1961), to print ἐν τῷ κατὰ δύναμιν rather than ἐν τῇ κατὰ δύναμιν at 426ᵃ4. All our manuscripts except one (the 13th-/14th-cent. Parisinus gr. 2043) read the latter; 'Philoponus' (perhaps the 6th-/7th-cent. commentator Stephanus) cites and comments on the latter; and

change comes to be in that which is affected; which is why it is not necessary for that which effects change to undergo change. (*DA* 3. 2, 426ᵃ2–6)

According to Aristotelian doctrine, the operation of the agent of change and that of the patient both occur in the patient.³² For example, the teacher's operation of teaching and the student's operation of learning both occur in the student. In the present passage, Aristotle applies this doctrine to perception. In doing so, he specifies the sense of hearing as the patient of an affection that he takes an occurrent sound to bring about in a suitably placed perceiver.³³ He then generalizes his analysis to perception in general:

The same account applies also to the other senses and sense-objects. Just as acting and being affected are in what is affected but not in what acts, so also the operation of the sense-object and that of what perceives are in what perceives [ἐν τῷ αἰσθητικῷ]. (*DA* 3. 2, 426ᵃ9–11)

In this generalized statement Aristotle is using the expression τὸ αἰσθητικόν ('what perceives') to pick out what he regards as the patient of an affection that he takes sense-objects to bring about in suitably placed perceivers. In perception in general, τὸ αἰσθητικόν stands to what is perceptible in the way in which, in hearing, the auditory sense stands to what is audible. It would seem, then, that

both Themistius' paraphrase and Simplicius' commentary make the sense that in which the joint operation of sound and hearing occurs. Moreover, as I shall attempt to show presently (pp. 199–206), that it is the sense in which that operation occurs is readily intelligible.

³² U. Coope, 'Aristotle's Account of Agency in *Physics* III 3', *Proceedings of the Boston Area Colloquium in Ancient Philosophy*, 20 (2004), 201–21 at 203–5, offers helpful comments on the relevant terminology. I propose to take as read Coope's suggestion that what agency, for Aristotle, comes to is that a potentiality of the agent is fulfilled by a change that comes about in the patient (219). I only wish to add that the change in the patient is a matter of taking on a given form, whose origin is the agent (cf. *Phys.* 3. 2, 202ᵃ9–12). More on this presently (pp. 199–206).

³³ In the context, I take it to be clear that by τῇ κατὰ δύναμιν (sc. ἀκοῇ) at 426ᵃ4 Aristotle means specifically the sense of hearing rather than the organ of hearing. (It may be worth noting that this reading is accepted also in R. Sorabji, 'Intentionality and Physiological Processes: Aristotle's Theory of Sense-Perception', in Nussbaum and Rorty (eds.), *Essays on Aristotle's De anima* (1992), 195–225 at 213.) As noted earlier, Aristotle does occasionally use the word ἀκοή to refer to the organ of hearing. In the present passage, however, he plainly leaves that use out of consideration, presumably as being non-standard. At 426ᵃ6–8 he recognizes two uses of the word (διττὸν γὰρ ἡ ἀκοή), one in which it picks out the sense and one in which it denotes an act of hearing; in this latter use it is synonymous with the word ἄκουσις. These, then, are the uses of the word that he takes to be relevant to his purposes in the passage. Given that context, the only reasonable way of construing the expression 'ἡ ἀκοή in potentiality' is as picking out the sense of hearing.

in the present passage the expression τὸ αἰσθητικόν serves to denote the power to perceive in general or generically, rather than this or that particular sense. It is also worth noting that in the same passage Aristotle writes of what perceives by taste (τὸ γευστικόν, 426ᵃ14–15) in parallel with sight (ὄψις), clearly so as to denote the sense of taste. There should be nothing surprising in this kind of usage. Aristotle routinely uses language of this kind in referring to powers or parts of the soul, such as the part responsible for nutrition (τὸ θρεπτικόν), the part responsible for thought (τὸ διανοητικόν), or, as one might translate, the part responsible for perception (τὸ αἰσθητικόν).³⁴ Presumably he thinks of the senses as themselves parts or aspects of the part of the soul responsible for perception. So 'the part responsible for tasting' (etc.) would seem to be a fair alternative translation of expressions such as τὸ γευστικόν (etc.).

The passage is thus of help in three interrelated ways. First, it reinforces the idea that Aristotle thinks one thing that happens in perception is that specifically the sense in question is in some way affected by a suitable sense-object. Secondly, it seems to use the expression 'what perceives' (τὸ αἰσθητικόν) as a general term to denote the power to perceive, rather than this or that particular sense. And thirdly, it makes it clear that in acting on the sense in the relevant way, the sense-object activates the sense and thereby brings about perceptual awareness.

At this stage, some readers might be inclined to think that the evidence that has been adduced is sufficient to conclude that Aristotle takes the non-destructive alteration described at the end of *DA* 2. 5 to consist simply in an affection undergone by the power to perceive, whereby it is brought into operation or actuality by some suitable sense-object. Before concluding in this way, however, we should confront two more questions. First, is there reason to think that when a sensory power is brought into operation by a suitable sense-object, it undergoes not only a non-destructive transition of some kind or other, but specifically a non-destructive alteration or quasi-alteration? Secondly, is it clear that the assimilation described at the end of *DA* 2. 5 is meant to be exhausted by an affection undergone by the relevant sensory power? It is one thing to ascribe to Aristotle the claim that perception crucially involves a peculiar kind of affection undergone by a sensory power at the hands of a

³⁴ e.g. *DA* 2. 2, 413ᵇ11–16; 2. 3, 414ᵃ29–32; 2. 4, 415ᵃ16–20.

suitable sense-object.[35] It is another thing to accept that the assimilation described at the end of *DA* 2. 5 is meant to be exhausted by such an affection.

I begin with the first question. Alteration is change in the category of quality. In standard cases of alteration, something or other loses one quality and gains another from the same range delimited by a given pair of contraries. A change which is not a matter of losing a quality is obviously no standard case of alteration. In introducing the notion of non-destructive alteration, Aristotle is extending his ordinary notion of alteration. The question is whether the notion can intelligibly be extended far enough to cover changes or quasi-changes that the senses undergo at the hands of suitable sense-objects. In characterizing this kind of change or quasi-change, I have so far relied on the idea of a transition from potential being to operation or actuality. This, however, is only one aspect of Aristotle's conception of that peculiar kind of affection. It is also part of his conception that while the sense prior to the act of perceiving is only potentially such as the sense-object, in the act of perception it has come to be actually like the sense-object. The sense-object brings the sense into operation by assimilating it to itself.[36] That, I take it, is the doctrine. It is to this conception of assimilation of sense to sense-object that we should now turn.

A number of passages subsequent to *DA* 2. 5 shed light on how Aristotle takes the senses to be affected by suitable sense-objects. These later passages enable us to piece together a relatively clear picture of the likeness of sense to sense-object in the act of perception. Two relevant passages are already in play: the first half of *DA* 2. 12 (424ᵃ17–ᵇ3) with its general characterization of sensory powers as being such as to receive perceptible forms without the matter, and the application to perception of the *Physics* 3. 3 agent–patient analysis at *DA* 3. 2, 425ᵇ26–426ᵃ26. To those passage I now want to add *DA* 3. 8, which is a rather short chapter in which Aristotle concludes and recapitulates the discussion of cognition that begins in *DA* 2. 5[37] In that chapter, he says that the perceptual part

[35] I borrow this picturesque turn of phrase from C. Shields, 'Intentionality and Isomorphism in Aristotle', *Proceedings of the Boston Area Colloquium in Ancient Philosophy*, 11 (1995), 307–30 at 310.
[36] Recall *De sensu* 4, 441ᵇ20–1: flavour 'is such as to alter the sense of taste into operation' (τῆς γεύσεως τῆς κατὰ δύναμιν ἀλλοιωτικὸν εἰς ἐνέργειαν); note the word 'alter'.
[37] Note the announcement at the beginning of *DA* 3. 8: 'Now let us sum up what

of the soul (τῆς . . . ψυχῆς τὸ αἰσθητικόν) is potentially what is perceptible, as the part responsible for knowledge is potentially what is
knowable (431ᵇ26–8). 'They must either be the things themselves',
he continues,

> or the forms in question. They are not the things themselves: for the rock
> is not in the soul, but the form is. So that the soul is like the hand. For the
> hand is a tool of tools;³⁸ the intellect is a form of forms, and the power to
> perceive [ἡ αἴσθησις] is a form of perceptibles. (DA 3. 8, 431ᵇ28–432ᵃ3)

Here Aristotle is claiming that the perceptual part of the soul—in
other words, the power to perceive—is potentially, or has potentially in itself, the forms of perceptibles.³⁹ In an act of perception,
the power to perceive undergoes a transition whereby the relevant
perceptible form comes to be actually present in it.

   The various claims Aristotle makes in DA 2. 12 and 3. 8 connect
rather smoothly with the description of the assimilation of what
perceives to the sense-object at the end of DA 2. 5 In claiming that
the perceptual part of the soul potentially has in it the forms—no
doubt the perceptible forms—of what is perceptible, Aristotle can
be seen to be offering a somewhat more determinate version of

has been said about the soul' (431ᵇ20). While the chapter makes no reference to any
part of the discussion in 2. 1–4, it does cover both perception and thought, thus
recapitulating at least DA 2. 5–3. 7. Note also DA 3. 9, 432ᵃ15–16: one of the two
powers in terms of which animal soul has been defined is that of discernment (τὸ
κριτικόν), 'which is the function of thought and perception', and 432ᵃ17–18: 'let this
much be determined about perception and intellect'. De anima can thus be seen
to offer, at 2. 5–3. 8, a loosely unified discussion of discernment, sensory as well
as intellectual.
   ³⁸ ἡ χεὶρ ὄργανόν ἐστιν ὀργάνων. Cf. PA 4. 10, 687ᵃ20–1: the hand is not one tool but
many, 'as it is, so to speak, a tool for tools' (ἔστι γὰρ ὡσπερεὶ ὄργανον πρὸ ὀργάνων);
this is because the hand becomes 'a talon, a claw, and a horn, and again a spear, a
sword, and any other weapon and tool: for it will be all of these things because it
can grasp and hold all things' (πάντα γὰρ ἔσται ταῦτα διὰ τὸ πάντα δύνασθαι λαμβάνειν
καὶ ἔχειν αὐτήν). Likewise, the soul can become all forms by receiving and holding
all of them. (Note 431ᵇ21: ἡ ψυχὴ τὰ ὄντα πώς ἐστι πάντα.)
   ³⁹ In fact, the claim is that the perceptual part of the soul is potentially all that is
perceptible, just as the intellect is potentially all that is intelligible (431ᵇ21–3). He
seems to set aside, presumably as an insignificant complication, that the sense of
touch is blind towards certain tangible qualities, and so is not potentially all that is
tangible, or at any rate not potentially all degrees of heat, wetness, and hardness (DA
2. 12, 424ᵃ2–5). That the sense of touch has blind spots follows from Aristotle's claim
that acts of perception require that the relevant sense-organ be affected, together
with the principle that like is not affected by like. Since the organ of touch is
inevitably the bearer of qualities such as a given degree of heat, sense-objects with
the same degree of heat cannot affect it.

the claim, at *DA* 2. 5, 418ª3–4, that 'what perceives is potentially such as the sense-object is already in actuality'. The sense rises to being actually such as the sense-object if and when the relevant perceptible form comes to be actually present in it. That transition, it would seem, can equally well be described as the reception by the sense of perceptible form without the matter. The key question for our purposes is what to make of Aristotle's notion of the reception of perceptible form by the sense. Once we have a reasonably clear view of that notion, the related notions of assimilation and alteration of the sense will readily fall into place.

To answer that key question, we should revisit the agent–patient analysis of *DA* 3. 2. In its context and against the background of *Physics* 3. 1–3, it makes it clear that Aristotle's notion of the reception of perceptible form by the sense is a rather technical one, and that he conceives of such reception as being identical with the perceiver's transition to perceiving, or perhaps with that transition considered in a way that disregards any bodily process that may be involved.⁴⁰ As we have seen already, the passage applies the *Physics* 3. 1–3 analysis of change to the case of perception, treating the sense-object as the agent and the sense as the patient of a certain kind of change or quasi-change. It is part of the doctrine of *Physics* 3. 1–3 that the agent of change, in changing the patient, imparts a form to it, thereby making it, for instance, an object of a certain kind, such as a house, or the bearer of a certain quality, such as health or knowledge: 'That which effects change', Aristotle holds,

will always carry some form [εἶδος δὲ ἀεὶ οἴσεταί τι τὸ κινοῦν]—either a 'this' or 'such' or 'so much'—which, when it effects change, will be the principle and cause of the change: for example, what is actually a human being makes, out of what is potentially a human being, a human being. (*Phys.* 3. 2, 202ª9–12).⁴¹

Thus the application of the *Physics* 3. 1–3 analysis of change to perception brings with it the idea that the sense-object, in affecting the sense, imparts to it a certain form. The form in question is, of

---

⁴⁰ In what follows I shall sometimes omit the second alternative, but only for simplicity of exposition. The significance of that alternative will become clear in Section 4, pp. 212–14.

⁴¹ E. Hussey, *Aristotle:* Physics, *Books III and IV* (Oxford, 1983), 64, offers discussion of the principle that the agent's form is propagated in change, noting that 'the principle is that if A acts on B, and "A is F" gives the form which is the origin of B's change, then B changes so as to become F'.

course, the perceptible form that resides in the sense-object. The idea is, then, that a fragrant lavender bush, in affecting your sense of smell, imparts its own perceptible form to it. The sense, in being affected by the sense-object, receives its perceptible form. As you enjoy the scent of lavender, the same perceptible form is present in the lavender bush and in your sense of smell, though it is present in different ways.

To get clear about what exactly the reception of perceptible form by the sense is meant to come to, we need to distinguish between the activity of perceiving and the change or quasi-change that is the transition to perceiving. Aristotle's analysis in *DA* 3. 2 starts, at 425$^b$25, with remarks about the relation between the operation of the sense-object and that of the sense: for instance, sound in operation on the one hand and hearing in operation on the other. They are one and the same, he holds, but distinct in being. It is natural to interpret these remarks as being simply about perceptual activity, rather than about the transition to perceiving. He then locates this complex operation in the sense, offering an argument that it may be helpful to quote again:

εἰ δὴ ἐστιν ἡ κίνησις καὶ ἡ ποίησις καὶ τὸ πάθος ἐν τῷ ποιουμένῳ, ἀνάγκη καὶ τὸν ψόφον καὶ τὴν ἀκοὴν τὴν κατ' ἐνέργειαν ἐν τῇ κατὰ δύναμιν εἶναι· ἡ γὰρ τοῦ ποιητικοῦ καὶ κινητικοῦ ἐνέργεια ἐν τῷ πάσχοντι ἐγγίγνεται. διὸ οὐκ ἀνάγκη τὸ κινοῦν κινεῖσθαι.

If change and acting and being affected are in that which is acted on, it is necessary also that sound and hearing in operation are in the sense of hearing. For the operation of what is such as to act and to effect change comes to be in that which is affected; which is why it is not necessary for that which effects change to undergo change. (*DA* 3. 2, 426$^a$2–6)

This analysis, it would seem, takes into consideration not only a change or quasi-change in which a sound, for instance, acts on a perceiver's auditory sense, but also an open-ended operation which the sound brings about in the sense by acting on it in the relevant way.[42] In effect, Aristotle is extending the *Physics* 3. 3 agent–patient analysis from acting so as to bring about a change to acting so as to

---

[42] Aristotle does not think, I assume, that in ongoing perceptual activity in relation to an unchanging sense-object (say, a motionless red surface) the sense-object keeps acting on the senses, or that the sense keeps being affected by the sense-object. For in the act of perception, sense and sense-object are like one another, and Aristotle of course holds that like is not affected by like. I thus take it that it is specifically in the change or quasi-change that is the transition to perceiving that the sense-object acts on the sense. (Similarly Hicks, ad 425$^b$29, 438: 'The transition from dormant power

bring about an (unqualified) operation. In the *Physics* 3. 3 analysis the item in which the change occurs is the bearer or subject of the change in question.[43] For instance, when a teacher teaches a student, a complex operation that is both a case of teaching and a case of learning occurs in the student. The point is that it is the student who is changed in this way. Thus we will want to explicate the claim that, in perception, the relevant change or quasi-change occurs in the sense in terms of the idea that it is the sense in question that undergoes the change or quasi-change. It is the sense that is activated by being acted on in the relevant way by a suitable sense-object. As we turn from the activation of the sense to its operation, the question arises of what it might mean for the joint operation of sense-object and sense, sounding and hearing, to come to be in the sense. It presumably means that in the act of perception it is the sense that is in some suitable way the bearer of that operation. It is worth noting, though, that for the sense of hearing to be the bearer of that operation in the relevant way need not be a matter of the sense engaging in some auditory activity. It need not, and perhaps should not, be a matter of the auditory sense, and thereby of the soul, doing a bit of hearing. After all, Aristotle is on record as holding that it is better to say that the person feels pity, learns, thinks things through, and so forth, than that the soul does (*DA* 1. 4, 408ᵇ13–15).[44]

On the present construal of the *DA* 3. 2 agent–patient analysis of perception, Aristotle is significantly extending the analysis of *Physics* 3. 3 by taking into consideration not only a change or quasi-change in the patient brought about by the agent, but also an on-

to its actual exercise must be treated as equivalent to πάσχειν or κινεῖσθαι.') Nothing, however, prevents the operation of what is such as to act, e.g. an odour getting itself perceived, from continuing indefinitely beyond its instantaneously completed exercise of agency. The presence of an odour in the perceiver's environment may sustain the perceiver's operation of smelling without further exercises of agency; this may require only that a suitable condition of the perceiver's sense-organ is maintained, e.g. a condition of slight dryness that departs somewhat from the organ's neutral condition of moistness.

[43] This is emphasized by Coope, 'Aristotle's Account of Agency in *Physics* III', 205–6.

[44] I do not take myself here to offer anything like a decisive reason against ascribing to Aristotle the view that the soul can properly be said to engage in activities such as perceiving. (This view is ascribed to Aristotle, for instance, by R. Heinaman, 'Aristotle and the Mind–Body Problem', *Phronesis*, 35 (1990), 83–102.) My present concern is only to make it clear that my interpretation does not commit Aristotle to that view.

going state or operation that is in place once that change or quasi-change has been effected. The idea is that the patient is not only the bearer of the transition, but also, in some way or other, of the state or operation that is in place once the transition has been made. Now, on the face of it this is a perfectly natural extension. It is not only that the student, in being taught, is the bearer of a complex operation that is describable both as a case of teaching and as a case of learning. He or she is also the bearer of the state of knowledge that is the proper terminus of both teaching and learning. Moreover, this extended analysis has a noteworthy precedent in *DA* 2. 2. There Aristotle distinguishes between two ways in which we can be said to know by something or other (ᾧ ἐπιστάμεθα, 414ᵃ5), namely on the one hand by knowledge and on the other hand by the soul. This is parallel, he holds, to the way one can be said to be healthy on the one hand by health and on the other hand by some part of the body, or by the body as a whole. He adds that in the first way of specifying the thing by which one knows or is healthy, what is being appealed to, knowledge or health, is

μορφὴ καὶ εἶδός τι καὶ λόγος καὶ οἷον ἐνέργεια τοῦ δεκτικοῦ, ἡ μὲν τοῦ ἐπιστη-μονικοῦ, ἡ δὲ τοῦ ὑγιαστικοῦ· δοκεῖ γὰρ ἐν τῷ πάσχοντι καὶ διατιθεμένῳ ἡ τῶν ποιητικῶν ὑπάρχειν ἐνέργεια. ἡ ψυχὴ δὲ τοῦτο ᾧ ζῶμεν καὶ αἰσθανόμεθα καὶ διανοούμεθα πρώτως—ὥστε λόγος τις ἂν εἴη καὶ εἶδος, ἀλλ' οὐχ ὕλη καὶ τὸ ὑποκείμενον.

a shape and a form, an account and, so to speak, an operation of what is such as to receive the thing in question, in the one case what is responsible for knowledge, in the other case what is responsible for health. For the operation of the things that are such as to act seems to be in that which is affected and in what is disposed in the relevant way. The soul is that by which we are alive, perceive, and think in the first way; so that it would be an account and a form, but not matter and the substratum in question. (*DA* 2. 2, 414ᵃ9–14)

He is characterizing knowledge as a form or account and as a quasi-operation of what is such as to receive knowledge. He is reluctant to refer to it simply as an operation (ἐνέργεια), I take it, because, strictly speaking, it is a dispositional state rather than an operation. In the second way of specifying that by which one knows or is healthy, what is being appealed to is the matter or substratum of the thing in question. This need not in every case be some stuff or collection of materials. The substratum of knowledge, Aristotle implies, is the soul, or the part or aspect of it that is responsible for knowledge, and that, of course, is no kind of stuff or material. What is appealed to in this second way of specifying that by which one knows or is healthy is that which is the bearer of knowledge or health in virtue of having been in-formed or actualized in the relevant way. I shall refer to this item as the receptacle of knowledge, health, or whatever else it may be.[45]

The receptacle of knowledge is 'what is responsible for knowledge' (τὸ ἐπιστημονικόν), and by this Aristotle must mean the relevant part or aspect of the soul, since he quite plainly takes the view that it is by saying that someone knows by the soul that one is appealing to the receptacle of knowledge (414ª5–8). By 'that which is responsible for knowledge', then, Aristotle evidently means the intellect or its theoretical part or aspect.[46] Thus it is clear that the passage applies the *Physics* 3. 3 agent–patient analysis to one of the potentialities that constitute the soul, with the potentiality in question, the intellect, playing the role of the patient of a change or quasi-change.[47] Moreover, it extends that analysis by treating the

[45] I mean to capture a certain Aristotelian notion of being τὸ δεκτικόν ('what is receptive') of something or other. This is the notion of being the bearer of some attribute, form, or actuality. Examples include bronze as the receptacle of statue-form, the body as that of health or disease (1023ª12–13), the intellect as the receptacle of knowledge, and, I shall presently suggest, the senses as the receptacles of perceptual operation. Being in something as in a receptacle is a way of being in (ἐν) something that is recognized in Aristotle's philosophical lexicon at *Metaph.* Δ 23, 1023ª11–13 (note 1023ª23–5). Cf. *Phys.* 4. 3, 210ª20–1.

[46] Recall *DA* 3. 8, where Aristotle refers to the intellect as 'the part of the soul responsible for knowledge' (τῆς δὲ ψυχῆς . . . τὸ ἐπιστημονικόν, 431ᵇ26–7). This is said to be 'a form of forms' (εἶδος εἰδῶν, 432ª2).

[47] Note that the acquisition of knowledge is a destructive alteration, and is evidently treated as such in *DA* 2. 5. It is also, of course, treated as a case of alteration in *Physics* 3. 3. Thus if that change is ascribed to the soul, this raises a difficulty in the light of Aristotle's claims in book 1 of *De anima* that the soul does not engage in, or undergo, change, and arguably a more severe one than the ascription to the soul or its parts of non-destructive alterations or quasi-alterations. (This is noted in Heinaman, 'Aristotle and the Mind–Body Problem', 96 n. 26.) Recall, however, that *DA* 2. 5 treats the acquisition of knowledge as either no case of being affected, or as a special manner of being altered (417ᵇ12–16). His reason is that acquiring knowledge is a change into, or towards, the thing's nature. Burnyeat, '*De anima* II 5', 65 n. 97, refers to *Phys.* 5. 2, 226ª26–9, where Aristotle says that alteration is change with regard to quality, but not with regard to quality that is in the nature (οὐσία) of the thing in question. Thus it might be Aristotle's view that although the soul does not engage in, or undergo, standard forms of change, non-standard forms of alteration, such as the acquisition of knowledge, can properly be ascribed to it. Furthermore, and alternatively, Aristotle might hold that while acquiring knowledge, so far as the student is concerned, is, or may well be, a genuine alteration, so far as the student's intellect is concerned it is not, and cannot be, a genuine change at all, but only a transition, completed instantaneously, from merely potential to actual presence of

relevant part of the soul not only as the patient of the change or
quasi-change that is the acquisition of knowledge, but also as the
receptacle of the state, and quasi-operation, of knowledge that is
the terminus of that transition. In fact, it would seem that Aristotle means to explain the idea that the intellect is the receptacle of
knowledge by appealing to the doctrine that the operation of what
is such as to act is in the patient ($414^a11–12$). This makes good
sense. The teacher, in teaching, acts on the student's intellect and
thereby brings it into a new state. For the intellect to enter into
a new state in this way is to receive intelligible form. And so the
student's intellect is not only what undergoes this change or quasi-
change. It is also what receives the form and quasi-operation which
is the proper terminus of that transition. That quasi-operation is
the newly established state of knowledge.

In the case of the change or quasi-change that is the transition
to perceiving, what is in place once the transition has been made
is a perfectly good example of an operation. So far as hearing is
concerned, that operation can equally well be described as a case
of sounding. When Aristotle claims, in *DA* 3. 2, that this complex
operation is in the auditory sense, we have all the resources needed
to understand this, given the background of the application and
extension of the agent–patient analysis in *DA* 2. 2. What he has
in mind, I submit, is that the sense comes to be the bearer of perceptual operation by being in-formed in the appropriate way. In
other words, he takes the sense to be the (proximate) receptacle of
perceptual operation.[48] On this view, the senses stand to perceptual
operation as the body, or the relevant part of it, stands to health, and
as the intellect stands to knowledge. Perceptual operation, health,

intelligible form. The idea would be that in the process of learning, the student may
gradually approach the transition to the actual presence of intelligible form in his or
her intellect, which, when it comes about, is instantaneously complete. I owe this
suggestion to discussion with Ben Morison.

[48] If this is along the right lines, then the *DA* 3. 2 analysis is adding a layer of
complexity to the picture offered by the *DA* 2. 2 analysis. According to that simpler
picture, one is alive, perceives, and thinks by the soul in the sense that it is the
soul that is the form by which one is alive, perceives, and thinks (*DA* 2. 2, $414^a12–$
14). Note that in saying this, Aristotle may well have in mind, not perceptual or
intellectual operation, but preparedness for such operation: in one use of perception
terms, they pick out being able to perceive (*DA* 2. 5, $417^a9–12$). On that picture, the
receptacle of perception, or of the power to perceive, is a body of a certain kind. We
now learn that in an act of perceiving the relevant part or aspect of the soul has itself
received a further layer of form. But this is just what one expects, if the senses, being
forms, are themselves receptive of forms, as Aristotle evidently thinks they are.

and knowledge are formal aspects or features in virtue of whose presence in the relevant receptacle the person or animal in question is perceiving, is healthy, or knows. Knowledge is intelligible form in a distinctive manner of manifestation;[49] likewise, perceptual operation is perceptible form in a distinctive manner of manifestation. Note that it is no part of Aristotle's analysis, so understood, that the senses can, strictly speaking, be said to perceive things. The *DA* 2. 2 analysis is compatible with holding that, strictly speaking, it is Euclid who knows and understands geometry, in virtue of his intellect having been in-formed in the appropriate way. Likewise, the *DA* 3. 2 analysis is compatible with holding that, as you look at a red flag, the perceiving subject, strictly speaking, is you, and you are seeing red in virtue of your sense of sight having been in-formed in the appropriate way.

In any case, Aristotle holds that for a sound to activate the auditory sense of a suitably placed perceiver is a matter of bringing about a change or quasi-change by acting, and so, given his conception of agency, he must take it to be a case of imparting form to what is being acted on, the perceiver's auditory sense. It would, however, be a mistake to think that the agent's imparting form to the patient, in Aristotle's analysis, is meant to underlie the agent's action, or the patient's change, as matter to form. When a stove heats a kettle, its imparting the perceptible form of hotness to the kettle is not what underlies the heating of the kettle as matter to form. It just is the heating of the kettle. Likewise, the teacher's imparting intelligible form to the student just is his or her teaching the student. In the same way, when a lavender bush imparts its olfactory form to your sense of smell, this is not what underlies the activation of the sense as matter to form. It just is the activation of the sense. Such is the upshot of Aristotle's agent–patient analysis of perception.

The idea, then, that in the act of perception the sense has been altered by and likened to the sense-object rests on a technical notion of transmission and reception of perceptible form from sense-object to sense. That notion itself, moreover, seems to rest on a commitment that may well be a fundamental axiom of Aristotle's scientific psychology, namely that the senses, as well as the intellect, are potentialities that are open to being in-formed, in the one case by receiving perceptible form, in the other by receiving intel-

---

[49] Cf. *Metaph. Z* 7, 1032$^b$13–14: 'the art of medicine and that of building are the forms of health and house; I call the essence substance without matter.'

ligible form. That this commitment is axiomatic is suggested by a number of texts, such as the first half of *DA* 2. 12 with its general characterization of the senses as being such as to receive perceptible form, or the recapitulation in *DA* 3. 8, with its claim that the forms of perceptibles are potentially present in the perceptual part of the soul. Those claims are made and to some extent explained, but never, it seems, argued for. However that may be, once the notion of the reception of perceptible form by the sense is in place, it is easy to see that, in an act of perception, the sense in question has come to be like the sense-object.[50] In an act of perception, the same perceptible form—say, the scent of lavender—is present in both the sense-object and the sense, though it is present in rather different ways.[51]

We are now ready to appreciate more fully than in Section 2 the significance of the fact that Aristotle characterizes the assimilation of what perceives to the sense-object as an alteration that is non-destructive. What he focuses on in characterizing this kind of change is not that what undergoes the change does not genuinely take on the relevant perceptible quality. He leaves it indeterminate whether or not receiving perceptible form without the matter is a genuine case of taking on the quality in question, however non-standard it may be. He says that 'there is a way in which' what sees, when it sees, has come to be coloured:[52] 'for each sense-organ is such as to receive what is perceptible without the matter' (*DA* 3. 2, $425^b22$–4). One thing on which he does focus in characterizing this peculiar kind of change is that it is not a matter of suffering the

---

[50] This meets a challenge formulated by S. Everson in *Aristotle on Perception*, 94: 'unless there is some property of the object which τὸ αἰσθητικόν takes on, the notion of "becoming like" the object has lost all content' (I have taken the liberty of replacing 'the organ', which is a tendentious translation, with the word it is meant to represent).

[51] I thus agree wholeheartedly with Burnyeat's memorable picture in 'Aquinas on "Spiritual Change" in Perception', 141: 'For an Aristotelian, both sensible and intelligible forms are present to the world in two irreducibly different ways, one of which is cognitive of the other. The form of tiger, for example, is active in the forests as the organizing principle of the life of tigers, but it may also be present, differently, in the intellect of a zoologist who has reached a principled understanding of that kind of life. Similarly, the orange and black colouring of a tiger's striped coat will also be present, differently, in the eye of its mate as they hunt together, watching each other's movements.' I only wish to add, by way of clarification, that the perceptible forms in question are in the tiger's eye derivatively, in virtue of being in the sensory power that resides in the eye.

[52] τὸ ὁρῶν ἐστιν ὡς κεχρωμάτισται, $425^b22$–3.

loss or destruction of a quality. Prior to perceptual activity, there is no way at all in which the inactive sense is in actuality the bearer of any perceptible quality or form.[53] Thus one remarkable feature that clearly does characterize the transition that is the assimilation of sense to sense-object is that it is an alteration, or quasi-alteration, that is thoroughly non-destructive.

In this connection, it is worth noting what may well be a significant linguistic detail in *DA* 2. 5. In the general statement, early on in the chapter, of what is affected by what, Aristotle says that

all things are affected and changed by what is such as to act and what is in activity. Which is why there is a way in which what is affected is affected by what is like it, and there is a way in which it is affected by what is unlike it, as we said. That which is unlike is affected; having been affected, it is like [πάσχει μὲν γὰρ τὸ ἀνόμοιον, πεπονθὸς δ᾽ ὅμοιον ἐστιν]. (*DA* 2. 5, 417ᵃ17–21)

The back-reference at 417ᵃ19–20 seems to be to Aristotle's discussion, in *GC* 1. 7, of agency and patiency (ποιεῖν καὶ πάσχειν).[54] According to the model that emerges from that discussion, those things are such as to affect one another that are alike in genus but unlike and contrary in species. For example, bitter flavours are such as to affect sweet ones. This model requires that for one thing to be such as to alter another, agent and patient must, prior to the al-

---

[53] One might think that this is contradicted at *DA* 3. 4, 429ᵃ24–7, where Aristotle argues that the intellect cannot be 'mixed with' the body, since in that case 'it would acquire some particular quality, cold or heat, or indeed would have some organ, as the power to perceive has; but as a matter of fact it has none' (ποιός τις γὰρ ἂν γίγνοιτο, ἢ ψυχρὸς ἢ θερμός, ἢ κἂν ὄργανόν τι εἴη, ὥσπερ τῷ αἰσθητικῷ· νῦν δ᾽ οὐθὲν ἐστιν). It seems best to interpret this as envisaging two distinct ways in which the intellect might be 'mixed with' the body: (i) literally, as one material thing with another, or (ii) in an extended way, by having a bodily organ, the way the power to perceive has. Only on the first construal would the intellect acquire qualities such as cold or heat. Thus interpreted, the passage is perfectly compatible with thinking that prior to being in operation, the power to perceive is not in actuality the bearer of any perceptible quality, not even in the non-standard way in which it may come to be the bearer of qualities in acts of perception.

[54] An alternative candidate is 416ᵃ29–ᵇ9 in the preceding chapter on the nutritive faculty. There Aristotle discusses the question of whether animals are nourished by what is like them or what is contrary to them, concluding that in so far as they are nourished by unconcocted food they are nourished by what is contrary, but in so far as they are nourished by concocted food, by what is like. However, the only thing that is said to be affected in the passage is the (unconcocted) food, which, being contrary, is affected. The only kind of likeness that is mentioned in the passage is the likeness between animal and food after concoction. That likeness plays no explanatory role in Aristotle's characterization of the affection undergone by the food as it is concocted.

teration, bear different qualities from the same range. For the sake of simplicity, Aristotle treats such qualities as contraries. Clearly the model cannot be applied without modification to a kind of alteration, or quasi-alteration, whose patient, to begin with, does not bear any quality from the relevant range. It would be wrong to say that the sense, prior to perceptual activity, is contrary to any sense-object.[55] In the discussion in *GC* 1. 7, being unlike (ἀνόμοιον) something or other is closely associated with being contrary to it.[56] Perhaps for that reason, Aristotle does not say, at the end of *DA* 2. 5, that what perceives is affected as something that is unlike the sense-object. In what I suggest is a subtle shift of phrasing, he says that what perceives is affected as something that is not like (οὐχ ὅμοιον)[57] the sense-object.

Finally, we should turn to the question of whether the assimilation described at the end of *DA* 2. 5 is meant to be exhausted by a change or quasi-change undergone by, or anyhow ascribed to, the sense in question. There is strong textual evidence, in *De anima* and elsewhere,[58] that Aristotle takes at least some acts of percep-

---

[55] A further complication is that the sense, prior to perceptual activity, is not generically like any sense-object, either. Thus there is not only the problem of how to satisfy the model's requirement of specific unlikeness between agent and patient, but also a problem of how to satisfy the requirement of generic likeness. It seems that Aristotle means to solve the second problem by relying on the somewhat obscure idea that at least some forms of being potentially *F* in themselves render what is potentially *F* like what is actually *F* (*DA* 2. 5, 417ᵇ4–5). The same kind of problem arises for the application of the model to intellectual cognition; again Aristotle's attempted solution may seem less than perfectly satisfactory: *DA* 3. 4, 429ᵇ22–430ᵃ2.

[56] *GC* 1. 7, 323ᵇ30–4: 'that which acts and that which is affected must be alike and the same in genus, but in species unlike and contrary' (τῷ δ᾽ εἴδει ἀνόμοιον καὶ ἐναντίον); note also 324ᵃ5–9 (τῷ μὲν γένει ταὐτὰ καὶ ὅμοια, τῷ δ᾽ εἴδει ἀνόμοια, τοιαῦτα δὲ τἀναντία).

[57] One might compare the distinction, at *NE* 3. 1, 1110ᵇ18–24, between the person who acts involuntarily or 'counter-voluntarily' (ἄκων) and the one who acts non-voluntarily (οὐχ ἑκών).

[58] A text that deserves special attention is *GA* 5. 1, 780ᵇ29–33, where Aristotle explains differences among perceivers in accuracy of visual discernment in terms of differences in purity of the perceiver's liquid eye-jelly: 'just as small stains are distinct on a pure, clean shirt, so small changes are distinct in a pure, clean sight, and they bring about perception' (ὥσπερ γὰρ ἐν ἱματίῳ καθαρῷ καὶ αἱ μικραὶ κηλῖδες ἔνδηλοι γίνονται, οὕτως καὶ ἐν τῇ καθαρᾷ ὄψει καὶ αἱ μικραὶ κινήσεις δῆλαι καὶ ποιοῦσιν αἴσθησιν). The 'pure, clean sight' mentioned here contrasts with the 'impure liquid in the eye' (τὸ δ᾽ ἐν τῇ κόρῃ ὑγρὸν μὴ καθαρόν) mentioned just before at 780ᵇ24; so it would seem that Aristotle is using the word 'sight' to pick out the organ of sight. The passage distinguishes clearly between acts of perception and changes in the eye-jelly, which depending on their extent, and on the purity of the organ, may or may not

tion to involve alterations that are undergone specifically by the relevant sense-organs. For example, the perception of flavour requires that the perceiver's tongue passes from being somewhat dry to being moist (*DA* 2. 10, 422ª34–ᵇ5).⁵⁹ That is because flavours reside in suitable moist materials, as Aristotle states in *DA* 2. 10⁶⁰ and explains in detail in *De sensu* 4. The organ of taste, prior to perceptual activity, must be in a condition of moderate dryness, so that it can be acted on by what is tasteable, which Aristotle evidently takes to be moist not incidentally, but precisely in so far as it is tasteable.⁶¹ When a perceiver's tongue enters into contact with something tasteable, the actually moist sense-object will assimilate the potentially moist organ to itself precisely as the *GC* 1. 7 model of agency and patiency predicts. This, I take it, is at least part of the material cause of flavour perception, much as boiling of the pericardial blood is at least a crucial part of the material cause of anger (*DA* 1. 1, 403ª29–ᵇ2).⁶²

Thus one might think that the assimilation of what perceives to the sense-object that is described at the end of *DA* 2. 5 is meant to have two aspects, a change undergone by a sense-organ and

bring about perceptions. If such a change is too faint or the organ is too impure, what occurs is an alteration in the organ without a corresponding activation of the sense.

⁵⁹ Note especially 422ᵇ3–5: ἀναγκαῖον ἄρα ὑγρανθῆναι . . . τὸ γευστικὸν αἰσθητήριον ('the organ of taste needs to be moistened'). R. Bolton, 'Perception Naturalized in Aristotle's *De anima*', in Salles (ed.), *Metaphysics, Soul, and Ethics in Ancient Thought*, 209–44 at 226 n. 12, offers detailed discussion of the explanatory role in Aristotle's theory of the tongue's being moistened by the object of taste.

⁶⁰ *DA* 2. 10, 422ª10–11: καὶ τὸ σῶμα δ᾽ ἐν ᾧ ὁ χυμός, τὸ γευστόν, ἐν ὑγρῷ ὡς ὕλῃ ('the body in which flavour resides, that which is tasteable, is in something moist as in matter').

⁶¹ This is made clear at *DA* 2. 10, 422ᵇ2–5, where Aristotle infers from the fact that taste is affected by the tasteable as such that the organ of taste must be capable of being moistened: 'the sense of taste is in some way affected by what is tasteable, in so far as it is tasteable. The organ of taste, then, which needs to be moistened, must be capable of being moistened while being preserved, while at the same time it must not be moist' (πάσχει γάρ τι ἡ γεῦσις ὑπὸ τοῦ γευστοῦ, ᾗ γευστόν. ἀναγκαῖον ἄρα ὑγρανθῆναι τὸ δυνάμενον μὲν ὑγραίνεσθαι σωζόμενον, μὴ ὑγρὸν δέ, τὸ γευστικὸν αἰσθητήριον). I owe this point to discussion with Rob Bolton.

⁶² Burnyeat, '*De anima* II 5', 83, claims that *DA* 2. 5–3. 2 'leaves no textual space for further material changes underlying the alteration which is perceiving'. What Aristotle says in *De anima* leaves it open, I think, whether, for instance, the moistening of the tongue by tasteables or, more probably, the condition of moistness thereby produced underlies flavour perception as matter to form. However, it is clear that Aristotle thinks flavour perception requires some suitable moistening of the tongue, and also that such moistening is part of Aristotle's explanatory account of flavour perception, no doubt under the rubric of the material cause.

a certain kind of alteration or quasi-alteration undergone by the sensory power that resides in the organ. However, that particular kind of assimilation is conceived of as a non-destructive alteration akin to the transition from possessing knowledge to the activity of contemplation. Only one of the two aspects of assimilation just mentioned qualifies as a non-destructive alteration. The other one, by contrast, is a matter of losing a suitable attribute, such as a given quality, by having it replaced with another. In tasting a strawberry, for instance, the perceiver's tongue undergoes a change that partly consists in losing the moderate level of dryness characteristic of a tongue that is currently inactive as an organ of taste, but fully prepared for operation.[63] It would seem, then, that the assimilation described at the end of *DA* 2. 5 is meant to consist in, and be exhausted by, an alteration or quasi-alteration that is undergone by, or at any rate ascribed to, the sense in question.

This also provides another reason in favour of interpreting the expression 'what perceives' (τὸ αἰσθητικόν) in the description of that assimilation in *DA* 2. 5 as denoting specifically the perceiver's power to perceive, rather than the perceiver, or sense-organ, conceived of as a form–matter composite. At the end of *DA* 2. 5, as we have seen, Aristotle says that what perceives is affected by the sense-object, so that it passes from not being like it to being such as it. What he has in mind is no doubt that this happens always or for the most part when certain conditions are in place: the sense-object must be appropriately located in relation to the perceiver, the perceiver must be in a suitable state of preparedness for perceptual activity, and so forth. The context, when interpreted properly, makes it clear that he takes 'what perceives', in suitable circumstances, to be affected by the sense-object in a non-destructive way, in a way that is not a matter of losing a given quality by having it replaced with another. But then the expression 'what perceives', in that statement at the end of *DA* 2. 5, should be interpreted, as it certainly can be, as denoting the perceiver's power to perceive, rather than the perceiver, or the sense-organ, considered as a form–matter composite. For it is true only with regard to the power to perceive, considered by itself, that the transition from perceptual inactivity to occurrent perception is a change or quasi-change that is non-destructive. For the form–matter composite that is the per-

---

[63] That is why a given act of tasting can interfere with a subsequent one, as Aristotle notes at *DA* 2. 10, 422[b]6–8.

ceiver, or the sense-organ in question, undergoing that transition, for instance in flavour or odour perception, is in important part a matter of losing a given quality by having it replaced with another. This consideration should be added to the arguments already offered for interpreting the expression 'what perceives', at *DA* 2. 5, 418ᵃ3, as denoting the power to perceive. Those arguments are, first, that in all ten occurrences prior to *DA* 2. 5 of that expression, used in the singular, it denotes the power to perceive; and, secondly, that a number of passages subsequent to *DA* 2. 5 enable us to piece together a clear, though rather intricate, conception of the likeness between sense and sense-object in the act of perception, in expounding which Aristotle uses the expressions τὸ αἰσθητικόν ('what perceives') and τῆς ψυχῆς τὸ αἰσθητικόν ('the perceptual part of the soul') to denote the power to perceive in general or generically, rather than this or that particular sense.⁶⁴

4. Perception, change, and the soul

According to the theory of perception that emerges from my reconstruction, there are two distinct aspects to the likeness between perceiver and sense-object in the act of perception. When a perceiver encounters a suitable sense-object, the sense-object affects both the relevant sense-organ and the sense that resides in it. It affects the organ by causing it to undergo an ordinary change—for instance, an alteration in which the organ loses one quality and acquires another from the same range. It affects the sense by 'altering it into operation', to use Aristotle's own expression. That second kind of affection is not only a transition from potentiality to operation or actuality. It is also a non-standard case of alteration, in which the sense in question in a certain way receives a perceptible form without suffering the loss of any quality.⁶⁵

⁶⁴ Recall also *De sensu* 4, 441ᵇ19–22, where Aristotle makes what looks to be the same step as in *DA* 3. 2 from a particular sense to τὸ αἰσθητικόν, meaning 'the power to perceive': he says of the affection in the wet that he takes flavour to be that it is 'such as to alter the sense of taste into operation: for it brings into operation that which perceives, which, prior to this, exists potentially; for perceiving is in accord not with learning but with contemplating' (τῆς γεύσεως τῆς κατὰ δύναμιν ἀλλοιωτικὸν εἰς ἐνέργειαν· ἄγει γὰρ τὸ αἰσθητικὸν εἰς τοῦτο δυνάμει προϋπάρχον· οὐ γὰρ κατὰ τὸ μανθάνειν ἀλλὰ κατὰ τὸ θεωρεῖν ἐστι τὸ αἰσθάνεσθαι). Note the clear recapitulation of the doctrine of *DA* 2. 5

⁶⁵ It is worth pointing out that on this reconstruction of Aristotle's mature theory

This reconstruction raises a number of questions concerning the two kinds of affection that it takes to be involved in Aristotle's analysis of what happens when a perceiver encounters a suitable sense-object. Questions arise both about each of the two kinds of affection by itself and about how they are related to one another. I shall not attempt to articulate, let alone resolve, all of those questions. But I would like to close by addressing two issues that seem particularly urgent. The first concerns the nature of perception, as Aristotle conceives of it. The second concerns the apparent ascription of changes or quasi-changes to the soul and its parts or aspects.

Aristotle begins *DA* 2. 5 by recalling that perception 'comes about in being changed and affected, for it seems to be some kind of alteration' (416ᵇ33–5). It would seem that the chapter proceeds to explain what kind of alteration perception is.⁶⁶ Now, one curious feature of the discussion is that it presents a conception not so much of perceiving as of becoming perceptually aware, or of perceptually noticing. After all, the alteration or quasi-alteration in question is the transition from perceptual inactivity to occurrent perceiving. This, however, is a point I wish to note only to get it out of the way.⁶⁷ My first question is this. Should we conclude that Aristotle takes perceiving, in the sense of becoming perceptually aware, to be exhausted by a non-destructive alteration or quasi-alteration that the relevant sensory power undergoes by the agency of a suitable sense-object? He could coherently hold that while what happens

of perception in *De anima*, there may be no need to posit that the remarks about perception in *Phys.* 7. 2–3 reflect an early and subsequently superseded stage of Aristotle's thought (*contra* S. Menn, 'Aristotle's Definition of Soul and the Programme of the *De anima*', *Oxford Studies in Ancient Philosophy*, 22 (2002), 83–139 at 86–91; similarly Heinaman, 'Aristotle and the Mind–Body Problem', 86–7). According to those remarks, acts of perception crucially involve some kind of alteration of the sense, or of the perceptual part of the soul (7. 2, 244ᵇ10–12: 'the senses, too, are in a way altered: for perception in operation is a change through the body, with the sense being in some way affected', ἀλλοιοῦνται γάρ πως καὶ αἱ αἰσθήσεις· ἡ γὰρ αἴσθησις ἡ κατ' ἐνέργειαν κίνησίς ἐστι διὰ τοῦ σώματος, πασχούσης τι τῆς αἰσθήσεως; 7. 3, 248ᵃ6–9: 'it is clear from what has been said that being altered and alteration occur in perceptibles and in the perceptual part of the soul, but in nothing else except incidentally').

⁶⁶ Note also *DA* 2. 4, 415ᵇ23–5, and *MA* 7, 701ᵇ17–18, where Aristotle says that perceptions are alterations of some kind (ἀλλοιώσεις τινες).

⁶⁷ It is explained by Burnyeat, '*De anima* II 5', 66–73. In short: Aristotle wants to ground the cognitive accuracy of perception by showing it to be a form of receptivity, of openness to being acted on by the very aspects of reality that (proper object) perception is of. In keeping with his conception of agency as set out in *Physics* 3. 1–3 and *GC* 1. 7, he locates the agency of perceptibles in a certain kind of change or quasi-change, namely in the perceiver's transition to perceiving.

when a perceiver advances from inactivity to an act of perception is not exhausted by that kind of alteration, it is none the less the case that the act of perceiving itself just is the non-destructive alteration or quasi-alteration of the sense in question. Still, that need not be his view, for all that has been said.

That is because he can reasonably expect that readers of *De anima* are familiar with the principle that terms which in one of their uses denote a form–matter composite can also correctly be used to denote the form, or the matter, of the thing in question. After all, he has said in *GC* 1. 5 that 'flesh and bone and each of the parts of this kind are twofold, as is the case with the other things that have their form in matter: for the form as well as the matter are called flesh or bone' (321ᵇ20–3).⁶⁸ Suppose that he thinks acts of perception, like episodes of anger, are things that have their form in matter. That would not prevent him from using the words 'perception', 'to perceive', and the like, to pick out specifically the formal aspect of an act of perception.⁶⁹ In that case, he might sometimes, though not necessarily always, use those words to pick out the various forms of perceptual awareness, considered in a way that disregards any bodily process or state that may be involved in, or associated with, them. That would be especially appropriate in the context of *De anima*, which evidently is meant to make determinations about the soul 'by itself' (περὶ ψυχῆς καθ' αὐτήν: *De sensu* 1, 436ᵃ1) and its capacities, rather than about the form–matter composites that are the animals and other living things.⁷⁰ On this view, Aristotle can consistently hold (i) that perception is a non-destructive alteration or quasi-alteration of the sense in question, and (ii) that perception

---

⁶⁸ σὰρξ καὶ ὀστοῦν καὶ ἕκαστον τῶν τοιούτων μορίων ἐστὶ διττόν, ὥσπερ καὶ τῶν ἄλλων τῶν ἐν ὕλῃ εἶδος ἐχόντων· καὶ γὰρ ἡ ὕλη λέγεται καὶ τὸ εἶδος σὰρξ ἢ ὀστοῦν. That *GC* 1 is important background to Aristotle's psychology is emphasized and amply illustrated by Burnyeat in his 'Introduction: Aristotle on the Foundations of Sublunary Physics', 9–11. Note also *Metaph. H* 3, 1043ᵃ29–36: the term 'animal' can be used so as to mean 'soul' as well as 'soul in a body'; likewise the term 'house' might be used so as to mean 'covering' as well as 'covering consisting of bricks and stones laid thus and thus'.

⁶⁹ In this regard I agree with Heinaman, 'Aristotle and the Mind–Body Problem', 97.

⁷⁰ *De sensu* begins the *Parva naturalia* by looking back to *De anima*: 'since determinations have previously been made about the soul by itself and about each of its capacities in turn [περὶ ψυχῆς καθ' αὐτὴν . . . καὶ περὶ τῶν δυνάμεων ἑκάστης κατὰ μόριον αὐτῆς], the next thing to do is to study animals and all living things, in order to ascertain which of their functions are peculiar and which ones are common' (436ᵃ1–5).

is a common attribute of body and soul,[71] involving both an ordinary change or modification in a sense-organ and a certain kind of change or quasi-change undergone by a sensory power. If he thinks that the relevant kind of modification in a sense-organ is the material aspect of an act of perception, he might also say (iii) that that kind of modification is perceiving.[72] To see that the three claims are consistent, one would only have to appreciate that in claim (i) the term 'perception' is used to denote the formal aspect of perception, in claim (ii) it picks out the form–matter composite, and in claim (iii) it denotes the material aspect. It should be noted that, for present purposes, I do not mean to claim that Aristotle does in fact conceive of acts of perception as form–matter composites, only that this is a possibility that remains open, for all that has been said.[73]

This takes me to the second, and last, issue on which I would like to comment before closing. According to my reconstruction of Aristotle's theory, he holds that perception is, or at any rate crucially involves, a certain kind of change or quasi-change undergone

---

[71] The idea that perception is an attribute that is common to body and soul is in play at *DA* 1. 1, 403$^a$3–7. Aristotle there seems to presuppose that the soul acts and is affected in certain ways (403$^a$6–7), though it does not appear to act or be affected without the body. That perception importantly involves both body and soul is also repeatedly insisted on in the *Parva naturalia*—for instance, at the beginning of *De sensu* (1, 436$^a$6–11; 436$^b$1–8), and in an important passage of *De somno*, in which Aristotle says that perceiving is not an attribute private to either the soul or the body, since perception in operation is 'some kind of change of the soul through the body' (κίνησίς τις διὰ τοῦ σώματος τῆς ψυχῆς, 454$^a$9–10). Cf. *Phys.* 7. 2, 244$^b$11–12.

[72] Aristotle might well think that suitable modifications in the sense-organs form the material aspect of a given act of perception. This at any rate is strongly suggested by *GA* 5. 1, 780$^a$4–5, where he says that the change of the liquid stuff in the eye, in so far as it is transparent, is seeing (ἐστι δ᾽ ἡ τούτου τοῦ μορίου κίνησις ὅρασις ᾗ διαφανές). This kind of change or modification is clearly distinguished from perception a little later, at 780$^b$29–33, where the idea is that relatively slight changes in the eye-jelly bring about perception only if the organ is sufficiently pure (see above, n. 58). There is no contradiction if Aristotle is using the word 'seeing' at 780$^a$4 to denote the material aspect of seeing.

[73] I have presented what I regard as strong reasons for thinking that Aristotle takes at least some forms of perception, such as flavour perception, to involve ordinary alterations that form part of the material cause of the perceptual act in question. This is enough to pose a serious challenge to, for instance, Burnyeat's spiritualist interpretation of Aristotle's theory of perception. But there is in principle room for the view that although acts of perception have material causes, they are not unified composites of matter and form, the way perceptible substances are. One might adopt such a view for the reason that ordinary changes and the activities that are acts of seeing, hearing, and so forth, differ in kind in a way that makes it impossible for them together to constitute unified composite items. (Cf. Everson, *Aristotle on Perception*, 254–5; Burnyeat, '*De anima* II 5', 82 n. 143.) This is a topic I leave for another occasion.

by the sense in question. But it would seem that the senses, for Aristotle, are parts or aspects of the soul.[74] Should we conclude that Aristotle's mature theory of perception in *De anima* ascribes changes or quasi-changes to the soul?

The main prima facie difficulty for that view is posed by Aristotle's repeated and emphatic claims, in book 1 of *De anima*, to the effect that the soul does not engage in, or undergo, change. His commitment to the changelessness of the soul motivates the famous assertion in *DA* 1. 4 that 'it is perhaps better not to say that the soul feels pity, learns, or thinks things through, but that the person does in virtue of the soul' (*DA* 1. 4, 408$^b$13–15). At one stage in his discussion of pleasure in *NE* 10. 1–5, he writes of a given sense as being in operation, and then interrupts himself, adding that it should make no difference 'whether one says that the sense itself is in operation, or that in which it is',[75] the sense-organ or the perceiver. Thus one might think that when Aristotle, in *De anima* and related writings, ascribes changes to the soul or to its parts or aspects, this is only a manner of speaking. An accurate statement of Aristotle's theory, on that view, will require suitable rephrasing. Some will insist, for instance, that when Aristotle says that flavours bring the sense of taste into operation by altering it in a certain way, he has in mind that flavours affect and activate the organ of taste, or the perceiver, precisely in so far as it is equipped with the sense of taste (or something like that).[76] It is, I think, worth noting that

[74] It is worth noting that Aristotle could consistently hold that (i) the senses are (in a way) parts or aspects of the soul, and (ii) the soul is not affected when the senses are (in a way) affected by suitable sense-objects. One way of defending that apparently inconsistent pair of claims is to distinguish between two ways of considering the senses, one 'flat' and one variable (I borrow those terms from P. Grice, *Aspects of Reason* (Oxford, 2001), 20–1): (i) as states of preparedness for perceptual operation and thereby as static first actualities; (ii) as dynamic potentialities, capable of rising from first to second actuality, and thereby of advancing into the fullness of their being. What are parts or aspects of the soul, Aristotle might hold, are the senses considered as static first actualities; what is altered into operation and actuality is the sense in question, considered as a dynamic potentiality. Interesting and perhaps viable though the idea may be, I see no evidence that Aristotle means to rely on such a distinction between two ways of considering the senses. It is conceivable, though, that he takes some such distinction for granted.

[75] *NE* 10. 4, 1174$^b$17–18: αὐτὴν δὲ λέγειν ἐνεργεῖν, ἢ ἐν ᾧ ἐστί, μηθὲν διαφερέτω.

[76] Note the expression 'being altered with regard to the senses' (ἀλλοιοῦσθαι κατὰ τὰς αἰσθήσεις) at *Phys.* 7. 2, 244$^b$14–15 and 245$^a$2. 'The animal's senses are altered' and 'the animal is altered with regard to its senses' are alternative forms of expression. The question remains, however, which form of expression ascribes the alteration in question to its proper subject.

much of the substance of the interpretation that I have offered in the present paper is open to that kind of reformulation.[77] In order to show this to be the case, let me recapitulate the main features of that interpretation in a suitably rephrased form.

It is part of Aristotle's theory of perception that when a perceiver encounters a suitable sense-object, it is acted on in two rather different ways, and in ways that exercise two rather different capacities of the perceiver. In virtue of having sense-organs composed of certain materials with certain features, the perceiver is open to being acted on by sense-objects in straightforward ways. For instance, its organ of smell is open to being altered so as to lose its neutral condition of moistness by being made somewhat dry. In virtue of being equipped with the power to perceive, organisms of many kinds are endowed with a distinctive kind of receptivity to perceptible form. When a perceiver encounters a sense-object in suitable circumstances, it is acted on by having the relevant sense-organ changed in some way or other. For instance, a fragrant lavender bush has dried the surrounding air in a certain way, and the air in turn brings about a certain drying in the perceiver's organ of smell. But this is not yet a complete account of what happens when a perceiver encounters a sense-object in suitable circumstances, since it leaves out of consideration the fact that the perceiver's power to perceive is engaged. In engaging the perceiver's sensibility, the sense-object

---

[77] One feature of my interpretation that cannot simply be 'formulated away' is my view that Aristotle, at any rate in *DA* 2. 5–3. 8, regards the senses as the proper subjects of certain extraordinary changes or quasi-changes. However, as indicated before (n. 18), I remain agnostic about whether this is what he would want to say on the final and most careful analysis. It is conceivable, and cannot be ruled out, that in *DA* 2. 5–3. 8 he is, perhaps for didactic purposes, systematically indulging in some form of quasi-personification of cognitive capacities in a way that is comparable to the quasi-personifications of desiderative capacities familiar from his ethical writings. (Note, for instance, *NE* 7. 6, 1149$^a$29–$^b$1, where anger or spirit gets upset and rushes to vengeance, and appetite rushes off to enjoy whatever reason or perception says is pleasant.) This, however, is a large assumption to make; and I see no decisive reason to make it. Even if one makes an assumption along such lines, one will still need to take seriously the precise terms and details of Aristotle's exposition in *DA* 2. 5–3. 8, in an effort to extract his theory of perception from that exposition. Even if the relevant non-destructive changes or quasi-changes are ultimately to be ascribed, not to the senses, but to the animal in virtue of the senses, the fact remains that Aristotle conceives of those changes or quasi-changes both as non-destructive and as in some way quality-imparting. Another fact that remains is that the drying of the organ of smell and the moistening of the tongue, envisaged at *DA* 2. 9 and 10, plainly are changes that consist in one quality being replaced with another. Hence the characterization of Aristotle's theory of perception that I am about to offer in the main text.

brings about a certain kind of change or quasi-change which Aristotle conceives of as a non-destructive alteration or quasi-alteration. It is an alteration or quasi-alteration in that it involves imparting perceptible form in a certain way. It is non-destructive in that it is not a matter of replacing a given quality, or perceptible form, with another—except incidentally, if the perceiver is switching from, say, seeing one colour to seeing another, rather than from not seeing to seeing.

In engaging the perceiver's power to perceive, the sense-object carries out a distinctive form of agency and hence imparts form in a certain way. For instance, it whitens or sweetens the perceiver in a distinctive and non-standard way. On the other hand, when an appropriately equipped organism encounters a suitable sense-object, it is subjected to a distinctive form of patiency and hence takes on form in a certain way. For instance, it is whitened or sweetened in a distinctive and non-standard way. This distinctive way of imparting and receiving perceptible form is a certain kind of interaction between sense-objects and perceivers which is crucially characterized in terms of the engagement of sensory powers by suitable sense-objects. Aristotle takes the view that this kind of interaction is perceiving, or that it is perceiving considered in a certain way, namely in a way that disregards any bodily process that may be involved.

It is unclear, however, whether, for purposes of adequately representing Aristotle's theory, all that rephrasing is called for. That is because it is unclear whether anything that Aristotle says in book 1 of *De anima* rules out the ascription, to the soul or its parts, of changes or quasi-changes of the kind introduced in *DA* 2. 5. This applies also to the *DA* 1. 4 passage about how to ascribe mental states.[78]

The context of the passage is a difficulty for Aristotle's view that the soul does not undergo change, at any rate not in its own right. According to a line of argument that he professes not to find completely unreasonable, the soul does undergo certain kinds of change:

---

[78] Menn, 'Aristotle's Definition of Soul and the Programme of the *De anima*', 99–102, offers an interpretation of the passage according to which it does not even rule out ascribing mental states or acts to the soul: 'Aristotle's intention', he holds, 'is simply to deny *motions* to the soul, redescribing all apparent motions of the soul either as non-kinetic activities or as motions of the body that are causally connected with the soul' (emphasis original). Similarly Heinaman, 'Aristotle and the Mind–Body Problem', 97 n. 28.

'for we say that the soul is pained, delighted, feels confidence and fear, is upset, perceives, and thinks things through; and all these things are changes' (408$^b$1–4). He concedes, perhaps only for the sake of the argument, that those mental states or acts are changes 'as much as you like', such as motions or alterations of the heart or some other bodily parts (408$^b$5–11). He then shows the way out of the difficulty by recommending the view that it is the person, not the soul, that is the proper subject of the relevant kinds of mental states or acts.

In the context, he is evidently concerned to reject, and reject emphatically, the ascription of change to the soul (*DA* 1. 4, 408$^b$30–1). However, the kinds of change that are under consideration in book 1 of *De anima* are the kinds familiar from the *Physics* and *De generatione et corruptione*, with a heavy focus on locomotion. Given Aristotle's conception of the soul as unextended and immaterial, it is easy to see why he rejects the ascription to it of locomotion, growth, diminution, and at least many forms of alteration, such as alteration from one perceptible quality to another. However, book 1 contains not even the faintest hint of the non-destructive form of alteration or quasi-alteration that is introduced and explained in *DA* 2. 5. Moreover, it may well be Aristotle's considered view, and the view to which he means eventually to guide his readers, that that kind of transition really is only a quasi-alteration, and no genuine case of change at all. In what looks to be a fragment on perception preserved in *DA* 3. 7, he says:

φαίνεται δὲ τὸ μὲν αἰσθητὸν ἐκ δυνάμει ὄντος τοῦ αἰσθητικοῦ ἐνεργείᾳ ποιοῦν· οὐ γὰρ πάσχει οὐδ' ἀλλοιοῦται. διὸ ἄλλο εἶδος τοῦτο κινήσεως· ἡ γὰρ κίνησις τοῦ ἀτελοῦς ἐνέργεια, ἡ δ' ἁπλῶς ἐνέργεια ἑτέρα, ἡ τοῦ τετελεσμένου.

The sense-object manifestly acts so as to bring what perceives from capacity into operation; for it is not affected or altered. This is why this is something different from change [*alternatively*: this is why this is a different kind of change]: for change is the operation of what is incomplete, but unqualified operation—that is, operation of what has been perfected— is different. (*DA* 3. 7, 431$^a$4–7)

The fragment suggests that the transition to perceiving, as it is undergone by the sense in question, is a case of being acted on in a certain way without being genuinely changed at all. In any case, Aristotle conceives of that transition either as a non-standard form of alteration or as a quasi-alteration that is no genuine form of change at all. As a result it is far from clear whether the remarks about the soul and change in *DA* 1, which presumably are about standard or at any rate genuine kinds of change, have any impact on the question whether non-destructive changes or quasi-changes of the kind identified in *DA* 2. 5 can properly be ascribed to the soul or to its parts or aspects. Thus Aristotle may well mean precisely what he says when, in *DA* 3. 2, he identifies the sense of hearing as what is in a certain way acted on by sound and what, in being so acted on, receives auditory form. After all, by the time we come to *DA* 3. 2, we have been introduced to entirely novel ways of being acted on, and thereby also to entirely novel ways of receiving form.

*Princeton University*

## BIBLIOGRAPHY

Barbotin, E. (trans.), *Aristote: De l'âme* (Paris, 1966).
Bolton, R., 'Perception Naturalized in Aristotle's *De anima*', in Salles (ed.), *Metaphysics, Soul, and Ethics in Ancient Thought*, 209–44.
Broadie, S., 'Aristotle's Perceptual Realism', in J. Ellis (ed.), *Ancient Minds* (*Southern Journal of Philosophy*, 31, suppl; 1993), 137–59.
Burnyeat, M., 'Aquinas on "Spiritual Change" in Perception', in D. Perler (ed.), *Ancient and Medieval Theories of Intentionality* (Leiden, 2001), 129–53.
—— '*De anima* II 5', *Phronesis*, 47 (2002), 28–90.
—— 'How Much Happens When Aristotle Sees Red and Hears Middle C? Remarks on *De anima* 2. 7–8', in Nussbaum and Rorty (eds.), *Essays on Aristotle's* De anima (1995 edn.), 421–34.
—— 'Introduction: Aristotle on the Foundations of Sublunary Physics', in F. De Haas and J. Mansfeld (eds.), *Aristotle: On Generation and Corruption, Book 1* (Oxford, 2004), 7–24.
—— 'Is an Aristotelian Philosophy of Mind Still Credible? (A Draft)', in Nussbaum and Rorty (eds.), *Essays on Aristotle's* De anima (1992), 15–26.
Caston, V., 'The Spirit and the Letter: Aristotle on Perception', in Salles (ed.), *Metaphysics, Soul, and Ethics in Ancient Thought*, 245–320.
Coope, U., 'Aristotle's Account of Agency in *Physics* III 3', *Proceedings of the Boston Area Colloquium in Ancient Philosophy*, 20 (2004), 201–21.
Everson, S., *Aristotle on Perception* (Oxford, 1997).
Frede, M., 'Introduction', in M. Frede and D. Charles (eds.), *Aristotle's Metaphysics Lambda* (Oxford, 2000), 1–52.
Grice, P., *Aspects of Reason* (Oxford, 2001).

220     *Hendrik Lorenz*

Heinaman, R., 'Aristotle and the Mind–Body Problem', *Phronesis*, 35 (1990), 83–102.

Hicks, R. D., *Aristotle:* De anima (Cambridge, 1907).

Hussey, E., *Aristotle:* Physics, *Books III and IV* (Oxford, 1983).

Johansen, T., *Aristotle on the Sense-Organs* (Cambridge, 1998).

Menn, S., 'Aristotle's Definition of Soul and the Programme of the *De anima*', *Oxford Studies in Ancient Philosophy*, 22 (2002), 83–139.

Murphy, D., 'Aristotle on Why Plants Cannot Perceive', *Oxford Studies in Ancient Philosophy*, 29 (2005), 295–339.

Nussbaum, M., and Rorty, A. (eds.), *Essays on Aristotle's* De anima (Oxford, 1992; paperback edn. 1995).

Ross, W. D., *Aristotle:* De anima (Oxford, 1961).

—— *Aristotle's* Physics: *A Revised Text* (Oxford, 1961).

Salles, R. (ed.), *Metaphysics, Soul, and Ethics in Ancient Thought: Themes from the Work of Richard Sorabji* (Oxford, 2005).

Shields, C., 'Intentionality and Isomorphism in Aristotle', *Proceedings of the Boston Area Colloquium in Ancient Philosophy*, 11 (1995), 307–30.

Sisko, J., 'Alteration and Quasi-Alteration', *Oxford Studies in Ancient Philosophy*, 16 (1998), 331–52.

Slakey, T., 'Aristotle on Sense Perception', *Philosophical Review*, 70 (1961), 470–84.

Sorabji, R., 'Body and Soul in Aristotle', *Philosophy*, 49 (1974), 63–89.

—— 'Intentionality and Physiological Processes: Aristotle's Theory of Sense-Perception', in Nussbaum and Rorty (eds.), *Essays on Aristotle's* De anima (1992), 195–225.

Waterlow, S., *Nature, Change, and Agency in Aristotle's* Physics (Oxford, 1982).

# EUDAIMONIA AS AN ACTIVITY IN NICOMACHEAN ETHICS 1. 8–12

## ROBERT HEINAMAN

### 1. Introduction

GIVEN the attention it has received, students of Aristotle may well be weary of the debate over inclusivist and non-inclusivist interpretations of the *Nicomachean Ethics*' account of *eudaimonia*. But I believe the issue is worth revisiting because evidence favouring the non-inclusivist view has yet to be appreciated. While attention has focused on *Nicomachean Ethics* 1. 7, there is strong support for the non-inclusivist view in the immediately following chapters of book 1.

Repeatedly, throughout the *Eudemian Ethics*, the *Nicomachean Ethics* and the *Politics*, Aristotle expresses his view on the identity of *eudaimonia*:[1]

(1) '. . . human good turns out to be *activity*[2] of soul in accordance with virtue, and if there are several virtues, ⟨human good is *activity* of soul⟩ in accordance with the best and most perfect virtue' (*NE* 1098ᵃ16–18).

(2) '. . . and we say that happiness is these [the best *activities*: 1099ᵃ29], or one—the best—of these ⟨activities⟩' (*NE* 1099ᵃ29–30).

(3) Happiness 'has been said to be a kind of *activity* of soul according to virtue' (*NE* 1099ᵇ26).

(4) '. . . happiness is an *activity* of soul in accordance with perfect virtue' (*NE* 1102ᵃ5).

© Robert Heinaman 2007

[1] I am concerned with the *Eudemian Ethics*, the *Nicomachean Ethics*, and the *Politics*, which, on the issue that concerns me, express the same view. But, as we shall see, that position can be instructively contrasted with a view set out in the *Rhetoric*.

[2] The word is ἐνέργεια, which in some of the quoted passages might be better translated as 'actuality'. Apart from a few remarks (n. 30), the present paper does not address the point that Aristotle counts *eudaimonia* as an activity in a sense to be contrasted with change (*Metaph.* 1048ᵇ25–6).

(5) 'Happiness, too, we say is *activity* of soul' (*NE* 1102ᵃ17–18).

(6) '. . . whether happiness is the *activity* of all [our dispositions] or ⟨the *activity*⟩ of one of them . . .' (*NE* 1153ᵇ10–11).

(7) '. . . the *activity* of this [intellect] according to its peculiar virtue is perfect happiness' (*NE* 1177ᵃ16–17).

(8) '. . . the *activity* of reason . . . the perfect happiness of man would be this' (*NE* 1177ᵇ19–24).

(9) '. . . happiness is a kind of contemplation' (*NE* 1178ᵇ32).

(10) '. . . happiness would be *activity* according to perfect virtue . . .' (*EE* 1219ᵃ38–9).

(11) 'If we are right in our view, and happiness is assumed to be *acting well* [εὐπραγίαν] . . .' (*Pol.* 1325ᵇ14–15).

(12) 'Since happiness is the best thing, but it is the perfect *activity* and use [χρῆσις] of virtue . . .' (*Pol.* 1328ᵃ37–9).

(13) 'We say (and have determined in the *Ethics* . . .) that *eudaimonia* is the perfect *activity* and use [χρῆσιν] of virtue' (*Pol.* 1332ᵃ7–9).[3]

While some of these passages raise serious problems, on the point that concerns me here they are uniform and unambiguous: happiness is—as a matter of identity—a certain kind of virtuous activity (where 'virtue' covers intellectual excellence as well as excellence of character).

After reading these passages (and the others cited in n. 3), an intelligent person unfamiliar with recent scholarship on Aristotle's ethics would, I believe, be shocked to learn that despite their number, uniformity, and clarity (on the point that *eudaimonia* is an activity), many, probably most, commentators on the *Nicomachean Ethics deny* that Aristotle identifies *eudaimonia* with virtuous activity. On the common, inclusivist interpretation, Aristotle rather identifies *eudaimonia* with virtuous activity plus all or at least some other human goods which are not activities, such as health and

---

[3] Other passages which identify *eudaimonia* as an activity: *NE* 1100ᵃ14, 1169ᵇ28–9, 30–1, 1176ᵃ35–ᵇ4, 1177ᵃ9–11, 12; *Pol.* 1325ᵃ31. Cf. *Metaph.* 1048ᵇ22–6, 1050ᵃ35–ᵇ2; *Phys.* 197ᵇ5; *Poet.* 1450ᵃ16–22; *NE* 1176ᵃ22–9. Daniel Graham, on the basis of Aristotle's classification of *eudaimonia* as an activity as opposed to a change in *Metaph.* Θ 6 (1048ᵇ22–6), claims that *eudaimonia* is a *state* ('States and Performances: Aristotle's Test', *Philosophical Quarterly*, 30 (1980), 117–30, at 123). Whatever Graham may mean by 'state', it cannot be that activities, as Aristotle understands them, are states, as Aristotle understands them (whether his ἕξεις or διαθέσεις). For Aristotle, states are qualities, and Aristotle's activities are not qualities (cf. *NE* 1173ᵃ13–15) but instances of doing (ποιεῖν, κινεῖν) or suffering (πάσχειν, κινεῖσθαι). See C. Hagen, 'The Energeia–Kinesis Distinction and Aristotle's Conception of Praxis', *Journal of the History of Philosophy*, 22 (1984), 263–80 at 269–74. Cf. *Top.* 125ᵇ15–19.

beauty.[4] On some versions, often motivated by a desire to avoid egoism, *eudaimonia* is even said to include the good states and activities of other human beings.[5] On this position, however important or central virtuous activity is in relation to other human goods, it is just one of several goods that constitute *eudaimonia*.[6] The works of Aristotle with which I am concerned (see n. 1) contain roughly 210,000 words (in English translation), but not one sentence in this sea of words expresses the inclusivist view. The usual interpretation must say that, even though Aristotle's central question in ethics is 'what is *eudaimonia*?', and the *Politics*' starting-point is his account of *eudaimonia*, his explicit statements on the identity of *eudaimonia* never succeed in saying what he believes *eudaimonia* to be. At best, they merely point out the 'principal component of happiness',[7] 'the life and soul of happiness'.[8]

---

[4] See e.g. W. F. R. Hardie, 'The Final Good in Aristotle's Ethics', in J. M. E. Moravcsik (ed.), *Aristotle* (Garden City, NY, 1967), 297–322; J. L. Ackrill, 'Aristotle on *Eudaimonia*', in A. Rorty (ed.), *Essays on Aristotle* (Berkeley, 1980), 15–33; A. Price, 'Aristotle's Ethical Holism', *Mind*, 89 (1980), 338–52; D. Devereux, 'Aristotle on the Essence of Happiness', in D. J. O'Meara (ed.) *Studies in Aristotle* (Washington, 1981), 247–60; T. Irwin, 'Aristotle on Reason, Desire and Virtue', *Journal of Philosophy*, 72 (1975), 567–78; id., 'Permanent Happiness: Aristotle and Solon', *Oxford Studies in Ancient Philosophy*, 3 (1985), 89–124; id., 'Stoic and Aristotelian Conceptions of Happiness', in M. Schofield and G. Striker (eds.), *The Norms of Nature* (Cambridge, 1986), 205–44; id., 'The Structure of Aristotelian Happiness' ['Structure'], *Ethics*, 101 (1991), 382–91; id., 'Ethics in the *Rhetoric* and in the *Ethics*', in A. Rorty (ed.), *Aristotle's* Rhetoric (Berkeley, 1996), 142–74; J. Annas, 'The Good Life and the Good Lives of Others', *Social Philosophy and Policy*, 9 (1992), 133–48, and *The Morality of Happiness* (Oxford, 1993), 367; S. Meyer, *Aristotle on Moral Responsibility* (Oxford, 1993), 25, 27; N. White, 'Conflicting Parts of Happiness in Aristotle's Ethics' ['Conflicting Parts'], *Ethics*, 105 (1995), 258–83; A. Gomez-Lobo, 'The Ergon Inference', in L. Gerson (ed.), *Aristotle: Critical Assessments* (London, 1999), 170–83. S. Broadie in S. Broadie and C. Rowe, *Aristotle:* Nicomachean Ethics [*Nicomachean Ethics*] (Oxford, 2002), 278, 283, 286, 288; ead., 'Aristotle's Elusive *Summum Bonum*' ['*Summum Bonum*'], *Social Philosophy and Policy*, 16 (1999), 233–51. Instrumental goods are not in question since only intrinsic goods are possible constituents of *eudaimonia*.

[5] As White points out ('Conflicting Parts', 282–3), inclusivism by itself cannot avoid the problem of egoism since it remains true on an inclusivist account of happiness that the good of others can conflict with one's own good, and it remains unclear why in such circumstances the agent should favour the good of others over his own good.

[6] Some inclusivists contrast virtuous activity with other goods by saying that it is the essence of, or central to, happiness; or that it is the core or focus of happiness. Nevertheless, they make other goods constituents of happiness as well and that suffices to put their positions in range of my objections.

[7] Broadie, in Broadie and Rowe, *Nicomachean Ethics*, 286.

[8] S. Broadie, *Ethics with Aristotle* [*Ethics*] (Oxford, 1991), 315.

Defenders of at least one variation of inclusivism will object that, in a way, they do allow that *eudaimonia* is constituted by virtuous activity alone, but then further claim that the other intrinsic goods that constitute *eudaimonia* should be understood to constitute virtuous activity itself.[9] While, in a way, reconciling an inclusivist interpretation with the evidence quoted above, this version of inclusivism faces its own special problems as well as more general objections to the inclusivist account.

So we can distinguish two forms of inclusivism:

> *First Version*: *Eudaimonia* is virtuous activity + other goods such as health.
>
> *Second Version*: *Eudaimonia* is virtuous activity alone; and virtuous activity is constituted from other goods such as health.

Either version can be extreme or moderate. The extreme version, *comprehensivism*, affirms that *eudaimonia* comprises all human goods, the weaker version only that it is constituted by some goods other than virtuous activity, including bodily goods such as health and/or external goods such as friends.[10]

The present paper argues that inclusivist views conflict with a

---

[9] J. Whiting, '*Eudaimonia*, External Results, and Choosing Virtuous Actions for Themselves' ['*Eudaimonia*'], *Philosophy and Phenomenological Research*, 65 (2002), 270–90 at 280–1, makes the external results of virtuous action—for example, others' possession of goods such as money—constituents of *the agent's* virtuous action and hence constituents of the agent's *eudaimonia*. R. Crisp, 'Aristotle's Inclusivism' ['Inclusivism'], *Oxford Studies in Ancient Philosophy*, 12 (1994), 111–36, and 'Kraut on Aristotle on Happiness', *Polis*, 10 (1993), 129–61 at 155, claims that while Aristotle believes that *eudaimonia* is 'one good', and that virtuous activity is 'the only component of *eudaimonia*', virtuous activity 'includes' other intrinsic goods ('Inclusivism', 119 n. 21, 133). In criticizing this view I will understand it to mean what it says. However, when Crisp explains the relation of the other intrinsic goods to virtuous activity, it turns out that the intrinsic goods other than virtuous activity are only 'involved' in virtuous activity in the way that seeing might be 'involved' in virtuous action ('Inclusivism', 129). This hardly suffices to make seeing a constituent of virtuous activity—certainly it would not in Aristotle's metaphysics—and does not justify the claim that the seeing and the virtuous activity are 'one good'.

[10] I do not count as 'inclusivist' interpretations which claim that virtuous activities other than contemplation constitute *eudaimonia* but limit the entities that constitute *eudaimonia* to such activities. On the contrary, that is the position I defend. Apart from the view of Irwin to be discussed shortly, I understand 'inclusivist' interpretations to claim that not only virtuous activity but (1) goods of the body and/or (2) external goods and/or (3) goods of the soul which are states or conditions (as opposed to activities) constitute *eudaimonia*. Aristotle clearly holds that such goods are necessary for *eudaimonia* (*NE* 1099ᵃ31–ᵇ8, 1099ᵇ27–8, 1100ᵇ26–8, 29–30, 1153ᵇ17–19; *Pol.* 1332ᵃ19–21). The issue in dispute is whether they are also constituents of *eudaimonia*.

substantial part of what Aristotle has to say about *eudaimonia* in *Nicomachean Ethics* 1. 8–12. These are the chapters in which Aristotle seeks confirmation of chapter 7's definition and develops some points which depend on that definition.

Before examining those chapters, I wish to point out one conclusion we can draw from the list of quotations in (1)–(13). On T. H. Irwin's 'regulative' interpretation, the description of *eudaimonia* as 'actuality in accordance with virtue' (ἐνέργεια κατ᾿ ἀρετήν) (at the conclusion of the function argument in *NE* 1098ª16–18; cf. *EE* 1219ª38–9) 'refers to a regulation by virtue, as distinct from full manifestation of the virtues'.¹¹ On this view, actions such as walking which are neither virtuous nor vicious, neither good nor evil, may nevertheless constitute *eudaimonia*. We know that, for Aristotle, not all human actions are manifestations of virtues or vices (*NE* 1173ª5–13, ᵇ26; *Poet.* 1450ᵇ8–10). On Irwin's proposal, actions which are not virtuous but do not violate the requirements of virtue can be 'in accordance with virtue' and constitute *eudaimonia*. But the list of quotations shows that this cannot be right. (2), (9), and in particular (12) and (13) identify *eudaimonia* with *virtuous* activities alone. Walking which exemplifies no virtue could not be a 'use' (χρῆσις) of virtue. If (1)–(13) all express the same view, 'actuality in accordance with virtue' cannot be interpreted in Irwin's weak sense.

The same is shown by Aristotle's assertion that the activity with which he identifies *eudaimonia* is 'of' virtue (*NE* 1098ᵇ31: ταύτης [sc. ἀρετῆς] γάρ ἐστιν ἡ κατ᾿ αὐτὴν ἐνέργεια; cf. 1101ᵇ32, 1176ᵇ18–19): the actuality *of* a virtue can only be a manifestation of that virtue. Drumming my fingers on the desk while reading the newspaper is not an actuality of courage, temperance, or any other virtue. Thus, at 1106ᵇ16–23, the actualities 'of' virtue are those actions that hit the mean in action between excess and deficiency. Hitting the mean evidently suffices to make an action a manifestation of virtue, not merely a non-violation of virtue. And, as Roger Crisp has pointed out,¹² there are still other passages that are incompatible with Irwin's interpretation: if, as Aristotle says, actions 'in accordance with virtue' (κατ᾿ ἀρετήν) are 'fine' (*NE* 1120ª23–4, 1176ᵇ7–9, 1179ª3–8) and are especially stable (*NE* 1100ᵇ12–17), they must be virtuous actions. So the activities constituting *eudaimonia* do not include actions which do not themselves exemplify virtue.

¹¹ 'Structure', 390.        ¹² 'Inclusivism', 117 n. 17.

Nor, I believe, should we accept Sarah Broadie's attempt to explain away Aristotle's statements by saying that they are merely examples of synecdoche, using the name of the main component of happiness to refer to the whole.[13] If *NE* 1. 7's assertion that *eudaimonia* is virtuous activity is an example of synecdoche, meaning merely that virtuous activity is the principal component of happiness, then presumably 1. 7's denials that *eudaimonia* is growth, nutrition, and perception mean merely that they are not the principal components of *eudaimonia*. This seems implausible. Further, since, for Aristotle, 'what is *eudaimonia*?' is the main question in ethics, it is hard to believe that he might be so unconcerned to distinguish happiness itself—on the inclusivist view happiness *plus* health, *plus* beauty, etc.—from one of its many components (virtuous activity) that he cannot be bothered *even once* to make the distinction explicit. Aristotle says that 'it makes no small difference whether we place the chief good in possession or in use, in state or in activity' (*NE* 1098[b]31–3). Presumably, then, it is also important if *eudaimonia* is *both* possession and use, the view which, on Broadie's account, Aristotle does not mention even though it is his own.

While synecdoche is of course a real linguistic phenomenon, it would be bizarre to use a word '*x*' in such a way when the issue under discussion was to specify exactly *what x is*.

## 2. *Nicomachean Ethics* 1. 7

Following various introductory points and a review of other positions in *Nicomachean Ethics* 1. 1–6, chapter 7 begins Aristotle's exposition of his answer to the question 'what is *eudaimonia*?' After laying down that *eudaimonia* is (1) the supreme good and not chosen for the sake of another good, (2) self-sufficient, and (3) most choiceworthy without being added to other goods,[14] the function

[13] Broadie, in Broadie and Rowe, *Nicomachean Ethics*, 278. It is not clear whether her claim is restricted to the statements she refers to (*NE* 1098[a]16, 1102[a]5–6, 1177[a]12) or would apply to all the passages listed above. If the former, a further argument against her view would be that, assuming that all the passages make the same claim about the relation between *eudaimonia* and virtuous activity, since some of (1)–(13) are not examples of synecdoche, none are.

[14] Aristotle's points about self-sufficiency and choiceworthiness are the usual basis for inclusivist interpretations. I discuss them elsewhere ('*Eudaimonia* and Self-Suf-

argument aims for a more specific description of *eudaimonia*. Since its concluding identification of *eudaimonia* with virtuous activity is clear, I wish merely to make one point of special relevance for my purposes here.

Aristotle's conclusion identifies happiness with the life of the rational soul, but 'life' can refer either to actual life or to potential life.[15] Aristotle explains ($1098^a5-7$) that he understands the function of man to be the former, what the *Eudemian Ethics* ($1244^b23-4$) calls 'living in actuality' (τὸ ζῆν τὸ κατ᾽ ἐνέργειαν).[16]

His conclusion, then, as quoted above, is that '. . . human good turns out to be *activity* of soul in accordance with virtue, and if there is more than one virtue, ⟨human good is *activity* of soul⟩ in accordance with the best and most perfect virtue' (*NE* $1098^a16-18$).

## 3. *Nicomachean Ethics* 1. 8

Chapter 8 offers further support for 1. 7's identification of *eudaimonia* with virtuous activity. Following his standard dialectical procedure, Aristotle begins by pointing out that what is commonly said about *eudaimonia* should 'harmonize' with the conclusion of 1. 7's argument ($1098^b9-11$): 'we should consider it [viz. *eudaimonia*], however, in the light not only of our conclusion and our premisses, but also of what is commonly said about it'. His mention of premisses and conclusion refers to the function argument and its claim that *eudaimonia* is virtuous activity, not to some implied and unstated conclusion of the self-sufficiency criterion which—being inconsistent with the assertion that *eudaimonia* is virtuous activity alone—is supposed somehow to override the conclusion of the function argument. Hence, as we shall now see in detail, the points he is about to make are designed to fit the 'conclusion' that *eudaimonia* is virtuous activity.

---

ficiency in the *Nicomachean Ethics*', *Phronesis*, 33 (1988), 31–53; 'The Improvability of *Eudaimonia* in the *Nicomachean Ethics*' ['Improvability'], *Oxford Studies in Ancient Philosophy*, 21 (2002), 99–147.

[15] See *NE* $1170^a16-19$; *Protr.* B 79–83; *EE* $1244^b23-4$.

[16] A similar point is made in the function argument's parallel in the *Eudemian Ethics* at $1219^a23-5$. Cf. the use of ζῆν and ζωή in *Metaph.* $1048^b25-6$, $1050^a35-^b2$.

228    *Robert Heinaman*

(*a*)  *The best goods are the goods of the soul* ($1098^{b}12$–20; cf. *EE*
$1218^{b}32$–6, $1219^{a}29$–30; *Pol.* $1323^{a}24$–6, $1323^{b}13$–18; *Protr.*
B 2–4; *Top.* $116^{b}2$–3)

Aristotle divides goods into goods of the soul, goods of the body,
and external goods. Goods *of* (περί) the soul are of two kinds. First,
they include goods such as knowledge whose proper subject is the
soul, goods which are present in the soul as their subject (cf. *EE*
$1218^{b}32$–7). By the 'proper subject' of an entity *y* I mean what *y* is
present in, where that subject is *y* in itself, non-accidentally. Thus,
the soul is the proper subject of thought, virtue, and knowledge
while the body is the proper subject of health and locomotion.

Second, action whose proper subject is not its agent's soul can
be a good *of* the agent's soul. For Aristotle, an agent's action, a
change, is not present *in* the agent (understanding 'agent' in a strict
sense) but in the patient of the action, what undergoes the action
as bricks and stones undergo the action which is a housebuilder's
building.[17] The proper subject, the patient, of such an action can
be the soul or body of another living thing, the agent's own body,
or an inanimate object.[18] But, though present in the patient, it will
be an action and, if it is a good, a good of (περί) the *soul* of the *agent*.

For Aristotle, an agent causes a voluntary action only if the
agent's soul is the efficient cause of the action, which consists in
some *desire* efficiently causing that movement (*DA* 3. 9–11; cf. *Rhet.*
$1369^{a}1$–4). Not everything caused by an agent's soul is an action in
the relevant sense. Thus, nourishment, though caused by the soul,
is a good of the body.

Clearly, goods of the body such as health cannot be goods of the
soul in either of the two specified ways. The subject in which health
exists is the body, not the soul; and health is not a kind of action.
Similarly, at least many external goods for a person *x* are goods
such as friends which have neither the soul nor the body of *x* as a
subject; nor are they actions.

The common view Aristotle refers to states that goods of the soul
are the best goods, and psychic activities and actions are goods of
the soul. He points out that this common view of different kinds

[17] See *Phys.* 3. 3. *DA* $411^{a}26$–30 explains that knowledge, perception, belief, and
wish belong to the soul, while the change *in the body* which is locomotion is brought
about by the soul.
[18] Examples of the four cases: teaching, healing another person, running, housebuilding.

of good and their value fits his own position since 'we are positing *actions* and *activities* of the soul' as constituting *eudaimonia*. So his definition puts happiness, the best good, into the class into which the common saying puts the best goods.

What can Aristotle's argument mean on the inclusivist view? It cannot mean what it says since inclusivist views affirm that external goods and/or goods of the body such as friends, health, and beauty as well as goods of the soul constitute *eudaimonia*. The fact that a collection of goods including health, friends, etc. would include goods of the soul would hardly warrant the claim that the entire collection—happiness—is a good of the soul any more than it would warrant the claim that it is a good of the body. Rather, obviously, on the inclusivist view happiness is a good of the soul *and* of the body *and* an external good.

The same problem exists for the second version of inclusivism, which says that the virtuous activity constituting *eudaimonia* is itself constituted from goods of the body and external goods. It is no easier to understand how the good of the soul that is virtuous activity could be constituted from bodily goods and external goods than it is to understand how the good of the soul that is happiness could be constituted from bodily goods and external goods.

*NE* 10. 3 ($1173^b7$–13) argues that pleasure cannot be replenishment because replenishment is a material change, and hence has the body as its primary subject, whereas the primary subject of pleasure is the soul ($1099^a7$–8; cf. $1117^b27$–31). Aristotle assumes that what has the soul as its primary subject cannot also have the body as its primary subject.[19] But on an inclusivist understanding of *eudaimonia* it does have the body as well as the soul as a primary subject since it includes goods such as health.

These arguments in *NE* 10. 3 and 1. 8 rest on Aristotle's standard metaphysical doctrine, a permanent fixture throughout his writings, that, for any non-substance, there is a substance for which it is true both that that kind of non-substance must be defined in terms of that kind of substance, and that such a substance is the proper sub-

---

[19] Although Aristotle only gives an explicit account of identity for changes (*Phys.* 5. 4 and $242^a31$–$^b8$, $242^a66$–$^b1$, $249^a16$–21, $^b12$–14, $261^b36$–$262^a5$), it can be taken for granted that, as in the case of change, any non-substances *x* and *y* are identical only if they have the same subject. When, as here, we are concerned with the identity of kinds of entity, the subjects must be of the same kind; when we are concerned with individual entities, the subjects must be one in number.

ject for that non-substance.[20] This position excludes the possibility that non-substance *x* might be identical with non-substance *y* when *x* and *y* have distinct proper subjects. It thereby excludes the inclusivist account of happiness since goods such as health and beauty have the body rather than the soul as their proper subject.[21] Just as, from the point of view of Aristotle's metaphysics, it is absurd to suppose that an attribute of the soul could be identical with an attribute of the body, so it is absurd to suppose that an attribute of the soul—happiness—could be constituted by features of the body.

The very division of goods into the three classes makes no sense on the inclusivist interpretation. Aristotle claims that every good falls into one of three classes: goods of the body, goods of the soul, and external goods. There is no fourth class of goods available as, on the inclusivist view, there must be since its own candidate for the greatest good falls into none of the three classes. The inclusivist view rather maintains that the greatest good—happiness—is a type of good that is a good of the soul *and* the body *and* an external good. So on the inclusivist interpretation Aristotle's classification of goods unaccountably fails to distinguish the type of good into which the greatest good falls, even though his subject is precisely the question of what that greatest good is, and he is appealing to his classification of goods to claim that happiness as he has defined it falls into the best of his three classes.

Aristotle's argument at the start of *NE* 1. 8 is usefully contrasted with the inclusivist position set out in *Rhetoric* 1. 5 (1360$^b$14–30). There, as in *NE* 1. 8, goods are divided into goods of the soul, goods of the body, and external goods (1360$^b$26–8). But, unlike what we find in *NE* 1. 8, happiness is not classified as a good of the soul or as belonging to any of these classes. Instead, an inclusivist position is set out according to which happiness is constituted from 'such

---

[20] *Post. An.* 73$^a$37–$^b$4; *Top.* 131$^b$33–6, 134$^a$18–25, $^b$10–13, 145$^a$33–7, 150$^a$26–33; *Phys.* 186$^b$18–23, 210$^a$29–$^b$6, 248$^b$21–249$^a$3, $^b$12–13; *GC* 321$^b$2–5; *Parva nat.* 453$^b$27–31; *Metaph.* 1022$^a$16–17, 29–32, 1028$^a$31–6, 1029$^a$15–16, $^b$16–17, 1045$^b$27–32. Cf. *Top.* 126$^a$3–13.

[21] Some might resist the argument of the last few paragraphs by appealing to *DA* 408$^b$11–15, which is often misinterpreted as denying that the soul can be the subject for any attributes (cf. F. Nuyens, *L'Évolution de la psychologie d'Aristote* (Louvain, 1973), 195–6). Then the many passages where Aristotle speaks of the soul as a subject are ignored or taken to be overridden by 408$^b$11–15. In response to such an appeal I can only refer to what I have said elsewhere ('Aristotle and the Mind–Body Problem', *Phronesis*, 36 (1990), 83–102 at 97 n. 27; and at http://www.archelogos. com/, comment on *Metaph.* 1028$^b$36–1029$^a$1).

*bodily* excellences as health, beauty, strength, large stature, athletic powers' ($1360^b21-2$) and external goods such as good birth and friends. Evidently, Aristotle has no difficulty in clearly expressing a position (whether or not it is his own) which both identifies happiness with a class of goods and counts bodily goods and external goods as members of the class. Likewise in *EE* $1214^b4-6$, Aristotle distinguishes between views which identify happiness with a collection of goods and views which identify it with a single good. The same distinction is drawn at *Protr.* B 94–5. How can it be, then, that in the *Nicomachean Ethics* Aristotle finds himself unable to express what, according to the inclusivists, he means? If he can explain this sort of position in the *Protrepticus*, the *Rhetoric*, and the *Eudemian Ethics*, why should we believe that some paralysis in his powers of expression seized him when he came to state his own view in the *Nicomachean Ethics*?

(*b*)  *The happy man lives well and does well* ($1098^b20-2$; cf. $1095^a$
        18–20; *EE* $1219^a39-^b4$; *Protr.* B 52)

Next, Aristotle affirms that his view conforms with the common belief that the happy man lives well and does well since he has said that *eudaimonia* is 'a kind of living well and doing well'.

As explained above, in the function argument ($1098^a5-6$) Aristotle distinguished two ways in which 'life' could be understood—referring to potentiality or actuality—and said that the life identified with *eudaimonia* must be the actuality. A disposition or potentiality such as a virtue of character is only a potentiality to 'live'—to act or behave or experience some kind of mental *event* in a certain way. Such a potentiality could not possibly constitute *eudaimonia* (cf. $1095^b30-1096^a2$, $1176^a33-^b2$, $1178^b18-20$).

This contradicts the inclusivist view since that interpretation must affirm that, as well as the actuality, the potentiality to live, in particular the virtues of character and intellect, constitute *eudaimonia*. For, being among the greatest human goods, virtues of character and intellect[22] cannot on the inclusivist view be excluded from the collection of goods making up *eudaimonia*.

It is also clear that the common view that *eudaimonia* is a kind

[22] Whenever Aristotle discusses the issue, he asserts that, *as excellent states of their subjects*, i.e. independently of the valuable activities they give rise to, virtues have intrinsic value (*Top.* $106^a1-8$, $149^b29-33$; *NE* $1097^a30-^b2$, $1144^a1-3$, $1145^a2-4$, $1174^a4-6$; *EE* $1248^b16-23$; *Rhet.* $1362^b2-4$).

of living well jars with the inclusivist idea that other goods such as health or friends constitute *eudaimonia*. From Aristotle's point of view, it would be absurd to suppose that these entities could constitute the *living* that the happy man does.

(*c*) *Happiness is virtue* (1098ᵇ23–1099ᵃ7; cf. 1095ᵇ29–1096ᵃ2, 1176ᵃ 33–5; *EE* 1215ᵃ20–5, 1216ᵃ37–ᵇ2)

Despite his rejection of the identification of *eudaimonia* with virtue, Aristotle says that his position fits the view that happiness is virtue. Not because he wants somehow to identify happiness with virtue— either in whole or in part—but because '*to* excellence *belongs* activity in accordance with it' (1098ᵇ31: ταύτης [sc. ἀρετῆς] γάρ ἐστιν ἡ κατ' αὐτὴν ἐνέργεια; cf. 1101ᵇ32, 1106ᵇ16–23, 1176ᵇ18–19). He immediately adds that it is crucial to distinguish between the assertion that *eudaimonia* is a kind of activity and the assertion that it is a virtue (1098ᵇ31–1099ᵃ3):

> But it makes, perhaps, no small difference whether we place the chief good in possession or in use, in state or in activity. For the state may exist without producing any good result, as in a man who is asleep or in some way quite inactive, but the activity cannot; for one who has the activity will of necessity be acting, and acting well.[23]

As Aristotle explains in the *Eudemian Ethics* (1220ᵃ4–8), there are activities *of* the virtues but the virtues themselves are not activities.

Suppose Aristotle identified happiness with virtuous activity + other intrinsic goods. He regards virtue of character as one of the greatest intrinsic goods (see n. 22), so this view must say that happiness is virtuous activity + virtue, plus, perhaps, other intrinsic goods, whether all or some.[24] Then Aristotle's present comment makes no sense. He says that it matters whether we place 'the chief

---

[23] When Aristotle resumes the topic of happiness in *NE* 10. 6, his first point, referring back to 1. 5, 1095ᵇ29–1096ᵃ2, is that happiness is not a state such as virtue: 'We said then that it is not a state [ἕξις]; for if it were it might belong to someone who was asleep throughout his life, living the life of a plant . . .' (1176ᵃ33–5). Note also *Poet.* 1450ᵃ16–22: 'Tragedy is an imitation not of men but of action [πρᾶξις] and life, of happiness and misery [κακοδαιμονία]. All human happiness or misery [κακοδαιμονία] *is action* [ἐν πράξει ἐστίν], and the end is some action, *not a quality*. Men are of a certain quality because of character [κατὰ τὰ ἤθη], but they are happy or the opposite because of actions.' Cf. *NE* 1152ᵇ33, 1173ᵃ13–15; *Pol.* 1325ᵃ31–2.

[24] Inclusivists often say that Aristotle regards virtue as a constituent of *eudaimonia*. See e.g. Whiting, '*Eudaimonia*', 282. Stephen A. White appears to identify the 'essence' of happiness with the virtues alone while happiness is virtue plus other

good in possession *or* [ἤ] in use, in state *or* in activity'. But on the inclusivist view Aristotle incomprehensibly fails to mention a third view which is the position his argument is supposed to be defending: happiness is possession *and* use.

If Aristotle placed happiness in both possession and use he would be able to confirm his position more directly by appeal to the view that happiness is virtue by saying, as of course he does not, that virtue actually constitutes happiness, even if it is not its principal component.

A special problem for the second version of inclusivism which makes virtue a constituent of virtuous activity is its conflict with Aristotle's metaphysics. His emphatic distinction between virtue and activity rests, in part, on the fundamental metaphysical distinction between actuality and potentiality. Students of Aristotle will know that he distinguishes different forms of potentiality and actuality in *De anima* 2. 5 (cf. also *Phys.* 8. 4). The differences are illustrated with the example of knowledge. We can distinguish *A*'s potentiality to acquire knowledge (first-level potentiality), the knowledge which *A* acquires which is a kind of actuality of that potentiality (first-level actuality/second-level potentiality), and *A*'s contemplation of what he knows (second-level actuality), the actuality of the acquired knowledge. Aristotle's identification of *eudaimonia* as a kind of activity means that it is an event of the same sort as the second-level actuality[25] of knowledge. It is clear that he would not allow such a second-level actuality, a kind of occurrence or event, to be constituted by either sort of potentiality.

It is true that at the end of *Metaphysics H*, when Aristotle is struggling with certain problems of unity in the case of substance, he says: 'the proximate matter and the shape are one and the same; the one existing potentially, and the other actually'. But whatever the correct interpretation of such difficult statements, they will not help an inclusivist interpretation of *eudaimonia*. For whatever sort

goods such as money, health, family, and friends ('Is Aristotelian Happiness a Good Life or the Best Life?', *Oxford Studies in Ancient Philosophy*, 8 (1990), 103–43 at 126, 132).

[25] My concern here is to be clear that in calling *eudaimonia* a kind of actuality Aristotle is not merely saying that it is a first-level actuality such as acquired knowledge that is not being used. But nor is describing *eudaimonia* as a second-level actuality sufficient to get across the point that *eudaimonia* is an event and not a state. In *Physics* 8. 4, *being high up* (τὸ ποῦ εἶναι καὶ ἄνω), which is not an event, is the second-level actuality of fire (255ᵇ11, 15–17).

of unity Aristotle has in mind, it cannot contradict his contention that form is primary substance while matter is not primary substance. This requires form and matter to be, in some important sense, different beings, and, of course, it is evident from Aristotle's entire philosophy that they are very different kinds of entity that play vastly different roles.

Further, what he is talking about in the *Metaphysics* is form and matter being, in some way, the same. One may be called actuality and the other potentiality, but they are not actualities and potentialities of the right sort. *Eudaimonia* is an actuality of the sort that contemplation is, an actuality that is not any kind of potentiality. But the form which Aristotle identifies as primary substance in the *Metaphysics*, the soul, is the sort of actuality that is also a potentiality. The contention that there is some kind of unity between such an actuality/potentiality and matter does not imply what would be for Aristotle the absurd idea that an *event*[26] could be *made out of a potentiality* for that event.

So what Aristotle says about the Megarians in *Metaphysics* Θ 3 (1047ᵃ18–20) can, in a way, also be applied to those who say that virtue constitutes *eudaimonia*: 'It is clear that potentiality and actuality are different, but these views make potentiality and actuality the same, and so it is no small thing they are seeking to destroy' (cf. *NE* 1098ᵇ31–3).[27]

A further metaphysical problem for the second version of the inclusivist account is its conflict with Aristotle's doctrine of categories. Whatever else Aristotle's distinction between kinds of category may amount to, it does, in part, draw fundamental distinctions between kinds of entity when it contrasts substances, qualities, quantities, and instances of doing or suffering. It is impossible for a being in the categories of doing (ποιεῖν) and/or suffering (πάσχειν) to be identified with or constituted out of beings from any other category.[28] Virtuous activity of soul must be an occurrence falling

---

[26] In Aristotle's universe, either a κίνησις or an ἐνέργεια in *Metaphysics* Θ 6's restricted sense; and falling into the category of doing (ποιεῖν, κινεῖν), or the category of suffering (πάσχειν, κινεῖσθαι), or both.

[27] Crisp would claim that this problem does not apply to his own position since he is not committed to making virtue a constituent of *eudaimonia*. On his view Aristotle allows only intrinsic goods to constitute *eudaimonia* and, he says, Aristotle does not regard virtue as an intrinsic good (Crisp, 'Inclusivism', 125–6). But there is no doubt that Aristotle considers virtue an intrinsic good. See n. 22.

[28] Some clarifications are needed here. (1) Aristotle allows that some things fall under different categories: a body, for example, is a quantity as well as a substance

into one of the two categories of doing or suffering.[29] But if it were constituted out of virtue, an instance of doing or suffering would be constituted out of a quality.

Aristotle never explicitly considers the, to him, self-evidently absurd suggestion that an event—a κίνησις or an ἐνέργεια, an instance of doing or suffering—could be composed from an entity falling under a different category. But he regularly dismisses any idea that an item from one category could be constituted from entities in other categories, or that the same thing could be a substance and quality and/or a quantity, etc. (*Phys.* 185ᵃ27–9, 186ᵇ14–18; *DA* 410ᵃ13–22; *Metaph.* 1038ᵇ23–7, 1039ᵃ30–2, 1070ᵃ33–ᵇ10, 1086ᵇ37–1087ᵃ4, 1088ᵇ2–4; cf. *Top.* 125ᵇ15–19). Even when two items fall under the same category, there may be no possibility of their being combined to form a single entity (*Parva nat.* 447ᵇ1–3).

When an inclusivist view of *eudaimonia* is set out in the *Rhetoric* (1. 5 and 6) and Aristotle lists its constituent parts, the question 'what kind of entity is *eudaimonia*?' is not raised. The explana-

(*Cat.* 4; *Metaph.* Δ 13). (2) He allows that a change is a quantity because the magnitude which is the path of change is a quantity, but then it is only in an accidental sense that the change itself can be called a quantity (*Metaph.* 1020ᵃ28–32). (3) Aristotle argues in *Physics* 3. 3 that the numerically same thing is an instance of doing and suffering. But both are what we would call occurrences or events. (4) On at least one of his explanations of relatives (*Cat.* 6ᵃ36–7; contrast 8ᵃ28–32; *Top.* 142ᵃ28–31, 146ᵇ3–4), he must allow that anything at all is—or is when described in a certain way (e.g. 'thinkable', *DA* 429ᵃ18)—a kind of relative (πρός τι) since all things are what they are (or, for some predicate '*F*', are *F*) only in relation to another entity (see e.g. *Metaph.* Δ 15; *Phys.* 194ᵇ8–9; cf. *Cat.* 11ᵃ37–9). This is connected to the tenuous, derivative reality of relatives as kinds of being (*Metaph.* 1088ᵃ21–ᵇ4; *NE* 1096ᵃ21–2). My argument assumes that, however Aristotle's doctrine of categories is to be interpreted, it is, *for him*, a metaphysical absurdity to suggest that an instance of doing or suffering could be or be constituted out of qualities or substances. This does not mean that it *is* a metaphysical absurdity. Some philosophers, such as Jaegwon Kim, correctly for all I know, hold that an event consists in an object having a property at a time. See e.g. his paper 'Causation, Nomic Subsumption, and the Concept of Event', *Journal of Philosophy*, 70 (1973), 217–36.

[29] Contemplation is an instance of πάσχειν, virtuous action at least often an example of ποιεῖν. On some occasions, e.g. when acting temperately, virtuous action will be a 'static event', e.g. *refraining* from positive action. It is not clear whether Aristotle would count this as '*activity* in accordance with virtue'. He may well consider it an instance of *rest* (ἠρεμεῖν), which he defines (*Phys.* 239ᵃ26–9) as a substance's possessing the same feature for a period of time. In at least some cases, Aristotle holds that rest is due to an *efficient cause* of rest (*Phys.* 194ᵇ29–30), and it is reasonable to think he would regard the temperate man's refraining from action as just such an example. Perhaps Aristotle regarded rest resulting from an efficient cause as a kind of πάσχειν, and if so, refraining from the action, doing what is temperate, might also count as a kind of ποιεῖν, a kind of activity.

tion is clear: the question 'what kind of being is happiness?' makes no sense for a list of the sort we find there, just as it makes no sense for a collection of the sort that inclusivists find in the *Nicomachean Ethics*. By contrast, in the *Nicomachean Ethics* Aristotle is very interested in the kind of entity *eudaimonia* is, stressing that it is *not* a quality such as virtue and *is* an activity, an instance of doing or suffering. Above all, it is not a quality or potentiality. Inclusivists must either say that *eudaimonia* is constituted out of virtue, or that virtue + virtuous activity constitute *eudaimonia* where there is no suggestion that the activity is constituted by the virtue. The former view leads to the metaphysical absurdities pointed out above. The second conflicts with the fact that Aristotle—always and consistently—identifies *eudaimonia* as an activity and nothing else. Nor could such a collection of activities, qualities (such as virtue) and substances (such as friends) constitute any kind of entity. Thus, in *De anima* ($410^a13-22$), a view's commitment to the absurdity that the same thing would be constituted from a quantity, a quality, and a substance is taken to be sufficient to refute it.

There is more to be said as to why Aristotle could not allow the virtuous activity that constitutes *eudaimonia* to be constituted from a quality such as virtue. As an activity, *eudaimonia* is an event. Aristotle distinguishes between two kinds of event—change and *energeia* (used here in the narrow sense of *Metaph. Θ* 6). When Aristotle defines happiness as activity according to virtue, 'activity' covers both types of event. For example, thinking of god will be an *energeia*, and many actions arising from virtue of character will be changes.[30] Although his discussions are very brief, it is plain that the

---

[30] So I argue in 'Activity and Praxis in Aristotle' ['Activity and Praxis'], *Proceedings of the Boston Area Colloquium in Ancient Philosophy*, 12 (1996), 71–111. Actions are events, and, apart from the possible case of rest, the only events available in Aristotle's ontology are changes and activities in the strict sense. His writings provide no account of action identity beyond his account of identity for changes. Unclarity does result from *NE* 10. 5's position that pleasures differ in species and value as the activities on which they supervene differ in species and value. Aristotle emphasizes that, for example, the just man will enjoy (perceiving himself) acting justly, and this pleasure will therefore differ in species and value from the pleasure of the unjust agent in acting unjustly. Since the actions of the just and unjust man might be the *same* in species according to *Physics* 5. 4's account of specific identity for change (they might both be walks along the same path from *x* to *y*), *NE* 10. 5 may imply an account of species of action that goes beyond *Physics* 5. 4's account of specific identity for change.

If so, however, Aristotle never explains it. And it would conflict with *NE* 10. 4's explanation of the species of actions. There ($1174^a19-{}^b5$) Aristotle explains the

features that Aristotle ascribes to *energeiai*[31] preclude the possibility that they could be constituted by or identified with items from other Aristotelian categories. An *energeia* is an *event* having no temporal parts or magnitude, though it may last for a period of time.[32] The idea of such an entity being made out of a substance, quality, or quantity makes no sense in Aristotle's metaphysics. Aristotle's god may be a substance which is also an *energeia*, but any *energeia* which human beings undergo is not a substance but rather must be present in a substance as its subject.

As for changes, which he explains at much greater length, and with which he must often identify virtuous actions, Aristotle dismisses the suggestion that a change could be constituted from anything other than changes (*Phys.* 232ᵃ8–9, 17, 234ᵇ21–235ᵃ13) and affirms that changes are divisible into the changes (or potential changes) that constitute them (*Phys.* 234ᵇ21–235ᵃ13, 31–3, 240ᵇ13– 17; *NE* 1174ᵃ19–ᵇ2; cf. *Phys.* 231ᵇ15–16, 238ᵃ1–4). A change is a continuous entity and hence, just as continuous magnitudes are infinitely divisible into magnitudes (not points or anything else), and time is infinitely divisible into periods of time (not indivisible

species of actions such as walking and leaping (1174ᵃ31) in terms of, and with reference to (1174ᵇ2–4), *Phys.* 5. 4's account of species of change (τὸ πόθεν ποῖ εἰδοποιόν). Elsewhere the question of whether a just action has been done is not a question of what happens but only of how what happens should be described (*NE* 5. 8: οὐ γὰρ . . . περὶ τοῦ γενέσθαι ἀμφισβητοῦσιν, . . . ἀλλ' ὁμολογοῦντες περὶ τοῦ πράγματος, περὶ δὲ τοῦ ποτέρως δίκαιον ἀμφισβητοῦσιν. Similarly at *Rhet.* 1373ᵇ37– 1374ᵃ17).

'Activity and Praxis' (96–9) also addresses the problem resulting from the fact that *Metaphysics* Θ 6 (1048ᵇ25–6) calls *eudaimonia* an activity in the narrow sense. Briefly, I understand Aristotle to mean that the highest form of *eudaimonia*, contemplation, is an activity. This does not mean that changes that are virtuous actions do not count as *eudaimonia*, just as Aristotle's statement at the close of *NE* 10. 8 that *eudaimonia* 'is a kind of contemplation' (1178ᵇ32) does not contradict what 10. 8 has just explained: that virtuous action is a secondary kind of *eudaimonia*. Similarly, *Metaph.* Θ 6, 1048ᵇ25–6's assertion that living is an *energeia* can only mean that the highest forms of living are *energeiai* (cf. *Protr.* B 78–85), and so it does not contradict Aristotle's belief that the changes of nutrition and growth are also kinds of living. (See e.g. *NE* 1098ᵃ1 and *DA* 413ᵃ22–5: πλεοναχῶς δὲ τοῦ ζῆν λεγομένου, κἂν ἕν τι τούτων ἐνυπάρχῃ μόνον, ζῆν αὐτό φαμεν, οἷον νοῦς, αἴσθησις, κίνησις καὶ στάσις ἡ κατὰ τόπον, ἔτι κίνησις ἡ κατὰ τροφὴν καὶ φθίσις τε καὶ αὔξησις.)

[31] I discuss the characteristics of *energeiai* in 'Activity and Change in Aristotle' ['Activity and Change'], *Oxford Studies in Ancient Philosophy*, 13 (1995), 187–216, and 'Alteration and Aristotle's Activity–Change Distinction', ibid. 16 (1998), 227– 57. The first paper explains why activities and changes must be understood to be mutually exclusive classes of events.

[32] See 'Activity and Change', 200–4.

moments or anything else), so changes are infinitely divisible into changes and nothing else.[33] Therefore changes cannot be made out of, or divisible into, items from categories other than doing or suffering.

Aristotle divides changes into four kinds corresponding to the categories of substance, quality, quantity, and place: generation and corruption, alteration, growth and diminution, and change of place. He dismisses out of hand the idea that one change could be divisible into different kinds of change, for example that one change could be constituted from an alteration, an increase in size, and a locomotion (*Phys.* 241$^b$16–18). It should be even clearer that a change could not be constituted from entities belonging to categories other than doing or suffering.

To see how absurd it would be to propose that a change could be constituted out of anything other than change (such as a quality like health), consider Aristotle's view that any change has a *path*, a stretch or distance between the starting- and end-points of the change which is 'traversed' by the subject which changes. The continuity of a change reflects and is determined by the continuity of its path (*Phys.* 207$^b$21–5, 219$^a$10–14), a change is divisible into 'parts' that will be matched by a corresponding divisibility of its path into corresponding parts with a positive 'size', which will themselves be further divisible into divisible parts, etc. The idea that a quality, quantity, or substance could possess such a path makes no sense.[34] Since only an entity possessing such a path can constitute a change, it is impossible for a change to be 'made out of' a quality, quantity, or substance.

Again, as a continuum, a change is infinitely divisible into parts whose extremities are 'one' (*Phys.* 231$^a$22, $^b$15–18, 232$^b$24–5). So if a change constituting *eudaimonia* were composed of a quality, one of the parts into which it is divisible would have to be a quality whose extremities were one with its adjacent parts. But the idea of qualities having such extremities makes no sense, and, whatever one might imagine such extremities to be, they could not be one with the extremities of a change (cf. *Phys.* 228$^a$22–6). Again, a continuum is divisible into parts which are themselves infinitely

---

[33] *Phys.* 207$^b$21–5, 219$^a$10–14, $^b$15–16, 220$^a$24–6, $^b$24–8, 231$^b$18–232$^a$22, 233$^a$10–12, 235$^a$13–$^b$5, 239$^a$20–3, 241$^a$2–4, 263$^a$27–8; *Metaph.* 1020$^a$26–32.

[34] A magnitude can of course *be* a path, but that is quite different from *having* a path in the way a change over the magnitude has that magnitude as its path.

divisible. If a change were divisible into a part which was a quality, the quality would have to be divisible into continuous entities which are themselves infinitely divisible, etc. For Aristotle, at any rate, the idea of infinite divisibility makes no sense in the case of qualities such as health or beauty.

The fact that, for Aristotle, a change can be constituted only out of changes rules out Whiting's view that the results of actions, which include items in categories other than doing and suffering, are constituents of the actions themselves.[35] Of course, as noted above, in *Phys.* 3. 3 (cf. *DA* 414$^a$11–12, 426$^a$2–11; *Metaph.* 1050$^a$30–4) Aristotle argues that $x$'s doing $y$ to $z$ is one in number with $z$'s suffering 'being $y$-ed' by $x$. For example, $x$'s moving $z$ from $S$ to $E$ is identical with $z$'s being moved from $S$ to $E$.[36] But this in no way suggests that the *end-point*, the terminus, of a change could itself be a constituent of the change. On the contrary, that is the *limit* of the change: when the limit is reached the change no longer exists. For example, the place to which Socrates walks is not itself a part of Socrates' walk. That is why Aristotle can say that, for any change $x$, one necessarily $x$es and has $x$ed at different times.[37] The perfect reports that the end-point of the change has been reached. When the change exists its end does not exist, and when the end of the change exists the change does not exist. So the end of the change could not be a constituent of the change.

Since Aristotle emphasizes that the non-change that is the limit of a change is not a part of the change, and that the change is over when that limit is reached, he could hardly consider some entity caused by and occurring *after* the limit is reached to be part of the change. Such effects might, of course, make the action valuable for its consequences, and explain why the action is chosen for its consequences as well as for itself. Whiting, however, claims that if $A$ gives $B$ money for $B$'s education, then $B$'s education is part of $A$'s generous action and hence (possibly) of $A$'s *eudaimonia*.[38] If $A$'s giving money to $B$ is an example of *doing* (ποιεῖν) and, as in *Phys.* 3. 3, one in number with $B$'s reception of the money (πάσχειν), then, perhaps, 3. 3 could be understood to mean that $B$'s possession of

---

[35] 'Eudaimonia', 280–1, 284.
[36] Since they are one in number, they are also one in species (*Phys.* 5. 4, 227$^b$20–32), but Aristotle would probably also describe them as different in being (*Phys.* 5. 5, 229$^a$16–20, 28–30).
[37] *Metaph.* Θ 6; *Phys.* 231$^b$28–232$^a$6, 235$^b$25–6, 236$^a$1–2, 240$^b$27–8.
[38] Whiting, 'Eudaimonia', 273–4.

money is (not a part of but) the end-point of the action, and thus the *limit* of the action beyond which no part of the action occurs. But it does not suggest that *B*'s education—a causal effect of *B*'s possession of money—is a *part of A*'s action of giving money to *B*. Similar points apply to Whiting's suggestions that the safety of one's family aimed at by a courageous action, or the health aimed at by a temperate action, might be part of the courageous and temperate actions themselves.[39]

Whiting finds evidence for her view at *NE* 1115$^b$21–2: 'courage is *kalon* to a courageous man and so also is its end, for each thing is defined by its end'. She says that

his point here seems to be that *courage* is *kalon* because its end is and not vice versa. This is striking, given Aristotle's requirement that *virtuous actions* be chosen for themselves. For it suggests that he does not take this requirement to be based on the claim that the value of virtuous activity is independent of the value of the results at which it aims.[40]

She appears to understand this passage to imply that choosing an action for itself at least includes choosing the action for the sake of its *kalon* results; hence, the passage implies that those results are parts of the action itself. One reason why Whiting's understanding of the passage should be rejected is that she evidently understands 'courage' to refer to courageous *action*. For her second sentence about virtuous action is based on her first sentence's assertion about courage. But courage (ἡ ἀνδρεία) is a virtue of character, a state, not an action.

The view that Whiting wants to reject does not suggest that the value of a virtuous action is independent of the value of its results. It says that the *intrinsic* value of a virtuous action is independent of its results, in accordance with all of Aristotle's explanations of intrinsic value.[41] And there is nothing in her passage to suggest that the intrinsic value of a virtuous action is not independent of its consequences or effects. It simply says that for both courage and activity arising from courage (e.g. standing and fighting the enemy) the end is action according to courage, that is, acting coura-

[39] Ibid. 279.
[40] Ibid. 281. My italics except for *kalon*.
[41] *Protr.* B 42, 44, 70, 72; *Top.* 106$^a$1–8, 116$^a$29–39, 117$^a$2–4, 118$^b$20–6, 149$^b$31–9; *NE* 1096$^a$7–9, $^b$13–19, 1097$^a$30–$^b$6, 1144$^a$1–6, 1145$^a$2–4, 1172$^b$20–3, 1174$^a$4–6, 1176$^b$6–7; *EE* 1248$^b$16–25; *Rhet.* 1362$^a$21–2, $^b$26–7, 1363$^b$13–14, 1364$^b$23–4.

geously.[42] There is no suggestion that the effects of an action could be constituents of the action itself.

Whiting goes so far as to *identify* choosing a courageous action for itself with choosing the causal consequences of the action for *their own sake*.[43] If there is nothing more to choosing a courageous action for itself than choosing, say, the safety of one's friends and fellow citizens for itself, then in a threatening situation I can do what is courageous for its own sake by valuing the safety of my friends and fellow citizens for itself, aim to secure that end for its own sake, and do so by hiring a replacement to take my place in the battle line.[44]

Whiting's attempt to make the causal consequences of an action constituents of the action itself leaves Aristotle open to the charge of absurdity that afflicts all accounts of action which try to squeeze its effects into the action itself. If the causal effect of my doing what is generous—*B*'s being educated—is part of my action of doing what is generous, then I can be doing what is generous after I cease to exist. Plainly, Aristotle would dismiss the idea that an action of doing could be going on when there was no agent in existence who

---

[42] We can see this by going over the passage in detail ($1115^b17$–24). My comments are inserted in brackets:

The man, then, who stands fast [ὑπομένων] and fears the right things and for the sake of the right end in the right way [etc., i.e. the man who *is active* in a certain way] . . . is courageous [i.e. is in a certain state]. Now the end of every activity [e.g. standing fast (ὑπομένων), etc.] is [for that activity] to be according to the state of character [κατὰ τὴν ἕξιν, quality; so, for example, the end of the activity of standing fast, etc. arising from the state of courage is to be according to courage, i.e. *courageous* action]. This is true, therefore, of the courageous [quality] man . . . but *courage* [quality] *is kalon to a courageous man and so also is its end* [sc. courageous action], *for each thing* [e.g. courage] *is defined by its end* [thus courage is defined by its end of acting courageously]. Therefore it is for a noble end [sc. acting courageously] that the courageous man [quality] stands fast [ὑπομένει] and acts as courage directs [cf. $1104^a27$–$^b3$; see also *EE* $1248^b18$–22].

[43] Whiting, '*Eudaimonia*', 280: 'choosing a virtuous action *just is* choosing that action simply in so far as it aims at a certain sort of external result. So *what is chosen for itself is* ultimately *the external result* at which one aims. Talk of choosing a virtuous *action* for itself is thus elliptical for talk of aiming at a certain sort of *result* for *it*self.'

[44] My action can be cowardly even if my feelings of fear and confidence match those of a courageous man. Nor can Whiting explain away this case by appeal to the 'countergoals' of courage. She says that 'seeking to secure the safety of one's friends and fellow citizens without running the risk of death and wounds is not courageous' (279). But I may know that in hiring someone to take my place I risk death and wounds from my outraged fellow citizens when they discover what I have done. It remains that my action was not courageous. Even if the risk is less, courage does not require that one always choose the riskiest option.

was doing it.⁴⁵ Since he holds that the doing and suffering that are one in number are simultaneous and cease to exist at the same time (*Phys.* 195ᵇ17–20; *DA* 425ᵇ26–426ᵃ19), any effect occurring in the patient after the agent ceases to exist could not be a constituent of the agent's action.

To conclude, apart from the special problems facing Whiting's account, the second version of inclusivism which tries to make virtuous action an activity somehow constituted out of non-substances violates two of Aristotle's basic metaphysical doctrines: (1) no actuality can be or be constituted out of a potentiality; (2) no instance of doing or suffering can be constituted out of any being found in a category other than the categories of doing and suffering.

(*d*) *The happy life is pleasant* (1099ᵃ7–31; cf. 1152ᵇ6–8, 1153ᵇ14–
     15, 1169ᵇ30–3, 1170ᵃ4, 1177ᵃ22–7, ᵇ20–1; *EE* 1214ᵃ7–8, 1249ᵃ
     17–21; *Pol.* 1339ᵇ32–3)

Another common view which is said by Aristotle to confirm his own account is the belief that pleasure belongs to happiness. Aristotle explains how his view fits this claim by noting that 'just *acts* are pleasant to the lover of justice and in general excellent *acts* to the lover of excellence' (1099ᵃ10–11).⁴⁶ And, while many men find that their pleasures conflict, this will not be so on Aristotle's account of happiness since, according to it, the happy man will find pleasant the things that are by nature pleasant, viz. excellent *actions*. Hence, the life of those who are happy is pleasant in itself since it will consist in performing *actions* which are by nature pleasant. They rejoice in noble *actions*, and will take pleasure in *doing* what is just and what is liberal. Hence excellent *actions* are pleasant in themselves. Citing the inscription from Delos, he says that the best *activities* are most noble, best, and most pleasant. He concludes (1099ᵃ29–31): 'and these [the best *activities*, ταῖς ἀρίσταις ἐνεργείαις], or one—the best—of these [*activities*], we identify with happiness [ταύτας δέ [ἐνεργείας], ἢ μίαν τούτων τὴν ἀρίστην, φαμὲν εἶναι τὴν εὐδαιμονίαν]'.

This is straightforward, at least with regard to the issue that con-

---

⁴⁵ Unaware of the Law of Inertia, Aristotle believed that a change can exist only if an existing agent is acting on the changing subject.

⁴⁶ The Greek speaks only of τὰ δίκαια and τὰ κατ' ἀρετήν, but the ensuing discussion shows that it is actions that Aristotle has in mind (1099ᵃ14, 21: αἱ κατ' ἀρετὴν πράξεις; 1099ᵃ17–18: ταῖς κάλαις πράξεσιν; 1099ᵃ19: δικαιοπραγεῖν; 1099ᵃ20: ταῖς ἐλευθερίοις πράξεσιν).

cerns us. Aristotle's points are based on the claim that *eudaimonia* is an activity. He identifies *eudaimonia* with the best activities, which constitute the life of the happy man. These best activities—virtuous activities—are what is most pleasant. Hence, on Aristotle's account of *eudaimonia*, the living that the happy man does is most pleasant. So his account of happiness as a kind of activity explains the common belief that the happy life is pleasant. While not providing a positive argument against the inclusivist view, Aristotle's argument clearly fits in well with my main contention.

(*e*) *Happiness is external prosperity* (τὰ ἐκτὸς ἀγαθά, εὐτυχία) (1099ᵃ 31–ᵇ9⁴⁷)

Aristotle points out (1099ᵇ7–8) that some people identify *eudaimonia* with good fortune, and he agrees that happiness needs external goods. One reason is that '*to do noble acts* without the proper equipment' is impossible or difficult. 'In many *actions* we use friends and riches and political power as instruments.' So in this respect Aristotle's view that *eudaimonia* is virtuous activity 'harmonizes' with the view that happiness is external prosperity, not in the sense that external prosperity is a constituent of *eudaimonia* but because external goods are often needed as instruments for the virtuous actions that constitute *eudaimonia*. If I am poor and friendless, for example, I will have to forgo opportunities to act generously.

Another reason offered for saying that the view that happiness is external prosperity harmonizes with Aristotle's account of happiness as virtuous activity is that such activity constitutes *eudaimonia* only in a context where certain important external goods are possessed (and certain external evils are absent). It is unlikely, he says, that someone could be happy 'if he had thoroughly bad children or friends or had lost good children or friends by death'. As Aristotle pointed out in I. 5 (1095ᵃ31–1096ᵃ2), only someone defending a thesis at all costs would describe a person sustaining severe misfortunes as happy. And 'nobody' would consider someone suffering the misfortunes of Priam happy (*NE* 1101ᵃ1–5; cf. *Pol.* 1332ᵃ19– 21). External prosperity is a necessary condition for *eudaimonia*,

---

⁴⁷ Cf. *NE* 1099ᵃ31–ᵇ8, 1099ᵇ25–8, 1100ᵃ5–9, 1100ᵇ22–33, 1101ᵃ14–16, 1153ᵇ16– 25, 1178ᵃ25–ᵇ7, 1178ᵇ33–1179ᵃ17; *EE* I. 2; *Pol.* 1323ᵇ23–9, 1331ᵇ39–1332ᵃ1, 1332ᵃ 7–27; *Phys.* 197ᵇ4.

and in this respect, too, Aristotle's view 'harmonizes' with the view that *eudaimonia* is external prosperity.[48]

But of course the fact that certain external goods are necessary if virtuous activity is to count as *eudaimonia* does not make it the case that those external goods constitute *eudaimonia*; just as the fact that *A*'s having given *B* $500 in 1992 is a necessary condition for *B*'s doing what is just in giving *A* $500 in 2003 does not make it the case that *A*'s action is a part of *B*'s action of doing what is just.[49]

The *Eudemian Ethics* (1. 2) explicitly distinguishes necessary conditions for *eudaimonia* from *eudaimonia* itself, and Aristotle's discussions of the last three points assume that distinction. He says explicitly in the *Nicomachean Ethics* that the presence of some external goods is 'necessary' (ἀναγκαῖον, 1099[b]27) if happiness is to exist.[50] Aristotle has claimed that the three different positions on

[48] I discuss the requirement that good circumstances be present if virtuous activity is to count as *eudaimonia* in 'Rationality, *Eudaimonia* and *Kakodaimonia* in Aristotle', *Phronesis*, 38 (1993), 31–56 at 46–55, and 'Improvability', 133–41. The point that some goods necessary for happiness are beyond our control lies behind Aristotle's argument at *NE* 1111[b]28–30. Broadie objects to the identification of virtuous activity with *eudaimonia* ('*Summum Bonum*', 248–9) on the grounds that the identification entails that 'no one can reasonably want a good whose absence does not hamper his or her excellent activity'. But since Aristotle believes that virtuous activity in the absence of important intrinsic, non-instrumental goods does not count as happiness, it is, on the contrary, clear why one must secure such goods (as well as instrumental goods and virtuous activity) in order to secure happiness.

[49] John Cooper argues that the passage under discussion does not mean that external goods are necessary for happiness (conflating this with their being constituents of happiness) since Aristotle's definition of happiness in 1. 7 does not mention such goods ('Plato and Aristotle on "Finality" and "(Self-)Sufficiency"', in R. Heinaman (ed.), *Plato and Aristotle's Ethics* (London, 2003), 117–47 at 130). But nor does 1. 7's definition, described as a first sketch whose details are to be filled in later (1098[a]20–2), mention the requirement that, in order to count as happiness, virtuous activity must occur over a complete life. None the less, following his definition, Aristotle affirms that it is necessary for happiness (1098[a]18–20). 1. 8 asserts that *eudaimonia* must be examined not only in terms of the argument just given but with the help of common beliefs. One of those common beliefs is that happiness requires fortunate circumstances of life, and as a result, in 1. 10, 1101[a]14–16, Aristotle defines as happy the man sufficiently furnished with external goods who acts (ἐνεργοῦντα) in accordance with perfect virtue in a complete life. *Pol.* 1332[a]7–27 reports 'the *Ethics*' view as being that *eudaimonia* is the ἁπλῶς, *not* the conditional (ἐξ ὑποθέσεως, cf. *EE* 1238[b]6), exercise of virtue. That is, the exercise of virtue must be an intrinsic good occurring in fortunate circumstances of life. See also n. 50.

[50] Aristotle has just defined *eudaimonia* as 'a kind of actuality according to virtue' (1099[b]26) before going on to say (1099[b]27–8): 'of the *remaining* goods [and thus goods other than happiness], some (τὰ μέν) are necessary conditions ⟨of happiness⟩, while others (τὰ δέ) are naturally useful and co-operative as instruments'. This constitutes evidence against Cooper's view (see n. 49) that, since Aristotle's definition of happiness in *NE* 1. 7 does not mention such goods, external goods are not ne-

the identity of *eudaimonia* which 'harmonize' with his own view do so because they specify necessary conditions for *eudaimonia* as he understands it, but at the same time he makes it plain that they fail to identify anything that constitutes *eudaimonia*.

Likewise in the *Politics* (7. 3), after identifying *eudaimonia* with virtuous activity in 1332$^a$7–9 and explaining that to count as happiness virtuous activity must occur in a context in which certain goods are present and certain evils are absent, Aristotle goes on to say that it is absurd to identify happiness with external goods that are necessary for happiness (1332$^a$25–7): 'This [viz. the necessity of external goods for happiness] makes men think that external goods provide the explanation of happiness, just as they might say that a brilliant performance on the lyre was to be explained by the instrument rather than the skill of the performer.'

One source of the inclusivist view seems to be the supposition that there are only two possibilities for what Aristotle can say about the intrinsic goods necessary for *eudaimonia* other than virtuous activity: either they are constituents of *eudaimonia*, or they are of merely instrumental value for virtuous activity. Since the second option is clearly not Aristotle's view, he must make them constituents of *eudaimonia*.[51] But this is a false choice because there is also a third option: some of the goods other than virtuous activity which Aristotle counts as necessary for *eudaimonia* are neither constituents of *eudaimonia* nor of merely instrumental value. Rather, the presence of such goods is required if the fortunate circumstances of life are to exist in which virtuous activity can be considered *eudaimonia*.

Suppose the inclusivist interpretation were correct. Then the view that external goods constitute happiness would confirm his

cessary for happiness. Aristotle specifies as necessary conditions for happiness (at 1099$^b$27–8) the other 'remaining' goods immediately after defining happiness solely in terms of virtuous activity (at 1099$^b$26). So the fact that Aristotle does not mention these other goods when defining happiness solely in terms of virtuous activity in *NE* 1. 7 cannot show that 1. 7's definition rules them out as necessary for happiness.

Likewise in our present passage, immediately after identifying *eudaimonia* with the best activity or the best of the best activities (1099$^a$29–31), Aristotle says that '*nevertheless*'—that is, despite the fact that *eudaimonia* is to be identified with the best activity alone—external goods are, 'as we said', also necessary for happiness (1099$^a$31–2). Likewise again in 1. 9, after appealing to the point that *eudaimonia* is virtuous activity (1099$^b$33–1100$^a$3), Aristotle adds that a complete life and good fortune are also necessary for happiness (1100$^a$4–9; cf. *Pol.* 1323$^a$24–7).

[51]  See e.g. D. Scott, 'Aristotle on Posthumous Fortune' ['Fortune'], *Oxford Studies in Ancient Philosophy*, 18 (2000), 211–29 at 212.

view much more directly than Aristotle allows. If, as the inclusivist view has it, health and beauty,[52] for example, are not merely necessary for but constitutive of happiness, what prevents Aristotle from saying just that rather than limiting himself to the point that external goods are needed if happiness is to exist?

This review of Aristotle's arguments for his definition of happiness in *Nicomachean Ethics* 1. 8 shows that, in this chapter, the idea that *eudaimonia* is an activity is central to every point he makes in appealing to common beliefs to confirm his definition of *eudaimonia* from 1. 7. At the same time those arguments frequently demonstrate the incompatibility of Aristotle's position with the inclusivist interpretation which identifies *eudaimonia* with a wider collection of intrinsic human goods, or constitutes virtuous activity from such goods. The same is true for much of the rest of Aristotle's discussion in *NE* 1.

## 4. *Nicomachean Ethics* 1. 9

*NE* 1. 9 examines the question 'how is happiness to be acquired?' Since happiness is the end of virtue, and—as Aristotle will explain in *NE* 2. 1—virtue is acquired by habituation and training, he says that happiness will be acquired by such habituation and training.

He supports this by saying (1099$^b$25–7):

> The answer to the question we are asking is plain also from the definition of happiness; for it has been said to be a virtuous activity of soul of a certain kind. Of the remaining goods, some must necessarily pre-exist as conditions of happiness, and others are naturally co-operative and useful as instruments.

As virtuous activity, happiness is the actualization of virtue, and since virtue is acquired in the way mentioned, happiness is acquired in the same way. However, Aristotle qualifies his answer by pointing out that certain other goods must also exist if virtuous activity is to count as happiness, and he does not suggest that they are acquired by training and habituation. For example, as we have already seen, he thinks that good birth and the absence of extreme ugliness are necessary for happiness, and these are not acquired

[52] The reference to beauty and ugliness at 1099$^b$3–4 shows that 'external goods' is being used in the present context to include bodily goods.

by habituation but are goods of fortune. And other goods must be present as instruments if virtue is to be exercised.

Here, then, Aristotle appeals to his definition of *eudaimonia* as virtuous activity in order to support his view. At the same time he makes it clear that the necessary conditions for happiness he refers to are not parts of happiness: 'it [viz. happiness] has been said to be a virtuous activity of soul . . . Of the *remaining* goods [τῶν δὲ λοιπῶν ἀγαθῶν]'—that is, of the goods *other than* happiness or virtuous activity which are needed for happiness—some must pre-exist and some are instruments of virtuous activity.

The chapter concludes with Aristotle saying that it is natural— given the definition of *eudaimonia* as virtuous activity—that no other animals should be called happy (1099ᵇ33–1100ᵃ1): 'for none of them can share in such activity'. Suppose that *eudaimonia* consisted in other human goods. Perception and other goods are shared with other animals (1097ᵇ33–4, 1098ᵃ2–3) but as one of the greatest human goods perception would have to be part of any inclusivist account of *eudaimonia*. Given that on the inclusivist view some of the goods that make up human happiness are shared with other animals, one would expect Aristotle's explanation of why other animals cannot be happy to be more complicated. He ought to point out that even though some goods constituting happiness are shared by other animals, not all goods are so shared, and all the constituents are needed for happiness.

Of course, the inclusivist might say that this is implied by what Aristotle actually says: since virtuous activity is not shared by other animals, they cannot have all the goods constituting human happiness. But why should we take this unmentioned implication of what Aristotle says to be his argument rather than what he does say, which is perfectly understandable as it stands?

## 5. *Nicomachean Ethics* 1. 10

At the start of this chapter Aristotle raises the question whether the dead can be said to be happy. He immediately dismisses the idea as absurd, 'especially for us who say that happiness is an activity' (1100ᵃ12–13).

He goes on to discuss two further difficult questions: (1) should a man be called happy only after he has died? (2) can the fortunes of a man's descendants so affect his own fortunes as to alter our description of him as happy or unhappy?

In examining the first question Aristotle points out that non-catastrophic swings of fortune should not be thought to affect a man's happiness, for happiness is durable and 'virtuous activities are responsible for happiness, and the opposite sort of activities are responsible for the opposite ⟨of happiness⟩' ($1100^b9$–$10$).[53]

He immediately adds ($1100^b11$–$20$):

> The question we have now discussed confirms our definition. For of human functions none has so much permanence as virtuous activities (these are thought to be more durable even than knowledge of the sciences), and of these themselves the most valuable are more durable because those who are happy spend their life most readily and most continuously in these; for this seems to be the reason why we do not forget them. The attribute in question, then, will belong to the happy man, and he will be happy throughout his life; for always, or by preference to everything else, he will be engaged in virtuous action and contemplation . . .

Aristotle's definition of happiness as virtuous activity is taken to explain why, as he has just said, happiness is something durable rather than something which varies with varying fortunes: happiness is virtuous activity and virtuous activity is durable. The happy man will be constant in his happiness precisely because happiness is the kind of activity it is.

Aristotle's discussion in this chapter contains a difficulty for the comprehensivist view. He is addressing Solon's question of whether a man can be called happy while he is alive. Solon thought not (and Aristotle agreed in the *Eudemian Ethics*, $1219^b6$–$8$) because happiness should not be subject to fluctuations, but as long as a man is alive it is possible that he will suffer severe misfortunes incompatible with happiness.

Aristotle's solution to the problem rests on two claims:

(1) Happiness is not subject to frequent fluctuation.
(2) A person's fortunes often fluctuate.

The passage quoted above ($1100^b11$–$20$) argues that Aristotle's account of happiness as virtuous activity explains why (1) is true: happiness consists in virtuous activity and this is something that is stable. However, the argument may wrongly suggest that happi-

---

[53]  Cf. *Poet.* $1450^a16$–$22$, quoted in n. 23.

ness has more stability than Aristotle actually thinks, that happiness cannot be lost (*NE* 1100$^b$18–20). But the ensuing discussion (*NE* 1100$^b$22–1101$^a$13) accommodates (2) by making it clear that misfortune of sufficient severity can destroy a man's happiness. Small changes in fortune will not destroy happiness, thus recognizing the truth of (1), but happiness is destroyed when the misfortunes are of sufficient gravity.

It is this further point that the extreme comprehensivist interpretation of happiness cannot explain. For on that view, all of its components must be present if happiness is to exist. So the comprehensivist cannot explain the difference on which Aristotle insists between small misfortunes and great misfortunes, for small misfortunes will often involve the loss of goods, not merely possessing a lesser version of a type of good. Hence, small misfortunes will often mean the loss of the comprehensive set of goods which the comprehensivist identifies with happiness. On the extreme comprehensivist view, then, many minor misfortunes and not merely severe ones should destroy happiness.

Aristotle's answer to the second question of whether the fortunes of the dead's descendants can affect their happiness is 'no': the good and evil that affects the dead's descendants can affect their welfare only in a minimal sense that cannot change the fact that they were or were not happy. The apparent strangeness in Aristotle's allowing that the dead can be affected even in this minimal sense[54] can, perhaps, be reduced when we recall (i) his comparison of the effect on the dead of the good and evil fortune of their descendants with the effect of good and evil on the living when they are unaware of it (1100$^a$18–21); and (ii) the importance of good and evil fortune for the possibility of happiness (1100$^b$22–1101$^b$5). Changes in the circumstances of life can affect one's happiness even when they have

---

[54] Cf. 1115$^a$26–7. One interpretation says that the dead can be affected to a certain degree after death because they, or their actions or effects, or certain aspects of these things, can survive in their descendants and friends (Scott, 'Fortune'; Crisp, 'Inclusivism', §14). But Aristotle believes that the well-being of the dead can equally be affected by their being honoured or dishonoured, and that the effect on the dead of their descendants' good or bad fortune is comparable to the effect of such fortune, honours and dishonours, on the living when they are unknown to the affected person (1100$^a$18–21). Clearly, the effect of honours and dishonours on the dead and the unknowing living involves no tenuous form of survival beyond death, and there is no reason to suppose that the effect on the dead of the good or bad fortune of their descendants is any different.

no effect on a man's virtuous activity.[55] Aristotle evidently thinks that the good or bad fortune of relatives is one of the circumstances of life that can affect one's happiness. Thus, he said at the end of chapter 8 ($1099^b3$–6) that a person is most unlikely to be happy if he has had good children who have died. Aristotle does not think that the man's well-being will persist as long as he is ignorant of his misfortune. Happiness requires excellence in the circumstances of one's life, not merely the belief that they are excellent. Regardless of one's awareness of the change, one's happiness will be destroyed if those circumstances are blighted to a sufficient degree. However, in the case of the dead, Aristotle holds, since happiness is determined primarily by the character of the activity that is the living one does, and that activity ceases when one dies, what happens to a man's descendants cannot affect his possession or lack of happiness. But, Aristotle appears to hold, the circumstances of one's life, to a diminishing degree over time, do extend beyond the term of one's life. So just as disasters that afflict a man's children destroy his happiness even when he is unaware of the misfortunes, so such disasters changing the circumstances of the dead may affect their well-being to a small degree.

## 5. *Nicomachean Ethics* 1. 12

This chapter is based on a distinction between things that are praised and things that are honoured. What is praised is not the best thing, and it is praised because it has a quality of a certain type ($\tau\tilde{\omega}$ $\pi o\iota\acute{o}\nu$ $\tau\iota$ $\epsilon\tilde{\iota}\nu\alpha\iota$) and is related to something better than it. For example, virtuous people and virtue are praised because of the virtuous actions they produce. But then what is best does not likewise produce some superior good and hence is not praised but is rather honoured. Both virtuous actions and *eudaimonia* are honoured while potentialities such as virtue of character are not. Aristotle's point is clearly that both virtuous actions and happiness are honoured because they are identical. (Cf. *Rhet.* $1367^b28$–36; *EE* $1219^b8$–16; for a very different account of the praiseworthy, see *EE* $1248^b16$–26.)

Suppose that *eudaimonia* were virtuous activity + virtue or vir-

[55] See Heinaman, 'Improvability', 137–41. Cf. *Pol.* $1265^a31$–2: 'it is possible to live temperately yet miserably'.

tuous activity + virtue + some or all other intrinsic goods. Then by being happy (that is, because of what, as a matter of definition, happiness is) one would—in part—be of a certain quality that produces superior goods. According to Aristotle's distinction, such qualities are the sorts of thing that are to be praised rather than honoured. Hence, if such a quality were a constituent of happiness, one ought to be, at least in part, praised because of one's happiness. But Aristotle says that happiness is something that is not praised but honoured, and that not virtue but actions and ἔργα are honoured (1101ᵇ32–4). His point assumes the identity of virtuous activity and happiness, and excludes the possibility that happiness could comprise intrinsic goods such as virtue which are not activities.

## 7. Conclusion

In the *Eudemian Ethics*, *Nicomachean Ethics*, and *Politics* Aristotle frequently, in fact over twenty times, makes the claim that happiness is a certain kind of entity. *Always*, in those works, he asserts that happiness is an activity. In *NE* 1. 7 he presents his main argument—the function argument—for his claim that *eudaimonia* is a certain kind of activity. The present paper has explained how the rest of book 1 supports the contention that, for Aristotle, happiness is nothing but a certain kind of activity. Whether confirming 1. 7's conclusion in chapter 8, or assuming it in succeeding chapters, the whole of book 1 provides compelling evidence that inclusivist interpretations of Aristotle's account of happiness are untenable.

*University College London*

### BIBLIOGRAPHY

Ackrill, J. L., 'Aristotle on *Eudaimonia*', in A. Rorty (ed.), *Essays on Aristotle* (Berkeley, 1980), 15–33.
Annas, J., 'The Good Life and the Good Lives of Others', *Social Philosophy and Policy*, 9 (1992), 133–48.
—— *The Morality of Happiness* (Oxford, 1993).
Broadie, S., *Ethics with Aristotle* [*Ethics*] (Oxford, 1991), 315.
—— 'Aristotle's Elusive *Summum Bonum*' ['*Summum Bonum*'], *Social Philosophy and Policy*, 16 (1999), 233–51.

—— and Rowe, C., *Aristotle:* Nicomachean Ethics [*Nicomachean Ethics*] (Oxford, 2002).

Cooper, J., 'Plato and Aristotle on "Finality" and "(Self-)Sufficiency"', in R. Heinaman (ed.), *Plato and Aristotle's Ethics* (London, 2003), 117–47.

Crisp, R., 'Aristotle's Inclusivism' ['Inclusivism'], *Oxford Studies in Ancient Philosophy*, 12 (1994), 111–36.

—— 'Kraut on Aristotle on Happiness', *Polis*, 10 (1993), 129–61.

Devereux, D., 'Aristotle on the Essence of Happiness', in D. J. O'Meara (ed.), *Studies in Aristotle* (Washington, 1981), 247–60.

Gomez-Lobo, A., 'The Ergon Inference', in L. Gerson (ed.), *Aristotle: Critical Assessments* (London, 1999), 170–83.

Graham, D., 'States and Performances: Aristotle's Test', *Philosophical Quarterly*, 30 (1980), 117–30.

Hagen, C. , 'The Energeia–Kinesis Distinction and Aristotle's Conception of Praxis', *Journal of the History of Philosophy*, 22 (1984), 263–80.

Hardie, W. F. R., 'The Final Good in Aristotle's Ethics', in J. M. E. Moravcsik (ed.), *Aristotle* (Garden City, NY, 1967), 297–322.

Heinaman, R., 'Activity and Change in Aristotle' ['Activity and Change'], *Oxford Studies in Ancient Philosophy*, 13 (1995), 187–216.

—— 'Activity and Praxis in Aristotle' ['Activity and Praxis'], *Proceedings of the Boston Area Colloquium in Ancient Philosophy*, 12 (1996), 71–111.

—— 'Alteration and Aristotle's Activity–Change Distinction', *Oxford Studies in Ancient Philosophy*, 16 (1998), 227–57.

—— Analysis of *Metaphysics Z*, *Archelogos Project* 2000 ⟨http://www.archelogos.com/⟩.

—— 'Aristotle and the Mind–Body Problem', *Phronesis*, 36 (1990), 83–102.

—— '*Eudaimonia* and Self-Sufficiency in the *Nicomachean Ethics*', *Phronesis*, 33 (1988), 31–53.

—— 'Rationality, *Eudaimonia* and *Kakodaimonia* in Aristotle', *Phronesis*, 38 (1993), 31–56.

—— 'The Improvability of *Eudaimonia* in the *Nicomachean Ethics*' ['Improvability'], *Oxford Studies in Ancient Philosophy*, 21 (2002), 99–147.

Irwin, T., 'Aristotle on Reason, Desire and Virtue', *Journal of Philosophy*, 72 (1975), 567–78.

—— 'Ethics in the *Rhetoric* and in the *Ethics*', in A. Rorty (ed.), *Aristotle's Rhetoric* (Berkeley, 1996), 142–74.

—— 'Permanent Happiness: Aristotle and Solon', *Oxford Studies in Ancient Philosophy*, 3 (1985), 89–124.

—— 'Stoic and Aristotelian Conceptions of Happiness', in M. Schofield and G. Striker (eds.), *The Norms of Nature* (Cambridge, 1986), 205–44.

—— 'The Structure of Aristotelian Happiness' ['Structure'], *Ethics*, 101 (1991), 382–91.

Kim, J., 'Causation, Nomic Subsumption, and the Concept of Event', *Journal of Philosophy*, 70 (1973), 217–36.

Meyer, S., *Aristotle on Moral Responsibility* (Oxford, 1993).

Nuyens, F., *L'Évolution de la psychologie d'Aristote* (Louvain, 1973).

Price, A., 'Aristotle's Ethical Holism', *Mind*, 89 (1980), 338–52.

Scott, D., 'Aristotle on Posthumous Fortune' ['Fortune'], *Oxford Studies in Ancient Philosophy*, 18 (2000), 211–29.

White, N., 'Conflicting Parts of Happiness in Aristotle's Ethics' ['Conflicting Parts'], *Ethics*, 105 (1995), 258–83.

White, S. A., 'Is Aristotelian Happiness a Good Life or the Best Life?', *Oxford Studies in Ancient Philosophy*, 8 (1990), 103–43.

Whiting, J., '*Eudaimonia*, External Results, and Choosing Virtuous Actions for Themselves' ['*Eudaimonia*'], *Philosophy and Phenomenological Research*, 65 (2002), 270–90.

# ARISTOTLE'S *POETICS* WITHOUT *KATHARSIS*, FEAR, OR PITY

## CLAUDIO WILLIAM VELOSO

*In memory of Wilma and Hildebrando, my parents*

THERE is no room for *katharsis* in the definition of tragedy as it occurs in chapter 6 of Aristotle's *Poetics*. The passage is corrupt. At least three scholars—Petruševski, Freire, and Scott—have shown that intervention in the text is justified and necessary, and I have already argued this case elsewhere.[1] I take it for granted here that κάθαρσις in line 1449ᵇ28 cannot remain. Instead, I ask (1) whether it is a matter of simple elimination or whether some other word should replace it; (2) what portion of the text should be considered corrupt; and, most important, (3) why.

## 1. Testimonies

Those who believe that κάθαρσις has no place in the definition of tragedy need not allow any later testimony as to tragic Aristotelian

© Claudio William Veloso 2007

I am indebted to Bernard Besnier, Luc Brisson, Vincent Carraud, Pier Luigi Donini, Marwan Rashed, Michelle Lacore, Carlos Lévy, and David Sedley for their comments and support. I should also like to thank Andrew Dalby and Alexandra Slaby for this meticulous translation. A first version of this paper was delivered at a seminar organized by the Centre for Research on Myth and Psyche (CERLAM) at the University of Caen in 2006.

[1] M. D. Petruševski, '*Παθημάτων κάθαρσιν* ou bien *πραγμάτων σύστασιν*?' ['*Παθημάτων*'], *Ziva antika*, 4 (1954), 237–44 (French précis of the Macedonian text published at 209–36; selected passages from *Poetics* at 245–50); A. Freire, *A catarse em Aristóteles* [*Catarse*], 2nd edn. (Braga, 1996; 1st edn. 1982); G. Scott, 'Purging the *Poetics*' ['Purging'], *Oxford Studies in Ancient Philosophy*, 25 (2003), 233–63; C. W. Veloso, 'Critique du paradigme interprétatif "éthico-politique" de la *Poétique* d'Aristote' ['Critique'], *Kentron*, 21 (2005), 11–46 (earlier version: 'Crítica del paradigma interpretativo "ético-político" de la *Poética* de Aristóteles', *Izta-palapa*, 59 (2005), 117–50).

catharsis to shake their faith.[2] In the first place, there is no evidence that these later testimonia refer to our *Poetics*. The most important witness is Proclus, *In Remp.* i. 42, 49–50 Kroll, but he does not use the word κάθαρσις and does not name the *Poetics* or any other Aristotelian text; some commentators are convinced that he is alluding to Aristotle's lost dialogue (?) *De poetis* (fr. 5 Ross),[3] but that is mere conjecture. Iamblichus, *Myst.* i. 11 Parthey (cf. i. 12–13; iii. 7–10), refers to tragedy and *katharsis*, but does not mention Aristotle; I see no justification for counting the passage as an Aristotelian fragment.[4] Olympiodorus, *In Alc. I* 145. 12–13 Westerink, speaks in general terms of an Aristotelian form of *katharsis* 'that cures evil with evil and by means of a battle between opposites leads to a state of equilibrium [συμμετρίαν]'. Elsewhere, however (54. 15–16), Olympiodorus calls this form of *katharsis* 'Peripatetic or Stoic' and characterizes it in a way that suggests the driving out of one passion by another (of fear by anger, for example) as described by Seneca (*De ira* 1. 8. 7; 1. 10. 1–2), who prefers total liberation by reason (cf. 2. 6. 3; 2. 13. 3);[5] but all this seems a long way from the *Poetics*.[6] As for *Tractatus Coislinianus*, it gives every sign of being a summary of some other text, but definitely not of the *Poetics*, still less of the so-called lost second book.[7] However, it does echo another text in the same manuscript (Par. Coisl. 120), namely the Περὶ παθῶν

---

[2] See Petruševski, 'Παθημάτων', 239, and Scott, 'Purging', 253–5.

[3] See e.g. R. Janko, 'From Catharsis to the Aristotelian Mean' ['Mean'], in A. O. Rorty (ed.), *Essays on Aristotle's Poetics* [*Essays*] (Princeton, 1992), 341–58 at 347 ff., and 'Philodemus' *On Poems* and Aristotle's *On Poets*' ['Philodemus'], *Cronache ercolanesi*, 21 (1991), 5–64 at 48 ff.; R. Laurenti (ed.), *Aristotele: i frammenti dei dialoghi* (Naples, 1987).

[4] See D. Lanza (trans.), *Aristotele: La poetica* [*Poetica*] (Milan, 1987), 237.

[5] See A. Ničev, *L'Énigme de la catharsis tragique dans Aristote* (Sofia, 1970), 184.

[6] *Pace* E. S. Belfiore, *Tragic Pleasures: Aristotle on Plot and Emotion* [*Tragic Pleasures*] (Princeton, 1992), 328.

[7] *Pace* R. Janko, *Aristotle on Comedy: Towards a Reconstruction of Poetics 2* [*Comedy*] (London, 2002; 1st edn. 1981); *contra* D. Lanza, 'La simmetria impossibile: commedia e comico nella *Poetica* di Aristotele', in C. Questa (ed.), *Studi offerti a Francesco Della Corte* (Filologia e forme letterarie, 5; Rome, 1987), 65–80. Marwan Rashed (in M. Trédé (ed.), *Traités théoriques anciens sur la comédie* (forthcoming)) points out that the signs appearing at the left of the text of *Tract. Coisl.* are abbreviations of ὅτι, 'that'; one of these might have been inserted by mistake into the text, before συμμετρίαν, after the initial sentence about tragedy. In so far as one can read them as something like 'the author says that', this discovery buttresses the idea that this text may be the work of an excerptor rather than a 'free' summary. But, in my opinion, it goes against the idea that the original work was the *Poetics*. For if the *Tract. Coisl.* consisted in a series of excerpts from the *Poetics*, it would be even more difficult to explain the lexical and conceptual differences between the two texts such

(*De passionibus*) attributed to Andronicus of Rhodes (wrongly according to Glibert-Thirry, who believes its author to be an eclectic or perhaps even a rhetor).[8] Still according to Glibert-Thirry, the second part of this text may be a version of the *De virtutibus et vitiis* attributed to Aristotle but actually Stoic in origin.[9] Both texts seem to me to show similarities to the author discussed in P.Herc. 1581, a text which may be part of book 4[10] or 5[11] of Philodemus' *De poematis*.[12] Janko[13] identifies him, mistakenly in my opinion, with the Aristotle of the *De poetis*. I shall come back later to some of these claimed testimonia.

Secondly, even if these were references to the text known to us as the *Poetics*, they refer to a text which was already corrupt.

It may be objected that if the word κάθαρσις is not to stand in *Poetics* 6, another Aristotelian passage will need to be cleaned out as well, the allusion to the *Poetics* in *Pol.* 8. 7; and two emendations may seem too many. One possible reply is that this passage may not after all allude to the *Poetics*, where Aristotle in fact fails to clarify the term in question; this strategy is actually adopted by Scott ('Purging', 252–3), for whom *Pol.* 8. 7 probably refers to a text on comedy, perhaps the alleged 'lost second book' of the *Poetics*.[14] My approach is quite different: there are powerful reasons within the

as the expression φοβερὰ παθήματα, differences which Janko, *Comedy*, persistently underrates—see below, n. 104.

   [8] A. Glibert-Thirry (ed.), *Pseudo-Andronicus de Rhodes: Περὶ παθῶν [Pseudo-Andronicus]* (Leiden, 1977), 30–4. In Περὶ παθῶν (1. 2 and 1. 3) one finds the nouns δέος and οἶκτος, also seen at the beginning of *Tract. Coisl.* on tragedy, in place of the usual φόβος, fear, and ἔλεος, pity. Yet in Aristotle's works the second is used only once (*Rhet.* 3. 16, 1417ᵃ12) and the first is not attested at all, *pace* Janko, *Comedy*, 136: this term appears only in a passage by David, *In Porph.* 116. 22–8 Busse, which has been considered a fragment of Aristotle (fr. 182 Rose) but seems to be a reference to the *Oeconomica*, which is no longer considered genuine.
   [9] Glibert-Thirry, *Pseudo-Andronicus*, 2–5. Its author may be an eclectic Peripatetic, according to M. Cacouros, 'De virtutibus et vitiis', in R. Goulet (ed.), *Dictionnaire des philosophes antiques*, suppl. (Paris, 2003), 506–46 at 515–21 and 528–30.
   [10] M. L. Nardelli, 'La catarsi poetica nel *PHerc.* 1581' ['Catarsi'], *Cronache ercolanesi*, 8 (1978), 96–103 at 99.
   [11] Janko, 'Philodemus', 60–1.
   [12] Note e.g. the presence of the word ἀφροσύνη in the three texts: Περὶ παθῶν 2. 10. 1; *VV* 1249ᵇ30; 1250ᵃ16; 1250ᵇ43–1251ᵃ4; P.Herc. 1581, fr. 2—see below, n. 106. This word is rarely used by Aristotle and the context is never significant (*Pol.* 3. 11, 1281ᵇ27; *NE* 7. 3, 1146ᵃ27).
   [13] 'Philodemus', 59–60; 'Mean', 349.
   [14] Against the necessity of the hypothesis of a second book of *Poetics*, a hypothesis which has quite unjustifiably become a certainty among commentators, see e.g. R. Cantarella, 'I "libri" della *Poetica* di Aristotele', *Rendiconti, Classe di scienze*

text of *Politics* 8 for suspecting that this passage is corrupt as well.
Before returning to the *Poetics* (Section 3 below), let us first look
at *Politics* 8.[15]

## 2. *Politics* 8. 5–7

[1] Since we accept the distinction made by some theoreticians, who divide
melodies into ethical, practical,[16] and inspiring melodies—they also relate the nature of the harmonies to each of these melodies, one harmony
being appropriate to one melody[17]—and since we say that music must
not be used for the sake of one benefit but for many—it must be used for
the sake of education and purification [παιδείας ἕνεκεν καὶ καθάρσεως]
(for the present we speak of purification without qualification, but we
will discuss it again more precisely in our discourses on composition
technique [ἐν τοῖς περὶ ποιητικῆς]), and thirdly, it must be used for pursuits [τρίτον δὲ πρὸς διαγωγήν], for repose, and for the relaxation of
tension [πρὸς ἄνεσίν τε καὶ πρὸς τὴν τῆς συντονίας ἀνάπαυσιν]—it is clear
that, although all of the harmonies should be used, they should not
all be used in the same manner. For education we should use ethical
ones, whereas for listening while others are performing we should use
practical and inspiring ones. (*Pol.* 8. 7, 1341ᵇ32–1342ᵃ4)[18]

Now the words 'for repose, and for the relaxation of tension', as
they appear in the manuscripts and in Aubonnet's edition, simply refuse to attach themselves to the words 'thirdly, it must be
used for pursuits', which end the preceding line. Several solutions
have already been proposed,[19] for example that of introducing a
fourth aim by inserting a disjunction. However, not only is there
no τέταρτον, fourth, in the manuscripts at this point, but there is
never any reference to a fourth aim in *Politics* 8.

At the beginning of chapter 5 Aristotle finally develops answers

*morali storiche filologiche, Accademia dei Lincei*, 30/7–12 (1975), 289–97, and Lanza,
*Poetica*, 20–1.

[15] I am revisiting the main points of my study of this text in Veloso, 'Critique'.

[16] These two terms must be considered in a more restricted and specialized sense,
as suggested by S. Halliwell, 'La psychologie morale de la *catharsis*: un essai de
reconstruction' ['Psychologie'], *Études philosophiques*, 4 (2003), 499–517 at 501–2.

[17] Reading μέλος, according to a correction made by Tyrwhitt ap. J. Aubonnet
(ed.), *Aristote: Politique*, vol. iii/2 [book 8] [*Politique*] (Paris, 1996).

[18] [*Translator's note*: translations from the Greek in this paper are based on the
French versions in the author's manuscript, sometimes drawing on published English translations.]

[19] See Aubonnet, *Politique*, app. crit. and note ad loc.

to the question why, under the best constitution, children must learn μουσική, meaning here quite simply 'music'. He considers three reasons:

[2] About music, it is not easy to determine what power it has, or the reason why one should participate in it, whether (1) for the sake of amusement and relaxation [παιδιᾶς ἕνεκα καὶ ἀναπαύσεως], like sleep and drink (for these things are not in themselves worthwhile [σπουδαίων],²⁰ but pleasant, and at the same time 'they ease our cares', as Euripides says; and this is why people class it as they do, and use all such things in the same way—sleep, drink, music, and they also include dancing); or whether we should think that (2) music to some degree concerns virtue [πρὸς ἀρετήν τι τείνειν], in the belief that, just as gymnastics gives a certain quality to the body, so music too has the power to give a certain quality to the character, accustoming it to take pleasure in the right way; or that (3) music contributes something to pursuits and to discernment [πρὸς διαγωγήν . . . καὶ πρὸς φρόνησιν]—which must be considered a third aim. (*Pol.* 8. 5, 1339ᵃ14–26)

It seems quite clear that in line 25 the word φρόνησις, 'discernment', does not refer to the excellence of practical reasoning as described in *Nicomachean Ethics* 6.²¹ Used along with διαγωγή, 'pursuits', 'life', *phronēsis* refers rather to thought without qualification.²² This may be a hendiadys,²³ which would explain why φρόνησις is no longer mentioned beside διαγωγή in the remainder of *Politics* 8. In this case, the phrase should be translated as something to the effect of 'intellectual pursuits [*or* activities]'.²⁴ Although διαγωγή on its own can refer to amusements (*NE* 10. 6, 1176ᵇ9–14), that is obviously not the case here, for then the first reason would be repeated. Besides, the distinction between pursuits and amusements already appears in chapter 3, which discusses the best way to fill one's leisure, σχολή, which is the ultimate goal of all work, ἀσχολία (1337ᵇ33 ff.). It should certainly not be with amusements, because that would then be our end in life,

²⁰ These are necessary things: see *NE* 4. 14, 1128ᵇ3–4; *Metaph.* Δ 5, 1015ᵃ20–6. Obviously, these are cases of 'hypothetical necessity'; on this concept see *PA* 1. 1, 639ᵇ21 ff.
²¹ *Pace* P. Donini, '*Mimèsis* tragique et apprentissage de la *phronēsis*' ['*Mimèsis*'], *Études philosophiques*, 4 (2003), 436–50 at 446–7; L. Golden, *Aristotle on Tragic and Comic Mimesis* [*Aristotle*] (Atlanta, 1992), 9.
²² Cf. *Metaph.* Λ 7, 1072ᵇ14 ff.; *De caelo* 2. 1, 284ᵃ31–2.
²³ See P. Pellegrin (trans.), *Aristote: Les Politiques* (Paris, 1993).
²⁴ R. Kraut (trans.), *Aristotle: Politics, Books 7 and 8* (Oxford, 1997), translates 'leisure time' or 'leisure activity'.

which is impossible. Amusements should rather be resorted to as a break from work, because work brings exhaustion and stress, and one who works needs relaxation, which is the goal of amusements ($1337^b36$–40). Thus amusements must be dispensed at the proper time, as a medicine, φαρμακείας χάριν (40–2). The best way to fill one's leisure is then with intellectual pursuits, that is to say things which are 'for their own sake' ($1338^a10$), such as listening to a bard ($1338^a21$–30).

Aristotle adds, still in chapter 5, that intellectual pursuits are inappropriate to the education of children, because 'the end is unsuited to one who is not yet complete' ($1339^a29$–31), in other words, the goal for an adult is not suitable for a child. This goal is leisure (3, $1337^b33$), which involves happiness and pleasure ($1338^a1$ ff.); amusement and relaxation are never an end in themselves (*NE* 10. 6, $1177^b28$ ff.), and nor is education.[25] Yet, given certain conditions, children may practise music in view of the pursuits they will enjoy in adulthood because the practice makes them good judges of music (6, $1340^b20$–5, 33–9), and listening to music is one of the pursuits that befit free men (5, $1339^b4$–10).[26] Although the contribution made by music to intellectual pursuits has some connection to the education which makes children capable of feeling joy or pain and judging correctly (5, $1340^a14$–18),[27] the two cannot be assimilated, because with intellectual pursuits one goes in a certain sense beyond the practical sphere; they fill the spare time of a happy life (*NE* 10. 7).

But excellence of practical reasoning is a part of excellence of character, and that is another possible reason for children to devote themselves to music. There is no excellence of character without φρόνησις, discernment, defined here as in *Nicomachean Ethics* 6. Better still, without discernment there is no *achieved* excellence of character, as distinct from the 'natural' one a child may possess, which is not, properly speaking, excellence of character (*NE* 6. 1, $1138^b20$ ff.; 13, $1144^a6$ ff.; $1144^b1$ ff.). The converse is also true (*NE* 6. 13, $1144^b30$–2). It is not surprising, then, that music may contribute to the emergence of excellence in practical reasoning, and we

---

[25] See Golden, *Aristotle*, 13.

[26] Practising music to a certain extent is not unworthy of a free man if he practises it for himself or his friends (*Pol.* 8. 2, $1337^b17$–23).

[27] Cf. Halliwell, 'Psychologie', 504.

need not look for this contribution where it cannot be found—in the third aim.[28] We must specify at this stage how music can make a character excellent (*Pol.* 8. 5, 1339ᵃ41 ff.).[29] Virtue and vice are habitual states of the faculties of desiring and reasoning concerning actions and emotions (*NE* 2. 5, 1106ᵇ14 ff.; 3. 1, 1109ᵇ30). We become virtuous or vicious by habituation and by learning,[30] i.e. by repeating certain movements[31] (and perceptions)[32] which once executed in a habitual state will constitute an act of virtue or vice. Action, properly speaking, consists not merely in doing certain things, but in doing them by choice, προαίρεσις; hence it is possible to perform just actions without oneself being just (*NE* 5. 10, 1135ᵃ8 ff.; 13, 1137ᵃ21–5; 6. 13, 1144ᵃ13–17). Even if emotions are not, properly speaking, chosen as actions are (*NE* 2. 4, 1106ᵃ2 ff.), one can habituate oneself to performing certain movements upon perceiving certain things on certain conditions, and this depends also on certain judgements.[33] It is through performing correct movements, though as yet lacking the correct habitual state of the faculties of the soul, that we become virtuous. Now music includes similarities to or imitations of characters (*Pol.* 8. 5, 1340ᵃ12 ff.):[34] it contains certain movements—physical movements[35]—in common with actions and emotions (1340ᵇ7–10), so that when children hear and perform music they are going through the very process of habituation through which one perfects oneself.

Let us return to the text of *Pol.* 8. 7 [1]. If intellectual pursuits are a 'third' element, education and purification are two separate elements. But we cannot consider pursuits—if these are the same pursuits mentioned at the beginning of chapter 5—and repose/

---

[28] *Pace* Donini, '*Mimèsis*', 446–7, 440.
[29] See *Pol.* 8. 5, 1339ᵃ41–1440ᵇ12.
[30] See also *NE* 2. 1, 1109ᵇ12.          [31] See *EE* 2. 2, 1220ᵇ1–2.
[32] See *Metaph. A* 1, 980ᵃ27–8; *Post. An.* 2. 19, 99ᵇ35–6.
[33] See B. Besnier, 'Aristote et les passions', in B. Besnier, P.-F. Moreau, and L. Renault (eds.), *Les Passions antiques et médiévales* (Paris, 2003), 29–94 at 67 and 76–8. An interpretation according to which judgement and reasoning come only 'afterwards' does not account for the virtuous or vicious character which Aristotle attributes to emotions.
[34] By 'imitation' one must understand *simulation*, as I explain in '*Phantasia* et *mimesis* chez Aristote' ['*Phantasia*'], *Revue des études anciennes*, 106/2 (2004), 455–76, and especially *Aristóteles mimético* (São Paulo, 2004).
[35] *Pace* S. Halliwell, *The Aesthetics of Mimesis: Ancient Texts and Modern Problems* [*Aesthetics*] (Princeton, 2002), 159–63, 238, 245, 253, 256.

262        *Claudio William Veloso*

relaxation as constituting jointly a subdivision of purification,[36] because nothing in *Politics* 8 represents intellectual pursuits as a form of purification. On the other hand, reason can be found for linking purification to repose and relaxation.[37]

The 'benefits' in [1] ought to recapitulate the three 'reasons' in [2]. The terms and the order in which they appear have been partly modified, but the three reasons can still be identified. At the beginning of chapter 5 the reasons are (1) amusement and relaxation, (2) virtue, (3) intellectual pursuits. In chapter 7 they are (1) education, (2) purification, (3) pursuits. In the meantime (5, 1339ᵇ13–14, not quoted above) the list had already become: (1) education, (2) amusement, (3) pursuits. In chapter 7, therefore, 'education' must be understood as formation in virtue and 'purification' as amusement and relaxation,[38] because Aristotle also says that relaxation, the aim of amusement, is a kind of therapy (ἰατρεία τις) for the pain caused by hard work (5, 1339ᵇ17), while at 7, 1342ª10–11, purification is associated with therapy. So the phrase 'for repose, and for the relaxation of tension' must apply to the second reason, i.e. purification (1341ᵇ38). Purification does indeed cover 'amusement and relaxation'. Therefore line 41 clarifies what is meant in that context by 'purification'; *thus the reference in that line to an explanation of 'purification' in another work is supererogatory, and the text must be suspect.* In any case this is already the second occurrence of the word κάθαρσις in *Politics* 8: when it first occurs (6, 1341ª23), where it is opposed to μάθησις, 'learning' (musical education, but it merges into education in general),[39] it does not call for any clarification. Moreover, Aristotle had already said that relaxation was a kind of therapy.

Against what harm would amusement offer a therapy? As it forms good habits, education imposes upon us certain movements to which we are not yet accustomed, and these result in pain.[40] Hence it is not possible to be educated all the time, just as it is not possible to stay awake all the time, sleep offering a relaxation which preserves

---

[36] By correcting τρίτον δέ to ταύτης δ' ἥ and inserting ἥ before πρὸς ἄνεσιν, as suggested by F. Susemihl (ed.), *Aristotelis politicorum libri octo cum vetusta translatione Guilelmi de Moerbeka* (Leipzig, 1872), app. crit.

[37] *Pace* Halliwell, 'Psychologie', 515. See G. Carchia, *L'estetica antica* (Rome and Bari, 2005; 1st edn. 1999), 107.

[38] Amusement and relaxation can also concern character, since the influence of music on character is not necessarily educational. Cf. the influence of the melodies of Olympos (5, 1340ª5–12), which are 'inspiring' (1342ª7 ff.); see also Halliwell, 'Psychologie', 501.

[39] See Halliwell, 'Psychologie', 503.        [40] See *Rhet.* 1. 11, 1370ª12–16.

our capacity to stay awake (*De somno* 3, 458ᵃ25–32). *Recreation* is then (hypothetically) necessary to all education. As it offers a break from the pains of educational work, amusement saves from an excess of education and comes as a relief. Music can and must be used as amusement. The musical therapy of *Pol.* 8. 7 consists in giving free vent to one's 'natural tendencies' concerning emotions, at least to a certain extent; this therapy seems to be 'homoeopathic', although Aristotle states elsewhere that therapies and punishments are effected by opposites (*NE* 2. 2, 1104ᵇ13–18; cf. *EE* 2. 1, 1220ᵃ35–7),[41] are in fact 'allopathic'. Beyond that, we must note that—contrary to what might be argued from an easy analogy between health of the body and virtue of the soul—κάθαρσις appears in *Pol.* 8. 7 as the physical analogue not of education,[42] but of recreation, that is, as the 'redress of a redress'. Of course, the need for a respite is not reserved solely for pathological cases, but is common to all, albeit in different degrees (*Pol.* 8. 7, 1342ᵃ11 ff.).[43] Besides, whereas the contribution of music to education includes musical performance, recreation lies in listening to music performed by others (*Pol.* 8. 5, 1339ᵃ26–9). Performance eventually creates tension, notably among those who are still learning; but resting from performance, listening, and perhaps dancing, offer relaxation.[44] This may explain why a differentiated use of harmonies is called for: ethical harmonies for education, practical and inspiring ones for other performers to listen to.[45]

Thus as regards the text of line 41 of [1], πρὸς ἄνεσίν τε καὶ πρὸς τὴν τῆς συντονίας ἀνάπαυσιν ('for repose, and for the relaxation of tension'), we have several possibilities. We can:

(1) delete line 41 as a gloss—and perhaps also τρίτον δὲ πρὸς δι- αγωγήν ('and thirdly . . . for pursuits') in line 40, given that there is a difference in construction between this and the first two elements; or

(2) move line 41

---

[41] See Olymp. *In Alc. I* 54. 18–55. 1 Westerink; also Belfiore, *Tragic Pleasures*, 324 n. 76.

[42] On this point Belfiore, *Tragic Pleasures*, 326 and 336, seems to be inconsistent.

[43] *Pace* Belfiore, *Tragic Pleasures*, 326, the πᾶσι in 1342ᵃ14 does not refer only to the παθητικοί, but also includes *the* (the article is missing from the translation, 320) others.

[44] See Plato, *Laws* 2, 653 D 7–654 A 5; 672 B–D; 7, 790 E 8–791 B 1.

[45] With other interpreters, at *Pol.* 8. 7, 1342ᵃ15, I read πρακτικά, not καθαρτικά: the practical harmonies also offering a certain therapy and enjoyable relief.

(2*a*) to follow παιδείας ἕνεκεν καὶ καθάρσεως ('for the sake of education and purification', line 38); or

(2*b*) to precede τρίτον δὲ πρὸς διαγωγήν (line 40); or

(2*c*) between the two, removing the reference to another text in lines 38–40; or

(3) insert a negative between the τρίτον δὲ πρὸς διαγωγήν and πρὸς ἄνεσίν τε καὶ . . .; or, finally,

(4) delete as a gloss the whole text from lines 38 to 41, including the reference.

Text [1] is, at any rate, corrupted by the intervention of someone who has not correctly identified the three reasons developed in *Politics* 8. If the reference to another text is not Aristotle's but inserted by another, this other may well have our *Poetics* in mind— either because the text known to him was already corrupt and he, in common with many modern interpreters, supposes that the rest of the book offers some kind of explanation of κάθαρσις; or because the text is unknown to him and he assumes for his own reasons that a book on poetics should be concerned to a large extent with *katharsis*.

Aubonnet (ad loc.), arguing to retain the manuscript reading, claims that 'παιδιά, amusement (ἄνεσις, repose), ἀνάπαυσις, relaxation, and διαγωγή, pursuits, are linked by their meaning'. This does not help. Although it is true that pursuits and relaxation are both pleasant, pleasure can only at best share some characteristics with the end ($1339^b31$–8), which is indeed pursuits, which also incorporate the good, τὸ καλόν ($1339^b17$–19). Further on, Aristotle also refers to an 'enjoyable relief' along with 'a kind of purification' (7, $1342^a14$–15). But a therapy which relieves us from pain is pleasant only *per accidens* (*NE* 7. 13, $1152^b33$ ff.; 15, $1154^a28$ ff.), just as learning is (*Pol.* 8. 5, $1339^a28$–9; *NE* 10. 7, $1177^a26$–7). In itself, pleasure is something which supervenes to an activity of the soul (10. 3, $1174^a14$ ff.; 10. 4, $1174^b34$), cognitive activities notably, i.e. perception and intellection (10. 4, $1174^a14$ ff.; 10. 2, $1173^b20$ ff.). That is why pleasure itself is not produced by any technique (*NE* 7. 13, $1153^a23$). Yet pursuits, which are part of good life, consist in an *activity* (or better still, in the conjoint exercise of two activities: perception and intellection); purification on the other hand, religious, medical, or other, is rather a *movement* which does not contain its own end (*Metaph.* Θ 6, $1048^b18$ ff.);[46] the same applies

---

[46] Cf. *Metaph.* Δ 1; *Phys.* 2. 3; 3. 1. That is why it is surprising that Golden, *Aris-*

to learning.[47] However pleasant pursuits may be, they are in no way a relaxation or repose (as relief, therapy, or purification may be). Thus, finally, the text of [1] makes nonsense and must be emended. Meanwhile we have a better sense of the relationship between the three aims of [2]: (1) *amusement* is for the sake of *relaxation*, which is (hypothetically) necessary to (2) *education*, which in its turn is for the sake of *excellence of character*, which fulfils itself in a *good life*, the best part of which is (3) *leisure*, which is spent, in the best way, carrying out *intellectual pursuits*.

If at this stage we wished to identify the 'external' aim of tragedy with one of the three key notions of *Politics* 8, it would be with intellectual pursuits. The 'mimetic pleasure' referred to in *Poetics* 4 must be that of intellectual pursuits, stemming as it does from the recognition of that which imitation is an imitation of, that is, the recognition of an intellective content through perception of the means by which imitation is effected, as I have shown elsewhere.[48] Thus, if Aristotle has to reply to the Platonic ban on imitative poetry (*Rep.* 10, 607 A–C), as many commentators think (following, more or less consciously, Proclus, *In Remp.* i. 49. 13 ff. Kroll), *Politics* 8 and the *Poetics* together give us a very good reply, without the need to regret a 'lost' book. This reply does not consist in a catharsis, however. Since they relate to the intellectual pursuits of the spectator, imitative techniques aim not at pleasure only, as Plato's Socrates believes, but also at the good, τὸ καλόν.

In fact, in *Politics* 8 Aristotle distinguishes between two types of theatre audiences: the free, educated spectator and the vulgar spectator. He implies that the vulgar audience, made up of craftsmen, wage-earners, and the like, attends the theatre for the sake of

*totle*, claims to identify the pursuits of *Politics* 8 with learning and a certain intellectual *katharsis*; likewise, Belfiore, *Tragic Pleasures*, 45–8, 58, 258, 268–9, 345 ff. Naturally, as M. F. Burnyeat specifies ('*De anima* II 5', *Phronesis*, 37 (2002), 29–90 at 67 n. 99), it is the immediate goal, in so far as Aristotle does not deny that, for instance, vision could be the means towards another end; see *Metaph. A* 1, 980ª22–6; *NE* 1. 4, 1096ᵇ16–19; *DA* 3. 12, 434ᵇ3–8. In any case, the ultimate end consists in an activity.

[47] At best, it is an improvement (*NE* 2. 1; *Phys.* 7. 3, 246ª13–16).

[48] See e.g. Veloso, '*Phantasia*' and 'Critique'. μανθάνειν at *Poet.* 4, 1448ᵇ16, should be understood not as 'learning' but as 'understanding'. One should also refrain from transposing what Aristotle says of recognition in tragedy as a shift from ignorance to knowledge (*Poet.* 11, 1452ª29–31; 16, 1454ᵇ19 ff.) to the recognition underlying *Poetics* 4. On the intellectual meaning of the verb προοράω, 'to foresee', 'to guess', or 'to recognize' (and not 'to have seen before') in *Poet.* 4, 1448ᵇ17, see Veloso, 'Critique', 28 n. 78.

relaxation (7, 1342ᵃ23 ff.). At least for the free, educated spectator (and such is the spectator Aristotle has in mind in the *Poetics*: see chapters 13 and 26), tragedy will be one of the intellectual pursuits, at least principally (it need not be that exclusively, just as for the vulgar spectator it need not be exclusively a source of relaxation). That tragedy may educate the free, educated spectator is to be ruled out because he is already educated. Aristotle may indeed allow a 'continuing education', notably as regards emotions (*NE* 10. 10, 1179ᵇ11 ff.; cf. 2. 2, 1104ᵃ14–26),⁴⁹ but no education, in childhood or in adulthood, may be an end in itself, since its goal is an excellent habitual state of certain capacities of the soul. But our pleasure in imitations seems to relate to activities of the soul which are ends in themselves.

If indeed tragedy has a main 'external' aim, this aim consists in the spectator's intellectual pursuits, which can be described neither as *katharsis* nor as education. The reflections Aristotle develops in the *Poetics* belong to this same pleasurable theoretical activity, since he acts as a judge of composition technique (*Poet.* 1, 1447ᵃ9–10)— an intellectual pursuit quite befitting the leisure of a free, educated man like himself.

This excursus on *Politics* 8 has shown both that the reference to a work on composition technique to clarify κάθαρσις is, to say the least, very suspect, and that there is no room for κάθαρσις in the definition of tragedy.

## 3. *Poetics* 6

[3] But let us discuss tragedy by drawing the definition of its essence which derives from what has been said: tragedy is then an imitation of a serious and complete action [μίμησις πράξεως σπουδαίας καὶ τελείας]⁵⁰ having a given extension, worded in a seasoned language [ἡδυσμένῳ] each form of which [is used] distinctly according to its various parts, [carried out] by agents [δρώντων] and not by means of a narrative; [*what follows I quote only in Greek:*] δι' ἐλέου καὶ φόβου περαίνουσα τὴν τῶν τοιούτων παθημάτων κάθαρσιν. (*Poet.* 6, 1449ᵇ22–8).⁵¹

---

⁴⁹ Not only for *hoi polloi*, who would not be truly educated and virtuous, but also for those who would be truly educated and virtuous. See Belfiore, *Tragic Pleasures*, 214–16.

⁵⁰ On the basis of *Poet.* 7, 1450ᵇ24 ff. (cf. 8, 1451ᵃ31–2; 23, 1459ᵃ20), Petruševski, '*Παθημάτων*', 240, assumes that ὅλης, whole, is missing from line 25.

⁵¹ S. Halliwell (ed.), *Aristotle: Poetics* [*Poetics*] (Cambridge, Mass., 1995), trans-

The presence of κάθαρσις in this definition is neither foreshadowed in the preceding chapters nor clarified in the remainder of chapter 6 (though its purpose is precisely to clarify the elements of the definition); nor indeed is it clarified in the rest of the work.[52] The hypothesis of a lacuna after the definition[53] does not account for this silence, because, in the event, nothing in the *Poetics* calls for *katharsis*. In any case we saw from *Politics* 8—to which commentators often go for help—that on a general theoretical level, the notion of *katharsis* cannot have a prominent place among the external aims of tragedy.[54] Yet the very presence of κάθαρσις in the definition should imply a prominent role for it, external or internal to tragedy; thus an explanation that plays down the importance of *katharsis* will not do, because a 'deflated' catharsis would not deserve its place in the definition.[55] In truth the real main external aim of tragedy need not appear in the definition at all: tragedy is for us an opportunity to engage in intellectual pursuits and thus pleases us *as imitation* (*Poet.* 4, 1448$^b$4 ff.), which does appear in the definition; and the fact that this pleasure is a determined pleasure derives from the media, mode, and objects of the imitation in question (see *Poet.* 13 [**5**] and 14 [**10**]), which are also represented in the definition. The formal final cause of tragedy is indeed imitation; we shall come back to that. In any case, any interpretation that relies on too specific a sense of the terms used in this passage—not only

lates this final clause as 'and through pity and fear accomplishing the catharsis of such emotions'; M. Heath (trans.), *Aristotle:* Poetics [*Poetics*] (London, 1996): 'effecting through pity and fear the purification of such emotions.'

[52]   There is a second occurrence of κάθαρσις in chapter 17 (1455$^b$15), where it refers to ritual practice, but it is of no help in making sense of the presence of this term in the definition of tragedy.

[53]   See e.g. A. Gudeman (ed.), *Aristoteles: Περί ποιητικῆς* (Berlin and Leipzig, 1934), who places it in line 31.

[54]   The parallelism put forward by Belfiore, *Tragic Pleasures*, 258, between *Poetics* 6 and *Metaph. H* 1, 1042$^a$3–4, seems a little unwarranted to me and plays on the meaning of τέλος, which at the beginning of *Metaphysics H* means something like a finishing touch and not a final cause.

[55]   Claiming a very specialized meaning for the verb περαίνω, P. Donini, 'La tragedia senza la catarsi' ['Tragedia'], *Phronesis*, 43 (1998), 26–41 at 37 ff., understands that tragedy 'completes' the musical catharsis discussed in *Pol.* 8. 7, a catharsis which takes place before tragedy and outside it. The final clause then becomes something totally insignificant. Halliwell, 'Psychologie', 514 n. 2, also notes that this interpretation makes the presence of catharsis in the definition seem rather strange, but the interpretation he offers (511 ff.) is also 'deflationary': he makes catharsis an added value or an extra benefit coming on top of the pleasure arising from tragedy. See also Heath, *Poetics*, xl–xliii, for whom it benefits vulgar audiences only.

κάθαρσις, but also the participle περαίνουσα, 'accomplishing'—must be set aside in view of *Top.* 6. 2, with its condemnation of the use of metaphors and obscure or rare words in definitions (139ᵇ32 ff.; cf. 10, 148ᵇ16–22).⁵⁶ So what are we to do?

The presence of κάθαρσις is not the only oddity in this passage, nor the only novelty.⁵⁷ The term ἡδυσμένος, 'seasoned', is also new for the reader, even if, right after the definition, Aristotle 'decompresses' it by 'translating' it into the language of chapter 1.⁵⁸ What is most relevant here, even ἔλεος and φόβος (commonly translated 'pity' and 'fear') are not mentioned in the preceding chapters. It is usually said⁵⁹ that their association with tragedy was already well established.⁶⁰ Some commentators argue that their occurrence here follows naturally from Aristotle's preceding discussion, notably in the course of the 'historical' study in chapters 4 and 5 and the contrast with comedy:⁶¹ therefore the presence of ἔλεος and φόβος is justified by the 'serious' nature (σπουδαῖον) of the action mentioned, already foreshadowed in chapter 2. There may be something in this, but if so, the presence of the adjective 'serious' should make the mention of ἔλεος and φόβος redundant in the remainder of the definition. We shall come back to that.

In order to clear up the mystery surrounding catharsis, Petruševski ('*Παθημάτων*', 238) proposed to correct the text, replacing the expression παθημάτων κάθαρσιν, commonly translated 'purification of emotions', with πραγμάτων σύστασιν, 'arrangement of events', an expression which has the same number of letters. In fact, παθημάτων κάθαρσιν is the reading only of manuscript B, Riccardianus 46 (four-

---

⁵⁶ See Petruševski, '*Παθημάτων*', 240; but he goes too far, claiming, for instance (243, 238), that the participle περαίνουσα cannot here have its generic meaning 'fulfilling'. However, that meaning is sufficiently clear and widespread to legitimate its use in a definition; περαίνεσθαι occurs with that same meaning three lines later (1449ᵇ30). Donini's interpretation ('Tragedia', 32–3 and 38) is based on a very specific meaning of this verb which would have required further explanation by Aristotle.

⁵⁷ See D. W. Lucas (ed.), *Aristotle: Poetics [Poetics]* (Oxford, 1968), 96; Veloso, '*Phantasia*', 462–3, and 'Depurando as interpretações da *kátharsis* na *Poética* de Aristóteles' ['Depurando'], *Síntese*, 99 (2004), 13–25 at 15–16 (first version in R. Duarte, V. Figueiredo, V. Freitas, and I. Kangussu (eds.), *Kátharsis: reflexos de um conceito estético* (Belo Horizonte, 2002), 70–9).

⁵⁸ See Scott, 'Purging', 241.

⁵⁹ See e.g. R. Dupont-Roc and J. Lallot (eds.), *Aristote: Poétique* (Paris, 1980), 189.

⁶⁰ See e.g. Plato, *Phaedr.* 268 c–d; *Gorgias, Hel.* 9.

⁶¹ See e.g. H. Haefliger, 'La *Poétique* d'Aristote: une synthèse et une intégration dans la méthodologie d'Aristote', *Kairos*, 9 (1997), 97–119 at 109–10, and Halliwell, *Aesthetics*, 219.

teenth century), while manuscript A, Parisinus 1741, which is the oldest (tenth–eleventh century), reads μαθημάτων κάθαρσιν, 'purification of learnings'.[62] The confusion between παθημάτων and μαθημάτων is easily explained, given the similarity of their respective initials in majuscules, Π and M.[63] There is no doubt that B offers many useful readings (though it is careless in this passage),[64] but, like Scott ('Purging', 242), I find it curious that its reading should be thought obviously preferable, despite the fact that there is no consensus on the meaning of κάθαρσις and some take the word to mean '(intellectual) clarification'. The expression proposed by Petruševski has the indisputable advantage over the other two of being well attested in the *Poetics*.[65] A few lines later in this same chapter, when Aristotle identifies plot (μῦθος), imitation of action (πράξεως μίμησις), and construction of events (σύνθεσις τῶν πραγμάτων, 6, 1450ᵃ2–5),[66] he goes so far as to claim that events and plot are the end, τέλος, of tragedy (1450ᵃ22–3; cf. 13, 1452ᵇ29–30, ἔργον, 'task').

This contention has been pursued by Freire, who claims to 'go further than Petruševski by bringing out the absurdities contained in the catharsis one supposes present in the definition' (*Catarse*, 42). In an earlier paper, while defending Petruševski and Freire against unfair criticism, I judged the emendation arbitrary and partly unnecessary.[67] I no longer regard it as arbitrary, but I still think it partly unnecessary, since πάθημα can be equivalent to πρᾶγμα 'event'.[68] In the only other occurrence of this word in the *Poetics*,

[62] On the independence of B in relation to A, see E. Lobel, *The Greek Manuscripts of Aristotle's* Poetics (*Transactions of the Bibliographical Society*, suppl. 9; Oxford, 1933).

[63] Both can be inscribed in a square or a rectangle: see J. Irigoin, 'Dédoublement et simplification des lettres dans la tradition d'Aristote: *Du ciel* II, *Métaphysique* Z', in id., *La Tradition des textes grecs: pour une critique historique* (Paris, 2003), 283–93 at 283.

[64] The word σπουδαίας, 'serious', does not occur here. Could a 'clever copyist' have considered it redundant, given the presence of δι' ἐλέου καὶ φόβου, 'through pity and fear'?

[65] *Poet.* 6, 1450ᵃ15, 32; 7, 1450ᵇ22; 14, 1453ᵇ2; 1454ᵃ14; 15, 1454ᵃ34. On the other hand, the expression παθημάτων κάθαρσις is attested nowhere else in the Greek corpus, apart from the definition of comedy in *Tract. Coisl.* See Petruševski, 'Παθημάτων', 237.

[66] Petruševski, 'Παθημάτων', 241 and 245, suggests reading σύστασιν, arrangement, instead of σύνθεσιν, construction, in this passage.

[67] Veloso, 'Depurando', 21.

[68] Cf. *EE* 2. 1226ᵇ30–1227ᵃ1. See among others G. F. Else (ed.), *Aristotle's* Poetics: *The Argument* [Poetics] (Cambridge, Mass., 1957), 228 ff., and A. Nehamas, 'Pity and

and still in the plural, it refers to 'external' events (or their imitations) and not to emotions (*Poet.* 24, 1459ᵇ11). In the *Poetics*, for 'emotion' we have rather πάθος (19, 1456ᵃ38); sometimes the latter word also refers to an event, notably the 'grievous event', a destructive or painful action[69] that constitutes the third part of the plot alongside recognition and reversal (*Poet.* 11, 1452ᵇ10–12; 14, 1454ᵃ12).[70] This is precisely the type of event that παθήματα refers to in our treatise. What is needed is to replace κάθαρσιν by σύστασιν 'arrangement', a change of five letters—not much, especially when one remembers that in majuscules kappa and the lunate sigma are often confused. The price to pay for this emendation is low if one takes into account the huge difficulties over which translators and commentators have stumbled in their struggles to retain κάθαρσιν. Unfortunately, even thus modified, the Petruševski–Freire proposition does not solve all our problems.

First, however important the notion of 'construction of events' may be, one can doubt whether it belongs in the definition in chapter 6. In the following lines of this same chapter, Aristotle writes:

[4] And the imitation of action is the plot [μῦθος], for what I mean here by 'plot' is the construction of events [σύνθεσιν τῶν πραγμάτων]. (*Poet.* 6, 1450ᵃ3–6)

This remark renders the hypothetical presence of περαίνουσα τὴν τῶν τοιούτων πραγμάτων [or παθημάτων] σύστασιν, 'which accomplishes the arrangement of such events', in the definition totally redundant, which is indeed the major weakness of the Petruševski–Freire proposition. Petruševski (241) himself anticipates this objection, but his reply does not seem satisfactory to me. While Petruševski accepts that μίμησις πράξεως, 'imitation of action', and σύστασις τῶν πραγμάτων, 'arrangement of events', are two periphrases for μῦθος, plot, he argues that they are not identical: in μίμησις πράξεως the μῦθος is envisaged as the imitation of a whole, complete action,

Fear in the *Rhetoric* and the *Poetics*', in Rorty (ed.), *Essays*, 291–313 at 307. Belfiore, *Tragic Pleasures*, 264, 354 ff., rejects this reading, but does not argue the case. Read in this manner, the presence of τοιούτων, 'of such', no longer raises any problem, while it constitutes an insurmountable problem for almost every other interpretation—see Belfiore, 268–9. In any case, refusing to accept the identification τοιούτων=τούτων ('of these') need not imply that other types of παθήματα are concerned.

[69] *Pace* Heath, *Poetics*, xxi, who, to explain the passage, has to resort to the broad sense of πρᾶξις.

[70] Cf. *Metaph.* Δ 21, 1022ᵇ19–21; *NE* 1. 11, 1101ᵃ30–1; *Rhet.* 2. 8, 1386ᵃ7 ff.

whereas in σύστασις τῶν πραγμάτων the μῦθος is envisaged as an arrangement of the parts of this action—a construction of separate events. We may agree that the two expressions are not identical, but the main difference between them consists in the fact that the expression σύστασις τῶν πραγμάτων says something about imitation itself. The events, πράγματα, arranged in a certain order, are an *imitation*; action, πρᾶξις, is the object of this imitation in the terms of *Poetics* 1–2 (see Petruševski, 242).[71] To say that the construction of events is the end of tragedy (its 'soul': see *Poet.* 6, 1450ᵃ38) amounts to saying that its end is imitation. Thus there is a redundancy in the definition; in other words, the 'arrangement of events' has no place in it.

What we have here is, quite simply, a gloss. At the very least we must delete the clause περαίνουσα τὴν τῶν τοιούτων παθημάτων κάθαρσιν, 'which accomplishes the purification of such emotions [*or* events]'; and we note that the infinitive περαίνεσθαι, occurring as it does three lines after the definition (1449ᵇ30), might well have suggested the participle περαίνουσα to the author of the gloss.

Secondly, the presence of ἔλεος, pity, and φόβος, fear, in the definition remains an enigma; which is why Scott ('Purging', 250) suggested removing the whole final clause: δι' ἐλέου καὶ φόβου περαίνουσα τὴν τῶν τοιούτων παθημάτων κάθαρσιν.[72]

That chapters 1–5 are silent on ἔλεος and φόβος is admittedly less important than their silence about κάθαρσις, given that one may appeal to the serious nature of tragic action, and, moreover, ἔλεος and φόβος (unlike κάθαρσις) are to be discussed in later chapters. *Pace* Scott (250–1), it does not matter very much either that Aristotle employs elements in the definition that have not previously been mentioned in chapters 1–5[73] or that he claims that they have

[71] Of course, this terminological distinction is arbitrary; see *Poet.* 11, 1452ᵇ11; 14, 1453ᵇ27; 15, 1454ᵃ18. There is a systematic homonymy between things and their imitations: πρόσωπον, face and mask; ἦθος, the character of a person and of a dramatis persona; δρᾶμα, action and dramatic action; etc. See e.g. *PA* 1. 1, 640ᵇ29–641ᵃ5.

[72] Else, *Poetics*, 231–2, suggests that the final clause was added by Aristotle later. Others (quoted by Else) believe that the final clause belongs to an earlier state of the text, but was added later. D. de Montmollin, *La Poétique d'Aristote: texte primitif et additions ultérieures* (Neuchâtel, 1951), 50 ff. (cf. 175–6), seems to not consider the final clause an anomaly.

[73] M. Pakaluk, review of *Oxford Studies in Ancient Philosophy*, 25 ['Review'], in *Bryn Mawr Classical Review* (2006) ⟨http://ccat.upenn.edu/bmcr/2006/2006-06-18.html⟩, gives two other examples: the clause 'also, in an accomplished life' in the definition of happiness in *NE* 1. 6, 1098ᵃ18, and the mention of the good in the

been (especially considering the generally poor state of the text). But it is undeniable that the *Poetics* suddenly becomes more unified and consistent when the final clause of the definition of tragedy is removed; and its removal does no violence to the syntax of the passage. In short, we can agree with Scott that the whole final clause may well be an interpolation.

And yet, as he points out (255–6), two objections internal to the *Poetics* may be raised against removing the whole clause:

(1) in the remainder of the *Poetics* we are repeatedly given to understand that ἔλεος and φόβος are essential to tragedy;
(2) *Poetics* 9 [6] seems to look back to the mention of ἔλεος and φόβος in the definition.

Scott's own response is to deny both objections. According to him (256–7), the first six chapters (with the exception of the definition itself) never restrict tragedy to ἔλεος and φόβος[74]—in due course, chapter 19 (1456[b]1–2) adds other emotions—while chapters 7–14 regard ἔλεος and φόβος as emotions applying only to a certain form of tragedy, the *best* (257 ff.). So ἔλεος and φόβος do not serve to characterize all tragedy; tragedy may trigger other emotions than these two. Scott goes on to say (259–60) that the passage in *Poetics* 9 concerns only this form of tragedy and in that case does not refer to *Poetics* 6.

However, Scott's argument is inadequate; and the stakes are high, because his proposal (which I consider valid) to delete the final clause risks rejection if inadequately justified. But his contention (258 ff.; cf. 245) that the ἔλεος and φόβος pair applies only to the *best* tragedy faces textual as well as theoretical difficulties.

First, the text. To support his contention, Scott quotes a passage which seems at first sight to tell against it, the opening of chapter 13:

[5] Following on from what has been said so far, one would have to state what must be aimed at and what must be avoided in arranging plots, as well as where the task [ἔργον] of tragedy comes from. Since indeed the construction [σύνθεσιν] of the best tragedy [καλλίστης τραγῳδίας] should be complex rather than simple—and it [ταύτην] should imitate fearful and pitiable events [φοβερῶν καὶ ἐλεεινῶν . . . μιμητικήν],

definition of courage in 3. 10, 1115[b]21–2. The parallels are imperfect, because these additions are accompanied by some explanation.

[74] Scott seems to imply that in the final clause τοιούτων, 'of such', does not allude to other kinds of emotions.

for this is the distinctive feature [ἴδιον] of such an imitation [τοιαύτης μιμήσεως]—then it is clear that one must . . . (*Poet.* 13, 1452ᵇ28–34)

According to Scott (258), the antecedent of ταύτην and τοιαύτης is the whole phrase καλλίστης τραγῳδίας, and not only τραγῳδίας (most commentators have seen no problem here). His view might find confirmation in a passage in *Poetics* 11 [7], where there is even a disjunction between ἔλεος and φόβος.[75] The imitation of fearful and pitiable events would then be a distinctive feature of the best tragedies, as opposed to lesser tragedies. We may concede that [5] reads more easily if καλλίστης τραγῳδίας is considered the antecedent of ταύτην;[76] this cannot apply to τοιαύτης, however. If Aristotle had wished to restrict the imitation of fearful and pitiable events to the best tragedy, it would have been more natural to write that this is the distinctive feature of such a *tragedy*, and not of such an imitation.

Now the theoretical difficulty. Aristotle asserts that the citharist and the good citharist perform the same task, ἔργον (*NE* 1. 7, 1098ᵃ8–12).[77] Elsewhere he concedes that sometimes we say of someone who does not do something well that he simply does not do it (*Metaph.* Δ 12, 1019ᵃ24–6; 1019ᵇ13–15);[78] even Aristotle himself does not always respect his own rule.[79] Even after ways of speaking and Aristotle's possible inconsistency have been accounted for, the problem remains, and it is only resolvable if we say that both tragedy and good tragedy are to imitate a serious action, but only the best tragedy is to imitate a serious action which is also fearful and pitiable. This solution assumes that what is fearful and pitiable is the most serious thing possible, which I think is defensible (see *Rhet.* 2. 8).[80] But then, in this case, the superiority of the best tragedy is conferred by the object it imitates, just as is the case with tragedy in general in relation to comedy, so that the good tragedian's task will no longer be exactly the same as that of the tragedian *tout court*.

---

[75] It is the only case of a non-negative disjunction of the two in the *Poetics*. See Lucas, *Poetics*, 132.

[76] Actually, ταύτην refers to the whole phrase τὴν σύνθεσιν τῆς καλλίστης τραγῳδίας.

[77] Pakaluk, 'Review', notes this difficulty.

[78] See Scott, 'Purging', 260 n. 33.

[79] Aristotle says that truth is the task (ἔργον) of the thinking faculty (*NE* 6. 2, 1139ᵃ28–9; cf. ᵇ12); truth ought rather to equate with excellence in achieving the task.

[80] See Halliwell, *Aesthetics*, 216–30. In common with Belfiore, *Tragic Pleasures*, 187–9, and P. Destrée, 'Éducation morale et *catharsis* tragique', *Études philosophiques*, 4 (2003), 518–35 at 527 ff., I do not think that fear is secondary to pity or parasitic on it; rather the contrary.

Scott (258) adds that in the following lines of chapter 13, three of the four types of envisaged arrangements of events are not fearful or pitiable, the criteria being the character of the agent and the direction of changes of fortune.[81] However, at least two of these types of plot are not tragic at all, given that they deal with the actions of an evil man, μοχθηρός, or of someone who is very wicked, σφόδρα πονηρός, already excluded from the scope of tragedy back in chapter 2. One of these types, when an evil man exchanges bad fortune for good fortune, contains 'the least tragic of all things' (13, 1452ᵇ36–8). There is a third, which, while it concerns a virtuous character, contains not the pitiable and fearful, but the disgusting, μιαρόν, that is to say a plot in which the ἐπιεικής, the virtuous man, exchanges good fortune for bad fortune;[82] however, excluding this type creates a tension between chapters 13 and 2, because it requires a distinction between ἐπιεικής, virtuous, and σπουδαῖος, good, which is never made explicitly (though we may argue that chapter 13 is engaged in refining the 'seriousness' laid down in chapter 2: tragedy concerns a virtuous man, but not excessively virtuous as the ἐπιεικής is).

Whether or not we accept the contention that only the best tragedy is an imitation of an action which is also fearful and pitiable, it is possible and preferable, without committing oneself to this contention, to show that there is no place for ἔλεος or for φόβος in the final clause of the definition of tragedy. Of the two objections identified by Scott to the removal of the final clause, (1) is not real, since something may be an element of the essence of tragedy without appearing in the definition in chapter 6; although Aristotle claims that this definition derives from the earlier chapters, nothing rules out later refinement, and that is exactly the purpose of the remainder of chapter 6 and of the following chapters,[83] quite in accord with the process of definition found in the *Posterior Analytics* (*Post. An.* 2. 8–10). The only real objection is (2). But I intend to show (Section 4) that, precisely because the passage in *Poetics* 9 refers to the defi-

---

[81]  The shift from bad to good fortune on the part of the ἐπιεικής is not examined.

[82]  The 'second-best', allowing a double end (good for the good man, bad for the evil man), can imitate something pitiable and fearful, in spite of its 'happy end'; see Heath, *Poetics*, xxxiv.

[83]  In the course of chapter 6 Aristotle mentions two plot elements, reversal and recognition (1450ᵃ33–4), which are not mentioned in the definition. Later one reads that all plots do not have these elements (10, 1452ᵃ12–16) and that there is also a third, the grievous event, πάθος (1452ᵇ9–13).

nition in *Poetics* 6, it adequately demonstrates that ἔλεος and φόβος have no place in a final clause of this definition. Our study of this passage will additionally guide us to a partial reconciliation (Section 5) of Scott's proposition with that of Petruševski and Freire.

## 4. *Poetics* 9 and 11

[6] Of simple plots and actions, the episodic ones are the worst. By 'episodic' I mean a plot in which the episodes follow one another without probability or necessity. Such plots are composed by bad playwrights through their own fault, and by good playwrights on account of the actors: for in composing showpieces, and drawing out the plot beyond its capacity, they are often forced to distort the sequence. However,[84] the imitation is not just of a complete action [οὐ μόνον τελείας ἐστὶ πράξεως], but also of fearful and pitiable events [*or* actions] [ἀλλὰ καὶ φοβερῶν καὶ ἐλεεινῶν], and these occur above all when they come about contrary to expectation because of one another. (*Poet.* 9, 1451$^b$33–1452$^a$4)

This is the first passage, after the definition of tragedy, that makes explicit reference to fear and pity. It does not employ the words φόβος and ἔλεος, but φοβερῶν and ἐλεεινῶν, plural adjectives which either are being used as neuter nouns, 'fearful and pitiable events', or qualify the understood noun πράξεων, 'actions'. In the *Poetics*, occurrences of φοβερόν and ἐλεεινόν are more numerous than those of φόβος and ἔλεος, notably in reference to the task assigned to tragedy (see [5]), and they are almost always used together.[85] In that sense, *tragedy is not meant to be fearful or pitiable, but to imitate what is fearful and pitiable.*[86] This point is important and tells in several ways against the presence of a 'catharsis of emotions'; but there is more to come. The words φόβος and ἔλεος can in themselves be

---

[84] I leave ἐπεί in 1452$^a$1 untranslated because it is syntactically redundant. The alternative of treating ἐπεί as active but δέ in 1452$^a$3 as redundant (thus apparently Halliwell, *Poetics*) would require the clause introduced by ἐπεί to be explanatory of the one following it (3–4), which it clearly is not.

[85] The φοβερόν–ἐλεεινόν pair: 9, 1452$^a$2–3; 13, 1452$^b$32, 36; 1453$^a$1, 6; 14, 1453$^b$1. φοβερόν on its own: 14, 1453$^a$9. ἐλεεινόν on its own: 14, 1453$^b$17; 19, 1459$^b$3 (with δεινά). The φόβος–ἔλεος pair: 6, 1449$^b$27 (definition of tragedy); 11, 1452$^a$38–$^b$1 (events); 13, 1453$^a$3–4 (events), 5 (emotions, in no direct relation to tragedy); 14, 1453$^b$12 (events?); 19, 1456$^b$1 (emotions, in no direct relation to tragedy). φόβος on its own: 11, 1452$^a$26 (the emotion felt by Oedipus). The φρίττειν–ἐλεεῖν pair: 14, 1453$^b$5 (the emotion felt by the listener). See also *Poet.* 14, 1453$^b$14, δεινά–οἰκτρά.

[86] See L. Mouze, 'Se connaître soi-même: tragédie, bonheur et contingence', *Études philosophiques*, 4 (2003), 483–98 at 489.

equivalent to φοβερόν and ἐλεεινόν.[87] This appears to be the norm in the *Poetics*, at least when it comes to the task assigned to tragedy. In *Poetics* 11 there is a telling passage which seems precisely to look back to *Poetics* 9:

[7] For such a recognition accompanied by reversal will include ἔλεος or φόβος—the type of actions of which tragedy is said to be an imitation [οἵων πράξεων[88] ἡ τραγῳδία μίμησις ὑπόκειται]. (*Poet.* 11, 1452ᵃ38–ᵇ1)

We are told here that the nouns ἔλεος and φόβος refer to *actions*; and it was established in *Poetics* 9 [6] that tragedy is an imitation of fearful and pitiable things, φοβερὰ καὶ ἐλεεινά.

However, when not in reference to tragedy, the terms ἔλεος and φόβος refer to emotions, as is the case with another occurrence of φόβος in *Poetics* 11 (shortly before the one just quoted) concerning Oedipus' fears about (πρός) his mother (1452ᵃ26; cf. Soph. *OT* 1002 ff.). The same applies to a passage where Aristotle discusses the object of ἔλεος and of φόβος (*Poet.* 13, 1453ᵃ2–6; but this is commonly regarded as a gloss[89]). Finally, *Poetics* 19 undoubtedly refers to emotions:

[8] We have discussed the other parts [of tragedy]; it remains to speak about language and thought. What has been said about thought in our treatise on rhetorical [technique] remains valid; that is rather the study where it belongs. Everything effected by language falls under thought. Among its elements are proof, refutation, and the effecting of emotions (such as pity [ἔλεος], fear [φόβος], anger, and all others of that kind), as well as enhancement and belittlement. (*Poet.* 19, 1456ᵃ33–ᵇ2)

First, rhetorical discourse is capable of triggering emotions (πάθη), whereas tragedy can offer only an imitation of it: in a tragedy there

[87] Cf. e.g. A. Rostagni (ed.), *Aristotele: Poetica*, 2nd edn. (Turin, 1945), 32; Else, *Poetics*, 226 ff. For φόβος, see e.g. Soph., *OT* 917, *OC* 1652; Xen. *Anab.* 4. 1. 23; for ἔλεος, Eur. *Or.* 832.

[88] I consider the underlying structure of the second sentence to be πράξεις (τοιῶνδε) οἵων . . . (cf. τοιούτων at *Poet.* 6, 1449ᵇ27) and the term πράξεις to have slipped into the relative clause, taking the case of the relative.

[89] For good reason. The fear for one's fellow creatures (περὶ τὸν ὅμοιον) in *Poet.* 13 (1453ᵃ6) resists assimilation to the fear for oneself (ἐφ' αὑτῶν) occurring in *Rhet.* 2. 8 (1386ᵃ27–8; this applies rather to pity, 2. 5, 1383ᵃ10), in spite of Belfiore's exegetic efforts in *Tragic Pleasures*, 230–1. She suggests understanding περί as 'concerning' or 'in the case of', and not 'for': 'we feel fear (for ourselves) in the case of the sufferings of someone who is like us.' In any case, the personae are not to be considered fellow creatures, *pace* Halliwell, *Aesthetics*, 216: they are not human beings but imitations of human beings.

are not people thinking and talking, but *personae* imitating people thinking and talking (cf. *Poet.* 6, 1450ᵇ4–8).⁹⁰ A character, though it may be something, is nobody.⁹¹

At least once, however, Aristotle explicitly discusses the emotional reaction of the audience:

[9] What is fearful and pitiable [τὸ φοβερὸν καὶ ἐλεεινόν] may then arise from the spectacle, but it may equally arise from the arrangement of events [ἐξ αὐτῆς τῆς συστάσεως τῶν πραγμάτων], which is definitely preferable and the mark of a better playwright. The plot should be constructed so that even without seeing it performed, one who hears of the events taking place shudders and feels pity [καὶ φρίττειν καὶ ἐλεεῖν] at what happens, just as he would when hearing the story of Oedipus [τὸν τοῦ Οἰδίπου μῦθον].⁹² (*Poet.* 14, 1453ᵇ1–7)

The verb is not φοβεῖσθαι 'to be frightened' (which never occurs in the *Poetics*), but φρίττειν, 'to shudder', which may be significant in view of some passages of the 'psychological' works where Aristotle distinguishes not only between the 'material' and 'formal' aspects of emotions (indeed, from an ontological point of view, emotions are categorial complexes, like actions: see *Rhet.* 1. 13, 1374ᵃ9–17), but also between emotions concerning only perceptible things and those rationally motivated (*DA* 1. 1, 403ᵃ22 ff.; *MA* 7, 701ᵇ16–23; 11, 703ᵇ3–9). The verb ἐλεεῖν may be used in *Poetics* 14, by homonymy, to refer to tearfulness or some other manifestation of pity not rationally motivated.⁹³

In the lines that follow directly, where ἔλεος and φόβος must probably be understood as being equivalent to ἐλεεινόν and φοβερόν, there is an ellipsis:

[10] Setting this out [i.e. what is fearful and pitiable] through spectacle has nothing to do with [sc. composition] technique and depends on production [χορηγίας]. Those who use spectacle to set out not what is fearful [μὴ τὸ φοβερόν] but only what is monstrous have nothing to

---

⁹⁰ I discuss this point further in Veloso, 'La *Poetica*: scienza produttiva o logica?', in D. Lanza (ed.), *La Poetica di Aristotele e la sua storia* (Pisa, 2003), 93–113.

⁹¹ Hence the idea of tragedy as something showing 'other people's sufferings (or business)', ἀλλότρια πάθη (or πράγματα), has no meaning (Gorg. *Hel.* 9; Plato, *Rep.* 10, 606 A–B; P.Herc. 1581, fr. 5; Iambl. *Myst.* i. 11 Parthey). On the ontological aspect of the question see Veloso, 'Signifier ce qui n'est pas, selon Aristote', in J. Laurent (ed.), *Dire le néant* (=*Cahiers de philosophie de l'Université de Caen*, 43 (2007)), 49–84.

⁹² It is not clear whether 'the story of Oedipus' refers to a tragedy.

⁹³ See *Rhet.* 2. 8, 1386ᵃ19–21; 13, 1390ᵃ19–23; cf. Plato, *Ion* 535 D.

do with tragedy. One must not look for every pleasure from tragedy, but only the pleasure that is appropriate to it [οἰκείαν]. And since the playwright must procure the pleasure deriving from what is fearful and pitiable [*or* from pity and fear] by means of imitation [τὴν ἀπὸ ἐλέου καὶ φόβου διὰ μιμήσεως . . . ἡδονήν], clearly it must be effected by the events [πράγμασιν]. (*Poet.* 14, 1453$^{b}$7–14)

The words 'the pleasure deriving from what is fearful and pitiable [*or* from pity and fear] by means of imitation' are an elliptical alternative to 'the pleasure deriving from *the recognition of what is pitiable and fearful* by means of imitation', in the terms of *Poetics* 4. The emotions of fear and pity are not pleasant (*Rhet.* 2. 5 and 8), which is the root of the (false) 'paradox of tragedy'. Our pleasure must consist in the recognition, by means of imitation, of an event which is pitiable and fearful,[94] or still better in the recognition, by means of imitation, of an event which is *judged* pitiable and fearful, by us or by others (see *Poet.* 25, 1460$^{b}$9 ff.).

If we continue to insist on the central role of emotions and their intellective aspect in the *Poetics*, we will be in the same uneasy position as Belfiore (*Tragic Pleasures*, 240) when it comes to explaining why a virtuous person does not take action immediately on the basis of the emotions he experiences during a performance or while reading;[95] Belfiore (245) is compelled to invoke a last-minute intervention from judgement, forestalling action. This explanation is unsatisfactory because it turns imitation into a sort of deceit. Setting aside exceptional cases, the spectator-listener-reader knows from the outset that what is before him cannot be pitiable or fearful, except by homonymy. If we are to account for the emotional reactions of the spectator-listener-reader, we must explain why one experiences emotions *in spite of* some of one's judgements. It is no good arguing, as some critics do,[96] that a tragedy triggers emotions based on judgement; that these judgements regarding the tragedy are true, and therefore that the emotional reactions are right. One who habitually judges tragic events to be things capable of arousing fear is simply a coward, because these judgements are false. The fundamental error of this interpretation consists in not

[94] *Pace* Halliwell, *Aesthetics*, 204–5.

[95] The idea that pity is a 'theatrical' emotion, not directed towards action (Halliwell, *Aesthetics*, 212–13) is not Aristotelian; otherwise there would be no reason why the orator should be concerned with this emotion (as, according to Aristotle, he is). Such an idea serves only to hide the difficulty to which I refer.

[96] See e.g. Halliwell, *Aesthetics*, 202–3.

distinguishing—or not sufficiently—between the different levels of the desiderative and cognitive elements of what we call 'emotions'. One must distinguish between, on the one hand, the emotion itself and its perceptible counterpart, and on the other, possible intellective motivations; and also between general and particular judgements. This does not, of course, compromise the intellectual character of the experience in question, which consists, according to *Poetics* 4, in recognizing that which imitation is an imitation of, a recognition that gives us pleasure in spite of the pain we may feel on perceiving the imitation. Through imitation, the spectator-listener-reader merely recognizes things which may play the role of subject in some of his general judgements. And thought is always accompanied by φαντάσματα, 'apparitions' (*DA* 3. 7–8; *Mem.* 1), which, deriving from perception (*DA* 3. 3), are particulars and retain some powers of the perceived thing (*MA* 7, 701$^b$13–23; 8, 701$^b$33–702$^a$7). I have discussed these questions elsewhere and I cannot enlarge on them here,[97] but I need to emphasize that the 'tragic effect', the arousal of pity and fear, is not in itself the aim of *any* tragedy; it is rather a 'collateral effect'. Tragedy is in the first place the imitation of a fearful and pitiable action.[98] Whether the imitation is or is not also capable of arousing fear and pity, or in what sense it is capable of doing so, is another question (whether these emotions are or are not to be purified by something, or are or are not to purify something, is another question still).

We come back to *Poetics* 9 [**6**]. Although there is no phrase resembling 'as has been said', the passage does seem to look back to the definition of tragedy in chapter 6 [**3**]. But what exactly does it take up from that definition? First, the idea of the imitation of a complete action; to this Aristotle has already returned, and with a clear reference to the definition (*Poet.* 7, 1450$^b$24–6; 8, 1451$^a$31–2).[99] However, while in *Poetics* 6 the action which tragedy imitates is said to be 'serious and complete', here Aristotle only says that it is 'complete', and, we may say, replaces 'serious' with 'fearful and pitiable'. Not all serious actions are fearful and pitiable, but all fearful and pitiable actions are undoubtedly 'serious'; we feel pity only if we believe that virtuous people are concerned, because pity

---

[97] In Veloso, 'Critique'.
[98] On this point, there is no disagreement between chapters 13 and 14, in spite of (apparent or real) incongruities between them.
[99] Aristotle also omits the extension referred to in chapter 7.

is a response to undeserved harm (*Rhet.* 2. 8, 1385ᵇ34–1386ᵃ1; cf. *Poet.* 13, 1453ᵃ2–6). Thus in *Poetics* 9 [6] Aristotle is adding something to the definition of tragedy—all tragedy—or rather making the definition more precise;[100] the pitiable and fearful nature of the action imitated by tragedy is linked to the unity of plot, which is discussed in chapters 8 and 9.[101] And, finally, if the 'serious' attribute applied to actions in chapters 1–5 can, according to some critics, foreshadow ἔλεος and φόβος in chapter 6, the 'serious' attribute in chapter 6[102] can just as well foreshadow φοβερόν and ἐλεεινόν in *Poetics* 9. Thus we have no cause to insist that the words must occur in chapter 6.

5. Return to *Poetics* 6

The conclusion is that if ἔλεος and φόβος are to be present in the definition of tragedy, their presence can only serve to specify more precisely the serious nature of the action of which tragedy is an imitation; so the nouns ἔλεος and φόβος or the adjectives ἐλεεινόν and φοβερόν ought either to appear alongside 'serious', or replace it, 'serious' being implied rather than stated.[103] In the text we have, ἔλεος and φόβος are not in the right place; nor is the preposition διά, which has little meaning here. These seem sufficient reason to me for deleting δι' ἐλέου καὶ φόβου, 'through pity and fear', or in fact for deleting the whole final clause, which we must see as a gloss inserted into the text.

It seems possible now to attempt a *diachronic* reconciliation of Scott's proposition with that of Petruševski and Freire. The text may have undergone a first interpolation, adding the words δι' ἐλέου καὶ φόβου περαίνουσα τὴν τῶν τοιούτων πραγμάτων σύστασιν, 'which, through pity and fear, accomplishes the arrangement of such events', and these last words may have been changed later, either because they were no longer legible or in a deliberate attempt to improve the text. In either case, the phrase δι' ἐλέου καὶ φόβου was perhaps misunderstood: in the first state of the gloss, the terms

---

[100] Petruševski, 'Παθημάτων', 241–2, 246, believes in fact that in this passage of *Poetics* 9 τελείας should be changed into σπουδαίας, which would make the specification totally explicit.

[101] See Halliwell, *Aesthetics*, 222.        [102] See also *Poet.* 6, 1450ᵃ33–5.

[103] Note the omission of 'serious' in the comparison between epic and tragedy at *Poet.* 23, 1459ᵃ17–20; cf. 3, 1448ᵃ25–7.

ἔλεος and φόβος probably referred to events, as they usually do in the *Poetics*; the second interpolator might have understood them not as external events but as 'emotions'. Perhaps, either from the very first or as a later stage, the phrase was already παθημάτων σύστασιν, which might have eased the passage to παθημάτων κάθαρσιν. In this case, a misunderstanding such as I have just illustrated might have happened with πάθημα as well.[104] In any case, the gloss may well have been suggested by a combination of *Poetics* 11 [**7**] and 14 [**10**].

The hypothesis of a first state of the gloss reading πραγμάτων (or παθημάτων) σύστασιν, 'arrangement of events', has advantages in that the insertion of κάθαρσις becomes more plausible. The *Poetics* has no room for κάθαρσις even in a gloss, unless the interpolator is expressing a personal idea or one heard elsewhere. In this case everything is possible, even the reading of manuscript A. But if the interpolator had in mind the idea of a 'tragic catharsis of passions', and if he did not invent it, where could he have possibly found it? And whose invention was it? Needless to say, we cannot be certain, but we can hypothesize.

First, if he got it from another surviving text by Aristotle, it can only be *Pol.* 8. 7; if so, clearly, it is irrelevant here. I cannot exclude the possibility that it was in the lost dialogue *De poetis* or in the alleged second book of the *Poetics*, nor the possibility that *Pol.* 8. 7 may refer to one of these texts, but I am sceptical. It seems more likely that the interpolator got the idea from a Neoplatonist, or that he is a Neoplatonist himself; or, if the gloss is older—as I prefer to believe—the interpolator may be someone like the author discussed in P.Herc. 1581. For reasons I cannot develop here, I do not think this author is Aristotle, or some ghostly Peripatetic;[105] he is more likely a Stoic[106] or an 'eclectic' Stoic,[107] or perhaps even a rhetor;

---

[104] Similar confusions may underlie the beginning of *Tract. Coisl.*: 'tragedy eliminates the frightening emotions of the soul through compassion and fright', ἡ τραγῳδία ὑφαιρεῖ τὰ φοβερὰ παθήματα τῆς ψυχῆς δι' οἴκτου καὶ δέους. To minimize the strangeness of the expression τὰ φοβερὰ παθήματα, 'the frightening emotions', Janko, *Comedy*, 136, argues that φοβεροί has a passive sense too in *Rhet.* 2. 5, 1382ᵇ7, which is wrong, as Belfiore also points out, *Tragic Pleasures*, 288 n. 98.

[105] As P. Kyriakou argues in 'Aristotle's *Poetics* and Stoic Literary Theory', *Rheinisches Museum für Philologie*, 140/3–4 (1997), 257–80 at 263, the 'Peripatetic school' is a ghost.

[106] *Pace* Nardelli, 'Catarsi', 96–8, and Janko, 'Philodemus', 59–60; against the attribution to Aristotle, see D. F. Sutton, '*P. Herc.* 1581: The Argument', *Philosophia*, 12 (1982), 270–6. For instance, fr. 2 seems to betray, on top of the vocabulary, the Stoic taste for paradox: τ]αῖς ψυχαῖς ἔνεστιν ἀ[φρο]σύνη μὲν ταῖς [σο]φωτάταις, 'there is even in the wisest souls a lack of discernment'. In any case, this is not an Aris-
[*See next page for n. 106 cont. and n. 107*]

and we may recall that Parisinus 1741, MS A of the *Poetics*, consists of a stylistic-rhetorical corpus. At least, on the basis of this text, we can assume that in the first century BC a theory of tragic catharsis of passions was already known. Whoever the author of this gloss may be, we can now at last purify the *Poetics* and, without fear or pity, read Aristotle's definition of tragedy without 'purification', 'fear', or 'pity'.

*Caen, France*

## BIBLIOGRAPHY

Aubonnet J. (ed.), *Aristote: Politique*, vol. iii/2 [book 8] [*Politique*] (Paris, 1996).

Belfiore E. S., *Tragic Pleasures: Aristotle on Plot and Emotion* [*Tragic Pleasures*] (Princeton, 1992).

Besnier B., 'Aristote et les passions', in B. Besnier, P.-F. Moreau, and L. Renault (eds.), *Les Passions antiques et médiévales* (Paris, 2003), 29–94.

Burnyeat, M. F., '*De anima* II 5', *Phronesis*, 37 (2002), 29–90.

Cacouros, M., 'De virtutibus et vitiis', in R. Goulet (ed.), *Dictionnaire des philosophes antiques*, suppl. (Paris, 2003), 506–46.

Cantarella, R., 'I "libri" della *Poetica* di Aristotele', *Rendiconti, Classe di scienze morali storiche filologiche, Accademia dei Lincei*, 30/7–12 (1975), 289–97.

Carchia, G., *L'estetica antica* (Rome and Bari, 2005; 1st edn. 1999).

Destrée, P., 'Éducation morale et *catharsis* tragique', *Études philosophiques*, 4 (2003), 518–35.

Donini, P., 'La tragedia senza la catarsi' ['Tragedia'], *Phronesis*, 43 (1998), 26–41.

—— '*Mimèsis* tragique et apprentissage de la *phronèsis*' ['*Mimèsis*'], *Études philosophiques*, 4 (2003), 436–50.

—— 'The History of the Concept of Eclecticism', in J. M. Dillon and A. A. Long (eds.), *The Question of 'Eclecticism': Studies in Later Greek Philosophy* (Berkeley, 1988), 15–33.

Dupont-Roc, R., and Lallot, J. (eds.), *Aristote: Poétique* (Paris, 1980).

totelian argument: the Aristotelian μέσον, mean, does not consist in a co-presence of virtue and vice—see rather Plato, *Rep.* 9, 571 B. Although the virtuous man may not always behave according to his habitual state, the latter cannot be good and bad at the same time.

[107] For a critical examination of the notion of eclecticism in antiquity, see P. Donini, 'The History of the Concept of Eclecticism', in J. M. Dillon and A. A. Long (eds.), *The Question of 'Eclecticism': Studies in Later Greek Philosophy* (Berkeley, 1988), 15–33.

Else, G. F. (ed.), *Aristotle's* Poetics: *The Argument* [*Poetics*] (Cambridge, Mass., 1957).

Freire, A., *A catarse em Aristóteles* [*Catarse*], 2nd edn. (Braga, 1996; 1st edn. 1982).

Glibert-Thirry, A. (ed.), *Pseudo-Andronicus de Rhodes:* Περὶ παθῶν [*Pseudo-Andronicus*] (Leiden, 1997).

Golden, L., *Aristotle on Tragic and Comic Mimesis* [*Aristotle*] (Atlanta, 1992).

Gudeman, A. (ed.), *Aristoteles:* Περὶ ποιητικῆς (Berlin and Leipzig, 1934).

Haefliger, H., 'La *Poétique* d'Aristote: une synthèse et une intégration dans la méthodologie d'Aristote', *Kairos*, 9 (1997), 97–119.

Halliwell, S., 'La psychologie morale de la *catharsis*: un essai de reconstruction' ['Psychologie'], *Études philosophiques*, 4 (2003), 499–517.

—— *The Aesthetics of Mimesis: Ancient Texts and Modern Problems* [*Aesthetics*] (Princeton, 2002).

—— (ed.), *Aristotle:* Poetics [*Poetics*] (Cambridge, Mass., 1995).

Heath, M., (trans.), *Aristotle:* Poetics [*Poetics*] (London, 1996).

Irigoin, J., 'Dédoublement et simplification des lettres dans la tradition d'Aristote: *Du ciel* II, *Métaphysique Z*', in id., *La Tradition des textes grecs: pour une critique historique* (Paris, 2003), 283–93.

Janko, R., *Aristotle on Comedy: Towards a Reconstruction of* Poetics 2 [*Comedy*] (London, 2002; 1st edn. 1981).

—— 'From Catharsis to the Aristotelian Mean' ['Mean'], in Rorty (ed.), *Essays*, 341–58.

—— 'Philodemus' *On Poems* and Aristotle's *On Poets*' ['Philodemus'], *Cronache ercolanesi*, 21 (1991), 5–64.

Kraut, R. (trans.), *Aristotle:* Politics, *Books 7 and 8* (Oxford, 1997).

Kyriakou, P., 'Aristotle's *Poetics* and Stoic Literary Theory', *Rheinisches Museum für Philologie*, 140/3–4 (1997), 257–80.

Lanza, D. (trans.), *Aristotele: La poetica* [*Poetica*] (Milan, 1987).

—— 'La simmetria impossibile: commedia e comico nella *Poetica* di Aristotele', in C. Questa (ed.), *Studi offerti a Francesco Della Corte* (Filologia e forme letterarie, 5; Rome, 1987), 65–80..

Laurenti, R. (ed.), *Aristotele: i frammenti dei dialoghi* (Naples, 1987).

Lobel, E., *The Greek Manuscripts of Aristotle's* Poetics (*Transactions of the Bibliographical Society*, suppl. 9; Oxford, 1933).

Lucas, D. W. (ed.), *Aristotle:* Poetics [*Poetics*] (Oxford, 1968).

Montmollin, D. de, *La Poétique d'Aristote: texte primitif et additions ultérieures* (Neuchâtel, 1951).

Mouze, L., 'Se connaître soi-même: tragédie, bonheur et contingence', *Études philosophiques*, 4 (2003), 483–98.

Nardelli, M. L., 'La catarsi poetica nel *PHerc.* 1581' ['Catarsi'], *Cronache ercolanesi*, 8 (1978), 96–103.

284                    Claudio William Veloso

Nehamas, A., 'Pity and Fear in the *Rhetoric* and the *Poetics*', in Rorty (ed.), *Essays*, 291–313.
Ničev, A., *L'Énigme de la catharsis tragique dans Aristote* (Sofia, 1970).
Pakaluk, M., review of *Oxford Studies in Ancient Philosophy*, 25 ['Review'], in *Bryn Mawr Classical Review* (2006) ⟨http://ccat.upenn.edu/bmcr/2006/2006-06-18.html⟩.
Pellegrin, P. (trans.) *Aristote: Les Politiques* (Paris, 1993).
Petruševski, M. D., '*Παθημάτων κάθαρσιν* ou bien *πραγμάτων σύστασιν*?' ['*Παθημάτων*'], *Ziva antika*, 4 (1954), 237–44.
Rashed, M., in M. Trédé (ed.), *Traités théoriques anciens sur la comédie* (forthcoming).
Rorty, A. O. (ed.), *Essays on Aristotle's* Poetics [*Essays*] (Princeton, 1992).
Rostagni, A. (ed.), *Aristotele: Poetica*, 2nd edn. (Turin, 1945).
Scott G., 'Purging the *Poetics*' ['Purging'], *Oxford Studies in Ancient Philosophy*, 25 (2003), 233–63.
Susemihl, F. (ed.), *Aristotelis politicorum libri octo cum vetusta translatione Guilelmi de Moerbeka* (Leipzig, 1872).
Sutton, D. F., '*P. Herc.* 1581: The Argument', *Philosophia*, 12 (1982), 270–6.
Veloso, C. W., *Aristóteles mimético* (São Paulo, 2004).
—— 'Critique du paradigme interprétatif "éthico-politique" de la *Poétique* d'Aristote' ['Critique'], *Kentron*, 21 (2005), 11–46; earlier version: 'Crítica del paradigma interpretativo "ético-político" de la *Poética* de Aristóteles', *Iztapalapa*, 59 (2005), 117–50.
—— 'Depurando as interpretações da *kátharsis* na *Poética* de Aristóteles' ['Depurando'], *Síntese*, 99 (2004), 13–25; first version in R. Duarte, V. Figueiredo, V. Freitas, and I. Kangussu (eds.), *Kátharsis: reflexos de um conceito estético* (Belo Horizonte, 2002), 70–9.
—— 'La *Poetica*: scienza produttiva o logica?', in D. Lanza (ed.), *La Poetica di Aristotele e la sua storia* (Pisa, 2003), 93–113.
—— '*Phantasia* et *mimesis* chez Aristote', *Revue des études anciennes*, 106/2 ['*Phantasia*'], 455–76.
—— 'Signifier ce qui n'est pas, selon Aristote', in J. Laurent (ed.), *Dire le néant* (=*Cahiers de philosophie de l'Université de Caen*, 43 (2007)), 49–84.

# THE EARLY STOIC DOCTRINE OF THE CHANGE TO WISDOM

RENÉ BROUWER

## 1. Introduction

THE early Stoics presented the sage as the crowning glory of their system of thought. Although they acknowledged the difficulty of achieving the ideal, this did not restrain them from describing how it could be attained. Here I wish to concentrate upon one small, but important aspect of the Stoics' theory of the long and strenuous process of achieving wisdom: the moment of becoming wise.

This aspect has drawn little attention in the scholarly literature. The best, although rather brief, description is still to be found in an essentially nineteenth-century handbook,[1] valuable observations were offered by Rist and more recently Bénatouïl.[2] Otherwise it was rejected as an early Stoic doctrine,[3] played down,[4] dealt with in passing,[5] described as a by-product of the Stoic theory of progress,[6]

© René Brouwer 2007

The first version of this paper was written during research leave at the Wiarda Institute of the University of Utrecht in the first semester of 2005. I am grateful to all who helped me to improve it, of whom I would like to mention in particular Malcolm Schofield for his continuous support and interest in my work, David Sedley for his many incisive comments, and Jörn Mixdorf for his careful proof-reading. All errors that remain are mine, of course.

[1] E. Zeller and M. Wellmann, *Die Philosophie der Griechen in ihrer geschichtlichen Entwicklung*, iii/1. *Die nacharistotelische Philosophie, erste Hälfte*, 5th edn. (Leipzig, 1923), 261–2.
[2] J. M. Rist, *Stoic Philosophy* [*Stoic*] (Cambridge, 1969), 90–3; T. Bénatouïl, 'Force, fermeté, froid: la dimension physique de la vertu stoïcienne' ['Force'], *Philosophie antique*, 5 (2005), 5–30 at 21, 24.
[3] K. Reinhardt, *Poseidonios* (Munich, 1921), 421, ascribing the doctrine to Posidonius; P. A. Heitmann, *Imitatio dei* (Rome, 1940), 36.
[4] E. G. Pembroke, 'Oikeiosis', in A. A. Long (ed.), *Problems in Stoicism* (London, 1971), 114–49 at 121.
[5] Described as a 'crisis' in B. Inwood, 'Hierocles: Theory and Argument in the Second Century AD', *Oxford Studies in Ancient Philosophy*, 2 (1984), 151–83 at 174.
[6] O. Luschnat, 'Das Problem des ethischen Fortschritts in der alten Stoa', *Philo-*

perfunctorily characterized—after the ancient critics of the Stoics—as notorious,[7] bizarre,[8] and (incorrectly in an important way, as we shall see) compared to Paul's Road to Damascus experience, Augustine's *tolle lege* experience,[9] or to the experience of a blinded man who has his bandage removed.[10] The lack of attention may be explained by the pitiful state of our sources, which is particularly precarious here. A snippet in Clement's *Stromata* or *Miscellanies*, 4. 28. 1 (*SVF* iii. 221), may illustrate the matter:

τὴν δὲ μεταστροφὴν τὴν ἐπὶ τὰ θεῖα οἱ μὲν Στωϊκοὶ ἐκ μεταβολῆς φασὶ γίνεσθαι μεταβαλλούσης τῆς ψυχῆς εἰς σοφίαν.

γίνεσθαι μεταβαλλούσης] von Arnim: γενέσθαι μεταβαλούσης codd.

The reversion to the divine the Stoics say happens out of a change, when the soul changes to wisdom.

Becoming wise is here described as a 'change' (μεταβολή). Clement connects it with a 'reversion' (μετασττροφή) to the divine. Clement's is but a miscellaneous remark (in keeping with the title of his work), and needs to be put into context in order to make sense of it. What kind of change will the Stoics have had in mind? How, if at all, does 'reversion to the divine' fit in?

Fortunately, two somewhat longer pieces of evidence which deal with becoming wise can be found in the Plutarchean corpus. The first passage is but a side topic in Plutarch's *How a Man May Become Aware of his Progress in Virtue*, at 75 C–F (*SVF* iii. 539[2]; *FDS* 1233; *LS* 61s (part)).[11] Despite its familiarity, I print it here, with my own subdivisions for ease of reference:

*logus*, 102 (1958), 178–214 at 195, 204; G. Roskam, *On the Path to Virtue* (Leuven, 2005), 29.

[7] D. Sedley, 'Diodorus Cronus and Hellenistic Philosophy', *Proceedings of the Cambridge Philological Society*, NS 23 (1977), 74–120 at 93.

[8] M. Mignucci, 'Logic 3: The Stoics 8: Paradoxes', in K. Algra *et al.* (eds.), *The Cambridge History of Hellenistic Philosophy* (Cambridge, 1999), 157–76 at 163; P. Veyne, 'Passion, perfection et âme matérielle dans l'utopie stoïcienne et chez saint Augustin', in id., *L'Empire gréco-romain* (Paris, 2005), 683–712 at 683.

[9] E. Bickel, 'Μετασχηματίζεσθαι: Ein übersehener Grundbegriff des Poseidonios', *Rheinisches Museum*, 100 (1957), 98–9 at 98.

[10] J. Passmore, *The Perfectibility of Man*, 3rd edn. (Indianapolis, 2000), 80.

[11] *SVF* = J. von Arnim (ed.), *Stoicorum veterum fragmenta* (3 vols.; Leipzig, 1903–5); *FDS* = K. Hülser (ed.), *Die Fragmente zur Dialektik der Stoiker* (4 vols.; Stuttgart, 1987–8)); *LS* = A. A. Long and D. N. Sedley, *The Hellenistic Philosophers* (Cambridge, 1987).

[i] καὶ γὰρ ἀκαρεῖ χρόνου καὶ ὥρας ἐκ τῆς ὡς ἔνι μάλιστα φαυλότητος εἰς οὐκ ἔχουσαν ὑπερβολὴν ἀρετῆς διάθεσιν μεταβαλὼν ὁ σοφός, [ii] ἧς οὐδ᾽ ἐν χρόνῳ πολλῷ μέρος ἀφεῖλε κακίας, ἅμα πᾶσαν ἐξαίφνης ἀποπέφευγε. [iii] καίτοι ἤδη ταῦτά γε λέγοντας οἶσθα δήπου πάλιν πολλὰ παρέχοντας αὑτοῖς πράγματα καὶ μεγάλας ἀπορίας περὶ τοῦ διαλεληθότος, ὃς αὐτὸς ἑαυτὸν οὔπω κατείληφε γεγονὼς σοφός, ἀλλ᾽ ἀγνοεῖ καὶ ἀμφιδοξεῖ τῷ κατὰ μικρὸν ἐν χρόνῳ πολλῷ τὰ μὲν ἀφαιροῦντι τὰ δὲ προστιθέντι γιγνομένην τὴν ἐπίδοσιν καθάπερ πορείαν τῇ ἀρετῇ λαθεῖν ἀτρέμα προσμίξασαν. [iv] εἰ δέ γ᾽ ἦν τάχος τοσοῦτον τῆς μεταβολῆς καὶ μέγεθος, ὥστε τὸν πρωῒ κάκιστον ἑσπέρας γεγονέναι κράτιστον, [v] ἢ ἂν οὕτω τινὶ συντύχῃ τὰ τῆς μεταβολῆς, καταδαρθόντα φαῦλον ἀνεγρέσθαι σοφὸν καὶ προσειπεῖν ἐκ τῆς ψυχῆς μεθεικότα τὰς χθιζὰς ἀβελτερίας καὶ ἀπάτας

"ψευδεῖς ὄνειροι, χαίρετ᾽· οὐδὲν ἦτ᾽ ἄρα",

[vi] τίς ἂν ἀγνοήσειεν ἑαυτοῦ διαφορὰν ἐν αὑτῷ τοσαύτην γενομένην καὶ φρόνησιν ἀθρόον ἐκλάμψασαν; ἐμοὶ μὲν γὰρ δοκεῖ μᾶλλον ἄν τις, ὡς ὁ Καινεύς, γενόμενος κατ᾽ εὐχὴν ἀνὴρ ἐκ γυναικὸς ἀγνοῆσαι τὴν μετακόσμησιν, [vii] ἢ σώφρων καὶ φρόνιμος καὶ ἀνδρεῖος ἐκ δειλοῦ καὶ ἀνοήτου καὶ ἀκρατοῦς ἀποτελεσθεὶς [viii] καὶ μεταβαλὼν εἰς θεῖον ἐκ θηριώδους βίον [ix] ἀκαρὲς διαλαθεῖν αὐτόν.

[i] The wise man changes in a moment or a second of time from the lowest possible inferiority to an unsurpassable character of virtue; [ii] and all his vice, of which he has not over a long time succeeded in removing even a small part, he instantaneously flees for ever. [iii] Yet, you doubtless know that, on the other hand, those who say these things make for themselves much trouble and great difficulties over the doctrine of the man who has not noticed, who has not yet grasped that he has become wise, but is ignorant and hesitates to believe that his advancement, which has been effected by the gradual and long-continued process of getting rid of some things and adding others, has, as on a march, unnoticed and quietly brought him to virtue. [iv] But if there were such a swiftness and magnitude of the change that the man who was the very worst in the morning should have become the very best at evening, [v] or should the change so come about that he who was a fool when he fell asleep should awake wise, and could say, having dismissed from his soul yesterday's gross stupidities and false conceptions:

'False dreams, goodbye! You are nothing'—

[vi] who would fail to recognize that a great difference like this had been generated in his own self, and that practical wisdom had all at once poured out its beams? For, it seems to me more likely that anyone who, like Caeneus, was made man from woman in answer to prayer would fail to recognize that make-over, [vii] than that anyone moderate, wise, and brave, from being cowardly, foolish, and weak-willed, [viii] and having changed from a bestial to a divine life, [ix] should for a single moment not notice what had happened to him.

As Plutarch's title already indicates, the treatise and indeed this passage concentrate not so much upon the moment of change as such as upon moral progress in general, and this from the perspective of the (un)awareness that goes with it. In the other, longer passage in the *Synopsis of the Treatise 'The Stoics Talk More Paradoxically than the Poets'* (1057 C–1058 E), becoming a sage is the central topic. Nothing from this passage, or indeed the *Synopsis* as a whole, has ended up in *SVF*, *FDS*, or LS. This neglect may partly have been caused by the obscurity of the treatise,[12] partly by the extravagant doctrines it contains.[13] Of the latter cause the first chapter of the *Synopsis* is a splendid example. The Stoic sage is compared with Pindar's description of the Lapith Canaeus. Whereas the sage and Canaeus have invincibility in common, the sage, unlike Canaeus, remains invincible even when 'wounded, in pain, on the rack' etc.[14]

In what follows I shall present and discuss the material on the moment of becoming a sage in the *Synopsis*, see whether it can be taken seriously by looking for Stoic parallels in *Progress* and elsewhere, and—even more importantly—deal with the question whether and how the evidence fits the Stoic system of thought. Restricting myself to the *Synopsis*, I shall thus not discuss the doctrine of unawareness as it occurs in *Progress*, leaving that topic for another occasion.

---

[12] The text is after all only three Teubner pages long. Furthermore, its authorship is disputed as the title does not occur in the Lamprias catalogue, the ancient list of Plutarch's writings. However, the title *The Stoics Talk More Paradoxically than the Poets* occurs there as no. 79, and our treatise indeed qualifies as a *synopsis* rather than an *epitome* or summary by giving a flavour of the main text offering some examples out of it (on this distinction see M. Casevitz and D. Babut (eds.), *Plutarque: Œuvres morales*, xv/1 [*Plutarque*] (Paris, 2004), 97). It thus seems likely that Plutarch is at least the author of the separate passages, the style and language of which have been characterized by H. Cherniss (ed.), *Plutarch's* Moralia, xiii/2. 1033 A–1086 B [*Moralia*] (Cambridge, Mass., 1976), 607, as thoroughly Plutarchean.

[13] It has been described as an exaggeration that should not be taken seriously by K. Ziegler, 'Plutarch von Chaironeia', in *RE* xxii/1 (1951), 636–962 at 760, and as a piece of writing that was to be read aloud in a banquet to amuse Plutarch's friends by M. Pohlenz, 'Plutarchs Schriften gegen die Stoiker', *Hermes*, 74 (1939), 1–33 at 2, and M. Pohlenz and R. Westman (eds.), *Plutarchi Moralia*, vi/2, 2nd edn. (Leipzig, 1959), 59.

[14] Pindar's description 'survived' as fr. 128F. 7–9 Maehler. (Casevitz and Babut, *Plutarque*, 103, have a typo here.)

2. The characteristics of the change in the *Synopsis*

As the title already indicates, the author of the *Synopsis* tries to show that what the Stoics talk about is even more absurd than what can be found in works of fiction.

In chapter 2 a comparison is offered between the Stoic sage-to-be and the depiction of Iolaus by Aeschylus and Euripides. In order to kill Eurystheus, who chased Heracles' children, old Iolaus, Heracles' nephew, got his strength and youth back from Zeus and Hebe, whereas

[2.1] ὁ δὲ τῶν Στωϊκῶν σοφὸς χθὲς μὲν ἦν αἴσχιστος ἅμα καὶ κάκιστος τήμερον δ᾿ ἄφνω μεταβέβληκεν εἰς ἀρετήν, [2.2] καὶ γέγονεν ἐκ ῥυσοῦ καὶ ὠχροῦ καὶ κατ᾿ Αἰσχύλον "ἐξ ὀσφυαλγοῦς κὠδυνοσπάδος λυγροῦ | γέροντος" εὐπρεπὴς θεοειδὴς καλλίμορφος.

[2.1] the sage of the Stoics, though yesterday he was most ugly and at the same time most vicious, today all of a sudden has changed to virtue, [2.2] and from being a wrinkled and sallow and, as Aeschylus says 'lumbago-ridden, wretched, pain-distraught | old man', has become seemly, of godlike form and good-looking.

In chapter 3 the Stoic sage is compared to Homer's Odysseus. The chapter picks up on the notion of 'wrinkled' in [2]. In the first sentence Odysseus is said to have had his wrinkles removed by Athena, whereas the Stoic sage has not: nevertheless the sage should not be considered ugly. The second and last sentence is badly connected with the preceding one. Yet again an absurd doctrine is expressed in it. The lover will turn away from the person he loves, once that person has become a sage: 'like beetles preferring bad smell and avoiding perfume', lovers prefer to be together with persons who are very ugly, and turn away

[3] ὅταν εἰς εὐμορφίαν καὶ κάλλος ὑπὸ σοφίας μεταβάλωσιν.

[3] when they change by wisdom into good looks and beauty.

The reaction of these non-sages may surprise, as it surprised Plutarch in the parallel passage of *Comm. not.* 1073 A–B (*SVF* iii. 719). What matters is that we yet again find becoming a sage described as a 'change'.

Chapter 4 picks up on 'most vicious' from [2]:

[4.1] ὁ παρὰ τοῖς Στωϊκοῖς κάκιστος, ἂν οὕτω τύχῃ, πρωῒ δείλης ἄριστος,

290     *René Brouwer*

[4.2.1] καὶ καταδαρθὼν [a] ἔμπληκτος καὶ ἀμαθὴς καὶ [b] ἄδικος καὶ ἀκόλαστος
καὶ [c] ναὶ μὰ Δία δοῦλος καὶ [d] πένης καὶ ἄπορος [4.2.2] αὐθημερὸν ἀνίσταται
[a] βασιλεὺς καὶ [b] πλούσιος καὶ ὄλβιος γεγονώς, [c] σώφρων τε καὶ δίκαιος καὶ
[d] βέβαιος καὶ ἀδόξαστος, [4.3.1] οὐ γένεια φύσας οὐδὲ ἥβην ἐν σώματι νέῳ καὶ
ἁπαλῷ, [4.3.2] ἀλλ᾽ ἐν ἀσθενεῖ καὶ ἁπαλῇ ψυχῇ καὶ ἀνάνδρῳ καὶ ἀβεβαίῳ, [a] νοῦν
τέλειον, [b] ἄκραν φρόνησιν, [c] ἰσόθεον διάθεσιν, [d] ἀδόξαστον ἐπιστήμην καὶ
[e] ἀμετάπτωτον ἕξιν ἐσχηκώς [4.4.1] οὐδὲν ἐνδούσης πρότερον αὐτῷ τῆς μο-
χθηρίας, [4.4.2] ἀλλ᾽ ἐξαίφνης, ὀλίγου δέω εἰπεῖν, ἥρως τις ἢ δαίμων ἢ θεὸς ἐκ
θηρίων τοῦ κακίστου γενόμενος. [4.5] ἐκ τῆς Στοᾶς γὰρ λαβόντα τὴν ἀρετὴν
ἔστιν εἰπεῖν

εὖξαι εἴ τι βούλει· πάντα σοι γενήσεται.

πλοῦτον φέρει, βασιλείαν ἔχει, τύχην δίδωσιν, εὐπότμους ποιεῖ καὶ ἀπροσδεεῖς
καὶ αὐτάρκεις, μίαν οἴκοθεν δραχμὴν οὐκ ἔχοντας.

[4.1] Among the Stoics the man who is most vicious in the morning, if so it
chance to be, is virtuous in the afternoon, [4.2.1] and having fallen asleep
[a] unstable, ignorant, [b] unjust, and licentious, [c] and even, by Zeus, a
slave, [d] poor, and without means, [4.2.2] he gets up the very same day,
having become [a] a king, [b] rich, and blessed, as well as [c] moderate, just,
[d] firm, and unopining, [4.3.1] not having grown a beard yet or pubic hair
in a body young and soft, [4.3.2] but having got, in a soul that was feeble and
soft and unmanly and not firm, [a] perfect insight, [b] the highest practical
wisdom, [c] a character equal to the gods, [d] unopining knowledge, and
[e] an unshakeable tenor, [4.4.1] and this not by any previous alleviation
of depravity, [4.4.2] but instantaneously, one could almost say, by having
become from the most vicious of wild beasts some hero or *daimōn* or god.
[4.5] For, if one has received virtue from the Stoa, it is possible to say

'Ask, if there's aught you wish, all will be yours.'

It brings wealth, it comprises kingship, it gives luck, it makes men pros-
perous and free from all other wants as well as self-sufficient, though they
have not a single drachma of their own.

Here, as well as in [2] and [3], and in *Progress*, in [i], [iv], [v], and
[viii] the standard term to describe what happens to someone who
becomes a sage is the same as used by Clement: change. Otherwise
these passages seem to offer a rather mixed bag of characterizations
associated with becoming a sage. In what follows I shall therefore
organize its contents by discussing three features: the change as
instantaneous (2.1), as between opposite states (2.2), and as radical (2.3).

## 2.1. *Instantaneous*

A first feature of the change as described in the *Synopsis* is the apparent speed with which it occurs. In [2] the suddenness of becoming a sage is put centre stage. Being compared to Iolaus, who from being weak suddenly changes into being young, strong, and prepared for battle, the sage of the Stoics also suddenly changes from a state of vice and ugliness to a state of virtue and beauty. In [4] the suddenness is mentioned again. In [4.1] the change occurs between morning and afternoon; in [4.2] between the time of going to bed and waking up. The suddenness can also be found in the implicit contrast expressed in the simile of [4.3.1] and [4.3.2]: other than the youth who slowly grows a beard and gets pubic hair [4.3.1], the sage-to-be suddenly has perfect intelligence etc. [4.3.2].[15] This implicit contrast between [4.3.1] and [4.3.2] is explained in [4.4.1] and [4.4.2]: the change happens suddenly without any previous alleviation.

In *Progress* the swiftness of the change is recorded in comparable variety: 'in a moment or even a second of time' in [i], 'instantaneously' in [ii], 'morning' and 'evening' in [iv], and 'falling asleep' and 'awaking' in [v]. In yet another piece of evidence, Plut. *Comm. not.* 1062 B (not in *SVF*; LS 61U; *FDS* 1235), the timespan is 'a little later', as the sage has 'now become both prudent and supremely happy when a little earlier he was utterly wretched and foolish'.[16]

In the *Synopsis* we thus find a characteristic that is confirmed in other sources, albeit of Plutarchean origin only.

## 2.2. *The opposite states*

A second feature of the change as described in the *Synopsis* is that it is a change between opposite states. In chapter 2 Plutarch starts off with the ugliness and badness of the sage-to-be. He thereupon tells us that the badness of the sage-to-be is transformed into virtue with the newly born sage. Plutarch then returns to the former state of the sage-to-be as the ugliest being, who is transformed into a being that is seemly, godlike in form, and good-looking.

Chapter 4 offers an even richer variety of changes. After the in-

---

[15] Cf. Cherniss, *Moralia*, ad loc.

[16] μικρῷ πρόσθεν ἀθλιώτατος ὢν καὶ ἀφρονέστατος νῦν ὁμοῦ φρόνιμος καὶ μακάριος γέγονεν.

troductory [4.1], which is all but a repetition of [2], in [4.2] the state before and the state after the change are characterized by two sets of opposite states, which—based upon their positions in the text—could be described as internal and external respectively. In the internal set of opposites, [4.2.1*c–d*] and [4.2.2*a–b*], the state before is characterized as one of a slave, a pauper, someone without means, and the state after as of a king, a rich and blessed man. The pair of opposites here are in fact two: in [4.2.1*c*] and [4.2.2*a*] slave and king are opposed, in [4.2.1*d*] and [4.2.2*b*] poor and rich. In the external set, [4.2.1*a–b*] and [4.2.2*c–d*], we find two subsets of opposites. In the first subset the state before is in [4.2.1*a*] characterized as unstable and ignorant, and the state after in [4.2.2*d*] as unopining and firm. In the second subset the change is described as from unjust and licentious [4.2.1*b*] to just and moderate [4.2.2*c*]. In [4.4.2] another set of opposites is added: the sage-to-be changes from the most vicious of wild beings into a hero, a *daimōn*, or a god. The change leads to an encompassing state of positive qualities, enumerated in [4.3.2] and appropriately illustrated in [4.5]. According to [4.3.2], next to [*a*] perfect insight and [*d*] unopining knowledge, the sage has [*b*] the highest practical wisdom, [*e*] an 'unchangeable tenor', and [*c*] a 'character equal to the gods'. In [4.5] wealth and kingship are repeated, and the gift of good fortune[17] and self-sufficiency are added. The quotation (from Menander, fr. 838. 6 KA) at the beginning of [4.5] is an apt illustration of this enumeration of positive qualifications, as the sage will have them all.

These bewildering sets of states can most easily be classified on the basis of the well-known Stoic tripartition of 'philosophy' into ethics, logic, and physics,[18] to which I shall now turn.

*2.2.1. Ethics*  Most of the states are to be placed within the ethical part of philosophy. The states are presented in terms of virtue and vice in general as well as in terms of specific virtues and vices. Those in terms of the virtues and vices *in general* are to be found in *Synopsis* [2] and [4.1]. In either passage the state of the sage-to-be changes from vice to virtue. *Progress* contains a similar account: in [i] and [ii] the change is from vice to a state of virtue, in [iv] it is from worst to best. The states in terms of the specific virtues

---

[17] Referred to by the words τύχη and πότμος.
[18] See Aëtius 1, pref. 2 (*SVF* ii. 35; LS 26A; *FDS* 15); Plut. *Stoic. repugn.* 1035 A–B (*SVF* ii. 42; LS 26C; *FDS* 24); D.L. 7. 39 (*SVF* ii. 37; LS 26B; *FDS* 1).

and vices are in [4.2.1*b*] and [4.2.2*c*]. Before he changed to wisdom
the sage was unjust and licentious, while after the change he is just
and moderate. In *Progress* [vii] we also find the change described
in relation to two specific virtues. As in the *Synopsis*, the virtue of
moderation occurs again; here the other specific virtue is bravery:
the inferior person is a coward, the sage is brave. The contrast
between sage and inferior person as a contrast between virtue(s)
and vice(s) respectively is well known.[19]

Two expressions in the *Synopsis* can be understood as implicit
references to the virtuous state of the sage. They occur in [4.3.2]:
'unshakeable tenor' and a 'character (equal to the gods)'.[20] In *Progress* [i] Plutarch makes the relation explicit, when he speaks of the
character of virtue. This is soundly Stoic. Virtue is often defined
as a character.[21] In Stoic usage both tenor and character relate to a
state or disposition. Character is a special kind of tenor: a tenor can
be intensified and relaxed, whereas a character cannot.[22] Virtue as
a character is thus also 'unshakeable tenor'.

Other variants of the change from one extreme state to the other
to be found in the *Synopsis* can be discussed under the heading
of ethics too. These variants include the change from ugliness to
beauty in [2], from slavery to kingship in [4.2.1*c*] and [4.2.2*a*], and
from poverty to wealth in [4.2.1*d*] and [4.2.2*b*]. All these variants
are yet again soundly Stoic. The beauty of the sage and the ugliness
of the inferior person are mentioned in e.g. Cic. *Fin.* 3. 75 (*SVF* i.
221, iii. 591), albeit implicitly in the statement that only the sage
is beautiful.[23] A similar implicit usage can be seen with regard to
the kingship of the sage, but here we find the contrast with the
slavery of the inferior person explicitly too.[24] The wealth of the

---

[19] See the passages assembled in *SVF* iii. 657–84.

[20] On 'equal to the gods' see below, sect. 2.2.3.

[21] See e.g. Plut. *Virt. mor.* 441 c (*SVF* i. 202, iii. 459; LS 61b): τὴν ἀρετὴν τοῦ
ἡγεμονικοῦ τῆς ψυχῆς διάθεσίν τινα καὶ δύναμιν, γεγενημένην ὑπὸ λόγου; D.L. 7. 89
(*SVF* iii. 197): τήν τ' ἀρετὴν διάθεσιν εἶναι ὁμολογουμένην. Cf. Stob. 2. 60. 7–8 (*SVF*
iii. 262), 2. 70. 21–6 (*SVF* iii. 104; LS 60l), Cic. *Tusc.* 4. 34 (*SVF* iii. 198).

[22] Simpl. *In Cat.* 237. 29–31 Kalbfleisch (*SVF* ii. 393; LS 47s): καὶ γὰρ τὰς
μὲν ἕξεις ἐπιτείνεσθαί φασι δύνασθαι καὶ ἀνίεσθαι· τὰς δὲ διαθέσεις ἀνεπιτάτους εἶναι καὶ
ἀνανέτους.

[23] Further evidence on the beautiful sage is in Cic. *Mur.* 61 (*SVF* i. 221), *Acad.*
2. 136 (*SVF* iii. 599); Philo, *QG* 4. 99 (*SVF* iii. 592).

[24] The implicit usage can be found in e.g. Plut. *Comm. not.* 1060 b (not in *SVF*),
*Tr. an.* 472 a (*SVF* iii. 655). Further evidence on the sage as king: Cic. *Fin.* 3. 75
(*SVF* iii. 591): the sage has a better claim to the title of king than Tarquinius; in
Philo see esp. *Somn.* 2. 244 (not in *SVF*), 'a doctrine laid down by those who occupy

sage and the poverty of the inferior person (cf. *Synopsis* at [4.5] and 1058 C) are explicitly contrasted at Stob. 2. 101. 14–20 (*SVF* iii. 593); the implicit distinction that only the sage is rich (and hence all non-sages are poor) is also a Stoic commonplace.²⁵

The *Synopsis* makes it abundantly clear (if only because of its title) that it is not according to common sense that the sage is a king, rich, or beautiful, or the inferior person a slave, poor, or ugly. With regard to beauty the sage may be hunch-backed, toothless, and one-eyed, but he is nevertheless not ugly or misshapen or unhandsome of face (1058 A). Nor is it according to common sense that the sage is king, or that the sage is rich. On the contrary: he may not even possess a drachma of his own [4.5], he may beg his bread from others, may analyse logical arguments for pay, and pay rent and buy his bread by borrowing or asking alms of those who have nothing (1058 C). For the Stoics these values of beauty, power, and wealth in their commonsense interpretations are of no importance, but are all to be understood in terms of virtue.²⁶ In the *Synopsis*,

themselves with philosophy', and also *Mut.* 152 (*SVF* iii. 620), ascribed to Moses, and *Sobr.* 57 (*SVF* iii. 603), *Migr.* 197 (*SVF* iii. 621); other sources include: Lucian, *Vit. auct.* 20 (*SVF* iii. 622); Clem. *Strom.* 2. 19. 4 (*SVF* iii. 619); Procl. *In Alc.* 165. 1 Creuzer/Westerink (*SVF* iii. 618); Olymp. *In Alc.* 55. 23–56. 1 Creuzer/Westerink (*SVF* iii. 618). The explicit contrast between the sage and the inferior person can be found at Stob. 2. 102. 11–19 (*SVF* iii. 615), 2. 108. 26–7 (*SVF* iii. 617), and D.L. 7. 122 (*SVF* iii. 617; LS 67M). The last passage apparently contains information from Chrysippus' lost *On the Fact that Zeno Used Terms in their Proper Significations*, in which 'kingship being answerable to no one' is attributed to the sage and denied to the inferior person.

²⁵ Further evidence on the rich sage includes Plut. *Stoic. repugn.* 1043 E (*SVF* iii. 153), *Comm. not.* 1060 B (not in *SVF*), *Tr. an.* 472 A (*SVF* iii. 655); Cic. *Mur.* 61 (*SVF* i. 221), *Parad.* 6 (not in *SVF*), *Acad.* 2. 136 (*SVF* iii. 599), *Fin.* 3. 75 (*SVF* iii. 591): richer than Crassus; Philo, *Sobr.* 56 (*SVF* iii. 603): the sage is even πάμπλουτος; Lucian, *Vit. auct.* 20 (*SVF* iii. 622); Alex. Aphr. *In Top.* 134. 13–16 Wallies (*SVF* iii. 594), 147. 12–17 Wallies (*SVF* iii. 595); S.E. *M.* 11. 170 (*SVF* iii. 598); Clem. *Strom.* 2. 19. 4 (*SVF* iii. 619); Procl. *In Alc.* 165. 2 Creuzer/Westerink (*SVF* iii. 618); Olymp. *In Alc.* 56. 1–3 Creuzer/Westerink (*SVF* iii. 618).

²⁶ The beauty of the sage is explained in Cic. *Fin.* 3. 75 (*SVF* iii. 591): it is the beauty of the sage's virtuous soul that counts. The wealth of the sage is explained in the same manner: only virtue makes one rich and self-sufficient, independent of fortune, for which see Cic. *Fin.* 3. 75 (*SVF* iii. 591); D.L. 7. 125 (*SVF* iii. 590); Philo, *Plant.* 69 (*SVF* iii. 596); Stob. 2. 101. 14–20 (*SVF* iii. 626; LS 60P). The paradox of the sage as king was, according to D.L. 7. 122 (*SVF* iii. 617), explained by Chrysippus as that the sage alone has knowledge of good and bad, which is one of the definitions of the virtue of practical wisdom (see e.g. Plut. *Comm. not.* 1066 D (*SVF* ii. 1181); D.L. 7. 92 (*SVF* iii. 265); Stob. 2. 59. 5–6 (*SVF* iii. 262; LS 61H); Ps.-Andronicus, *Pass.* 2. 2 (*SVF* iii. 266); S.E. *M.* 9. 162 (*SVF* iii. 274), 11. 170 (*SVF* iii. 598); Simpl. *In Cat.* 389. 19–20 Kalbfleisch (*SVF* ii. 174; *FDS* 945)).

however, and as a matter of course in a treatise entitled [*Synopsis of the Treatise*] *'The Stoics Talk More Paradoxically than the Poets'*, the paradoxes are exploited to the full.

2.2.2. *Logic* In the *Synopsis* becoming a sage is expressed from the perspective of logic too: that is, if logic is understood in a broad sense, as (not only) the Stoics did, to include epistemology.[27] Plutarch's description of the transition in epistemological terms is short. He uses the opposition between 'unstable and ignorant' in [4.2.1a] on the side of the inferior person and 'firm and unopining' in [4.2.2d] on the side of the sage.

'Firm' and 'unopining' used with regard to the sage are well-established Stoic notions. Although the word 'unopining' is associated with Aristo, Zeno's pupil and later rival, Aristo attached most importance precisely to this 'Stoic doctrine', as it is called in D.L. 7. 162 (*SVF* i. 347; *FDS* 139). What is more, the conviction that the sage does not have opinions is a well-known Stoic doctrine.[28] 'Firm' clearly also occurs in an epistemological context, as in the definition of knowledge, only to be found in the sage, as at S.E. *M*. 7. 151–2 (*SVF* ii. 90; LS 41C; *FDS* 370).[29] 'Unstable' and 'ignorant' used with regard to the inferior person do not, as far as I know, occur in Stoic texts. 'Ignorant' (ἀμαθής), however, will in Greek often be used as the standard adjective in relation to the noun 'ignorance' (ἄγνοια) and the verb 'to be ignorant' (ἀγνοῶ). For the

---

[27] See D.L. 7. 41–2 (*SVF* ii. 48; LS 31A; *FDS* 33). S.E. *M*. 7. 24 simply ascribes this broad sense to the Dogmatists, thus also to the Stoics. This is not to say that the change could not also have been formulated in terms of logic proper. The sage is characterized as the only dialectician in the conclusion of Diogenes Laertius' account of Stoic logic in D.L. 7. 83 (*SVF* ii. 130; LS 31C; *FDS* 87), Stob. 2. 67. 14 (*SVF* iii. 654; not in *FDS*), and Alex. Aphr. *In Top*. 1. 8–14 Wallies (*SVF* ii. 124; LS 31D; *FDS* 57), which, as with beauty, wealth, and kingship, suggests that by becoming a sage someone who is not at all a dialectician changes into someone who is. On the sage as the (only) true dialectician see A. A. Long, 'Dialectic and the Stoic Sage', in J. M. Rist (ed.), *The Stoics* (Berkeley, 1978), 101–24, repr. in Long, *Stoic Studies* (Cambridge, 1996), 85–106.

[28] Most of the evidence is collected in *SVF* i. 54: Cic. *Mur*. 61, *Acad*. 2. 113 (*FDS* 339); Lact. *Inst*. 3. 4 (also in *SVF* iii. 553; *FDS* 377); Aug. *Acad*. 2. 11 (*FDS* 338, 376); Stob. 2. 112. 2 (*FDS* 89; cf. also 2. 113. 10–11: *SVF* iii. 548; *FDS* 89). Other evidence includes P.Herc. 1020, fr. In ll. 12–13 (*SVF* ii. 131; *FDS* 88); Cic. *Acad*. 1. 42 (*SVF* i. 53; *FDS* 256); D.L. 7. 121 (*SVF* i. 54, iii. 549; *FDS* 375A); the Sphaerus anecdote in D.L. 7. 177 (*SVF* i. 625; LS 40F; *FDS* 381); S.E. *M*. 7. 157 (*SVF* iii. 550; not in *FDS*).

[29] ἐπιστήμην . . . τὴν ἀσφαλῆ καὶ βεβαίαν καὶ ἀμετάθετον ὑπὸ λόγου κατάληψιν. . . . ἐπιστήμην ἐν μόνοις ὑφίστασθαι λέγουσι τοῖς σοφοῖς.

Stoics ignorance or to be ignorant is one of the distinctive characteristics of the inferior person: every inferior person is ignorant,[30]
whereas the sage is not.[31] 'Unstable' seems to be the equivalent of
'weak' (ἀσθενής): ignorance is changeable and weak assent, only to
be found with the non-sage.[32]

Plutarch in these few words may have intended to offer a characterization of the state before and after the change on two epistemological levels: one level referring to the epistemological state
of the inferior person and sage as such, i.e. in terms of 'unopining' vs. 'ignorant' respectively, the other being an explanation of
these states, i.e. in terms of 'unstable' vs. 'firm' respectively. The
inferior person is ignorant, because he deals with his perceptions
in an unstable manner, or—in the technical expression used by the
Stoics—has weak cognitions. The sage has unopining knowledge,
as he has firm cognitions.

2.2.3. *Physics*    At first sight the *Synopsis* does not seem to contain
a description of the change in terms of physics. What we do find,
however, is a change to the divine. As the Stoics considered theology
a part of physics,[33] the change can thus be discussed in relation
to physics. In the *Synopsis* three references to the divine or the
gods can be found. In [2] the sage is described as 'divine in form'.
Here one could perhaps say that this reference should not be taken
literally. After all, the context is a description of the beauty of the
sage, and 'divine' could simply reinforce that claim metaphorically.
However, in [4.4.2] and [4.3.2] reference is yet again made to the
gods. In [4.4.2] the change is from beast to hero, *daimōn*, or god, in
[4.3.2c] a 'character equal to the gods' is ascribed to the newly born
sage. In *Progress* [viii] the change is from a bestial to a divine life.

Should we thus after all take these expressions literally? And if
so, how? Let us begin with the phrase 'a character equal to the
gods' in [4.3.2c]. The most obvious interpretation is that sages are
*like* the gods. This seems confirmed by the Clement passage with
which I started off, and by a variety of passages in which the sage

---

[30] S.E. *M*. 7. 434 (*SVF* iii. 657), presented by Sextus as a Chrysippean doctrine.
[31] P.Herc. 1020 Ox Ld ll. 1–2 (*SVF* ii. 131; *FDS* 88): μηδὲν ἀγνοεῖν τὸν σοφόν.
[32] Stob. 2. 111. 20–2 (*SVF* iii. 548; LS 41G; *FDS* 89): τὴν γὰρ ἄγνοιαν μετα-
πτωτικὴν εἶναι συγκατάθεσιν καὶ ἀσθενῆ. μηδὲν δ' ὑπολαμβάνειν ἀσθενῶς, ἀλλὰ ἀσφαλῶς
καὶ βεβαίως, διὸ καὶ μηδὲ δοξάζειν τὸν σοφόν.
[33] The 'final' (ἔσχατος) part according to Chrysippus in *On Lives* 4 ap. Plut. *Stoic.
repugn.* 1035 A (*SVF* ii. 42; LS 26C; *FDS* 24).

is either declared to be as happy as the gods,[34] or as virtuous as the gods[35] or as Zeus.[36] The expression in [4.3.2c] and the confirmation thereof in these other sources sit uneasily with the other expression on the divine in the *Synopsis*, 'the change from beast to hero, or *daimōn*, or god' in [4.4.2], or for that matter in *Progress* [viii]. The expression in [4.4.2] goes a step further, as the sage is not *like* a god or Zeus any more: he *is* divine. Are we dealing with a deliberate exaggeration here?

[34] See Stob. 2. 98. 19–99. 2 (*SVF* iii. 54³): καὶ ⟨ἐκείνων⟩ τὴν εὐδαιμονίαν μὴ διαφέρειν τῆς θείας εὐδαιμονίας (μηδὲ τὴν ἀμεριαίαν ὁ Χρύσιππός φησι διαφέρειν τῆς τοῦ Διὸς εὐδαιμονίας) ⟨καὶ⟩ κατὰ μηδὲν αἱρετωτέραν εἶναι μήτε καλλίω μήτε σεμνοτέραν τὴν τοῦ Διὸς εὐδαιμονίαν τῆς τῶν σοφῶν ἀνδρῶν. For the reading see J. von Arnim, *SVF* vol. i, p. xliii: only the bracketed part can safely be ascribed to Chrysippus (followed by C. Viano, *Etica stoica* [*Etica*] (Rome and Bari, 1999), but not by A. J. Pomeroy, *Arius Didymus*: Epitome of Stoic Ethics [*Epitome*] (Atlanta, 1999)); Cic. *ND* 2. 153 (not in *SVF*): 'animus accipit [*Davies*: accedit ad *codd.*] cognitionem deorum, e qua oritur pietas, cui coniuncta iustitia est reliquaeque virtutes, e quibus vita beata existit, par et similis deorum, nulla alia re nisi immortalitate (quae nihil ad bene vivendum pertinet), cedens caelestibus'; Orig. *Cels.* 6. 48 (*SVF* iii. 248): τὴν αὐτὴν ἀρετὴν λέγοντες ἀνθρώπου καὶ θεοῦ οἱ ἀπὸ τῆς Στοᾶς φιλόσοφοι μὴ εὐδαιμονέστερον λέγωσιν εἶναι τὸν ἐπὶ πᾶσι θεὸν τοῦ ἐν ἀνθρώποις κατ' αὐτοὺς σοφοῦ, ἀλλ' ἴσην εἶναι τὴν ἀμφοτέρων εὐδαιμονίαν.

[35] Procl. *In Tim.* 2. 106F, i. 351. 11–14 Diehl (*SVF* i. 564², iii. 252): οἱ δὲ ἀπὸ τῆς Στοᾶς καὶ τὴν αὐτὴν ἀρετὴν εἶναι θεῶν καὶ ἀνθρώπων εἰρήκασιν; Alex. Aphr. *Fat.* 74. 10–14 Thillet (*SVF* iii. 247) in his criticism of Stoic doctrine: οὐ γὰρ τὰς αὐτὰς ἀρετὰς οἷόν τε λέγειν εἶναι τῶν ἀνθρώπων καὶ τῶν θεῶν. οὔτε γὰρ ἄλλως ἀληθὲς τὸ τὰς τῶν τοσοῦτον ἀλλήλων κατὰ τὴν φύσιν διεστώτων τὰς αὐτὰς τελειότητάς τε καὶ ἀρετὰς λέγειν, οὔθ' οἱ πρὸς αὐτῶν περὶ αὐτῶν λεγόμενοι λόγοι εὔλογόν τι ἐν αὐτοῖς ἔχουσιν; Cic. *Leg.* 1. 25 (*SVF* i. 564³, iii. 245): 'iam vero virtus eadem in homine ac deo est, neque alio ullo in genere [*Davies*: ingenio *codd.*] praeterea; Sen. *Const.* 8. 2 (not in *SVF*): 'sapiens autem vicinus proximusque dis consistit, excepta mortalitate similis deo'; Ep. 59. 14 (not in *SVF*): '[sapiens] cum dis ex pari vivit'; Clem. *Strom.* 7. 88. 5–6 (*SVF* iii. 250) οὐ γὰρ καθάπερ οἱ Στωϊκοί, ἀθέως πάνυ τὴν αὐτὴν ἀρετὴν ἀνθρώπου λέγομεν καὶ θεοῦ; Orig. *Cels.* 4. 29 (*SVF* iii. 249): ἡ αὐτὴ ἀρετὴ ἀνθρώπου καὶ θεοῦ; Them. *Or.* 2. 27c (*SVF* i. 564³, iii. 251): in the context of the reliability of oracles the Stoics say that τὴν αὐτὴν ἀρετὴν καὶ ἀλήθειαν ἀνδρὸς καὶ θεοῦ.

[36] Plut. *Comm. not.* 1076 A (*SVF* iii. 246; LS 61J): against the common conception that men and gods differ in virtue Chrysippus maintained that οὐδὲ τοῦτο περίεστιν αὐτοῖς [sc. θεοῖς τὸ εὐδαιμονεῖν]· ἀρετῇ τε γὰρ οὐχ ὑπερέχειν τὸν Δία τοῦ Δίωνος ὠφελεῖσθαι θ' ὁμοίως ὑπ' ἀλλήλων τὸν Δία καὶ τὸν Δίωνα, σοφοὺς ὄντας; Chrysippus, *On Motion* 3 ap. Plut. *Stoic. repugn.* 1038 D (*SVF* iii. 526): τοῖς ἀγαθοῖς . . . κατ' οὐδὲν προεχομένοις ὑπὸ τοῦ Διός; Sen. *Ep.* 73. 13 (not in *SVF*): 'Iuppiter quo antecedit virum bonum? diutius bonus est: sapiens nihilo se minoris aestimat quod virtutes eius spatio breviore cluduntur'; *NQ* praef. 6 (not in *SVF*): 'effugisti vitia animi? . . . multa effugisti, te nondum. virtus enim ista quam adfectamus magnifica est non quia per se beatum est malo caruisse, sed quia animum laxat et praeparat ad cognitionem caelestium, dignumque effecit qui in consortium ⟨cum⟩ deo veniat.' More passages can be found in J. Lipsius, *Manuductionis ad Stoicam philosophiam libri tres* [*Manuductio*] (Antwerp, 1604), repr. in M. N. Bouillet (ed.), *L. Annaei Senecae pars prima sive opera philosophica* (Paris, 1827), vol. iv, pp. li–ccxliii), bk. 3, ch. 14.

Yet again there is evidence outside the Plutarchean texts for the reading that sages *are* divine. Stob. 2. 68. 3 (*SVF* iii. 604) records that the sage is the only priest, as for a priest it is not only necessary to be experienced in the regulations concerning sacrifices, prayers, etc., but also 'to be inside divine nature'.[37] Furthermore, S.E. *M*. 7. 423 (not in *SVF* or *FDS*), emphatically conveying the doctrine as Stoic, tells us that the Stoics have described the sage as divine, this time because of the sage's ability to distinguish between truth and falsehood:

ἀπλανὲς γὰρ εἶχε κριτήριον κατ' αὐτοὺς ὁ σοφός, καὶ κατὰ πάντα ἐθεοποιεῖτο διὰ τὸ μὴ δοξάζειν, τουτέστι ψεύδει συγκατατίθεσθαι, ἐν ᾧ ἔκειτο ἡ ἄκρα κακο-δαιμονία καὶ ἡ τῶν φαύλων διάπτωσις.

according to them [i.e. the Stoics] the sage possesses an infallible criterion, which makes him in all respects divine because he never opines, i.e. assents to what is false, wherein lies the height of unhappiness and the ruin of the inferior person.

It may, of course, be maintained that the expression 'to make divine' should not be given too much weight here, and is simply used metaphorically, as an expression of the sage's excellence.[38] Further evidence for the sage as divine is ascribed to Cleanthes in the admittedly not always very reliable doxography by Epiphanius, *De fide* 9. 41, p. 508. 28 Holl–Dümmer (*SVF* i. 538; fr. 58 Watanabe),[39] who is reported to have said that 'those who are possessed by the divine are initiates'.[40] Although the connection with

---

[37] καὶ ⟨τοῦ⟩ ἐντὸς εἶναι τῆς φύσεως τῆς θείας. Some interpreters, however, have rendered the Greek more freely as 'to have knowledge of the divine nature'. Among the defenders of the strong reading may be counted Pomeroy, *Epitome*, n. 51. Among the more liberal interpreters are B. Inwood and L. P. Gerson, *Hellenistic Philosophy*, 2nd edn. (Indianapolis, 1997), 208, who translate 'to be intimate with the nature of divinity', and Viano, *Etica*, 42, who gives 'saper penetrare ⟨nel⟩ profondo della natura divina'.

[38] Only J. A. Fabricius (ed.), *Sexti Empirici opera Graece et Latine* (Leipzig, 1718), ad loc., seems to have taken the expression seriously by giving a reference to Lipsius, *Manuductio*, bk. 3, ch. 14 (see above, n. 36).

[39] On the reliability see H. Diels, *Doxographi Graeci* [*Doxographi*] (Berlin, 1879), 175, 177, followed by A. Pourkier, *L'Hérésiologie chez Épiphane de Salamine* (Paris, 1992), 96–9.

[40] τοὺς κατόχους τῶν θείων τελεστὰς ἔλεγε. The manuscripts have τελετάς, but all modern editors, starting with C. A. Lobeck, *Aglaophamus sive de theologiae mysticae Graecorum causis* (Königsberg, 1829), 130 (overviews in K. Holl and J. Dümmer (eds.), *Epiphanius*, iii: *Panarion haer. 65–80. De fide*, 2nd edn. (Berlin, 1985), ad loc., or A. T. Watanabe, 'Cleanthes: Fragments. Text and Commentary' (diss. Urbana, Ill., 1988), 171–2 ad fr. 58), alter it to τελεστάς.

wisdom is not obvious, the Stoics sometimes refer to the sage as the 'initiated'. Chrysippus interpreted initiation as perfection, and hence, we may infer, the initiated as the perfected.[41] In Greek the words 'initiation' (τελετή) and 'fulfilment' (τελευτή) differ by only one letter, which will not have escaped Chrysippus. The relation of the sage to the divine is thus that he is filled with the divine, and hence 'fulfilled' (to preserve the etymological association in the translation). Cleanthes would thus have said that sages are divine. Moreover, D.L. 7. 119 (*SVF* iii. 606), giving an overview of the sages' qualities, informs us:

θείους τ᾽ εἶναι· ἔχειν γὰρ ἐν ἑαυτοῖς οἱονεὶ θεόν. τὸν δὲ φαῦλον ἄθεον. διττὸν δὲ εἶναι τὸν ἄθεον, τὸν τ᾽ ἐναντίως τῷ θείῳ λεγόμενον καὶ τὸν ἐξουθενητικὸν τοῦ θείου· ὅπερ οὐκ εἶναι περὶ πάντα φαῦλον.

they are divine; for they have god in themselves as it were, but the inferior person is godless. The word 'godless' has two senses: the first sense is 'opposite to divine', the other sense is 'one who denies the divine'. In this latter sense the term does not apply to every inferior person.

While 'godless' in the latter sense of being an atheist 'does not apply to every inferior person' (since in the Greek world most people will have honoured the (Olympian) gods), by contrast 'godless' in the former sense will apply to every inferior person, who will hence be 'the opposite of the divine man'. The conclusion must thus be that the sage is a divine man.[42]

What we find is that the two ways in which the sage is related to the divine in the *Synopsis* (and in *Progress*) are *both* reflected in other sources on Stoicism. This apparent contradiction would be explained by the Stoics with reference to their allegorical interpretation of popular religion. On the one hand they would of course have admitted that the sage would surely never become a god in the sense of the beings worshipped in popular rites. He would at best be *like* these gods. On the other hand they would have pointed out that the divinities of traditional religion should in fact be understood as parts of the cosmos. In Philodemus' *On Piety*, in which some information about Chrysippus' first book *On Gods* (*SVF* ii. 1076) is given,[43] we find a particularly telling example of this alle-

---

[41] See esp. the *Etymologicum Magnum* s.v., p. 751. 16–22 Kallierges, col. 2108 Gaisford (*SVF* ii. 1008; *FDS* 650). Cf. Plut. *Stoic. repugn.* 1035 A–E, from Chrysippus' *On Lives* 4 (*SVF* ii. 42; LS 26C; *FDS* 24), and Sen. *Ep.* 90. 28; 95. 64.

[42] Cf. D. S. Du Toit, *Theios anthropos* (Tübingen, 1997), 94 ff.

[43] The standard edition of this text is still A. Henrichs, 'Die Kritik der stoischen

gorical method, which at the same time is linked with a description of men becoming divine. It should already be noted that the title of the work lacks the definite article, and that therefore the traditional translation *On the Gods* is at least inaccurate. This may seem a small point, but the absence of the article suggests that the book deals with a wider phenomenon than the traditionally acclaimed set of Olympian gods.[44] This suggestion is confirmed by what Philodemus tells us about its contents. Chrysippus explains in allegorical fashion that not only are the Olympian gods such as Zeus, Ares, and Hephaestus to be 'assimilated' respectively to reason that rules over everything, war or the principle of order and disorder, and fire, but furthermore the sun and moon are gods. What we thus seem to have is an interpretation of the gods of traditional religion in terms of natural phenomena and an interpretation of natural phenomena in terms of the divine. Philodemus ends his summary of Chrysippus' *On Gods* 1 with the remark (col. 6. 14–16 Henrichs): 'He says also that men change into gods.'[45] Unfortunately Philodemus does not elaborate.[46] Notwithstanding the lack of further information, in this context of reinterpreting traditional religion it seems unlikely that Chrysippus is talking about traditional deification of human beings for services to (parts of) mankind, such as the examples in conformity with popular usage given by Cicero in *ND* 3. 49–50. It seems rather more likely that he is talking about a man becoming a divine sage. The description of the sage in the *Synopsis* as having a character equal to the popular gods and even being transformed into a god is thus wholly in line with the Stoic position.

The description of the change in physico-theological terms in [4.4.2] and [viii] seems to run into trouble, however, from a Stoic

Theologie im *PHerc.* 1428', *Cronache ercolanesi*, 4 (1974), 5–32, but parts of it, in improved readings, can now also be found in D. Obbink, '"All gods are true" in Epicurus', in D. Frede and A. Laks (eds.), *Traditions of Theology* (Leiden, 2002), 183–221. Our text (no. 5 in Obbink's numbering) is on pp. 199–200.

[44] A similar phenomenon can be discerned with regard to the book-title *On Cosmos*. See J. Mansfeld, '*Περὶ κόσμου*: A Note on the History of a Title', *Vigiliae Christianae*, 46 (1992), 391–411.

[45] καὶ ἀ[ν]θρώπους εἰς θεούς φησι μεταβάλλειν. Obbink's reading (silently returning to the reading by T. Gomperz (ed.), *Philodem: Über Frömmigkeit*, pt. 1. *Der Text* (Leipzig, 1866), 80 of the apographs) is different from μεταβαλεῖν in Diels, *Doxographi*, 574ᵇ15–16 (without acknowledgement) or in *SVF* ii. 1076.

[46] Nor does the parallel account in Cic. *ND* 1. 39 (*SVF* ii. 1077; LS 54B): 'iam vero Chrysippus . . . magnam turbam congregat ignotorum deorum . . .; atque etiam homines eos qui immortalitem esse consecuti.'

point of view. The notion of a change from beast to god is not Stoic, as the Stoics would object to an immediate transition from an animal to a perfect human being (or god for that matter). The important point for the Stoics is that human beings should first develop reason, before they can take on the next step to perfection.[47] (I shall return to this in Section 2.3.3.) Nevertheless, this objection is rebutted if we understand 'beast' here in a metaphorical sense, as referring to a most immoral human being. The adjective 'most vicious' that Plutarch actually uses in combination with beast makes this suggestion of an exaggeratedly expressed reference to a very immoral person rather likely. Taking the phrase in [4.4.2] as a metaphor, we yet again find the *Synopsis* (and *Progress*) to be a reliable (albeit hostile) source on Stoicism.

## 2.3. *The radical change*

A third feature of becoming wise is the radicalism of the change. In the *Synopsis* the change is not only characterized under its temporal aspect as sudden, it is moreover characterized as a change from the one extreme state to the other, most clearly in [4.4.1]: 'and this not by any previous alleviation of depravity'. In *Progress* the radicalism comes out clearly in [ii]: over a long time the sage-to-be has not succeeded in removing even a small part of his vice; only at the moment of change does he leave vice behind for ever.

This radicalism is yet again perfectly Stoic and can be found formulated both in general terms and in terms of the parts of philosophy—in general terms in a central passage in the last part of Arius Didymus' exposition of Stoic ethics in Stobaeus.[48] It is central because it forms the introduction to the long description of the qualities of the sage, which are in most cases accompanied by a short reference to the absence of these qualities in the inferior person.[49] At 2. 99. 3–5 (*SVF* i. 216; LS 59N) we read:

[47] Moreover, in a more technical sense the combination of most vicious and beast is not meaningful for the Stoics, as 'vicious' can be applied only to human beings, who, owing to the fact that they possess reason, are able to make a choice between good and bad. See e.g. Alex. Aphr. *Quaest.* 122. 3 Bruns (*SVF* iii. 537): children and animals are neither just nor unjust. Only if they become rational *can* they become good. This implies that human beings, once having become rational, are *not yet* good and hence are inferior. Cf. Philo, *Opif.* 73 (*SVF* iii. 372); D.L. 7. 129 (*SVF* iii. 367); Cic. *Fin.* 3. 67 (*SVF* iii. 371).

[48] Chapter 11 in Wachsmuth's edition.

[49] Cf. the division in D. Hahm, 'The Diaeretic Method and the Purpose of Arius'

ἀρέσκει γὰρ τῷ Ζήνωνι καὶ τοῖς ἀπ' αὐτοῦ Στωικοῖς φιλοσόφοις δύο γένη τῶν
ἀνθρώπων εἶναι, τὸ μὲν τῶν σπουδαίων, τὸ δὲ τῶν φαύλων· καὶ τὸ μὲν τῶν
σπουδαίων διὰ παντὸς τοῦ βίου χρῆσθαι ταῖς ἀρεταῖς, τὸ δὲ τῶν φαύλων ταῖς
κακίαις.

Zeno and the other Stoic philosophers after him hold that there are two
kinds of human being, the excellent and the inferior, and that the class of
the excellent uses the virtues during their whole life, and that the inferior
uses the vices.

From this distinction it follows, as Stob. 2. 99. 7–8 says, that to
sages and inferior persons belong respectively 'doing everything
they undertake rightly and doing everything wrongly'.[50]

As with my discussion of the opposed states in 2.2, I shall employ
the organizational principle of tripartition to discuss the radical
nature of the change.

2.3.1. *The radical change in ethics*   With Stobaeus we have in fact
already moved on towards the distinction in ethics. The radicalism
was not only expressed in the doctrine that the sage does everything
well and the inferior person everything badly. Virtue too was presented as an all-or-nothing matter and expressed in formulas such as
'there is nothing in between virtue and vice' and 'all sins are equal'.
Various images, both familiar and less well known, were used to
get the point across. The formula 'nothing in between virtue and
vice' was explained by the images of the stick and the unfinished
verse. Just as a stick is either straight or crooked, justice is an all-
or-nothing affair. There is not a more just or a less just. The same
goes for the other virtues.[51] According to Stob. 2. 65. 7–11 (*SVF* i.
566; fr. 87 Watanabe), Cleanthes compared human beings who have
natural impulses to virtue to an unfinished verse: just as the metre
of the verse which has not been brought to completion is not good,
so human beings who have not brought their natural impulses to
completion are not good either.[52] The formula 'all sins are equal',

Doxography', in W. W. Fortenbaugh (ed.), *On Stoic and Peripatetic Ethics* (New
Brunswick, 1983), 41–65 at 57 ff., followed by C. Viano, 'L'*Epitomê de l'éthique
stoïcienne* d'Arius Didyme (Stobée, *Eclog.* II, 5, 7, 57, 13–116, 18)', in J.-B. Gourinat
(ed.), *Les Stoïciens* (Paris, 2005), 335–55 at 346.

[50] τὸ μὲν ἀεὶ κατορθοῦν ἐν ἅπασιν οἷς προστίθεται, τὸ δὲ ἁμαρτάνειν.
[51] D.L. 7. 127 (*SVF* iii. 536; LS 611): μηδὲν μεταξὺ εἶναι ἀρετῆς καὶ κακίας· . . .
ὡς γὰρ δεῖν φασιν ἢ ὀρθὸν εἶναι ξύλον ἢ στρεβλόν, οὕτως ἢ δίκαιον ἢ ἄδικον, οὔτε δὲ
δικαιότερον οὔτ' ἀδικώτερον, καὶ ἐπὶ τῶν ἄλλων ὁμοίως.
[52] ἀρετῆς δὲ καὶ κακίας οὐδὲν εἶναι μεταξύ. πάντας γὰρ ἀνθρώπους ἀφορμὰς ἔχειν ἐκ

already ascribed to Zeno and his pupil Persaeus (D.L. 7. 120; *SVF* i. 224, 450), was explained with the images of the pilgrim, the blind, and the drowning. According to Chrysippus in his fourth book *On Ethical Questions* (in D.L. 7. 120, *SVF* iii. 527), just as it does not matter whether the pilgrim is a hundred or a few miles away from Canopus (a sanctuary in the Nile Delta which flourished in the third century BC), as both positions are equally not in Canopus, so it does not matter whether one makes a big or a small mistake: in either case one is not virtuous.[53] The other two images are attested by Plutarch at *Comm. not.* 1063 A (*SVF* iii. 539; LS 61T): just as the blind person who is later going to recover his sight is until then still blind,[54] and just as it does not matter whether a drowing person is in water one foot or a hundred feet deep, it does not matter whether one makes a big or small moral mistake: one is equally vicious and inferior in either case.

### 2.3.2. *The radical change in logic*    In logic (or epistemology for that matter[55]) we find a similar radical approach.[56] It is knowledge that counts; everything else, whether it is called opinion or ignorance, does not. Presenting it as the cardinal point in Zeno's epistemology (or perhaps even in Zeno's contribution to philosophy in general—

φύσεως πρὸς ἀρετήν, καὶ οἱονεὶ τὸν τῶν ἡμιαμβείων λόγον ἔχειν κατὰ τὸν Κλεάνθην· ὅθεν ἀτελεῖς μὲν ὄντας εἶναι φαύλους, τελειωθέντας δὲ σπουδαίους. The expression τὸν τῶν ἡμιαμβείων λόγον has been interpreted by Pomeroy, *Epitome*, 109 n. 38, as a reference to comedy, where a series of iambic dimeters may be used to conclude a scene. If the dimeters are only half finished, the scene is not completed, and laughter will not ensue. Another interpretation is that the expression refers to an unfinished account in a specific type of metre (e.g. the iambic trimeter described by Aristotle, *Poet.* 4, 1449ᵃ24, as best suited to natural speech). This interpretation is not only simpler, but also in line with Cleanthes' interest in metre, rhythm, and melody, not just for their own sake, but also with respect to divine things, for which the most important piece of evidence is Philodemus, *Mus.* col. 28. 3–22 Kemke–Neubecker (*SVF* i. 486 (part); fr. 5 Watanabe), esp. ll. 10–15: τὰ μέτρα καὶ τά μέλη καὶ τοὺς ῥυθμοὺς ὡς μάλιστα προσκινεῖσθαι πρὸς τὴν ἀλήθειαν τῆς τῶν θείων θ[ε]ωρίας. K.-H. Rolke, *Die bildhaften Vergleiche in den Fragmenten der Stoiker von Zenon bis Panaitios* [*Vergleiche*] (Hildesheim, 1975), 69, 294, is unhelpful here.

⁵³ On the image see further Rolke, *Vergleiche*, 162–3. It also occurs in the doxographical PMilVogliano 1241, ll. 11–19 (in the revised reading by F. Decleva Caizzi and M. Serena Funghi, 'Dossografia stoica: riposta a Marcello Gigante', in F. Decleva Caizzi *et al.* (eds.), *Varia papyrologica* (Florence, 1991), 127–34 at 132). In the papyrus reference is made to a 'city' (ἄστυ) rather than Canopus.
⁵⁴ Cic. *Fin.* 3. 48 (*SVF* iii. 530) uses the image of a puppy about to be born.
⁵⁵ See above, sect. 2.2.2.
⁵⁶ See C. Meinwald, 'Ignorance and Opinion in Stoic Epistemology' ['Ignorance'], *Phronesis*, 55 (2005), 215–31.

the context leaves that open), Cic. *Acad.* 1. 42 (*SVF* i. 53 and i. 60 (part); LS 41B; *FDS* 256) informs us that Zeno 'removed error, rashness, ignorance, opinion, and conjecture from virtue and wisdom, and in a word, everything foreign to firm and consistent assent'.[57] The same radical distinction had been expressed a little earlier, at *Acad.* 1. 41 (*SVF* i. 60; LS 41B; *FDS* 256), in terms of the definitions of knowledge and ignorance, which are presented as complementing each other: knowledge as sense-perception so grasped as not to be disrupted by reason; ignorance as otherwise.

This simple binary picture seems to be complicated by two other accounts, which suggest a less clear-cut picture: the famous image of Zeno's hands and the account of Stoic epistemology in Arcesilaus' critique of it. In the hand simile in Cic. *Acad.* 2. 145 (*SVF* i. 66; LS 41A; *FDS* 369) Zeno is said to have compared the open palm of his hand with an impression, the fingers of his hand a bit contracted with assent to the impression, his fingers made into a fist with a cognition, and the tight and forceful gripping of his other hand over the fist with knowledge. This simile may be understood in a developmental sense, as offering a description of the various phases in the process of gaining knowledge. This, however, seems an over-interpretation of a passage that not only offers to students of Stoicism[58] a mnemonic device to get to grips with Stoic terminology, but also—and more importantly—is used to get the point across that only the sage has knowledge. For this is how Cicero introduces the simile in the dialectical setting of *Academica* 2: 'You deny that anyone knows anything, except the sage. And this Zeno demonstrated with gestures.'[59]

In the other problematic passage, S.E. *M.* 7. 151 (*SVF* ii. 90; LS 41C; *FDS* 370), in the context of Sextus' overview in *M.* 7. 89–260 of the various epistemological theories since Thales, the Stoics make a surprise appearance in the discussion of Arcesilaus' theory (the account of Stoic epistemology proper is at the end, 227–60). But as Arcesilaus' theory, Sextus explains, was only formulated in response to the Stoics, Stoic doctrine has to be brought up at this stage. In what is therefore a multi-layered account Sextus informs

---

[57] 'errorem autem et temeritatem et ignorantiam et opinationem et suspicionem, et uno nomine omnia quae essent aliena firmae et constantis adsensionis, a virtute sapientiaque removebat.'

[58] Note that the setting seems to be a lecture, or at any rate a conversation.

[59] 'at scire negatis quemquam rem ullam nisi sapientem. et hoc quidem Zeno gestu conficiebat.'

us that according to Arcesilaus 'the Stoics say there are three things that are linked together, knowledge, opinion, and cognition stationed between them'.[60] This passage might be taken as a description of three successive epistemological phases, in which opinion becomes cognition, and cognition becomes knowledge. However, Meinwald rightly pointed to the usage of 'linking' or—as it can also be translated—'yoking'.[61] If this image of the yoke between two oxen is taken seriously, cognition is not an intermediate stage between opinion and knowledge, but rather functions as a yoke between the two: if used badly it is opinion, if well, knowledge. Yet again, this passage would confirm the radical opposition between the inferior person and the sage that we have thus far encountered, and hence the radical nature of the change from the state of ignorance to the state of knowledge.

2.3.3. *The radical change in physics* Finally, the radical character of the change can be expressed in physical terms. This is best approached through the Stoic theory of the taxonomy of natural kinds. The basic tenets of this hierarchical scheme of nature or *scala naturae* are clear, although our sources offer different versions, especially where the lowest and highest levels are concerned.[62] The lowest level is that of 'tenor' (ἕξις), as the power of holding together, such as can be found in stones.[63] At the second level, which the Stoics call 'nature' (*physis*), the power of holding together is

[60] τρία γὰρ εἶναί φασιν ἐκεῖνοι τὰ συζυγοῦντα ἀλλήλοις, ἐπιστήμην καὶ δόξαν καὶ τὴν ἐν μεθορίῳ τούτων τεταγμένην κατάληψιν.

[61] 'Ignorance', 15–16.

[62] Complete taxonomies are offered by Cic. *Off.* 2. 11 (not in *SVF*); Philo, *Leg.* 2. 22–3 (*SVF* ii. 458; LS 47P with the highest kind in vol. ii only; cf. Philo, *Aet.* 75 (*SVF* ii. 459), *Opif.* 73 (*SVF* iii. 372—D. T. Runia, *Philo of Alexandria: On the Creation of the Cosmos according to Moses* (Leiden, 2001), ad loc., doubts its Stoic character: 'The passage is sufficiently general to be subscribed by Stoics, Platonists and Aristotelians'). A complete taxonomy is implied in a passage on kinds of movement by Simpl. *In Cat.* 306. 13–27 Kalbfleisch (*SVF* ii. 499), although the account is contaminated with Aristotelian terminology. The taxonomy without the lowest—inanimate—kind is given in Cic. *ND* 2. 33–6 (referred to at *SVF* i. 529), and used by Cleanthes according to S.E. *M.* 9. 88 (*SVF* i. 529). The taxonomy without the highest kind (for reasons that will become apparent below, sect. 3) is offered by Clem. *Strom.* 2. 110. 4–111. 2 (*SVF* ii. 714), Orig. *Princ.* 3. 1. 2–3 (*SVF* ii. 988; LS 53A; cf. Orig. *Or.* 6. 1, *SVF* ii. 989, as with Simplicius in a passage on the kinds of movement). The best modern discussion of the *scala naturae* is B. Inwood, *Ethics and Human Action in Early Stoicism* (Oxford, 1985), 21–6, 209 ff., but cf. also J. A. Akinpelu, 'The Stoic *scala naturae*', *Phrontisterion*, 5 (1967), 7–16 at 8, who however restricts himself to *ND* 2. 33–6.

[63] It has sometimes been doubted whether the first level had already been in-

supervened upon by the capacity to grow and to generate, as can be found in plants. The third level is the level of the 'soul', which brings the power to perceive and to act, as can be found in animals. The fourth level is the level of mature human beings, whose souls have a rational faculty, or as it is usually called, 'commanding faculty' (ἡγεμονικόν).[64] Finally, the fifth level is ascribed to gods and sages alike, and is characterized by 'mind' (νοῦς) or virtue.[65] Reason on level 4 differs from reason on level 5, succinctly characterized by Seneca, *Ep.* 92. 27, as 'reason which is capable of being perfected' (*ratio consummabilis*) and 'reason brought to perfection' (*ratio consummata*) respectively.

As the higher levels supervene upon the lower levels, a human being will not only have the peculiar characteristic of reason, but also the characteristics that belong to the level of tenor (to be found in bones and sinews[66]), *physis*, and soul. The higher level is said to guide the lower level, e.g. reason guiding perception. A rational being perceives the world in a totally different manner from a non-rational being: that is, he perceives it by means of reason, he accepts or rejects impressions by using substantive conceptions about the world.[67]

The taxonomical accounts do not deal with possible transitions between the levels. However, the Stoics *were* interested in them, especially where human beings are concerned. Best known are the Stoic descriptions of two of these transitions: the transition from the level of *physis* to the level of soul, and the transition from the level of soul to the level of the soul becoming rational. The moment of getting a soul occurs at birth: when the foetus leaves the womb, its breath, which till that point is still characterized as *physis*, becomes chilled by air and tempered, which brings about the change to the level of soul (like Plato, at *Crat.* 399 D–E, and Aristotle, at *DA*

troduced by Zeno, but it seems likely: according to Themistius, *In DA*. 35. 32–4 Heinze (*SVF* i. 158), the Zenonians, as the Stoics are called here, unanimously held this opinion.

    [64]  See e.g. Aëtius 4. 21. 1 (*SVF* ii. 836; LS 53H).
    [65]  Gods and sages: Cic. *Off.*, *ND*; mind: Philo, *Leg.*; virtue: Philo, *Aet.*, *Opif.*, and Simpl. (as referred to in n. 62 above).
    [66]  See D.L. 7. 139 (*SVF* ii. 634; LS 470): δι’ ὧν μὲν γὰρ ὡς κέχρηκεν, ὡς διὰ τῶν ὀστῶν καὶ τῶν νεύρων· δι’ ὧν δὲ ὡς νοῦς, ὡς διὰ τοῦ ἡγεμονικοῦ.
    [67]  On the rational being perceiving rationally or having a rational impression see D.L. 7. 51 (*SVF* ii. 61; LS 39A; *FDS* 255); on the definition of a rational impression see S.E. *M*. 8. 70 (*SVF* ii. 187; LS 33C; *FDS* 699).

405$^b$28–9, the Stoics preserve the etymological link between 'soul' (ψυχή) and 'cold' (ψυχρός)).[68] The transition to the next level starts at the age of about seven and ends at the age of about fourteen, when the body starts to emit seminal fluids.[69] In each case the change is described as a physical process.

These accounts show that the Stoics related the changes between the natural kinds to qualities such as cold and warm. They distinguished four of these basic qualities (cold, warm, moist, and dry) and identified these qualities with the four elements (air, fire, water, and earth respectively).[70] The former two elements were considered to be the active qualities or elements: fire was thought to expand, and air to contract.[71] The latter two were considered to be passive, to be acted upon by the active elements.[72] The natural kinds are hence explained as combinations of the active elements of air and fire, which in different quantities pervade parts of the combinations of the passive elements water and earth. (Presumably the lowest kind is characterized by the active element air going through (contracting) the passive elements of water and earth.[73]) The Stoics call this combination of fire and air (or of warm and cold) 'breath' (πνεῦμα).[74] The changes may hence have been understood as changes of the composition of these elements within these bodies.

The change to wisdom is of a different nature from the other changes that befall human beings earlier in their development. For

---

[68] The sources are conveniently assembled in *SVF* ii. 806, esp. Plut. *Stoic. repugn.* 1052 E–F (*SVF* ii. 806$^1$; *FDS* 680); *Comm. not.* 1084 D–E (*SVF* ii. 806$^5$); to these can be added Hierocles, *Elem. Eth.* 1. 25–6 Bastianini–Long (LS 53B): φύσις ἐμβρύου πέπον[ος] ἤδη γεγονότ[ο]ς οὐ βραδύνε[ι τ]ὸ μ(ετα)βα[λ]λεῖν εἰς ψυχὴν ἐμ[πε]σοῦσα τῷ π[(ερι)έ]χον(τι).

[69] See Aëtius 4. 11. 4 (*SVF* ii. 83; LS 39E), 5. 23. 1 (*SVF* ii. 764). Cf. Iambl. *De anima* ap. Stob. 1. 317. 21–4 (*SVF* i. 149$^2$, ii. 835). The completion at the age of fourteen is already ascribed to Zeno in the *Scholia vetera in Alc. I* 121 E, p. 99 Greene (*SVF* i. 149$^1$), and is ascribed to Diogenes of Babylon too at D.L. 7. 55 (*SVF* fr. 17). See further A. A. Long, 'Soul and Body in Stoicism', *Phronesis*, 27 (1982), 34–57 at 50, repr. in id., *Stoic Studies* (Cambridge, 1996), 224–49 at 246; M. Frede, 'The Stoic Conception of Reason', in K. Boudouris (ed.), *Hellenistic Philosophy*, ii (Athens, 1994), 50–63 at 56–63.

[70] See e.g. D.L. 7. 137 (*SVF* ii. 580; LS 47B, cf. LS i. 287).

[71] See e.g. Galen, *Nat. fac.* 106. 13–16 Helmreich (*SVF* ii. 406; LS 47E).

[72] See e.g. Nemes. *Nat. hom.* 5. 52. 18–19 Morani (*SVF* ii. 418; LS 47D).

[73] The tenor of iron, stone, or silver is air according to Chrysippus in *On Tenors* ap. Plut. *Stoic. repugn.* 1053 F–1054 B (*SVF* ii. 449; LS 47M).

[74] For breath as a mixture of fire and air (or of warm and cold) see e.g. Galen, *PHP* 5. 3. 8 (*SVF* ii. 841; LS 47H); Alex. Aphr. *Mixt.* 224. 15–17 Bruns (*SVF* ii. 442; LS 47I).

evidence we may look to the Stoic definitions of soul, which is defined in two distinct ways. Firstly, soul is defined as a mixture of the elements of fire and air in sources as varied as Galen,[75] Alexander of Aphrodisias,[76] and Macrobius.[77] Secondly, soul is defined as fire (or warmth), without the mention of air (or coldness for that matter). This definition is attributed to Zeno by Cicero, *Tusc.* 1. 19 (*SVF* i. 134),[78] and to the Stoics in general by Plutarch, Alexander of Aphrodisias, Porphyry, and in the *Scholia in Lucanum.*[79] The definition of soul as warmth also occurs several times.[80] Since fire corresponds to the quality of warmth (as we have seen), this is not surprising.[81]

How can these different definitions of the soul be accounted for? If we look more carefully at the passages that offer the definition of soul as fire or warmth, we find that this definition is related to virtue or the divine.[82] It thus seems reasonable to suppose that the soul in its highest state is characterized as fire or warmth, and that the first definition of the soul is a description of the soul in its non-virtuous,

---

[75] *Quod animi mores* 4. 45. 22–3 Müller (*SVF* ii. 787).

[76] *DA* 26. 16–17 Bruns (*SVF* ii. 786).

[77] *In Somnium Scipionis* 1. 14. 20 (Boethus *SVF* iii fr. 10).

[78] D. Hahm, *The Origins of Stoic Cosmology* (Columbus, Oh., 1977), 159, seems overcautious when he states that 'we do not know know whether Zeno tried to integrate the notions of fire and pneuma'. By defining soul as fire as well as warm breath Zeno must have integrated the notions. The question is rather: exactly how did he do that?

[79] Plut. *De facie* 926 C (*SVF* ii. 1045): the soul is swift and fiery (and a divine thing, traversing instantaneously in its flight all heaven and earth and sea); Alex. Aphr. *Mantissa* 115. 6–7 Bruns (*SVF* ii. 785): 'Soul is either fire or a breath consisting of fine particles.' There is no need to consider the first view as Heraclitean and the second as Stoic, as suggested by J. Mansfeld, 'Doxography and Dialectic: The *Sitz im Leben* of the "Placita"', in W. Haase (ed.), *Aufstieg und Niedergang der römischen Welt*, 2.36.4 (Berlin, 1990), 3056–229 at 3109 n. 220: as lines 8 and 11 make clear, fire and breath are simply put on a par. Hence the soul as fire is simply explained as breath; Porphyry, *De anima* ap. Euseb. *PE* 15. 11. 4 (*SVF* ii. 806⁴): soul as thinking fire (immediately followed by an account of its birth, in a set of 'scandalous' views on the soul); *In Lucani Bellum civile* 9. 7, p. 290. 25–6 Usener (*SVF* ii. 775).

[80] D.L. 7. 157 (*SVF* i. 135): soul is warm breath; Aëtius 4. 3. 3 (*SVF* ii. 779): the soul as breath, thinking and warm; Stob. 2. 64. 22–3 (*SVF* iii. 305): soul as breath which is warm.

[81] The definition of the soul offered by Nemesius, *Nat. hom.* 2. 16. 17 Morani (*SVF* ii. 773), as the kind of breath that is 'warm as well as thoroughly fiery' (ἔνθερμον καὶ διάπυρον), is hence pleonastic from a Stoic point of view.

[82] Stob. 2. 64. 22–3 (*SVF* iii. 305); *In Lucani Bellum civile* 9. 7, p. 290. 25–6 Usener (*SVF* ii. 775): according to the scholiast, virtue in Lucan's phrase 'quos ignea virtus innocuos vita' means virtue of the soul, as the Stoics call the soul fire; Plut. *De facie* 926 C (*SVF* ii. 1045).

i.e. inferior, state. Unlike the changes at birth or in the period of puberty, which are explained in terms of combinations of fire and air, the change to wisdom should thus apparently be understood as a physical change to the level of fire only.[83] This change does not only involve the elimination of the cold (after all, this might still imply gradualism[84]), it also involves a radical transformation: undiluted, the human soul (or its commanding faculty for that matter) consisting out of pure fire will have become 'in a sense identical with' or rather part of the divine active principle in the world.[85] Seneca characterizes this kind of radical change, brought about 'after many additions' ('post multa incrementa', *Ep.* 118. 16), and unique to human beings,[86] as a change in 'property' (*proprietas*, *Ep.* 118. 13).[87]

[83] The role of fire is obscured by the fact that the Stoics distinguished between ordinary consuming fire and 'creative' (*technikon*) fire (see Stob. 1. 213. 17–20, Aëtius fr. 33, *SVF* i. 120, LS 46D; Cleanthes according to Cic. *ND* 2. 40–1, *SVF* i. 504, fr. 24B Watanabe; Aëtius 1. 7. 33, *SVF* ii. 1027, LS 46A; Clem. *Ecl. proph.* 26. 3, not in *SVF*). The change to pure fire can hence be understood as (i) the change from the element of consuming fire to the principle of technical fire (see e.g. M. Lapidge, 'Ἀρχαί and στοιχεῖα: A Problem in Stoic Cosmology', *Phronesis*, 18 (1973), 240–78 at 270; M. J. White, 'Stoic Natural Philosophy', in B. Inwood (ed.), *The Cambridge Companion to the Stoics* (Cambridge, 2003), 124–52 at 134), or (ii)—if fire is already technical fire on the lower levels (see R. W. Sharples, 'On Fire in Heraclitus and in Zeno of Citium' ['Fire'], *Classical Quarterly*, NS 34 (1984), 231–3 at 232), less or in a lesser amount with regard to plants, but more on the level of animals, as in Stob. 1. 213. 19–20—as the change to the level of pure technical fire.

[84] Cf. Sen. *Ep.* 66. 9: 'crescere posse imperfectae rei signum est.' Note that we are a long way from Aristotelian (or Hippocratic or Galenic) notions of correct ratios or balances here: cf. e.g. *SVF* ii. 789, where the second part is not Stoic, but rather Galen.

[85] Sharples, 'Fire', 232, who for god as the active principle refers to Stob. 1. 35. 9 (*SVF* i. 157): Ζήνων ὁ Στωϊκὸς νοῦν κόσμου πύρινον [sc. θεὸν ἀπεφήνατο], but see also e.g. Aëtius 1. 7. 33 (*SVF* ii. 1027; LS 46A): god as νοερός, πῦρ τεχνικόν, ὁδῷ βαδίζον ἐπὶ γενέσει κόσμου.

[86] See *Ep.* 66. 11: 'una inducitur humanis virtutibus regula'.

[87] Seneca in *Ep.* 118. 16 gives the example of an archway: only after the addition of the keystone are two rows of stones transformed into an archway. On the origin and afterlife of the 'qualitative change' see esp. E. G. Schmidt, 'Eine Frühform der Lehre vom Umschlag Quantität-Qualität bei Seneca', *Forschungen und Fortschritte*, 34 (1960), 112–15, repr. as 'Der Umschlag von Quantität und Qualität bei Seneca und Hegel', in id., *Erworbenes Erbe* (Berlin, 1988), 392–404. Bénatouïl, 'Force', 21, suggested a role for coldness here: like the change to (or birth of) the soul, the change to wisdom might be understood in terms of chilling, which in either case would bring a kind of firmness of the soul. However, apart from the fact that there is no support for this parallel in the sources (as Bénatouïl himself acknowledged), the firmness of the commanding faculty seems rather the result of the qualitative change to fire only and to consist in the commanding faculty having become part of the fiery divine active principle in the world.

A well-known phrase ascribed to Cleanthes in Plutarch's summary of Cleanthes' *Physical Treatises*, at *Stoic. repugn.* 1034 D (*SVF*
i. 563; fr. 84 Watanabe), may also be understood in this context of
the change to wisdom as a change to fire only. Cleanthes is reported
to have said that 'tension is a stroke of fire'.[88] In his *Hymn to Zeus*
10–11 (*SVF* i. 537; LS 541; fr. 57 Watanabe) he had used the same
phrase referring to the strokes of the obviously fiery thunderbolts
with which Zeus accomplishes all works of nature. These lines in
the prayer in the fashion of traditional popular religion may be
translated thus in terms of Stoic physics: fire plays an active role in
the formation of nature as a whole. In the soul this stroke of fire,
in Plutarch's formulation, is at some point apparently 'enough for
fulfilling what comes in one's path'.[89] If so, it is called strength and
power. The strength and power are explained by Plutarch (ibid.)
with a quotation from Cleanthes' book, in which Cleanthes says
that this strength and power is manifested as virtue. Cleanthes thus
seems to describe a state in which the role of fire at some point
becomes enough, and with it the change to virtue. The formulation
'enough' is (deliberately?) opaque here, but the likelihood is that
Cleanthes may have described the change to virtue as a change to
fire only.[90]

This interpretation of the change to wisdom as a physical change
should not obscure the fact that it must be prepared by a long
strenuous process of improving one's rational faculty. The pivotal
point here is that towards the end of that process the sage-to-be
apparently undergoes a qualitative, physical change to fire. This interpretation can now be seen to serve the explanation of the change
in the parts of ethics and indeed logic too.[91] With regard to ethics we

[88] πληγὴ πυρὸς ὁ τόνος ἐστί.
[89] κἂν ἱκανὸς ἐν τῇ ψυχῇ γένηται πρὸς τὸ ἐπιτελεῖν τὰ ἐπιβάλλοντα.
[90] In von Arnim's reading of Cornutus' *ND* 31 (*SVF* i. 514; fr. 33 Watanabe),
which von Arnim ascribed to Cleanthes, Heracles is allegorically interpreted as
tension at its highest level and identified with strength and power. However, rather
than tension, the manuscripts have λόγος, which is retained by R. S. Hays, 'Lucius
Annaeus Cornutus' *Epidrome*' (diss. Austin, Tex., 1983), ad loc.
[91] The point made by F. Solmsen, *Cleanthes or Posidonius: The Basis of Stoic
Physics* (Amsterdam, 1961), 20, that 'Stoic originality lies not in the creation of such
[biological] concepts . . .; where they did break new ground was in transferring them
to physics, cosmology, and even theology', should hence be extended with 'and even
ethics and logic'. Even more to the point are Rist, *Stoic*, 89: 'All moral . . . must
be related to physical facts . . . It is necessary to understand the physical structure
of man in order to grasp the nature of moral problems', and especially Bénatouïl,
'Force', who rightly stresses the physical dimension of virtue and knowledge.

have already seen in Section 2.2.1 that the Stoics described virtue (also) as the state of the soul that does not allow a more or less, or as the state that in contrast to non-virtuous states can no longer be intensified or relaxed. The change from vice to virtue is in physical terms, then, the change to the state of unmixed, pure fire. With regard to 'logic' the Stoics define knowledge in familiar fashion as a system of cognitions, but also as a firm and unshakeable grasp of reason, and as a tenor that is receptive of impressions and unshakeable by reason, something that exists in tension and power.[92] As Zeno, Cleanthes, and their followers identified fire with reason, the physical character of knowledge becomes even more apparent. The change from opinion to knowledge is then presumably yet again a change to the unmixed state of fire.

## 3. Conclusion

Taking as our starting-point the passage in the Plutarchean *Synopsis*, which turned out to be a reliable piece of evidence for our reconstruction of Stoic doctrine, we have seen that the Stoics described the change to wisdom as a radical change in the nature of a rational being. The immediate change from the one extreme state to the other could be explained as a qualitative change to the state of the soul that has been brought to perfection. As such, this state is characterized as virtue, as (perfect) reason, or as divine fire.

The Stoic interpretation of the change to wisdom can be interestingly compared with Plato's interpretation of the final moment of achieving wisdom: Plato's philosopher-king has reverted towards a different, transcendent world,[93] whereas for the Stoics the person who has become a sage has become an active part of this world.[94]

---

[92] See D.L. 7. 47 (*SVF* i. 68; *FDS* 33): τὴν ἐπιστήμην φασὶν ἢ κατάληψιν ἀσφαλῆ ἢ ἕξιν ἐν φαντασιῶν προσδέξει ἀμετάπτωτον ὑπὸ λόγου; Stob. 2. 73. 19–74. 5 (*SVF* iii. 112; *FDS* 385; LS 41H): εἶναι δὲ τὴν ἐπιστήμην . . . ἕξιν φαντασιῶν δεκτικὴν ἀμετάπτωτον ὑπὸ λόγου, ἥν τινά φασιν ἐν τόνῳ καὶ δυνάμει κεῖσθαι.

[93] See *Rep.* 532 B: ἡ . . . λύσις τε ἀπὸ τῶν δεσμῶν καὶ μεταστροφὴ ἀπὸ τῶν σκιῶν ἐπὶ τὰ εἴδωλα καὶ τὸ φῶς καὶ ἐκ τοῦ καταγείου εἰς τὸν ἥλιον ἐπάνοδος.

[94] Cf. Tatian, *Adv. Gr.* 4, p. 5. 2–3 Schwartz (presumably referred to at *SVF* ii. 1035, reading p. 5 rather than p. 4): 'God is breath, not going through matter, but the constructor of material breath and of the shapes in matter' (trans. Whittaker, without the quotation marks, of πνεῦμα ὁ θεός, οὐ διήκων διὰ τῆς ὕλης, πνευμάτων δὲ ὑλικῶν καὶ τῶν ἐν αὐτῇ σχημάτων κατασκευαστής), thus opposing the Stoic and Platonic view, respectively. The difference can also be formulated in terms of the

The difference in terminology, 'reversion' (μεταστροφή) vs. 'change' (μεταβολή) respectively, is wholly explicable in this context.⁹⁵ In the Western tradition the transcendent approach has been very influential, if only because of Christianity. It may explain why Clement (see above, Section 1) connected the change with a reversion to the divine, and not to becoming divine. It may also explain why Bickel and Passmore (ibid.) incorrectly used Christian examples or formulated their interpretations in transcendent language.

*University of Utrecht*

## BIBLIOGRAPHY

Akinpelu, J. A., 'The Stoic *scala naturae*', *Phrontisterion*, 5 (1967), 7–16.

Arnim, J. von (ed.), *Stoicorum veterum fragmenta* [*SVF*] (3 vols.; Leipzig, 1903–5).

Bénatouïl, T., 'Force, fermeté, froid: la dimension physique de la vertu stoïcienne' ['Force'], *Philosophie antique*, 5 (2005), 5–30.

Bickel, E., 'Μετασχηματίζεσθαι: Ein übersehener Grundbegriff des Poseidonios', *Rheinisches Museum*, 100 (1957), 98–9.

Casevitz, M., and Babut, D. (eds.), *Plutarque: Œuvres morales*, xv/1 [*Plutarque*] (Paris, 2004).

Cherniss, H. (ed.), *Plutarch's* Moralia, xiii/2. 1033 A–1086 B [*Moralia*] (Cambridge, Mass., 1976).

Decleva Caizzi, F., and Serena Funghi, M., 'Dossografia stoica: riposta a Marcello Gigante', in F. Decleva Caizzi *et al*. (eds.), *Varia papyrologica* (Florence, 1991), 127–34.

Diels, H., *Doxographi Graeci* [*Doxographi*] (Berlin, 1879).

Du Toit, D. S., *Theios anthropos* (Tübingen, 1997).

Fabricius, J. A. (ed.), *Sexti Empirici opera Graece et Latine* (Leipzig, 1718).

Frede, M., 'The Stoic Conception of Reason', in K. Boudouris (ed.), *Hellenistic Philosophy*, ii (Athens, 1994), 50–63.

Gomperz, T. (ed.), *Philodem: Über Frömmigkeit*, pt. 1. *Der Text* (Leipzig, 1866).

good life. For Plato the good life consists in becoming like god so far as is possible for a human being, for the Stoics the ideal is to become god in the sense of becoming part of the divine power that structures the world.

⁹⁵ Cf. N. P. White, 'The Basis of Stoic Ethics', *Harvard Studies in Classical Philology*, 83 (1979), 143–78 at 178, who notes that in contrast to Plato's depreciation of the sensible world relative to another intelligible world, the Stoics appreciated the sensible world as exhibiting perfect order, making it central to their ethical doctrine.

Hahm, D., 'The Diaeretic Method and the Purpose of Arius' Doxography', in W. W. Fortenbaugh (ed.), *On Stoic and Peripatetic Ethics* (New Brunswick, 1983), 41–65.

—— *The Origins of Stoic Cosmology* (Columbus, Oh., 1977).

Hays, R. S., 'Lucius Annaeus Cornutus' *Epidrome*' (diss. Austin, Tex., 1983).

Heitmann, P. A., *Imitatio dei* (Rome, 1940).

Henrichs, A., 'Die Kritik der stoischen Theologie im *PHerc.* 1428', *Cronache ercolanesi*, 4 (1974), 5–32.

Holl, K., and Dümmer, J. (eds.), *Epiphanius*, iii. *Panarion haer. 65–80. De fide*, 2nd edn. (Berlin, 1985).

Hülser, K. (ed.), *Die Fragmente zur Dialektik der Stoiker* (4 vols.; Stuttgart, 1987–8).

Inwood, B., *Ethics and Human Action in Early Stoicism* (Oxford, 1985).

—— 'Hierocles: Theory and Argument in the Second Century AD', *Oxford Studies in Ancient Philosophy*, 2 (1984), 151–83.

—— and Gerson, L. P., *Hellenistic Philosophy*, 2nd edn. (Indianapolis, 1997).

Lapidge, M., '*Ἀρχαί* and *στοιχεῖα*: A Problem in Stoic Cosmology', *Phronesis*, 18 (1973), 240–78.

Lipsius, J., *Manuductionis ad Stoicam philosophiam libri tres* [*Manuductio*] (Antwerp, 1604); repr. in M. N. Bouillet (ed.), *L. Annaei Senecae pars prima sive opera philosophica* (Paris, 1827), vol. iv, pp. li–ccxliii.

Lobeck, C. A., *Aglaophamus sive de theologiae mysticae Graecorum causis* (Königsberg, 1829).

Long, A. A., 'Dialectic and the Stoic Sage', in J. M. Rist (ed.), *The Stoics* (Berkeley, 1978), 101–24; repr. in Long, *Stoic Studies* (Cambridge, 1996), 85–106.

—— 'Soul and Body in Stoicism', *Phronesis*, 27 (1982), 34–57; repr. in id., *Stoic Studies* (Cambridge, 1996), 224–49.

—— and Sedley, D. N., *The Hellenistic Philosophers* [LS] (Cambridge, 1987).

Luschnat, O., 'Das Problem des ethischen Fortschritts in der alten Stoa', *Philologus*, 102 (1958), 178–214.

Mansfeld, J., 'Doxography and Dialectic: The *Sitz im Leben* of the "Placita"', in W. Haase (ed.), *Aufstieg und Niedergang der römischen Welt*, 2.36.4 (Berlin, 1990), 3056–229.

—— '*Περὶ κόσμου*: A Note on the History of a Title', *Vigiliae Christianae*, 46 (1992), 391–411.

Meinwald, C., 'Ignorance and Opinion in Stoic Epistemology' ['Ignorance'], *Phronesis*, 55 (2005), 215–31.

Mignucci, M., 'Logic 3: The Stoics 8: Paradoxes', in K. Algra *et al.* (eds.),

314 René Brouwer

The Cambridge History of Hellenistic Philosophy (Cambridge, 1999), 157–76.

Obbink, D., ' "All gods are true" in Epicurus', in D. Frede and A. Laks (eds.), Traditions of Theology (Leiden, 2002), 183–221.

Passmore, J., The Perfectibility of Man, 3rd edn. (Indianapolis, 2000).

Pembroke, E. G., 'Oikeiosis', in A. A. Long (ed.), Problems in Stoicism (London, 1971), 114–49.

Pohlenz, M., 'Plutarchs Schriften gegen die Stoiker', Hermes, 74 (1939), 1–33.

——and Westman, R. (eds.), Plutarchi Moralia, vi/2, 2nd edn. (Leipzig, 1959).

Pomeroy, A. J., Arius Didymus: Epitome of Stoic Ethics [Epitome] (Atlanta, 1999).

Pourkier, A., L'Hérésiologie chez Épiphane de Salamine (Paris, 1992).

Reinhardt, K., Poseidonios (Munich, 1921).

Rist, J. M., Stoic Philosophy [Stoic] (Cambridge, 1969).

Rolke, K.-H., Die bildhaften Vergleiche in den Fragmenten der Stoiker von Zenon bis Panaitios [Vergleiche] (Hildesheim, 1975).

Roskam, G., On the Path to Virtue (Leuven, 2005).

Runia, D. T., Philo of Alexandria: On the Creation of the Cosmos according to Moses (Leiden, 2001).

Schmidt, E. G., 'Eine Frühform der Lehre vom Umschlag Quantität-Qualität bei Seneca', Forschungen und Fortschritte, 34 (1960), 112–15; repr. as 'Der Umschlag von Quantität und Qualität bei Seneca und Hegel', in id., Erworbenes Erbe (Berlin, 1988), 392–404.

Sedley, D., 'Diodorus Cronus and Hellenistic Philosophy', Proceedings of the Cambridge Philological Society, NS 23 (1977), 74–120.

Sharples R. W., 'On Fire in Heraclitus and in Zeno of Citium' ['Fire'], Classical Quarterly, NS 34 (1984), 231–3.

Solmsen, F., Cleanthes or Posidonius: The Basis of Stoic Physics (Amsterdam, 1961).

Veyne, P., 'Passion, perfection et âme matérielle dans l'utopie stoïcienne et chez saint Augustin', in id., L'Empire gréco-romain (Paris, 2005), 683–712.

Viano, C., Etica stoica [Etica] (Rome and Bari, 1999).

——'L'Epitomê de l'éthique stoïcienne d'Arius Didyme (Stobée, Eclog. II, 5, 7, 57, 13–116, 18)', in J.-B. Gourinat (ed.), Les Stoïciens (Paris, 2005), 335–55.

Wachsmuth, C., and Hense, O. (eds.), Stobaeus (Berlin, 1884–1923).

Watanabe, A. T., 'Cleanthes: Fragments. Text and Commentary' (diss. Urbana, Ill., 1988).

White, M. J., 'Stoic Natural Philosophy', in B. Inwood (ed.), The Cambridge Companion to the Stoics (Cambridge, 2003), 124–52.

White, N. P., 'The Basis of Stoic Ethics', *Harvard Studies in Classical Philology*, 83 (1979), 143–78.

Zeller, E., and Wellmann, M., *Die Philosophie der Griechen in ihrer geschichtlichen Entwicklung.* iii/1. *Die nacharistotelische Philosophie, erste Hälfte*, 5th edn. (Leipzig, 1923).

Ziegler, K., 'Plutarch von Chaironeia', in *RE* xxii/1 (1951), 636–962.

# PARTICULARISM, PROMISES, AND PERSONS IN CICERO'S *DE OFFICIIS*

## RAPHAEL WOOLF

## I

COULD Cicero have been an ethical particularist?[1] Could he, that is, have believed that ethics should proceed without rules or principles?[2] The answer, at first blush, looks like an obvious no. After all, Cicero's main work on practical ethics, the *De officiis*, seems precisely aimed at setting out ethical principles. Early on in the work he speaks of passing on 'rules of duty' (*officii praecepta*, 1. 5)

© Raphael Woolf 2007

A version of this paper was read at a conference on particularism held at the University of Texas at Austin in February 2006. My thanks to all participants for a stimulating and educational experience. I owe a special debt of gratitude to Paul Woodruff for suggesting the topic of Cicero and particularism. Any shortcomings in this attempt to address it are my responsibility.

[1] The question is prompted from two main directions, the first of which is the growing contemporary literature on particularism in ethics. For a recent full-length study by a leading proponent see J. Dancy, *Ethics without Principles* (Oxford, 2004). A useful collection of articles for and against can be found in B. Hooker and M. O. Little (eds.), *Moral Particularism* (Oxford, 2000). See therein, for a historical perspective, T. H. Irwin, 'Ethics as an Inexact Science: Aristotle's Ambition for Moral Theory' (100–29), which rejects a particularist reading of the *Nicomachean Ethics*. A second source of motivation is the lively debate among scholars of Hellenistic philosophy over the place of rules in Stoic ethics. See e.g., in ascending order of importance allotted to rules, P. Vander Waerdt, 'The Original Theory of Natural Law', *Studia Philonica Annual*, 15 (2003), 17–34; B. Inwood, 'Rules and Reasoning in Stoic Ethics' ['Rules and Reasoning'], in K. Ierodiakonou (ed.), *Topics in Stoic Philosophy* (Oxford, 1999), 95–127; P. Mitsis, 'Seneca on Reason, Rules, and Moral Development', in J. Brunschwig and M. Nussbaum (eds.), *Passions and Perceptions* (Cambridge, 1993), 285–312. Vander Waerdt offers a strongly particularist reading of early Stoic theory as 'one dispensing entirely with rule-based moral reasoning' (17), though he thinks the later Stoa adopted a more rules-based approach.

[2] Dancy characterizes particularism rather more weakly as the thesis that ethics *can* get along without principles (*Ethics without Principles*, 1). But he implies the stronger thesis—that it *should* do without them—in suggesting that 'the imposition of principles on an area that doesn't need them is likely to lead to some sort of distortion' (2).

and emphasizes that these items have a pervasive scope,[3] since 'No part of life . . . can be free from duty' (1. 4).[4] The ethical vision implied seems to be one in which rules of conduct inform every aspect of our existence. How could this be a prologue to a position that would deny a role for rules?[5]

Things are not quite so straightforward. One may, for example, note the exemption granted by Cicero to exceptional individuals such as Socrates and Aristippus from acting in accordance with customs and civil codes, which Cicero insists are themselves rules (1. 148). This indicates, presumably, that the ideal moral agent is in a position to transcend rules. Cicero also contrasts the operation of laws with that of, respectively, a just and good king (2. 42) and the philosopher's reason and intelligence (3. 68). The contrast seems out of place if moral reasoning is itself supposed to consist in the application of rules. Cicero does not say explicitly that a rules-based system is inferior; but he does imply that it is not what we would get were a perfect individual in charge.

Now *De officiis* is, naturally, aimed at the imperfect: it concerns *officia—kathēkonta—*the duties or appropriate actions that all can perform, rather than the sage's proprietary right actions— *katorthōmata* (see 1. 8 with 3. 14). We are warned that those of us lacking in the 'great and divine goods' of a Socrates have no licence to follow suit when it comes to ignoring convention (1. 148). Yet Cicero bids us in the next paragraph to look up to those with 'great and honourable achievements' to their credit; and Socrates himself has been presented as a model at 1. 90, albeit for lifelong equanimity, not rule-flouting.

Evidently we should aspire to the condition of such exceptional individuals.[6] If we keep to the spirit of his implicit human/divine

---

[3] I use 'rules' and 'principles' interchangeably (and without prejudice to the distinction between *praecepta* and *decreta* explored most notably in Sen. *Ep.* 94 and 95), though a category of basic principles will play a special role in Cicero's theory.

[4] Translations of *De officiis* are taken from M. T. Griffin and E. M. Atkins (eds.), *Cicero:* On Duties (Cambridge, 1991), with occasional amendment.

[5] A further reason for initial scepticism might be Cicero's curt dismissal of the Stoic Aristo (1. 4), who we know mounted a severe attack on the utility of rules. But the basis of the dismissal (as frequently also in *De finibus*) is not Aristo's attitude to rules but that he held nothing to be of value (and so worth going after) except virtue itself. One who holds this may well see no point in concrete rules. But one who rejects it is not required, nor need be inclined, to endorse a rules-based system.

[6] Virtue is the province of the wise (3. 13), but we can make progress towards its acquisition (3. 17).

contrast, Cicero perhaps takes it as obvious that we moral children should not dispense with rules, as ordinary children should not cross busy streets unaccompanied. None the less, the state of moral adulthood, in the attainment of which we will have earned the entitlement to make our own way, is paradigmatic. So it should not be a surprise if Cicero's theoretical commitments turn out to envisage a more circumscribed place for rules than may first appear.

What could be wrong with a rules-based system? On several occasions in *De officiis* Cicero shows himself sensitive to ethical variability—the idea, at its most basic, that rules admit of exceptions, and so cannot, to that extent, be reliable guides to action.[7] For example, it may be wrong in general to kill another human being, but there will, plausibly, be circumstances when to do so is permissible or even obligatory. The particularist in ethics argues that no given description can exceptionlessly ground a prescription.[8] The fact that this was a killing—descriptive—does not in itself allow us to conclude that this was wrong—prescriptive (cf. 3. 19); the fact that this was a protecting of one's parent does not allow us to conclude, off the bat, that this was right (cf. 3. 90); and so on for any description whatsoever.

From this perspective, the particularist may find Cicero's position rather congenial. Cicero is adamant that action of a given kind may be right in some circumstances, wrong in others. Thus there are times in which actions most befitting a just individual 'alter and become the opposite [*contraria*] . . . duty alters likewise, and is not invariable [*non semper est idem*]' (1. 31).[9] Examples he gives

---

[7]  In the light of this, it might seem odd that Cicero should apparently be aiming at 'steady and stable rules' (*praecepta firma, stabilia*) at 1. 6. But the sense of this is explained by the context. Cicero is excluding philosophical schools—he evidently has Epicureanism particularly in mind—that, in his view, can make room for virtue only on pain of inconsistency with their official theory of the good (1. 5). Any moral precepts they offer will thus be unstable not because of exceptions but because the purported content would inherently be in tension with the background theory.

[8]  The precise import of the contrast here can be hard to specify, and controversial in terms of ancient ethics, which (arguably) did not deal in such distinctions. But some such contrast needs to be given for debate to get off the ground, as even critics of particularism concede: 'All we can do here is presume some reasonable conception of the distinction and note that particularists do likewise' (F. Jackson, P. Pettit, and M. Smith, 'Ethical Particularism and Patterns', in Hooker and Little (eds.), *Moral Particularism*, 79–99 at 81). Cicero's examples indicate, I think, a reasonable application to the *De officiis*.

[9]  Cf. also 3. 19: 'Often the occasion arises when something that is generally and customarily considered to be dishonourable is found not to be so.'

of things which 'from time to time it becomes just to set aside and not to observe' (ibid.) are the return of a deposit and the keeping of a promise. These examples are descriptive: one can lay down factual conditions, as it were, for something's being a return of a deposit or a keeping of a promise. If one concedes, as Cicero does, that such descriptions have variable ethical valence, then one is a potential ally of particularism.

Cicero does not draw from the examples the moral that ethics is better off without rules or principles, nor is this the only moral that can legitimately be drawn. It is a step, or a number of steps, on from recognizing that principles have exceptions to concluding that there are not really principles at all. Rules of thumb are still rules (of a kind), though presumably needing supplementation if our goal is correct action. Moreover, the examples that Cicero has mentioned might strike one as obviously too simple. A possible anti-particularist response is that exceptions be incorporated into a more complex, hopefully invariant, principle: 'Keep your promises except . . .', with the dots filled out by the circumstances in which the rule unqualified may be breached.

Cicero's response is somewhat different. What he recommends is that such principles as 'Keep your promises' be regulated by an ordered pair of basic principles of justice (*fundamenta iustitiae*): 'Harm no one' and 'Serve the common good' (1. 31).[10] And this raises the following question: do more specific principles such as 'Keep your promises' have, for Cicero, any independent normative force? Are we to keep our promises *only* to the extent that doing so harms no one, promotes the common good, or both? (I leave aside for now questions about relations, and possible conflicts, between the two basic principles.) If so, then the particularist continues to have a claim on Cicero. For what we would have here, in effect, is a system consisting of just two principles, each of which, it might be argued, is insufficiently concrete to serve as action-guiding. 'Harm no one' is negative; and 'Serve the common good' leaves the agent needing to discover what counts as serving the common good before being able to make good decisions. Perhaps, then, the quality of our ethical lives will be determined not by a set of action-guiding rules

[10] 'primum ut ne cui noceatur, deinde ut communi utilitati serviatur.' Cicero had also labelled 'faith' (*fides*) a *fundamentum iustitiae* at 1. 23, but it actually seems to be subordinate given that at 1. 31 promise-keeping and other items that pertain to faith (*quaeque pertinent . . . ad fidem*) are said to require regulation by the two principles laid out there.

but by the 'experience and practice' that, as Cicero later stresses
(1.60), is an important component in our being able to do the right
thing.

I want to suggest that this reading is, in broad outline, correct,
and that the outlook of *De officiis* tends markedly in a particularist
direction. Backing for this claim will come, firstly, from a more detailed examination of what Cicero has to say about the keeping of
promises and its relation to the basic principles (Sections II–VI).
Further support will then be offered via an investigation of the
ethical importance that the treatise allots to the character of persons or agents (Sections VII–X). According to Cicero, an agent's
individual character should play a prominent role in the determination of what counts as right or wrong action. Character differences
being potentially unlimited, a fact Cicero himself draws our attention to, we may regard general rules as having a correspondingly
questionable status in Cicero's ethical scheme.

## II

At *De officiis* 1.32 Cicero states that 'promises should not be kept
[*nec promissa . . . servanda sunt*] if they are disadvantageous to
those to whom you have made them'. The force of this statement
is noteworthy. It is not simply that promises need not be kept in
case of harm (to the promisee); they should not be. This sense is
secured by Cicero's illustrative example, in which he is evidently
privileging the counterfactual 'if Neptune had not done what he
had promised Theseus', the doing of which resulted in the death
of Theseus' son Hippolytus.[11] 'Keep your promises' apparently
lacks independent normative force here.[12] The governing criterion
is that one should do no harm.

The picture is reinforced by a later example (3.92) in which,
interestingly, a promise is rightfully breached if harm would be
done, were it kept, even to the promisor (a point I shall return
to). Cicero discusses the case of someone with a disease who is

---

[11] This is even clearer in a parallel passage at 3.94, where Cicero, as well as
repeating the Theseus tale, tells the story of Sol and his son Phaethon and exclaims:
'How much better it would have been if the father's promise had not been kept
in this case!'

[12] It may, though, be significant that the promisor in both the Theseus and the
Sol examples is a god; on the divine nature of promising see further sect. v below.

given a cure on condition he promise not to use it again should he fall ill in future. In Cicero's view the patient 'should consider his own life and safety' and use the cure again if necessary. One might give this a topical twist by imagining a drug company that licensed its treatment for a serious disease to a developing country on condition that the country only manufacture a certain quantity of the treatment. Would the country be right to manufacture a greater quantity in case of need, having promised not to do so? Given the evident harm that would result from its not doing so, Cicero would answer in the affirmative, one may plausibly infer. The fact that a promise was made appears to bear no countervailing weight.

In a world of intellectual property rights, the drug company may itself suffer harm of a financial nature from the licence being breached. Cicero implies that in these sorts of case (his actual example here is different: a lawyer who because of a sick child has to break a promise to defend a client) one is still entitled (*nec . . . contra officium est*) to break promises 'if they harm you more than they benefit the person whom you have promised' (1. 32) and, *a fortiori*, one would think, if they harm third parties more. Whatever the right way of assessing and balancing benefits and harms, it is the issue of benefit and harm that dominates. Although he does not say that one should (rather than one may) break one's promise here, Cicero's focus on the calculus reinforces the sense that assessment of harm and benefit is what matters in the determination of whether to keep a promise and, in general, how to act correctly.[13]

The example of the cure is introduced by Cicero as a response to the question whether promises not extracted by force or fraud should always be kept; and it is possible that he is making a point about coercion. If we assume that the recipient of the cure was already ill, then one might argue that the extracted promise was coerced. So the moral would be not that it is all right to break a promise, but that the promise was defective in the first place because coerced. Cicero had earlier ruled that a promise was non-binding if one is tricked into it or 'is compelled to make it through fear' (1. 32). So although it would be possible to claim that this applied to the case of the cure—fear of pain or death being the

---

[13] Cf. 1. 59: we must be 'good calculators of our duties' (*boni ratiocinatores officiorum*). Note that this is followed by the remarks on the importance of practice and experience: we do not achieve anything great by rules (*praecepta*) alone (1. 60). By implication, appeal to the basic principles will not suffice either. How much of a role this actually leaves for rules or principles is a question to be further addressed.

operative notion—the case is specifically said by Cicero not to fall under the heading of force (*nec vi*, 3. 92). Presumably he is thinking of this category as being restricted to the extraction of promises by either the use of force or the threat of force, or of harm more generally; and it would indeed be a stretch to read the non-repeat clause as being a threat of this (or any) sort. The promise, then, was not, by Cicero's lights, compelled or coerced and so is not, as such, defective. Rather, it seems that *qua* promise it did not carry normative force independent of the harm/benefit calculus.

Carrying the day thus far are the basic principles 'Harm no one' and 'Serve the common good'. Admittedly, Cicero says (3. 92) that the promise may be breached given that the supplier of the cure would be 'inhuman' in having failed to grant permission for it to be used again, the promise notwithstanding, and given that, in his version, the supplier is not suffering any injury from its reuse. Still, the inhumanity is in turn plausibly explicated as a wilful failure to serve the common good, if not an actual commission of harm, to the extent that the apparently gratuitous withholding of available medical treatment may be regarded as such.

Now since the discussion is about whether one is entitled to break one's promises, it would seem that the issue of abiding by the basic principles is one for the maker of the promise. That person should be prepared to breach the promise if harm is done by keeping it, or the common good not served. Part of the mix is that harm not be done to the promisee; but it is not that, in the case of the cure, the promise is being breached in *order* not to harm the promisee, say the supplier of the cure. Rather, in the absence of harm, or at least greater harm, to the promisee (no doubt an important constraint) what really gives the green light is that, as noted earlier, keeping the promise would harm the *promisor*. Similarly, the promisee's refusal to release the promisor from his pledge may well stand as a failure to serve the common good. But what is at stake is the *promisor's* entitlement to breach a promise for the sake of serving the common good; and the representative beneficiary in the case at hand is himself!

It is striking that avoidance of harm and promotion of benefit to the agent (as opposed to others) can serve to mandate the breach of a more specific principle such as keeping one's promise. In fact, Cicero is quite explicit about this. When spelling out the circumstances in which such principles may be set aside, he writes (1. 32):

'It can happen that something that has been promised and agreed, if carried out, would be disadvantageous to the person to whom the promise has been made, *or else to him who gave the promise*.' That is, in respecting the basic principles, the interests of the agent carry weight. For a proper assessment of the scope of these principles we now need to ask: How much weight? And how does it compare with what is owed to others?

## III

The Stoic view, on which Cicero bases much of *De officiis*,[14] is that each individual has a natural impulse for self-preservation (cf. 1. 11), and given that nature is, on this view, normative, it follows that it is legitimate to protect and promote one's own interests. One should do so with care, however. Cicero observes that

> We tend to notice and feel our own good and bad fortune more than that of others, which we see as if a great distance intervenes; accordingly, we do not make the same judgements about them and about ourselves . . . good advice . . . prevents you from doing anything if you are unsure whether it is fair. (1. 30)

He means, at a minimum, that we must not understate the condition of others relative to our own: decide, say, that we are worse off than others (and perhaps thus deserving of more) when proper reflection would show this is not the case.

Now it does not follow from one's taking an *accurate* view of one's condition that one gives any particular *weight* to that condition. I could, for example, accurately gauge that I was worse off than others but still believe that others' interests had precedence over mine. None the less, it seems reasonable to take Cicero's talk of 'the same judgements' as indicating, or perhaps presupposing, that if a person is in a certain condition, then if I judge one in that condition to be deserving of certain benefits (or whatever it may be), the judgement should be invariant as to whether the person in question is me or not. For he is talking about how to make sure one is *acting* fairly; and what he offers as a basis for fair action is that

---

[14] As he tells us at 3. 20 (cf. 1. 6). His chief individual source is Panaetius (2. 60; 3. 7). In all these places Cicero affirms that he retains the independence of judgement befitting a follower of the sceptical Academy. I shall not here consider further the question of Cicero's relation to his source material.

we judge others as we do ourselves. The default inference is surely that we then *treat* others in the same way as we would ourselves, in a given situation.

Impartiality cuts both ways for Cicero. If it is true that we need to make sure we do not privilege ourselves unduly, nor profit at another's expense (3. 21),[15] we are equally not required to sacrifice our interests for the sake of another.[16] Liberality is a virtue, but it should not result in the agent's impoverishment (2. 64). Cicero cites with approval Ennius' recommendation to the effect that one should help others so long as it is not to the detriment of oneself (1. 51–2). He offers as examples the giving of fresh water (presumably regarded as being in ample supply), fire from one's fire, and good advice. It is even 'permitted [*concessum*] . . . that each man should prefer to secure for himself rather than another anything connected with the necessities of life' (3. 22). Note the relatively weak formulation: apparently it would be permitted *not* to prefer one's own securing of the necessities; or perhaps common sense in any event dictates that it is hard to provide for others if one does not have the necessities of life oneself. Still, Cicero tells us (3. 42) that 'we are not to neglect benefits to ourselves and surrender them to others when we ourselves need them', and he broadens the thought in proceeding to commend Chrysippus' dictum that in a race we should try our best to win but not trip up our fellow competitors.

We are, then, entitled to pursue our own interest so long as we do not unfairly hamper others from doing the same. And this, one might add, is something every person could do in principle. There is something of a Kantian flavour about Cicero's stance not just here, but also in the notion that others have a claim on one just in so far as they are human, Cicero endorsing the following conditional: 'if nature prescribes that one man should want to consider the interests of another, whoever he may be, for the very reason that he is a man . . .' (3. 27). By the same token, my own humanity entitles my interests to carry weight with others to an equivalent degree, and

---

[15] Indeed, Cicero regards this latter as a 'rule of procedure' (*formula*) for deciding how to act, though he goes on to delimit it with the rather uncontentious cases of theft and violence.

[16] On the other hand, Cicero opposes the charging of high prices by a corn-dealer who neglects to mention to his customers that other dealers are on their way (3. 50–3; 3. 57). For interpretation and discussion of this case see J. Annas, 'Cicero on Stoic Moral Philosophy and Private Property', in M. T. Griffin and J. Barnes (eds.), *Philosophia Togata* (Oxford, 1989), 151–73; M. Schofield, *Saving the City* (London, 1999), 160–77; Inwood, 'Rules and Reasoning', 122–5.

entitles me to pursue those interests without undue interference,
and with whatever else may be mandated by the requirement that
my fellow humans take account of them.


## IV

If impartiality between self and other is in a clear sense to the
forefront here,[17] while offering a position that can continue to smile
on the healthy pursuit of one's own interest, there is also a strain
of altruism at work which can be admitted without affecting the
overall point. Its pithiest formulation comes at 3. 90, where Cicero
famously tackles the question of what the outcome should be if
two shipwrecked sages only have a plank large enough for one
of them. Cicero states that the plank should be given up 'to the
one whose life most matters for his own or the republic's sake'.
Now the notion that an individual should put the interests of his
country or political community ('the republic') before his own is
prevalent in *De officiis* (see e.g. 1. 83; 1. 85). For most practical
purposes (though one should obviously not regard it as an identity)
the republic stands as the entity in service of which we can take
ourselves to be fulfilling our duty to serve the common good, this
being, we may recall, one of the basic principles. But that does not
necessarily affect the question of how my interests weigh relative
to those of other individuals. One can consistently maintain that
each individual should be prepared to put the common good before
their own good, but that their own good has a claim equal to that
of other individuals.

Cicero in fact allows that in pursuit of the common good one
may harm the interests of another (3. 30–2); but his example of the
recipient of harm, 'Phalaris, a cruel and monstrous tyrant' (3. 29),
suggests that an individual who has damaged the common good can
*forfeit* a claim to equal treatment, not that one can override the interests of other (blameless) individuals for the sake of the common
good.[18] A similarly restrictive moral is drawn from a later example:

[17] I leave aside the question, of some interest to Cicero, of differential duties:
those 'owed to one group of people rather than to another' (1. 59)—family or friends,
for example. This introduces complications about how to characterize 'other', but
does not undermine the basic thought that one should not give special treatment
(positive or negative) to oneself.
[18] The case of Collatinus, removed from office by his fellow consul Brutus, is also

one should not return money deposited by someone who subsequently makes war on one's country (3. 95). It is also permitted to save one's own life by taking goods from another if one's continuing to live would serve the common good (3. 30), where the other is 'an inactive and useless person' (3. 31). But there is no general rule that a greater capacity to serve the common good entitles one to a greater claim than, or on, others.

Cicero is mostly rather conservative about private property rights, and indeed in an initial formulation of the principles of justice (1. 20), after 'Harm no one' (except a wrongdoer) we are given: 'Treat common goods as common and private ones as one's own.' In the discussion of promises the second principle appears merely as 'Serve the common good', as we have seen. The question of how to weigh private and public interest is a sensitive one for any social theorist. Cicero has gone on to make it clear that there are important limits to the extent to which one can use the goods of individuals to further a common good. Perhaps this explains why 'Harm no one' is ranked first in both places (cf. *primum . . . deinde*, 1. 20; 1. 31), with the mention of the status of private goods even in the second principle (as initially formulated) making it explicit that there is a careful balance to be struck.

It is, then, to save a life (which may be one's own), where doing so would enhance the common good, that one is entitled to appropriate another's goods.[19] Cicero gives no indication that one may thereby deprive the *other* party of life to save that of the common benefactor, or that goods may be transferred from one to another just because they would be better used in the hands of the latter for furthering the common good. And only in a situation, such as the shipwreck, where someone has to die does greater capacity to benefit the community function as a tie-breaker.

So we yield the plank to the one who can best serve the common

approved of by Cicero as a benefit to the republic, apparently on the grounds of Collatinus' family connection with the deposed monarchy (3. 40). The limiting of the exemption clause to the need to deal with tyranny is thus maintained, albeit tenuously.

[19] And not in every case in which appropriation would serve the common good, as Tad Brennan erroneously infers in *The Stoic Life* (Oxford, 2005): 'A is justified in confiscating B's property for the sake of the common welfare' (208). Cicero's example is carefully confined to saving the life of the benefactor (3. 30; 3. 31). He does assert that it is unjust to neglect the common good (3. 30); but this is to breach the second of the two principles of justice, the first being to harm no one.

good—though without a corresponding right to commandeer the plank, even sage from non-sage (3. 89). But why also defer to the other, as Cicero says we ought, merely because his life is more important to him than mine is to me? If we accept that this kind of differential may exist and can be ascertained, then it seems to me that impartiality is being upheld by Cicero's rule. A third party, forced to choose who lives in these circumstances, and with other things being equal, would surely be rationally compelled to choose the one who cared more about living. (The example now concerns sages, who are thus perfectly rational themselves.) As for the one who cared less, it is no doubt right to call altruistic his ceding of the plank to the other, since one assumes his life has *some* value to him. But there is no asymmetry, since he would have been entitled to claim the plank, and the other obliged to cede it, if instead he had been the one who cared more.


# V

We can see that the basic principles of justice are hardly intended to exclude the agent's own interests from consideration. I may break a promise if keeping it would harm me, so long as others would be harmed less or not be harmed by my breaking it (as we are to take it applies in the case of the cure). The weight given to the agent's interest in such circumstances is a bold and perhaps contentious element in the operation of the basic principles that Cicero establishes. But it does no more than round out a picture in which we have seen little evidence of more specific principles having normative force independent of the basic ones. As Cicero declares at 3. 96: 'To keep promises, to stand by agreements, and to return deposits become no longer honourable, if what is beneficial changes.' However, there is evidence yet to consider, and it suggests that specific principles do retain a degree of independence. Sticking to our core example, we can discern Cicero at times working with the idea that something may have normative weight just in virtue of its being a promise.

This is most evident in the case of the consul Regulus, whom Cicero discusses at 3. 99 ff. Regulus, a prisoner of war in Carthage, is sent back to Rome to negotiate the release of enemy prisoners held there, having promised to return to captivity if the release of the prisoners were not secured. At Rome, Regulus argues successfully *against* the release of the prisoners, as being useful to the enemy, and duly returns to captivity. Should he have done so? Cicero is clear that it would have been wrong for Regulus to break his promise to the enemy, and the question is why.

Cicero imagines a number of objections to Regulus' decision, including a cluster reacting to the idea that one who swears in god's name (as we presume was the case with Regulus) will incur god's wrath if the oath is breached. The objector wonders if god is in the business of being wrathful, and even if so, how a wrathful god could have harmed Regulus more than he harmed himself in returning to certain (and rather unpleasant) death (3. 102). Cicero responds by *conceding* that god is not in the business of getting angry. None the less, 'a sworn oath is a religious affirmation; and if you have promised something by affirmation with the god as witness you must hold to it . . . anyone who violates a sworn oath violates Faith'—and Faith, Cicero reminds his readers, occupies a shrine on the Capitol next to the temple of Jupiter (3. 104).

What should deter one from breaking an oath, then, is not that one will incur god's wrath by so doing, but just the very fact that it will be a breach of faith. We would not these days necessarily try to capture what I take Cicero to be after here by appeal to divinity, but this should not lead us to miss the fact that divinity is being used to represent the idea that to make a promise is an act of binding oneself to do what one has promised. It is precisely not because of divine consequences—there are none—that promises bind. Rather, in putting oneself before the divine, one thereby enters the realm of the normative. A promise binds not because of what will or will not flow from it, but because of the kind of act it is.

Promises, Cicero acknowledges, are as such binding. But it must be admitted that the binding is not wound very tight. For to acknowledge this is really no more than to recognize that there is such a thing as promising. If one were dealing with something unconnected with the idea of imposing a distinct element of obligation on an agent, it would not qualify, whatever else it might be, as a promise. One can of course say this without holding that the obligation imposed by making a promise is indefeasible.

On the other hand, Cicero's description of the divine bonds of promising is rhetorically rather intense. Perhaps we should take him to be attributing a correspondingly robust moral weight to the very act of promising. And yet, the question remains: does the rhetoric signify or amount to a softening of the position that the calculus of benefit and harm determines whether a promise should be kept or broken? It is not clear to me that it does. The case of Regulus, however rhetorically stirring, is far from decisive, in part because Cicero presents his decision as one that, if anything, benefited the republic (3. 101). Although it is not quite the same as saying that keeping his promise did this, Cicero at least emphasizes how Regulus, once back in Rome, was intent on preventing the return of the captives in the interests of his country. Cicero elides the utility-maximizing possibility of both Regulus and the captives staying put in Rome, which would have thrown into high relief the issue of conflict between keeping a promise and serving the republic. He presents Regulus as believing that it would damage his country if the captives were returned and he stayed, and as proceeding on that basis (3. 110). Cicero is even prepared to argue, on the grounds that pain is not a genuine evil, that Regulus brought no harm on himself by returning to Carthage (3. 105).

Regulus' sticking to his promise, and the serving of the common good, are treated as pulling in the same direction. And that the common good was served is presented, in effect, as a point in favour of his doing what he had promised. For all the rhetoric about the divine nature of promising, then, it seems to me that Cicero's overall position, on the balance of the evidence in *De officiis*, is the following: that a promise was made is a reason to do what was promised; but if to do what was promised would cause harm or go against the common good, that is sufficient reason to break the promise. So 'Keep your promises' has strictly limited normative independence, just enough to retain the idea that we are still talking about promises at all. One must always consider if keeping a promise would breach the duties to do no harm and serve the common good. If so, the promise should be broken. If not, but only if not, it should be kept.[20]

---

[20] Hence it is a mistake to speak, with Martha Nussbaum, of Cicero's 'insistence that all promises be preserved' ('Duties of Justice, Duties of Material Aid: Cicero's Problematic Legacy' ['Duties of Justice'], *Journal of Political Philosophy*, 8 (2000), 176–206 at 185). *Pace* Nussbaum, who focuses exclusively on the Regulus case, promise-keeping is an area in which Cicero is no Kantian.

## VI

And this, I take it, provides considerable comfort to the particularist who would claim Cicero as ally. True, a thoroughgoing particularist, intolerant of invariance, may want to claim, with suitably ingenious examples, that something's being a promise is not always even *a* reason to do it.[21] Here, I think, Cicero would disagree. But this verges on being a distinction without a difference, in that promise-keeping does not thereby gain any practical independent weight; it is not able to break through to the top level—the level of action—on its own. The Ciceronian agent is instead called upon to abide by principles that, despite the filling out that Cicero provides, are not themselves specific enough to be action-guiding. So in making decisions the Ciceronian will resemble the particularist more than the generalist. The generalist must operate with principles that are sharp enough, in virtue of their content, to enable the agent to identify what actions would serve to meet them. Once one knows, say, that one ought to keep one's promises, there is no real extra work to be done in being able to tell that doing this would be a promise-keeping, doing that a promise-breaking.

Particularists, by contrast, have as such no principles to draw on to enable them to home in on the correct action. The Ciceronian deliberator is in much the same boat. From a Ciceronian perspective, if one tries to sharpen the basic principles to get a set concrete enough to enable straightforward identification of particular cases, sharpness is bought at the cost of variable ethical valence—promises should sometimes be broken, and so on—and thus of rules which fail to be action-guiding for that reason. One must return on each occasion to the basic principles, none the wiser thereby as to what constitutes adherence to them. This aspect is reflected in the debate over the corn-dealer (n. 16 above) that Cicero stages between the two Stoic scholarchs Antipater and Diogenes of Babylon. Each is said to acknowledge the fundamental Stoic principle that there is a common fellowship between human beings (3. 53), but disagree over what this entails in the particular case.[22] It is not that Cicero

---

[21] Strictly speaking, a particularist can accept reasons of invariant polarity so long as this feature is regarded as a contingent fact and not a reflection of the logical structure of such reasons (Dancy, *Ethics without Principles*, 77–8).

[22] I am not sure that Inwood is right to infer here that 'Stoics can legitimately disagree on the application of principles which they share' ('Rules and Reasoning',

thinks there is no right answer (he sides firmly with Antipater's view that the dealer should not raise his prices, 3. 57); but the principle itself, as the debate indicates, cannot tell you what it is.[23]

Ethical success may thus have to depend on what Dancy has called 'a skill of discernment',[24] a sentiment with which Cicero would be in substantial accord, to judge by his use of perceptual verbs and his emphasis on particulars in describing, early in the treatise (1. 16), wisdom and prudence as exemplified by one who 'best perceives what is most true in each individual thing and who can most acutely and swiftly both see and explain the reason'.[25] Cicero's declaration is readily accounted for on the interpretation I have been advancing.[26] Ciceronian basic principles tell one what has to be true of an action for it to count as ethically successful, but do not help one, other than as bare starting-points, to achieve that success. What gets the Ciceronian from there to the right decision will not be the following of a principle.

I do not mean to suggest that whenever we require something other than rote consultation of a principle to get things right we are on a particularist path. That would be to caricature non-particularist ethics. Leaving aside issues of conflict between principles, one could presumably conjure up examples in which, say, deciding what would count as a keeping of one's promise required some deliberation—the same might go for any case in which the issue is the meeting of a certain standard. It is, rather, a point about determinacy. Tell a competent agent to keep his promises, and we want to say that the agent will be well placed, in virtue of having

123). At any rate, the mere fact of the disagreement cannot show this; there can be a definite right answer without consultation of the principle being able to provide it.

[23] Inwood ('Rules and Reasoning', 124) suggests that Cicero goes about settling the case by appeal to the rule of procedure (*formula*) earlier established to the effect that one must not profit at another's expense. Yet any back-reference to that is inexplicit and less prominent than Cicero's insistence that the dealer's behaviour manifests an unsavoury character (note the catalogue of pejorative adjectives towards the end of 3. 57)—a matter of judgement rather than rule.

[24] *Ethics without Principles*, 143.

[25] 'maxime perspicit quid in re quaque verissimum sit quique acutissime et celerrime potest et videre et explicare rationem.' Reasons are of course no less the province of particularists than of anyone else, particularism being largely a theory about reasons which claims that there need be nothing about a feature counting as a reason to do something in one context that means its presence will so count (or will not count against) in another.

[26] We are, for example, supposed to 'see' (cf. 'quis non videt?') that the corn-dealer who raised his prices would be a bad sort (3. 57).

that maxim, to know what to do to fulfil it. Tell the same agent to go out into the world and serve the common good, and possession of the maxim hardly seems to equip an agent for ethical success at all, even on its own terms—not because the maxim is wrong (though it might be) or complicated (it is not), but because it simply lacks the sort of determinate content that could do more. Principles of this sort play a categorically thin role.

Not that it will always fail to be obvious what counts as serving the common good. A potentate deciding whether to allocate the latest oil revenues either to the building of a new palace for himself or to the improvement of his country's rickety water supply could not, without considerable self-deception, choose other than the latter, and will choose it without hesitation if his aim is to serve the common good. But this sort of case, which works in part by ignoring other possible welfare needs, will be an exception, and not contingently so, a fact derived from the principle's lack of determinacy. What the indeterminacy gives is a corresponding generality: 'serve the common good' offers a matrix that might subsume any circumstance whatsoever in a way that a more determinate principle such as 'keep your promises' cannot aspire to. But then we are confronted with the world of scarce resources and competing demands, the world, therefore, of hard choices however sincerely devoted one may be to upholding the principle at hand. It is for just such a world that this type of principle is supposed to have its salience in the first place.

So we are committed to good judgement playing the kind of decisive role in right action that Cicero's scheme implies, whether basic or more determinate principles are in play. Though not yet equivalent to a particularist position, given that the basic principles retain an independent status (which we shall see come under pressure below), Cicero's theory none the less pictures systemic weakness where principles are concerned. Those that are general enough to avoid at least immediate problems of variable valence fail to be action-guiding because of their indeterminacy. Those that are specific enough to be, on that score, action-guiding fall at the hurdle of variable valence.[27]

---

[27] I have appealed to determinacy to generate the question about valence, rather than a contrast between prescriptive and descriptive as such. There is, however, a fairly tight connection. In speaking of what is good or right, we eliminate variable valence by using terms that necessarily commend at the cost of the descriptive

It is, moreover, doubtful whether even the 'easy' cases are properly characterized as ones where rule-following gets us to correct
decisions. For it seems a feature of such cases that one finds it correspondingly unproblematic to discern, without further specification
to provide guidance, what counts, in full generality, as doing the
right thing.[28] The limitedly specific content of 'serve the common
good' is not called upon to play an informative role. Too indeterminate to resolve complexity, it is now beset from, so to speak, the
other side, as unnecessarily specific. It is not that we need just that
maxim, or any of equal (let alone greater) determinacy, to enable
us to see what constitutes the right option between, say, palace and
water supply. If we do not already see it, one is tempted to say that
no amount of maxim-giving will help. But then with regard to such
cases, on pain of vacuity, we are no longer operating with a rules-
based ethic. What I have tried to argue thus far is that the overall
structure of Cicero's theory lends itself to a similar conclusion.


## VII

In the remainder of this paper I want to pursue the idea that the
viewpoint of *De officiis* has much to commend it to the particularist by exploring the question of variable ethical valence from a
somewhat different angle. The ethics of the treatise is virtue-based
in the sense that it derives our ethical obligations by considering
what actions count as expressions of the virtues. Our obligations, as
Cicero puts it, 'have their origin' (*nascuntur*) in the virtues (1. 15).[29]
Four broad categories of virtue are laid down, the two most significant for our purposes being that of social virtue, subdivided into

---

specificity required for action guidance. In speaking of what is e.g. a promise-
keeping, we introduce a determinacy of description sufficient to guide action at the
cost of variable valence. 'Serve the common good' retains a level of determinacy that
could allow one to take issue with it; but it is not accidental that what makes it at
the same time only limitedly action-guiding is its proximity to a simple injunction
to do good.

[28] Again this seems borne out by the corn-dealer scenario, Cicero's rhetorical
question (cf. n. 26 above) suggesting that no one could fail to see that raising the
price would be wrong. Cicero has somewhat dizzyingly managed to turn what began
as a case over which even experts might clash into an apparently straightforward
matter; either way, it is not the following of a rule that leads to the answer.

[29] Cf. 2. 1: 'Duties are based on [*ducerentur ab*] what is honourable and on every
type of virtue.'

justice and liberality (1. 20), and that of what Cicero terms 'order and limit' (1. 15), which includes most prominently the virtue of 'seemliness' (*decorum*).

Justice Cicero calls 'mistress and queen of virtues' (2. 28),[30] and we have spent some time examining the role of his two basic principles of justice, with the status of justice seeming to entitle us to regard the principles as holding sway over others across the ethical board. But justice turns out to have a rival for the crown in seemliness;[31] and seemliness in turn importantly embodies the idea of being true to oneself or one's nature. It represents in this aspect what we might call a notion of integrity, and one can therefore ask what ethical weight Cicero places on that notion. If being true to oneself does have a certain ethical weight, one can then ask to what extent the ethical valence of an action may vary with the character of the agent. Might it be the case that what would be right if done by a person of one sort of character would be wrong if done by a person of another sort?

The answer, we may think, is not an obvious yes. It seems unlikely, for example, that a source of the variable valence of promise-keeping could lie in the character of the agent, such that it would be right for one kind of character to keep promises, a different kind not to.[32] But let us keep an open mind pending a review of Cicero's position, and turn to a type of case that is of great importance to him, what one might call life decisions.

Consider military service. One might take the view that everyone ought to serve in the military (assuming presumably a certain age range, physical and mental ability, and so on). Or one might take the contrary view, that no one ought to serve. One might also quite sensibly think that certain types of character ought to serve, and certain types ought not. The question 'Is it right or wrong to serve

---

[30] For discussion of the status of justice (from a perspective rather different from mine), see E. M. Atkins, '*Domina et regina virtutum*: Justice and *Societas* in *De officiis*', *Phronesis*, 35 (1990), 258–89.

[31] Cf. 1. 94: seemliness is not just one part of virtue but manifests itself in all the parts; the seemly and the honourable are coextensive.

[32] Examples are not out of reach, however. We might be inclined to indulge the promise-breaking of a flighty person who tends to rush into commitments more than that of a sober type who incurs obligations only after careful weighing. Cicero makes a comparable point, to somewhat different effect, at 1. 49: favours granted on impulse should not weigh as heavily, from the point of view of our obligation to return them, as those given with thought.

in the military?' cannot be answered comprehensively, on this view, without reference to character.

Now this need not be a question simply of *competence*. It is plausible that some types of character tend to make good (competent) soldiers, others not. Human beings, though, can be resourceful and resilient to an amazing degree: often one can perfectly successfully perform that which is quite alien to one's temperament, values, or beliefs. It then becomes a question of integrity. One can argue that the truth of the statement 'This isn't me' may be part of what legitimizes an agent's decision not to do something—serve in the military, for example; and the truth of the statement 'This is me' be part of what legitimizes a contrary decision.[33] Integrity may have significant ethical weight, such that the rightness or wrongness of decision and action is sensitive to how what is being proposed fits or fails to fit with the agent's character.

## VIII

I shall argue that this view, or something like it, can be gleaned from Cicero's exposition in *De officiis*. In the course of his discussion of seemliness he remarks that nature has given human beings two roles (*personae*):[34] 'One is common, arising from the fact that we all have a share in reason . . . The other . . . is that assigned specifically to individuals [*proprie singulis*]' (1. 107). He goes on to note that just as there are great bodily differences between individuals, so too there are great differences in character. Running through a list of notables, he observes that some were jolly, others serious, some cunning, others straightforward, some affable, others haughty, and so on (1. 108–9).

[33] This can be regarded as an aspect of a larger debate about whether differences in agent identity can morally legitimize contrary responses to a given situation. For a suggestive defence, see P. Winch, 'The Universalizability of Moral Judgements', in id., *Ethics and Action* (London, 1972), 151–70.

[34] A third and fourth role are added at 1. 115: that arising from circumstance and from our will respectively. For a useful discussion of the theory and its ethical implications see C. Gill, 'Personhood and Personality: The Four-*Personae* Theory in Cicero, *De officiis* I', *Oxford Studies in Ancient Philosophy*, 6 (1988), 169–99. See also A. A. Long, *Stoic Studies* (Cambridge, 1996), 164–7; Inwood, 'Rules and Reasoning', 125–6; M. Forschner, 'Le Portique et le concept de personne', in G. Romeyer Dherbey and J.-B. Gourinat (eds.), *Les Stoïciens* (Paris, 2005), 293–317 at 298–306; G. Reydams-Schils, *The Roman Stoics* (Chicago, 2005), 93–7; R. Sorabji, *Self* (Oxford, 2006), 158–60.

Cicero concludes that 'Each person should hold on to what is his as far as it is not vicious, but is peculiar [*propria*] to him, so that the seemliness that we are seeking might more easily be maintained' (1. 110). Clearly our common role takes precedence. Character cannot be used to justify vicious behaviour. At the same time, seemliness is itself a virtue, and one way to manifest it, Cicero has just told us, is to act in accordance with our particular character. So he recognizes that there are actions whose ethical valence, in particular whose wrongness, is insensitive to the character of the agent. At the same time, he implies that there are cases in which to act with integrity—to hold on to what is ours—is itself a factor that contributes to making an action virtuous, with the corresponding possibility that failing to do so may detract from an action's virtue. The virtuousness of an action, that is, can be sensitive to its fit with the agent's character.

Matters are pushed further when Cicero turns to the example of Cato, who having been part of the losing side against Julius Caesar killed himself rather than accept Caesar's pardon. He says (1. 112):

Surely the case of Marcus Cato was different from that of the others who gave themselves up to Caesar in Africa. Indeed it would perhaps have been counted as a fault if they had killed themselves, for the very reason that they had been more gentle in their lives . . . But since nature had assigned to Cato an extraordinary seriousness . . . he had to die rather than look upon the face of a tyrant.

Cato had to die: his character required it. His companions would, if anything, have been at fault had they pursued the same course, since they were more gentle and lacked Cato's ferocious earnestness. Here we have presented with some vividness the thesis that variance in character can determine the ethical valence of an action. When Cicero speaks of the companions' gentleness as expressed in their lives, this is no doubt supposed to communicate the idea that their gentleness was a firm trait. Cato was right to kill himself because of the way it matched his character, the others would quite possibly have been wrong because it failed to fit with theirs.

One can extend the thought without betraying the spirit of Cicero's remarks. What applies to the killing of oneself might apply also to the killing of others. The type of case brought to philosophical prominence, with regard to agent integrity, by Bernard Williams can be considered under the rubric presented by Cicero.

Is it right to kill one innocent person to save the lives of many innocent others?[35] One can only speculate about what Cicero's answer would have been, though, as we have seen, he is generally averse to sanctioning the harm of an individual for a (perceived) greater good.[36] But the structure of his view certainly allows us to grant that integrity may be a factor in determining the correct answer. Indeed, one moral of the Williams case is, I think, that integrity cuts both ways. An agent for whom the idea of killing an innocent human being (even) in these circumstances was repugnant may be right not to do so. An agent who possesses the character to, as it were, live with such an action may be permitted, or even obliged, to perform the killing. We do not have to declare in advance that, say, only one who refrained from the killing would be doing the right thing, or in possession of good character. One might regard preparedness to go through with the killing as a manifestation of good character, at least of a certain sort—the more so, perhaps, as one increases the number of lives that would be saved.

## IX

How important is integrity in Cicero's ethical scheme? Previously, we have seen him work with the idea that the two basic principles of justice are in control. Nothing that breaches either of those ought to be done. How does seemliness, the kind that Cicero at one point calls being 'constant to ourselves' (*constare . . . nobismet ipsis*, 1. 119), line up? One can easily imagine Cato's decision to kill himself as damaging the common good. Cicero does not assess the case from that perspective, so we cannot infer from it that integrity trumps justice on his view.

There are, however, cases he presents in which he commends a decision that apparently goes against the common good. Thus he approves the consul Fabricius' decision not to accept an enemy deserter's proposal to poison, for a fee, the enemy king. Cicero has a tendency, here and elsewhere, to head off awkward questions by claiming that anything dishonourable is thereby not beneficial. He

---

[35] I refer to the famous thought-experiment involving Jim and the captives discussed in J. J. C. Smart and B. Williams, *Utilitarianism: For and Against* (Cambridge, 1973), 93–117.

[36] Cf. also 2. 51, in which the hounding of an innocent person through the courts is decisively ruled out. Scapegoating would have no place in Cicero's theory.

does, though, admit that 'if we are looking for the appearance of benefit [*speciem utilitatis*]', a serious foe of Rome might have been dispensed with at a stroke, but adds that to accept the deserter's offer 'would have been a great disgrace and an outrage' (3. 86), and we may take the sternness of the language to indicate that this alone should have sufficed for rejection.

Does this mean that for Cicero integrity can trump justice? His association of common benefit with benefit to one's country can render the issue rather blurry. So if we do not want to squeeze a surreptitious poisoning into the category of justice, we can at least ask whether integrity is capable of trumping utility. We cannot push Cicero too hard here since he refuses even in these terms to admit that there is a genuine conflict in the Fabricius case—only the 'appearance' of benefit. None the less, we should probably answer in the affirmative. At any rate, he states explicitly that 'some things are so disgraceful . . . that a wise man would not do them even to protect his country' (1. 159). This does imply that an action could be disgraceful and still worth doing for the sake of the common weal. Cicero gives a later example of an otherwise dishonourable act that would be justified for the sake of the republic—dancing in the forum (3. 93), whose register is a little hard to gauge. To judge by his remarks on the presumably equal offence of singing in the forum (1. 145), we are dealing with grave impropriety, though one imagines this leaves a degree of space for more heinous acts which utility would not suffice to condone.

But there is a deeper problem about cases such as that of Fabricius. The integrity we are talking about clearly falls into the general rather than specific category. The idea is that it would simply not be worthy of a human being to accept the deserter's offer. And this is perilously close to the tautology that no human ought to do what no human ought to do. It is only when we have moved under the radar, so to speak, to cases where we cannot say, just given a description of the action, whether it would be unworthy or not, that questions of conflict arise. The Cato- and Williams-type cases are of this kind and, not coincidentally, are cases in which specific integrity is at issue.

The scope of Cicero's radar is narrower than the Fabricius case may suggest. One of the things that enables Cicero to fulminate unreservedly against the idea of accepting the deserter's offer is, presumably, the thought that acceptance is unjustified regardless of the accepter's character. In similar vein, he is able to offer whole-hearted approval of the Athenian assembly's rejection of Themis-tocles' proposal to torch the Spartan fleet in secret (3. 49). Yet when he is focusing on specific integrity, a different picture emerges. In the pageant of notables, Themistocles features as a representative of the crafty and cunning sort, along with such stalwarts as Hanni-bal and Solon (1. 108). And the purpose of the pageant is to help suggest that the virtue of acting in character is sustainable across a broad spectrum of character types, as Cicero concludes with a flourish: 'There are countless other dissimilarities of nature and conduct, which do not in the least deserve censure' (1. 109).

One guesses that Cicero's own preference leans markedly towards the straightforward types, given his attitude towards Fabricius' de-cision and Themistocles' proposal, and given the lengthy negative discussion of concealment and pretence at 3. 50–74. But this should not blot out the pageantry, nor lead us to posit inconsistency with the theory of seemliness as concerns an agent's character. The bulk of the cases treated in the book 3 discussion are those in which the agent is out for monetary gain, which Cicero might reasonably feel introduces no tension with a theory whose aim is evidently not to license in blanket fashion any action that happens to accord with its agent's character. Moreover, it is interesting to note that Cicero does not condemn Themistocles as agent of the slippery proposal; he commends the Athenians for their rejection of it (cf. 'melius hi quam nos', 3. 49), a subtle but significant difference. If the underhandedness of Themistocles might have inclined Cicero to condemn him outright, the theory he has laid out gives pause. Its point is not the downbeat one that Themistocles' proposal is all we would expect from someone of that sort. It is that Themistocles *ought* to be making this kind of proposal, given the character he is. Even if the assembly finds it, all things considered, unacceptable, Themistocles is doing right by them in having brought it forward. One might even hazard, to pick up an earlier theme, that breach of promise could serve as part of any cunning operator's full arsenal, an arsenal that may include, as Cicero is happy to relate of that doughty general Quintus Maximus, the ability 'to conceal, or to keep silent, to dissemble, to lay traps' (1. 108). Let the straightfor-ward types make their own proposals.

# X

Cicero, then, is in a position to allow quite a generous range of cases in which the ethical valence of an action may be sensitive to differences in the character of the agent. But seemliness as manifested in particular actions and decisions is if anything its lesser aspect for him. He writes: 'Just as in each specific thing that we do we seek what is seemly according to what and how each of us has been born . . . we must exercise much more care when establishing our whole way of life' (1. 119). The question of what kind of life to live is ethically central. Cicero recognizes the possibility of a person having 'made a mistake in choosing his type of life. If that happens . . . he ought to change his behaviour and his plans' (1. 120).

Remarks like these throw up some fruitful tensions with regard to the ethical weight to be placed on integrity. Cicero inherits, ultimately from Plato and Aristotle, a keen debate about whether a life devoted to intellectual pursuits or one dedicated to practical activity, in particular public service, is the more worthy. Cicero has a strong inclination to favour the latter: 'It is . . . contrary to duty to be drawn by such a devotion [to learning] away from practical achievements' (1. 19), and 'the achievements which are greatest . . . are those of the men who rule the republic' (1. 92). There is a poignant autobiographical element, as the era of republican government fades at Rome: 'I pursue leisure because I am barred from public life' (3. 1).

Public service is the noblest career; but a person should make sure to have 'adopted a plan of life entirely in accordance with his nature' (1. 120). What if one's nature is unsuited to a life on the public stage? Cicero is willing to concede that there are those who are not fitted for the public arena, and therefore need not participate (1. 121); and his criticism of reluctance to enter that arena is confined to 'those who are equipped by nature to administer affairs' (1. 72).

Now this may seem no more than common sense, but such a reaction is too quick. One need only think of societies in which, say, martial virtues predominated (Sparta springs immediately to mind). Cicero is no radical, and shows little interest in the status of women, for example. But he takes himself to be opposing the views of most in denying that military affairs are of greater importance than civic (1. 74);[37] and he is ready to insist that virtue can be displayed even by those who do not participate in public life (1. 121). The notion that the field of virtue need not be restricted to a set of activities that many may not be especially suited (even if eligible) for is not one to be taken for granted.

We have not, though, got to the crux of the issue where integrity is concerned. What if one is able well enough to do a job one is totally out of sympathy with? Battle is joined if we add the assumption that one would be enhancing general utility in doing the job. Cicero, I think, does not pose the question so starkly. None the less, there are indications that he believes integrity can come apart from serving the common good, even to the extent of being able to defeat it in a decision about which path one should follow.

Part of the way Cicero conceives of seemliness is as having normative force independent of questions of utility. He bids us to 'follow our own nature . . . even if other pursuits may be weightier and better' (1. 110). This surely implies, in principle, that it might be legitimate to pursue a course that would benefit the common good less if it meant being truer to oneself. Cicero goes on to advise against pursuing what one cannot attain, so perhaps sheer competence is still in the foreground and with it the idea that acting against one's nature harms patients no less than the agent. And yet Cicero, so fond in general of asserting that the honourable and the beneficial go hand in hand, does not choose to press this line when discussing seemliness.

The latter in fact is treated as quite autonomous, and as concerned with the state of the agent, not the agent's effects on the world. Even when it would have been rather easier than in some of his examples to make a case for a connection between the honourable and the beneficial, he refrains from doing so. Thus in speaking of occasions on which we are 'pushed . . . beyond our natural talents' (1. 114), where there must be an obvious danger of just doing damage, Cicero simply bids us try as best we can to avoid unseemliness. There is certainly a strong external component, but one that remains centred on the agent. Cicero notes at 1. 111 that unseemliness is liable to 'draw well-justified ridicule upon ourselves'. The problem is the way the agent is affected, not those whom he may be trying to serve.

Though not directly concerning benefit to others, a similar moral

[37] Doubtless there is an element of self-serving here, unmistakable in the boasting of 1. 77–8.

is applicable to the contrast that Cicero draws between Odysseus and Ajax (1. 113). Odysseus had the stomach for slights and humiliations undergone to achieve his ultimate goal; Ajax, that proud spirit, would rather have died a thousand deaths than submit to such indignities. Judged by outcome, Odysseus will presumably be the more successful. But results may have to take a back seat when integrity is at issue. Cicero concludes not that one figure rather than the other is to be emulated, but that one should be oneself.

In keeping with this approach, Cicero makes the intriguing remark that 'assuming a role that we want ourselves is something that proceeds from our own will', and he uses this to explain why some choose philosophy, others law or oratory, and even why different people select different virtues to excel in (1. 115). Although the kind of role that is just a matter of our will (or wish, *voluntas*) is only the fourth (out of four) in order, Cicero makes no claim that our choice must line up with contribution to the common benefit, or that the pursuits from which we may choose, though they must doubtless all be worthy (as his examples indicate), need rank equally in this regard.

This had already been confirmed in Cicero's discussion of 'greatness of spirit' (*magnitudo animi*), before the official treatment of seemliness. Cicero permits someone of 'outstanding ability' to choose study over public life (1. 71), despite affirming that those in public service 'lead lives more profitable to mankind' (1. 70), only much later giving thinkers their due as benefactors of humanity (1. 155–6).[38] Interestingly, he speaks of those 'who have adapted themselves' ('qui se . . . accommodaverunt', 1. 70) to achievement on the public stage, as if to acknowledge that the performance may require some sacrifice of integrity, confronted as one is with 'the behaviour of the populace or its leaders' that a number of worthy individuals have been unable to endure (1. 69). The tone is that of one who, without necessarily sharing it, can identify imaginatively enough with the dilemma. Fear of the disrepute engendered by failure is a bad reason for steering clear of the public arena (1. 71); desire for one's freedom (*libertas*) is not (1. 70). Cicero is to be sure unequivocal at 1. 72 that those equipped to do so should participate

[38] As we saw, Cicero had initially declared bluntly that it was 'contrary to duty' to let intellectual pursuits pull one away from public business (1. 19). The sequence reflects a more general broadening of viewpoint as Cicero takes the range of virtues into account.

in public life. Yet it would be odd if he had intended the much more nuanced previous paragraphs to be cancelled out by this sentiment. They appear to leave room, in advance of the forces of seemliness, for the view that, though the decision will be a delicate one, integrity is capable of outranking service to the common good.[39]

What I hope to have shown is that there is a strand in Cicero's thinking that recognizes integrity as having independent normative force, and that this is largely based on the idea of being true to one's individual character. Cicero declares that differences in character between individuals are greater than their already 'enormous bodily differences' (1. 107). We might say that the potential variation is unlimited—Cicero calls the differences 'countless' (*innumerabiles*) at 1. 109—and that correspondingly so will be the permutations in character that might make a difference as to whether a given action would be out of step or not. If the agent's character is indeed an ethically significant factor in determining what counts as the right thing to do, then the prospect of constructing general principles of conduct looks, from this point of view, futile.[40]

## XI

Was Cicero, then, a particularist? On the weight of the evidence examined here, it is fair to conclude that in several key areas his sympathies flow in that direction. A Ciceronian agent who strives to serve the common good will not, as we have seen, be able to do so by following rules. The goal of serving the common good is in

[39] Nussbaum ('Duties of Justice', 195) offers a reading of this material that strikes me as too one-sided when concluding that, with the exception of the sick, the philosophically gifted, and so forth, it is in Cicero's view 'wrong to pursue a life that does not involve service to others though political action . . . Clearly he means to blame people who will not serve their own nation.' Nussbaum is right to regard Cicero's earlier remarks at 1. 28–9, when he is elaborating justice, as a reproach to those who consider that refraining from the commission of injustice suffices to make one fully just—as if, so to speak, only the first of the basic principles were in force. The question of what are the criteria for justice is, however, distinct from the question whether considerations of justice must always prevail.

[40] One might offer a principle such as 'Only act in ways consistent with one's character', but this would resemble 'Serve the common good' in being insufficiently concrete to be action-guiding. What would be needed are rules spelling out, for any permutation of character, what counted as appropriate action. The matter seems ripe for attention to the particulars of a given case, rather than the application of a rule book. Cicero stresses the need to be a 'keen judge' ('acrem . . . iudicem') of one's own character as the basis for correct choices (1. 114).

turn answerable to the demand that integrity be upheld. A theorist who attempted to construct rules of action without reference to the character of the agent would, from Cicero's point of view, have missed something important that is not presented as rectifiable in terms of rules. In these ways, *De officiis* lays down serious challenges to a rules-based ethic. If not a particularist treatise, it provides early ammunition in the particularist cause.

*King's College London*

## BIBLIOGRAPHY

Annas, J., 'Cicero on Stoic Moral Philosophy and Private Property', in M. T. Griffin and J. Barnes (eds.), *Philosophia Togata* (Oxford, 1989), 151–73.

Atkins, E. M., '*Domina et regina virtutum*: Justice and *Societas* in *De officiis*', *Phronesis*, 35 (1990), 258–89.

Brennan, T., *The Stoic Life* (Oxford, 2005).

Dancy, J., *Ethics without Principles* (Oxford, 2004).

Forschner, M., 'Le Portique et le concept de personne', in G. Romeyer Dherbey and J.-B. Gourinat (eds.), *Les Stoïciens* (Paris, 2005), 293–317.

Gill, C., 'Personhood and Personality: The Four-*Personae* Theory in Cicero, *De officiis* I', *Oxford Studies in Ancient Philosophy*, 6 (1988), 169–99.

Griffin, M. T., and Atkins, E. M. (eds.), *Cicero:* On Duties (Cambridge, 1991).

Hooker, B., and Little, M. O. (eds.), *Moral Particularism* (Oxford, 2000).

Inwood, B., 'Rules and Reasoning in Stoic Ethics' ['Rules and Reasoning'], in K. Ierodiakonou (ed.), *Topics in Stoic Philosophy* (Oxford, 1999), 95–127.

Irwin, T. H., 'Ethics as an Inexact Science: Aristotle's Ambition for Moral Theory', in Hooker and Little (eds.), *Moral Particularism*, 100–29.

Jackson, F., Pettit, P., and Smith, M., 'Ethical Particularism and Patterns', in Hooker and Little (eds.), *Moral Particularism*, 79–99.

Long, A. A., *Stoic Studies* (Cambridge, 1996).

Mitsis, P., 'Seneca on Reason, Rules, and Moral Development', in J. Brunschwig and M. Nussbaum (eds.), *Passions and Perceptions* (Cambridge, 1993), 285–312.

Nussbaum, M., 'Duties of Justice, Duties of Material Aid: Cicero's Problematic Legacy' ['Duties of Justice'], *Journal of Political Philosophy*, 8 (2000), 176–206.

Reydams-Schils, G., *The Roman Stoics* (Chicago, 2005).

Schofield, M., *Saving the City* (London, 1999).

Smart, J. J. C., and Williams, B., *Utilitarianism: For and Against* (Cambridge, 1973).

Sorabji, R., *Self* (Oxford, 2006).

Vander Waerdt, P., 'The Original Theory of Natural Law', *Studia Philonica Annual*, 15 (2003), 17–34.

Winch, P., 'The Universalizability of Moral Judgements', in id., *Ethics and Action* (London, 1972), 151–70.

# ASPASIUS ON *NICOMACHEAN ETHICS* 7: AN ANCIENT EXAMPLE OF 'HIGHER CRITICISM'?

## CARLO NATALI

### 1. Received opinions

I N *NE* 7. 14 Aristotle seems to identify pleasure and happiness:

Presumably it is even necessary, given that there are unimpeded activities of each state, and happiness is the activity of all of them or of one of them, that this activity, provided that it is unimpeded, is most desirable; but this is pleasure. ($1153^b9$–12)

On this passage, Aspasius notes in his commentary (*In NE* 151. 18–27 Heylbut):[1]

διὰ μὲν οὖν τούτων δοκεῖ ταὐτὸν ἀποφαίνεσθαι τἀγαθὸν καὶ τὴν ἡδονήν· οὐ μὴν οὕτως ἔχει, ἀλλὰ πρὸς τοὺς λέγοντας γένεσιν εἶναι ἢ φαύλας τινὰς τῶν ἡδονῶν, οἷς[2] καὶ δι' αὐτὸ τὸ μὴ εἶναι αὐτὴν[3] τὸ ἀγαθὸν ἐπιγίνεται [καὶ][4] ἐπιχειρεῖ ἐνδόξως ὡς ἐνὸν αὐτὴν τὸ ἄριστον λέγειν, ἐπεὶ ἔν γε τοῖς Νικομαχείοις, ἔνθα διείληπται καὶ περὶ ἡδονῆς Ἀριστοτέλης σαφῶς εἴρηκεν αὐτὴν μὴ ταὐτὸν εἶναι τῇ εὐδαιμονίᾳ ἀλλὰ παρακολουθεῖν "ὥσπερ τοῖς ἀκμαίοις τὴν ὥραν". σημειωτέον[5] δὲ τοῦ μὴ εἶναι τοῦτ' Ἀριστοτέλους ἀλλ' Εὐδήμου τὸ ἐν τῷ[6] λέγειν περὶ ἡδονῆς ὡς οὐδέπω περὶ αὐτῆς διειλεγμένου· πλὴν εἴτε Εὐδήμου ταῦτά ἐστιν εἴτε Ἀριστοτέλους,

My thanks to David Sedley and David Charles for help with the improvement of my English text.

[1] References are to G. Heylbut, *Aspasii in Ethica Nicomachea quae supersunt commentaria* [Heylbut] (Berlin, 1889).

[2] οἷς Rose: ἇς codd.; del. Spengel.         [3] αὐτὴν Spengel: αὐτὸ codd.

[4] Secl. Hayduck.

[5] σημειωτέον codd.: σημεῖον L. Spengel, 'Über die unter den Namen des Aristoteles erhaltenen Ethischen Schriften' ['Ethische Schriften'], *Bayer. Ak. der Wiss., Sitzung phil.-hist. Kl.*, 24/4 (1841), 1–115 at 85, and all subsequent editors. I maintain the text of the manuscripts, on the basis of a similar passage in Olympiodorus (*In Cat.* 75. 11–12 Busse).

[6] MS Z (Parisinus gr. 1903) has a lacuna here, supplemented with δεκάτῳ by Spengel and others; see Spengel, 'Ethische Schriften', 86.

348                          *Carlo Natali*

ἐνδόξως εἴρηται· διὰ τοῦτο λέγεται τὸ ἄριστον ἡδονή, ὅτι σὺν τῷ ἀρίστῳ καὶ
ἀχώριστον αὐτοῦ.[7]

With these words, then, he seems to say that the good and pleasure are
one and the same. But this is not the case. Rather, against those who say
that pleasure is a process or that some pleasures are base, for whom it also
follows, for this reason, that pleasure is not the good, he argues on the
basis of reputed opinion that it is possible to call pleasure the supreme
good. For at least in the *Nicomachean Ethics*, in the place where he does
make distinctions on pleasure, he says clearly that pleasure is not the same
thing as happiness, but accompanies it 'as the bloom accompanies the cheek
of youth' [*NE* 1174$^b$33]. As evidence that this is not by Aristotle but by
Eudemus one should cite the fact that in ⟨book 10⟩ he [=Aristotle] talks
about pleasure as if he had not yet discussed it. But whether those words
express Eudemus' or Aristotle's view, this is an argument drawn from
reputed opinion; he says that pleasure is the supreme good for the following
reason: it accompanies the supreme good and cannot be separated from it.

The passage attracted discussion in the nineteenth century, because
it seems to attribute a section of the *Nicomachean Ethics* (τοῦτο, 151.
24) to Eudemus and not to Aristotle. Spengel maintained that Aspasius was still close enough to the rediscovery of Aristotle's works
to be able to discuss the attribution of books of the *Nicomachean
Ethics*, and suggested that the passage presents its argument as 'nur
ein dialektischer Versuch'.[8] But a bolder interpretation emerged in
the twentieth century. According to Paul Moraux, Aspasius in this
passage touches on a problem of interest to 'higher criticism', one
concerned, that is, with the attribution of authorship—in this case,
the question whether the so-called common books (*NE* 5–7 = *EE* 4–
6) should be attributed to the *Nicomachean Ethics* or the *Eudemian
Ethics*. He maintains that the author of the passage argues on the
basis of common opinions (ἐνδόξως, 21 and 26), but also cites the
*Nicomachean Ethics* as a work different from the one that contains

---

[7] This section of Aspasius' commentary (150. 31–151. 27) is very difficult and
full of lacunae. It has been edited many times: by H. Hase, '*Aspasiou scholiōn
eis ta Ethica tou Aristotelous epitomē*', *Classical Journal*, 28 (1823), 306–17, and
29 (1824), 104–18 at 117; Spengel, 'Ethische Schriften', 84–5; V. Rose, 'Über die
griechischen Commentäre zur Ethik des Aristoteles', *Hermes*, 5 (1871), 61–113 at
107; and Heylbut. There is a modern translation only for the commentary on book 8,
in D. Konstan, *Commentators on Aristotle on Friendship* [*Commentators*] (London,
2001) (Aspasius at 13–57). A complete translation of Aspasius' commentary by
Professor Konstan is in preparation. I would like to thank him very warmly for
allowing me to read it in draft, and for many useful comments on a first version
of the present article.

[8] L. Spengel, 'Ethische Schriften', 84; 'nich mehr als eine Conjectur', he adds (85).

the present passage. Moraux takes lines 24–5 to mean that Aspasius is uncertain whether the common books belong to the *Eudemian* or *Nicomachean Ethics*.[9] He adds that it is not certain whether Aspasius considered all the common books to belong to the *Eudemian Ethics*, or only the final chapters of book 7, 12–15. Further, Moraux quotes a comment by Aspasius on *NE* 8, 1155[b] 13–16, which states: 'Even things different in species admit of degree. We have discussed this matter [ὑπὲρ αὐτῶν] previously.'[10] Aspasius' comments:

ἔοικε δὲ εἰρῆσθαι ἐν τοῖς ἐκπεπτωκόσι τῶν Νικομαχείων. (*In NE* 161. 9–10)

It appears that they were discussed in the books that have fallen out of the *Nicomachean Ethics*.

Moraux thinks that Aspasius is here referring to the lacuna that must be admitted to exist between *NE* 4 and 8, if the common books are attributed to the *Eudemian Ethics*.

Moraux's interpretation has been revived by Anthony Kenny, in an important book about the relationship between the *Eudemian* and *Nicomachean Ethics*.[11] Kenny claims, *inter alia*, that (i) the common books belong to the *Eudemian Ethics*, and (ii) before the second century AD, the *Eudemian Ethics* was preferred to the *Nicomachean Ethics* by ancient authors. According to Kenny, the situ-

[9] P. Moraux, *Der Aristotelismus bei den Griechen*, ii. *Der Aristotelismus im I. und II. Jh. n. Chr.* [*Aristotelismus*] (Berlin and New York, 1984), 258–61.

[10] Modern editions of the *Nicomachean Ethics* have ὑπὲρ αὐτῶν. This use of ὑπέρ is quite rare in Aristotle, and for this reason Ramsauer, Grant, Stewart, Tricot, and Gauthier think that it is a spurious interpolation. But Aspasius' text here has περὶ αὐτῶν. Regarding the point referred to, among those scholars who accept the passage as authentic Susemihl and Dirlmeier follow Aspasius, Irwin thinks that the allusion is to *Cat.* 6[b]10–17 or to *NE* 2. 8, Burnet and Broadie just say that the reference is uncertain. E. Berti, 'Amicizia e "Focal Meaning"', in A. Alberti and R. W. Sharples (eds.), *Aspasius: The Earliest Extant Commentary on Aristotle's Ethics* [*Aspasius*] (Berlin and New York, 1999), 176–90 at 178, thinks that the reference is to 1096[b]8–16.

[11] A. Kenny, *The Aristotelian Ethics* [*Ethics*] (Oxford, 1978), 29–36. Shorter or more prudent versions of the same interpretation can be found in C. Rowe, *The Eudemian and Nicomachean Ethics* (Cambridge, 1971); R. Bodeüs, 'Contribution à l'histoire des œuvres morales d'Aristote: les testimonia', *Revue philosophique de Louvain*, 71 (1973), 451–67 at 452–3; H. B. Gottschalk, 'Aristotelian Philosophy in the Roman World from the Time of Cicero to the End of the Second Century AD' ['Aristotelian Philosophy'], in W. Haase and F. Temporini (eds.), *Aufstieg und Niedergang der römischen Welt*, 2.36.2 [*Aufstieg*] (Berlin and New York, 1987), 1079–174 at 1158; F. Becchi, 'Aspasio commentatore di Aristotele' ['Aspasio'], in Haase and Temporini (eds.), *Aufstieg*, 5365–96 at 5368; J. Barnes, 'An Introduction to Aspasius', in Alberti and Sharples (eds.), *Aspasius*, 1–50 at 19–21.

ation had radically changed by the time of Alexander of Aphrodisias, and since then the supremacy of the *Nicomachean* to the
*Eudemian Ethics* has been taken for granted. In general, Kenny
thinks (iii) that the *Eudemian Ethics* is the more important treatise,
from both a philosophical and a historical point of view.

In this paper I shall discuss only Kenny's interpretation of the
passage quoted above from Aspasius' commentary. Kenny mainly
follows Moraux's interpretation, with just a few changes, and in-
serts it into his reconstruction of the history of the *Nicomachean*
and *Eudemian Ethics* in the period between the fourth century BC
and the second century AD. He writes:

> In Aspasius' writing we find the situation with which we have been fa-
> miliar for centuries: the *Nicomachean Ethics* is the undoubted treatise of
> Aristotle, the *Eudemian Ethics* is the problematic treatise whose attribu-
> tion fluctuates, regarded now as authentic Aristotle, now as the work of
> his disciple Eudemus. But if Aspasius departs from the earlier tradition
> in his ranking the two *Ethics*, he is at one with it—as we shall see—in
> regarding the disputed books as belonging essentially to the Eudemian
> version. (29–30)

Kenny quotes the passage 151. 18–27, and follows Moraux's interpretation: Aspasius is in doubt as to whether this passage of *NE* 7,
and by implication the common books in general, belongs to the
*Nicomachean* or to the *Eudemian Ethics*. He repeats Moraux's argument according to which the phrase 'in the *Nicomachean Ethics*'
(ἐν τοῖς Νικομαχείοις, 151. 21–2) implies that Aspasius takes himself to be commenting on a work different from the *Nicomachean
Ethics*. But his reading of the text is more accurate than Moraux's
and he sees the implications of the argument more clearly. First, he
notes that the attribution of book 7 (and the others) to Eudemus
is only one of the possible explanations considered by Aspasius;
second, he points out that in his interpretation Aspasius attributes
book 7 not to the *Eudemian Ethics* but to Eudemus himself. This
implies that Aspasius thinks that Eudemus is the author of the *Eudemian Ethics*. But such a conjecture has damaging consequences
for the unity of Aspasius' commentary itself. If *NE* 7 belongs to
the *Eudemian Ethics* and that work is by Eudemus, how could the
commentary on this book and the commentary on *NE* 1–4 and 8 be
part of the same work? Kenny lists two possibilities. According to
the first, we have fragments of two Aspasian commentaries, one on

the *Nicomachean Ethics*, to which the comments on books 1–4 and 8 belong, and one on the *Eudemian Ethics*, to which the fragment of the commentary on book 7 belongs. But Kenny thinks rather that, when commenting on *NE* 1–4, Aspasius found many forward references to the common books, and suggests that, since in his time there were copies of the *Eudemian Ethics* containing the common books, the following may be hypothesized:

In these circumstances Aspasius, having commented on books 1–4 of the *NE*, proceeded to comment on books 5–6 of the *Eudemian Ethics*, in order to have a full commentary on Aristotle's ethical system, in spite of the lacuna in the *Nicomachean* version. (32, cf. 33)

But how could Aspasius have produced such a 'full commentary on Aristotle's ethical system' by adding some Eudemian books to the *Nicomachean Ethics*, if he clearly thought that Eudemus and Aristotle had different ethical theories, at least on pleasure?

Kenny recalls Moraux's observation on the passage 161. 9–10 and discusses the cross-references between the parts of the commentary in order to find some difference between the way in which Aspasius quotes the common books and his commentary on the undisputed *Nicomachean Ethics* books (34–5). This is a point we shall discuss later.[12]

At the end of his discussion, however, Kenny remarks that Aspasius is not certain whether the common books are by Eudemus, and notes that there are passages of the commentary where Aspasius refers to some of the common books as the work of Aristotle, whereas in other passages he attributes them to Eudemus (35).

There should be a simpler way to interpret this passage. In my view, (1) in lines 151. 24 and 26 the pronouns 'this' (τοῦτο) and 'these' (ταῦτα) refer not to the passage, or to the entire seventh book, let alone to the three common books, but only to the specific argument of *NE* 1153ᵇ7–12. Aspasius is not saying that the text he is commenting on was written by Eudemus; rather he is saying that here Aristotle is not speaking in his own name but is reporting someone else's argument, namely Eudemus'. (2) In the remaining parts of Aspasius' commentary there is no indication that he takes

---

[12] Becchi, 'Aspasio', 536₉, sees the weakness of the hypothesis and maintains rightly that the passage 161. 9–10 could be interpreted as a reference to a lost passage or section of the *Nicomachean Ethics*, and not to an entire book, as Kenny suggests (*Ethics*, 34).

the common books to belong to a treatise different from the *Nicomachean Ethics* or not to be by Aristotle. (3) An examination of his comments on the first two arguments of 7. 14 (150. 3–151. 27) can help to explain why Aspasius thinks that Aristotle is here quoting someone else's opinion.

To argue in favour of these three claims, I shall first examine some external and general features of the whole commentary, and then discuss the passage 150. 3–151. 27 in detail.

## 2. The authorship of the books commented on by Aspasius

Let us consider the passage in which Aspasius' comments occur, and his view on the authorship and constitution of Aristotle's ethical treatise. In the manuscripts the commentary has a title for every book. They always say: 'Aspasius' comments on book . . . of Aristotle's *Ethics*',[13] but in two cases there is a variant reading: 'Aspasius on book 7 of the *Nicomachean Ethics* of Aristotle' and 'Aspasius' scholia on book 8 of Aristotle's *Nicomachean Ethics*'.[14] To be sure, the evidence is weak because these titles could be late. But perhaps the commentary itself provides better clues.

There is some evidence that Aspasius took all the material he was commenting on to be by Aristotle, including book 7. He often says in his comments: 'Aristotle says/adds/wants/does not say', etc. The name of Aristotle as author of the relevant material appears in his commentaries on all of the books: seven times in the commentary on book 1, three times on book 2, seven times on book 3, twelve times on book 4, and three times on book 8.[15] This applies also to book 7, where Aspasius quotes Aristotle as the author of the sections on *akrasia* (133. 15–16; 19–20; 136. 7–8; 138. 19–20; 139. 12–13) and on pleasure (150. 5; 154. 20–1). It is impossible to interpret the above-quoted passage, 151. 18–27, as indicating that some part of

[13] Book 1, 'Aspasius' scholia on Aristotle's *Ethics*' (1. 1); book 2, 'On book 2 of Aristotle's *Ethics*' (37. 1), or 'On the second of Aristotle's ethical books' (in app., p. 37 Heylbut); book 3, 'On book 3 of Aristotle's *Ethics*' (58. 1); book 4, 'The scholia of the philosopher Aspasius on book 4 of Aristotle's *Ethics*' (95. 1); book 7, 'Aspasius on book 7 of Aristotle's *Ethics*' (127. 1); book 8, 'Aspasius on book 8 of Aristotle's *Ethics*' (158. 1).

[14] According to Heylbut's apparatus, the variant title for book 7 is to be found in MS Z. In fact it is in Parisinus gr. 1902 (sec. xvi, very close to Z), fo. 115ᵛ; the variant title for book 8 is in the Aldine edition (1536).

[15] See the references in Heylbut's *Index nominum* s.n. Ἀριστοτέλης.

book 7, or the entire book, is by Eudemus. In fact, three pages later, commenting on 1154ᵃ15–16, Aspasius tells us that '*Aristotle* says in general that all the goods of the body have an excess [καθόλου δέ φησιν ὁ Ἀριστοτέλης σωματικῶν ἀγαθῶν πάντων εἶναι ὑπερβολήν]' (154. 20–1). He clearly considers Aristotle to be the author of the entire book.

## 3. Cross-references in Aspasius

There is, it seems, enough evidence to show that Aspasius considers the *Ethics* on which he is commenting to form a continuous whole, composed of books 1, 2, 3, 4, 5, 6, 7, 8, (9), and 10. This is clear from his way of citing the other books of the *Nicomachean Ethics* when he is commenting on one of them. The most quoted book is 6, which is referred to in his surviving comments on all the other books except book 8. This preference is understandable because book 6 contains many of the central doctrines of Aristotle's ethics and many definitions which are needed to explain the doctrines of the other books. But Aspasius seems to have used book 6 in a systematic way, as the key to understanding the meaning of Aristotle's expressions in other books, disregarding the nuances that arise from the usage of a term in books other than 6. The most important element absent from Aspasius' commentary is the progression implicit in Aristotle's analysis. Aristotle starts in the first pages of the *Nicomachean Ethics* by using terms in their more common meaning, and refines them as the discussion proceeds. Aspasius, on the contrary, takes the results of the analysis for granted already at the beginning, and so imposes on Aristotle's procedures a systematic aspect that is far from the dialectical and rhetorical procedures of the *Nicomachean Ethics*.

But let us confine ourselves to the raw data. Book 6 is cited eight times in the commentary on the other books, books 1 and 10 five times, books 2 and 5 four times, and book 3 just once.[16] The commentaries on books 7 and 8 have internal citations but are not cited in the commentaries on the other books. They do, however, often quote the other books: the commentary on book 7 has nine citations,[17] that on book 8 five citations,[18] that on book 1 seven,

---

[16] See the list of passages on p. 243ᵃ of Heylbut's edition.
[17] Two of book 1 (141. 26–7; 146. 15–16), one of book 2 (123. 2–3), one of book 3
[*See next page for* n. *17 cont. and* n. *18*]

that on book 2 only two, that on book 3 none, and that on book 4 four. This adds up to a network of reciprocal references, with some gaps (Table 1).

TABLE 1

| Comm.: | 1 | 2 | 3 | 4 | 7 | 8 | TOTAL |
|---|---|---|---|---|---|---|---|
| **Book** | | | | | | | |
| 1 | × | | | × | × × | × | 5 |
| 2 | | | | × × | × | ×(?) | 4 |
| 3 | | | | | × | | 1 |
| 4 | | | | | | | 0 |
| 5 | ×(?) | | | | | × × × | 4 |
| 6 | × × × | × | | × | × × × | | 8 |
| 7 | | | | | | | 0 |
| 8 | | | | | | | 0 |
| 9 | | | | | | | 0 |
| 10 | × × | × | | | × × | | 5 |
| TOTAL | 7 | 2 | 0 | 4 | 9 | 5 | |

As might be expected, the commentaries on the first books often cite the subsequent books with expressions meaning 'later', and those on the later books cite the earlier ones with expressions meaning 'before' or 'at the beginning'. When commenting on book 1, Aspasius cites book 10 with the words 'on which he will speak *later*' (περὶ ἧς ὕστερον ἐρεῖ)[19] or 'he will be more specific about it

(152. 22–7, the only citation of this book in the commentary outside the commentary to book 3 itself), three of book 6 (136. 28–137. 3; 140. 23–7 and 29–31), and three of book 10 (141. 24–6; 151. 18–19).

[18] Three of them, understandably, of book 5 on justice, because friendship and justice are closely connected subjects (160. 11–12; 175. 3–4; 178. 19–22), one of book 1 (162. 1–6), and one of book 2 (158. 5–11).

[19] There is a problem in this passage: at 19. 2–3, having quoted *NE* $1098^a17$–18, Aspasius adds: 'that is, the virtue of contemplation, concerning which he will speak later—the presence of complete virtue clearly being presupposed' (περὶ ἧς ὕστερον ἐρεῖ, προϋπαρχούσης δηλονότι τῆς καλοκαγαθίας). Here the mention of *kalokagathia* seems to be a reference to *EE* 8. 3 and not only to *NE* 10. But in any case *NE* 10. 7 is clearly being cited, because it would not be accurate to say that in *EE* 8. 3 there is an analysis of ἀρετὴ θεωρητική. It seems that, while Aspasius was providing a forward reference to *NE* 10. 7, *EE* 8. 3 also came into his mind.

*later'* (ὕστερον δὲ ἀκριβώσει περὶ αὐτῆς: 19. 2; 23. 28–9). Regarding book 6, some of the citations we find in book 1 are only implicit (6. 27), and others limit themselves to quoting the text of book 6 verbatim, without reference to its position. For example:

ἰδίως δὲ καλεῖν εἰώθασι τέχνην τὴν ποιητικήν. ἀποδίδωσι δὲ αὐτῷ λόγον ὁ Ἀριστοτέλης λέγων "τέχνη ἐστὶν ἕξις μετὰ λόγου ποιητική" (2. 23–5)

In the strict sense people are accustomed to call the productive art *technē*. Aristotle provides it with a definition, when he says 'art is the productive habit, involving reasoning'—

the reference being to *NE* 1140ª10. But there is also a passage of the commentary on book 1 where Aspasius cites book 6 thus:

ἀλλὰ ταύτην γε λύει τὴν ἀπορίαν προϊών· φησὶ γὰρ τὸ μηδὲν κωλύειν τὴν ἐλάττω προστάσσειν περὶ τῶν κρειττόνων, οἷον ⟨προστάσσει⟩ ἡ πολιτικὴ καὶ ναοὺς θεῶν κατασκευάζεσθαι καὶ σέβειν αὐτούς (8. 32–4)

But he solves that *aporia* later: for he says that nothing prevents the inferior from giving orders about the superior: for instance politics ⟨enjoins⟩ that temples of the gods be built and that people worship them—

the reference being to book 6, 1145ª6–11.

From these passages we can infer that the commentary on book 1 does not discriminate between book 10, an undisputed part of the *Nicomachean Ethics*, and book 6, one of the common books. Both texts alike are ones that the reader will encounter 'later'. There is no sign that Aspasius considers *NE* 6 to be part of another work or its commentary to be distinct from the commentary on book 1.

This suggestion is confirmed by Aspasius' commentary on book 2, where book 6 is again referred to as a text that will be read 'later'. He finds a passage where Aristotle refers forward to chapters 1 and 13 of book 6, and paraphrases it by saying:

τίς δέ ἐστιν ὁ ὀρθὸς λόγος ὕστερον ῥηθήσεται καὶ πῶς ἔχει πρὸς τὰς ἄλλας ἀρετάς (40. 7–8)

It will be said *later* what right reason is and how it is related to other virtues.[20]

Aristotle himself in book 2 refers to *NE* 6. 1 and 13 as something

---

[20] Cf. *NE* 1103ᵇ32–4: ῥηθήσεται δ' ὕστερον . . . τί ἐστιν ὁ ὀρθὸς λόγος, καὶ πῶς ἔχει πρὸς τὰς ἄλλας ἀρετάς. Ramsauer, Dirlmeier, Gauthier, and Tricot think that the reference is to 6. 1 and 13. Stewart and Broadie refer to book 6 or to 'what may have corresponded to it in the original *NE* treatise'. Bywater and Burnet delete the passage.

which will come later, and Aspasius picks up this indication without expressing any doubt about Aristotle's authorship.

The commentary on book 4 refers back to books 1 and 2 as something already read. At 120. 25–6 Aspasius paraphrases Aristotle again, and refers back to book 1, calling it 'the first discussions':

ἔλεγε δὲ καὶ ἐν τοῖς πρώτοις λόγοις ὅτι περὶ τῶν πρακτῶν τύπῳ μὲν ἔστι λέγειν.

He said in the first discussions as well that in practical matters you can give an approximate account.[21]

Later, at 121. 15–16, he quotes the list of virtues in book 2, 1108ª26–9, saying:

πρότερον μὲν γὰρ ἐν τῇ διαγραφῇ κοινότερον αὐτὴν φιλίαν εἶπε.

*Earlier*, in the diagram, he has called it 'friendship' using the term in a general way.

Book 1 is indicated as the beginning of the entire ethical work, and book 2 as something that precedes book 4.

Later, in the commentary on books 7–8, both book 1 and book 2 are indicated with phrases such as 'at the beginning', and book 6 is mentioned as something which comes 'earlier'. In fact, the commentary on book 7 refers to book 2 as 'in the first discussions' and to book 6 as 'before' or 'in the previous discussion'. Let us examine the passages.

*Citation of book 2*
. . . ὃν ἐν τοῖς κατ' ἀρχὰς λόγοις ἀναίσθητον ἔλεγε. (132. 2–3, referring to 1104ª2, ἀναίσθητός τις)
. . . whom in the first discussions he called 'insentient'.

*Citations of book 6*
ὥσπερ καὶ πρότερον ἔλεγεν, ἠθικὴ ἀρετὴ τίθεται ἐνίοτε μὲν ἡ φυσική, ἔστι δὲ ὅτε ἡ ἐκ τοῦ ἔθους (136. 31–2 referring to 1144ᵇ2 + 1144ª6–7)
But, as he said also before, sometimes it is natural virtue that is posited as ethical virtue, but also sometimes the virtue derived from habituation.

δέδεικται γὰρ ἐν τοῖς ἔμπροσθεν λόγοις (140. 23, referring to 1145ª1–2)
It has been demonstrated in the previous discussions.

But in his commentary on book 7, as Kenny noticed, Aspasius quotes book 2 with the expression 'elsewhere':

[21] See *NE* 1126ª31–2: ὃ δὲ καὶ ἐν τοῖς πρότερον εἴρηται κτλ., the reference being to 1094ᵇ24.

ἰδίως δὲ νῦν τὸν χαῦνον εἶπεν ἐοικέναι τῷ ἐλευθερίῳ, ἐν ἄλλοις εἰπὼν τὸν ἄσωτον
αὐτῷ ὅμοιον εἶναι κατὰ τὴν φαντασίαν. (138. 22–3, referring to 2, 1108ᵇ22)

In a peculiar sense he says now that the vain resemble the liberal, *elsewhere*
he says that it is the spendthrift that resembles them in appearance.

According to Kenny, Aspasius here cites book 2 as if it were part
of a different work. Kenny also says that the passage of the commentary on (*NE*) book 8, 178. 19–22, where Aspasius refers to the
(common) book 5 with the expression 'elsewhere', indicates the
same relationship between the two sets of books:

λέγει δὲ ἐν ἄλλοις ἴσον τὸ κατ' ἀριθμόν.

Elsewhere he calls 'equal' that which is equal according to number—

the reference being to 5, 1134ᵃ28. In Kenny's view the commentaries on the *Nicomachean Ethics* books and those on the common
books each refer to books of the other group as belonging to a different work. But his conclusion is not necessary. It is true that in
Aristotle the expression 'elsewhere' (ἐν ἄλλοις) usually means 'in
another work',[22] but this does not apply to Aspasius, who uses the
expression in a freer way. For instance, in the commentary on book
1 he uses it to refer to another part of that same book:

ἐν ἄλλοις δὲ τὸ ὡς πεφυκὸς πείθεσθαι ἄλογον καλεῖ διὰ τὸ μὴ ἔχειν ἴδιον λόγον.
(18. 6–9, referring to 1, 1102ᵇ25–34)

Elsewhere he calls that which can be persuaded (by reason) 'irrational'
because it does not possess its own reasoning capacity.

I turn now to the commentary on book 8. Aspasius there cites
book 1 by means of the expression 'at the beginning':

... ὥσπερ καὶ ἐν τοῖς κατ' ἀρχὰς λόγοις ἔλεγε. (162. 2–3, referring to 1096ᵃ6)[23]

... as he said in the discussions at the beginning.

At 158. 9–14 he refers back to *NE* 2. 7, 1108ᵃ26–30, and 4. 12,
1126ᵇ10–20, without any explicit indication. But the commentary
on book 8 refers most to book 5, because of their similarity of
content and the connection between the concepts of 'friendship'
and 'justice': cf. 175. 3–4, where the phrase 'equality according to

---

[22] Cf. M. Burnyeat, *A Map of* Metaphysics *Z* (Pittsburgh, 2001), 29. But there
are exceptions in Aristotle as well: *Metaph.* 1017ᵇ9, 1046ᵃ6, 1055ᵇ7, 1056ᵇ35.
[23] The passage is quoted verbatim immediately after.

proportion' (ἡ κατὰ ἀναλογίαν ἰσότης, cf. *NE* 5, 1134ᵃ5–6) is cited. It is true that at 160. 11 Aspasius refers to *NE* 5, 1134ᵇ9–19, with the words 'in the (discussions) on justice':

πολλὰ γὰρ εἴδη τοῦ δικαίου, καθάπερ ἐλέχθη ἐν τοῖς περὶ δικαιοσύνης.

For there are many kinds of just thing, as was said in the (discussions) on justice.

But the expression 'in the (discussions) on justice' does not necessarily indicate that Aspasius is referring to book 5 as another work. It is simply a different way of referring to a preceding book, used for *variatio*. Further, in his commentary on *NE* 2. 7, when Aspasius encounters a phrase by which Aristotle refers to the common books 5 and 6 as later parts of the same work,[24] he is not surprised and paraphrases it without any problem:

περὶ δὲ δικαιοσύνης ὕστερον ἐρεῖν ἐπαγγέλλεται καὶ περὶ τῶν λογικῶν ἀρετῶν. (55. 27–8)

About justice he promises to speak later, and about the rational virtues.

In modern times many have doubted the authenticity of this passage, but Aspasius has no problems with it and, when commenting on book 2, he quotes books 5 and 6 as belonging to the same work. He finds it natural that the discussions about justice and rational virtue in books 5 and 6 should follow the discussion of particular virtues in book 4.

In sum, in his commentary on the *Nicomachean Ethics* we have a series of references which indicate that Aspasius considers all the different books to be on the same level and to belong to the same work.[25] In his comments on the first books he often cites the last books as something that will come later, and in the comments on the last books he cites the first and second as something already read, or read at the beginning. To be sure, the network of quotations is not complete. There are books never cited in the commentary on

[24] 'With regard to justice, since it has more than one meaning, *we shall distinguish* those meanings *and say* how each one is a mean, after describing the other states; and we shall do the same also with regard to the rational virtues' (περὶ δὲ δικαιοσύνης, ἐπεὶ οὐχ ἁπλῶς λέγεται, μετὰ ταῦτα διελόμενοι περὶ ἑκατέρας ἐροῦμεν πῶς μεσότητές εἰσίν· ὁμοίως δὲ καὶ περὶ τῶν λογικῶν ἀρετῶν, 1108ᵇ8–10). Grant, Ramsauer, Stewart, Burnet, and Gauthier consider the *Nicomachean Ethics* passage interpolated, because for Aristotle the rational virtues are not μεσότητες. Dirlmeier, Tricot, Rackham, Irwin, and Broadie and Rowe accept the received text.

[25] Cf. Becchi, 'Aspasio', 5368.

some other book (for instance, that on book 1 never refers to book 2)
or never cited at all (9). There are books with plenty of citations
(7, 8) and books whose commentaries scarcely cite others at all
(2). There are books much cited (6) and books scarcely referred to.
The commentary on book 3 never cites other books and book 3
itself is cited only in the commentary on book 7. This evidently
depends partly on the content, and partly on the necessity Aspasius
felt to refer to some parts of the *Nicomachean Ethics* more than
to others. It is not an indication of the situation of the text in
his time.

It is extremely unlikely that Aspasius wanted to attribute to Eudemus either book 7 or the entire group of books 5–7. But what
did he want to say in the passage I quoted at the beginning? An
analysis of the context may provide an answer.

### 4. Aspasius' comments on *NE* 1153$^b$1–12

To understand Aspasius' commentary on 1153$^b$1–12, where the
section quoted at the beginning of this article is to be found, we
must bear in mind that his general interpretation is different from
ours, and that he takes many unsound positions in his commentary
on the last part of *NE* 7. According to Aspasius, the defender of
the thesis that pleasure is not a good is Antisthenes (142. 9) and
not Speusippus. He thinks that Speusippus is a hedonist, and that
Aristotle agrees with him but wants to replace one of his arguments
with a better one in the first lines of *NE* 7. 14.

On Aspasius' interpretation, the argument of *NE* 1153$^b$1–7 is to
be reconstructed as follows:

(1) People say that Speusippus maintained that the opposite of
*evil* is good; but pain is an evil; so its opposite, pleasure, is
a good (150. 3–4).
(2) Aristotle corrects Speusippus' argument and says: the opposite of *what is to be avoided* is good; pain is to be avoided;
pleasure is not an evil and it is the opposite of pain; therefore
pleasure is good (150. 4–8).
(3) The preceding argument is against those who maintain that
pleasure is neither a good nor an evil (150. 8–9).

By contrast, at the beginning of *NE* 7. 14, according to modern interpretations,

(1′) Aristotle accepts the common opinion that pain is an evil, absolutely or because it is an obstacle ($1153^b1-3$).

(2′) Aristotle, following an argument by Eudoxus,[26] affirms that the opposite of what is evil is good; necessarily, then, pleasure is a good ($^b3-4$).

(3′) Aristotle quotes Speusippus as being opposed to point (2′), saying that one excess is opposed to the other excess and to the right intermediate (Speusippus' point seems to be that there is more than one opposite: pleasure and pain are two excesses, to which the right intermediate, absence of both pleasure and pain, is equally opposed, $^b4-6$). This solution, adds Aristotle, does not work: in fact not even Speusippus could admit that pleasure is an evil ($^b6-7$).[27]

Aspasius attributes to Aristotle a version of Speusippus' double opposition theory, whereby to an evil both another evil and a good are opposite. To confirm this, he quotes the example of an ethical virtue, where two bad states are opposed to the right intermediate: 'For example, not only is courage, which is a good thing, the opposite of rashness, but so too is a bad thing, cowardice' (150. 23–4). To arrive at his conclusion Aristotle must assume both that pleasure is opposed to pain and that pleasure is not an evil (150. 25–30).

Aspasius attributes to common opinion what Aristotle attributes to Speusippus, and takes as subject of the phrase 'for [he] would not have said that pleasure is something ⟨essentially evil⟩' (*NE* $1153^b6–$7) not Speusippus, but 'anybody' (οὐδείς, 150. 7). The premiss, which appears to be *ad hominem* against Speusippus, becomes an endoxic premiss which applies universally. Therefore, if the contrary of pain, which is an evil, is either an evil or a good and if pleasure is the contrary of pain and is not an evil, necessarily pleasure is a good.

The controversy between Speusippus and Aristotle does not depend on an opposition between theories (pleasure is good/pleasure

---

[26] Cf. *NE* 10, $1172^b18–20$: 'He [Eudoxus] believed that the same conclusion followed with the same clarity from the contraries: because pain *per se* is a thing to be avoided for everybody, in the same way its contrary [pleasure] is choiceworthy for all.'

[27] I follow the interpretation given by J. Burnet, *The Ethics of Aristotle* (London, 1900), 336, and others.

is bad), but becomes merely a difference in their ways of arguing, Aristotle's argument being judged by Aspasius more effective than Speusippus'. This is Aspasius' strange interpretation of the first argument. It is paradoxical that Aspasius, who knows *NE* 10. 1–5 and quotes it verbatim a few pages later, did not realize that argument (2′) is not by Speusippus but by Eudoxus. Evidently he took the reference to Speusippus at 1153ᵇ5 to refer to the preceding lines.

In his analysis of Aristotle's second argument Aspasius fares no better. The text of his commentary here is full of lacunae and difficult to understand. Editors have tried to amend it by conjecture, but the results are uncertain.

Aspasius finds a difficulty in the argument of lines 1153ᵇ7–12: he thinks that the argument proves too much, namely, not only that pleasure is a good, but also that some pleasure is the supreme good, i.e. happiness. He is not alone in thinking this. It is possible to interpret the argument, taken literally, in this way. However, since such an interpretation is fully hedonistic and conflicts with the theory of *NE* 10. 1–5, nearly all interpreters reject it.[28] They take the passage to mean simply that the supreme good is pleasant, and not that some pleasure is the supreme good.[29] But let us return to Aspasius.

The opposing parties in this dispute are not, according to Aspasius, Aristotle and those who maintain that pleasure is an evil (as in chapter 13),[30] nor two groups of philosophers who think that pleasure is a good but defend this position with different arguments (as at 1153ᵇ1–7). They are, on the one side, those who deny that pleasure is the supreme good, and on the other those hedonists, not to be identified with Aristotle, who allow that it is.

The hedonist's argument is against a view which is not in the list of anti-hedonist positions catalogued at 142. 29–33:

ἀλλ᾽ οὖν τοῖς μὲν δοκεῖ μηδεμία ἡδονὴ εἶναι ἀγαθόν, τοῖς δὲ μία μὲν ἀγαθή, αἱ δὲ πολλαὶ φαῦλαι, τοῖς δὲ εἰ καὶ πᾶσαι ἀγαθὸν ὅμως μὴ εἶναι τὴν ἡδονὴν τὸ ἄριστον, τουτέστιν μὴ εἶναι εὐδαιμονίαν, οἷς ἐναντιοῦνται οἱ λέγοντες τὴν εὐδαιμονίαν ἡδονὴν εἶναι.

---

[28] See e.g. the discussion by F. Dirlmeier, *Aristoteles: Nikomachische Ethik* (Berlin, 1956), 503.

[29] This is the opinion of Stewart, Gauthier, Irwin, and Broadie. Burnet thinks that it is only an *ad hominem* argument against the anti-hedonists.

[30] Aspasius takes Aristotle to be the opponent of the anti-hedonists at 148. 2, 15, 23, 30; 149. 8, 20, 28.

362      *Carlo Natali*

Now then, some believe (*a*) that no pleasure is a good, others (*b*) that one is good but many are base, and still others that (*c*) though all pleasures are a good, nevertheless pleasure is not the best, that is, it is not well-being, while (*d*) those who say that well-being is pleasure are opposed to these last.[31]

The anti-hedonist in question says (*e*) that pleasure is not the best thing and the supreme good because some pleasures are base—a very weak position, it seems to me. After setting out their position Aspasius seems to refer to an argument in favour of (*e*), but in the text there is at least one lacuna, and the argument itself is unintelligible.[32]

That the argument in these lines is one in favour of those who support (*e*) and not against them is demonstrated by the fact that some unknown hedonists object to this very argument by introducing another. They say (ἐνίστανται, 151. 1–2), (*f*):

τί γὰρ κωλύει φαύλων ἡδονῶν οὐσῶν εἶναί τινα ἡδονὴν τὸ ἄριστον τῶν ἀνθρωπί-
νων ἀγαθῶν, ὥσπερ καὶ ἐπιστήμη τίς ἐστιν ἡ ἀρίστη τῶν ὄντων, οἷον ἡ σοφία,
καίτοι πολλῶν τεχνῶν φαύλων οὐσῶν, οἷον τῶν βαναύσων; (151. 2–4)

For even though there are base pleasures, what prevents some pleasure from being the best among human goods?—just as a certain kind of knowledge is best of those that exist, for example wisdom, even though there are many base arts, such as the artisanal ones.[33]

Here Aspasius paraphrases *NE* 1153[b]7–9 without attributing it to Aristotle.

Instead, Aspasius attributes to Aristotle the position expressed in the following lines, 1153[b]9–12, but seems to have doubts as to whether Aristotle is right:

ἃ δ᾽ ἑξῆς ἐπιφέρει, τάχα ἄν τῳ δόξειεν ἀληθῆ ἀποφαινόμενα τὸ μέγιστον καὶ
ἄριστον τὴν ἡδονήν. λέγει γὰρ ἴσως δὲ καὶ ἀναγκαῖον αἱρετώτατον εἶναι, δηλονότι
τὴν ἡδονήν, τὸ δὲ αἱρετώτατόν τι εἶναι ἐπὶ τέλει ἐστὶ τοῦ λόγου καὶ συνηγορεῖται
τῷ λόγῳ πάντων αἱρετώτατον εἶναι τὴν ἡδονὴν λέγοντι. (151. 6–10)

What he [Aristotle] adduces next may perhaps seem to someone to be true,

---

[31] This repeats what Aristotle says at *NE* 1152[b]8–12, with the addition of the last position (ἐναντιοῦνται, 32).

[32] ὅσον γὰρ ἐπὶ τούτῳ τῷ λόγῳ ἔστι τινὰ ἡδονὴν * ἡγεῖται τὸ ἄριστον [τὸ ἄριστον N; ἄριστον Parisinus gr. 1902, fo. 116[r]] καὶ ταὐτὸν τῇ εὐδαιμονίᾳ (150. 33–151. 1).

[33] The example of the bad type of science, the arts of manual workers, although not found in the *Nicomachean Ethics*, is present in *MM* 1205[a]32. However, direct influence of *Magna moralia* on Aspasius seems not to be possible, because in *Magna moralia* the argument tends to show only that pleasure is a good thing, whereas in the *Nicomachean Ethics* the thesis is that pleasure is the supreme good.

affirming that pleasure is the greatest and the best thing. For he says that 'perhaps it is also necessary' [1153$^b$9] that it—pleasure, obviously—be the most choiceworthy thing.

The argument for this is given in lines 10–15, according to Aspasius (*g*):

- if 'unimpeded activities' of the best states occur when there is nothing impeding them,
- if happiness is the unimpeded activity of all the habitual states or of one of them,
- and if pleasure is the unimpeded activity of some habitual state,
- then it is clear that some pleasure would be the supreme good, i.e. happiness.

Next, at 151. 16–18 Aspasius concludes:

ἔστι δέ, ὥς φησι, τὰ ἑξῆς τῆς φράσεως· ἴσως δὲ ἀναγκαῖον αἱρετωτάτην εἶναι τὴν ἡδονήν, εἴπερ ἑκάστης ἕξεως καὶ τὰ ἑξῆς· διὰ μὲν οὖν τούτων δοκεῖ ταὐτὸν ἀποφαίνεσθαι τἀγαθόν.

This is the rest of the sentence, as he says: 'perhaps it is necessary' that pleasure be most choiceworthy, 'if in fact for each habitual state' etc. With these words, then, he seems to say that the good and pleasure are one and the same.

We have, in effect, three positions, the anti-hedonists' (*e*), the hedonists' (*f*), and Aristotle's argument (*g*), which seems to support (*f*). But Aspasius sees a danger in attributing to Aristotle the theory that 'it is evident that some pleasure would be the best and the most final good, even if it happens that there are bad pleasures'.[34] And it is at this point that he makes the comments quoted at the beginning of the paper. Having attributed 1153$^b$7–9 to an unknown hedonist, Aspasius here goes on to inform us that Aristotle's argument is only one from reputed opinion (*endoxa*), and is perhaps not endorsed by Aristotle himself. In saying (151. 26) that 'whether those words [ταῦτα] express Eudemus' or Aristotle's view, this is an argument drawn from reputed opinion', it is clear that he can only be referring to argument (*f*), and not to the whole passage or to the whole of book 7.[35] There is no hypothesis here about the authorship of book 7, still less of the three common books. Aspasius says:

[34] 151. 15: φανερὸν ὡς ἂν εἴη τις ἡδονὴ τὸ ἄριστον καὶ τελειότατον τῶν ἀγαθῶν, εἰ οὕτως ἔτυχε φαύλων οὐσῶν ἡδονῶν.
[35] Kenny, *Ethics*, 30–1 and n. 2; Gottschalk, 'Aristotelian Philosophy', 1158.

in *NE* 10, where his true doctrine of pleasure is set out, Aristotle discusses pleasure as if he had never before discussed it. If so, all the discussion of pleasure in 7. 12–15 might in fact have been seen as purely endoxical, but there is no sign in the preceding part of his commentary of any such interpretation. His interpretation seems to be confined to the argument at *NE* 1153ᵇ9–12 (referred to by τοῦτο, 151. 24, and ταῦτα, 151. 26).

Let us take stock. In this section of the commentary Aspasius has discussed first (150. 3–30) what he takes to be two arguments against the anti-hedonists, one by Speusippus and one by Aristotle, and has observed that the second is the better. Next (150. 31–151. 18) he has discussed argument (*f*), which seems to identify pleasure with the supreme good and happiness. He finds that Aristotle appears to agree with (*f*), to back it with (*g*), and to consider its conclusions 'necessary'. At this point, however, he refuses to accept Aristotle's words at face value, and looks for a way out of the problem. His solution consists in saying that

(1) the argument (*g*) which supports (*f*) is based on popular opinion;

(2) in *NE* 10 Aristotle says the opposite, and there is no reference in that book to this argument, or in general to the book 7 discussion;

(3) perhaps (*g*) is by Eudemus, not Aristotle, and is anyway based only on 'popular opinion';

(4) 'Some pleasure is the supreme good' in reality means 'Pleasure accompanies the supreme good and cannot be separated from it.'

Why refer (*g*) to Eudemus, and not to Eudoxus? This remains unclear, but the preceding mistake about Speusippus' position at lines 150. 3–4 implies that Aspasius' information about the position of Aristotle's associates and the Academics is thoroughly confused. The source of his information is unknown (cf. 'they say', 150. 3), as is the reason why at some point he attributes (*g*), with some hesitation, to Eudemus. But at all events, his choice is to all appearances unrelated to the fact that in our manuscripts book 7 of the *Nicomachean Ethics* is identical to book 6 of the *'Eudemian' Ethics*.

There are other puzzling attributions in this section of Aspasius' commentary. Later, when commenting on chapter 15, he quotes a

passage from *NE* 7, 1154ᵇ13–14, as if it were part of Theophrastus'
*Ethics*:

καὶ τὸν Ἀναξαγόραν αἰτιᾶται Θεόφραστος ἐν Ἠθικοῖς λέγων ὅτι ἐξελαύνει ἡδονὴ
λύπην ἢ γε ἐναντία. (156. 16–17)

Theophrastus too, in his *Ethics*, criticizes Anaxagoras, saying that *'pleasure,
or at least the opposite pleasure, drives out pain'*.[36]

Aspasius' ways of citing other philosophers deserve to be studied
more carefully. He often quotes Plato, and does so with great precision, but when he refers to other philosophers—Pythagoreans,
Anaxagoras, the Socratics, Xenophon, Theophrastus, Eudemus,
Andronicus, Boethus, the early Peripatetics, the Stoics—he fails
to maintain the same level of precision in every citation.[37] His commentary on the last part of book 7 seems somewhat negligent.
Perhaps Konstan is right to say that at the end of his work Aspasius
appears to have been a little tired.[38]

The only puzzling point that remains to be explained in 151. 18–
26 is the references there to book 10. In the commentary on book 1,
book 10 is referred to simply with a 'later' (ὕστερον, 19. 2 and 23. 28–
9). In the commentary on book 7 there is another implicit reference
to book 10, when Aspasius says that 'the politician is the guide
as to how happiness could come into being';[39] this refers to *NE*
1177ᵇ12–14:

ἔστι δὲ καὶ ἡ τοῦ πολιτικοῦ ἄσχολος, καὶ παρ' αὐτὸ τὸ πολιτεύεσθαι περιποιου-
μένη δυναστείας καὶ τιμὰς ἢ τήν γε εὐδαιμονίαν αὐτῷ καὶ τοῖς πολίταις.

The life of the politician is also unleisurely, and, apart from the governing
itself, procures power, honour and at least happiness for himself and the
other citizens.

There is no indication here that the thesis is being derived from

---

[36] The italicized clause is identical to *NE* 1154ᵇ13–14. Diels in app. corrects to
ὡς Θεόφραστος. W. W. Fortenbaugh, *Quellen zur Ethik Theophrasts* (Amsterdam,
1984), 79 and 309, and in his edition of Theophrastus' fragments, places a lacuna
after λέγων ὅτι (see W. W. Fortenbaugh *et al.*, *Theophrastus of Eresus: Sources for his
Life, Writings, Thought and Influence* (Leiden, 1992), 555), which would mean that
the verbatim quotation from Theophrastus' *Ethics* has been lost. Likewise Moraux,
*Aristotelismus*, 266; Gauthier, 'Introduction', in R. A. Gauthier and J. Y. Jolif (trans.
and comm.), *Aristote: Éthique à Nicomaque*, 2nd edn. (Louvain and Paris, 1970),
92, thinks that Theophrastus repeated Aristotle's expression word for word. But
those are *ad hoc* solutions.
[37] See Heylbut's *Index nominum*, 242–5.          [38] Konstan, *Commentators*, 9.
[39] 141. 25–6: ὁ δὲ πολιτικὸς ὑφηγεῖται ὅπως ἂν γένοιτο εὐδαιμονία.

a work other than the _Nicomachean Ethics_, especially as another internal citation, this time of book 6, immediately follows:

ἔτι φρόνησις ἀρχιτεκτονικὴ λέγεται, διότι τὸν λόγον παρέχει ταῖς ἠθικαῖς ἀρεταῖς. (141. 26–7)

Furthermore, prudence is called architectonic because it endows the ethical virtues with reason.[40]

The commentary on book 7 seems here to be referring to _NE_ 10 and to another common book, 6, in just the same way, as if they were parts of the same work.

How, then, are we to interpret the expression 'in the _Nicomachean Ethics_' (151. 21–2)? It may simply be an example of stylistic _variatio_, like 'in the discussions concerning justice' (ἐν τοῖς περὶ δικαιοσύνης, 160. 11), which we met earlier. It does not necessarily indicate that Aspasius is referring to the _Nicomachean Ethics_ as a work which is different from the one on which he is here commenting. This is confirmed by the fact that in the commentary on book 8, which is an undisputed part of the _Nicomachean Ethics_, Aspasius refers to some lost part of the same _Nicomachean Ethics_ with the expression 'in the parts of the _Nicomachean Ethics_ that have fallen out' (ἐν τοῖς ἐκπεπτωκόσι τῶν Νικομαχείων, 161. 9–10). If so, Moraux's claim, that when commenting on the _Nicomachean Ethics_ Aspasius could not refer to another part of the same work with the words 'in the _Nicomacheans_', loses its apparent basis. For if Aspasius at 161. 9–10 refers to other parts of the _Nicomachean Ethics_ with this very expression, 'in the parts of the _Nicomachean Ethics_ that have fallen out', he can very well use the expression 'in the _Nicomachean Ethics_' at 151. 21–2 to refer to another passage of that work. It is strange that this passage has been used to support an argument to the contrary.

_Università di Venezia 'Ca' Foscari'_

## BIBLIOGRAPHY

Alberti, A., and Sharples, R. W. (eds.), _Aspasius: The Earliest Extant Commentary on Aristotle's_ Ethics [_Aspasius_] (Berlin and New York, 1999).
Barnes, J., 'An Introduction to Aspasius', in Alberti and Sharples (eds.), _Aspasius_, 1–50.

---

[40] The reference is to 1141[b]22–3.

Becchi, F., 'Aspasio commentatore di Aristotele' ['Aspasio'], in Haase and Temporini (eds.), *Aufstieg*, 5365–96.

Berti, E., 'Amicizia e "Focal Meaning"', in Alberti and Sharples (eds.), *Aspasius*, 176–90.

Bodeüs, R., 'Contribution à l'histoire des œuvres morales d'Aristote: les testimonia', *Revue philosophique de Louvain*, 71 (1973), 451–67.

Burnet, J., *The Ethics of Aristotle* (London, 1900).

Burnyeat, M., *A Map of* Metaphysics *Z* (Pittsburgh, 2001).

Dirlmeier, F., *Aristoteles: Nikomachische Ethik* (Berlin, 1956).

Fortenbaugh, W. W., *Quellen zur Ethik Theophrasts* (Amsterdam, 1984).

—— *et al.*, *Theophrastus of Eresus: Sources for his Life, Writings, Thought and Influence* (Leiden, 1992).

Gauthier R. A., and Jolif J. Y. (trans. and comm.), *Aristote: Éthique à Nicomaque*, 2nd edn. (Louvain and Paris, 1970).

Gottschalk, H. B., 'Aristotelian Philosophy in the Roman World from the Time of Cicero to the End of the Second Century AD', in Haase and Temporini (eds.), *Aufstieg*, 1079–174.

Haase, W., and Temporini, F. (eds.), *Aufstieg und Niedergang der römischen Welt*, 2.36.2 [*Aufstieg*] (Berlin and New York, 1987).

Hase, H., '*Aspasiou scholiōn eis ta Ethica tou Aristotelous epitomē*', *Classical Journal*, 28 (1823), 306–17, and 29 (1824), 104–18.

Heylbut G., *Aspasii in Ethica Nicomachea quae supersunt commentaria* (Berlin, 1889).

Kenny, A., *The Aristotelian* Ethics [*Ethics*] (Oxford, 1978).

Konstan, D., *Commentators on Aristotle on Friendship* [*Commentators*] (London, 2001).

Moraux, P., *Der Aristotelismus bei den Griechen* ii. *Der Aristotelismus im I. und II. Jh. n. Chr.* [*Aristotelismus*] (Berlin and New York 1984).

Rose, V., 'Über die griechischen Commentäre zur Ethik des Aristoteles', *Hermes*, 5 (1871), 61–113.

Rowe C., *The Eudemian and Nicomachean Ethics* (Cambridge, 1971).

Spengel L., 'Über die unter den Namen des Aristoteles erhaltenen Ethischen Schriften' ['Ethische Schriften'], *Bayer. Ak. der Wiss., Sitzung phil.-hist. Kl.*, 24/4 (1841), 1–115.

# GALEN'S TELEOLOGY AND FUNCTIONAL EXPLANATION

MARK SCHIEFSKY

## 1. Introduction

THE importance of functional analysis in contemporary biology and social science is widely recognized. By *functional analysis* I mean an approach in which the parts of a complex system are studied in order to determine their contribution to the continued existence or operation of the system as a whole. Thus we may say that the *function* of the heart in an organism is to circulate the blood, and in doing so we identify the contribution of the heart to the organism's continued existence.[1] When we cite the function of an organ such as the heart to explain its presence or its distinctive structure we are giving a functional explanation, and such an explanation will involve teleological language. Why does the heart have four chambers and a set of precisely fitting valves? *In order to* fulfil its function of circulating the blood. The status of such functional explanations is a major concern in contemporary philosophy

I would like to express my thanks to Peter McLaughlin, Francesca Schironi, David Sedley, and Gisela Striker for their very helpful comments on earlier versions of this paper, which was completed under the ideal working conditions provided by the Institute for Advanced Study, Princeton.

[1] C. Hempel, *Aspects of Scientific Explanation* (New York, 1965), 304–5: 'The kind of phenomenon that a functional analysis is invoked to explain is typically some recurrent activity or some behaviour pattern in an individual or a group, such as a physiological mechanism, a neurotic trait, a culture pattern, or a social institution. And the principal objective of the analysis is to exhibit the contribution which the behaviour pattern makes to the preservation or the development of the individual or the group in which it occurs. Thus, functional analysis seeks to understand a behaviour pattern or a sociocultural institution by determining the role it plays in keeping the given system in proper working order or maintaining it as a going concern.' For E. Nagel, functions are analysed in terms of the contributions of parts of a system to the maintenance of its global properties or modes of behaviour, and the function-bearer is viewed as supporting the 'characteristic activities' of the system (*The Structure of Science: Problems in the Logic of Scientific Explanation* [*Structure*] (New York, 1961), 403, 409, 421–2).

of science, in which key issues include the precise understanding of terms such as 'function', the possibility of reformulating functional explanations in non-teleological language, and the question whether the prevalence of functional explanations in biology and the social sciences reflects inherent differences between those disciplines and the physical sciences. The question 'what functions explain' is a matter of ongoing debate.[2]

Whatever position one takes on these foundational issues, there seem to be at least two major reasons why functional analysis is important in the study of living things. (1) First, organisms have capacities for self-maintenance and reproduction, and these capacities imply a certain plasticity of behaviour. That is, whatever the changes in the environment, a living organism will behave in ways that promote its own survival and reproduction. Since the organism consistently engages in these activities despite changes in the environment, it is natural to take the activities as basic *explananda* and to enquire into the roles of the various parts in promoting them. (2) Moreover, living things are organic wholes whose parts interact with one another in complex ways; organisms are not systems of independently functioning parts. As Nagel put it, the parts of the organism are 'internally related'; they 'mutually influence one another, and their behaviour regulates and is regulated by the activities of the organism as a whole'.[3] For these reasons, among others, functional explanations are prevalent in contemporary biology. Such explanations, of course, do not imply any reference to animate agents; to say that the heart is structured in a certain way in order to circulate the blood is not to say that an intelligent agent *designed* it for this purpose, *intended* it to do so, or *makes* it circulate the blood.

The aim of this paper is to argue that Galen adopted a functional approach to the study of living organisms and that he did so for rea-

[2] Nagel, *Structure*, ch. 12, argues for the possibility of reducing teleological to non-teleological explanations, while recognizing the importance of functional explanation as a mode of investigation in the biological sciences. See also Hempel, *Aspects of Scientific Explanation*, 297–330; J. Canfield, 'Teleological Explanation in Biology', *British Journal for the Philosophy of Science*, 14/56 (1964), 285–95; F. J. Ayala, 'Teleological Explanations in Evolutionary Biology', *Philosophy of Science*, 37/1 (1970), 1–15; L. Wright, 'Functions', *Philosophical Review*, 82/2 (1973), 139–68; and for a full review of the contemporary literature and all the major issues P. McLaughlin, *What Functions Explain: Functional Explanation and Self-Reproducing Systems* [*What Functions Explain*] (Cambridge, 2001).
[3] Nagel, *Structure*, 401.

sons similar to those that have just been described. Galen's method in works such as *On the Use of the Parts* (*De usu partium*) and *On the Natural Faculties* (*De naturalibus facultatibus*)[4] reflects a keen awareness of the complexity of the ways in which the parts of the body work together to promote activities such as self-maintenance and reproduction. The basic idea that governs his approach in *De usu partium* is that the existence, structure, and attributes of all the parts must be explained by reference to their functions in promoting the activities of the whole organism; this means that functions have an ineliminable role in the explanation of the parts.

In *De usu partium* and other works, Galen describes the construction of the human body as the result of the effort of a supremely intelligent and powerful divine Craftsman or Demiurge, who exerts foresight or providence (*pronoia*) on behalf of living things. Galen also frequently attributes the construction of the body to a personified nature or *physis*, which is said to be 'craftsmanlike' (*technikē*), i.e. capable of art or craft (*technē*). Galen was obviously committed to the view that the structure of the body is a result of intelligent design. To argue that his Demiurge is only a device of exposition would be going too far, and that is not my claim. Nevertheless, Galen's descriptions of the ways in which the Demiurge devised the structure of the human body reflect a highly sophisticated, functional analysis of the organism, and there are good reasons to adopt such an approach that are independent of belief in a divine artificer. Sections 2–5 below describe the background and main features of Galen's functional approach; I return to the question of the relationship between functions and design in Section 6.

## 2. Aristotle

Although the Hippocratic writings of the fifth and fourth centuries BC are rich in descriptions of the human body and its parts,

[4] For *De usu partium* and *De naturalibus facultatibus* I use the Greek text of G. Helmreich: *Galeni De usu partium libri XVII* (2 vols.; Leipzig, 1907–9); *Claudii Galeni Pergameni scripta minora*, vol. iii (Leipzig, 1893), with reference to volume (for *UP*), page, and line of his edition (H.), followed by the reference to volume and page in the edition of C. G. Kühn (*Claudii Galeni opera omnia* (20 vols. in 22; Leipzig, 1821–33; repr. Hildesheim, 1965)). For all other Galenic works I give the volume and page reference to Kühn (K.) along with references to more recent editions where available. Translations are my own unless otherwise indicated, but I have drawn extensively on the excellent translation of M. T. May (*Galen: On the Usefulness of the Parts of the Body* [*Usefulness*] (2 vols.; Ithaca, NY, 1968)).

the first thinker to apply functional analysis consistently to the study of living things is Aristotle.[5] I therefore begin with a brief account of his methodology, based largely on *De anima* and *De partibus animalium*.[6] For Aristotle, what distinguishes the living from the lifeless is the possession of soul, viewed as the source of a set of 'powers' or 'faculties' (*dynameis*) to engage in activities such as nutrition, reproduction, appetite, perception, locomotion, and thought (*DA* 413[a]20–[b]13; 414[a]29–32). The most basic faculty of the soul is that of self-nutrition and reproduction; it is common to all living things, and so also serves to distinguish the living from the lifeless (*DA* 412[a]13–15; 415[a]23–[b]3, [b]26–8; 416[b]17–20). All other faculties of the soul, such as perception, locomotion, and thought, presuppose the capacity for nutrition (i.e. self-maintenance) and reproduction (*DA* 415[a]1–13). In identifying self-maintenance and reproduction as the distinctive activities of living things, Aristotle focuses on the tendency of organisms to respond to the environment in ways that promote their own survival. The growth of plants is not explained by reference to the natural tendencies of fire to move upward and earth downward; rather, plants grow in a way that is directed at maintaining their existence, and it is because of this that they count as alive (*DA* 413[a]25–31; cf. 415[b]28–416[a]9). Since survival and reproduction are the most fundamental activities of living things, we must take them as the starting-point of explanation and investigate the ways in which the organism is able to perform them.

The same issues are approached from a slightly different angle in the opening chapters of *De partibus animalium* (i. 1–5). A major theme in this work is the idea that the parts of an organism can be understood only with reference to the whole; in other words, the whole organism is prior to its parts in the order of explanation. The processes that go on during embryonic development make up

---

[5] In general the Hippocratics conceive of the parts of the body in structural rather than functional terms: they are 'forms' or 'conformations' (σχήματα, Hipp. *VM* 22) rather than 'organs' or 'instruments' (*organa*). For the general point see J. Jouanna, *Hippocrates* (Baltimore, 1999), 310–11; see also B. Gundert, 'Parts and their Roles in Hippocratic Medicine', *Isis*, 83/3 (1992), 453–65. The sole Hippocratic treatise that can be said to adopt a consistently functional approach is *On the Heart*, but this feature is generally regarded as a sign of its Hellenistic date; see I. M. Lonie, 'The Paradoxical Text *On the Heart*', *Medical History*, 17 (1973), 1–15, 136–53 at 4–5, 143–7. Cf. esp. *De corde* 8, ix. 84–6 Littré, on the auricles as 'instruments' (*organa*) with which nature captures the air, like the bellows in a blacksmith's furnace.

[6] On Aristotle's functional approach see M. Nussbaum, *Aristotle's* De motu animalium *[De motu]* (Princeton, 1978), 76–85, and M. R. Johnson, *Aristotle on Teleology* (Oxford, 2005), 159–78.

a complex, interrelated progression whose order is intelligible only from the point of view of the resulting organism, just as, in the case of housebuilding, the steps in the process make sense only in reference to the finished house. Explanations of development must therefore begin with a specification of the form (*eidos*) or definition (*logos*) of the finished product or organism (*PA* 1. 1, 640ᵃ33–ᵇ4). In *PA* 1. 5 Aristotle explains the implications of this kind of approach for the study of the parts of the fully developed organism:

> Since every instrument [*organon*] is for the sake of something [ἕνεκά του], and each of the parts of the body is for the sake of something, viz. some activity [πρᾶξις], it is clear that also the whole body is constituted for the sake of some complex activity [πράξεώς τινος ἕνεκα πολυμερούς]. For sawing has not come to be for the sake of the saw, but the saw for the sake of sawing, because sawing is a use [χρῆσις]. Hence also the body in a certain way has come to be for the sake of the soul, and the parts for the sake of the functions [*erga*] to which each of them is naturally adapted [πρὸς ἃ πέφυκεν ἕκαστον]. First, then, we must state the activities [πράξεις] common to all, then those which belong to a genus and a species. (*PA* 1. 5, 645ᵇ14–22)

Just as the saw exists 'for the sake of' sawing, so the body exists 'for the sake' of the soul and its characteristic activities. The basic idea is the adaptation of structure to function. The saw is constructed in such a way as to make it good for sawing, just as any tool or instrument is made to perform its function well; similarly, the parts of the body, and the body as a whole, are constructed in such a way as to perform the activities (πράξεις) of the soul. All the parts contribute to the achievement of a particular set of activities which make up an intelligible pattern, the characteristic life of the organism; in this sense, they exist 'for the sake of' these activities. Once again the method is clear: we must begin with an enumeration of the organism's activities, then go on to consider the parts that enable it to perform them.

Aristotle consistently describes the parts of the organism as 'instruments' or 'organs' (*organa*) distinguished by their 'works' or 'functions' (*erga*), i.e. the contributions they make to the organism's characteristic activities. What makes the eye an eye is its capacity to see, just as an axe is defined by its capacity to chop; an eye without the capacity to see is an eye only in name (*DA* 412ᵇ9–22).[7] In many cases, the function (*ergon*) of a part will be its contribution to the or-

---

[7] Even the parts of plants are organs, albeit very simple ones: the leaf protects the pericarp, and the roots attract nutriment like a mouth (*DA* 412ᵇ1–4). Cf. *DA*

ganism's self-maintenance or reproduction. Some organs, however, are present in order to make life better, not just to make it possible. Thus the kidney, for example, exists to improve the functioning of the bladder, and the senses other than touch are present 'not for the sake of being, but for well-being'.[8] In every case, however, the functions are understood as contributions to the organism's characteristic activities. And, crucially, the analysis stops there: Aristotle does not conceive of organisms or their parts as having functions in some larger order or system.[9]

A final important aspect of Aristotle's conception of the organism is the notion of functional organization, the ways in which the parts work together to promote the activities of the whole. In *De motu animalium* ($703^a29-^b2$) he compares the organism to a well-governed city in which each part performs its allotted function (*ergon*). But it is not as though the function of each of the parts can be specified independently of the others. The organism is a system in which the parts interact with one another to produce results that are beneficial for the whole. Respiration, for example, occurs when the lungs expand due to the increase in innate heat caused by the process of nutrition. But the function of respiration is to cool the innate heat, and thus to enable the organism's continued self-maintenance and nutrition (*Resp.* $474^a25-^b24$ and $480^a16-^b20$). In this way the functions of the organs of respiration (the lungs) and of the innate heat (the heart) are interdependent.

$416^a4-6$: 'The head in animals is analogous to the roots in plants, if we are to identify and distinguish organs [*organa*] by their functions [*erga*].'

[8] *DA* $435^b17-25$, esp. $435^b20-1$ (οὐ τοῦ εἶναι ἕνεκα ἀλλὰ τοῦ εὖ). Cf. *PA* $640^a33-^b1$ and $670^b23-7$: the kidneys are present 'for the sake of what is good and fine' (τοῦ εὖ καὶ καλῶς ἕνεκεν), i.e. 'so that the bladder might perform its function [*ergon*] better'. On this category of parts see Johnson, *Aristotle on Teleology*, 188–9 and 197–8. Cf. also Plato, *Tim.* 75 D 5–E 5, on the dual role of the mouth and tongue as both serving a necessary purpose and contributing to the best life.

[9] I take this to be a consequence of the fact that for Aristotle, the final cause must be an end of whatever it is meant to explain: the cause 'for the sake of which' is always referred to the nature (*physis*) or essence (*ousia*) of the individual thing in question (cf. *Phys.* $198^b8-9$). This is not to deny that the various natural kinds may be so ordered as to benefit one another by the fulfilment of their individual ends (cf. *Metaph.* Λ 10), or that the lower creatures may be instrumentally useful to man (cf. *Pol.* $1256^b10-22$). The point is just that the good that is relevant to the final cause is the good of the organism as specified in its definition or *logos*, not the good of anything outside it. See Nussbaum, *De motu*, 95–7, and Johnson, *Aristotle on Teleology*, for a comprehensive and (I think) convincing defence of this interpretation. For the contrary view see D. Sedley, 'Is Aristotle's Teleology Anthropocentric?', *Phronesis*, 36 (1991), 179–96.

Four interconnected features of Aristotle's approach have emerged from this brief survey: (1) the fundamental importance of self-maintenance and reproduction; (2) the explanatory priority of the whole organism to its parts; (3) the emphasis on the functions of the parts, understood as their contributions to the organism's activities; (4) the notion of functional organization and the interdependence of the various organs. Let us now turn to Galen and see how these features are reflected in his approach.

## 3. An Aristotelian approach

Like Aristotle, Galen identifies self-maintenance and reproduction as the fundamental activities of living things. In *De naturalibus facultatibus* he conceives of the organism's *physis* or 'nature' as an entity responsible for managing (διοικεῖν) activities which do not involve cognition or voluntary motion, such as growth and nutrition; cognition and voluntary motion, by contrast, are assigned to the soul (*psychē*) rather than nature. Plants have a nature but not a soul, reflecting the status of self-maintenance and reproduction as marking off the living from the lifeless (*Nat. fac.* i. 1, 101. 1–15 H., ii. 1–2 K.).[10] The investigation of *physis* begins from an enumeration of its characteristic 'works' (*erga*) and 'activities' (*energeiai*); to each activity there corresponds a particular faculty (*dynamis*) as its cause (*aitia*). Galen explains that 'works' (*erga*) refers primarily to products, such as flesh, blood, and bone, while 'activities' refers to processes or, more specifically, 'active changes' (δραστικαὶ κινήσεις). The scope of *ergon* is wider than *energeia*, since all activites (e.g. digestion or blood production) can be considered products, but not all products (e.g. flesh, blood, bone) are activities (*Nat. fac.* i. 2, 105. 13–106. 3 H., ii. 6–7 K; i. 4, 107. 20–3 H., ii. 10 K.). The most fundamental activities of *physis* are those that make possible the organism's continued existence and promote its development: generation (γένεσις), growth (αὔξησις), and nutrition (θρέψις). Galen emphasizes both the interdependence of these activities and their contribution to the organism's self-maintenance. The faculty of generation is responsible for the formation of the organism in the womb, that of growth for its development to full

---

[10] In dividing up the activities of soul and nature in this way Galen follows Stoic usage.

size once born, and that of nutrition for its continued existence. Generation is 'compounded' (σύνθετος) from alteration (ἀλλοίωσις) and shaping (διάπλασις) (*Nat. fac.* 1. 5, 107. 24–108. 20 H., ii. 10–11 K.). The faculties of growth and nutrition are present in the embryo, but only as 'handmaids' (ὑπηρέτιδες) to the generative faculty; from the time of birth until the organism reaches its full size, the faculty of growth is dominant, while alteration and nutrition are its 'handmaids' (*Nat. fac.* 1. 7, 112. 6–15 H., ii. 16 K.). Once the various activities and their interrelationships have been analysed, Galen turns to an examination of the organs that perform them. Nutrition, defined as 'assimilation of that which nourishes to that which is nourished' (ὁμοίωσις τοῦ τρέφοντος τῷ τρεφομένῳ), requires organs which alter food so that it can be assimilated, others which dispose of the inevitable residues formed during this process, and still others which convey the nutriment through the body; a large number of organs will be needed to perform these activities, and the investigation should begin from those which are most closely related to the end (*telos*) to be achieved, i.e. nutrition (*Nat. fac.* 1. 10, 117. 17–118. 2 H., ii. 23–4 K; 1. 11, 118. 7–8 H., ii. 24 K.). In this way the investigation of the principal activities of *physis* leads directly to the investigation of the parts of the body and their activities.

Just as *De naturalibus facultatibus* takes off from *De anima*, so *De usu partium* picks up from *De partibus animalium*.[11] After a brief introductory paragraph setting out the notion of a part as that which is neither totally distinct from nor entirely fused with its surroundings, Galen continues with a statement that is of fundamental significance for understanding his method throughout the work:

The use [*chreia*] of all of them [sc. the parts] is for the soul. For the body is its instrument [*organon*], and for this reason, the parts of animals differ greatly from one another, because their souls also differ. For some are brave and others timid; some are wild and others tame; and some are, so to speak, political and craftsmanlike [πολιτικά τε καὶ δημιουργικά], whereas others are, as it were, asocial. But for all of them, the body is suited to the character [ἤθεα] and faculties [*dynameis*] of the soul. (*UP* 1. 2, i. 1. 13–2. 2 H., iii. 2 K.)

Like Aristotle, Galen identifies the body as the 'instrument' (*organon*) of the soul, the tool that enables it to carry out its characteristic

[11] Cf. P. Moraux, 'Galen and Aristotle's *De partibus animalium*', in A. Gotthelf (ed.), *Aristotle on Nature and Living Things: Philosophical and Historical Studies Presented to David M. Balme on his Seventieth Birthday* (Pittsburgh, 1985), 327–44.

activities. The body and its parts are for the sake of the soul, in the sense that they are adapted to the performance of the organism's activities. If one is to understand why an organism has the parts it does, it is necessary to have knowledge of its characteristic activities, as expressed in the 'character and faculties' of its soul. Galen elaborates by considering the appropriateness of various creatures' bodies to their souls: the lion is strong and fearless and has teeth and claws to match, while the timid deer has a body that is sleek but also defenceless (*UP* 1. 2, i. 2. 2–11 H., iii. 2–3 K.). Human beings, though they lack defensive organs, make up for this by the possession of hands; with these they construct tools to compensate for their natural inferiority to animals in qualities such as speed and strength (*UP* 1. 2, i. 2. 11–3. 24 H., iii. 3–5 K.). Galen goes on to praise Aristotle for rejecting Anaxagoras' suggestion that human beings are intelligent because they possess hands; rather, they possess hands because they are intelligent (*UP* 1. 3, i. 4. 2–5 H., iii. 5 K.; cf. Arist. *PA* 687ᵃ7–23). In all of this the underlying idea, as in Aristotle, is the explanatory priority of the whole organism to its parts. The organism's activities are not explained by reference to its parts; rather, the parts are explained by reference to the total pattern of the organism's activities, as expressed in the character and faculties of its soul.

Like Aristotle, Galen conceives of all the parts as existing for the sake of three primary ends: life, a better life, and reproduction.[12] Furthermore the Galenic body, as well as being the 'instrument' of the soul, is also a collection of instruments or organs (*organa*) which are distinguished from one another by their activities (*energeiai*). What makes an organ an organ, as opposed to just a 'part' (*morion*), is its ability to perform an activity. Thus the eye is both an organ and a part, since it is a functional system that produces a single activity, sight; on the other hand the retina and the cornea are parts (both of the eye and, secondarily, of the face) but not organs.[13] Galen indi-

---

[12] *UP* 14. 1, ii. 284. 20–285. 1 H., iv. 142 K.: 'Nature had three principal aims [*skopoi*] in constructing the parts of the animal; for she crafted them either for the sake of life [ἕνεκα τοῦ ζῆν] (the brain, heart, and liver), or for a better life [τοῦ βέλτιον ζῆν] (the eyes, ears, and nostrils), or for the continuance of the species [τῆς τοῦ γένους διαδοχῆς] (the pudenda, testes, and uteri).'

[13] *De methodo medendi* 1. 6, x. 47 K.: 'I call an organ [*organon*] a part of the animal that is productive of a complete activity [*energeia*], as the eye is of vision, the tongue of speech, and the legs of walking; so too arteries, veins, and nerves are both organs [*organa*] and parts [*moria*] of animals.'

cates his indebtedness to Aristotle for this functional conception of the organs, and is if anything more strict than Aristotle in insisting that organs must be identified in purely functional terms. He often remarks in *De usu partium* that organs should be named according to their activities rather than their visible structure or form, and criticizes Aristotle for failing to do so.[14]

As an example of Galen's functional approach we may consider *UP* 1. 8–10. These chapters set out what Galen describes as a general method for determining the 'use' (*chreia*) of any part—a problem which, he says, had led to extensive disagreement among doctors and philosophers alike (*UP* 1. 8, i. 12. 13–19 H., iii. 17 K.). Galen takes his start from a cryptic remark found in the Hippocratic text *On Nutriment*, a work which is now generally considered to reflect Stoic influence, but which for Galen was a key source of genuine Hippocratic doctrine:

> Taken as a whole, all in sympathy, but taken severally, the parts in each part for its work [*ergon*].[15] (*UP* 1. 8, i. 12. 24–5 H., iii. 17 K. = Hipp. *Alim.* 23, ix. 106 Littré)

Galen offers a typically creative exegesis of this remark, which he says 'is rather obscure for most people because it is written in the archaic style and with his [sc. Hippocrates'] customary conciseness':

> All the parts of the body are in sympathy with one another, that is to say, all co-operate [ὁμολογεῖ] in producing one work [*ergon*]. The large parts, main

---

[14] For recognition of the Aristotelian background see *PHP* 1. 8, i. 92. 23–94. 10 De Lacy, v. 202–3 K. Cf. *UP* 8. 4, i. 454. 8–11 H., iii. 627 K., criticizing Aristotle for being deceived by 'names which are established not from the very essence [οὐσία] of the thing, but from some accidental characteristics [ἀπό τινων συμβεβηκότων]'.

[15] κατὰ μὲν οὐλομελίην πάντα συμπαθέα, κατὰ μέρος δὲ τὰ ἐν ἑκάστῳ μέρει μέρεα πρὸς τὸ ἔργον. However, this differs slightly from the standard modern text of *On Nutriment* (R. Joly, *Hippocrate*, vol. vi/2 (Paris, 1972), 143): σύρροια μία, σύμπνοια μία, συμπαθέα πάντα· κατὰ μὲν οὐλομελίην πάντα, κατὰ μέρος δὲ τὰ ἐν ἑκάστῳ μέρει μέρεα πρὸς τὸ ἔργον. This might be rendered: 'Conflux one, conspiration one, all things in sympathy; all the parts as forming a whole, and severally the parts in each part, with reference to the work' (so W. H. S. Jones, *Hippocrates*, vol. i (Cambridge, Mass., 1923), 351). Galen was fond of the aphorism and refers to it on a number of occasions as expressing the essence of Hippocrates' teaching about the body; see *Nat. fac.* 1. 12, 122. 6–10 H., ii. 29 K.; 1. 13, 129. 7–9 H., ii. 39 K.; 3. 13, 238. 4–7 H., ii. 189 K.; 3. 13, 243. 10–13 H., ii. 196 K.; *De causis pulsuum* 2. 12, ix. 88 K.; *De tremore* 6, vii. 616 K.; and *De methodo medendi* 1. 2, x. 16 K. (where the doctrine is ascribed to both Aristotle and the Stoics as well as Hippocrates). For the Stoic influence on *On Nutriment* see H. Diller, 'Eine Stoisch-pneumatische Schrift im Corpus Hippocraticum', *Sudhoffs Archiv*, 29 (1936), 178–95, repr. in G. Baader and H. Grensemann (eds.), *Hans Diller: Kleine Schriften zur antiken Medizin* (Berlin, 1973), 17–30.

divisions of the whole animal, such as the hands, feet, eyes, and tongue, came to be for the sake of the activities [*energeiai*] of the animal as a whole and all co-operate in performing them [πρὸς ταύτας . . . ὁμολογεῖ]. But the smaller parts, the components of the parts I have mentioned, have reference to the work [*ergon*] of the whole organ. The eye, for example, is the instrument of sight, composed of many parts which all co-operate [ὁμολογοῦντα] in one work [*ergon*], vision; it has some parts by means of which we see, others without which sight would be impossible, others for the sake of better vision, and still others to protect all these. This, moreover, is also true of all the other parts. (*UP* 1. 8, i. 13. 7–20 H., ii. 18–19 K.)

As Galen has it, 'Hippocrates' is remarking on the way in which the parts of the body work together or 'co-operate' (ὁμολογεῖν) to produce the characteristic activities (*energeiai*) of the organism.[16] First there are the larger parts such as the hands or eyes, which have come to be for the sake of the activities (*energeiai*) of the body as a whole, and co-operate (ὁμολογεῖ) with one another in bringing them about. But each individual organ such as the eye is also composed of many component parts, and these also co-operate (ὁμολογεῖ) towards producing the work (*ergon*) of the entire organ: the eye has some parts 'by means of which' (δι᾽ ὧν) we see, others for the sake of seeing better, others as necessary conditions of seeing, and still others for protection. Knowledge of the activities (*energeiai*) of the various organs (*organa*) is thus essential for understanding the uses (*chreiai*) of the parts, their beneficial contributions to the organism's activities. In the case of the hand, Galen claims, it is evident that its work (*ergon*) is grasping; but earlier thinkers have failed to understand the way in which all its parts have been constructed with a view towards performing this activity (*UP* 1. 8, i. 13. 22–14. 2 H., iii. 19 K.). In the case of many other organs the *ergon* is not at all clear, and this explains many of the errors that have been made concerning the uses (*chreiai*) of the parts (*UP* 1. 8, i. 14. 9–13 H., iii. 19–20 K.). In sum, when studying the uses of the parts, activity or *energeia* is 'the starting-point [ἀρχή] of investigation and the criterion [κριτήριον] of what is discovered' (*UP* 1. 10, i. 20. 2–4 H., iii. 27 K.).

[16] I follow May in translating ὁμολογεῖν as 'co-operate' (rather than, say, 'agree') since I take Galen's point to be not just that the parts 'agree' or 'accord' with one another (i.e. that they fit together well, making compatible but distinct contributions to the organism's activities), but also that they actively work together to promote the organism's activities. The ideas of active assistance and interdependence between the parts are suggested by the references to 'sympathy' (συμπάθεια), 'conspiration' (σύμπνοια), and 'conflux' (σύρροια) in the Hippocratic passage that Galen is expounding here.

There is much more to be said about the distinction between 'use' (*chreia*) and 'activity' (*energeia*), and I shall return to this in the next section. But it should now be clear that the co-ordinated activity of the various organs was a major factor that motivated Galen's functional approach to the body. The organs all work together to enable the organism to perform its characteristic activities, just as the parts of each organ work together to enable it to function normally. As in Aristotle, more is involved than just a high level of structural organization. The major organs and bodily systems not only work together towards the maintenance of the whole; they also depend on one another and influence one another's behaviour. In *On the Formation of the Embryo* Galen claims that while the parts can perform their activities (*energeiai*) independently of one another, they depend on 'assistance' (ἐπικουρία) from one another for their continued operation; this is because the substance of the parts is constantly changing in both quantity and quality (*De foetuum formatione* 5, 88. 13–21 Nickel, iv. 684 K.). He goes on to describe the interdependence of the three most important organs of the body, the brain, heart, and liver:

Now the heart (which some believe to be solely responsible for managing [διοικεῖν] the animal) when deprived of breathing ceases its motion, and with it the whole animal dies. It is deprived of breathing not just in cases of strangulation or when the path for inhalation is shut off due to inflammation of the parts around the larynx, but also when the nerves that move the chest are damaged (whether by cutting, crushing, or ligation), the spinal cord being the source of all these nerves, and the brain in turn of it. So just as the brain is useful [χρήσιμος] to the heart in order for the latter to sustain itself [εἰς τὴν διαμονήν]—it moves the chest through the nerves, and it is by expansion of the chest that inhalation takes place and by contraction, exhalation— in the same way, the heart provides a use [*chreia*] to the brain and the liver to both of these, as has been shown in the accounts of these matters. But it is not only these three principal organs [ἀρχαί] that are helped by one another; this is characteristic of all the other parts as well. For the present, let a single reminder suffice of all the other individual points that were made in *On the Use of the Parts.* (*De foetuum formatione* 5, 88. 25–90. 7 Nickel, iv. 685 K.)

The activity of the heart depends on the brain, but the heart also serves the brain as the source of the arteries, which maintain the innate heat and nourish the psychic pneuma. The liver serves both heart and brain, but it is also dependent on them for its continued activity.[17] The analysis of major bodily systems thus involves a kind of feedback in which each both sustains and is sustained by the others. Evidently Galen considers this kind of functional interdependence to be one of the essential points of *De usu partium*.[18]

### 4. Use and activity

One way in which Galen goes beyond anything found in Aristotle's biological works is in developing a systematic distinction between the notions of 'use' (*chreia*) and 'activity' (*energeia*).[19] At the beginning of the last book of *De usu partium* Galen offers his most explicit characterization of this distinction:

Now the activity [*energeia*] of a part differs from its use [*chreia*], as I have said before, because activity is active change and use is the same as what is commonly called utility [εὐχρηστία]. I have said that activity is *active* change because many changes occur passively [κατὰ πάθος], and indeed they are called 'passive' [παθητικαί]—all those which occur in things when other things change them. (*UP* 17. 1, ii. 437. 8–15 H., iv. 346–7 K.)

The idea of *energeia* as a specifically active (δραστικός) change or motion (*kinēsis*) is one that can be paralleled in other Galenic works, where we also find the contrast with 'passive' (παθητική) change arising from an external source; it is clear in these passages that *kinēsis* covers both change of quality and change of place or local motion. Thus when food becomes blood this is a passive change

---

[17] For the heart as the source of the arteries and their role in maintaining the vital heat and nourishing the psychic pneuma see *UP* 1. 16, i. 32. 23–33. 10 H., iii. 45–6 K. For the dependence of the liver on the brain and heart see *UP* 4. 13, i. 227. 4–23 H., iii. 309–10 K.: arteries from the heart arrive at the liver in order to preserve the due measure of heat in it, and a nerve is inserted into its outer tunic to prevent it from being completely without sensation. For ἐπικουρία cf. *De propriis placitis* 10, with the new text of V. Boudon-Millot and A. Pietrobelli, 'Galien ressuscité: édition *princeps* du texte grec du *De propriis placitis*' ['Galien ressuscité'], *Revue des études grecques*, 118 (2005), 168–213 at 181. 26–182. 15.

[18] The discussion of R. E. Siegel, *Galen on Psychology, Psychopathology, and Function and Diseases of the Nervous System: An Analysis of his Observations and Experiments* (Basel, 1973), 31–53, has the merit of drawing attention to Galen's conception of functional integration or interdependence, though his translations and analyses are often unreliable.

[19] On Galen's use/activity distinction see D. Furley and J. S. Wilkie, *Galen on Respiration and the Arteries* [*Galen on Respiration*] (Princeton, 1984), 58–69; R. J. Hankinson, 'Galen Explains the Elephant', in M. Matthen and B. Linsky (eds.), *Philosophy and Biology* (Calgary, 1988), 135–57.

of the food but an active change of the veins; similarly, when the muscles move the limbs, the motion of the muscles is active and that of the limbs passive.[20] Galen's extensive deployment of *energeia* and its correlate *dynamis* obviously reflects the pervasive influence of Aristotle on Greek medical and biological thought, though the extent to which his use of these concepts is genuinely Aristotelian is not immediately clear.[21]

The remark that *chreia* is equivalent to 'what is commonly called utility [εὐχρηστία]' is the closest Galen comes to defining the term in *De usu partium*. LSJ gives a wide range of meanings, including 'need', 'want', 'use', 'advantage', and 'service', and examples of all these senses can be found in the hundreds of instances of *chreia* in *De usu partium*.[22] Despite this variation, however, the basic idea expressed by *chreia* in a large number of passages is that of a beneficial contribution to the organism's characteristic activities, especially self-maintenance and reproduction. The importance of a part is judged by its *chreia*, its beneficial contribution to the organism's life:

This can be decided in both cases by the use [*chreia*]. But since there are three kinds of use—for life itself [εἰς αὐτὸ τὸ ζῆν], or for living well [εἰς τὸ καλῶς ζῆν], or for preserving the species [εἰς τὴν τοῦ γένους φυλακήν] . . . (*UP* 6. 7, i. 318. 8–11 H., iii. 435 K.)

Again we have the Aristotelian tripartite schema: all the parts contribute to life, reproduction, or the improvement of life.[23] In so far

---

[20]  *Nat. fac.* 1. 2, 105. 13–23 H., ii. 6–7 K. Cf. *De methodo medendi* 1. 6, x. 45–6 K.; 2. 3, x. 87 K.; and *PHP* 6. 1, ii. 360. 22–3 De Lacy, v. 506 K.: 'Now activity is active change, and I mean by "active" a change arising from the thing itself, while "affection" is change in one thing that arises from another' (ἡ μὲν οὖν ἐνέργεια κίνησίς ἐστι δραστική, δραστικὴν δ' ὀνομάζω τὴν ἐξ ἑαυτοῦ, τὸ δὲ πάθος ἐν ἑτέρῳ κίνησίς ἐστιν ἐξ ἑτέρου). Galen goes on to say that the active and passive changes are often the same process, but viewed in two different ways; for example, the separation of a cut object is an activity of the cutter but an affection of what is cut. But then he adds that according to another usage *energeia* is change 'according to nature' (κατὰ φύσιν) and πάθος change 'contrary to nature' (παρὰ φύσιν), and that when the terms are used in this sense it does not matter whether the source of the change is internal or external (ii. 360. 23–362. 9 De Lacy, v. 506–7 K.).

[21]  The term 'active' (δραστικός) is not found in Aristotle, and its use by Galen probably reflects Stoic influence. Moreover, while Aristotle recognizes a close association between *energeia* and *kinēsis*, he also draws important distinctions between the two concepts (see esp. *Metaph.* 1048ᵇ18–35 ).

[22]  A TLG search for the various forms of *chreia* in the treatise yields some 467 instances.

[23]  See also *UP* 6. 7, i. 318. 15–19 H., iii. 436 K.: those parts of the heart are most

as *chreia* refers primarily to the beneficial contribution of the parts rather than to their 'suitability' or 'fitness' to make such contributions, the translation 'use' is preferable to 'utility' or 'usefulness'.[24]

Understood in this way, *chreia* is clearly distinct from *energeia* understood as 'active change'. Galen writes of the *chreiai* of *energeiai*, where what is in question is the contribution of the active motion or change in question to the organism's life. For example, the *energeia* of the arteries is their active, pulsating motion, caused by the 'pulsative faculty' (σφυγμικὴ δύναμις) transmitted by the heart through the arterial coats; but the *chreia* of this activity is the preservation of the vital heat and nourishing of the psychic pneuma.[25] Where a part does have an activity of its own, its principal contribution to the organism's life will be made through that activity. An example of this is the elephant's trunk: Galen says he thought it was useless and superfluous until he saw the elephant performing many useful actions with it; in this case 'the use of the part is bound up with the usefulness of the activity'.[26] Nevertheless, the concepts of *chreia* and *energeia* remain distinct. The *chreia* of some parts consists in providing security or the necessary conditions for activities, or in making it possible for them to be performed better.[27]

important [κύριον] whose *chreiai* preserve the life of the whole organism; and 8. 6, i. 471. 11–16 H., iii. 650 K.: the pores of the nostrils have two *chreiai*, one of which is necessary for life itself (the discharge of residues from the brain), the other for a better life (the transmission of odours to the organ of smell).

[24] *Pace* May, *Usefulness*, i. 9, who takes the basic meaning to be 'the suitability or fitness of a part for performing its action'. The translation 'use' is in keeping with the traditional Latin title, *De usu partium*; cf. also the titles Περὶ χρείας ἀναπνοῆς (*De usu respirationis*) and Περὶ χρείας σφυγμῶν (*De usu pulsuum*). In Harvey's usage, the terms *usus* and *actio* correspond to Galen's *chreia* and *energeia*; see Furley and Wilkie, *Galen on Respiration*, 61.

[25] *UP* 1. 16, i. 32. 23–33. 10 H., iii. 45–6 K.; cf. *De usu pulsuum* 3, v. 160–1 K. See also *UP* 6. 4, i. 308. 15–18 H., iii. 422 K.: 'Where the use of the activity [ἡ τῆς ἐνεργείας . . . χρεία] of each of two organs is of equal importance [ὁμότιμος], as for the eyes and ears and hands and feet, nature has made the ones on the right exactly equal to those on the left.'

[26] συναφθείσης τῷ τῆς ἐνεργείας χρησίμῳ τῆς χρείας τοῦ μορίου (*UP* 17. 1, ii. 438. 19–20 H., iv. 348 K.). Cf. *UP* 11. 16, ii. 167. 15–16 H., iii. 918 K.: 'when the activity [*energeia*] of this muscle has been discovered, its use [*chreia*] is also immediately clear'.

[27] *UP* 6. 4, i. 307. 25–308. 1 H., iii. 421 K.: 'Indeed, the use [*chreia*] of the respiratory organs would rightly come about through movement [διὰ κινήσεως], while that of organs of support would come about through rest [δι' ἡσυχίας]'; 7. 12, i. 407. 7–14 H., iii. 559–60 K.: 'Now when parts act, their use [*chreia*] straightway becomes evident at the same time, and anyone who is explaining use [*chreia*] need only mention their activity [*energeia*]. But for those parts which perform no activity manifestly useful to the animal as a whole (for this is how you should always

The distinction between use and activity is also reflected on the methodological level. The investigation of *energeiai* involves the attempt to discern the specific causes of motions or changes in the parts, e.g. whether the pulsation of the arteries is caused by a faculty (*dynamis*) transmitted by the heart through the arterial coats or by the heart acting as a pump.[28] Since Galen holds that a part's activity depends on the character of the substance from which it is made (i.e. the particular blend of hot, cold, wet, and dry), the investigation of activities will also involve a study of the material substance of the parts.[29] The study of the *chreia* of a bodily process or part, on the other hand, involves a general consideration of its role in the overall economy of the organism. In particular, it requires the systematic examination of the contribution of all the part's attributes (including substance, shape, and arrangement in relation to other parts) to the life of the organism as a whole.[30]

In many passages the *chreia* of a part is closely associated with the purpose for which it was constructed:

Now nature in providing for their [sc. the fingernails'] safety made them moderately hard, so as not to detract in any way from the use for which they have come to be [τὴν χρείαν, ἧς ἕνεκα γεγόνεσαν], and also to keep them from being easily harmed. (*UP* 1. 11, i. 21. 6–10 H., iii. 29 K.)

If the leg were completely without movable joints it could not be extended or flexed, and so would lose all the use for which it has come to be [τὴν χρείαν, ἧς ἕνεκα γέγονεν]. (*UP* 3. 14, i. 185. 4–7 H., iii. 252 K.)

Since the whole arm was constructed for many, varied movements, it needed to have the head of the humerus rounded . . . and to have a concavity associated with it that was not very deep and did not end in large rims. For if the joint of the humerus were enclosed in a shallow concavity but still restrained all around by large rims, it could not be rotated easily in every direction, though this rather than safety was its use [*chreia*], since it

understand use) but which subserve parts that do act, I must give in this treatise an explanation in greater detail; for this is its special purpose.'

[28] For Galen's discussion of this question see *PHP* 6. 7, ii. 404. 38–406. 24 De Lacy, v. 560–2 K.; *An in arteriis natura sanguis contineatur* 8, iv. 733–4 K.

[29] For the dependence of *energeiai* on the substance of the organs see e.g. *Nat. fac.* 1. 3, 106. 4–6 H., ii. 7 K.

[30] See *UP* 1. 9, i. 19. 9–24 H., iii. 26–7 K., and 4. 13, i. 220. 19–25 H., iii. 300 K., on the need to study not just the distinctive substance of the parts but also their placement, number, size, contexture (πλοκή), shaping (διάπλασις), connection (ξύμφυσις), and interrelationships (ἡ πρὸς ἄλληλα κοινωνία ἅπάση).

was for the sake of this [τούτου γὰρ ἔνεκα] that the whole arm was created. (*UP* 13. 12, ii. 276. 1–12 H., iv. 129–30 K.)

In contexts such as these, to specify the *chreia* of a part is to state the reason why it is present in the organism; the terminology [οὗ ἔνεκα, 'for the sake of which'] obviously recalls the Aristotelian final cause. The connection between *chreia* and purpose is reinforced by an association between *chreia* and *skopos* ('aim', 'goal'). *Chreia* is the 'primary aim' (πρῶτος σκοπός) of the construction of all the parts; the most important 'cause' (*aitia*) to consider in explaining an organ is 'the aim of its activity' (σκοπὸς τῆς ἐνεργείας).[31] In passages where *chreia* refers to the reason why a part is present in the organism or the purpose for which it came to be, it retains the connotation of 'need': to state the reason why a part is present is also to say why it is needed. Galen sometimes uses the phrase ἀναγκαία χρεία ('necessary use') to refer to this sort of essential contribution to the organism's life. For example, the fibula 'provides a use [*chreia*] to the animal: the primary and necessary one is twofold, but there is a third use for good measure' (*UP* 3. 13, i. 180. 20–2 H., iii. 246 K.).[32]

As this remark suggests, however, parts may have uses that are not necessary or essential for the organism's life. Galen frequently distinguishes between the *chreia* 'for the sake of which' (ἧς ἔνεκα) a part has been created and its other beneficial contributions to the organism's activities:

It was, then, for the sake of these activities [ἔνεκα μὲν δὴ τούτων] that the convexities at the ends of the ulna and radius came to be; but nature also makes use of them to secure another advantage [χρῆται δ᾽ αὐταῖς καὶ πρὸς ἄλλο τι χρηστόν], just as she is accustomed frequently to make something that has come to be on account of one thing serve other uses as well [τῷ δι᾽ ἕτερόν τι γεγονότι συγχρῆσθαι καὶ πρὸς ἄλλα]. For she located the heads of the tendons moving the fingers in the concavity between these eminences, thus establishing as if with a wall or tower a safe refuge for the tendons. (*UP* 2. 11, i. 97. 19–98. 2 H., iii. 133 K.)

The purpose 'for the sake of which' (ἔνεκα) the convexities were made (the mobility of the hand) is clearly distinct from the ancil-

---

[31] *UP* 11. 13, ii. 153. 19–26 H., iii. 899 K.; 6. 12, i. 338. 20–2 H., iii. 464 K; cf. also 6. 4, i. 308. 18–27 H., iii. 422 K.; 5. 9, i. 276. 26–277. 4 H., iii. 378 K.

[32] See also *De anatomicis administrationibus* 7. 1, ii. 590 K.: 'All these things nature made in the first instance [κατὰ πρῶτον λόγον], some of them for the sake of necessary uses [ἀναγκαίων ἔνεκα χρειῶν], for life itself, but others for uses that are indeed beneficial to living things, but not necessary to them.'

lary or spin-off benefit that they confer (protection of the tendons). These spin-off benefits are also *chreiai*, and they are in fact one of the most important indications of nature's craftsmanship:

For the greatest evidence of a resourceful craftsman, as has been said many times before, lies in using what has come to be for the sake of one thing also for other uses [τὸ συγχρῆσθαι τοῖς ἑτέρου τινὸς ἕνεκα γεγονόσι καὶ πρὸς ἄλλας χρείας], instead of seeking to make a special part for each use. (*UP* 9. 5, ii. 17. 18–22 H., iii. 706 K.)

How, then, would this too not be among the most wondrous works of nature, namely that she is eager to craft each of the organs that has come to be for the sake of some use to the animal [ἕνεκά τινος χρείας τῷ ζῴῳ] straightaway also for some other benefit [πρὸς ἄλλο τι . . . ὠφέλιμον]? (*UP* 7. 22, i. 439. 20–3 H., iii. 605 K.)

In contexts where Galen emphasizes the distinction between 'primary' or 'necessary' *chreiai* and such spin-off benefits, *chreia* is more general than purpose; it refers to any contribution that a part makes to the organism's activities.

One way in which Galen attempts to articulate the complex functional organization of the human body is by stressing the interdependence of uses and activities. For example, the *chreia* of a part of the hand will be its contribution to the *energeia* of the hand, grasping; but this activity also has many uses (*chreiai*) for the life of the organism as a whole. A more complex example comes in *UP* 6. 9 (i. 322. 13–323. 17 H., iii. 441–3 K.). Here Galen argues that the hearts of animals with a lung always have the right ventricle, while those of lungless animals lack the right ventricle. The right ventricle exists for the sake of (ἕνεκα) the lung (that is, its service to the lung is its *chreia*), while the lung itself is an organ of respiration and voice (i.e. its *energeiai*, which have further *chreiai* for the organism as a whole). Criticizing Aristotle's view that the number of chambers of the heart is correlated with the size of the organism, Galen writes:

Nature pays no attention to the large or small size of the body when she varies the form of the organs; on the contrary, her aim [*skopos*] in construction is difference of activity [*energeia*], and she measures the activities themselves in turn by their primary use [τῇ πρώτῃ χρείᾳ]. Thus there is produced a wonderful series [στοῖχος] of activities and uses succeeding one another, as I have demonstrated in what I have already said and as my present discourse will show no less clearly to those who will study it with some degree of care. (*UP* 6. 9, i. 323. 9–17 H., iii. 442–3 K.)

Elsewhere Galen writes that the 'association' or 'partnership' (κοινωνία) of *chreiai* and *energeiai* makes an important contribution to
the organism's life (*UP* 8. 7, i. 475. 20–8 H., iii. 655–6 K.).
The interdependence of *chreiai* and *energeiai* is also reflected on
the methodological level. It is a recurrent theme in *De usu partium*
that the study of *chreiai* presupposes a knowledge of *energeiai*, which
itself is sometimes said to be based on the results of dissection.[33]
Galen often remarks that it is not his purpose in *De usu partium* to
investigate *energeiai;* rather, for the knowledge of these one should
use the results established in other works such as *De naturalibus
facultatibus* or *De placitis Hippocratis et Platonis* as 'foundations'
(ὑποθέσεις).[34] On the other hand, he sometimes suggests that knowledge of *chreiai* can confirm accounts of *energeiai* where the latter
are unclear or disputed.[35] It is possible to grasp the usefulness of
some part to the organism as a whole without grasping the nature
of its activity, just as an activity can be grasped independently of
its contribution to the overall economy of the organism. Accounts
of *chreiai* and *energeiai* thus confirm one another, leading to a more
complex methodological situation than some of Galen's explicit
remarks might suggest.[36] Where the *chreia* of a part or process is
known, it can help to determine the nature of the *energeiai* involved;
where an *energeia* is known, it can be used to find *chreiai*. Again, activities are both 'the starting-point of investigation and the criterion
of what is discovered' (*UP* 1. 10, i. 20. 2–4 H., iii. 27 K.).
The sequence of *chreiai* and *energeiai* revealed by the study of the
parts must explain their role in promoting the primary activities of
the organism. This is relatively straightforward in some cases: the
parts of the hand are useful because they promote the activity of the
hand, which has many uses for the animal in attempting to survive
in a changing environment. In the case of bodily processes such as

[33] e.g. *UP* 2. 7, i. 86. 1–4 H., iii. 117 K.; 2. 16, i. 114. 6–12 H., iii. 155 K.; 6. 12,
i. 337. 22–338. 1 H., iii. 463 K.; 7. 4, i. 379. 23–380. 1 H., iii. 522–3 K.; 7. 12, i.
407. 4–7 H., iii. 559 K.
[34] e.g. *UP* 4. 13, i. 226. 7–15 H., iii. 308 K.; 4. 17, i. 241. 19–242. 1 H., iii. 329 K.;
8. 4, i. 453. 11–18 H., iii. 625–6 K.; 8. 11, i. 484. 15–23 H., iii. 667–8 K.
[35] e.g. *UP* 5. 5, i. 266. 24–267. 4 H., iii. 364 K.; 7. 5, i. 382. 15–18 H., iii. 526 K.;
7. 8, i. 391. 24–5 H., iii. 539 K.
[36] Cf. *UP* 7. 5, i. 383. 25–384. 3 H., iii. 528 K.: 'But now, since I have shown that
all the true statements I have made about uses [*chreiai*] in this exposition and about
activities [*energeiai*] in earlier ones are consistent and corroborate one another [πάντ'
ἀλλήλοις ὁμολογεῖ τε καὶ μαρτυρεῖ τἀληθῆ], let us proceed to discuss the remaining
parts of the lung.'

respiration and the pulse, however, the sequence tends towards circularity: the uses of these activities consist partly of contributions to their own continued performance. Thus the pulse is the *energeia* of the arteries, and is caused by the pulsative faculty transmitted by the heart; the existence of this faculty depends on the constitution of the flesh of the heart, which is the seat of the innate heat. The primary *chreia* of the pulse, Galen says, is maintenance of the innate heat. But the innate heat itself also has many uses, including nutrition and digestion, and these activities contribute to preserving the distinctive mixtures of the various organs (including the heart) so that they can continue to exercise their faculties. Thus the primary use of the activity of the arteries is to create the conditions necessary for its continued performance by maintaining the innate heat, and the uses of the innate heat include the activities that help to sustain it. Such circularity is in no way vicious; it is, rather, just what we should expect from a sophisticated attempt to explain the feedback inherent in a self-maintaining system such as the human body.[37]

## 5. Functions

I now want to consider the extent to which Galen's concepts of *chreia* and *energeia* capture the notion of function as it is used in contemporary biology and philosophy of science. At first sight it is perhaps natural to think that *energeia* corresponds to function, for the idea of function seems closely linked to activity: an account of a thing's function is, very crudely, an account of something that it *does*.[38] But the function of a part of a complex system need not be an

---

[37] The circularity is noted by Wilkie (*Galen on Respiration*, 66–7), but he does not connect it with the need to account for the organism as a self-maintaining system. For the role of the innate heat in causing nutrition and digestion see *Nat. fac.* 2. 4, 165. 23–166. 12 H., ii. 89–90 K. Galen sometimes identifies it as the cause of the motion of the arteries, as at *PHP* 8. 7, ii. 524. 10–13 De Lacy, v. 702 K. At *De causis pulsuum* 1. 2, ix. 4–5 K., however, he refuses to state whether the cause of the pulse is the innate heat, the peculiar blend of qualities in the heart, or a number of other possibilities; he is willing only to assert the existence of a faculty (*dynamis*) that causes the pulse. For the self-maintaining character of the innate heat see *De tremore* 6, vii. 616 K., where it is identified with nature and soul: 'And nature and soul are nothing other than this, so that if you think of it as a self-moving, ever-moving substance [οὐσίαν αὐτοκίνητόν τε καὶ ἀεικίνητον], you will not be in error.'

[38] May thinks that *energeia* is closer to 'function' than *chreia* (*Usefulness*, i. 9). M. Beckner, 'Function and Teleology', *Journal of the History of Biology*, 2 (1969), 151–64, restricts functions to activities.

activity: it is reasonable to say that the function of the windows in a house is to let in light, but this is not an activity.[39] In fact it is *chreia* that corresponds more closely than *energeia* to the modern notion of function, as can be seen from two consderations in particular. (1) Giving an account of a part's *chreia* involves specifying its beneficial contribution to the organism's activities, chief among them survival and reproduction. Specifying the *chreia* of a part thus carries an implicit reference to the good or benefit of the organism as a whole. The notion that function ascriptions imply a reference to the organism's good, and in particular its survival or reproduction, is fundamental to many modern discussions of biological function. One modern attempt to set out a conception of biological function that is especially close to Galen's notion of *chreia* is that of John Canfield.[40] For Canfield, to give a functional analysis of a structure, part, or feature of an organism is to state what the item in question 'does' that is 'useful' to the organism (where 'does' need not imply activity but includes verbs such as 'store' or 'prevent', and 'useful' is glossed as 'contributing to survival and reproduction'). Canfield notes further that the class of items for which functions should be specified includes processes such as the heartbeat or the secretion of bile, and also that functions can be understood as contributing not only to the organism as a whole but also to 'subsystems' such as the homeostasis of blood sugar.[41] All this is entirely in the spirit of Galen: compare the notion that the use of the pulse (which is itself the activity of the arteries) is the maintenance of the innate heat.[42] (2) The second point concerns the kinds of question that an account of *chreia* is meant to answer. An account of the *chreia* of a part explains its contribution to the organism's activities; it

---

[39] The example is taken from Wright, 'Functions', 139; cf. ibid. 152 (objecting to Beckner): 'It is not at all clear that functions—even natural functions—have to be activities at all . . . Making seconds easier to read is an example, but there are many others: preventing skids in wet weather, keeping your pants up, or propping open my office door. All of these things are legitimate functions (of tire treads, belts, and doorstops, respectively); none are activities in any recognizable sense.'

[40] Canfield, 'Teleological Explanation in Biology'.      [41] Ibid. 287 n. 1.

[42] R. Sorabji, 'Function', *Philosophical Quarterly*, 14/57 (1964), 289–302, identifies contribution to a good as an essential attribute of functions in living organisms and social systems. Various authors (e.g. Wright) have attacked the view that a contribution to the organism's good is essential to function ascriptions; but see McLaughlin, *What Functions Explain*, for a defence of the view that function ascriptions, if they are to be genuinely explanatory, demand an (Aristotelian) metaphysical commitment to the existence of the organism as the beneficiary of a good.

answers the question 'What is this part good for?' But in giving the *chreia* of a part Galen may also be explaining why it is present in the organism or why it has the particular set of attributes that it does; it is these questions, in fact, that seem to be Galen's primary concern throughout *De usu partium*. The important point is that the scope of functional explanation in modern philosophy of science covers both sorts of question: both 'What is this part good for?' and 'Why is this part here?' To say that the function of the liver is to secrete bile is to specify the liver's contribution to the animal's survival, but it may also be part of an explanation of the presence of livers in animals (for example, because the presence of an organ to secrete bile was favoured by natural selection).[43] For these reasons, Galen's accounts of *chreia* can reasonably be viewed as functional explanations.

To be sure, Galen's use of *chreia* is broader than some contemporary conceptions of function in at least two respects. First there is the issue of the kinds of activity to which *chreiai* are viewed as contributing: these include more than just survival and reproduction, for Galen says that *chreia* can be understood as a contribution to living well (τὸ καλῶς ζῆν). In this he follows both Plato and Aristotle.[44] Second, there is the more problematic question of whether utility alone is an adequate criterion for the identification of functions. Much of the recent literature is based on the idea that functions must be distinguished from accidental benefits. The importance of the distinction between function and accident has been urged especially by Wright, who remarks: 'Something can do something useful purely by accident, but it cannot have, as its function, something it does only by accident.'[45] Since for Galen *chreia* can refer

---

[43] Wright is a leading proponent of the view that function ascriptions explain the presence of the function-bearer in biological systems, via the mechanism of natural selection. Thus, the function of the liver is what the liver does in an organism that also explains (via natural selection) why livers are there: 'If an organ has been naturally differentially selected-for by virtue of something it does, we can say that the reason the organ is there is that it does that something' ('Functions', 159). On his view, we can say that *Y* is the function of a part *X* if and only if *X* does *Y* and *X* is there *because* it does *Y*. For the alternative view that what functions explain is not the presence of the function-bearer but rather its role in a complex system see esp. R. Cummins, 'Functional Analysis', *Journal of Philosophy*, 72 (1975), 741–65.

[44] As Sorabji has noted ('Function', 293–5), both Plato and Aristotle recognize the distinction between activities essential for the preservation of life and those that make it possible to live well (cf. n. 8 above). He makes a good case for regarding contributions to the latter kind of activity as 'luxury functions'.

[45] Wright, 'Functions', 147, objecting to the view of Canfield mentioned above.

to any beneficial contribution to the organism's life, it would seem that he lacks the means for distinguishing genuine functions from accidental benefits.

In fact, however, the situation is both more complicated and more interesting. As we have seen, Galen's concept of *chreia* is richly differentiated, and he frequently distinguishes between 'spin-off' benefits and the 'primary *chreia*' for which a part was created. Building on this distinction, one might develop a view on which the functions of the parts would be limited to their primary *chreiai*, as reflected in the need for the Demiurge or nature to bring them into existence in the first place. But it is also possible to take Galen's wide-ranging application of the concept of *chreia* to support the idea that *any* contribution a part makes to the organism's activities may be considered one of its functions. It is not at all clear that the distinction between functions and accidental benefits is as fundamental as some modern authors have taken it to be. If functions are understood as contributions to the welfare of the organism as a whole, there is no obvious reason to rule out *any* such contribution from counting as a genuine function.[46]

However this may be, it should be clear that Galen's use of the concept of *chreia* shares a good deal of common ground with modern discussions of biological function, as it does with Aristotelian functional analysis. The basic reason for this is that for Galen, ascriptions of *chreia* are always referred back to the organism's good, understood as survival, reproduction, or a better life. Galen may be a lot more generous than Aristotle in ascribing functions to the parts and their attributes (see next section), but it can hardly be said that his ascriptions are arbitrary or piecemeal. Rather, they flow from a sophisticated analysis of the organism's activities and the various ways in which the parts contribute to their performance.

6. From functions to design

So far I have emphasized the close similarities between Galen's and Aristotle's functional approach to the study of living things.

---

[46] Wright, who has emphasized the importance of the function/accident distinction, also rejects the notion that functions can be understood as contributions to the organism's welfare.

But there are of course major differences as well, and it is important to take note of them. First of all, Galen's argument in *De usu
partium* is not only that the parts of the body are adapted to the
performance of the organism's activities, but also that they are so
well adapted to carrying out those activities that no better construction is possible. At the beginning of *UP* 1. 5, immediately after his
introductory discussion of the human hand, Galen goes on to give
the first of many statements of this fundamental thesis:

Come now, let us investigate this very important part of man's body, examining it to determine not simply whether it is useful or whether it is
suitable for an intelligent animal, but whether it is in every respect so
constructed that it would not have been better had it come into being
differently. (*UP* 1. 5, i. 6. 18–22 H., iii. 9 K.)

Galen's attempts to discern purpose in the structure and arrangement of the parts of the body are nothing less than an effort to
demonstrate this sweeping claim. Now while Aristotle is certainly
concerned to show that the parts of a human being are 'useful' and
'suitable for an intelligent animal', it is no part of his project to argue that the parts are so well constructed that they could not be any
better. For Aristotle, the goal is just to show that a certain feature
or structure makes some contribution to the organism's activities,
especially survival or reproduction; for Galen this is only the beginning. This explains the abundance of counterfactual argument
in *De usu partium*: Galen often argues that if a certain part were any
larger or smaller, or placed differently in any way, the activities of
the organism would somehow be impaired.[47] Such arguments play
no role in Aristotle's accounts of living things. In general Galen's
teleology is comprehensive in a way that Aristotle's is not. Galen is
committed to finding a use for virtually every part of the body, and
every attribute; Aristotle, by contrast, is more willing to acknowledge that some parts are present for no purpose.[48]

Thus Galen, as well as adopting a functional approach to the

[47] As R. J. Hankinson notes ('Galen and the Best of All Possible Worlds', *Classical
Quarterly*, NS 39/1 (1989), 206–27 at 220–1), such arguments are open to objection
in that they presuppose that all the parts other than the one in question are fixed,
so that only variation in that particular part needs to be considered when evalu-
ating whether it is structured as well as it could possibly be. But this ignores the
possibility that a radically different structural plan might enable the organism to
perform its activities better.

[48] The spleen is a case in point (*PA* 670ᵃ30–1); cf. also the remarks on bile at *PA*
677ᵃ11–19. Such parts or constituents, Aristotle thinks, follow necessarily from the

study of the parts, also argued for the claim that the human body displays optimal construction. As he sees it, this is largely a matter of the best possible adaptation of structure to function. But it is important to see that an argument for optimal construction is independent of a concern with functional explanation *as such*. As the example of Aristotle shows, one can adopt a functional approach to the study of the parts without arguing for their optimal construction. And one might also argue that the parts are structured as well as they could possibly be without grounding this in a notion of functional organization. Galen's concern to argue for optimal construction thus reflects commitments different from those which motivate his functional approach.

In fact, this concern is connected with a feature of Galen's thought that is Platonic rather than Aristotelian: the notion that a divine Craftsman or Demiurge is ultimately responsible for the order discernible in the world as a whole and living things in particular. That the human body is constructed 'as well as it could possibly be' is for Galen a major piece of evidence for the existence of the Demiurge. In the last book of *De usu partium*, he discusses the purpose of studying the uses of the parts. This study has several uses for the doctor, including diagnosis and prognosis (*UP* 17. 2, ii. 449. 20–450. 26 H., iv. 363–4 K.), but the main reason to pursue it is for what it reveals about the beneficent intelligence that is responsible for the design of the human being:

Thus, when anyone looking at the facts with an open mind sees that in such a slime of fleshes and juices there is yet an indwelling intelligence and sees too the structure of any animal whatsoever—for they all give indication

presence of parts that *do* have a purpose; cf. Johnson, *Aristotle on Teleology*, 197. It is sometimes said that Galen refuses to acknowledge the existence of *any* parts of this kind in the body (e.g. Hankinson, 'Galen and the Best of All Possible Worlds', 214). See, however, *UP* 5. 3 on the jejunum or νῆστις, which provides no *chreia* to the organism but 'follows by necessity on parts which have come to be for a purpose [ἐξ ἀνάγκης ἕπεσθαι τοῖς ἕνεκά του γεγονόσιν]', i. 254. 6–7 H., iii. 346 K.; cf. also ibid. 5. 16, i. 297. 21–4 H., iii. 406 K. (the obliquity of the neck of the bladder follows of necessity on purposive structures), and 11. 14, ii. 160. 20–161. 1 H., iii. 908–9 K. (hair in the armpits is due not to the providence [*pronoia*] of the Demiurge, but rather to the nature of the fluids there). Galen says that such features are simply not his concern in *De usu partium*: 'For in these commentaries I am explaining not the necessary consequences of things that have come to be for a purpose [τῶν ἐξ ἀνάγκης ἑπομένων τοῖς ἕνεκά του γεγονόσιν], but those things that have been crafted by nature in the first instance [τῶν κατὰ πρῶτον λόγον ὑπὸ τῆς φύσεως δεδημιουργημένων]' (5. 3, i. 257. 4–8 H., iii. 350–1 K.). None of this is to deny, of course, that Galen is much more systematic and comprehensive than Aristotle in his search for uses of the parts.

[ἔνδειξις] of a wise craftsman—he will understand the superiority of the intelligence in the heavens. Then a work on the use of the parts, which at first seemed to him a thing of scant importance, will be truly established as the starting-point [ἀρχή] of a precise theology [θεολογίας ἀκριβοῦς], which is a thing far greater and far more honourable than all of medicine. Hence such a work is useful not only for the doctor, but much more so for the philosopher who is eager to gain an understanding of the whole of nature. (*UP* 17. 1, ii. 447. 16–448. 3 H., iv. 360–1 K.)

The crucial step in the argument is the move from optimal construction to the existence of the Demiurge—a classic example of 'inference to the best explanation', which is strictly speaking no inference at all. Galen views the situation as a choice between two exhaustive alternatives: *either* the marvellous construction of living things is due to the random collision of elementary particles, *or else* it is the result of divine intelligence (*UP* 17. 1, ii. 440. 3–441. 10 H., iv. 350–1 K.). Given this choice, Galen opts for the latter alternative as the best explanation. It is not my intention to evaluate the plausibility of this move here; I want only to point out that it too is independent of a functional approach to the study of the parts. Just as one can argue for optimal construction on grounds other than functional organization, so too the move from optimal construction to design does not itself imply a concern with functional explanation. This suggests that it was not the assumption of design that motivated Galen's functional approach, but rather the Aristotelian notion of the organism as a unified whole manifesting a coherent pattern of activities such as self-maintenance and reproduction.

Now it is true that, for Galen, functional considerations do enter into the arguments for the optimal construction of the body and the existence of the Demiurge. They do so via the notion of craftsmanship (*technē*). The human body, Galen claims, displays a superlative degree of craftsmanship; hence it must be the work of a divine Craftsman, even if we cannot perceive his existence directly.[49] Galen's notion of craftsmanship involves a number of features, in-

---

[49] The claim that the human body displays skilled craftsmanship is a constant refrain throughout *De usu partium*; Galen elaborates on it at length in *UP* 17. 1, ii. 441. 10–446. 7 H., iv. 351–8 K. In *PHP* 9. 8 he presents the inference from the craftsmanship of the body to the existence of the Demiurge as a paradigm example of inductive reasoning (ii. 590–6 De Lacy, v. 782–91 K.). At *PHP* 9. 8, ii. 596. 5–20 De Lacy, v. 789–90 K., he argues that to doubt the existence of the Demiurge simply because he cannot be perceived directly would be as absurd as doubting that an artefact such as a bed or couch was made by a craftsman just because he has never been seen.

cluding symmetry (συμμετρία), equality (ἰσότης), proportion (ἀναλογία), and beauty, but the most important feature is the adaptation of structure to function.[50] Just as the craftsman constructs all the parts of a complex artefact with a view to the uses they must serve in the whole, so all the parts of the human body are constructed to perform their functions in the whole organism. The perfect adaptation of the parts of an artefact to their uses is a reliable indication of craftsmanship, and this holds no less of the human body than of an artefact such as a ship or a couch. Of those who fail to recognize the craftsmanship manifest in living things, Galen writes:

They completely forget the judgement that all men naturally make about the arts [*technai*], and they forget the very great similarity between our formation and the arts; and yet they see many men working with materials who are not called shoemakers or builders or moulders unless it is evident that every object they fashion has been made for some useful purpose [χρησίμου ἔνεκά τινος], since there is no other mark of an art besides the use [*chreia*] of each part of the product it fashions. (*PHP* 9. 8, ii. 590. 30–592. 1 De Lacy, v. 784 K.)

Thus, grasping the supposedly perfect adaptation of structure to function in the body reveals that it is the product of craftsmanship, which in turn reveals the existence of the Demiurge.

However, even though Galen believes that the complex functional organization of living things could never have arisen without divine intelligence, it does not follow that the uses of the parts can be understood only with reference to the Demiurge's intentions. This is because Galen, like Aristotle, holds that organisms have internal rather than external teleology: that is, the end subserved by the parts of an organism is the continued existence of the organism as a whole, rather than any purpose external to it. The teleology of artefacts, by contrast, is external: an artefact is created by an intelligent agent to serve some purpose that lies outside the artefact itself.[51] Now it is

---

[50] For these features of the craftsmanship of the body see esp. *UP* 17. 1, ii. 441. 10–446. 7 H., iv. 351–8 K., and *PHP* 9. 8, ii. 592. 22–596. 4 De Lacy, v. 786–9 K. For beauty as the adaptation of structure to function see *UP* 1. 9, i. 17. 20–18. 5 H., iii. 24–5 K.: 'And so, if you are seeking to discover the proper form for the eye or nose, you will find it by correlating their structure [κατασκευή] and activities [*energeiai*]. In fact, this is your standard, measure, and criterion of proper form and true beauty [κάλλος], since true beauty is nothing but excellence of structure, and in obedience to Hippocrates you will judge that excellence from activities [*energeiai*], not from whiteness, softness, or other such qualities, which are indications of a beauty meretricious and false, not natural and true.'

[51] For the distinction between external and internal teleology see Ayala, 'Teleo-

certainly possible to conceive of organisms as having external teleology in this sense. The Stoics, for example, argued that living things
are part of a hierarchy in which each kind of organism serves a purpose external to it that is established by God: the purpose of grass is
to be eaten by sheep, just as that of sheep is to be eaten by man.[52] On
such a view, the functions of the parts of an organism are determined
by their contributions to the purpose of the organism as a whole: as
Chrysippus put it, the pig has a soul to keep it fresh for the slaugh-
terhouse.[53] But Galen does not think that organisms have purposes
external to themselves, and his version of the argument from design makes no appeal to such considerations.[54] In arguing that living
things display craftsmanship, Galen does not appeal to the idea that
an artefact *as a whole* has a use; instead what he emphasizes is that all
the parts are optimally useful *with respect to* the whole.[55] While the

logical Explanations in Evolutionary Biology', esp. 13: 'A feature of a system will be
teleological in the sense of internal teleology if the feature has utility for the system
in which it exists and if such utility explains the presence of the feature in the systems. Utility in living organisms is defined in reference to survival or reproduction.
A structure or process of an organism is teleological if it contributes to the repro-
ductive efficiency of the organism itself, and if such contribution accounts for the
existence of the structure or process. Man-made tools or mechanisms are teleological
with external teleology if they have utility, i.e., if they have been designed to serve
a specified purpose, which therefore explains their existence and properties.' What
Galen offers in the case of organisms is internal teleology that is the result of design.

[52] Cf. Cic. *ND* 2. 37 (*SVF* ii. 1153; LS 54H): 'As Chrysippus cleverly put it, just
as the shield-cover was made for the sake of the shield and the sheath for the sake
of the sword, so too with the exception of the world everything else was made for
the sake of other things: for example, the crops and fruits which the earth brings
forth were made for the sake of animals, and the animals which it brings forth were
made for the sake of men (the horse for transport, the ox for ploughing, the dog for
hunting and guarding)' (trans. Long and Sedley).

[53] See Porph. *Abst.* 3. 20. 1 (*SVF* ii. 1152; LS 54P): 'It was certainly a persuasive
idea of Chrysippus' that the gods made us for our own and each other's sakes, and
animals for our sake: horses to help us in war, dogs in hunting, and leopards, bears
and lions to give us practice in courage. As for the pig, that most appetizing of
delicacies, it was created for no other purpose than slaughter, and god, in furnishing
our cuisine, mixed soul in with its flesh like salt' (trans. Long and Sedley).

[54] Cf. *De semine* 1. 15, 132. 16–19 De Lacy, iv. 581 K., discussing the tension of
strings on a musical instrument: 'But let us not suppose that because their tension
is useful [χρήσιμος] to performers, this state is natural [κατὰ φύσιν] for the cords.
The natural state [τὸ κατὰ φύσιν] of each thing that exists is not measured by usefulness to us [ταῖς ἡμετέραις χρείαις]; for by that reckoning even the death of animals
slaughtered for food will be natural [κατὰ φύσιν], as they are about to become useful
to us' (trans. De Lacy).

[55] The only passage I have found where Galen seems to appeal to the *chreia* of an
artefact as a whole is *UP* 17. 1, ii. 438. 2–7 H., iv. 347 K., which reads as follows in
May's translation (slightly modified): 'there is no part which we desire for its own

functions of the parts of an externally teleological system depend on the purpose for which the system has been designed, the functions of the parts of an internally teleological system can be understood independently of the intentions of its designer—if there is one. The parts have functions, understood as contributions to the system's continued existence, whether or not the system was designed by an intelligent agent.[56] In this way, even though Galen thinks that living organisms are so complex that they could never have arisen without intelligent design, the *chreiai* of their parts can be understood independently of any reference to the Demiurge's intentions.

Moreover, it is not the case that the parts are useful just *because* the Demiurge created them or gave them a certain structure; rather, the Demiurge creates the parts and structures them as he does because such an arrangement is maximally beneficial to the organism. It is *chreia* that determines the Demiurge's intentions, not the other way round.[57] The Demiurge simply reasons as any good craftsman would; if we are able and apply ourselves to the study of the parts, we can reconstruct his reasoning. The uses of the parts of course *correspond* to the Demiurge's intentions, but that is just because he is supremely intelligent and therefore able to grasp what sort of construction would be most useful to an organism of a certain kind. And because he is supremely powerful (though not omnipotent), he is largely able to realize this construction.[58] In an important sense, then, Galen's functional explanations are independent of the thesis

sake, and a part deprived of its activity would be so superfluous that we should cut it off rather than wish to keep it. Indeed, if there were any such part in the body of an animal, *we would not say that the whole had any certain use* [οὐκ ἂν ἁπάντων ἐλέγομεν εἶναί τινα χρείαν]. But since neither man nor any other animal has such a part, we say that nature is skilful.' But the italicized sentence could better be translated 'we would not say that all the parts had a use', and there is in any case some uncertainty about the reading ἁπάντων (the alternatives include both αὐτοῦ and ἀπ' αὐτοῦ according to Helmreich's apparatus).

[56] Cf. McLaughlin, *What Functions Explain*, 142–50.
[57] See esp. *De constitutione artis medicae ad Patrophilum* 2, 58. 34–60. 6 Fortuna, i. 231 K.: 'Just as the person who wishes to know precisely what sort of thing a house that has already come to be is attains knowledge of it from analysis and decomposition, in the same way we too will come to know the body of a human being from dissection. Now god and nature know the parts in advance, like the one who originally constructed the house, since use furnishes them with the model [τῆς χρείας αὐτοῖς τὸ παράδειγμα γεννώσης], but we [know the parts] like one who investigates the house that has already come to be. And yet for us too, if we do not make our knowledge as similar as possible to god's, it will be impossible to discern whether all [the parts] have come to be on account of some use [*chreia*], or some of them in vain.'
[58] Galen's Demiurge is limited by the nature of the matter he has to work with; in

of design. What they tell us is *why* the Demiurge structured the parts in a certain way. That the Demiurge *intended* to act as he did is indeed fortunate; it tells us something about him and about how the body came to be structured as it is. But in itself it is irrelevant to the fact that the parts structured in this way are useful; *that* is because of their beneficial contributions to the organism as a whole.[59]

It would no doubt be over-simplistic to suppose that Galen adopted the thesis of design purely on the basis of his investigation of the correspondence between structure and function in the organism. He obviously had many reasons for his commitment to the existence of a Platonic Demiurge, some of them religious or theological, others connected with his own education and the intellectual prestige of Plato in the philosophical tradition.[60] The assumption that the body is the result of providential design must have functioned as a heuristic principle legitimating the search for uses of the parts even where others had seen none: once it is accepted that the design of the human body is the result of the activity of a Demiurge who is supremely good, powerful, and intelligent, there is every reason to suppose that he will have left no part without a use in so far as this is possible.[61] As a guide to anatomical investigation such a principle is undeniably fruitful, even if it did sometimes

this sense he is fundamentally distinct from the Judaeo-Christian God, who could 'make a horse or a cow out of ashes' (*UP* 11. 14, ii. 158. 23–6 H., iii. 906 K.).

[59] Of course it is presumably the Demiurge who conceives of the various kinds of living things, so in this sense the uses of all the parts do ultimately depend on his intentions. But once the forms of living organisms have been established (i.e. by specifying the 'character and faculties' of their souls), the plan of construction follows immediately. The point is that even though Galen thinks that organisms, like artefacts, are the result of intelligent design, the teleology of the organism does not depend on the intentions of its designer in the same way as the teleology of an artefact. In the case of artefacts, the functions of the parts are dependent on the purpose for which the artefact was designed. In the case of organisms, which are their own ends, the functions of the parts depend solely on their contributions to the whole; the designer is invoked only because matter would never come to possess an appropriate level of structural organization if left to its own accord.

[60] In *De propriis placitis* 2 Galen says that the existence of the gods can be inferred from their 'works' (*erga*), which include: the 'construction' (κατασκευή) of living things; omens, portents, and dreams; cures (Galen refers to an occasion on which he was cured by Asclepius); and help at sea (Galen claims personal experience of the providence (*pronoia*) and power (*dynamis*) of the Dioscuri). See the recently rediscovered Greek text as presented in Boudon-Millot and Pietrobelli, 'Galien ressuscité', at 173. 1–8.

[61] On the heuristic role of teleology in Galen see Hankinson, 'Galen and the Best of All Possible Worlds', 223–7.

lead to excesses. Nevertheless, the fact remains that Galen's explicit argument in *De usu partium* and *PHP* 9 is *from* optimal construction, understood as consummate craftsmanship, *to* the existence of the Demiurge. Craftsmanship is chiefly a matter of the adaptation of structure to function, and so the starting-point of the whole argument is a grasp of the complex functional organization of living things. As I have tried to show, Galen had good reasons to adopt this as a starting-point for his biological investigations—reasons which were independent of some of the bolder and more sweeping conclusions he attempted to draw from them.

*Harvard University*

## BIBLIOGRAPHY

Ayala, F. J., 'Teleological Explanations in Evolutionary Biology', *Philosophy of Science*, 37/1 (1970), 1–15.

Beckner, M., 'Function and Teleology', *Journal of the History of Biology*, 2 (1969), 151–64.

Boudon-Millot, V., and Pietrobelli, A., 'Galien ressuscité: édition *princeps* du texte grec du *De propriis placitis*' ['Galien ressuscité'], *Revue des études grecques*, 118 (2005), 168–213.

Canfield, J., 'Teleological Explanation in Biology', *British Journal for the Philosophy of Science*, 14/56 (1964), 285–95.

Cummins, R., 'Functional Analysis', *Journal of Philosophy*, 72 (1975), 741–65.

De Lacy, P. (ed.), *Galeni De placitis Hippocratis et Platonis* (3 vols.; Corpus Medicorum Graecorum, 5.4.1.2; Berlin, 1978–84).

—— *Galeni De semine* (Corpus Medicorum Graecorum, 5.3.1; Berlin, 1992).

Diller, H., 'Eine Stoisch-pneumatische Schrift im Corpus Hippocraticum', *Sudhoffs Archiv*, 29 (1936), 178–95; repr. in G. Baader and H. Grensemann (eds.), *Hans Diller: Kleine Schriften zur antiken Medizin* (Berlin, 1973), 17–30.

Fortuna, S., *Galeni De constitutione artis medicae ad Patrophilum* (Corpus Medicorum Graecorum, 5.1.3; Berlin, 1997).

Furley, D., and Wilkie, J. S., *Galen on Respiration and the Arteries* [*Galen on Respiration*] (Princeton, 1984).

Gundert, B., 'Parts and their Roles in Hippocratic Medicine', *Isis*, 83/3 (1992), 453–65.

Hankinson, R. J., 'Galen and the Best of All Possible Worlds', *Classical Quarterly*, NS 39/1 (1989), 206–27.

—— 'Galen Explains the Elephant', in M. Matthen and B. Linsky (eds.), *Philosophy and Biology* (Calgary, 1988), 135–57.

Helmreich, G. (ed.), *Claudii Galeni Pergameni scripta minora*, vol. iii (Leipzig, 1893).

—— *Galeni De usu partium libri XVII* (2 vols.; Leipzig, 1907–9).

Hempel, C., *Aspects of Scientific Explanation* (New York, 1965).

Johnson, M. R., *Aristotle on Teleology* (Oxford, 2005).

Joly, R., *Hippocrate*, vol. vi/2 (Paris, 1972).

Jones, W. H. S., *Hippocrates*, vol. i (Cambridge, Mass., 1923).

Jouanna, J., *Hippocrates* (Baltimore, 1999).

Kühn, C. G. (ed.), *Claudii Galeni opera omnia* (20 vols. in 22; Leipzig, 1821–33; repr. Hildesheim, 1965).

Littré, É. (ed.), *Œuvres complètes d'Hippocrate* (10 vols.; Paris, 1839–61).

Long, A. A. and Sedley, D., *The Hellenistic Philosophers* [LS] (Cambridge, 1987).

Lonie, I. M., 'The Paradoxical Text *On the Heart*', *Medical History*, 17 (1973), 1–15, 136–53.

McLaughlin, P., *What Functions Explain: Functional Explanation and Self-Reproducing Systems* [*What Functions Explain*] (Cambridge, 2001).

May, M. T. (trans.), *Galen: On the Usefulness of the Parts of the Body* [*Usefulness*] (2 vols.; Ithaca, NY, 1968).

Moraux, P., 'Galen and Aristotle's *De partibus animalium*', in A. Gotthelf (ed.), *Aristotle on Nature and Living Things: Philosophical and Historical Studies Presented to David M. Balme on his Seventieth Birthday* (Pittsburgh, 1985), 327–44.

Nagel, E., *The Structure of Science: Problems in the Logic of Scientific Explanation* [*Structure*] (New York, 1961).

Nickel, D. (ed.), *Galeni De foetuum formatione* (Corpus Medicorum Graecorum, 5.3.3; Berlin, 2001).

Nussbaum, M., *Aristotle's* De motu animalium [*De motu*] (Princeton, 1978).

Sedley, D., 'Is Aristotle's Teleology Anthropocentric?', *Phronesis*, 36 (1991), 179–96.

Siegel, R. E., *Galen on Psychology, Psychopathology, and Function and Diseases of the Nervous System: An Analysis of his Observations and Experiments* (Basel, 1973).

Sorabji, R., 'Function', *Philosophical Quarterly*, 14/57 (1964), 289–302.

Wright, L., 'Functions', *Philosophical Review*, 82/2 (1973), 139–68.

# INDEX LOCORUM

$417^a$17–21: 207
$417^a$19–20: 207
$417^a$21–$^b$2: 181
$417^b$2–7: 185 n. 12
$417^b$2–5: 185 n. 11
$417^b$2–4: 183
$417^b$3–5: 183, 185 n. 12, 186
$417^b$3–4: 182
$417^b$4–5: 208 n. 55
$417^b$6–7: 181, 182, 184
$417^b$8–9: 186 n. 14
$417^b$12–16: 185, 185 n. 11, 203–4 n. 47
$417^b$14: 185 n. 11
$417^b$15: 185 n. 13
$417^b$16–17: 192 n. 26
$417^b$16: 184
$417^b$33–$418^a$3: 181
$418^a$3–6: 181, 192
$418^a$3–4: 199
$418^a$3: 211
$418^a$8–9: 193 n. 29
$418^a$23–4: 193 n. 29
$418^a$24: 193 n. 29
$422^a$6–7: 191 n. 22
$422^a$10–11: 209 n. 60
$422^a$34–$^b$10: 189–90 n. 20
$422^a$34–$^b$5: 191, 209
$422^b$2–5: 209 n. 61
$422^b$3–5: 209 n. 59
$422^b$6–8: 210 n. 63
$423^b$17–26: 189–90 n. 20
$424^a$2–5: 198 n. 39
$424^a$17–$^b$3: 197
$424^a$17–24: 190
$424^a$21–4: 193
$424^a$24–8: 189, 189 n. 19, 190
$424^a$24: 193 n. 29
$424^a$25–6: 189 n. 19
$425^a$4–5: 190 n. 21
$425^b$22–4: 206
$425^b$23–4: 190, 206 n. 52
$425^b$25: 200
$425^b$26–$426^a$26: 197
$425^b$26–$426^a$19: 242
$425^b$29: 200–1 n. 42
$426^a$2–11: 239
$426^a$2–6: 194–5, 200
$426^a$4: 194–5 n. 31, 195 n. 33
$426^a$6–8: 195 n. 33
$426^b$7–12: 189
$426^a$9–11: 195
$426^a$14–15: 196
$429^a$18: 234–5 n. 28

$429^a$24–7: 207 n. 53
$429^b$22–$430^a$2: 208 n. 55
$431^a$4–7: 218
$431^b$20: 197–8 n. 37
$431^b$21–3: 198 n. 39
$431^b$21: 198 n. 38
$431^b$26–8: 198
$431^b$26–7: 203 n. 46
$431^b$28–$432^a$3: 198
$432^a$2: 203 n. 46
$432^a$15–16: 197–8 n. 37
$432^a$17–18: 197–8 n. 37
$434^a$3–8: 264–5 n. 46
$434^a$32: 159 n. 35
$435^b$17–25: 374 n. 8
$435^b$20–1: 374 n. 8
*De caelo*
$284^a$31–2: 259 n. 22
$292^b$6–7: 159 n. 34
*De interpretatione*
$17^a$38–$^b$1: 125
*De generatione animalium*
$715^a$4: 159 n. 35
$744^a$2–5: 190 n. 21, 191 n. 22
$744^b$12–27: 174 n. 61
$778^b$13: 159 n. 35
$780^a$4–5: 214 n. 72
$780^a$4: 214 n. 72
$780^b$24: 208–9 n. 58
$780^b$29–33: 208–9 n. 58, 214 n. 72
*De generatione et corruptione*
1. 5: 213
1. 7: 207, 208, 209, 212 n. 67
2. 11: 169 n. 53
$319^b$11–16: 183 n. 8
$319^b$34: 183 n. 8
$321^b$2–5: 230 n. 20
$321^b$20–3: 213
$323^b$30–4: 208 n. 56
*De memoria*
1: 279
*De motu animalium*
$700^b$26–7: 159 n. 35
$701^b$13–23: 279
$701^b$16–23: 277
$701^b$17–18: 212 n. 66
$701^b$33–$702^a$7: 279
$703^a$29–$^b$2: 374
$703^b$3–9: 277
*De partibus animalium*
1. 1–5: 372
3. 2: 173
$639^a$12–15: 168

$1023^a12-13$: 203 n. 45
$1023^a23-5$: 203 n. 45
$1028^a31-6$: 230 n. 20
$1028^b36-1029^a1$: 230 n. 21
$1029^a15-16$: 230 n. 20
$1029^b16-17$: 230 n. 20
$1032^b6-8$: 162 n. 39
$1032^b13-14$: 205 n. 49
$1038^b11-12$: 126–7 n. 3
$1038^b23-7$: 235
$1039^a30-2$: 235
$1041^a24-32$: 157
$1042^a3-4$: 267 n. 54
$1043^a29-36$: 213 n. 68
$1045^b27-32$: 230 n. 20
$1046^a6$: 357 n. 22
$1047^a18-20$: 234
$1048^b18$ ff.: 264
$1048^b18-35$: 382 n. 21
$1048^b22-6$: 222 n. 3
$1048^b25-6$: 221 n. 2, 236–7 n. 30
$1050^a30-4$: 239
$1050^a35-{}^b2$: 222 n. 3, 227 n. 16
$1051^a21-9$: 156
$1051^a22-3$: 156 n. 27
$1055^b7$: 357 n. 22
$1056^b35$: 357 n. 22
$1065^a31$: 159 n. 35
$1070^a33-{}^b10$: 235
$1071^b17-19$: 192 n. 24
$1072^b14$ ff.: 259 n. 22
$1086^b37-1087^a4$: 235
$1088^a21-{}^b4$: 234–5 n. 28
$1088^b2-4$: 235
*Meteorologica*
$369^b12-24$: 155 n. 25
*Nicomachean Ethics*
1. 7: 226 ff.
1. 8–12: 221 ff.
1. 9: 246 ff.
1. 10: 247 ff.
1. 12: 250–1
2. 1: 265 n. 47
2. 7: 358
2. 8: 349 n. 10
5. 8: 236–7 n. 30
6. 1: 355, 355 n. 20
6. 13: 355, 355 n. 20
7. 12–15: 349, 364
7. 14: 31, 35, 347, 352, 359, 360
10. 1–5: 215, 361
10. 5: 236–7 n. 30
10. 7: 260, 354 n. 19

$1094^b24$: 356 n. 21
$1095^a18-20$: 231
$1095^a31-1096^a2$: 243
$1095^b29-1096^a2$: 232, 232 n. 23
$1095^b30-1096^a2$: 231
$1096^a6$: 357
$1096^a7-9$: 240 n. 41
$1096^a21-2$: 234–5 n. 28
$1096^b8-16$: 349 n. 10
$1096^b13-19$: 240 n. 41
$1096^b16-19$: 264–5 n. 46
$1096^b26-9$: 163 n. 42
$1097^a30-{}^b6$: 240 n. 41
$1097^a30-{}^b2$: 231 n. 22
$1097^b33-4$: 247
$1098^a1$: 236–7 n. 30
$1098^a2-3$: 247
$1098^a5-7$: 227
$1098^a5-6$: 231
$1098^a8-12$: 273
$1098^a16-18$: 221, 225, 227
$1098^a16$: 226 n. 13
$1098^a17-18$: 354 n. 19
$1098^a18-20$: 244 n. 49
$1098^a18$: 271–2 n. 73
$1098^a20-2$: 244 n. 49
$1098^b9-11$: 227
$1098^b12-20$: 228
$1098^b20-2$: 231
$1098^b23-1099^a7$: 232
$1098^b31-1099^a3$: 232
$1098^b31-3$: 226, 234
$1098^b31$: 225, 232
$1099^a7-31$: 242
$1099^a7-8$: 229
$1099^a10-11$: 242
$1099^a14$: 242 n. 46
$1099^a17-18$: 242 n. 46
$1099^a19$: 242 n. 46
$1099^a20$: 242 n. 46
$1099^a21$: 242 n. 46
$1099^a29-31$: 242, 244–5 n. 50
$1099^a29-30$: 221
$1099^a31-{}^b9$: 243
$1099^a31-{}^b8$: 224 n. 10, 243
$1099^a31-2$: 244–5 n. 50
$1099^b3-6$: 250
$1099^b3-4$: 246 n. 52
$1099^b7-8$: 243
$1099^b25-8$: 243 n. 47
$1099^b25-7$: 246
$1099^b26$: 221, 244–5 n. 50
$1099^b27-8$: 224 n. 10, 244–5 n. 50

**Augustine**
*Contra Academicos*

**Boethus,** ed. *SVF*

**Chrysippus**
*On Gods*
*On Lives*
*On Tenors*

**Cicero**
*Academica*
*De finibus*

# Notes for Contributors to Oxford Studies in Ancient Philosophy

1. Articles should be submitted with double or $1\frac{1}{2}$ line-spacing through-out. At the stage of initial (but not final) submission footnotes may be printed in small type at the foot of the page. Pages should be A4 or standard American quarto ($8\frac{1}{2} \times 11''$), and ample margins should be left.

2. Two identical printed copies, or a PDF attached to an e-mail, should be submitted to the editor. Authors are asked to supply an accurate word-count (*a*) for the main text, and (*b*) for the notes. The covering letter should provide a current e-mail address, if available, as well as a postal address. In the case of electronic submission, revised versions will not be accepted: the version first submitted will be the one adjudicated.

3. Typescripts will not normally be returned to authors. After all dealings have been concluded, typescripts will be disposed of and electronic files deleted.

*The remaining instructions apply to the final version sent for publication, and need not be rigidly adhered to in a first submission.*

4. Only one printed copy of the final version should be supplied, double-spaced and in the same typesize throughout, **including displayed quotations and notes**. Notes should be numbered consecutively, and may be supplied as either footnotes or endnotes. Any acknowledge-ments should be placed in an unnumbered first note. Wherever pos-sible, references to primary sources should be built into the text.

5. **Use of Greek and Latin.** Relatively familiar Greek terms such as *psychē* and *polis* (but not whole phrases and sentences) may be used in transliteration. Wherever possible, Greek and Latin should not be used in the main text of an article in ways which would impede comprehen-sion by those without knowledge of the languages; for example, where appropriate, the original texts should be accompanied by a transla-tion. This constraint does not apply to footnotes. Greek copy must be supplied in a completely legible and accurate form, with all diacritics in place both on the hard copy and in the computer file. A note of the system employed for achieving Greek (e.g. GreekKeys, Linguist's Software) should be supplied to facilitate file conversion.

6. For citations of Greek and Latin authors, house style should be fol-lowed. This can be checked in any recent issue of *OSAP* with the help of the Index Locorum.

7. In references to books, the first time the book is referred to give the ini-tial(s) and surname of the author (first names are not usually required), and the place and date of publication; where you are abbreviating the

title in subsequent citations, give the abbreviation in square brackets, thus:

> T. Brickhouse and N. Smith, *Socrates on Trial* [*Trial*] (Princeton, 1981), 91–4.

Give the volume-number and date of periodicals, and include the full page-extent of articles (including chapters of books):

> D. W. Graham, 'Symmetry in the Empedoclean Cycle' ['Symmetry'], *Classical Quarterly*, NS 38 (1988), 297–312 at 301–4.

> G. Vlastos, 'The Unity of the Virtues in the *Protagoras*' ['Unity'], in id., *Platonic Studies*, 2nd edn. (Princeton, 1981), 221–65 at 228.

Where the same book or article is referred to on subsequent occasions, usually the most convenient style will be an abbreviated reference, thus:

> Brickhouse and Smith, *Trial*, 28–9.

**Do *not* use the author-and-date style of reference:**

> Brickhouse and Smith 1981: 28–9.

8. Authors are asked to supply *in addition*, at the end of the article, a full list of the bibliographical entries cited, alphabetically ordered by (first) author's surname. Except that the author's surname should come first, these entries should be identical in form to the first occurrence of each in the article, including where appropriate the indication of abbreviated title:

> Graham, D. W., 'Symmetry in the Empedoclean Cycle' ['Symmetry'], *Classical Quarterly*, NS 38 (1988), 297–312.

9. If there are any unusual conventions contributors are encouraged to include a covering note for the copy-editor and/or printer. Please say whether you are using single and double quotation marks for different purposes (otherwise the Press will employ its standard single quotation marks throughout, using double only for quotations within quotations).

10. Authors should send a copy of the final version of their paper on a compact disk (CD) or 3.5″ high density (HD) floppy disk (Macintosh or IBM format), indicating on the disk or in an accompanying note the program in which the text is written, including the system employed for achieving Greek (see point 5 above). This version must be in a standard word-processing format **and not a typeset file or PDF**, though an accompanying PDF version may be included. **NB. The version on disk must be the *exact* version which produced the hard copy sent in for printing.**